Foundations *of* PSYCHOLOGICAL TESTING

3rd Edition

Leslie Miller dedicates this book to her husband, Robert Miller, and children, Zachary Kenneth Miller and Kia Anne Miller.
Sandra McIntire dedicates this book to her son, Jonathan McIntire Hart.
Robert Lovler dedicates this book to his wife, Patsy Lovler, his daughter, Lauren Lovler, and his mentor at Hofstra University, Dr. William Metlay.

Leslie A. Miller ▪ Sandra A. McIntire ▪ Robert L. Lovler

LanneM TM, LLC   Rollins College   Wilson Learning Corporation

Foundations *of* PSYCHOLOGICAL TESTING

A Practical Approach

3rd Edition

Los Angeles | London | New Delhi
Singapore | Washington DC

For information:

SAGE Publications, Inc.
2455 Teller Road
Thousand Oaks, California 91320
E-mail: order@sagepub.com

SAGE Publications Ltd.
1 Oliver's Yard
55 City Road
London EC1Y 1SP
United Kingdom

SAGE Publications India Pvt. Ltd.
B 1/I 1 Mohan Cooperative Industrial Area
Mathura Road, New Delhi 110 044
India

SAGE Publications Asia-Pacific Pte. Ltd.
33 Pekin Street #02-01
Far East Square
Singapore 048763

Printed in the United States of America

Library of Congress Cataloging-in-Publication Data

Miller, Leslie A.
Foundations of psychological testing : a practical approach / Leslie A. Miller, Sandra A. McIntire, Robert L. Lovler. -- 3rd ed.
        p. cm.
Includes bibliographical references and index.
ISBN 978-1-4129-7639-8 (cloth)
    1. Psychological tests--Textbooks. I. McIntire, Sandra A., 1944- II. Lovler, Robert L. II. Title.

BF176.M38 2011
150.28'7--dc22   2010032174

This book is printed on acid-free paper.

10   11   12   13   14   10   9   8   7   6   5   4   3   2   1

Acquisitions Editor:	Christine Cardone
Editorial Assistant:	Sarita Sarak
Production Editor:	Libby Larson
Copy Editor:	Sarah J. Duffy
Typesetter:	C&M Digitals (P) Ltd.
Proofreader:	Susan Schon
Indexer:	Wendy Allex
Cover Designer:	Candice Harman
Marketing Manager:	Stephanie Adams
Permissions Editor:	Karen Ehrmann

Brief Contents

Detailed Contents

Preface

Psychological testing is big business, and using psychological tests to make important decisions continues to increase. For example, educators are using tests to determine who will receive high school diplomas, who will be admitted to college, who will participate in special school programs (for example, gifted, remedial), and who will earn high and low grades. Clinicians are using tests to help diagnose psychological disorders and plan treatment programs. Industrial/organizational psychologists are using tests to select people for jobs, measure individual job performance, and evaluate the effectiveness of training programs. Students are using tests to gain greater insight into their personal interests, decide which college majors to pursue, and determine the graduate or professional schools to which they might apply. Professional organizations and governmental agencies are using licensing or certification tests to ensure that individuals engaged in certain occupations have the necessary qualifications to ensure that the safety of the public is protected.

In spite of widespread use, psychological tests continue to be misunderstood and used improperly. At one extreme, these misunderstandings and misuses have led many people to believe that psychological tests are useless or even extremely harmful. At the other extreme, many other people believe that psychological tests serve as ideal and extremely precise instruments of measurement. More commonly, these misunderstandings and misuses have led to the misconceptions that psychological testing is synonymous with diagnosing mental disorders, that psychological tests can and should be used as a sole means for making decisions, and that anyone can create, administer, or interpret a psychological test.

Our Mission

We originally wrote the first edition of *Foundations of Psychological Testing: A Practical Approach* in response to the growing need for a scholarly, yet pragmatic and easy-to-understand, introductory textbook for students new to the field of psychological testing and to the concepts of statistics and psychometrics that support its practice. As with the first two editions of this textbook, we had two primary objectives in writing the third edition. Our first objective was to prepare students to be informed consumers of psychological tests—as test users or test takers—rather than to teach students to administer or interpret individual psychological tests. To meet this objective, we have taken care to focus the first two-thirds of the textbook primarily on the basic concepts, issues, and tools used in psychological testing and their relevance to daily life. The last one-third of the book focuses on how tests are used in educational, clinical, and organizational settings.

Our second objective was to present the information in a way that is maximally conducive to student learning. Over the years, many of our students have lamented that textbooks do not always explain material as clearly as a professor would during a class lecture. They have also shared that textbooks lack practical application of the material. We have designed this textbook with those students' comments in mind. Not only does *Foundations of Psychological Testing* provide a fresh look at the field of psychological testing, but we have written it in a style that we believe will encourage and promote student learning and enthusiasm. First, we focus on communicating the basics of psychological testing clearly and concisely, and we relate these basics to practical situations that students can recognize and should be able to embrace. Second, we present this information at a comfortable reading level and in a conversational format. Although current textbooks on psychological testing are moving in this direction, we believe that some books are too complex and contain more detailed discussion of certain technical issues than is necessary.

New in This Edition

For the current edition, we added a third objective in response to feedback we received from our current and potential future adopters: to incorporate more discussion of specific tests while keeping the focus on the foundational elements of psychological testing. We accomplished this objective in two ways. First, we linked our discussion of testing concepts more directly with examples from published tests that demonstrate how each concept is actually used. Second, for many mentioned tests, we included more detail about the test in a Test Spotlight—a more in-depth account of the referenced test. For ease of reading, Test Spotlights are included in Appendix A.

One of the most substantial changes that we made for the third addition was updating all the chapters on test validity to reflect how the *Standards for Educational and Psychological Testing* treats validity as a unitary concept and no longer speaks of different types of validity. But because so many testing practitioners still use the more traditional concepts of content, criterion-related, and construct validity, we made sure that we explained these concepts and how they are connected to the more recent conceptualization. We also focused attention on the fact that the concept of validity concerns the appropriateness of the inferences that are made from test scores, rather than the older definitions that concentrated on whether or not the test "measured what it was supposed to measure."

In this new edition, we made a few additional changes to enhance readability, update critical information, and improve the learning process. We reformed the text boxes throughout the book to improve readability and flow of information. We also updated information to reflect the most recent current events and active URLs. Last, because more instructors are using discussion questions to guide classroom learning, we incorporated more discussion questions, leveraging Bloom's Taxonomy, to the section titled Engaging in the Learning Process at the end of each chapter.

Learning Strategies

As with the previous edition, to further promote student learning, we included multiple learning strategies. We preview, discuss, review, and reinforce important information in multiple ways at the text, section, and chapter levels. These learning strategies include the following:

- *Section Preview:* Each section of this textbook opens with a concept map that pictorially displays the chapters covered in that section and a preview of those chapters. We intend these previews to provide two tools that appeal to two very different learning styles—visual and verbal—and to prepare students to receive the material to be covered.
- *Chapter Opening Narratives:* Each chapter opens with narratives that pertain to the chapter topic. These narratives provide students with means to identify with the material by relating them to their own experiences.
- *Learning Objectives:* The introduction to each chapter includes clearly defined learning objectives that set expectations for what students should know and be able to do after studying the chapter.
- *Instruction Through Conversation:* In response to our students' cries of "Why couldn't the text have said it that way?" we have written each chapter the way our students best understand the information—at as simple a reading level as possible and, in most cases, in conversational style.
- *True to Life:* The concepts in each chapter are illustrated by real-life examples drawn from the testing literature and from our experiences.
- *For Your Information, In the News, and On the Web:* Each chapter contains the following boxes:

FYI	For Your Information provides relevant, interesting, or more detailed information about a particular concept or calculations relevant to a particular topic.
	In the News features testing stories from the print or news media.
	On the Web features web sources relating to issues discussed in the chapter.

- *Interim Summaries:* These summaries appear at varying intervals. They include important information within each chapter and serve as study aids for focusing on critical textbook content.
- *Key Words and Concepts:* Within each chapter, we have taken care to alert students to key words and concepts that are important for them to master. We introduce and define each term and concept within a logical structure to promote ease of comprehension. These appear at the end of each chapter and are provided in a Glossary located at the back of the book.
- *Experiential Activities:* At the end of each chapter, we have added a section titled "Engaging in the Learning Process." This section contains learning activities, study tips, and practice test questions to facilitate the learning process.

Organization of Material

Foundations of Psychological Testing: A Practical Approach is divided into four sections. The first section consists of four chapters that provide an overview of the basics of psychological testing. It includes discussions of what a psychological test is, where to find information about psychological tests, who uses psychological tests and for what reasons, the history of psychological testing, some concerns our society has about the use of psychological tests, the ethical and proper use of psychological tests, and testing with computers and special populations.

The second section consists of five chapters that cover psychometric principles. These chapters discuss the procedures we use to interpret test scores, the concepts of reliability and validity, and the methods for estimating reliability and validity.

The third section begins with two chapters in which we describe how to develop, pilot test, and validate psychological tests. Because there are many overlapping design principles between psychological tests and surveys, and because many of our adopters use this text as a part of a measurements course, we have also included a chapter on how to construct, administer, and use surveys.

The final section of the textbook consists of three chapters that discuss how tests are used in three important settings: education, clinical and counseling practice, and organizations.

Final Thoughts

We hope our audience will find this edition of the textbook to be a scholarly, informative, applicable, and appropriate undergraduate introduction to the field of psychological testing. Because we strongly believe that assessment and feedback are vital to development and improvement, we encourage professors and students to send their feedback to us.

Acknowledgments

We could not have written the third edition of our textbook without the assistance of various individuals. First, we would like to thank the reviewers who provided helpful suggestions and recommendations that resulted in improvements to the organization and contents of the book. The reviewers include Luis A. Cordón, Professor, Eastern Connecticut State University; Bo Zhang, University of Wisconsin—Milwaukee; Karen S. Martinkowski, PhD; Joseph F. Arnoult, PhD, Nicholls State University; and Linda D. Ladd, PhD, PsyD, Texas Woman's University. In addition, we wish to acknowledge those test authors who shared their photos and test information. We also wish to thank Lauren Lovler for her help researching test information and creating test spotlights.

Finally, we would like to express our sincere thanks to Christine Cardone (our editor), Sarita Sarak (our editorial assistant), Libby Larson (our production editor), and Sarah Duffy (our copy editor) at SAGE Publications, who have been particularly helpful during the editing and production of the textbook.

Leslie A. Miller, PhD, PHR (DrLeslieMiller@hotmail.com)

Sandra McIntire, PhD (drfiddler1@msn.com)

Robert Lovler, PhD (Bob_Lovler@wilsonlearning.com)

SECTION I

OVERVIEW OF PSYCHOLOGICAL TESTING

Overview of Section I

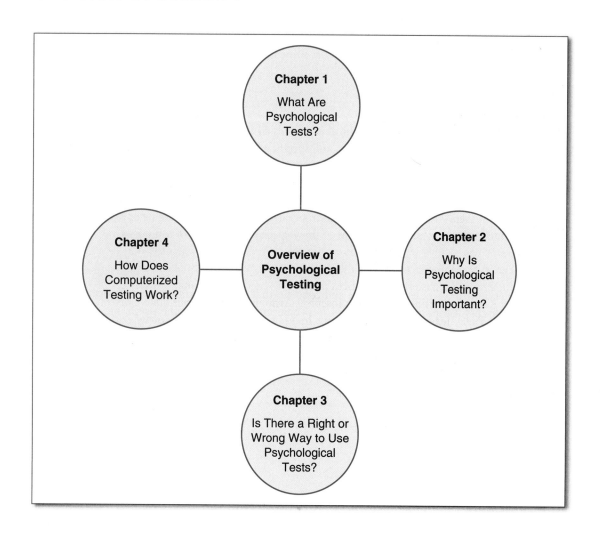

CHAPTER 1: WHAT ARE PSYCHOLOGICAL TESTS?

In Chapter 1, we discuss what a psychological test is and introduce you to some tests you might never have considered to be psychological tests. After exploring the history of psychological testing, we discuss the three defining characteristics of psychological tests and the assumptions that must be made when using psychological tests. We then discuss how tests are classified and distinguish four commonly confused concepts: psychological assessment, psychological tests, psychological measurement, and surveys. We conclude by sharing print and online resources for locating information about psychological testing and specific tests.

CHAPTER 2: WHY IS PSYCHOLOGICAL TESTING IMPORTANT?

In Chapter 2, we discuss why psychological testing is important. We explore who uses psychological tests and for what reasons. We also discuss some of the concerns society has about the use of psychological tests.

CHAPTER 3: IS THERE A RIGHT OR WRONG WAY TO USE PSYCHOLOGICAL TESTS?

In Chapter 3, we introduce you to ethical standards in psychological testing. We discuss what ethics are, the history of ethical standards, and specific ethical standards for psychological testing, including issues of privacy, anonymity, and informed consent. After highlighting various publications of ethical guidelines, we focus on the responsibilities of test publishers and test users. Finally, we discuss special considerations and requirements necessary for individuals who have impairments that interfere with taking a test. We address various types of impairments or disabilities and provide information on ethical treatment of these special populations of test takers.

CHAPTER 4: HOW DOES COMPUTERIZED TESTING WORK?

In Chapter 4, we look in depth at issues and concepts that are transforming psychological testing. First, we discuss computer-based testing—how computers are used in the psychological testing process. Second, we look at computerized adaptive testing, which can decrease the number of test questions and still provide reliable and valid scores. Third, we consider the advantages and disadvantages of psychological testing using the World Wide Web. Finally, we discuss the implications that web-based testing has for the testing and survey industry in the future.

CHAPTER 1

What Are Psychological Tests?

"When I was in the second grade, my teacher recommended that I be placed in the school's gifted program. As a result, the school psychologist interviewed me and had me take an intelligence test."

"Last semester I took a class in abnormal psychology. The professor had all of us take several personality tests, including the MMPI [Minnesota Multiphasic Personality Inventory].

It was awesome! We learned about different types of psychological disorders that the MMPI can help diagnose."

"This year I applied for a summer job with a local bank. As a part of the selection process, I had to participate in a structured interview and an assessment center."

"Yesterday I took my driving test—both the written and the road test. I couldn't believe everything they made me do. I had to parallel park, switch lanes, and make both right and left turns."

I f your instructor asked whether you have ever taken a psychological test, you would probably report the intelligence test you took as an elementary school student or the personality test you took in your abnormal psychology class. If your instructor asked what the purpose of psychological testing is, you would probably say its purpose is to determine whether someone is gifted or has a psychological disorder. Intelligence tests and personality tests are indeed psychological tests—and they are indeed used to identify giftedness and diagnose psychological disorders. However, this is only a snapshot of what psychological testing is all about. There are many types of psychological tests, and they have many different purposes.

In this chapter, we introduce you to the concept of psychological testing. We discuss what a psychological test is and introduce some tests you might never have considered to be psychological tests. Then, after exploring the history of psychological testing, we discuss the three defining characteristics of psychological tests and the assumptions that must be made when using these tests. We then turn our attention to the many ways of classifying tests. We also distinguish four concepts that students often get confused: psychological assessment, psychological tests, psychological measurement, and surveys. We conclude this chapter by sharing with you some of the resources (print and online) that are available for locating information about psychological testing and specific psychological tests.

Why Should You Care About Psychological Testing?

Before discussing what a psychological test is, we would like you to understand just how important it is for you to understand the foundations of psychological testing. Psychological testing is not just another subject that you may study in college; rather, it is a topic that personally affects many individuals. Each day, psychological tests are administered by many different professionals to many different individuals, and the results of these tests are used in ways that significantly affect you and those around you. For example, test scores are used to diagnose mental disorders, to determine whether medicines should be prescribed (and, if so, which ones), to treat mental and emotional illnesses, to select individuals for jobs, to select individuals for undergraduate and professional schools (for example, medical school, law school), and to determine grades. Good tests facilitate high-quality decisions, and bad tests facilitate low-quality decisions.

The consequences of bad decisions can be significant. For example, a poor hiring decision can dramatically affect both the person being hired and the hiring organization. From the organization's perspective, a poor hiring decision can result in increased absenteeism, reduced morale of other staff, and lost productivity and revenue. From the employee's perspective, a poor hiring decision may result in a loss of motivation, increased stress leading to depression and anxiety, and perhaps loss of opportunity to make progress in his or her career. Although you might never administer, score, or interpret a test, it is very likely that you or someone you know may have a life-altering decision made about him or her based on test scores. Therefore, it is important that you understand the foundations of psychological testing, specifically how to tell whether a decision is a good or bad one. Being able to do this requires that you understand the foundations of psychological testing.

What Are Psychological Tests?

Each anecdote at the beginning of this chapter involves the use of a psychological test. Intelligence tests, personality tests, interest and vocational inventories, college entrance exams, classroom tests, structured interviews, assessment centers, and driving tests all are psychological tests. Even the self-scored tests that you find in magazines such as *Glamour* and *Seventeen* (tests that supposedly tell you how you feel about your friends, stress, love, and more) can be considered psychological tests. Although some are more typical, all meet the definition of a psychological test. Together, they convey the very different purposes of psychological tests. For a continuum of some of the most and least commonly recognized types of psychological tests, see Figure 1.1.

Similarities Among Psychological Tests

Psychological testing is best defined as "the process of administering, scoring, and interpreting psychological tests" (Maloney & Ward, 1976, p. 9). But what exactly is a psychological test? We can easily answer this question by considering what all psychological tests do.

First, all **psychological tests** require a person to perform some **behavior**—an observable and measurable action. For example, when students take a multiple-choice midterm exam, they must read the various answers for each item and identify the best one. When individuals take an intelligence test, they may be asked to define words or solve math problems. When participating in a structured job interview, individuals must respond to questions from the interviewer—questions such as "Tell me about a time when you had to deal with an upset customer. What was the situation, what did you do, and what was the outcome?" In each of these cases, individuals are performing some observable and measurable behavior.

Figure 1.1   A Continuum of Psychological Tests

More Typical	←――――――――――――――――――――→		*Less Typical*
Personality tests Intelligence tests	Vocational tests Interest inventories Achievement tests Ability tests	Self-scored magazine tests Classroom quizzes and exams	Road portion of driving test Structured employment interviews Assessment centers

Second, the behavior an individual performs is used to measure some personal attribute, trait, or characteristic that is thought to be important in describing or understanding human behavior. For example, the questions on a multiple-choice exam might measure your knowledge of a particular subject area such as psychological testing. The words you defined or the math problems you solved might measure your verbal ability or quantitative reasoning. It is also important to note that sometimes the behavior an individual performs is also used to make a prediction about some outcome. For example, the questions you answered during a structured job interview may be used to predict your success in a management position.

So, what is a psychological test? It is something that requires you to perform a behavior to measure some personal attribute, trait, or characteristic or to predict an outcome.

Differences Among Psychological Tests

Although all psychological tests require that you perform some behavior to measure personal attributes, traits, or characteristics or to predict outcomes, these tests can differ in various ways. For example, they can differ in terms of the behavior they require you to perform, what they measure, their content, how they are administered and formatted, how they are scored and interpreted, and their psychometric quality (**psychometrics** is the quantitative and technical aspect of mental measurement).

Behavior Performed

The behaviors a test taker must perform vary by test. For example, a popular intelligence test, the Wechsler Adult Intelligence Scale–fourth edition (WAIS-IV), a general test of adult intelligence, requires test takers to (among other things) define words, repeat lists of digits, explain what is missing from pictures, and arrange blocks to duplicate geometric card designs. The Thematic Apperception Test (TAT), a widely used and researched projective personality test designed at Harvard University in the 1930s, requires test takers to look at ambiguous pictures showing a variety of social and interpersonal situations and to tell stories about each picture. The Graduate Record Examinations (GRE) General Test, a graduate school admissions test that measures verbal and quantitative reasoning, critical thinking, and analytical writing skills, requires test takers to answer multiple-choice questions and respond to two analytical writing tasks. The road portion of an auto driving test typically requires test takers to do things such as start a car, change lanes, make right and left turns, use turn signals properly, and parallel park. Assessment centers require job applicants to participate in simulated job-related activities (that mimic the activities they would perform in the job) such as engaging in confrontational meetings with disgruntled employees, processing e-mail and paperwork, and conducting manager briefings.

Attribute Measured and Outcome Predicted

What a test measures or predicts can vary. For example, the WAIS-IV asks individuals to explain what is missing from pictures to measure verbal intelligence. The TAT requires individuals to tell stories about pictures to identify conscious and unconscious drives, emotions, conflicts, and so on in order to ultimately measure personality. The road portion of a driving test requires individuals to perform various driving behaviors to measure driving ability. The GRE requires students to answer different types of questions to predict success in graduate school.

Some of the characteristics, attributes, and traits commonly measured by psychological tests include personality, intelligence, motivation, mechanical ability, vocational preference, spatial ability, and anxiety. Some of the outcomes that tests typically predict include success in college, worker productivity, and who will benefit from specialized services such as clinical treatment programs.

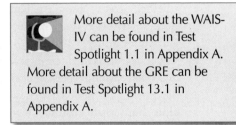

More detail about the WAIS-IV can be found in Test Spotlight 1.1 in Appendix A. More detail about the GRE can be found in Test Spotlight 13.1 in Appendix A.

Content

Two tests that measure the same characteristic, attribute, or trait can require individuals to perform significantly different behaviors or to answer significantly different questions. Sometimes how the test developers define the particular characteristic, attribute, or trait affects how the test is structured. For example, the questions on two intelligence tests may differ because one author may define intelligence as the ability to reason and another author may define it in terms of **emotional intelligence**—one's ability to understand one's own feelings and the feelings of others and to manage one's emotions (Gibbs, 1995).

The difference in content may also be due to the theoretical orientation of the test. (We talk more about theoretical orientation and its relation to test content in Chapter 8.)

Administration and Format

Psychological tests can differ in terms of how they are administered and their format. A test can be administered in paper-and-pencil format (individually or in a group setting), on a computer, or verbally. Similarly, a psychological test may consist of multiple-choice items, agree/disagree items, true/false items, open-ended questions, or some mix of these. There are also tests that ask respondents to perform some behavior such as sorting cards, playing a role, or writing an essay.

Scoring and Interpretation

Psychological tests can differ in terms of how they are scored and interpreted. Some tests are completed on scannable sheets and are computer scored. Some are hand-scored by the person administering the test. Others are scored by the test takers themselves. In terms of interpretation, some tests generate results that can be interpreted easily by the test taker, and others require a knowledgeable professional to explain the results to the test taker.

Psychometric Quality

Last, but extremely important, psychological tests can differ in terms of their psychometric quality. For now, let us just say that there are a lot of really good tests out there that measure what they say they measure and do so consistently, but there are also a lot of really poor tests out there that do not measure what they say they measure. Good tests measure what they claim to measure, and any conclusions that are drawn from the test scores about the person taking the test are appropriate (they are what we call *valid*). Good tests also measure whatever they measure consistently (they are what we call *reliable*). The concepts of reliability and validity are central to determining whether a test is "good" or "bad" and are covered in detail later in this textbook. These concepts are so important that four chapters are devoted to them (Chapter 6 covers reliability, and Chapters 7–9 discuss validity).

Because tests can differ in so many ways, to make informed decisions about tests, you must know how to properly critique a test. A critique of a test is an analysis of the test. A good critique answers many of the questions in Table 1.1. (These questions are also in Appendix B.) Your instructor may have additional ideas about what constitutes a good critique.

INTERIM SUMMARY 1.1
SIMILARITIES AND DIFFERENCES AMONG PSYCHOLOGICAL TESTS

Similarities

- All psychological tests require an individual to perform a behavior.
- The behavior performed is used to measure some personal attribute, trait, or characteristic.
- This personal attribute, trait, or characteristic is thought to be important in describing or understanding behavior.
- The behavior performed may also be used to predict outcomes.

Differences

Psychological tests can differ in terms of the following:

- The behavior they require the test taker to perform
- The attribute they measure
- Their content
- How they are administered and formatted
- How they are scored and interpreted
- Their psychometric quality

The History of Psychological Testing

Some scholars believe that the use of psychological tests can be traced to 2200 BCE in ancient China. For a summary of this history, see For Your Information Box 1.1. Most scholars agree that serious research efforts on the use and usefulness of psychological tests did not begin until the 20th century with the advent of intelligence testing.

Intelligence Tests

Alfred Binet and the Binet–Simon Scale

Late in the 19th century, Alfred Binet founded the first experimental psychology research laboratory in France. In his lab, Binet attempted to develop experimental techniques to measure intelligence and reasoning ability. He believed that intelligence was a complex characteristic that could be determined by evaluating a person's reasoning, judgment, and problem-solving abilities. Binet tried a variety of tasks to measure reasoning, judgment, and problem solving on his own children as well as on other children in the French school system.

Binet was successful in measuring intelligence, and in 1905 he and Théodore Simon published the first test of mental ability, the Binet–Simon Scale. Parisian school officials used this scale to decide which children, no matter how hard they tried, were unable to profit from regular school programs (Binet & Simon, 1905).

Table 1.1	Guidelines for Critiquing a Psychological Test

General descriptive information

- What is the title of the test?
- Who is the author of the test?
- Who publishes the test, and when was it published? (Include dates of manuals, norms, and supplementary materials)
- How long does it take to administer the test?
- How much does it cost to purchase the test? (Include the cost of the test, answer sheets, manual, scoring services, and so on)
- Is the test proprietary or nonproprietary?

Purpose and nature of the test

- What does the test measure? (Include scales)
- What does the test predict?
- What behavior does the test require the test taker to perform?
- What population was the test designed for (for example, age, type of person)?
- What is the nature of the test (for example, maximal performance, behavior observation, self-report, standardized or nonstandardized, objective or subjective)?
- What is the format of the test (for example, paper-and-pencil or computer, multiple choice or true/false)?

Practical evaluation

- Is the test manual comprehensive (does it include information on how the test was constructed, its reliability and validity, composition of norm groups, whether it is easy to read)?
- Is the test easy or difficult to administer?
- How clear are the administration directions?
- How clear are the scoring procedures?
- What qualifications and training does a test administrator need to have?
- Does the test have face validity?

Technical evaluation

- Is there a norm group?
- Who comprises the norm group?
- What types of norms are there (for example, percentiles, standard scores)?
- How was the norm group selected?
- Are there subgroup norms (for example, by age, gender, region, occupation, and so on)?
- What is the estimate of the test's reliability?
- How was reliability determined?
- What is the evidence for the validity of the test?
- How was the evidence for validity gathered?
- What is the standard error of measurement?
- What are the confidence intervals?

Test reviews

- What do reviewers say are the strengths and weaknesses of the test?
- What studies that use the test as a measurement instrument have been published in peer-reviewed journals?
- How did the test perform when researchers or test users, other than the test developer or publisher, used it?

Summary

- Overall, what do you see as being the strengths and weaknesses of the test?

FOR YOUR INFORMATION BOX 1.1

Psychological Tests: From Ancient China to the 20th Century

2200 BCE: Xia Dynasty

Some scholars believe that the use of psychological tests dates back approximately 4,000 years to 2200 BCE, when the Chinese emperor Yushun examined officials every third year to determine whether they were suitable to continue in office (DuBois, 1970; Martin, 1870). However, modern scholars of ancient China say that there is little archaeological evidence to support these claims. Reliable writing systems were developed by the Chinese somewhere between 1766 and 1122 BCE (Shang dynasty; Bowman, 1989). Nowhere in these writings were there any hints suggesting that leaders were examined as just described. Even in 1115 BCE, with the advent of more elaborate writing systems, there were no inscriptions or writings to suggest the existence of such an examination process (Martin, 1870).

200–100 BCE: Late Qin, Early Han Dynasty

Most modern scholars of ancient China agree that royal examinations began around 200 to 100 BCE, in the late Qin (Ch'in) or early Han dynasty (Eberhard, 1977; Franke, 1960; Pirazzoli-t'Serstevens, 1982; Rodzinski, 1979). Hucker (1978) believes that the first written examinations in world history began in 165 BCE, when the emperor administered written examinations to all nominees. Pirazzoli-t'Serstevens also believes that this was the beginning of all examination systems. Eberhard, on the other hand, admits that there may have been some assessment procedures before 165 BCE for selecting officials, who were probably tested more for literacy than for knowledge.

618–907 CE: T'ang Dynasty

Such examination systems seem to have been discontinued until the T'ang dynasty, when their use increased significantly (Bowman, 1989).

1368–1644: Ming Dynasty

During the Ming dynasty, the examinations became more formal. There were different levels of examinations (municipal, county, provincial, and national), and the results of examinations became associated with granting formal titles, similar to today's university degrees. On passing each level of examination, people received more titles and increasingly more power in the civil service (Bowman, 1989). These examinations were distressful, and this distress became a part of Chinese culture and also a part of folk stories and the literature (poems, comedies, and tragedies). Nonetheless, this examination system seemed to work well. Today, many scholars believe that this examination system kept talented men in the national government (Kracke, 1963) and kept members of the national government from becoming nobility because of their descent.

Seeing the value of these examinations for making important decisions, European governments, and eventually the governments of the United Kingdom, the United States, Canada, and other countries, adopted the use of such examination systems.

1791: France and Britain

France initially began using this kind of examination system in 1791. However, soon after, Napoleon temporarily abolished them. The system adopted by France served as a model for a British system started in 1833 to select trainees for the Indian civil service—the beginning of the British civil service.

1860s: United States

Due to the success of the British system, Senator Charles Sumner and Representative Thomas Jenckes proposed to Congress in 1860 that the United States use a similar system. Jenckes's report, *Civil Service in the United States,* described the British and Chinese systems in detail. This report laid the foundation for the establishment of the Civil Service Act Health and Psychosocial Instruments (HAPI), passed in January 1883.

20th Century: Western Europe and the United States

In 1879, Wilhelm Wundt introduced the first psychological laboratory, in Leipzig, Germany. At this time, psychology was the study of the similarities among people. For example, physiological psychologists studied how the brain and the nervous system function, and experimental psychologists conducted research to discover how people learn and remember. Strongly influenced by James McKeen Cattell, an American researcher in Wundt's laboratory, psychologists turned their attention to exploring individual differences. Cattell and others realized that learning about the differences among people was just as important as learning about the similarities among people. They believed that developing formal psychological tests to measure individual differences could help solve many social problems, such as who should be placed in remedial programs, who should be sent to battlefields, and who should be hired for particular jobs. At this time, scientists were particularly interested in finding a quantitative way of measuring general intelligence.

During the early 20th century, serious research efforts began on the use and usefulness of various testing procedures. Research conducted by scholars in the United States and Germany eventually led to Alfred Binet's research on intelligence in children.

Lewis Terman and the Stanford–Binet

Binet's work influenced psychologists across the globe. Psychological testing became a popular method of evaluation, and the Binet–Simon Scale was adapted for use in many countries. In 1916, Lewis Terman, an American psychologist, produced the

More detail about the Stanford-Binet Intelligence Scales can be found in Test Spotlight 1.2 in Appendix A.

Stanford–Binet Intelligence Scales, an adaptation of Binet's original test. This test, developed for use with Americans ages 3 years to adulthood, was used for many years. A revised edition of the Stanford–Binet remains one of the most widely used intelligence tests today.

The Wechsler–Bellevue Intelligence Scale and the Wechsler Adult Intelligence Scale

By the 1930s, thousands of psychological tests were available, and psychologists and others were debating the nature of intelligence (what intelligence was all about). This dispute over defining intelligence prompted the development in 1939 of the original Wechsler–Bellevue Intelligence Scale (WBIS) for adults, which provided an index of general mental ability (as did the Binet–Simon Scale) and revealed patterns of a person's intellectual strengths and weaknesses. David Wechsler, the chief psychologist at Bellevue Hospital in New York City, constructed the WBIS believing that intelligence is demonstrated based on an individual's ability to act purposefully, think logically, and interact/cope successfully with the environment (Hess, 2001; Rogers, 2001; Thorne & Henley, 2001). Wechsler published the second edition, the WBIS-II, in 1946.

More detail about the fourth edition of the WAIS-IV can be found in Test Spotlight 1.1 in Appendix A.

In 1955, Wechsler revised the WBIS-II and renamed it the Wechsler Adult Intelligence Scale (WAIS). In 1981 and 1991 the WAIS was updated and published as the WAIS-R and WAIS-III, respectively. In a continuing effort to improve the measurement of intelligence, as well as the clinical utility and user-friendliness of the test, the fourth edition was published in 2008 (Pearson Education, 2009).

Personality Tests

In addition to intelligence testing, the early 1900s brought about an interest in measuring personality.

The Personal Data Sheet

During World War I, the U.S. military wanted a test to help detect soldiers who would not be able to handle the stress associated with combat. To meet this need, the American Psychological Association (APA) commissioned an American psychologist, Robert Woodworth, to design such a test, which came to be known as the Personal Data Sheet (PDS). The PDS was a paper-and-pencil psychiatric interview that required military recruits to respond *yes* or *no* to a series of 200 questions (eventually reduced to 116 questions) that searched for mental disorders. The questions covered topics such as excessive anxiety, depression, abnormal fears, impulse problems, sleepwalking, nightmares, and memory problems (Segal & Coolidge, 2004). One question asked, "Are you troubled with the idea that people are watching you on the street?" (cited in Cohen, Swerdlik, & Phillips, 1996). During a pilot study of the test, new recruits on average showed 10 positive psychoneurotic symptoms; recruits who were deemed unfit for service generally showed 30 to 40 positive psychoneurotic symptoms (Segal & Coolidge, 2004). Unfortunately, because Woodworth did not complete the final design of this test until too late in the war, the PDS was never implemented or used to screen new recruits.

After World War I, Woodworth developed the Woodworth Psychoneurotic Inventory, a version of the PDS. Unlike the PDS, the Woodworth Psychoneurotic Inventory was designed for use with civilians and was the first self-report test. It was also the first widely used personality inventory.

The Rorschach Inkblot Test and the TAT

During the 1930s, interest also grew in measuring personality by exploring the unconscious. With this interest came the development of two important projective tests: the Rorschach Inkblot Test and the TAT. The Rorschach, a projective personality test (described further in Chapters 2 and 14), was developed by Swiss psychiatrist Hermann Rorschach. The TAT, also a projective personality test, was developed by two American psychologists, Henry A. Murray and C. D. Morgan. Both tests are based on the personality theories of Carl Jung and continue to be widely used today for personality assessment.

Vocational Tests

During the 1940s, a need developed for **vocational tests** to help predict how successful an applicant would be in specific occupations. The Public Employment Services needed such tests because thousands of people had lost their jobs due to the Great Depression and thousands more were coming out of school and seeking work. Because there were not enough jobs, people were forced to look for new lines of work. As a result, psychologists developed large-scale programs to design vocational aptitude tests that would predict how successful a person would be at an occupation before entering it. In 1947, the Department of Labor developed the General Aptitude Test Battery (GATB) to meet this need. The GATB was used for a variety of purposes, including vocational counseling and occupational selection.

By the mid-20th century, numerous tests were available and they were used by many to make important decisions about individuals. (We talk more about these decisions in Chapters 2 and 8.) Because of the increased use of psychological tests, to help protect the rights of the test taker, the APA (1953) published *Ethical Standards of Psychologists*. (We discuss these ethical standards in more detail in Chapter 3.)

Testing Today

In the 21st century, psychological testing is a big business. There are thousands of commercially available, standardized psychological tests as well as thousands of unpublished tests. Tests are published by hundreds of test publishing companies that market their tests very proactively—on the web and in catalogs. Before the turn of this century, these publishers were earning close to $200 million per year (Educational Testing Service, 1996), and approximately 20 million Americans per year were taking psychological tests (Hunt, 1993). For the names and web addresses of some of the most well-known test publishers, as well as some of the most popular tests they publish, see On the Web Box 1.1. Publishing and marketing companies are capitalizing on the testing trend, creating and marketing a bonanza of new products and study aids. To read about some of these products and study aids, see In the News Box 1.1.

Today, psychological testing is a part of the American culture. Psychological tests are in use everywhere. For example, let us take a look at Sylvan Learning Center (SLC), a provider of personal instructional services to children from kindergarten through 12th grade that has more than 1,100 centers worldwide. You might be familiar with SLC because of the test preparation programs they offer (for example, preparation for the SAT). However, did you know that much of SLC's business is focused on personalized programs to help children develop skills in areas such as reading, math, and writing? These personalized programs are created by administering and combining the results of standardized tests to capture a student's academic strengths and weaknesses and to identify skill gaps (Sylvan Learning, 2010). SLC uses identified skill gaps, often the reason for underperformance in school, to create a blueprint for an individual child's unique tutoring program. SLC also administers learning style inventories to help instructors understand how each child learns best. Trained and certified instructors integrate these learning styles into their tutoring sessions to promote individual student learning (SLC, 2010).

Now let us take a look at the Society for Human Resources Management (SHRM). As the world's largest association devoted to human resources management, SHRM provides human resources professionals with essential information and resources (SHRM, 2010a). One of these resources is an online testing center, which provides SHRM members who are qualified testing professionals with electronic access to more than 400 tests, from over 50 test publishers, in areas such as personality and skills assessment, coaching and leadership, mechanical and technical skills, information technology skills, pre-employment screening, and career exploration (SHRM, 2010b). The testing center allows qualified testing professionals to purchase individual tests, administer the tests online, and receive electronic reports.

ON THE WEB BOX 1.1

Names and Web Addresses of Test Publishers

Open your web browser, go to your favorite search engine, and conduct a search for "test publishers" or "psychological test publishers." You will find pages and pages of websites dedicated to psychological testing and publishing. You will also find the websites of hundreds of test publishers. Although there are many different publishers, some of the most well-known, including some of the widely known tests they publish, are listed here:

Publisher	Website	Popular Published Tests
Educational Testing Service	www.ets.org	• Advanced Placement (AP) Program Tests • Graduate Management Admission Test (GMAT) • Graduate Record Examinations (GRE) • Scholastic Assessment Test (SAT) • Test of English as a Foreign Language (TOEFL)
Pearson	www.pearsonassessments.com	• BarOn Emotional Quotient Inventory • Bayley Scales of Infant and Toddler Development—III • Bender Visual-Motor Gestalt Test—II • Watson–Glaser Critical Thinking Appraisal
Hogan Assessment Systems	www.hoganassessments.com	• Hogan Personality Inventory (HPI) • Hogan Development Survey (HDS) • Hogan Business Reasoning Inventory (HBRI) • Motives, Values, Preferences Inventory (MVPI)
IPAT	www.ipat.com	• 16 Personality Factors (16PF)
PAR	www3.parinc.com	• Self-Directed Search • NEO Personality Inventory • Personality Assessment Inventory • Slosson Intelligence Test—Revised for Children and Adults
Psytech International	www.psytech.co.uk	• Occupational Interest Profile • Clerical Test Battery • Values and Motives Inventory
PSI	www.psionline.com	• Customer Service Battery • Firefighter Selection Test • Police Selection Test
Hogrefe	www.testagency.com	• Rorschach Inkblot Test • Trauma Symptom Inventory (TSI) • WPQ Emotional Intelligence Questionnaire
University of Minnesota Press Test Division	www.upress.umn.edu/tests/default.html	• Minnesota Multiphasic Personality Inventory (MMPI)
Wonderlic	www.wonderlic.com	• Wonderlic Personnel Test

IN THE NEWS

Box 1.1   SAT Prep Tools: From Cellphones to Handhelds to CDs

Early in 2005, the College Board introduced thousands of high school juniors to the new SAT. No longer containing the much-dreaded analogy questions, the new SAT is longer and more difficult and, for the first time, contains a writing section (College Board, 2010). The writing section contains multiple-choice questions that assess how well test takers use standard written English language and a handwritten essay to assess how well they can develop a point of view on a topic.

Not wanting to miss an opportunity, publishers capitalized on the updated SAT by creating and marketing a number of new and innovative products—products promising to appeal to today's technology-savvy, music-hungry, multitasking teens. In 2005, *The Wall Street Journal* published an article introducing some of these unique products. In 2009, the products are still being marketed to students preparing to take the SAT.

Princeton Review: This company offers private instruction and tutoring for standardized achievement tests. In partnership with Cocel, Princeton Review has developed a new software program called Prep for the SAT, which beams SAT practice questions, including reading passages, to cell phones so that students can prepare for the SAT at their convenience. Answers are quickly graded, and parents can even receive electronic reports. In 2005, Princeton Review also released Pocket Prep, an interactive, portable, handheld SAT prep device designed to help 21st-century high school students prepare for the SAT using a format and technology that suits their lifestyles and preferences. Pocket Prep features information about the new SAT; comprehensive verbal, math, and essay preparation; full-length timed practice exams; instant scoring; and personal diagnostic reports. It also includes practice drills, flash cards, and an extensive verbal and essay reference suite to help students maximize their grammar and essay scores.

Kaplan: Another test preparation company, Kaplan has designed software for cell phones and handheld devices and is publishing books, such as *Frankenstein* and *Wuthering Heights,* that contain SAT vocabulary words in bold print as well as their definitions. An example of a sentence containing an SAT vocabulary word (*desolation*) might be "Mr. Heathcliff and I are such a suitable pair to divide the desolation between us."

SparkNotes: This Internet-based, youth-oriented education product (owned by Barnes & Noble) has published several Spuzzles books containing crossword puzzles in which the answers are commonly occurring SAT vocabulary words. For example, in U.S. History Spuzzle No. 56, the clue to 8 Across is "English Quaker who founded Pennsylvania in 1681."

Wiley Publishing: A well-known publisher of print and electronic products, Wiley has published a teen novel, *The Marino Mission: One Girl, One Mission, One Thousand Words,* that contains 1,000 need-to-know SAT vocabulary words. Not only are vocabulary words defined at the bottom of each page, but there also are self-tests at the end of the novel to help readers retain what they have learned.

Defined Mind—These independent recording artists, along with Kaplan, have produced *Vocabulary Accelerator,* a 12-track CD full of rock, folk-funk, and techno beats. What is unique is that the lyrics are studded with SAT vocabulary.

SOURCE: Kronhold, J. (2005, March 8). To tackle the new SAT, perhaps you need a new study device. *The Wall Street Journal.* Retrieved May 20, 2010, from http://www.tilcoweb.com/wallstreetjournal01.htm

One of the most significant and controversial uses of psychological testing in the 21st century has been a result of the No Child Left Behind Act of 2001 (NCLB Act). The NCLB Act, which President George W. Bush signed into law on January 8, 2002, was intended to improve the performance of America's primary and secondary schools. The NCLB Act contains the following four basic strategies for improving the performance of schools—strategies that were intended to change the culture of America's schools by defining a school's success in terms of the achievement of its students (U.S. Department of Education, 2004):

1. Increase the accountability that states, school districts, and schools have for educating America's children by requiring that all states implement statewide systems that (a) set challenging standards for what children in Grades 3 to 8 should know and learn in reading and math, (b) test students in Grades 3 to 8 on a yearly basis to determine the extent to which they know and have learned what they should have according to state standards, and (c) include annual statewide progress objectives to ensure that all students are proficient by the 12th grade.

2. Ensure that all children have access to a quality education by allowing parents to send their children to better schools if their schools do not meet state standards.

3. Increase the amount of flexibility that high-performing states and school districts have for spending federal education dollars.

4. Place more emphasis on developing children's reading skills by making grants available to states to administer screening and diagnostic assessments to identify children who may be at risk for reading failure and by providing teachers with professional development and resources to help young children attain the knowledge and skills they need to be readers.

Years after the implementation of the NCLB Act, there remains significant controversy, some of which focuses on the overreliance on test scores that may "distort teaching and learning in unproductive ways" (Center for Public Education, 2006, para. 6). While tests have always played a critical role in the assessment of student achievement, the NCLB Act requires that students be tested more often and relies on test scores to make more important decisions than in the past. In Chapter 13, we talk more about how one state, Florida, has responded to the NCLB Act, focusing primarily on the role that psychological tests have played in assessing the extent to which children and schools measure up to state standards.

The Defining Characteristics of Psychological Tests

As we have already discussed, a psychological test is anything that requires an individual to perform a behavior for the purpose of measuring some attribute, trait, or characteristic or to predict an outcome. All good psychological tests have three characteristics in common:

1. They representatively sample the behaviors thought to measure an attribute or thought to predict an outcome. For example, suppose we are interested in developing a test to measure your physical ability. One option would be to evaluate your performance in every sport you have ever played. Another option would be to have you run the 50-meter dash. Both of these options have drawbacks. The first option would be very precise, but not very practical. Can you imagine how much time and energy it would take to review how you performed in every sport you have ever played? The second option is too narrow and unrepresentative. How fast you run the 50-meter dash does not tell us much about your physical ability in general. A better method would be to take a representative sample of performance in sports. For example, we might require you to participate in some individual sports (for example, running, tennis, gymnastics) and team sports (for example, soccer, basketball) that involve different types of physical abilities (for example, strength, endurance, precision). This option would include a more representative sample.

2. All good psychological tests include behavior samples that are obtained under standardized conditions. That is, a test must be administered the same way to all people. When you take a test, various factors can affect your score besides the characteristic, attribute, or trait that is being measured. Factors related to the environment (for example, room temperature, lighting), the examiner (for example, examiner attitude, how the instructions are read), the examinee (for example, disease, fatigue), and the test (for example, understandability of questions) all can affect your score. If everyone is tested under the same conditions (for example, the same environment), we can be more confident that these factors will affect all test takers similarly. If all of these factors affect test takers similarly, we can be more certain that a person's test score accurately reflects the attribute being measured. Although it is possible for test developers to standardize factors related to the environment, the examiner, and the test, it is difficult to standardize examinee factors. For example, test developers have little control over what test takers do the night before they take a test.

3. All good psychological tests have rules for scoring. These rules ensure that all examiners will score the same set of responses in the same way. For example, teachers might award 1 point for each multiple-choice question you answer correctly, and they might award or deduct points based on what you include in your response to an essay question. Teachers might then report your overall exam score either as the number correct or as a percentage of the number correct (the number of correct answers divided by the total number of questions on the test).

Although all psychological tests have these characteristics, not all exhibit these characteristics to the same degree. For example, some tests may include a more representative sample of behavior than do others. Some tests, such as group-administered tests, may be more conducive to administration under standardized conditions than are individually administered tests. Some tests may have well-defined rules for scoring, and others might have general guidelines. Some tests may have very explicit scoring rules, for example, "If Question 1 is marked true, then deduct 2 points." Other tests, such as those that include short answers, may have less explicit rules for scoring, for example, "Award 1 point for each concept noted and defined."

INTERIM SUMMARY 1.2
THE THREE DEFINING CHARACTERISTICS OF PSYCHOLOGICAL TESTS

All psychological tests have three common characteristics:

- First, a good test should representatively sample the behaviors thought to measure an attribute or predict an outcome. This ensures that the test measures what it says it measures.
- Second, the behavior samples should be obtained under standardized conditions. That

is, a test must be administered exactly the same way to all individuals so that we can be confident that a person's score accurately reflects the attribute being measured or the outcome being predicted.

- Third, there must be rules for scoring so that all examiners will score the test in the same way.

Assumptions of Psychological Tests

There are many assumptions that must be made when using psychological tests. The following are what we consider the most important assumptions:

1. *Psychological tests measure what they purport to measure or predict what they are intended to predict.* In addition, any conclusions or inferences that are drawn about the test takers based on their test scores must be appropriate. This is also called test validity. If a test is designed to measure mechanical ability, we must assume that it does indeed measure mechanical ability. If a test is designed to predict performance on the job, then we must assume that it does indeed predict performance. This assumption must come from a personal review of the test's validity data.

2. *An individual's behavior, and therefore test scores, will typically remain stable over time.* This is also called test–retest reliability. If a test is administered at a specific point in time and then we administer it again at a different point in time (for example, two weeks later), we must assume, depending on what we are measuring, that an individual will receive a similar score at both points in time. If we are measuring a relatively stable trait, we should be much more concerned about this assumption. However, there are some traits, such as mood, that are not expected to show high test–retest reliability.

3. *Individuals understand test items similarly* (Wiggins, 1973). For example, when asked to respond *true* or *false* to a test item such as "I am almost always healthy," we must assume that all test takers interpret "almost always" similarly.

4. *Individuals will report accurately about themselves* (for example, about their personalities, about their likes and dislikes; Wiggins, 1973). When we ask people to remember something or to tell us how they feel about something, we must assume that they will remember accurately and that they have the ability to assess and report accurately on their thoughts and feelings. For example, if we ask you to tell us whether you agree or disagree with the statement "I have always

liked cats," you must remember not only how you feel about cats now but also how you felt about cats previously.

5. *Individuals will report their thoughts and feelings honestly* (Wiggins, 1973). Even if people are able to report correctly about themselves, they may choose not to do so. Sometimes people respond how they think the tester wants them to respond, or they lie so that the outcome benefits them. For example, if we ask test takers whether they have ever taken a vacation, they may tell us that they have even if they really have not. Why? Because we expect most individuals to occasionally take vacations, and therefore the test takers think we would expect most individuals to answer *yes* to this question. Criminals may respond to test questions in a way that makes them appear neurotic or psychotic so that they can claim they were insane when they committed crimes. When people report about themselves, we must assume that they will report their thoughts and feelings honestly, or we must build validity checks into the test.

6. *The test score an individual receives is equal to his or her true ability plus some error, and this error may be attributable to the test itself, the examiner, the examinee, or the environment.* That is, a test taker's score may reflect not only the attribute being measured but also things such as awkward question wording, errors in administration of the test, examinee fatigue, and the temperature of the room in which the test was taken. When evaluating an individual's score, we must assume that it will include some error.

Although we must accept some of these assumptions at face value, we can increase our confidence in others by following certain steps during test development. For example, in Section III of this textbook, which covers test construction, we talk about how to design test questions that are understood universally. We also talk about the techniques that are available to promote honest answering. In Section II, which covers psychometric principles, we discuss how to measure a test's reliability and validity.

Test Classification Methods

As we have already discussed, there are tens of thousands of commercially available psychological tests, and professionals refer to these tests in various ways. Sometimes professionals refer to them as tests of maximal performance, behavior observation tests, or self-report tests. Sometimes professionals refer to tests as being standardized or nonstandardized, objective or projective. Other times professionals refer to tests based on what the tests measure. In this section, we discuss the most common ways that professionals classify and refer to psychological tests.

Maximal Performance, Behavior Observation, or Self-Report

Most psychological tests can be defined as being tests of maximal performance, behavioral observation tests, or self-report tests.

- **Tests of maximal performance** require test takers to perform a particular well-defined task such as making a right-hand turn, arranging blocks from smallest to largest, tracing a pattern, or completing mathematical problems. Test takers try to do their best because their scores are determined by their success in completing the task. Intelligence tests, tests of specific abilities (for example, mechanical ability), driving tests (road and written), and classroom tests all are good examples of tests of maximal performance.

- **Behavior observation tests** involve observing people's behavior and how people typically respond in a particular context. Unlike with tests of maximal performance, many times people do not know that their behavior is being observed and there is no single defined task for the individual to perform. Many restaurants use this technique to assess food servers' competence in dealing with customers. Sometimes managers hire trained observers to visit their restaurant disguised as a typical customer. In exchange for a free meal or some predetermined compensation, observers agree to record specific behaviors performed by a food server. For example, observers may document whether a food server greeted them in a friendly manner. Other examples of behavior observations include documenting job performance for performance appraisals or clinical interviews.

- **Self-report tests** require test takers to report or describe their feelings, beliefs, opinions, or mental states. Many personality inventories, such as the Hogan Personality Inventory (HPI), are self-report tests. The HPI, a test used primarily for personnel selection and individualized assessment, asks test takers to indicate whether each of more than 200 statements about themselves is true or false.

Most psychological tests fit one of the above categories, and some tests contain features of more than one category. For example, a structured job interview (which involves asking all job applicants a standard set of interview questions) could include both technical questions and questions about one's beliefs or opinions. Technical questions, which are well defined for the interviewee, qualify the interview as a test of maximal performance. Questions about beliefs and opinions qualify it as a self-report test. The interviewer may also observe the interviewees' behaviors, such as their greetings, which would qualify the interview as a behavioral observation.

Standardized or Nonstandardized

Standardized tests are those that have been administered to a large group of individuals who are similar to the group for whom the test has been designed. For example, if a test is designed to measure the writing ability of high school students, the test would be administered to a large group of high school students. This group is called the **standardization sample**—people who are tested to obtain data to establish a frame of reference for interpreting individual test scores. These data, called **norms**, indicate the average performance of a group and the distribution of scores above and below this average.

For example, if you took the SAT, the interpretation of your score included comparing it with the SAT standardization sample to determine whether your score was high or low in comparison with others and whether you scored above average, average, or below average. In addition, standardized tests always have specific directions for administration and scoring.

Nonstandardized tests do not have standardization samples and are more common than standardized tests. Nonstandardized tests are usually constructed by a teacher or trainer in a less formal manner for a single administration. For example, in many cases, the exams you take in your college courses are nonstandardized tests.

Objective or Projective

Sometimes people make a distinction between objective and projective tests. **Objective tests** are structured and require test takers to respond to structured true/false questions, multiple-choice questions, or rating scales. What the test taker must do is clear, for example, answer *true* or *false,* circle the correct multiple-choice answer, or circle the correct item on the rating scale. The GRE, Stanford-Binet Intelligence Scales, General Aptitude Test Battery, and most classroom tests are examples of objective tests.

 More detail about the GRE can be found in Test Spotlight 13.1 in Appendix A. More detail about the Stanford–Binet Intelligence Scales can be found in Test Spotlight 1.2 in Appendix A.

Another example of an objective test is the NEO Personality Inventory, an objective self-report instrument designed to identify what makes individuals unique in their thinking, feeling, and interaction with others. Although there are two forms of the inventory, both measure five broad personality dimensions: neuroticism, extroversion, openness, agreeableness, and conscientiousness. Test takers are asked to indicate whether they strongly disagree, disagree, are neutral, agree, or strongly agree with each of 240 statements. These statements are about their thoughts, feelings, and goals. For sample questions from the NEO Personality Inventory, see For Your Information Box 1.2.

On the other hand, **projective tests** are unstructured. They require test takers to respond to unstructured or ambiguous stimuli such as incomplete sentences, inkblots, and abstract pictures. The role of the test taker is less clear than with a standardized test. People who use projective tests believe that test takers project themselves into the task they are asked to perform and that their responses are based on what they believe the stimuli mean and on the feelings they experience while responding. These tests tend to elicit highly personal concerns. They are often used to detect

 More detail about the NEO Personality Inventory can be found in Test Spotlight 1.3 in Appendix A.

unconscious thoughts or personality characteristics, and they may be used to identify the need for psychological counseling. The TAT is an example of a projective test. (Chapter 14 contains more information on the TAT and other projective tests.)

Dimension Measured

Psychological tests are often discussed in terms of the dimensions they measure. For example, sometimes we distinguish among achievement tests, aptitude tests, intelligence tests, personality tests, and interest inventories. We refer to these as dimensions because they are broader than a single attribute or trait level. Often these types of tests measure various personal attributes or traits.

Achievement Tests

Achievement tests measure a person's previous learning in a specific academic area (for example, computer programming, German, trigonometry, psychology). A test that requires you to list the three characteristics of psychological tests would be considered an achievement test. Achievement tests are also referred to as tests of knowledge.

Achievement tests are used primarily in educational settings to determine how much students have learned or what they can do at a particular point in time. Many elementary schools and high schools rely

FOR YOUR INFORMATION BOX 1.2

Sample Items From the NEO Personality Inventory

The NEO Personality Inventory is an objective self-report instrument designed to identify what makes individuals unique in their thinking, feeling, and interaction with others. The inventory measures five broad personality dimensions: neuroticism, extroversion, openness, agreeableness, and conscientiousness. Test takers are asked to indicate whether they strongly disagree (SD), disagree (D), are neutral (N), agree (A), or strongly agree (SA) with each of 240 statements. These statements are about their thoughts, feelings, and goals. In the following, we list a sample item from three of the five scales:

Neuroticism

| Frightening thoughts sometimes come into my head. | SD | D | N | A | SA |

Extroversion

| I don't get much pleasure from chatting with people. | SD | D | N | A | SA |

Openness

| I have a very active imagination. | SD | D | N | A | SA |

SOURCE: Reproduced by special permission of the publisher, Psychological Assessment Resources, Inc., 16204 North Florida Avenue, Lutz, Florida 33549, from the NEO Personality Inventory-Revised, by Paul T. Costa, Jr., PhD, and Robert R. McCrae, PhD, Copyright 1978, 1985, 1989, 1991, 1992 by Psychological Assessment Resources (PAR). Further reproduction is prohibited without permission from PAR.

on achievement tests to compare what students know at the beginning of the year with what they know at the end of the year, to assign grades, to identify students with special educational needs, and to measure students' progress.

Aptitude Tests

Achievement tests measure a test taker's knowledge in a specific area at a specific point in time. **Aptitude tests** assess a test taker's potential for learning or ability to perform in a new job or situation. Aptitude tests measure the product of cumulative life experiences—or what one has acquired over time. They help determine what "maximum" can be expected from a person.

Schools, businesses, and government agencies often use aptitude tests to predict how well someone will perform or to estimate the extent to which an individual will profit from a specified course of training. Vocational guidance counseling may involve aptitude testing to help clarify the test taker's career goals. If a person's score is similar to scores of others already working in a given occupation, the test will predict success in that field.

Intelligence Tests

Intelligence tests, like aptitude tests, assess the test taker's ability to cope with the environment, but at a broader level. Intelligence tests are often used to screen individuals for specific programs (for example, gifted programs, honors programs) or programs for the mentally challenged. Intelligence tests are typically used in educational and clinical settings.

Interest Inventories

Interest inventories assess a person's interests in educational programs for job settings and provide information for making career decisions. Because these tests are often used to predict satisfaction in a particular academic area or employment setting, they are administered primarily to students by counselors in high schools and colleges. Interest inventories are not intended to predict success; rather, they are intended only to offer a framework for narrowing career possibilities.

Personality Tests

Personality tests measure human character or disposition. The first personality tests were designed to assess and predict clinical disorders. These tests remain useful today for determining who needs counseling and who will benefit from treatment programs. Newer personality tests measure "normal" personality traits. For example, the Myers–Briggs Type Indicator (MBTI) is often used by industrial/organizational psychologists to increase employees' understanding of individual differences and to promote better communication between members of work teams. Career counselors also use the MBTI to help students select majors and careers consistent with their personalities.

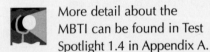

More detail about the MBTI can be found in Test Spotlight 1.4 in Appendix A.

Personality tests can be either objective or projective. The MBTI is an example of an objective personality test. Projective personality tests, such as the TAT, serve the same purpose as some objective personality tests, but they require test takers to respond to unstructured or ambiguous stimuli.

Subject Tests

Many popular psychological testing reference books also classify tests by subject. For example, the *Seventeenth Mental Measurements Yearbook* (Geisinger, Spies, Carlson, & Plake, 2007) classifies thousands of tests into 19 major subject categories:

- Achievement
- Behavior assessment
- Developmental
- Education
- English
- Fine arts
- Foreign languages
- Intelligence
- Mathematics
- Miscellaneous (for example, courtship and marriage, driving and safety education, etiquette)
- Multiaptitude batteries
- Neuropsychological
- Personality
- Reading
- Science
- Sensorimotor

- Social studies
- Speech and hearing
- Vocations

Reference books such as the *Mental Measurements Yearbook* often indicate whether a test is (a) a test of maximal performance, a behavior observation test, or a self-report test; (b) standardized or nonstandardized; and (c) objective or projective. We discuss the *Mental Measurements Yearbook,* as well as other reference books, later in this chapter.

INTERIM SUMMARY 1.3
ASSUMPTIONS AND TEST CLASSIFICATION METHODS

When using psychological tests, the following assumptions must be made:

- Psychological tests measure what they say they measure, and any inferences that are drawn about test takers based on their test scores are appropriate.
- An individual's behavior, and therefore test scores, will remain unchanged over time.
- Individuals understand test items similarly.
- Individuals can report about themselves accurately.
- Individuals will report their thoughts and feelings honestly.
- The test score an individual receives is equal to his or her true ability plus some error.

Psychological tests can be classified in many different ways:

- As tests of maximal performance, behavior observation tests, or self-report tests
- As standardized or nonstandardized
- As objective or projective
- Based on the dimensions they measure
- Based on subject

Psychological Assessment, Psychological Tests, Measurements, and Surveys

Before discussing much more, we should spend some time discussing some terms that students often confuse—psychological assessment, psychological tests, measurement, and surveys. Students often think of psychological assessment and psychological testing as one and the same. Similarly, students often do not understand the difference between psychological tests and surveys. This section is designed to help you distinguish among these terms that are commonly used in psychological testing.

Psychological Assessments and Psychological Tests

Psychological assessments and psychological tests both are methods of collecting important information about people, and both are also used to help understand and predict behavior (Kline, 2000, Maloney & Ward, 1976). Assessment, however, is a broader concept than psychological testing. **Psychological assessment** involves multiple methods, such as personal history interviews, behavioral observations, and psychological tests, for gathering information about an individual. Psychological assessment involves *both* an objective component and a subjective component (Matarazzo, 1990), and psychological tests are only one tool in the assessment process. For example, a clinical psychologist may conduct a psychological assessment of a patient and, as a part of this assessment, may administer a psychological test such as the MMPI.

Psychological Tests and Measurements

Although the meanings overlap, *psychological test* and *measurement* are not synonyms. **Measurement,** broadly defined, is the assignment of numbers according to specific rules. The concept of measurement is represented by the darker circle in Figure 1.2.

Psychological tests require test takers to answer questions or per- form tasks to measure personal attributes. The concept of a psycho- logical test is represented by the lighter circle in the figure. With psychological tests, test takers' answers to questions or their perfor- mance on some task is not initially expressed in physical units of any

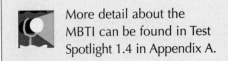

More detail about the MBTI can be found in Test Spotlight 1.4 in Appendix A.

kind; instead, scores are derived according to some predetermined method. In some cases, the end result of a psychological test is not a derived score at all, but rather a verbal description of an individual. For exam- ple, there are some personality tests that, although they have rules for scoring or summarizing information, do not produce overall scores. Instead, these tests yield profiles. The MBTI is an example of such a test.

Psychological tests can be considered psychological measurements when a sample of behavior can be expressed as a numerical score. This is represented by the overlapping section of the two circles in Figure 1.2.

You will find that many people use the terms *psychological test* and *psychological measurement* inter- changeably. Although most psychological tests are measurements, not all psychological tests, strictly defined, meet the definition of a measurement. Throughout the remainder of this text, we follow the common practice of referring to all psychological tests as measurements because most of them are, but keep in mind the distinctions we have drawn in this section.

Psychological Tests and Surveys

Surveys, like psychological tests (and psychological assessments), are used to collect important infor- mation from individuals. Surveys differ from psychological tests in two important ways. First, psychological tests focus on individual outcomes, and sur- veys focus on group outcomes. Psychological tests provide important information about individual differences and help individuals and institutions make important decisions about individuals. For example, a psycho- logical test may suggest that a child is unusually intelligent and therefore should be placed in a gifted or honors program. Surveys, on the other hand, provide impor- tant information about groups and help us make important decisions about groups. For example, an organizational survey may suggest that employees are displeased with a company benefits program and that a new benefits program is needed.

Figure 1.2	A Comparison of Measurement and Psychological Testing (the area of intersection represents samples of behavior expressed as numerical scores)

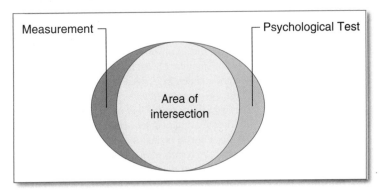

Second, the results of a psychological test are often reported in terms of an overall derived score or scaled scores. Results of surveys, on the other hand, are often reported at the question level by providing the percentage of respondents who selected each answer alternative. Of course, in some cases, surveys focus on individual outcomes and are constructed using scales. In such cases, the survey approximates a psychological test. (Chapter 10 is devoted to an in-depth discussion of surveys.)

Locating Information About Tests

With so many psychological tests available, we are sure you can imagine that finding the most appropriate one for your specific purpose can be a difficult task. To choose an appropriate test for a particular circumstance, you must know the types of tests that are available and their merits and limitations. Prior to the 1950s, test users had few resources for obtaining such information. Today, however, numerous resources are available. Although all have the same general purpose—to help test users make informed decisions—the information such resources contain varies. Some resources provide only general descriptive information about psychological tests, such as the test's name, author, and publisher, and others contain detailed information, including test reviews and detailed bibliographies. Some resources focus on commercially available, standardized published tests, and others focus on unpublished tests. Some references include information about tests for particular groups (for example, children), and others include a broad range of tests for various populations.

Some of the most commonly used resource books, including a brief synopsis of the contents as well as a library catalog number, are described in For Your Information Box 1.3. The first four resource books, the *Mental Measurements Yearbook* (*MMY*), *Tests in Print* (*TIP*), *Tests,* and *Test Critiques,* are often viewed as the most useful and popular (American Psychological Association, 2010b). Note that although different libraries may give a particular reference a different catalog number, the one we have supplied will direct you to the general area where you will find the book. If you cannot find a particular book, ask the librarian for assistance; your library might not carry the reference book, and the librarian can help you find the book at another location.

FYI

FOR YOUR INFORMATION BOX 1.3

Commonly Used Resource Books

Book Title	Contents	Reference Number
Tests in Print (multiple volumes)	*Tests in Print (TIP)* is published in multiple volumes. Each volume contains descriptive listings of commercially published psychology and achievement tests that are available for purchase. *TIP* also serves as a comprehensive index to the contents of previously published *Mental Measurements Yearbooks* (see below for a description of the *Mental Measurements Yearbook*). Each descriptive listing, or test entry, contains extensive information, including but not limited to the title of the test, the purpose of the test, the intended population, publication dates, the acronym used to identify the test, scores the test provides, whether the test is an individual test or group test, whether the test has a manual, the author(s), the publisher, the cost of the test, and available foreign adaptations. Each entry also contains brief comments about the test as well as cross-references to reviews in the *Mental Measurements Yearbooks*.	LB3051.T47

Book Title	Contents	Reference Number
Mental Measurements Yearbook (multiple volumes)	The *Mental Measurements Yearbook (MMY)* is published in multiple volumes. Each volume contains descriptive information and test reviews of new English-language, commercially published tests and tests that have been revised since the publication of the previous *MMY* edition. The *MMY* is cumulative, meaning that later volumes build on earlier ones rather than replace them. Each descriptive listing, or test entry, contains extensive information about a particular test. If the test is a revision of a previous test, the entry also includes the volume of the *MMY* in which the test was originally described. Each entry also typically includes information about the test's reliability and validity, one or two professional reviews, and a list of references to pertinent literature. For a guide to descriptive entries in the *MMY*, see Figure 1.3. The *MMY* is very likely accessible electronically through your college's library system.	LB3051.M4
Tests	*Tests* contains descriptions of a broad range of tests for use by psychologists, educators, and human resource professionals. Each entry includes the test title, the author, the publisher, the intended population, the test purpose, major features, the administration time, the cost, and the availability.	BF176.T43
Test Critiques (multiple volumes)	*Test Critiques* is published in multiple volumes. Each volume contains reviews of frequently used psychological, business, and educational tests. Each review includes descriptive information about the test (for example, author, attribute measured, norms) and information on practical applications and uses. *Test Critiques* also contains in-depth information on reliability, validity, and test construction.	BF176.T419
Personality Test and Reviews (multiple volumes)	*Personality Test and Reviews* is published in volumes. Each volume contains a bibliography of personality tests that are contained in the *MMY*. Each entry contains descriptive information about the test as well as test reviews.	BF698.5B87
Tests in Education	*Tests in Education* contains descriptive and detailed information about educational tests for use by teachers, administrators, and educational advisers.	LB3056.G7.L49
Measures for Psychological Assessment	*Measures for Psychological Assessment* contains annotated references to journal articles and other publications in which measures of primarily mental health are described.	BF698.5C45
Testing Children	*Testing Children* contains descriptions of tests available for children. These descriptions include the knowledge, skills, and abilities measured by each test; the content and structure of the test; the time required to administer the test; the scores that are produced; the cost; and the publisher.	BF722.T47
Test and Measurements in Child Development: A Handbook	*Tests and Measurements in Child Development* contains a listing of unpublished measures for use with children as well as detailed information about each measure.	BF722.J64
Measures for Psychological Assessment: A Guide to 3,000 Original Sources and Their Applications	*Measures for Psychological Assessment* is a guide that contains annotated references to thousands of less recognized assessment devices developed and described in journal articles.	155.28016.C559

Whether you are trying to locate tests that measure intelligence, self-esteem, or some other attribute, trait, or characteristic, we suggest that you begin your search with one of the first four resource books in For Your Information Box 1.3. *TIP* and the *MMY* are two of the most helpful references, and students often find it most helpful to begin with *TIP*. Figure 1.3 includes a descriptive guide of the type of information you will find in the *MMY*. Figure 1.4 includes a summary of how to use *TIP* to find tests. You can find more information on how to use both of these resources, as well as how to use the information contained in these resources to evaluate a test, on the Buros homepage discussed in On the Web Box 1.2.

Figure 1.3   A Guide to Descriptive Entries in the *Mental Measurements Yearbook*

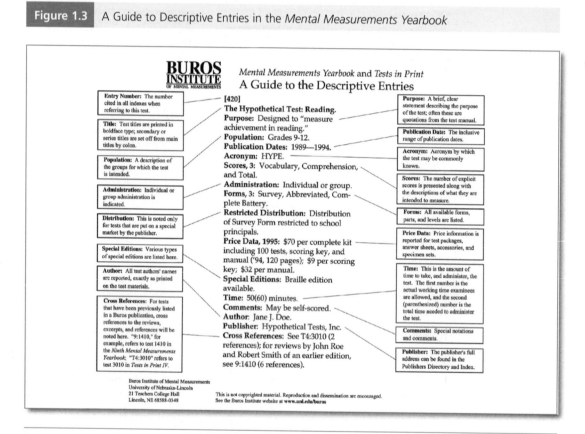

SOURCE: Buros Institute of Mental Measurements, University of Nebraska-Lincoln. www.unl.edu/buros

Because there is a wealth of psychological tests available, there is a wealth of resources available for you to use in gathering information about psychological tests. You are not limited to print resources; advances in technology now allow you to access the Internet and gather information about psychological tests on demand. On the Web Box 1.2 discusses some websites you can access to locate information on psychological tests. For Your Information Box 1.4 discusses where you can locate unpublished psychological tests.

Figure 1.4   How to Use *Tests in Print*

BUROS INSTITUTE OF MENTAL MEASUREMENTS

How to Use
Tests in Print

Tests in Print (TIP) *consists of descriptive listings, without reviews, of commercially published tests in print.* TIP *is also a comprehensive index to the contents of previously published* Mental Measurements Yearbooks.

1. If you know the TEST TITLE:

Use the "**Index of Titles.**" The index lists all tests in that volume plus all tests out of print since last being listed. "2458," for example, refers to test 2458 in that volume; "9:1128" refers to now out-of-print test 1128 in the *Ninth Mental Measurements Yearbook. Citation numbers refer to entry numbers, not to page numbers.*

Example from "Index of Titles":

> Short Tests of Clerical Ability, 2458
> Shortened Edinburgh Reading Test, 2459
> Shortened Aptitude Test, T4:2195
> Signals Learning Test, 2461
> Silver Burdett Music Competency Tests, 9:1128
> Silver Drawing Test of Cognitive Skills and Adjustment, 2462
> Simile Interpretations, T4:2198
> Similes, T4:2199

2. If you know the TYPE OF TEST:

Use the "**Classified Subject Index**" to locate various categories of tests, such as achievement, intelligence, personality, etc. This index organizes all tests into 18 major categories; tests appear alphabetically within each category. *Citation numbers refer to entry numbers, not to page numbers.*

Example from "Classified Subject Index, Education":

> Gifted Program Evaluation Survey, Gifted and talented programs, see 1040
> Graduate Records Examinations Education Test, Graduate School candidates, see 1063
> High School Characteristics Index, Grades 9-13, 4-13, see 1157
> How a Child Learns, Classroom teachers, see 1175
> Hudson Educational Skills Inventory, Grades K-12, see 1184

3. If you know the NAME OF THE TEST AUTHOR OR REVIEWER:

Use the "**Index of Names.**" This index includes test authors (for example, "test, 1460"), review authors ("rev, 2589"), and authors of referenced articles ("ref, 2222"). (Parenthesized numbers indicate the reference number.) *Citation numbers refer to entry numbers, not to page numbers.*

Example from "Index of Names":

> Caeglio, G.: test, 1460
> Caffey, C. A.: ref, 2222(1)
> Caggiula, A. A.: ref, 2563(449)
> Cahalane, J.: ref, 268(395), 1043(39)
> Cahen, L. S.: rev, 2589
> Cahill, C.: ref, 1705(65), 2937(935)
> Cahir, N.: ref, 1135(14), 2674(188)
> Cahn, T. S.: ref, 268(90)
> Cain, J.: ref, 93(84), 1690(84)
> Cain, L. F.: test, 2844

Buros Institute of Mental Measurements
University of Nebraska-Lincoln
21 Teachers College Hall
Lincoln, NE 68588-0348

This is not copyrighted material. Reproduction and dissemination are encouraged.
See the Buros Institute website at **www.unl.edu/buros**

SOURCE: Buros Institute of Mental Measurements, University of Nebraska-Lincoln. www.unl.edu/buros

---

ON THE WEB BOX 1.2

Locating Information About Tests on the Web

Computer technology lets us connect to the World Wide Web and locate websites containing valuable information about psychological tests. These websites include information such as the following:

- Frequently asked questions about psychological testing
- How to find a particular type of psychological test
- How to locate reviews of psychological tests
- How to select an appropriate test
- What qualifications are necessary to purchase psychological tests
- How to contact test publishers
- How to obtain copies of specific psychological tests

Although there are many available websites, here are four that we have found to be extremely valuable:

(Continued)

(Continued)

Website	Description
American Psychological Association www.apa.org/science /programs/testing/find -tests.aspx#findinfo	Although the American Psychological Association (APA) does not sell or endorse specific testing instruments, it does provide guidance on testing resources and how to find psychological tests. This website contains answers to the most frequently asked questions about psychological testing. One section focuses on questions about published psychological tests (those that can be purchased from a test publisher); here you will find advice on how to find information about a particular test and about the proper use of tests, how to contact test publishers and purchase tests, and available software and scoring services. Another section focuses on unpublished psychological tests and measures (those that are not commercially available); here you will find advice on how to find unpublished tests in your area of interest and important information regarding your responsibilities as a user of unpublished tests.
Buros Institute of Mental Measurement www.unl.edu/buros/ bimm/index.html	The Buros Institute of Mental Measurement promotes the appropriate use of tests and provides professional assistance, expertise, and information to those who use commercially published tests. This website contains a number of instructional resources, tools, and links. For example, it contains detailed instructions on what information can be found in two popular Buros publications that we have already discussed: the *Mental Measurements Yearbook* and *Tests in Print.* This site also contains some great "how to" resources such as how to use *Tests in Print* and the *Mental Measurements Yearbook* and how to use the information in these resources to evaluate a test. In addition, it contains a link to *Test Reviews Online,* a service that provides access to more than 2,000 test reviews, beginning with those that are published in the *Ninth Mental Measurements Yearbook.* Likewise, there are links to the *Code of Fair Testing Practices* (discussed further in Chapter 3) and the APA's frequently asked questions website mentioned previously.
Educational Testing Service Test Link www.ets.org/testcoll/	Educational Testing Service Test Link is the world's largest database of tests and measurement instruments that have been available since the early 1900s. This online database contains descriptions of more than 20,000 tests (published and unpublished) and research instruments, collected from test publishers and test authors from around the world. Each description includes the title of the test/instrument, the author, the publication date, availability (how to obtain the test or measurement), the intended population, and specific uses of the test/instrument. In addition to providing information about specific tests, this database contains valuable information on how to order tests.
O-Net Resource Center www.onetcenter.org/ guides.html	The Occupational Information Network (O-Net) is sponsored by the U.S. Department of Labor and is a primary source for occupational information. Consisting of a comprehensive database of worker attributes and job characteristics, O-Net also provides valuable resources on testing and assessment—resources intended to support public and private sector efforts to identify and develop the skills of the American workforce. This website provides access to three extremely valuable testing and assessment guides: • *Testing and Assessment: A Guide to Good Practices for Workforce Investment Professionals* includes information on how assessment instruments can be used to promote talent development in career counseling, training, and other talent development activities. It discusses how to evaluate and select assessment instruments, administer and score assessments to meet business and individual client needs, and accurately and effectively interpret assessment results. It also lists the professional and legal standards related to assessment use in talent development. • *Tests and Other Assessments: Helping You Make Better Career Decisions* includes an explanation of how assessment instruments are used in employment selection and career counseling and provides tips and strategies for taking tests and other assessments. • *Testing and Assessment: An Employer's Guide to Good Practices* helps managers and workforce development professionals understand and use employment testing and assessment practices to meet their organizations' human resources goals.

FOR YOUR INFORMATION BOX 1.4

Locating Unpublished Psychological Tests

Although there are thousands of commercially available tests, there are just as many, if not more, unpublished tests designed and used by researchers. A number of print and nonprint resources are available for locating information on unpublished tests.

Two of the most popular print resources are the *Directory of Unpublished Experimental Measures* and *Measures for Psychological Assessment: A Guide to 3,000 Original Sources and Their Applications*. Three of the most popular nonprint resources for locating information about unpublished or noncommercial tests are Tests in Microfiche, the PsycINFO database, and the Health and Psychosocial Instruments database.

Directory of Unpublished Experimental Measures (Goldman, Mitchell, & Egelson, 1997)

This directory provides easy access to more than 5,000 experimental mental measures, tests, and surveys that have been used by other researchers but are not commercially available. Topics range from educational adjustment and motivation to personality and perception. The measures, tests, and surveys are arranged in a 24-category system and grouped according to function and content, noting purpose, format, psychometric information (where available), and related research. First published in 1974 and currently in its seventh edition, this resource is updated periodically by the publisher.

Measures for Psychological Assessment: A Guide to 3,000 Original Sources and Their Applications (Chun, Cobb, & French, 1975)

This guide includes annotated references to psychological measures that have appeared in journal articles and other publications. Although a bit outdated, this can be a useful resource. It has two sections: primary references and applications. The primary references section includes the name of each measure, the reference in which the measure originally appeared, and one or more other researchers who have used the measure in experimental research. The applications section includes other research studies that have used the original measures and references other experimental tests.

Tests in Microfiche

This resource can be accessed through the Educational Testing Service Test Link. It contains a variety of educational and psychological instruments that are cited in the literature but are either out of date or unpublished. It contains more than 1,000 tests, and new tests are added each year. For more information, go to www.ets.org/testcoll or check with your college's library.

PsycINFO Database

This bibliographic database indexes published studies in psychology. By using the Form/Content field "Tests & Measures" to search the PsycINFO database, you can find tests that have been used in research and written about in the literature. For more information, go to www.apa.org/pubs/databases/psycinfo/index.aspx.

Health and Psychosocial Instruments Database (HAPI)

This computerized database includes citations to unpublished health and psychosocial evaluation and measurement tools (for example, questionnaires, interviews, tests, checklists, rating scales) that have appeared in journals and technical reports since 1985. HAPI is updated quarterly and contains more than 15,000 measurement instruments. HAPI is provided online by Ovid Technologies, which typically must be accessed through BRS Information Technologies at your college's library. Some libraries maintain the database on CD-ROM. For more information, see www.ovid.com/site/catalog/DataBase/866.jsp

Chapter Summary

By now, we hope you understand that psychological testing extends well beyond the use of intelligence and personality tests. Anything that requires a test taker to perform a behavior that is used to measure some personal attribute, trait, or characteristic or to predict an outcome can be considered a psychological test. The quizzes and exams you take in class are psychological tests. The written and road portions of driving exams are psychological tests. Even the structured job interviews you have participated in, or will participate in as you conduct your job search, qualify as psychological tests.

Psychological tests have various similarities and many differences. All psychological tests require an individual to perform one or more behaviors, and these behaviors are used to measure some personal attribute, trait, or characteristic thought to be important in describing or understanding behavior or to predict an outcome. However, psychological tests can and do differ in terms of the behaviors they require individuals to perform, the attributes they measure, their content, how they are administered and formatted, how they are scored and interpreted, and their psychometric quality.

Although the use of psychological tests can be traced to ancient China, most scholars agree that the advent of formal psychological testing did not begin until Binet published the first test of intelligence in 1905. Today, psychological testing is a big business, with tens of thousands of commercially available, standardized psychological tests as well as thousands of unpublished tests.

All good tests have three defining characteristics in common. First, they include a representative sample of behaviors. Second, they collect the sample under standardized conditions. Third, they have rules for scoring. When using psychological tests, we must make some assumptions. We must assume that a test measures what it says it measures, that any inferences that are drawn about test takers from their scores on the test are appropriate, that an individual's behavior (and therefore test scores) will remain stable over time, that individuals understand test items similarly, that individuals can and will report accurately about their thoughts and feelings, and that the test score an individual receives is equal to his or her true behavior/ability in the real world plus some error.

Testing professionals refer to psychological tests in various ways. Sometimes they refer to them as tests of maximal performance, behavior observations, or self-reports. Sometimes they refer to them as standardized or nonstandardized. Other times they refer to them as objective or projective. Professionals also refer to tests based on the dimensions they measure.

It is important to remember the distinctions among four commonly misunderstood terms: *psychological assessment, psychological test, measurement,* and *survey.* First, although both psychological assessments and psychological tests are used to gather information, a psychological test is only one of many tools in the psychological assessment process. Second, a psychological test can be considered to be a measurement when the sampled behavior can be expressed in a derived score. Third, psychological tests are different from surveys in that psychological tests focus on individual differences and often report one overall derived score (or scaled scores), and surveys focus on group similarities and typically report results at the question or item level.

Last, but not least, a number of resources are available, in print and online, to locate information about published and unpublished psychological tests and measures. The *Mental Measurements Yearbook* and *Tests in Print* are two of the most popular references for learning more about available tests.

Engaging in the Learning Process

KEY CONCEPTS

After completing your study of this chapter, you should be able to define each of the following terms. These terms are bolded in the text of this chapter and defined in the Glossary.

- achievement tests
- aptitude tests
- behavior
- behavior observation tests
- emotional intelligence
- intelligence tests
- interest inventories
- measurement
- nonstandardized tests
- norms
- objective tests
- personality tests
- projective tests
- psychological assessments
- psychological tests
- psychometrics
- self-report tests
- standardization sample
- standardized tests
- surveys
- tests of maximal performance
- vocational tests

LEARNING ACTIVITIES

The following are some learning activities you can engage in to support the learning objectives for this chapter.

Learning Objectives	Study Tips and Learning Activities
After completing your study of this chapter, you should be able to do the following:	*The following study tips will help you meet these learning objectives:*
Define what a psychological test is, and understand that psychological tests extend beyond personality and intelligence tests.	• Write your definition of a psychological test. List examples of psychological tests, from what comes to your mind first to what comes to your mind last. Compare your list of examples with Figure 1.1. • Ask various professionals, in and outside of the psychology field, to define what a psychological test is. Compare and contrast their definitions. Compare these definitions with the definitions provided in this textbook. Discuss why definitions might vary.
Trace the history of psychological testing from Alfred Binet and intelligence testing to the tests of today.	• Reflect on the history of testing. Create a timeline showing significant events in testing, beginning with testing in ancient China and ending with testing today.
Describe the ways in which psychological tests can be similar to and different from one another.	• Think about two exams you recently took. Make two lists: one of how they were similar and another of how they were different. Compare your lists with Interim Summary 1.1.
Describe the three characteristics that are common to all psychological tests, and understand that psychological tests can demonstrate these characteristics to various degrees.	• Recall the three characteristics common to all psychological tests. Make three columns, and label them Representative Sample of Behaviors, Standardized Conditions, and Rules for Scoring. Select one or two psychological tests that you have taken. Write how the test(s) demonstrate(s) each characteristic.

(Continued)

(Continued)

Learning Objectives	Study Tips and Learning Activities
	• Construct an eight-question quiz, with one question for each learning objective. Give the quiz to your classmates (your professor will determine the logistics of this). As a class, discuss whether the quiz meets all of the characteristics of a psychological test. What were the strengths of your quiz? How could your quiz have been improved?
Describe the assumptions we must make when using psychological tests.	• Describe the six assumptions we must make when using psychological tests. Without looking in your book, see how many assumptions you can write. Compare your written assumptions with the assumptions in the book. Explain why we must make these assumptions.
Describe the ways that psychological tests can be classified.	• Review the test classification methods in your book. Think about the road portion of the driving test, the SAT, a job interview, the NEO Personality Inventory, and a multiple-choice test you took recently. Classify each test using the different test classification methods.
Describe the differences among four commonly used terms that students often get confused: psychological assessment, psychological tests, measurement, and surveys.	• Draw a picture or diagram illustrating how these four commonly confused terms overlap.
Identify and locate printed and online resources that are available for locating information about psychological tests.	• Go to your college library and find *Tests in Print* and the *Mental Measurements Yearbook*. Write the names of three tests and what they measure. • Go to each of the websites referenced in your book. Compare and contrast the information found on these websites. • Select a psychological test that is mentioned in Chapter 1 or 2 or that is suggested by your instructor. Using reference books available at your college library and online, collect as much of the information as possible about your test. Keep track of where you found the information.

PRACTICE QUESTIONS

The following are some practice questions to assess your understanding of the material presented in this chapter.

Multiple Choice

Choose the one best answer to each question.

1. What do all psychological tests require that you do?
   a. Answer questions
   b. Fill out a form
   c. Perform a behavior
   d. Sign a consent form

2. According to the textbook, which one of the following is least typical of psychological tests?
   a. Personality tests
   b. Intelligence tests
   c. Structured interviews
   d. Classroom tests

3. Who published the first
   test of intelligence in 1905?
   a. Lewis Binet
   b. Alfred Simon
   c. Robert Woodworth
   d. Alfred Binet

4. Who published the Stanford–Binet?
   a. Henry Murray
   b. Robert Woodworth
   c. Lewis Terman
   d. Alfred Binet

5. What test did Robert Woodworth
   develop during World War I to help
   the U.S. military detect soldiers
   who would not be able to handle
   the stress associated with combat?
   a. Thematic Apperception Test
   b. Stanford–Binet
   c. Personal Data Sheet
   d. Rorschach Inkblot Test

6. What was the first widely used personality
   inventory?
   a. Woodworth Psychoneurotic Inventory
   b. Personal Data Sheet
   c. Rorschach Inkblot Test
   d. Thematic Apperception Test

7. A test that requires you to demonstrate your
   driving ability can best be classified as what
   type of test?
   a. Test of maximal performance
   b. Self-report test
   c. Behavior observation test
   d. Projective test

8. A test that requires you to
   respond to test questions about
   your feelings and beliefs can best be described
   as what type of test?
   a. Test of maximal performance
   b. Self-report test
   c. Behavior observation test
   d. Projective test

9. The role of the test taker is least clear in which
   one of the following?
   a. Objective tests
   b. Projective tests
   c. Standardized tests
   d. Self-report tests

10. What type of test is
    administered to a large
    group of individuals who
    are similar to the group for
    which the test has been designed?
    a. Nonstandardized test
    b. Standardized test
    c. Objective test
    d. Subjective test

11. What type of test would a classroom
    teacher most likely administer?
    a. Achievement test
    b. Aptitude test
    c. Intelligence test
    d. Interest inventory

12. What type of test assesses test
    takers' potential for learning or
    ability to perform in an area in
    which they have not been
    specifically trained?
    a. Achievement test
    b. Intelligence test
    c. Aptitude test
    d. Vocational test

13. What type of test requires
    test takers to respond to
    structured true/false questions,
    multiple-choice questions,
    and/or rating scales?
    a. Projective test
    b. Nonstandardized test
    c. Subjective test
    d. Objective test

14. What type of test would a
    career development counselor
    most likely administer?
    a. Achievement test
    b. Aptitude test
    c. Intelligence test
    d. Interest inventory

15. Which one of the following
    would be the best source for locating
    a professional test review for a
    commercially available published test?
    a. *Tests in Print*
    b. *Tests in Microfiche*
    c. *Mental Measurements Yearbook*
    d. *Measures for Psychological Assessment*

Short Answer/Essay

Read each of the following, and consider your response carefully based on the information presented in this chapter. Write your answer to each question in two or three paragraphs.

1. What is a psychological test?
2. Why should you care about psychological tests?
3. What three characteristics do all psychological tests have in common? Explain and provide an example of each.
4. Summarize the ways in which psychological tests can be similar to and different from one another.
5. When using a psychological test, what assumptions must be made? Why are these assumptions important?
6. What are the similarities and differences among intelligence tests, aptitude tests, and achievement tests? Provide an example of each.
7. How are psychological assessments, psychological tests, and measurement similar? How are they different?
8. How are psychological tests and surveys similar? How are psychological tests and surveys different?

ANSWER KEYS

Multiple Choice

1. c	2. c	3. d	4. c	5. c
6. a	7. a	8. b	9. b	10. b
11. a	12. c	13. d	14. d	15. c

Short Answer/Essay

Refer to your textbook for answers. If you are unsure of an answer and cannot generate the answer after reviewing your book, ask your professor for clarification.

CHAPTER 2

Why Is Psychological Testing Important?

"I have a 4.0 grade point average, but I didn't do so well on the LSAT. I'm going to apply to some top-rated law schools and, to be safe, to some law schools where LSAT scores aren't as important."

"The college I will be attending decided not to give me the scholarship I wanted. Because all the applicants had similar grade point averages and great letters of recommendation, the scholarship review committee decided to give the scholarship to the applicant who had the highest SAT score."

"I told my academic counselor that I did not know what I wanted to do with my life. She sent me to the college career services office. A career counselor talked with me for a long time, asking me about my likes and dislikes and my hobbies. She had me take several interest and vocational tests, and she used test scores to help me focus on what I should major in."

You have probably had to make some important decisions in your life, such as where to apply to college and what to major in. Likewise, others have probably made important decisions about you. For example, colleges may have decided to admit you, scholarship committees may have decided not to offer you a scholarship, organizations may have decided to hire you, or psychologists may have decided to place you in a gifted program. There is a good chance that psychological tests helped make most of these decisions.

In this chapter, we discuss why psychological testing is important. We look at who uses psychological tests and for what reasons. We also discuss some of the concerns society has about the use of psychological tests.

The Importance of Psychological Testing

As you learned in Chapter 1, psychological testing is important because people use test results to make important decisions such as those just mentioned. These decisions affect every one of us. Consider some of the decisions we (the authors) have made in our roles as professors, industrial/organizational practitioners, and managers using test scores:

- What grade to assign a student
- Whether to consider a job candidate for employment
- Whether to hire a job candidate
- Whether an employee will receive a merit increase (and if so, how much)
- What coaching advice to offer a business leader

Likewise, consider some of the decisions that have been made by others, about us or our families, based on the results of psychological tests:

- Whether we, or our children, will be admitted to a specific college
- Whether our children will be invited to participate in the elementary school gifted program
- Whether our children will receive a Florida high school diploma or a certificate of completion
- Whether our children will receive a Bright Futures College Scholarship

The fact is that many types of decisions are made using the results of psychological tests. These decisions are often classified as individual versus institutional and comparative versus absolute.

Individual and Institutional Decisions

Both individuals and institutions use the results of psychological tests to make decisions. If test takers use their test scores to make decisions about themselves, these are referred to as **individual decisions.** For example, in the future you may take the Law School Admissions Test (LSAT), a half-day standardized test required for admission to most law schools. Knowing that some law schools are more competitive than others, the score that you receive on this test might influence the law schools to which you apply. If you do very well on the test, you may apply to more competitive law schools. Or perhaps you are having a difficult time deciding what career you would like to pursue. You might seek assistance from a career counselor to explore and discuss various career options. As part of the process, the career counselor may ask you to complete an interest inventory. Based on the results of this inventory (as well as other information), you may decide to pursue a career in, for example, teaching or computer science. In this case, you (the individual who took the test) used the test results to make a decision about your career.

Institutional decisions, on the other hand, are those made by another entity (for example, a company, an organization, an institution) about an individual based on his or her test results. For example, let us say that because you did well on your LSAT, you decided to apply to a highly competitive law school. Administrators at the law school to which you apply will use your LSAT score, among other things, to help them make a decision about whether you will be offered admission to their law school. Likewise, let us say that an acquaintance of yours is attending counseling sessions with a mental health professional. As part of these counseling sessions, the mental health professional may administer a number of psychological tests and use the results to develop a treatment program for your acquaintance. In each of these cases, someone else—usually representing an institution—has used the results of a psychological test to make a decision about another individual.

Comparative and Absolute Decisions

When institutions use test scores to make decisions about those who took a test, they do so using either a comparative method or an absolute method. **Comparative decisions** are made by comparing the test scores of a number of people to see who has the best score. For example, imagine you applied to and were accepted into the law school of your choice. Now imagine that the law school is going to offer an academic scholarship to only one individual who was offered admission. Based on interviews and letters of recommendation, you advance as one of four finalists for the scholarship. Who will get the scholarship comes down to LSAT scores. Because you scored higher than the other three finalists, you receive the scholarship. This is a comparative decision because all of the finalists' LSAT scores were compared and the individual with the highest score was selected. Or perhaps you applied for a job at an organization where psychological tests were used as part of the selection process. If, after you took these tests, the organization decided to continue to consider your application because you scored better than 75% of the other applicants, the organization would be using the test results to make decisions using a comparative method.

Absolute decisions, on the other hand, are made by others (institutions) by looking at who has the minimum score needed to qualify. For example, let us consider the same scholarship example, with you advancing as one of four finalists for the scholarship. However, this time the school offers the scholarship to any finalist who has a score of at least 160 (where the minimum score is 120 and the maximum score is 180). Or suppose the organization to which you applied for a job called and informed you that the managers would like you to come in for an interview because you scored at least a 50 on one of the tests. In each of these cases, the institution made a decision about you not by comparing your score with the scores of other test takers but rather by basing their decision on some minimum score.

Who Uses Psychological Tests and for What Reasons?

Psychological tests are used by a variety of professionals for many different purposes in a number of different settings. Psychiatrists, psychologists, social workers, mental health counselors, career counselors, human resources directors, administrators, and many other professionals all use psychological tests. As you can see from Table 2.1, they use psychological tests in three primary settings: educational,

Table 2.1	Who Uses Psychological Tests and for What Purposes	
Educational Settings		
Who	*Where*	*Why*
Administrators Teachers School psychologists Career counselors	Primary schools Secondary schools Colleges Universities	To select students into schools To award scholarships To place students in programs To measure student learning To identify problems To identify career interests
Clinical Settings		
Who	*Where*	*Why*
Clinical psychologists Psychiatrists Social workers Counseling psychologists Licensed professional counselors Marriage and family counselors	Mental health clinics Residential programs Private practices	To diagnose disorders To plan treatment programs To assess treatment outcomes To counsel and advise
Organizational Settings		
Who	*Where*	*Why*
Human resources professionals Industrial/organizational consultants	Organizations Consulting practices	To make hiring decisions To determine training needs To evaluate employee performance

clinical, and organizational. We have devoted Chapters 13 to 15 to discussing how tests are used in these settings, and here we provide an overview to help you understand the importance of testing.

Educational Settings

Administrators, teachers, school psychologists, and career counselors in primary schools (elementary school), secondary schools (middle school and high school), and colleges and universities all use psychological tests. For example, in colleges and universities, administrators (for example, admissions officers, deans of admissions) use the results of tests such as the SAT to help make admissions decisions and award scholarships. Originally developed in 1926 by Carl Campbell Brigham for the College Examination Board, today the SAT is the most widely used standardized college admission test. It measures the critical thinking skills students are believed to need for academic success in college.

 More detail about the SAT can be found in Test Spotlight 2.1 in Appendix A.

In primary and secondary schools, teachers administer tests to measure student learning and assign course grades. The same is true for faculty at colleges and universities. In primary and secondary schools, school psychologists use the results of tests to determine eligibility for gifted programs and to identify developmental,

ON THE WEB BOX 2.1

Self-Directed Search

www.self-directed-search.com

 Developed by John Holland, the Self-Directed Search (SDS) is an interest inventory based on the theory that most people and organizations can be classified into six types: realistic, investigative, artistic, social, enterprising, and conventional (Reardon, 2001):

- *Realistic*: The **realistic (R) individual** generally likes to work with things more than with people. The R type is described as conforming, frank, genuine, hardheaded, honest, humble, materialistic, modest, natural, normal, persistent, practical, shy, and thrifty. Realistic people like realistic careers such as auto mechanic, air traffic controller, surveyor, electrician, and farmer. The R type usually has mechanical and athletic abilities and likes to work outdoors and with tools and machines.
- *Investigative*: The **investigative(I) individual** generally likes to explore and understand things or events rather than to persuade others or sell them things. The I type is described as analytical, cautious, complex, critical, curious, independent, intellectual, introverted, methodical, modest, pessimistic, precise, rational, and reserved. I people like investigative careers such as biologist, chemist, physicist, geologist, anthropologist, laboratory assistant, and medical technician. The I type usually has math and science abilities and likes to work alone and to solve problems.
- *Artistic*: The **artistic (A) individual** generally likes to work with creative ideas and self-expression more than with routines and rules. The A type is described as complicated, disorderly, emotional, expressive, idealistic, imaginative, impractical, impulsive, independent, introspective, intuitive, nonconforming, open, and original. Artistic people like artistic careers such as composer, musician, stage director, dancer, interior decorator, actor, and writer. The A type usually has artistic skills, enjoys creating original work, and has a good imagination.
- *Social*: The **social (S) individual** generally likes to help, teach, and counsel people more than to engage in mechanical or technical activity. The S type is described as convincing, cooperative, friendly, generous, helpful, idealistic, kind, patient, responsible, social, sympathetic, tactful, understanding, and warm. S people like social careers such as teacher, speech therapist, religious worker, counselor, clinical psychologist, and nurse. The S type usually likes to be around other people, is interested in how people get along, and likes to help other people with their problems.
- *Enterprising*: The **enterprising (E) individual** generally likes to persuade or direct others more than to work on scientific or complicated topics. The E type is described as acquisitive, adventurous, agreeable, ambitious, attention getting, domineering, energetic, extroverted, impulsive, optimistic, pleasure seeking, popular, self-confident, and sociable. Enterprising people like enterprising careers such as buyer, sports promoter, television producer, business executive, salesperson, travel agent, supervisor, and manager. The E type usually has leadership and public speaking abilities, is interested in money and politics, and likes to influence people.
- *Conventional*: The **conventional (C) individual** generally likes to follow orderly routines and meet clear standards and to avoid work that does not have clear directions. The C type is described as careful, conforming, conscientious, efficient, inhibited, obedient, orderly, persistent, practical, thrifty, and unimaginative. Conventional people like conventional careers such as bookkeeper, financial analyst, banker, tax expert, secretary, and radio dispatcher. The C type has clerical and math abilities, likes to work indoors, and enjoys organizing things.

Believing that people who choose careers that match their own types are more likely to be satisfied and successful, the SDS helps individuals understand more about themselves and explore careers that they are most likely to find satisfying based on their interests and skills. Individuals can complete the SDS online and receive an immediate personalized report. This report contains a three-letter Holland code to help individuals find careers that best match their interests and abilities, answers to frequently asked questions about the SDS, a list of occupations (and college majors) with codes identical or similar to the individual's three-letter Holland code, and suggestions and resources to assist individuals with educational and career planning.

SOURCE: Adapted from Reardon, R. (2001). *The Self-Directed Search interpretive report.* Retrieved July 5, 2010, from http://www.self-directed-search.com/sdsreprt.html

To learn more about one such test, the Self-Directed Search, see On the Web Box 2.1 and Test Spotlight 13.2 in Appendix A. To complete the SDS and receive a personalized report, go to www.self-directed-search.com.

visual, and auditory problems for which children might need special assistance. In colleges and universities, career counselors use the results of tests to help students identify career interests and select major areas of concentration and careers that are consistent with students' skills and interests. These are only some of the ways in which professionals use tests in educational settings. (Chapter 13 is devoted to discussing how educators use psychological tests.)

Clinical Settings

Clinical psychologists, psychiatrists, social workers, counseling psychologists, and other health care professionals use psychological tests in clinical settings such as mental health clinics, residential programs, and private practices. For example, clinical psychologists and psychiatrists administer psychological tests to help diagnose psychological disorders, plan treatment programs, and determine the effectiveness of treatment programs (for an example of some simple memory tests thought to be helpful in the early detection of Alzheimer's disease, see In the News Box 2.1). Counseling psychologists administer psychological tests to individuals and use the results to counsel and advise those seeking help in how to deal with problems of everyday living such as marital and relationship problems. Again, these are only some of the ways professionals use psychological tests in clinical settings. (Chapter 14 discusses how clinicians use psychological tests.)

IN THE NEWS
Box 2.1   A Precious Gift of Time

Alzheimer's disease, a brain disorder that gradually destroys a person's mental functioning and ability to perform daily activities, is the most common form of dementia in the United States. Over 30 million people have dementia (Alzheimer's Disease International, 2009), of which approximately 5.3 million are living with Alzheimer's (Alzheimer's Association, 2009). By 2030, more than 7 million people are expected to have Alzheimer's, and by 2050, it is estimated that 11–16 million people will be diagnosed with Alzheimer's.

With no known cure and a significant threat to the elderly population and health care system, early detection of Alzheimer's disease is critical to slowing the progress of the disease and delaying its disabling symptoms. One of the first symptoms of Alzheimer's is mild forgetfulness. During the beginning stages, many individuals report difficulty in remembering recent events, activities, or the names of familiar things and people. Eventually, this mild forgetfulness becomes more serious, with individuals forgetting how to comb their hair or brush their teeth. As the disease progresses, individuals might experience problems in writing, speaking, and understanding others. They may also become aggressive or wander away from home. During late stages of Alzheimer's, individuals need total care.

Although the only true diagnosis for Alzheimer's disease requires finding plaques and tangles in brain tissue during an autopsy, there are early detection techniques that doctors can use to diagnose the disease correctly 90% of the time (Alzheimer's Association, 2009). Neuropsychological tests that measure memory are among the techniques for making a probable diagnosis.

In 2005, *U.S. News & World Report* published an article titled "A Very Precious Gift of Time." In this article, Josh Fischman paints a bleak picture of Alzheimer's disease, but he also shares some perspectives on how early detection can gain precious time:

"I've spent the past year and a half sitting with these people," says Renee Beard, a medical sociologist at the University of California–San Francisco. "Yes, they're afraid when they hear the news. But they see positive things, too: They have time to plan, to take vacations with their families, to find support groups. And they're grateful for the time to do all this." (para. 1)

Fischman also shares,

Last week, at a major Alzheimer's research conference, doctors described simple, five-minute tests that general physicians can use to screen people for possible signs of the disease—something few doctors do now. Scientists also highlighted new ways to scan for Alzheimer's years before obvious symptoms appear: by measuring changes in the brain. Raising these prospects for detection has also raised researchers' optimism, even if medical options are limited. "If we want to be able to intervene as early as possible, we need to be able to identify people who are at high risk," says Marilyn Albert, co-director of the Johns Hopkins Alzheimer's Disease Research Center in Baltimore. (para. 2)

Fischman discusses the fact that people experiencing the early stages of Alzheimer's disease typically go to general physicians. Unfortunately, according to Henry Brodaty, a neuropsychiatrist at the University of New South Wales, in Australia, few general physicians screen their patients for Alzheimer's disease, with only roughly one-third of general physicians administering simple memory tests that are useful in tentatively diagnosing Alzheimer's. This lack of testing reduces the likelihood of early detection.

Why do general physicians not administer these simple memory tests? One of the most common tests administered in physicians' offices is the Mini-Mental State Examination (MMSE), a widely used 10-minute test of cognitive mental status. According to Brodaty, "since the average office visit doesn't last much longer than that, physicians just don't have the time" (quoted in Fischman, 2005).

Knowing the importance of early detection, Brodaty identified three other tests that require patients to recall the names of a few items (and sometimes to draw a picture) that are just as accurate as the MMSE. According to him, there is a clear advantage to conducting such tests: "Five minutes. . . . These other tests take five minutes or less to give, so doctors should have an easier time fitting them in" (quoted in Fischman, 2005). If a test indicates memory problems, the patient can be referred to a memory clinic for more specialized testing to confirm the diagnosis.

SOURCE: Adapted from Fischman, J. (2005, June 26). A very precious gift of time. *U.S. News & World Report.*

Organizational Settings

Human resources professionals and industrial/organizational practitioners use psychological tests in organizations. For example, they administer tests to job applicants to measure the applicants' knowledge, skills, abilities, and personalities, and they use the test results, along with other information, to make hiring decisions. Human resources professionals and industrial/organizational practitioners use psychological tests to identify employees' strengths and opportunities for development and ultimately to determine employees' training needs (for an example of such a test, the Leadership Practices Inventory, see On the Web Box 2.2). These professionals also use tests to measure employee performance and determine employee performance ratings. (Chapter 15 discusses how managers and others use psychological tests in organizational settings.)

ON THE WEB BOX 2.2

The Leadership Practices Inventory

www.lpionline.com

Developed by Jim Kouzes and Barry Posner, the Leadership Practices Inventory (LPI) is a 360-degree, or multirater, leadership assessment tool that helps individuals in organizations measure the extent to which they demonstrate the Five Practices of Exemplary Leadership. In a 360-degree process, surveys are sent to those people an individual works closely with, including managers, peers, subordinates, and customers, and these people are asked to provide feedback on the extent to which the individual demonstrates key behaviors.

The Five Practices of Exemplary Leadership (adapted from Kouzes & Posner, 2003, p. 4–6) are defined as follows:

Model the way: Credibility is the foundation of leadership. People will not believe the message until they believe in the messenger. And what is a behavioral example of credibility? The most frequent response to that question is, "Do what you say you will do" (or DWYSYWD). Embedded in this typical description of credibility are two essentials: *say* and *do*. Leaders must stand for something. They must find their voice by clarifying their personal values and express those values in their own style. Good leaders, however, do not force their views on others. Instead, they work tirelessly to build consensus on a set of common principles. Then they set the example by aligning their personal actions with shared values. When constituents know that leaders have the courage of their convictions, they become willingly engaged in following that example.

Inspire a shared vision: Leaders passionately believe they can make a difference. They envision the future by imagining exciting possibilities. But visions seen only by leaders are insufficient to mobilize and energize. Leaders enlist others in their dreams by appealing to shared aspirations. They breathe life into ideal and unique images of the future and get people to see how their own dreams can be realized through a common vision.

Challenge the process: The work of leaders is change. The status quo is unacceptable to them. Leaders search for opportunities by seeking innovative ways to change, grow, innovate, and improve. They also experiment and take risks by constantly generating small wins and learning from mistakes. Extraordinary things do not get done in huge leaps forward; they get done one step at a time.

Enable others to act: Leaders know they cannot do it alone. They foster collaboration by promoting cooperative goals and building trust. Leaders promote a sense of reciprocity and a feeling of "we're all in this together." They understand that mutual respect is what sustains extraordinary efforts. Leaders also strengthen others by sharing power and providing choice, making each person feel competent and confident.

Encourage the heart: The climb to the top is arduous and steep. People become exhausted, frustrated, and disenchanted. They are often tempted to give up. Leaders encourage the heart of their constituents to carry on. To keep hope and determination alive, leaders recognize contributions by showing appreciation for individual excellence. Genuine acts of caring uplift spirits and strengthen courage. In every winning team, the members need to share in the rewards of their efforts so that leaders celebrate the values and the victories by creating a spirit of community.

Believing that leadership is a measurable, learnable, and teachable set of behaviors, the LPI provides leaders with the opportunity to gather feedback from those they work with on a day-to-day basis on the extent to which they engage in 30 leadership behaviors associated with the Five Practices of Exemplary Leadership. Using a rating scale from 1 (almost never) to 10 (almost always), peers, direct reports (subordinates), others the individual works with, and the leader's manager rate the extent to which the individual leader demonstrates each of the 30 leadership behaviors. Individuals also rate themselves.

Available for electronic implementation through a web-based application, the LPI Online offers easy-to-use administrator and leader websites as well as a just-in-time, streamlined, and easy-to-interpret personalized report. This report presents 360-degree results in a number of ways, including the following:

- Self, individual observer (for example, manager, colleague, direct report, and others in the workplace), and overall average scores for each of the five practices as well as each of the behaviors within each practice, in both numeric and graphical form
- Ranking of all leadership behaviors from most frequently demonstrated to least frequently demonstrated
- A comparison of how self-scores and observers' scores compare with the scores of thousands of individuals who have taken the same version of the LPI
- All responses to any open-ended questions that were included in the survey

If you want to learn more about the LPI, go to www.lpionline.com/lpi/ and view the online demo.

INTERIM SUMMARY 2.1
WHO USES PSYCHOLOGICAL TESTS AND FOR WHAT REASONS?

- Psychological testing is important because people use tests to make important decisions.
- Individual decisions are those made by the person who takes a test, and institutional decisions are those made by others as a result of an individual's performance on a test.
- Comparative decisions involve comparing people's scores with one another to see who has the best score, and absolute decisions involve seeing who has the minimum score to qualify.
- Psychological tests are used by professionals for a variety of purposes in educational, clinical, and organizational settings.
- In educational settings, administrators, teachers, school psychologists, and career counselors use psychological tests to make a variety of educational decisions, including admission, grading, and career decisions.
- In clinical settings, clinical psychologists, psychiatrists, social workers, and other health care professionals use psychological tests to make diagnostic decisions, determine interventions, and assess the outcomes of treatment programs.
- In organizational settings, human resources professionals and industrial/organizational psychologists use psychological tests to make decisions such as whom to hire for a particular position, what training individuals need, and what performance rating an individual will receive.

The Social and Legal Implications of Psychological Testing

As we discussed in Chapter 1, psychological testing today is a big business and a part of the American culture. Thousands of psychological tests are available, and they are taken by many individuals and professionals to make informed decisions. In educational settings alone, more than 1.8 million students took the SAT in 2008 (College Board, 2008).

As you just learned, individuals and institutions use the results of psychological tests for many purposes, including making important decisions. These decisions, of course, are meant to benefit people. The widespread use of tests suggests that, in general, psychological tests do serve their purpose. Nonetheless, psychological testing has always been, and probably always will be, controversial. Although some of this controversy stems from the general public's misunderstandings about the nature and use of psychological tests and can be easily eliminated through education, some of the controversy is deeply rooted in ongoing debates and occurs among professionals themselves.

One of the largest and most deeply rooted controversies pertains to discrimination. For years, some members of society have been concerned that standardized psychological tests unfairly discriminate against certain racial and economic groups, resulting in qualified members of these groups being passed over for admission to educational programs or not being hired at the same rate as members of other groups. The American public really began to express its concern that psychological tests were discriminatory when psychological testing became widespread during the 20th century. Much of this concern was, and continues to be, targeted at standardized tests of intelligence, aptitude, and achievement. As shared by Lemann (1999) in his book *The Big Test,*

> In the 1940s standardized educational tests created a ranking of Americans, one by one from top to bottom on a single measure. If one analyzed the ranking by social or ethnic group, then at the bottom, always, were Negroes. Living mostly in the benighted, educationally inferior South, consigned to separate schools that operated only sporadically with ill-trained teachers, historically denied by law even the chance to learn to read and write and figure, disproportionately poor, ill-nourished, and broken-familied, Negroes as a group were in a uniquely bad position to perform well on tests designed to measure such school-bred skills as reading and vocabulary and mathematics fluency. So whenever goods were distributed on the basis of test scores, Negroes got a disproportionately low share of them. (pp. 155–156)

Today, the discrimination controversy continues. One of the most recent and visible cases started in 2003, when the city of New Haven, Connecticut, administered a promotional examination for firefighters aspiring to achieve the ranks of lieutenant and captain. When the tests were scored, the city made the decision to scrap the results for fear that the city would be sued for discrimination if it used the results because no African Americans and only 2 Hispanics had scores high enough to be eligible for promotion. Subsequently, 1 Hispanic and 19 White firefighters sued the city, claiming that they were discriminated against when they were denied promotions as a result of the city's refusal to use the test results. The firefighters claimed city officials denied them promotions due to the fear of potential Civil Rights Act violations rather than how they performed on the promotional exams

(Savage, 2009). The case was elevated to the Supreme Court in June 2009. We talk more about this case later in the text.

The Controversy Over Intelligence Tests

Intelligence Testing in Education

Researchers have documented that middle- and upper-class White people, on average, score higher on intelligence tests than do other economic and racial groups (Lemann, 1999). Early in the 20th century, believing that this difference in intelligence was due to heredity, elementary schools began administering intelligence tests to students and using the results to place those with higher IQ scores in special academic programs and those with lower scores in more vocationally related programs (Hunt, 1993). Individuals who believed that intelligence was inherited had no problem with using psychological tests in this manner. They believed that people who do better on such tests naturally have superior intellects. In their view, if intelligence is indeed inherited, using psychological tests in this manner is fair and in the best interest of individuals and society.

However, what if intelligence is not inherited but rather is the result of the environment in which one is raised? If this were the case, all people would be born with the same potential and only those who grew up in favorable backgrounds would, in general, score higher on intelligence and academic ability tests. Those who had disadvantaged backgrounds would score lower. In this case, using intelligence test scores, which are thought to reflect innate abilities, to determine an individual's educational opportunities would be unfair. Hence, we are sure you can understand the debate and the public's concern over the use of intelligence tests.

Over the years, activists who believe that intelligence is determined primarily by environment have worked to eliminate what they consider to be the unfair use of such tests. During the 1960s, in the heat of the civil rights movement, activist groups demanded that schools abandon the use of intelligence tests. New York, Los Angeles, and Washington, D.C., did just that (Hunt, 1993). For Your Information Box 2.1 includes discussion of a court case in which, for exactly this reason, schools in California were ordered not to use intelligence tests for student placement. However, continued efforts to eliminate intelligence testing failed when it became apparent that the placement of children with learning or physical disabilities in the same classrooms as average and gifted children slowed learning (Hunt, 1993).

Intelligence Testing in the Army

In an effort to improve the credibility of psychological testing and establish psychology as a true scientific movement, during World War I Robert Yerkes came across an opportunity to promote the use of mental testing. The American military gave Yerkes permission to administer mental tests to more than 1.75 million U.S. Army recruits. As a result, believing that individuals might be intelligent but not literate or proficient in English, Yerkes (1921) designed the Army Alpha and Beta tests, the first mental tests designed for group testing. The Army Alpha test was developed for use with literate groups, and the Army Beta test for use with those who were unable to read, write, or speak English. Yerkes argued that both tests measured native intellectual abilities—abilities unaffected by culture or educational opportunities. By the end of the war, the Army Alpha and Beta tests were being used to screen army recruits for officer training.

FOR YOUR INFORMATION BOX 2.1

Can IQ Tests Be Illegal?

Unless you live in California, you are probably not aware of the controversy surrounding the use of IQ scores as a method for placing children in Educable Mentally Retarded (EMR) classes. In 1979, in the case of *Larry P. v. Riles,* testimony suggested that IQ tests are biased against African American children. The plaintiff, the party bringing the suit, showed that six African American children who scored low on one intelligence test scored much higher on the same test when it was revised to reflect the African American children's cultural background. The African American children's first scores placed them in the range labeled "retarded"; however, the scores from the revised test labeled them as "normal." In addition, evidence was given that a higher proportion of African American children, compared with the rest of the student body, were in EMR classes. This information caused the judge to rule that schools in California may not use IQ test scores to place African American children in EMR classes or their "substantial equivalent."

California abolished EMR classes, and in 1986 the same judge modified his ruling, this time banning the use of IQ tests to evaluate African American children referred for any special assessment. This ruling did not please all parents. For instance, Wendy Strong, the mother of a 7-year-old, tried to get help for her daughter, Brianna, who had problems in learning. Because her race was shown as African American on school records, school psychologists were not able to administer an IQ test to Brianna. Brianna's mother threatened to have her daughter's racial category changed so that she could be tested. Such a change was possible because Brianna had one African American parent and one White parent.

Eventually, another suit was brought by African American parents who wished to have their children tested. In 1994, the appeals court ruled that parents such as the Strongs were not adequately represented in the 1986 proceedings. Therefore, the court canceled the 1986 ruling but upheld the original 1979 ruling.

SOURCE: Adapted from *Crawford v. Honig,* 9th Cir. 37 F.3d 485 (1994).

During the 1920s, Walter Lippmann, a popular newspaper columnist, criticized the Army Alpha and Beta tests as having a great potential for abusing the psychological testing process—a process that could be of great benefit to the army (Lippmann, 1922a–e). Like others, Lippmann questioned whether intelligence tests such as the Army Alpha and Beta tests actually measured "intelligence" and whether intelligence was determined by heredity or through life experiences—a question that came to be known as the **nature-versus-nurture controversy.** Data collected using army recruits suggested that average intelligence scores of African American males were much lower than average scores of White males. In addition, when scores of foreign-born recruits were sorted by their countries of origin, Eastern European recruits (for example, Turks, Greeks, Poles, Russians) produced large numbers of scores that indicated a mental age of younger than 11 years, which for an adult was an indication of low intelligence (Yerkes, 1921). Political groups who opposed the immigration of large numbers of families from Europe following World War I used these data to support their arguments that immigration was harmful to the United States.

Later in the 20th century, Gould (1982) also criticized such mass intelligence testing, claiming that the intelligence tests were culturally biased. For immigrants, the language and customs of the United States were unfamiliar and what appeared to be stupidity was just lack of cultural knowledge and experience. Consider the following three examples from the Army Alpha test (Gould, 1982, para. 21):

1. Crisco is a:

    a. patent medicine.
    b. disinfectant.
    c. toothpaste.
    d. food product.

2. *Washington* is to *Adams* as *first* is to _____.

3. Christy Mathewson is famous as a:

    a. writer.
    b. artist.
    c. baseball player.
    d. comedian.

How did you do on those questions? Did you know that Crisco was a popular vegetable shortening and butter substitute? Washington was the first president of the United States, and Adams was the second. At the time these questions were used, Christy Mathewson was a well-known baseball player; however, his name is no longer general knowledge.

Critics' concern was that immigrants would not have the cultural knowledge and experience to answer such questions correctly. In addition, the tests themselves and the instructions given when administering them were usually incomprehensible to uninformed test takers. The Army Alpha and Beta tests, for example, required test takers to follow directions and perform a series of ballet movements that were confusing and distracting.

The Army Alpha and Beta tests were discontinued following World War I, but the nature-versus-nurture debate continued. Its connection to psychological tests and intelligence raised public controversy again nearly 50 years later at a time when the civil rights movement was changing the American experience.

In 1969, Arthur Jensen published an article in the *Harvard Education Review* that again pointed out a difference in average intelligence scores between Blacks and Whites. Although there have been numerous explanations for these findings, Jensen caused an uproar by implying that this difference in intelligence was almost exclusively (80%) due to genetic factors. This time, Jensen used later and more sophisticated tests than those the army had used during World War I, but the basic "pro-heredity" argument was still the same.

The debate that followed Jensen's (1969) article led professionals and the public to question how psychologists and test developers define and measure intelligence. A number of psychologists (Eells, Davis, Havighurst, Herrick, & Tyler, 1951; Harrington, 1975, 1976) also have pointed out that the intelligence tests administered to Blacks were invalid for measuring the intelligence of Blacks because the tests had been developed for middle-class White children whose experiences are different from those of children from other ethnic groups and socioeconomic classes. Furthermore, Asa Hilliard (1984) questioned Jensen's underlying assumptions regarding an operational definition of race.

The same debate arose again in 1994 when Richard Herrnstein and Charles Murray published their book *The Bell Curve: Intelligence and Class Structure in American Life*, which reiterated many of the conclusions that Jensen drew in 1969. Herrnstein and Murray argue that IQ is extremely important, that it is somewhere between 40% and 80% heritable, and that it is related not only to school performance but also to jobs, income, crime, and illegitimacy. Herrnstein and Murray use intelligence research to substantiate their claim that some of the difference in average IQ scores between Whites and Blacks is likely attributable to genetic factors, suggesting that Blacks are genetically inferior in intellectual abilities and capabilities.

In response to the publication of *The Bell Curve,* the American Psychological Association (APA) convened a task force of psychologists representing the prevalent attitudes, values, and practices of the psychology profession. Based on the work of this task force, the APA published a report, *Intelligence: Knowns and Unknowns* (Neisser et al., 1995). The report did not disagree with the data presented in *The Bell Curve;* however, it interpreted the data differently and concluded that although no one knows why the difference exists, there is no support for the notion that the 15-point IQ difference between Black and White Americans is due to genetics (Neisser et al., 1995; Yam, 1998). Furthermore, in a review of *The Bell Curve* in *Scientific American,* Leon Kamin (1995) states, "The caliber of the data in *The Bell Curve* is, at many critical points, pathetic. Further, the authors repeatedly fail to distinguish between correlation and causation and thus draw many inappropriate conclusions" (p. 99).

The Controversy Over Aptitude and Integrity Tests

As with intelligence tests, the American public has expressed concern over the use of aptitude and integrity tests.

Aptitude Tests and the U.S. Employment Service

During the 1940s, before the Equal Employment Opportunity Act became law, the U.S. Employment Service (USES) developed the General Aptitude Test Battery (GATB) to assist with career counseling and job referral. An occupationally oriented, multiaptitude test, the GATB consists of 12 tests measuring nine cognitive and manual aptitudes: general learning ability, verbal aptitude, numerical aptitude, spatial aptitude, form perception, clerical perception, motor coordination, finger dexterity, and manual dexterity (Nelson Education, n.d.).

As with intelligence tests, research showed that average GATB scores of minority groups were well below those of the other groups. Because the USES and many of its state and local offices used GATB scores to make referrals to employers, more Whites were being referred for particular jobs than were African Americans or Hispanics (Hunt, 1993). The amended Civil Rights Act of 1991 made it illegal to use GATB scores in this way because national policy required giving the disadvantaged compensatory advantages (Wigdor, 1990). Rulings by the Equal Employment Opportunity Commission and several court decisions resulted in a solution called **within-group norming** or "race norming"—the practice of administering the same test to every test taker but scoring the test differently according to the race of the test taker. Using within-group norming, test users would not be able to refer test takers for jobs using their raw test scores—the scores calculated according to the test instructions—or based on how their scores compared with others in the overall norm group. Instead, the test users were required to compare each test taker's score with the scores of other test takers only within the same racial or ethnic group. (We talk more about norms in Chapter 5.) Using race norming, a minority test taker who scored the same as a White test taker would in fact rank higher than the White test taker. Employment services in 38 states used this race norming.

Many psychologists were outraged about the use of race norming. They claimed it was a disgrace to the psychological testing industry, a distortion of a test's measure of job fitness (Gottfredson, 1991), and an illegal quota system that unfairly discriminated against Whites. Nonetheless, in 1989 the National Research Council conducted a study that supported the use of race norming. However, the council recommended that referrals by employment services be based not only on an applicant's GATB score but also on the applicant's experience, skills, and education. Several years later, race norming was outlawed, but not because it was unfair. In a struggle to pass the Civil Rights Act of 1991, members of Congress who favored race norming needed to yield to those who did not. As passed, Section 106 of the Civil Rights Act of 1991 prohibited employers from adjusting scores on the basis of race, color, religion, sex, or national origin (Hunt, 1993) when the sole purpose was to refer or select people for jobs. Use of the GATB in the United States has declined considerably because it became evident that parts of the GATB discriminated against minorities. Canadians continue to use the GATB as a pre-employment test.

The U.S. Armed Forces now uses a similar instrument, the Armed Services Vocational Aptitude Battery (ASVAB), a series of tests used primarily by the military to help determine whether individuals qualify for service in certain military branches and, if so, what jobs they qualify for. For more information on the ASVAB, read On the Web Box 2.3.

The Armed Services Vocational Aptitude Battery

www.military.com/ASVAB

Developed by the Department of Defense during the 1960s, there are currently three versions of the Armed Services Vocational Aptitude Battery (ASVAB) available (Powers, n.d.):

1. *High School Version (Form 18–19)*: This version is a paper-based test typically administered to high school juniors and seniors. Offered by the Department of Defense and the Department of Education to more than 90,000 students in more than 13,000 high schools and postsecondary schools in the United States each year, this test is used primarily to help high school counselors and students identify where students' basic aptitudes lie.

2. *Paper ASVAB for Recruiting (Form 20–22)*: This version is also a paper-based test; however, it is administered by the armed forces only to military recruits for enlistment purposes. Although the questions on Form 20–22 are different from those on Form 18–19, the questions are of the same level of difficulty.

3. *CAT–ASVAB (computerized version of Form 20–22)*: This version is a computer-based test available at a number of Department of Defense Military Entrance Processing Stations. Although the questions on the CAT–ASVAB are the same as those on Form 20–22, this version is computer adaptive, meaning that when a recruit answers a question correctly, the computer automatically selects a more difficult question. When a recruit gets an answer wrong, the computer selects an easier question. (We discuss computer-based adaptive testing in more detail in Chapter 4.)

To learn more about these versions, take a free ASVAB sample test, and receive some tips and strategies, go to www.military.com/ASVAB. To find out more about minimum scores for military jobs in the Air Force, Army, Marine Corps, and Navy, go to www.military.com/ASVAB/0,,ASVAB_MOS.html.

In 1964, the U.S. Congress passed the Civil Rights Act. Intended to bring about equality in hiring, transfers, promotions, compensation, access to training, and employment-related decisions, Title VII of the act made it unlawful to discriminate or segregate based on race, color, national origin, or gender in all terms and conditions of employment. Issued as an interpretation of Title VII in 1978, the Uniform Guidelines on Employee Selection Procedures recommended that employers analyze their hiring and promotion processes to determine whether their selection procedures (including the use of tests) were discriminatory. If the selection rate for any race, sex, or ethnic group was less than four-fifths (or 80%) of the selection rate for the group with the highest selection ratio, the selection process could be considered potentially discriminatory, possibly causing adverse impact for the underselected groups. (Chapter 15 discusses using psychological tests in compliance with the Civil Rights Act of 1964 in more detail.)

Aptitude Testing in Education

During the 1970s, Americans noticed an apparent decline in SAT scores (Haney, 1981). National averages for the SAT between 1952 and 1963 stayed approximately the same despite the fact that 7% more students took the SAT during those years. However, between 1964 and 1970, national average scores began to decline significantly. By 1977, both the SAT math and verbal scores had declined (Dutch, 2009).

This time, the concern was not with how "intelligent" Americans were but rather with how much American students were learning in public schools. Between 1963 and 1975, the College Board reported that college-bound high school students answered approximately 5% fewer SAT questions correctly—a 60- to 90-scale point decline in aggregate SAT scores. As a result, the College Board and Educational Testing Service convened a special panel that concluded that a 14-year decline in average scores was due to two factors. First, more students were taking the SAT, and these students not only had weaker academic records but also were coming from more diverse backgrounds. Again, the implication was that the traditional test takers, middle- and upper-class White students, were more likely to make high grades. Second, the type of educational experience students had during the late 1960s and early 1970s had caused a decrease in performance on standardized tests. Among the reasons given for a decline in educational experience were a "diminished seriousness of purpose and attention" and a "marked diminution in young people's learning motivation" (Haney, 1981, p. 1026).

However, Berliner and Biddle (1995) state,

> So although critics have trumpeted the "alarming" news that aggregate national SAT scores fell during the late 1960's and the early 1970's, this decline indicates nothing about the performance of American schools. Rather, it signals that students from a broader range of backgrounds were then getting interested in college, which should have been cause for celebration, not alarm. (p. 21)

Integrity Testing in Organizations

Yet another concern has been integrity testing. **Integrity tests** measure individual attitudes and experiences toward honesty, dependability, trustworthiness, reliability, and prosocial behavior (Society for Industrial and Organizational Psychology, 2009). Typically, integrity tests require test takers to answer questions about the following:

- Illegal use of drugs or engagement in unacceptable theft or criminal activities
- Opinions about illegal or inappropriate activities
- Personality or beliefs
- Reactions to theoretical and/or hypothetical situations (Eisenberg & Johnson, 2009)

There are two basic types of integrity tests. One requires individuals to respond to questions about previous experiences related to ethics and integrity. These tests are overt and include very straightforward questions. The other type requires individuals to respond to questions about their preferences and interests. These tests are more personality based and measure propensity to engage in unacceptable work behaviors. From the preferences and interests, inferences are drawn about how the individual may behave in the future. Both types are used by organizations to identify individuals who are likely to engage in inappropriate, dishonest, and antisocial behavior at work.

Employers have used integrity tests for many years both to screen job applicants and to keep existing employees honest. According to research, their use is justified. Organizations lose anywhere from $10 billion (as reported by the American Management Association) to $150 billion (as reported by the Federal Bureau of Investigation) annually due to workplace behaviors such as theft and shoplifting (Net Industries, 2010). Results of employee surveys reveal the following:

- 56% of working people admit they have lied to their supervisors.
- 41% say they have falsified records.
- 64% admit using the Internet for personal reasons during working hours.
- 35% have stolen from their employers, by their own admission.
- 31% abuse drugs or alcohol. (Profiles International, n.d., para. 8)

According to Profiles International (n.d.), a company that provides assessment instruments to organizations, over one-third of organizations declaring bankruptcy report being "stolen out of business"

IN THE NEWS

Box 2.2   Controversy Over the Use of Personality Tests: Testing Tsunami

In a *Boston Globe* article titled "Against Types," Bennett (2004) discusses how many people are using personality tests for purposes different from the ones for which the tests
were developed. He refers to the exploding popularity of using personality tests for
decision making as a "testing tsunami." Furthermore, he contends that the controversy
over the use and abuse of personality tests may soon reach the level of controversy associated with intelligence testing and the SAT—a level that, as you know, has caused the
government to begin regulating the field of testing.

For example, Bennett notes that some tests ask test takers to respond to unusual stimuli such as inkblots or
to questions such as the following from the Minnesota Multiphasic Personality Inventory (MMPI):

- Do you prefer a bath to a shower?
- Are you fascinated by fire?
- At parties, do you sometimes get bored or always have fun?
- Do you sometimes feel like smashing things?
- Do you think Lincoln was greater than Washington?
- Do you feel uneasy indoors?

When the MMPI was first released, clinicians used it in psychiatric settings. However, by the 1960s, the use of the
MMPI had expanded and professionals were using it for decision making in job settings and court cases as much as
in psychiatric settings. According to Bennett, each year organizations administer the MMPI to as many as 15 million
individuals and use the results to screen applicants for jobs such as priest, police officer, and nuclear technician. (We
discuss the MMPI in Chapters 8, 12, and 14, and Test Spotlight 12.1 in Appendix A features the MMPI and explains
its development and interpretation.) After you learn more facts about the MMPI, you can decide for yourself
whether you believe its questions are appropriate and whether people always use it appropriately.

Bennett also writes that 8 out of 10 psychologists administer the Rorschach Inkblot Test to diagnose disorders and use the results as evidence in lawsuits and cases. The Rorschach is a projective test that asks test
takers to look at inkblots and describe what they see. (Chapter 14 and For Your Information Box 14.6
describe the theoretical basis of the test and research on the test's psychometric properties.) Again, after you
study more about projective tests and learn about the Rorschach Inkblot Test, you can decide for yourself
about its usefulness.

Finally, Bennett suggests that nearly 90% of Fortune 100 companies administer and use the results of the
Myers–Briggs Type Indicator (MBTI) to help employees learn how to work better with one another. You
learned about the MBTI in Chapter 1 and in Test Spotlight 1.1, and therefore you can judge for yourself
whether administering the MBTI is appropriate for helping employees learn how to understand each other.

Sometimes personality tests, such as those described above, have unusual test users such as dating services
to match prospective couples, organizational recruiters to match people to jobs, and security agencies to detect
people who are untrustworthy. In Section II, we discuss how testing professionals justify the use of any psychological test for a particular purpose.

We believe that Bennett, who writes for the general public, raises interesting and appropriate questions
regarding the use of psychological tests. The study of psychological testing is not only an academic endeavor
but also an important part of how we make decisions as individuals and as a society.

SOURCE: Bennett, D., "Against Types." *The Boston Globe*, September 12, 2004.

by their employees (para. 7). Further, the average shoplifter steals $59, and the average employee caught stealing takes $549! What do employees steal? If you define "employee theft" as the theft, use, or misuse of assets without permission, employees steal money, supplies, and merchandise or company property. Employee theft can also include the time employees are paid for time during which they did not work.

Although the use of integrity tests might be justified by alarming figures associated with employee theft, many individuals and labor groups oppose their use because they believe that integrity tests (a) are neither valid nor reliable and therefore falsely classify some honest people as dishonest, (b) are an invasion of privacy, and (c) have a different and more inhibiting effect on minorities, eliminating higher percentages of minorities than Whites from job opportunities (U.S. Congress, Office of Technology Assessment, 1990). In the early 1990s the APA expressed concern about the reliability and validity of such tests. After two years of research, an APA task force concluded that for most integrity tests, publishers have little information regarding whether the tests actually predict honesty. As a result, the APA urged employers to stop using those integrity tests for which little validity information was available (APA Science Directorate, 1991). Instead, the APA suggested employers rely on only those tests that have substantial evidence of their predictive validity. (Chapter 8 discusses predictive validity in more detail, and Chapter 15 provides more information on integrity testing in organizations.)

Although a history of controversy over the use of intelligence, aptitude, and integrity tests exists, today there is also an emerging controversy over the use of personality tests. For a review of some of this controversy, read In the News Boxes 2.2 and 2.3.

IN THE NEWS

Box 2.3   Can Your Personality Get You Hired or Fired?

In an ABC News report titled "Can Your Personality Get You Hired or Fired," Tory Johnson (2006) discusses how organizations use personality tests and his experience taking two such tests: the California Psychological Inventory and the Myers-Briggs Type Indicator. Johnson's article follows. What do you think?

Personality tests have been around for more than a century, but employers are using them now more than ever when hiring. The main reason: to select the best possible candidates and reduce turnover, which costs a company between a quarter to one-and-a-half times the departing worker's salary.

Even though the word "test" implies pass or fail, there's no such thing in personality assessments. There's no right or wrong, no numerical score. Instead, these tools assess our "soft" skills—personality types, strengths, styles and preferences.

More than 2,500 types of personality tests are used today, and they generally fall into two distinct categories for employment purposes: those used for selecting and hiring new workers and those used for developing and advancing existing staffers.

Last week I took two of these tests: the California Psychological Inventory, which is popular in hiring because it helps predict how an employee might interact with other people, and the Myers-Briggs, which is the gold standard for assessing preferences and styles useful for worker development.

A confession: I was incredibly nervous before starting the online assessments. I was fearful of the unknown. What if the tests revealed weaknesses I wasn't aware of? My mind wandered every which way.

But as I dived into the 350-plus questions between the two assessments, all of that fear dissipated. I very quickly realized it's all based on my opinions, with no right or wrong.

CPP.com, a leading publisher and administer [*sic*] of many of these tests, gave permission to share some of the questions I had to answer on each of the two tests I took. These are no by means mini tests but rather an illustrative sample of items that appear in each test.

From Myers-Briggs Type Indicator Instrument, by Katherine C. Briggs and Isabel Briggs-Myers:

Are you inclined to:

A) value sentiment more than logic, or

B) value logic more than sentiment?

Do you prefer to:

A) arrange dates, parties, etc, well in advance, or

B) be free to do whatever looks like fun when the time comes?

Would you rather work under a boss who is:

A) good-natured but often inconsistent, or

B) sharp-tongued but always logical?

At parties do you:

A) do much of the talking, or

B) let others do most of the talking?

When you start a big project that is due in one week, do you:

A) take time to list the separate things to be done and the order of doing them, or

B) plunge right in?

Which one word in each of the following pairs appeals to you more?

A) sensible

B) fascinating

A) imaginative

B) realistic

A) devoted

B) determined

From CPI 260 Assessment, by Harrison G. Gough, Ph.D.:

Answer TRUE or FALSE as to how you feel each statement applies to you.

- I have a natural talent for influencing people.
- I always see to it that my work is carefully planned and organized.
- People often expect too much of me.
- It is hard for me to just sit still and relax.
- The idea of doing research appeals to me.
- I enjoy hearing lectures on work affairs.
- I read at least 10 books a year.
- I always try to consider the other person's feelings before I do something.
- I like parties and socials.

As you can see from the examples, it's impossible to paint a picture of someone based on just a few answers, which is why so-called mini assessments have absolutely no value. However, when you've answered a comprehensive assessment featuring multiple questions on similar topics, a pattern of strengths and styles will emerge. Sophisticated scoring systems are used to generate meaningful results, and certified interpreters are able to tell you what it all means and how to apply it to your career development.

(Continued)

(Continued)

"Faking Good"

Many people are quick to ask if it's possible to cheat or beat the assessments. The answer is no. In fact, the CPI has a built-in mechanism designed to catch a test-taker who is trying to do what's called faking good. By this I mean people who take every opportunity to paint themselves in an exceptionally positive light will likely be flagged. One true/false question along these lines is: "I have never deliberately told a lie."

There are 25 questions that revolved around the same issue, and they are designed to get your honest answer, not just what you think makes you sound the best or most truthful. If you appear to be too good to be true, you'll likely be flagged by the test administrator.

It's best to be honest—not only for the employer's sake but really for yours too. Be true to yourself. If you don't get the job because of it, there's a good chance you wouldn't have been a good fit, and it's a blessing to know that before an offer is made.

A Critical Concern

The biggest criticism of personality tests stems from a fear that employers rely too heavily on them in making decisions. But every employer and interpreter I spoke to emphasized the importance of using these assessments as only one part of the decision-making process.

Think of it in terms of the SAT for college admittance. A student is so much more than a simple SAT score. The best colleges make decisions based on GPA, course loads, the high school profile, essays, recommendations and more, including the SAT score.

The same is true in hiring: Assessments are only one piece of a much more comprehensive process that includes interviews, role playing, recommendations and more. If you're asked to take a personality test by a prospective employer, ask how it will be used in the overall hiring process, and confirm that the information stays confidential. If you're passed over for a position and you believe it's because of your personality assessments, don't panic. Since assessments are specific to an individual employer and are measured against the position you're applying for and the company's culture and needs, the results do not follow you from position to position. Getting fired from a job sticks with your employment record, but these assessments do not.

SOURCE: Johnson, T. (2006, May 3). Can your personality get you hired or fired? *ABC News.* Retrieved July 5, 2010, from http://abcnews.go.com/GMA/TakeControlOfYourLife/Story?id=1915016

INTERIM SUMMARY 2.2
SOCIAL AND LEGAL IMPLICATIONS OF PSYCHOLOGICAL TESTING

- Even with their widespread use, psychological tests are not without their critics.
- Some individuals are very concerned that psychological tests are biased and do not result in the correct institutional decisions.

- Much of this controversy is focused on the use of intelligence, aptitude, and integrity tests.
- This controversy has influenced social movements, laws, and guidelines on how psychological tests should and should not be used.

Chapter Summary

By now, you should understand that psychological testing is important because psychological tests are used to make important decisions. Both individuals and institutions use the results of psychological tests to make decisions. Individual decisions are those made by the person who takes a test, and institutional decisions are made by others who use an individual's performance on a test to make a decision about that individual. Furthermore, institutions make decisions using either a comparative method or an absolute method. Comparative decisions involve comparing an individual's score with other people's scores to see who has the best score. Absolute decisions involve setting a minimum score that test takers must achieve to qualify.

Testing is also important because different professionals, in a variety of clinical, educational, and organizational settings, use psychological tests for many purposes. In educational settings, administrators, teachers, school psychologists, and career counselors use psychological tests to make a variety of educational decisions, including admissions, grading, and career decisions. In clinical settings, clinical psychologists, psychiatrists, social workers, and other health care professionals use psychological tests to make diagnostic decisions, determine interventions, and assess the outcomes of treatment programs. In organizational settings, human resources professionals and industrial/organizational psychologists use psychological tests to make decisions such as whom to hire for a particular position, what training an individual needs, and what performance rating an individual will receive.

Even given their widespread use, psychological tests are not without their critics. Many people have been, and continue to be, concerned that psychological tests discriminate against certain racial and economic groups, resulting in fewer educational and employment opportunities for these groups. During the 20th century, this concern influenced social movements and resulted in legislatures passing laws and courts setting case law that determined how psychological tests can and cannot be used.

Engaging in the Learning Process

KEY CONCEPTS

After completing your study of this chapter, you should be able to define each of the following terms. These terms are bolded in the text of this chapter and defined in the Glossary.

- absolute decisions
- Alzheimer's disease
- artistic individual
- comparative decisions
- conventional individual
- enterprising individual
- integrity tests

- individual decisions
- institutional decisions
- investigative individual
- nature-versus-nurture controversy
- realistic individual
- social individual
- within-group norming

LEARNING ACTIVITIES

The following are some learning activities you can engage in to support the learning objectives for this chapter.

Learning Objectives	Study Tips and Learning Activities
After completing your study of this chapter, you should be able to do the following:	*The following study tips will help you meet these learning objectives:*
Describe the different types of decisions that are made using the results of psychological tests.	• Make a list of all the psychological tests you have ever taken. Write down any decisions you made about yourself based on the results of each of these tests. Write down any decisions others made about you based on the results of these tests. Consider whether others used a comparative method or an absolute method when evaluating your test score.
Describe the different types of decisions that are made using the results of psychological tests. Explain which professionals use psychological tests in what settings and for what reasons.	• Schedule time to talk with three of the following professionals: a clinical psychologist, a career counselor, a secondary school administrator, a school psychologist, an industrial/organizational psychologist, and a human resources director. Interview these professionals and find out what tests they use on a day-to-day basis, why they use these tests, and how they use the test scores to make decisions. Be prepared to share your findings with your class.
Describe some concerns individuals have regarding the use of psychological tests as well as the social and legal implications of psychological testing, especially as they relate to intelligence, achievement, aptitude, and integrity testing.	• Find two news or journal articles: one discussing controversies in psychological testing prior to the 1980s and one discussing legal challenges associated with psychological testing after 1980. Compare and contrast these articles. Be prepared to share your articles and findings with your class. • On a piece of paper, create three columns: Intelligence and Achievement, Aptitude, Integrity. Write as many of the social and legal implications as you can remember in each of the categories.

PRACTICE QUESTIONS

The following are some practice questions to assess your understanding of the material presented in this chapter.

Multiple choice

Choose the one best answer to each question.

1. What type of decision is made when a high school administrator uses your test score to place you in a gifted program?
   a. Absolute
   b. Comparative
   c. Individual
   d. Institutional

2. Hector completed several interest inventories at the career center at his college. He used the results to decide on a college major. What kind of decision did Hector make?
   a. Institutional
   b. Individual
   c. Comparative
   d. Absolute

3. What method is an organization using to make a decision when it continues to consider your job application because your score was one of the highest on a pre-employment test?
   a. Absolute
   b. Comparative
   c. Individual
   d. Institutional

4. The XYZ Corporation administers an employment test to help determine which job candidate will be offered a job. It makes its decision by looking to see who performed at a minimum level. The XYZ Corporation uses the test to make what kind of decision?
   a. Individual
   b. Absolute
   c. Comparative
   d. Normative

5. A leader who passionately believes he or she can make a difference would be demonstrating which one of Kouzes and Posner's Five Practices of Exemplary Leadership?
   a. Model the way
   b. Inspire a shared vision
   c. Enable others to act
   d. Encourage the heart

6. The Self-Directed Search is based on the theory that most people and organizations can be classified into what six types?
   a. Realistic, Imaginative, Artistic, Social, Enterprising, and Conventional
   b. Realistic, Imaginative, Artistic, Social, Entrepreneurial, and Conventional
   c. Realistic, Investigative, Artistic, Social, Entrepreneurial, and Conventional
   d. Realistic, Investigative, Artistic, Social, Enterprising, and Conventional

7. In educational settings, teachers, administrators, school psychologists, and career counselors use psychological tests for all EXCEPT which one of the following purposes?
   a. Measure student learning
   b. Award scholarships
   c. Identify career interests
   d. Plan treatment programs

8. In organizational settings, human resources professionals and industrial/organizational psychologists use psychological tests for all EXCEPT which one of the following purposes?
   a. Make hiring decisions
   b. Diagnose disorders
   c. Determine training needs
   d. Evaluate employee performance

9. What has been a major concern of the general public regarding the use of psychological tests?
   a. Test publishing companies make too much money selling psychological tests.
   b. Psychological tests unfairly discriminate against certain racial groups.
   c. Psychological tests are neither reliable nor valid.
   d. Local and federal government regulation of psychological testing is too prevalent.

10. What debate centers around whether people are born with their intelligence or acquire their intelligence during their lives?
    a. Innate versus learned
    b. Mature versus learned
    c. Innate versus nurture
    d. Nature versus nurture

11. What test would you use if you were interested in determining whether individuals qualify for service in military branches?
    a. Rorschach Inkblot Test
    b. General Aptitude Test Battery (GATB)
    c. Armed Services Vocational Aptitude Battery (ASVAB)
    d. Leadership Practices Inventory (LPI)

12. What solution was introduced because an examination of GATB scores showed that more Whites were being referred for jobs than were African Americans and Hispanics?
    a. Ethnic norming
    b. Situational norming
    c. Within-group norming
    d. Between-group norming

13. What is the term used to describe when test takers' raw scores are compared with those of their own racial or ethnic group?
    a. Ethnic norming
    b. Situational norming
    c. Race norming
    d. Between-group norming

14. What do integrity tests claim to measure?
    a. Ability to perform a job
    b. Personality
    c. Individuals' ethics
    d. Honesty

Short Answer/Essay

Read each of the following, and consider your response carefully based on the information presented in this chapter. Write your answer to each question in two or three paragraphs.

1. Describe the different types of decisions that are made using the results of psychological tests. Provide an example of each.

2. How might individuals use the results of psychological tests? How might organizations use the results of psychological tests?

3. How do comparative decisions differ from absolute decisions?

4. Who uses psychological tests, and for what reasons do they use them?

5. What are some of society's concerns about intelligence, aptitude, and integrity testing?

6. How do past controversies over psychological testing compare to current controversies?

7. What concerns have been expressed regarding the use of the following personality tests: Rorschach Inkblot Test, Minnesota Multiphasic Personality Inventory (MMPI), and Myers–Briggs Type Indicator (MBTI)?

ANSWER KEYS

Multiple Choice

1. d	2. b	3. b	4. b	5. b
6. d	7. d	8. b	9. b	10. d
11. c	12. c	13. c	14. d	

Short Answer/Essay

Refer to your textbook for answers. If you are unsure of an answer and cannot generate the answer after reviewing your book, ask your professor for clarification.

Is There a Right or Wrong Way to Use Psychological Tests?

CHAPTER 3: IS THERE A RIGHT OR WRONG WAY TO USE PSYCHOLOGICAL TESTS?

After completing your study of this chapter, you should be able to do the following:

- Define ethics and discuss ethical issues of concern to testing professionals and consumers.
- Identify organizations concerned with ethical testing procedures and their ethical standards or codes of ethics.
- Describe how organizations can and cannot enforce compliance with their ethical standards.
- Differentiate between ethical standards and ethical guidelines.
- Define and understand the rights to privacy, anonymity, and informed consent.
- Explain the ethical responsibilities of test publishers and test users.
- Explain what test user qualifications are and why they are important.
- Explain what the *Ethical Standards of Psychologists* say about testing special populations.
- Describe what learning disabilities are and strategies for coping with them.

"My roommate is taking a personality class. Last week, after a long night of studying, she decided to give me a personality test. I came out neurotic. Since then, I've been too upset to go to class."

"My company hired a psychologist to assess all employees to determine their personality types. Instead of using information about personality type to train employees how to work together, my boss went around asking people to transfer to other areas, telling them that he did not want certain types working in his area."

"Can I please get a copy of the Wechsler intelligence test? My son is going to be taking the test next week to determine if he should be put in a gifted program. I'd like to show him the test and give him a little experience."

"I have a friend who wants to go to graduate school. Graduate schools require that you take the GRE. How can she take the GRE when she is blind?"

You might have personally experienced situations or heard of situations similar to those described in the anecdotes at the beginning of this chapter. At first, you might not see anything wrong; however, knowledgeable test users and consumers know that each one of these remarks illustrates a potential misuse of psychological tests.

Psychological tests are used by many professionals in a variety of settings, including educational, clinical, and organizational settings. Unfortunately, misuse by those administering and taking tests, as well as those scoring and interpreting test results, is a chronic and disturbing problem that can harm individuals and society. For individuals, test misuse may result in inappropriate decisions and improper diagnoses. Test misuse reflects poorly on professional organizations and properly trained test users, and it results in poor decisions that harm the public economically and mentally.

Often people who administer tests and people who take tests do not misuse tests intentionally; rather, they do so because of inadequate technical knowledge and misinformation about proper testing procedures. To prevent test misuse, psychologists have developed technical and professional standards for the construction, evaluation, administration, scoring, and interpretation of psychological tests.

Test misuse can be overcome by understanding the technical and professional standards that exist for psychological testing, as well as understanding the guidelines for the dissemination and use of psychological tests. This chapter introduces you to those standards and guidelines. The information in this chapter will enable you, at a very general level, to evaluate your own experience in taking psychological tests such as the SAT and the American College Test (ACT) to gain entrance into college, various intelligence tests to determine your eligibility for gifted or honors programs, and classroom tests to determine your mastery of course material.

To enhance your understanding of proper test use, we begin by introducing you to an important component of proper test use, namely, ethical standards in psychological testing. We discuss what ethics are, the history of ethical standards, and specific ethical standards for psychological testing, including issues of privacy, anonymity, and informed consent. Along the way, we introduce you to various publications of ethical guidelines. Then we introduce you to proper test use, focusing initially on the responsibilities of test publishers and then on the responsibilities of test users. Finally, we discuss special considerations and requirements necessary for individuals who have impairments that interfere with taking a test. We address various types of impairments or disabilities and provide information on ethical treatment of these special populations of test takers.

Ethical Standards for Psychological Testing

One day in 1954, Charlotte Elmore became concerned because her six-year-old son, Michael, was not receiving the same instruction in reading as was her neighbor's daughter. Both attended first grade at the same school, but Michael's class was just starting reading lessons, and the girl next door was already reading to her parents. Mrs. Elmore contacted the school principal, who made a shocking revelation. The school had administered an intelligence test to all students, and Michael's score, the principal said, indicated that he was borderline "retarded." Furthermore, the principal informed her that Michael would need to repeat first grade. When Mrs. Elmore asked why she and her husband had not been told of Michael's score, the principal explained that most parents have difficulty in really understanding intelligence tests and that it was best for their children if parents leave such matters to school authorities.

When Mrs. Elmore asked to have Michael retested, the principal refused, explaining that scores rarely change more than a few points.

Fortunately, Mrs. Elmore put more faith in her observations of Michael and his accomplishments than she did in the school's interpretation of one test score. She asked an outside psychologist to retest Michael, and the boy's IQ score on the retest was 90. Although 100 is the mean of most intelligence tests, 90 is not considered low. (We explain this concept in more detail in Chapter 5.) The outside psychologist did not agree that Michael needed to repeat first grade, and he contacted the principal on Mrs. Elmore's behalf. Eventually, with the help of remedial reading classes and a change of schools, Michael caught up with his classmates.

In high school, Michael was recommended for college preparatory classes, where he earned As and Bs and became a member of the honor society. In 1965, he was accepted as a pre-med student at Indiana University. While he was in medical school, he took another intelligence test and earned a score of 126—a "superior" score. He completed medical school and began practicing medicine as a gastroenterologist, a doctor who treats diseases of the digestive tract (Elmore, 1988).

Although Michael Elmore's story had a happy ending, a number of practices on the part of his elementary school could have prevented him from reaching his full potential and becoming a successful contributor to society. In this section, we examine the ethical standards that now guide psychologists and others who use psychological tests and that seek to protect children and adults from test misuse.

What Are Ethics?

Whenever professionals offer advice or intervene in the affairs of individuals, questions arise concerning honesty, fairness, and conflicts of interest. **Ethics** refers to issues or practices that influence the decision-making process in terms of "doing the right thing." In other words, ethics reflect the morals—what is considered "right" or "wrong"—of a society, a culture, or an organization.

Most professional societies, including the American Psychological Association (APA), have a set of professional practice guidelines or codes known as **ethical standards.** Members of professional societies vote on and adopt these codes after a good deal of discussion and debate. As you can imagine, it is often difficult for everyone to agree on the right thing to do.

For example, psychologists and other professionals often disagree about how to interpret a client's right to privacy. Should clients who have committed aggressive or sexually abusive acts be protected from legal inquiry about their psychological histories? What about clients who are likely to harm themselves or others in the immediate future? Such situations pose **ethical dilemmas**—problems for which there are no clear or agreed-on moral solutions.

At the APA's 2004 annual convention, psychologists pondered ethical dilemmas and how to resolve them. For example, they discussed this question: "A company has released a new edition of an assessment tool. Can a psychologist still use the older version that he or she knows and prefers?" The *Standards for Educational and Psychological Testing* (APA, 1985, Section 9.08) declare that psychologists should not use tests that are obsolete or "not useful for the current purpose." However, Ann Hess, an ethics committee member, interpreted the *Standards* as meaning that older tests are not automatically off the table. Psychologists, she said, "should note the norm groups for each version and from that determine which test is more appropriate for the client. For example, the norms of newer versions tend to include more diverse populations, but the content of an older intelligence test might be more appropriate for older adults or a specific population." On the other hand, Hess continued, "Being too lazy to learn the new test is not defensible" (cited in Bailey, 2004, p. 62).

Robert Kinscherff, a panelist at the same meeting, offered these suggestions to psychologists facing an ethical dilemma:

- Consult with a colleague or an ethics expert, and consider calling your state board or state psychology association for additional assistance.
- Document the steps you took, as well as those you considered but did not take, and your reasoning behind those decisions.
- Aspire to the general principles in the code of conduct and consider whether and how the five principles help inform the decision-making process.
- When the law and the code of conduct conflict, review Standard 1.02, which allows psychologists to follow the law after first making known their commitment to the code of conduct.
- If a conflict of interest, such as having a relationship with someone closely associated with a client, can reasonably be expected to jeopardize your objectivity, carefully consider your options, most notably refraining from the relationship.
- Any time you decide to terminate counseling, follow Standard 10.10 and offer the client a referral to another mental health professional.
- Above all, if you find yourself in an ethical decision-making process, "show that you were careful, reasonable, [and] prudent and that you did the best you could" (cited in Greer, 2004, p. 63).

Ethical standards are not laws established by governmental bodies. Violation of ethical standards, however, has various penalties—including expulsion from the organization. No one can be tried or sued in a court of law for violating ethical standards; rather, these standards are statements by professionals regarding what they believe are appropriate and inappropriate behaviors when practicing their profession.

Psychological testing plays an important role in individuals' opportunities for education, employment, and mental health treatment. When people use tests improperly, there is great potential for harm to individuals—often without the victims' awareness. Therefore, ethical use of psychological tests is of paramount importance to psychologists and other professionals who use or rely on them.

Ethical Principles of the APA

Although the history of psychological testing reaches into antiquity, the formulation of standards for proper use of tests was much longer in coming. In 1953, the APA published the first ethical standards for psychologists. This document, *Ethical Standards of Psychologists* (APA, 1953), was the result of much discussion and study by the APA committee that developed it as well as many persons in the general membership.

Since then, the ethical principles of the APA have been revised and updated several times. The most current, *Ethical Principles of Psychologists and Code of Conduct* (APA, 2010a), was approved and adopted by the members of the APA in December 2002. The *Ethical Principles* contain a preamble and five general principles that are goals to guide psychologists toward the highest ideals of psychology:

Principle A—Beneficence and Nonmaleficence: Psychologists strive to benefit their clients and to do them no harm. This includes safeguarding the welfare and rights of clients, research participants, and animals used in research. They guard against personal, financial, social, organizational, and political factors that might lead to misuse of their influence or services, and they strive to be aware of the possible effect of their own physical and mental health on their ability to help others.

Principle B—Fidelity and Responsibility: Psychologists establish relationships of trust, and they are aware of their professional and scientific responsibilities to society. They uphold professional standards of conduct, clarify their professional roles and obligations, accept appropriate responsibility for their behavior, and seek to manage conflicts of interest that could lead to exploitation or harm.

Principle C—Integrity: Psychologists seek to promote accuracy, honesty, and truthfulness in the science, teaching, and practice of psychology. In situations such as research studies, where deception may be ethically justifiable, they seek to maximize benefits and minimize harm.

Principle D—Justice: Psychologists recognize that all persons should have access to their services and to equal quality of those services. Psychologists exercise reasonable judgment and take precautions to ensure that their potential biases, the boundaries of their competence, and the limitations of their expertise do not lead to or condone unjust practices.

Principle E—Respect for People's Rights and Dignity: Psychologists respect the dignity and worth of all people and the rights of individuals to privacy, confidentiality, and self-determination. They respect cultural, individual, and role differences, including those based on age, gender, gender identity, race, ethnicity, culture, national origin, religion, sexual orientation, disability, language, and socioeconomic status.

In addition, there are 10 sets of ethical standards (APA, 2010a):

1. Resolving ethical issues

2. Competence

3. Human relations

4. Privacy and confidentiality

5. Advertising and other public statements

6. Record keeping and fees

7. Education and training

8. Research and publication

9. Assessment

10. Therapy

Although the ninth set of standards, Assessment, is most directly related to the use of psychological tests, the values set forth in the five general principles also are relevant for test users. And compliance with the standards for privacy and confidentiality is critical to ethical testing. While the complete *Ethical Principles* can be found online (www.apa.org/ethics/code/index.aspx) the complete ethical standards for Assessment appear in Appendix C.

The APA also collaborates with other organizations to provide detailed guidance on ethical issues associated with psychological tests. Perhaps the most important collaborative document is the updated *Standards for Educational and Psychological Testing* that was prepared in 1999 by the American Educational Research Association (AERA), the APA, and the National Council on Measurement in Education (NCME). The *Standards* provide direction for a variety of practices for test construction, administration, and interpretation.

The *Code of Fair Testing Practices in Education* is another important document that supports the *Standards*. The *Code* was revised in 2004 by the Joint Committee on Testing Practices, a consortium of professional organizations and test publishers. The *Code* is a guide for providing "tests that are fair to all test takers regardless of age, gender, disability, race, ethnicity, national origin, religion, sexual orientation, linguistic background, or other personal characteristics" (Joint Committee on Testing Practices, 2004, p. 2). The *Code* also describes the obligations of test developers and test users, and it guides our discussion in the next section. You can find a copy of the *Code* in Appendix D.

A number of professional associations related to the field of psychology have also expressed their concern about ethical standards. For instance, the National Association of School Psychologists (2000) published ethical standards that address the selection, use, and interpretation of psychological tests in elementary and secondary schools, and the American Counseling Association (ACA; 2005) adopted and published its own *Code of Ethics*. The Council of American Survey Research Organizations provides benchmarks of ethical standards for research and development of surveys. (Chapter 10 provides more information about this organization and ethical standards for surveys.)

Certification and Licensure

Many fields also offer **certification**—a professional credential based on meeting specific training objectives and passing a certification exam—and licensure. Certification is generally conducted by state or national organizations, and licensure is awarded to practitioners who meet criteria developed by the state legislature.

One organization that oversees certification for counselors is the National Board for Certified Counselors (NBCC), an independent nonprofit credentialing body for counselors. The NBCC was created by the ACA to establish and monitor a national certification system that would identify and maintain a register of counselors who have voluntarily sought and obtained certification (NBCC, 2005). Because certified counselors may have training in various fields, such as psychology, education, and counseling, the NBCC (2005) has its own *Code of Ethics,* which is a minimum ethical standard for all national certified counselors. Section D of the NBCC's *Code of Ethics* addresses measurement and evaluation.

Another organization that oversees certification for human resources professionals is the Human Resource Certification Institute (HRCI). In partnership with the Professional Examination Service and Prometric, HRCI screens for, administers, scores, and provides certificates to individuals wishing to obtain a Professional in Human Resources, Senior Professional in Human Resources, or Global

Professional in Human Resources credential (HRCI, n.d.-b). The HRCI has its own *Code of Ethics,* which is a set of standards for all who hold an HRCI credential (HRCI, n.d.-a).

Testing Guidelines

As you recall, ethical standards apply to the members of the organization that published the code of ethics. The APA's (2010a) *Ethical Principles* apply only to members of the APA, and the ACA's ethical standards apply only to members of the ACA. Many individuals who use psychological tests do not belong to any professional organization, and membership in such an organization is not a requirement. These people include test publishers, test administrators, managers, and teachers, among others. To provide those outside the membership of professional organizations with a set of standards, several organizations have developed guidelines that apply to everyone in the field of testing—licensed and unlicensed, professional as well as other test users.

The International Test Commission (ITC), which is made up of national psychological associations, test commissions, and test publishers, was established in 1978 to facilitate the exchange of information on problems related to the construction, development, and use of tests and other diagnostic tools. The ITC published its *International Guidelines for Test Use* in 2000 and *International Guidelines on Computer-Based and Internet-Delivered Testing* in 2005. These guidelines were developed for the following individuals (Coyne, 2005):

- The purchasers and holders of test materials
- Those responsible for selecting tests and determining the use to which tests will be put
- Those who administer, score, or interpret tests
- Those who provide advice to others on the basis of test results (for example, recruitment consultants, educational and career counselors, trainers, succession planners)
- Those concerned with the process of reporting test results and providing feedback to people who have been tested

Although the ITC's guidelines are not as extensive as the APA's *Standards* (AERA, APA, & NCME, 1999) or *Code* (Joint Committee on Testing Practices, 2004), they do call attention to the need for everyone involved in the testing process to take responsibility for ethical test use and fair testing practices.

In addition, in the 1980s, the APA Science Directorate published *Test User Qualifications: A Data-Based Approach to Promoting Good Test Use* (Eyde, Moreland, Robertson, Primoff, & Most, 1988), a 143-page technical report that examines various models for screening qualifications of test users. Later, it published the *Report of the Task Force on Test User Qualifications* (APA, 2000). The latter report contains guidelines that inform test users about the qualifications that the APA deems essential for the optimal use of psychological tests. The guidelines are relevant today and identify two kinds of qualifications: generic, which apply to most testing situations, and specific, which apply to specific situations such as testing people with disabilities. Unlike the APA's publications of ethical standards that it intends for compliance of its members, the *Report of the Task Force on Test User Qualifications* describes its guidelines as "aspirational"; that is, the purpose is to inspire achievement in best testing practices. For Your Information Box 3.1 contains the core knowledge and skills for test users taken from these guidelines. We address these generic qualifications throughout this textbook. On the Web Box 3.1 provides an overview of the APA Science Directorate's Testing and Assessment website.

FOR YOUR INFORMATION BOX 3.1

Report of the Task Force on Test User Qualifications

If you have looked ahead on your class syllabus or in this textbook, you may be wondering why there are chapters devoted to topics such as reliability and validity. In fact, the material covered in this book was chosen to provide you with the information you will need in order to use and understand psychological tests. As you recall from Chapter 1, we all are, at one time or another, users and consumers of the results of psychological testing.

As you review the following list of the knowledge and skills a test user should have, you might find it helpful to locate the chapter or passage in this book that addresses each requirement.

1. Psychometric and Measurement Knowledge

   It is important for test users to understand Classical Test Theory and, when appropriate or necessary, Item Response Theory (IRT). The essential elements of classical test theory are outlined below. When test users are making assessments based on IRT, such as adaptive testing, they should be familiar with the concepts of Item Parameters (e.g., item difficulty, item discrimination, guessing), Item and Test Information Functions, and Ability Parameters (e.g., theta).

   1.1. *Descriptive statistics.* Test users should be able to define, apply, and interpret concepts of descriptive statistics. For example, means and standard deviations are often used in comparing different groups on test scales, and correlations are frequently used for examining the degree of convergence and divergence between test user qualifications on two or more scales. Similarly, test users should understand how frequency distributions describe the varying levels of a behavior across a group of persons. Test users should have sufficient knowledge and understanding of descriptive statistics to select and use appropriate test instruments as well as score and interpret results. The most common descriptive statistics relevant to test use include the following:

      1.1.1. Frequency distributions (e.g., cumulative frequency distributions)
      1.1.2. Descriptive statistics characterizing the normal curve (e.g., kurtosis, skewness)
      1.1.3. Measures of central tendency (e.g., mean, median, and mode)
      1.1.4. Measures of variation (e.g., variance and standard deviation)
      1.1.5. Indexes of relationship (e.g., correlation coefficient)

   1.2. *Scales, scores, and transformations.* Test results frequently represent information about individuals' characteristics, skills, abilities, and attitudes in numerical form. Test users should understand issues related to scaling, types of scores, and methods of score transformation. For instance, test users should understand and know when to apply the various methods for representing test information (e.g., raw scores, standard scores, and percentiles). Relevant concepts include the following:

      1.2.1. Types of scales

         a. Nominal scales
         b. Ordinal scales
         c. Interval scales
         d. Ratio scales

      1.2.2. Types of scores

         a. Raw scores
         b. Transformed scores
            i. Percentile scores
            ii. Standard scores
            iii. Normalized scores

      1.2.3. Scale score equating
      1.2.4. Cut scores

   1.3. *Reliability and measurement error.* Test users should understand issues of test score reliability and measurement error as they apply to the specific test being used as well as other factors that may be influencing test results. Test users should also understand the appropriate interpretation and application of different measures of reliability (e.g., internal consistency, test–retest reliability, interrater reliability, and parallel forms reliability). Similarly, test users should understand the standard error of measurement, which presents a numerical estimate of the range of scores consistent with the individual's level of performance. It is important that test users have knowledge of the following:

1.3.1. Sources of variability or measurement error

    a. Characteristics of test taker (e.g., motivation)
    b. Characteristics of test (e.g., domain sampling, test length, and test heterogeneity)
    c. Characteristics of construct and intended use of test scores (e.g., stability of characteristic)
    d. Characteristics and behavior of test administrator (e.g., importance of standardized verbal instructions)
    e. Characteristics of the testing environment
    f. Test administration procedures
    g. Scoring accuracy

1.3.2. Types of reliability and their appropriateness for different types of tests and test use

    a. Test–retest reliability
    b. Parallel or alternative forms reliability
    c. Internal consistency
    d. Scorer and interrater reliability

1.3.3. Change scores (or difference scores)
1.3.4. Standard error of measurement (i.e., standard error of a score)

1.4. *Validity and meaning of test scores.* The interpretations and uses of test scores, and not the test itself, are evaluated for validity. Responsibility for validation belongs both to the test developer, who provides evidence in support of test use for a particular purpose, and to the test user, who ultimately evaluates that evidence, other available data, and information gathered during the testing process. Test users should understand the implications associated with the different sources of evidence that contribute to construct validity as well as the limits of any one source of validity evidence. Test users have a larger role in evaluating validity evidence when the test is used for purposes different from those investigated by the test developer. Contemporary discussions of validity have focused on evidence that supports the test as a measure of a construct (sometimes called *construct validity*). For example, evidence for the uses and interpretations of test scores may come through evaluation of the test content (content representativeness), through evidence of predictions of relevant outcomes (criterion-related validity), or from a number of other sources of evidence. Test users should understand the implications associated with the different sources of evidence that contribute to construct validity as well as the limits of any one source of validity evidence.

1.4.1. Types of evidence contributing to construct validity

    a. Content
    b. Criterion related
    c. Convergent
    d. Discriminant

1.4.2. *Normative interpretation of test scores.* Norms describe the distribution of test scores in a sample from a particular population. Test users should understand how differences between the test taker and the particular normative group affect the interpretation of test scores.

    a. Types of norms and relevance for interpreting test taker score (e.g., standard scores and percentile norms)
    b. Characteristics of the normative group and generalizability limitations of the normative group
    c. Type of score referent
        i. Norm referenced
        ii. Domain referenced (criterion referenced)
        iii. Self-referenced (ipsative scales)
    d. Expectancy tables

SOURCE: Sections 1 through 1.4.2 from *Report of the Task Force on the Test User Qualifications.* Copyright © 2000 by the American Psychological Association.

ON THE WEB BOX 3.1

APA Science Directorate: Testing and Assessment

www.apa.org/science/programs/testing/index.aspx

The American Psychological Association (APA) has a long and continuing interest in the ethical and effective use of psychological tests. This web page provides access to the APA's latest publications on ethics.

One of the most helpful and interesting links on this page is Frequently Asked Questions (FAQ)/Finding Information About Psychological Tests. This link provides "how to" information on locating and purchasing published tests as well as information on directories of unpublished tests.

Other links of interest in the Testing and Assessment area include the following:

- *The Report of the Task Force on Test User Qualifications*
- *APA's Guidelines for Test User Qualifications: Executive Summary*
- *Psychological Testing on the Internet, New Problems, Old Issues: The Report of the Task Force on Psychological Testing on the Internet*
- *Rights and Responsibilities of Test Takers: Guidelines and Expectations*

You are likely to find the *Rights and Responsibilities of Test Takers* to be particularly interesting because these apply to you. According to the preamble of this document, "the intent . . . is to enumerate and clarify the expectations that test takers may reasonably have about the testing process, and the expectations that those who develop, administer, and use tests may have of test takers" (para. 1). In other words, in this document the APA has set out to educate the test taker, the test user, and the test publisher about the responsibilities of each in ensuring that the assessment is developed, administered, scored, and interpreted with the highest ethical and professional standards in mind.

SOURCE: American Psychological Association. (2005). *Testing and Assessment.* Retrieved May 20, 2010, from http://www .apa.org/science/programs/testing/index.aspx

Issues of Primary Concern

The codes of conduct, ethical standards, and guidelines that we have described cover a multitude of ethical issues and concerns. Their common purpose is to protect the rights of individuals who are the recipients of psychological services that include testing. The *Ethical Principles* (APA, 2010a) affirm the importance of respect for individuals, establish the need to safeguard individual dignity and privacy, and condemn unfair discriminatory practices. These core values are so important that they apply in all situations, including testing.

Right to Privacy

The concepts of individual freedom and privacy are integral to the cultural heritage of Americans. The *Ethical Principles* (APA, 2010a) affirm the rights of individuals to privacy, confidentiality, and self-determination. **Confidentiality** means that individuals are assured that all personal information they disclose will be kept private and will not be disclosed without their explicit permission. As you recall, the latest *Ethical Principles* now allows psychologists to disclose test scores with the test takers' permission or in compliance with a court order.

Sometimes test users are tempted to violate ethical standards regarding confidentiality. Managers, for instance, may believe it is in the best interest of their companies to have psychological information about employees. Teachers may also seek test scores of students with the good intention of understanding students' performance problems. Sometimes researchers may simply be careless about safeguarding files that contain test scores and personal information about research participants. However, APA ethical standards emphasize that regardless of good intentions or the apparently trivial nature of data collected, test users should not disclose information without consent.

A related concept is **anonymity**—the practice of administering tests or obtaining information without obtaining the identity of the participant. Anonymous testing is often found in double-blind studies—those in which the researchers do not know the names of the participants. Some research suggests that persons who complete surveys or tests anonymously might be more honest about themselves. On the other hand, it is often important for researchers to identify individuals so as to correlate test scores with other variables. Hence, there is a strong temptation for investigators to code test materials or surveys in such a way that participants can be identified without the participants' knowledge. Such practices violate ethical standards that ensure individual privacy. The *Ethical Principles* (APA, 2010a) acknowledge that other obligations (for example, knowledge that failure to disclose information would result in danger to others) may lead to conflict of ethical standards. For most psychologists and test administrators, however, there are no ethical reasons for violating rights of confidentiality or anonymity.

Right to Informed Consent

Individuals have the right of self-determination. This concept means that individuals are entitled to full explanations of why they are being tested, how the test data will be used, and what their test scores mean. Such explanations, referred to as **informed consent,** should be communicated in language the test takers can understand. In the case of minors or persons of limited cognitive ability, both the test takers and their parents or guardians must give informed consent. In the case of Michael Elmore, school administrators did not inform his parents about administering the intelligence test, and they assumed that the Elmores were not capable of understanding the test and its implications. It is important to note that parental permission is not the same as informed consent. It is the test user's responsibility to confirm that both the child and the parent understand, to the best of their ability, the requirements and implications of the psychological test before the test is administered.

Right to Know and Understand Results

In addition, the test taker—or the child and parent—is entitled to a nontechnical explanation of the scores of all tests. Furthermore, because some test results might affect the test taker's self-esteem or behavior, a trained professional should explain the test results in a sensitive manner.

Right to Protection From Stigma

Likewise, in communicating test results to the test taker, guardian, or others, the test user should refrain from using stigmatizing labels such as "feebleminded" and "addictive personality." In other words, the test results provided to individuals, families, and/or managers should facilitate positive growth and development.

Ethical Use of Computer-Based Testing

As with traditional tests, it is crucial that the developers, distributors, and users of computer-based tests, scoring services, and interpretation services abide by the ethical, professional, and technical standards that we have discussed. Several organizations have developed guidelines that address ethical issues that arise with computer-based testing. As we mentioned earlier, the ITC (2005) published its *International Guidelines for Computer-Based and Internet-Delivered Testing*. In addition, the Association of Test Publishers (2005), a nonprofit organization representing providers of tests and services related to assessment, has published and made available to its members *ATP Computer Testing Guidelines*.

INTERIM SUMMARY 3.1
ETHICAL STANDARDS FOR PSYCHOLOGICAL TESTING

- Ethics reflect the morals—what is considered "right" or "wrong"—of a society or culture.
- Most professional societies have a set of ethical standards that have been discussed and adopted by their members.
- The APA, the ACA, and others have ethical standards that protect the rights of individuals who are the recipients of psychological testing.

- Most important, test takers have the rights to privacy, informed consent, and protection from stigma as well as the right to know and understand results.

Appropriate Use of Psychological Tests

Psychological testing can be very useful for clinicians, counselors, teachers, managers, and others. Inappropriate or incompetent use of testing—as in the case of Michael Elmore—can have undesirable and harmful consequences for individuals. The proper use of tests is so important that we have devoted this section to discussing it in detail. We discuss proper test use from both the test publisher's perspective and the test user's perspective.

Test Publisher Responsibility

Test publishers should follow professional standards and guidelines such as the guidelines published by the ITC and APA. The *Ethical Standards* (AERA, APA, & NCME, 1999) state that publishers should sell psychological tests only to qualified users, market psychological tests truthfully, provide all test information (including evidence of validity) to test users before purchase, and provide comprehensive test manuals for each psychological test after purchase. The *Standards* state that tests should include statements of **user qualifications,** such as certification or experience, that the test purchaser or test user must meet. Not all publishing firms place the same restrictions on the sale of psychological tests, but in general reputable publishers require purchasers to have appropriate credentials for test use. For Your Information Box 3.2 discusses the sale of tests to test users and provides a sample of a customer qualification form.

FYI

FOR YOUR INFORMATION BOX 3.2

The Sale of Psychological Tests to Test Users

Sometimes professionals and students (both undergraduate and graduate) need to purchase a psychological test for their business, for a research project, or for a class assignment. For example, a clinical psychologist may need to purchase a test to help diagnose disorders. An industrial/organizational psychologist may need to purchase a test to use as part of the organization's selection process. Likewise, students may need to purchase tests. In a tests and measurements class, for example, an instructor may ask you to evaluate a psychological test. A thorough evaluation requires not only library research but also access to the test and the test manual. Students also may be interested in conducting an independent research study. They may wish to explore the relationship between some psychological attribute and an outcome, for example, self-esteem and grade point average. To conduct this research, students might want to purchase a psychological test to measure self-esteem. (Note that many reliable and valid tests are also available at no charge in professional journals.)

To purchase most psychological tests, test users must meet minimum training, education, and experience qualifications. For example, Pearson, one test publishing company, has test user qualification levels for each of the tests it sells (Pearson Education, 2010). Pearson tests are classified into one of four levels:

- LEVEL 1: User has completed training in measurement, guidance, or an appropriate related discipline or has equivalent supervised experience in test administration and interpretation. Other professional degrees and certifications may also be considered.
- LEVEL 2: User has completed a bachelor's degree program that included coursework in principles of measurement and in the administration and interpretation of tests. If these qualifications have not been met, Users must provide proof that they have been granted the right to administer tests at this level in their jurisdiction. Level 2 purchasers can also select tests from qualification Level 1.
- LEVEL 3: User has a licensure to practice psychology independently, or User has completed a doctoral (or in some cases master's) degree program in one of the fields of study indicated for the test that included training (through coursework and supervised practical experience) in the administration and interpretation of clinical instruments. If neither of these qualifications are met, Users must provide proof that they have been granted the right to administer tests at this level in their jurisdiction. Level 3 purchasers can also select tests from Levels 1, 2 and M.
- LEVEL M: Level M purchasers must provide credentials indicating: a specialized degree in the healthcare field and accompanying licensure or certification, OR proof that they have been granted the right to administer tests at this level in their jurisdiction. Level M purchasers can also select tests from Qualification Levels 1 & 2. (Pearson Education, 2010, paras. 6–9)

(Continued)

(Continued)

Customer Qualification Levels

In accordance with the *Standards for Educational and Psychological Testing* and PAR's competency-based qualification guidelines, many tests and other materials sold by PAR are available only to those professionals who are trained to administer, score, and interpret psychological tests. If you have not already established a **Qualification Level** with PAR, please complete the form and send it with your first order.

Qualification Level: A

• No special qualifications required.

Qualification Level: B

• A degree from an accredited 4-year college or university in psychology or counseling related field, plus completion of coursework in test interpretation, psychometrics and measurement theory, educational statistics, or a closely related area;

• OR license or certification from an agency/organization that requires appropriate training and experience in the ethical and competent use of psychological tests.

Qualification Level: C

• All Level B qualifications, plus an advanced professional degree that provides appropriate training in the administration and interpretation of psychological tests;

• OR license or certification from an agency that requires appropriate training and experience in the ethical and competent use of psychological tests.

Qualification Level: S

• A degree, certificate, or license to practice in a physical or mental health care profession or occupation, plus training and experience in the ethical administration, scoring, and interpretation of clinical behavioral assessment instruments.

Certain health care providers may be eligible to purchase selected B and C level instruments within their area of expertise. Specifically, relevant supervised clinical experience using tests (i.e., internship, residency) in combination with formal coursework (i.e., tests and measurement, individual assessment, or equivalent) qualifies a health care provider to purchase certain restricted products.

PAR No-Risk Guarantee

"If you are not completely satisfied with your purchase, we will accept the return of any item."

R. Bob Smith III, PhD, Chairman and CEO

PAR Customer Qualification Form

Customer Information

☐Dr. ☐Mr. First
☐Ms. ☐Mrs. name _____ Last name _____

Customer no. _____ E-mail address _____

I would like to order via your Web site. Please send me a temporary password.
☐ Yes ☐ No (E-mail address required above.)

Mailing Address   Phone (_____) _____

Organization name _____

Street address _____ Suite/Apt. _____

City _____ State/Province _____

Zip/Postal code _____ Country _____

Educational Background

Highest degree attained _____ Year degree completed _____

Major field _____

Institution _____

Please check the appropriate Professional Organizational Memberships
(If you are a full member of any of the organizations listed below, you may simply provide your member number, then sign and date this form. Additional information is not required. If you are not a member of any of the organizations listed, please skip to Professional Credentials.)

☐ APA ☐ NASP ☐ National Register of Health Service Providers in Psychology

Membership Number _____

Professional Credentials

Certificate/License (type) _____

Certifying or licensing agency _____

Certificate/License no. _____ Exp. date _____

Coursework/Workshops Completed in Use of Tests
Please provide the following information about your training and/or coursework. For all that apply, indicate whether undergraduate (U) or graduate (G), name of institution or organization, and date completed.

Title _____ ☐G ☐U

Institution _____

Title _____ ☐G ☐U

Institution _____

I certify that all information contained in this form is accurate. I certify that I and/or other persons who may use any test materials I order have a general knowledge of measurement principles and of appropriate and ethical test use and interpretation as called for in the *Standards for Educational and Psychological Testing*. I also certify that I/we are qualified to use and interpret the results of these tests as recommended in the *Standards*, and I assume full responsibility for proper use of all materials I order from PAR.

Signature **X** _____ Date _____

☐ I am a graduate student. My professor has endorsed my order (see signature below).

☐ I agree to supervise this student's use of items ordered and endorse the statement above.

Professor's name _____

Department _____

Institution _____

Signature **X** _____ Date _____

Completed Qualification Forms may be submitted via fax (1.800.727.9329 or 1.813.968.2598) or mail (PAR, Inc., 16204 N. Florida Ave., Lutz, FL 33549).

PAR • 16204 N. Florida Ave. • Lutz, FL 33549 • 1.800.331.8378 • www.parinc.com

SOURCE: http://www4.parinc.com/webuploads/staticpages/Qualif_form.pdf

The qualification level required to purchase each test can be found in the test catalogue or on the web. While there are some exceptions, test purchasers must complete a qualification form in order to purchase a test. Once the form has been accepted, test users are allowed to purchase the test.

PAR, another test publisher, also classifies the tests they sell into one of four levels:

- Qualification Level: A—No special qualifications are required, although the range of products eligible for purchase is limited.
- Qualification Level: B—A degree from an accredited 4-year college or university in psychology, counseling, speech-language pathology, or a closely related field PLUS satisfactory completion of coursework in test interpretation, psychometrics and measurement theory, educational statistics, or a closely related area; OR license or certification from an agency that requires appropriate training and experience in the ethical and competent use of psychological tests.
- Qualification Level: C—All qualifications for Level B PLUS an advanced professional degree that provides appropriate training in the administration and interpretation of psychological tests; OR license or certification from an agency that requires appropriate training and experience in the ethical and competent use of psychological tests.
- Qualification Level: S—A degree, certificate, or license to practice in a healthcare profession or occupation, including (but not limited to) the following: medicine, neurology, nursing, occupational therapy and other allied healthcare professions, physician's assistants, psychiatry, social work; plus appropriate training and experience in the ethical administration, scoring, and interpretation of clinical behavioral assessment instruments. (PAR, 2010b, paras. 3–6)

To establish the qualification level, test users complete a customer qualification form. A sample of this form is on page 74.

Because publishers recognize how valuable reviewing and using psychological tests can be to the learning experience, they often allow a student to purchase a test if the student provides a letter from a qualified instructor or completes a qualification form signed by the instructor. By signing the letter or the qualification form, the instructor assumes responsibility for the proper use of the test purchased by the student. You can find qualification forms for various test publishers on their websites.

The Marketing of Psychological Tests

Test publishers should properly and truthfully market the psychological tests that they publish. They should ensure **test security** so that the content of psychological tests does not become public. Test security includes not publishing psychological tests in newspapers, magazines, and popular books. Not only does a lack of test security invalidate future use of the test, but it also may result in psychological injury to individuals who take and attempt to interpret the test. Such test misuse creates further resistance on the part of the public toward psychological testing.

An exception to this rule occurs when test developers wish to share their tests with the research community. In such cases, peer-reviewed journals will often publish test questions along with validation studies and scoring instructions. Tests published in scholarly journals are considered to be in the public domain.

It is common, however, for test publishers to print examples of outdated test items. For example, Educational Testing Service releases previously administered tests in the form of practice tests. All portions of tests shown in this textbook have been published with the permission of the respective test publishers.

Availability of Comprehensive Test Manuals

Publishers should ensure that every psychological test has an accompanying test manual, which should contain psychometric information based on research. The manual should include the following:

1. Information that a test purchaser can use to evaluate the psychometric characteristics of the test (for example, how the test was constructed, its reliability and validity, composition of norm groups)

2. Detailed information about proper administration and scoring procedures

3. Information about how to compare test scores with those of norm groups

(You can find more information on test manuals in Chapter 12.)

Although test publishers try to comply with these objectives, sometimes the system fails. Sometimes unqualified people may purchase and use psychological tests, or a test may be released before it is complete or may be released with misleading or incomplete information in the manual. For this reason, responsibility for proper test use ultimately resides with the individual using the psychological test.

Test User Responsibility

Test users have the responsibility to ensure that they have the necessary training and experience to purchase and use psychological tests. Psychologists should also do what they can to keep others from misusing the information that assessments, interventions, results, and interpretations provide. If a person who is misusing a test or does not have the proper qualifications belongs to a professional organization, a member may approach him or her and explain the ethical breach. If the person continues to act unethically, an appeal may be made to the organization's ethics committee to stop the unethical behavior. Test publishers also want to know when their tests are being misused.

Up to this point we have been referring to test users. Who exactly is a test user? A **test user** is anyone who participates in purchasing, administering, interpreting, or using the results of a psychological test. A **test taker** is the person who responds to test questions or whose behavior is being measured. It is easy to understand what is meant by test user if you think of the various stages that are involved in the psychological testing process:

1. An individual or group determines a need for psychological testing.

2. An individual or group selects the psychological test(s) to use.

3. An individual administers a test to the test taker.

4. An individual scores the test.

5. An individual interprets the test for the test taker.

Sometimes the same person carries out each step of this process. For example, in the case of Michael Elmore, the outside psychologist may have (a) determined that Michael's intelligence needed to be retested, (b) selected which intelligence test to administer, (c) administered the intelligence test, (d) scored the test, (e) interpreted the results, and (f) communicated the results to Michael's family and the school principal.

Sometimes there are various people involved. For example, the outside psychologist probably determined that Michael should be retested, and selected the appropriate intelligence test, and one of the psychologist's assistants may have administered the intelligence test. The test may have been mailed to a test publishing company for scoring. The psychologist may have taken Michael's raw score, along with other information, to interpret the test results. Michael's psychologist most likely communicated these results to Michael's parents and perhaps to the school principal.

Thus, there may be various professionals involved in the test administration process. Each of these parties is a test user and must act responsibly to contribute to the effective delivery of testing services. Acting responsibly means ensuring that each person in one or more of the roles just described is qualified to perform that role. The *Code* (Joint Committee on Testing Practices, 2004) in Appendix D lists specific responsibilities of the test developer and the test user.

On the Web Box 3.2 describes a website that gives the public access to many well-known psychological tests.

ON THE WEB BOX 3.2

Queendom

www.queendom.com/tests/index.html

Do you like to take personality tests? If so, you are not alone. Many people enjoy completing personality tests in magazines, in books, or on the web. They like to take a test, find out their score, and (if possible) compare themselves with others who have taken the test. What harm can there be in doing that?

Queendom is a website that allows you to self-administer tests on topics such as intelligence, relationships, personality, career, and health. The site presents these tests as "the largest variety of professionally developed and validated tests online" and claims that "over 250 tests have been taken in nine languages."

Now that you are familiar with various ethical codes regarding psychological testing, ask yourself how the codes relate to psychological tests offered to the public on a website. Refer to Appendixes C and D to help you remember the various ethical issues associated with psychological testing.

In addition, here are some questions about Queendom and similar sites that you can discuss with your classmates and friends:

1. How does Queendom address the test taker's right to privacy? How would you challenge or defend the site's approach?

2. How does Queendom address the ethical issue of providing feedback in a sensitive manner that the test taker can understand? How would you challenge or defend the site's approach?

3. How does Queendom fulfill (or not fulfill) its responsibilities as a test publisher? How would you challenge or defend the site's approach?

4. How does Queendom address the issue of test security? How would you challenge or defend the site's approach?

5. Queendom offers its psychological tests for enjoyment and entertainment. Is entertainment an ethical use of psychological testing? Why or why not?

INTERIM SUMMARY 3.2
APPROPRIATE USE OF PSYCHOLOGICAL TESTS

- Test publishers should follow professional standards and guidelines by marketing tests truthfully, selling tests only to qualified users, providing evidence of validity, developing a comprehensive test manual for each test, and maintaining test security.
- Test publishers have the responsibility to ensure that everyone who uses the test has the necessary

training and experience to carry out his or her obligations in regard to the test.
- A test user is anyone who participates in purchasing, administering, interpreting, or using the results of a psychological test.
- A test taker is the person who responds to test questions or whose behavior is being measured.

Testing Special Populations

As psychological testing becomes more prevalent in workplace, education, and clinical settings, people who have minority status in terms of disabilities or ethnicity might need special accommodations so that they can perform to the best of their abilities. Three of those special populations are people with physical or mental challenges, people with learning disabilities, and people who come from cultural backgrounds different from those for whom the test was designed.

Test Takers With Physical or Mental Challenges

Some people who have physical or mental challenges might need special accommodations during testing to ensure that their test scores are accurate. By physical and mental challenges, we mean sensory, motor, or cognitive impairments. **Sensory impairments** include deafness and blindness. **Motor impairments** include disabilities such as paralysis and missing limbs. **Cognitive impairments** include mental retardation, learning disabilities, and traumatic brain injuries.

The *Standards* (AERA, APA, & NCME, 1999) address testing individuals with disabilities. According to the *Standards*, test users should ensure that the test outcomes indicate the intended skills or attributes accurately and that the test scores have not been altered because of disabilities. When testing individuals with disabilities for diagnostic and intervention purposes, test users should not rely solely on test scores. Test users must consider other sources of information, such as interviews and behavioral measures, in addition to test scores. Various laws also protect persons who are physically or mentally challenged, for

example, the Rehabilitation Act of 1973 (which was amended in 1978, 1986, and 1987), the Americans with Disabilities Act of 1990, and the Education for All Handicapped Children Act of 1990.

These ethical standards and laws guide our understanding of what the test user must consider when testing someone who has physical or mental challenges. Often such test takers have special needs that require modifications to the testing process. Test users must modify the testing format and the test interpretation process to accurately reflect the skill or attribute that the psychological test measures. In other words, an individual's impairment must not influence the test outcome when the test is measuring a concept unrelated to the disability.

On the Web Box 3.3 provides some history and directions for online access to *Guidelines for Computer-Administered Testing* (Allan, Bulla, & Goodman, 2003), which provides information on modifying and adapting tests for individuals who are blind.

ON THE WEB BOX 3.3

Guidelines for Testing the Blind

www.aph.org/tests/access/index.html

 Larry Skutchan, a young college student in the 1970s who had lost his sight, quickly gained familiarity with the problems of assessing the blind. Traditional assessment methods in the 1970s relied on printed tests and handwritten answers. "I was very lucky that many of the professors at the University of Arkansas at Little Rock were patient and caring enough to provide alternate means of assessment, usually with the professor himself reading the questions and accepting my responses orally," Skutchan recalled (in Allan, Bulla, & Goodman, 2003, Foreword, para. 1). Skutchan, however, also experienced alternative techniques that were not nearly so comfortable or fair.

I particularly recall an assessment where a freshman work study student read me the questions and wrote my responses, and it was clear that the material was far above the knowledge level of that student. This situation is particularly troublesome in advanced course studies where the pool of candidates qualified to render such an examination shrinks in direct proportion to the complexity of the material on which the student is assessed. On the other hand, one has to wonder, especially with oral assessments, if the student or professor sometimes inadvertently conveys information about the material. None of these situations makes for an accurate assessment of the student's knowledge and ability. (Foreword, para. 2)

Skutchan was technology project leader for the American Printing House for the Blind when it published the *Guidelines for Computer-Administered Testing* (Allan et al., 2003). You can access the guidelines online by going to www.aph.org/tests/access/index.html. (In Chapter 4, we discuss computer-based testing in more detail.)

The modifications that the test developer or user makes depend on the specific disability. For Your Information Box 3.3 highlights some of the major administration and interpretation modifications for four categories of disabilities: visual impairment, hearing impairment, motor impairment, and cognitive impairment. Of course, not all psychological tests can be appropriately modified using these methods. Therefore, psychologists have designed some alternative tests for individuals with disabilities. Table 3.1 shows appropriate alternative tests for measuring various attributes in individuals with disabilities in one of the four categories.

Test Takers With Learning Disabilities

Some people have learning disabilities. Unlike the physical and mental disabilities already discussed, such as paralysis and visual impairment, a **learning disability** does not have visible signs. A learning disability is a difficulty in any aspect of learning. According to the National Institute of Neurological Disorders and Stroke (2010), "learning disabilities are disorders that affect the ability to understand or use spoken or written language, do mathematical calculations, coordinate movements, or direct attention (para. 1). There are a variety of learning disabilities, and Table 3.2 includes some examples of the most common ones.

FOR YOUR INFORMATION BOX 3.3

Guidelines for Accommodating Test Takers With Disabilities

Visual Impairment (Totally or Partially Blind)

- The room should be free of distractions because the visually impaired are easily distracted by extraneous events.
- The test taker should be given ample time for testing to allow for dictation of instructions, slower reading of instructions, or time for the test taker to touch the testing materials.
- All materials should be put within reach of the test taker.
- The room lighting should be modified for optimal vision for the partially blind.
- The size of the test print should be increased for the partially blind.
- The appropriate writing instruments and materials (for example, thicker writing pens) should be available for the partially blind.
- The test should be administered in Braille if the test taker uses Braille to read.
- Test scores of modified standardized tests should be interpreted cautiously unless there are norms for visually impaired test takers.

Hearing Impairment (Totally or Partially Deaf)

- The test taker who has a mild hearing impairment should be given the option of amplifying the test administrator's voice using an electronic amplification apparatus.
- The test taker who has a severe hearing impairment should be provided with the option of having written instructions and questions pantomimed or having an interpreter sign instructions, questions, and the test taker's responses. The test administrator, however, should be aware that substituting written instructions for verbal instructions introduces another variable (reading proficiency) into the testing situation and that pantomiming can compromise the standardization of instructions.
- When interpreting scores, test users should understand that the communication of the deaf is often fragmented, similar to that of individuals who are not very intelligent or who have a mental disability, but in this case the fragmentation does not indicate low intelligence or a mental disability.

Motor Impairment

- Test administrators should select tests that do not need to be modified due to the test taker's motor impairment or that require very little modification. (Often intelligence tests include verbal and motor performance measures. Not using the motor performance measures could put too much emphasis on verbal intelligence.)
- The test administrator should have a writer available to enter responses on paper-and-pencil tasks that require fine motor coordination.

Cognitive Impairment

- Test takers with cognitive impairments should, in many cases, be tested using a structured interview, usually with family members or friends of the test takers present.

SOURCE: Adapted from Cohen, R. J., Swerdlik, M. E., & Phillips, S. M. (1996). *Psychological Testing and Assessment: An Introduction to Tests and Measurements* (3rd ed.). Mountain View, CA: Mayfield.

Table 3.1	Tests Developed Specifically for Persons With Physical or Mental Challenges

Disability	Attribute Measured	Name of Test
Visual Impairment	Intelligence	Haptic Intelligence Scale
	Intelligence	Intelligence Test for Visually Impaired Children
	Intelligence	Perkins Binet Tests of Intelligence for the Blind
	Cognitive ability	Cognitive Test for the Blind and Visually Impaired
	Development	Skills Inventory
	Learning/job success	Non-Language Learning Test
	Learning potential	The Blind Learning Aptitude Test
	Personality	Adolescent Emotional Factors Inventory
	Personality	Sound Test
	Vocational functioning	Comprehensive Vocational Evaluation System
	Vocational functioning and interest	PRG Interest Inventory
Hearing Impairment	Cognitive ability	Test of Nonverbal Intelligence
	Intelligence	Child Behavior Checklist
	Behavior	Devereaux Adolescent Behavior Rating Scale
	Behavior disorders	Walker Problem Behavior Identification Checklist
Motor Disabilities	Perceptual-motor skills	Purdue Perceptual-Motor Survey
	Sensory-motor skills	Frostig Movement Skills Test Battery
Cognitive Disabilities	Adaptive behavior	Vineland Adaptive Behavior Scales
	Career assessment	Career Assessment Inventories for the Learning Disabled
	Sexual knowledge and attitudes	Socio-Sexual Knowledge and Attitudes Test
	Vocational preference	Reading Free Vocational Inventory

To compensate for physical and mental impairments and learning disabilities, students can develop learning and test-taking strategies. The specific strategies required depend on the type and severity of the impairment or disability and vary from one person to the next, with some people requiring more help than others. Given the appropriate resources and support, most people with learning disabilities are very capable of performing well in school.

Students with learning disabilities have an important resource in their instructors, who can make adjustments that allow these students to learn and test more effectively. However, instructors cannot help students who have not self-declared their disabilities—informed the school administration or their instructors—and presented their diagnoses by a professional in education, psychology, or medicine. Even physical impairments are not always apparent to teachers and testing administrators.

Persons applying for a job might not be as likely as students to have a trained professional advocate to assist them with test modifications. Therefore, applicants who have any types of disabilities, including learning disabilities, need to self-declare their disabilities and, when appropriate, present their diagnoses by a professional in education, psychology, or medicine to the school administration or their instructors.

Table 3.2	Three Broad Categories of Learning Disabilities

Learning disabilities affect the ability to learn. Some examples of learning disabilities include the following:

- *Reading disability* is a reading and language-based learning disability, also commonly called dyslexia. For most children with learning disabilities receiving special education services, the primary area of difficulty is reading. People with reading disabilities often have problems recognizing words that they already know. They may also be poor spellers and may have problems with decoding skills. Other symptoms may include trouble with handwriting and problems understanding what they read. About 15 percent to 20 percent of people in the United States have a language-based disability, and of those, most have dyslexia.
- *Dyscalculia* (dis-kal-**kyoo**-lee-*uh*) is a learning disability related to math. Those with dyscalculia may have difficulty understanding math concepts and solving even simple math problems.
- *Dysgraphia* (dis-**graf**-ee-*uh*) is a learning disability related to handwriting. People with this condition may have problems forming letters as they write or may have trouble writing within a defined space.
- *Information-processing disorders* are learning disorders related to a person's ability to use the information that they take in through their senses—seeing, hearing, tasting, smelling, and touching. These problems are not related to an inability to see or hear. Instead, the conditions affect the way the brain recognizes, responds to, retrieves, and stores sensory information.
- *Language-related learning disabilities* are problems that interfere with age-appropriate communication, including speaking, listening, reading, spelling, and writing.

SOURCE: National Institute of Child Health and Human Development. (2010). *Learning disabilities*. Retrieved June 19, 2010, from http://www.nichd.nih.gov/health/topics/learning_disabilities.cfm

Test Takers From Multicultural Backgrounds

Test takers vary considerably in terms of their experiences and backgrounds. The U.S. Census Bureau (n.d.) reports that 14.4% of the U.S. population was Hispanic in 2000 and that this percentage is growing rapidly. Other minority groups, especially those from Asia, are also growing. In this textbook, we refer to test takers from **multicultural backgrounds** as those who belong to various minority groups based on race, cultural or ethnic origin, sexual orientation, family unit, primary language, and so on. As we move further into the 21st century, identifying racial differences will become more difficult as the number of families with two or more racial backgrounds increases.

This advance in diversity requires test users and test developers to attend to the demographic characteristics of the people for whom a test was developed. When test takers differ from the original test takers that the developer used to develop the test, minority scores can differ significantly from the majority of test takers. For instance, a vocabulary test in English is likely to be more difficult for test takers whose primary language is not English, but rather is Spanish, Arabic, or Japanese. In this case, the test user should not compare English speakers with those who speak other languages. Decisions based on "high" or "low" scores or on "passing" or "failing" scores will depend on the purpose of the test.

 More detail about the Personality Assessment Inventory can be found in Test Spotlight 6.1 in Appendix A.

Although attention to multicultural clinical assessment and its accompanying ethical or measurement problems has grown, the quality and quantity of research studies do not match the current need for information. Studies of American minorities and non-Americans are scarce for many popular assessment techniques, ranging from well-researched objective tests, such as the Personality Assessment Inventory, to projective techniques, such as the Thematic Apperception Test.

Studies conducted on the Rorschach Inkblot Test provide a good example. The Rorschach, which was developed in the early 20th century by Swiss psychologist Hermann Rorschach, is a projective personality test that is often used to identify personality disorders and assess emotional functioning. While various methods for scoring the Rorschach are used, the Exner scoring system appears to be the most popular method in the United States as it addresses many criticisms of skeptics. Several studies indicate that scores for relatively normal community samples of Mexicans, Central Americans, and South Americans on the Rorschach often differ strikingly from the norms of Exner's system for scoring this test. These findings raise the issue of whether the test can be used ethically with Hispanic adults and children in the United States (Wood, Nezworski, Lilienfeld, & Garb, 2003).

 More detail about the Rorschach Inkblot Test can be found in Test Spotlight 3.1 in Appendix A.

A positive example of multicultural relevance is demonstrated by the Minnesota Multiphasic Personality Inventory–Revised (MMPI-2). The MMPI was originally developed in the 1930s at Minnesota University to help identify personal, social, and behavioral problems in psychiatric patients. The test takers who participated in the development of the original MMPI were White residents of Minnesota, a largely rural state. As the MMPI became widely used for people of all races from diverse backgrounds, psychologists questioned whether the test provided accurate information for persons of color and urban populations. A major impetus for revising the MMPI came from these questions. Recent research suggests that the revised test, the MMPI-2, is a suitable measure for Blacks and Hispanics in the United States because the distribution of scores for these minorities is similar to the distribution of scores for Whites. The revision of the original MMPI provides a model for improving older tests that are not suitable for use with minorities (Wood et al., 2003).

 More detail about the Minnesota Multiphasic Personality Inventory can be found in Test Spotlight 12.1 in Appendix A.

Although the tests discussed in this section are appropriate primarily for clinical diagnosis, these and other tests have also been administered in the workplace. Using tests that are inappropriate for test takers in the workplace can cause people to be refused jobs, passed over for promotions, or perceived as ineligible for merit increases. In educational settings, inappropriate testing of minorities can cause students to be denied access to college or assigned to remedial classes.

INTERIM SUMMARY 3.3
TESTING SPECIAL POPULATIONS

- Some people who have physical or mental challenges might need special accommodations during testing to ensure that their test scores are accurate.
- Test users should ensure that the test outcomes accurately indicate the intended skill or attribute and that the test score has not been altered because of a disability.
- Often test users must modify the testing format and the test interpretation process to accurately reflect the skill or attribute the psychological test measures.

- Unlike physical and mental disabilities, a learning disability does not have visible signs.
- To compensate for physical and mental impairments and learning disabilities, students can develop learning and test-taking strategies. Professors can also help students who have diagnosed learning disabilities.
- Special populations also include test takers from diverse backgrounds that were not used to develop a test. Using tests inappropriate for minorities can cause these test takers to suffer adverse consequences due to inaccurate test scores.

Chapter Summary

Most professional societies have a set of professional practice guidelines known as ethical standards. Because testing is an important and often misunderstood area of psychology, the APA and other professional societies have published numerous documents on ethical issues that relate to testing and assessment. One important document is the *Standards for Educational and Psychological Testing* (AERA, APA, & NCME, 1999). Another is the *Code of Fair Testing Practices in Education* (Joint Committee on Testing Practices, 2004), which describes the obligations of test developers and test users.

These ethical codes affirm the importance of respect for individuals, establish the need to safeguard individual dignity and privacy, and condemn unfair discriminatory practices. Particular issues of importance include maintaining confidentiality and anonymity, obtaining informed consent, and using tests appropriately.

Test publishers have ethical and professional standards that they should follow. Publishers should sell psychological tests only to qualified users, market psychological tests truthfully, and provide a comprehensive test manual for each psychological test. Test publishers have the responsibility to ensure that the persons who purchase and administer tests have the necessary training and experience to use psychological tests appropriately.

Persons who have physical or mental challenges might have special needs when taking tests that require modifying the testing process. The modifications that the test user makes depend on the specific disability of the test taker. When testing someone who has physical or mental challenges, ethical standards and certain laws require that the test user modify the test or the interpretation to ensure that the individual's impairment does not influence the test outcome. Another group whose members might need test modifications are those with learning disabilities. Students and their instructors can work together to develop learning and test-taking strategies.

Engaging in the Learning Process

Key Concepts

After completing your study of this chapter, you should be able to define each of the following terms. These terms are bolded in the text of this chapter and defined in the Glossary.

- anonymity
- certification
- cognitive impairments
- confidentiality
- ethical dilemmas
- ethical standards
- ethics
- informed consent

- learning disability
- motor impairments
- multicultural backgrounds
- sensory impairments
- test security
- test taker
- test user
- user qualifications

LEARNING ACTIVITIES

The following are some learning activities you can engage in to support the learning objectives for this chapter.

Learning Objectives	Study Tips and Learning Activities
After completing your study of this chapter, you should be able to do the following:	*The following study tips will help you meet these learning objectives:*
Define ethics and discuss ethical issues of concern to testing professionals and consumers.	• Look back in this chapter and make a list of the ethical dilemmas and problems that test publishers and test users might face.
Identify organizations concerned with ethical testing procedures and their ethical standards or codes of ethics.	• Make a list of all the organizations in this chapter that have published ethical standards or guidelines.
Describe how organizations can and cannot enforce compliance with their ethical standards.	• Write a case study in which a psychologist has not complied with one or more ethical points. As part of the study, describe what various parties were able to do about the psychologist's noncompliance.

Differentiate between ethical standards and ethical guidelines.	• Answer the following questions for ethical standards and for ethical guidelines:
	  ○ By whom are they written? ○ To whom do they apply?
	  ○ How are they enforced?

Define and understand the rights to privacy, anonymity, and informed consent.	• Write three case studies—one for each term.
Explain the ethical responsibilities of test publishers and test users.	• Think about each of the ethical responsibilities discussed in the chapter. Write a paragraph on why someone might choose or not choose to be responsible for each.
Explain what test user qualifications are and why they are important.	• Make a list of possible user qualifications in the *Standards* (AERA, APA, & NCME, 1999) and why each might be important.
Explain what the *Standards* say about testing special populations.	• Define each of the four types of impairments, and describe what kind of accommodations you think a person with that impairment might need.
Describe what learning disabilities are and strategies for coping with them.	• Interview someone who has been diagnosed as having a learning disability, and ask what accommodations that person needs when testing.

ADDITIONAL LEARNING ACTIVITIES

College students, particularly those majoring in psychology, take psychological tests often. Not only are you tested on your academic knowledge, but you also may be asked to participate in class exercises or research studies that call for testing. The following situations are adapted from a casebook on ethical teaching (Keith-Spiegel, Wittig, Perkins, Balogh, & Whitley, 1994). Answer the following questions for each situation:

1. Is there an ethical issue? If so, what is it?
2. Is there an ethical dilemma, or has an ethical standard clearly been violated? Explain your answer.
3. Propose how such a situation can be avoided.

   a. *Marketing Research Participation.* A professor teaching an introductory psychology course informs his students at the beginning of the semester that they will be required to either participate in a research study or complete another assignment that takes about the same amount of time and effort. The study is one that he is conducting on intelligence in which they will take a number of psychological tests, including IQ tests. He describes to the students the department's rules on test administration that follow American Psychological Association guidelines regarding confidentiality, informed consent, and debriefing. He then tells the students that he definitely prefers that they serve as research participants.

b. *Class Demonstrations of Secure Tests.* In an upper division undergraduate course on psychological testing, the professor demonstrates two psychodiagnostic tests designated as "secure": the Rorschach Inkblot Test and the Minnesota Multiphasic Personality Inventory (MMPI). Although she does not teach students how to score or interpret them, she does show actual Rorschach cards to the students and reads actual items from the MMPI.

c. *Student Disclosures in Class.* A professor in a social psychology class likes to give attitude scales as class demonstrations and exercises. His scales cover topics such as attitudes toward women and the "Just World" theory as well as personality traits such as locus of control and self-efficacy. He asks the students to complete a scale and then gives them the key for scoring it. (He uses only scales that are published in professional journals for public access.) After the students have determined their scores, he asks them to form groups and discuss their results. Often he also requires students to include their test results in their journals, which the professor reads at the end of the semester.

PRACTICE QUESTIONS

The following are some practice questions to assess your understanding of the material presented in this chapter.

Multiple Choice

Choose the one best answer to each question.

1. Which one of the following statements about ethical standards is FALSE?

    a. Members of professional organizations can be expelled from the organization for violating ethical standards.

    b. Ethical standards are laws passed by federal or local government agencies.

    c. Ethical standards are statements by professionals regarding appropriate behavior.

    d. No one can be tried or sued in a court of law for violating an ethical standard.

2. Misuse of psychological tests by those administering and using the tests is

    a. not a problem in today's society.

    b. sometimes a problem, but rarely with serious consequences.

    c. a chronic and disturbing problem that can result in serious harm.

    d. of most concern to researchers who are likely to be affected.

3. Test takers have the right to

    a. keep the test.

    b. understand what the test is measuring.

    c. review the test before administration.

    d. privacy.

4. A group of teachers at Alfred E. Newman High School decided that it would be helpful to administer intelligence tests to first-year students to be used for placing students in appropriate classes. They also decided that it would be best not to tell the students what they were being tested for and not to tell them their scores on the intelligence tests. When they discussed their plan with the school psychologist, he strongly opposed it because he said it violated students' right to

    a. assemble.

    b. withdraw.

    c. know their IQ.

    d. informed consent.

5. Belinda conducted a research project in which she interviewed workers about their work standards and integrity on the job. She assured her participants that all personal information they disclosed would be kept private and would not be disclosed without their permission. Which of the following was she guaranteeing her participants?

    a. Anonymity

    b. Reliability

    c. Confidentiality

    d. Obscurity

6. Phillip is a supervisor at the LMNOP Corporation. He is very concerned about helping his workers and meeting their needs. Therefore, he sent a request to the human resources department asking for the scores on pre-employment tests that his workers had taken. The human resources department replied that it could not give him the scores because the test takers had been assured of their

    a. right to informed consent.

    b. protection from invasion of privacy.

    c. protection from stigma.

    d. right to confidentiality.

7. Coding test materials in such a way that participants can be identified without their knowledge or consent would be a violation of test users' promise of

   a. anonymity.
   b. protection from invasion of privacy.
   c. protection from stigma.
   d. right to confidentiality.

8. Ethical standards are written for

   a. test publishers and test users.
   b. members of a professional organization.
   c. test takers with disabilities.
   d. everyone involved in the testing process.

9. Publishers should ensure that every psychological test has

   a. adequate marketing.
   b. an unlimited number of test users.
   c. a complete test manual.
   d. a record of satisfied test users.

10. When test questions are published or given to persons other than test takers, there may be a problem with test

    a. scoring.
    b. security.
    c. validity.
    d. reliability.

11. Which of the following is listed in your textbook as a responsibility of the test publisher?

    a. Ensure that only qualified persons purchase its psychological tests
    b. Market the psychological tests it publishes
    c. Give a copy of the test to each potential purchaser
    d. Give a copy of the test manual to each potential purchaser

12. Mental retardation, learning disabilities, and traumatic brain injuries are examples of

    a. cognitive impairments.
    b. motor impairments.
    c. sensory impairments.
    d. personality impairments.

13. Laws that protect people with physical and mental challenges

    a. require that the test user modify the testing form to prevent an individual's impairment from influencing the test outcome.
    b. require that all tests be given individually and orally.
    c. relieve the test user from the ethical standard of informed consent.
    d. dictate specific methods for administering tests to people with impairments.

14. A structured interview might need to be substituted for paper-and-pencil tests for individuals with what type of impairments?

    a. Visual
    b. Motor
    c. Hearing
    d. Cognitive

15. Learning disabilities

    a. are much like physical and mental disabilities.
    b. do not have visible signs.
    c. do not require special testing administration.
    d. do not affect test scores.

16. Which of the following can instructors do to help students with learning disabilities?

    a. Tape-record lectures
    b. Encourage learning-disabled students to self-disclose
    c. Request "reasonable accommodations"
    d. Determine how each individual learns best

17. Which one of the following is TRUE?

    a. Most psychological tests currently in use are appropriate for test takers from various cultures and backgrounds.
    b. The Rorschach Inkblot Test is appropriate for Blacks and Hispanics as well as for Whites.
    c. Tests appropriate for people with learning disabilities are also appropriate for normal Blacks and Hispanics.
    d. The revision of the original Minnesota Multiphasic Personality Inventory provides a model for revising older tests that were not developed with minorities in mind.

Short Answer/Essay

Read each of the following, and consider your response carefully based on the information presented in this chapter. Write your answer to each question in two or three paragraphs.

1. Discuss three ethical issues of concern to testing professionals and consumers.

2. What documents about ethics are published by the APA? Why is it important for test users to be familiar with these documents?

3. Describe how organizations can and cannot enforce compliance with their ethical standards.

4. Compare and contrast ethical standards and ethical guidelines.

5. What rights do test takers have regarding privacy, anonymity, and informed consent?

6. What are the ethical responsibilities of test publishers and test users?

7. Explain what test user qualifications are and why they are important.

8. What are the ethical responsibilities of test publishers?

9. Describe what learning disabilities are and strategies for coping with them.

10. Explain what the *Standards* (AERA, APA, & NCME, 1999) say about testing special populations.

11. If you thought you had a learning disability, what steps would you take to be eligible for test modifications?

12. Describe the issues associated with test takers from multicultural backgrounds.

Answer Keys

Additional Learning Activities

a. *Marketing Research Participation.* Although the professor has assured his students that the research study will conform to the APA's guidelines for ethical research, Keith-Spiegel and colleagues (1994) point out that when professors make their preferences known, students may interpret the situation as less than voluntary or even coercive. Insisting that there is no penalty for not complying with the professor's preference might not be enough to relieve the pressure that some students feel to conform to the instructor's preferences.

b. *Class Demonstrations of Secure Tests.* Making secure test items available to anyone who is not authorized to use them—outside of the standard testing situation described in the test manual—is inappropriate. Assessment demonstrations should be limited to those in the textbook because the professor can assume that items were released by the test publisher (as is the case in this textbook). Using secure materials in graduate courses for training purposes is an exception to this limitation (Keith-Spiegel et al., 1994).

c. *Student Disclosures in Class.* Requiring students to disclose personal information in class or to their instructor is a violation of their right to privacy. Such disclosures also have the potential for embarrassment and harm. Asking students to complete attitude scales in class without divulging the results is acceptable when the professor is careful to provide adequate debriefing regarding how the results can be interpreted. However, no student should be required to participate against his or her will. Scales for which there is no reliability or validity information should be clearly designated by the instructor as learning activities, not psychological tests.

Multiple Choice

1. b	2. c	3. d	4. d
5. c	6. b	7. a	8. b
9. c	10. b	11. a	12. a
13. a	14. a	15. b	16. d
17. d			

Short Answer/Essay

Refer to your textbook for answers. If you are unsure of an answer and cannot generate the answer after reviewing your book, ask your professor for clarification.

How Does Computerized Testing Work?

CHAPTER 4: HOW DOES COMPUTERIZED TESTING WORK?

After completing your study of this chapter, you should be able to do the following:

- Describe how computers have enhanced the development, administration, and scoring of psychological tests.
- Discuss the advantages and disadvantages of computerized testing.
- Explain the differences between adaptive testing and traditional testing.
- Discuss the advantages and disadvantages of administering tests using the web.
- Discuss the implications of web-based technology for testing in the future.

"I want to apply to graduate school this spring, but I understand that I have to take the GRE on a computer. I don't know much about computers, and I'm anxious about taking the GRE."

"I took a vocational interest inventory at our Career Services Center a couple of weeks ago. I spent three hours answering questions on a computer, but I learned that I have strong leadership and communication skills. I'm also an extrovert and a visionary."

"I've heard that many companies ask job applicants to apply and even take tests online. I'm really worried because I don't have much experience with computers."

"My teacher says that my test is her test and my grade is her grade. What's she talking about?"

Have you ever taken a computer-administered test or survey? Chances are good that you have completed a survey or test online. Advances in computer technology have added a new dimension to many areas of the psychological testing process, including the construction and administration of psychological tests. Using a computerized testing system can streamline the testing process, ensure standardized administration, decrease scoring errors, and enable test takers to apply and qualify for jobs outside the areas in which they live.

Advances in computer technology have also benefited the survey administration and scoring process. Many companies administer surveys online because online surveys are more convenient for respondents. When surveys are more convenient, they are likely to be completed by more people. In addition, computer software can often enable people with physical challenges to complete surveys or standardized tests that they could not complete in a paper-and-pencil format. Finally, current computer software allows the testing community to develop, administer, and score adaptive tests—a complicated type of test that was unfeasible before computers became a part of daily life.

Another capability that has changed the field of psychological testing is communication using the web. Traditionally, standardized testing was a lengthy process that relied on the postal service. Delivery of tests to test administrators and test takers, return of the tests to the scoring center, scoring and interpretation of the tests, and delivery of test results to the test takers and test users often took place over a period of two to three months. Now it is possible for a test taker and the test administrator to sign in to a website, pay for testing, take the test, and receive the test report (test score and interpretation) in half a day—often within a matter of hours.

In this chapter, we look in depth at issues and concepts that have transformed psychological testing and will likely continue to do so. First, we look at how computers are used in the psychological testing process. Second, we discuss computerized adaptive testing. Third, we highlight the advantages and disadvantages of online psychological testing. Finally, we discuss the implications that web-based testing has for the testing and survey industry in the future.

Computerized Testing

Computers are a very popular tool in the psychological testing industry. Although using computers for scoring and interpreting tests is not new, computers now facilitate and enhance all phases of the testing process. Some of the first computerized tests were used to make hiring decisions in organizational settings and included tests to see how well an individual typed, word-processed, and entered data into a spreadsheet. These tests replicated the types of tasks that are most often encountered in the automated office.

Today, many computerized tests are available. Professionals such as social workers, psychiatrists, psychologists, counselors, opinion surveyors, and human resources professionals rely on computers to assist them in developing, administering, scoring, and interpreting tests. In this section of the chapter, we discuss the use of computers in test development, administration, scoring, and interpretation. We also discuss the advantages and disadvantages of computerized testing.

Test Development

Computers make it easy to construct many types of tests, particularly classroom tests. In education, for example, textbook publishers now offer professors computerized test construction software programs to help them prepare course exams. These programs contain a **test bank**—a large number of multiple-choice, true/false, and short-answer questions that assess knowledge of a subject or group of subjects. The publisher categorizes the questions by chapter and sometimes also by difficulty. This classification helps professors increase evidence of content validity (which we discuss in more detail in

Chapter 7) by making it easier to choose a representative sample of questions from each chapter. Publishers also provide software for combining the questions and printing the test (for example, the Test Construction Kit published by JCG Software).

Test Administration

Now test users can administer many types of assessments on computers. During the early days of computer administration, computer-based tests were exact copies of their paper-and-pencil counterparts. For example, Vispoel, Boo, and Bleiler (2001) report on their use of a computerized personality test, the Rosenberg Self-Esteem Scale (SES). Rosenberg (1965, 1986) developed the SES in a paper-and-pencil format to measure self-esteem in adolescents during the early 1960s. Since then, many studies have used the scale to measure self-esteem in people of all ages. Vispoel and colleagues conducted a study to compare test administration of a computer-based version of the SES with the paper-and-pencil version. When they administered both versions to 224 college students, they found no differences in the students' scores on the two versions. Two major differences did exist, however: students took longer to complete the computerized test, and students reported the computerized version to be *less* fatiguing.

In addition, computerized administration allows test developers to use a more sophisticated type of assessment—**adaptive testing.** Adaptive tests are made up of questions chosen from a large test bank to match the skill and ability level of the test taker. We discuss computer adaptive testing in more detail later in this chapter.

Test Scoring and Interpretation

For decades, test users have mailed answer sheets to a service that scores, interprets, and writes reports using computer software. Today, however, many computer-administered tests are immediately scored or test users send assessment data to the scoring center using e-mail. For immediate scoring and interpretation, test users can purchase computerized scoring programs or ask test takers to respond directly on the test publisher's website. Your college's career services center probably has computerized vocational tests and the ability to score test takers' answers immediately.

Advantages of Computerized Testing

Computer-based tests have become popular because of their many advantages. Test publishers develop computerized tests for many of the following reasons:

- Computerized tests are efficient. Whether administering or scoring tests, computers save test users money (for example, the cost of shipping scoring sheets for analysis) and time (for example, test users and test takers receive their test results almost immediately).
- Computerized tests can be scheduled at a test taker's convenience. Rather than needing to wait for a group administration, as once was the case with most college entrance exams, test takers can schedule testing at a time that is convenient for the test administrator and the test user.
- Computerized tests can be administered individually in comfortable settings. Paper-and-pencil tests are often administered to groups in large rooms where it is difficult to control room temperature or to provide enough comfortable seats. Individuals can complete tests in a computer lab or even in their homes.
- Computerized tests facilitate standardized administration procedures by eliminating human error. Test administrators are not as involved in the computerized testing process (for example, most of the time they are not required to read instructions to test takers), and therefore standardized administration

procedures are less likely to be compromised. However, Potosky and Bobko (2004) point out that test takers can choose to read, scan, or skip directions when they appear only on the computer screen.

- Computerized tests allow for more technologically advanced testing procedures. Computers can simulate real-life situations, present three-dimensional graphics, respond to voice-activated responses, and provide on-screen calculators. They also can provide split screens that show reading passages and questions at the same time.

- Computerized tests allow more opportunities for testing people with physical or mental challenges. For example, in the mid 1980s Jackson (1986) described a test response device for people with hearing or physical impairments—a dental plate that allows test takers to use their tongues to depress certain areas on the plate to respond to test questions.

- Computerized tests can be administered in an adaptive format. With an adaptive format, a test taker's time is not wasted on questions that are too easy or too hard. More on adaptive testing follows in the next section of this chapter.

- Computerized tests decrease the errors associated with scoring. Once again, humans are not as involved in the process, and therefore it is less likely that a test taker's score will be affected by errors in data entry or calculations. Computers also provide better security for storing data than do paper files.

- Computerized tests can incorporate sound. One valuable feature of these tests is the ability of test developers to communicate using audio. Adding audio to a test has several advantages. For example, test takers might not attend to instructions on a computer screen as well as those who hear the instructions read by an administrator (Ployhart, Weekley, Holtz, & Kemp, 2003). More important, audio is a critical element in human cognition. Of a person's total time involved in communicating, research indicates approximately 45% is spent listening, 30% is spent speaking, 16% is spent reading, and 9% is spent writing (University of Missouri, 1993–2010). Therefore, test developers can enhance the accuracy of measurement, particularly for cognitive skills, by using speech and nonspeech audio appropriately. Using audio and video can also enhance the fidelity or realism of the assessment.

Disadvantages of Computerized Testing

Although some disadvantages of computerized testing remain, innovative test developers have found ways to overcome most difficulties that computerized testing presents.

Computer Anxiety

 More detail about the Computer Anxiety Scale can be found in Test Spotlight 4.1 in Appendix A.

Although computers are as familiar as telephones and televisions to many people, some people still experience anxiety about using computer technology. For example, disadvantaged persons who do not have access to computers might be anxious about taking a test administered on a computer. Protocols and software are now available to help those who are computer illiterate or who have computer anxiety to become comfortable with using a computer before testing begins. For Your Information Box 4.1 includes a description of one of the older measures of computer anxiety, Marcoulides's (1985) Computer Anxiety Scale. The box also includes a description of a study that examined whether computer anxiety has changed since it was first recognized nearly 25 years ago.

Interpretation of Computer-Based Tests

For a computer to interpret a raw test score, the test developer must load onto the computer a file of explanatory sentences matched to possible test scores. When the computer program scores a test, it selects the prearranged interpretation. Although programs can be created to take into account scores from other tests and demographic characteristics, such as sex and age, most programs simply provide the test taker with the prearranged interpretation. If the test developer groups a range of

FOR YOUR INFORMATION BOX 4.1

Computer Anxiety

Are you likely to experience anxiety when you use a computer? Do you find that you have sweaty palms and a feeling of fear when you try to learn something new about the computer? How would you rate your anxiety (not at all, a little, a fair amount, much, or very much) if you did the following?

1. Think about taking a class in computer programming.
2. Apply for a job that requires some training in computers.
3. Sit in front of a home computer.
4. Be around people who are "into" computers.
5. Watch a movie about an intelligent computer.
6. Get "error" messages from a computer.
7. Attend a workshop on the uses of computers.

If you answered "much" or "very much", you might be experiencing computer anxiety. You might be interested to know that although computers have become a part of our daily lives, a large percentage of the population continues to find using computers quite unpleasant.

The concept of computer anxiety was acknowledged during the 1980s when computers began being used in the workplace, in schools and colleges, and in homes. Simonson, Maurer, Montag-Torardi, and Whitaker (1987) define computer anxiety as "the fear or apprehension felt by individuals when they use computers or when they consider the possibility of computer utilization" (p. 238).

Another group of researchers (Rosen, Sears, & Weil, 1987) propose three types of individuals with computer anxiety. People of the first type react to computers with anxiety behaviors such as sweaty palms, heart palpitations, and headaches. People of the second type experience fear of computers and continually experienced negative cognitions regarding computers. People of the third type are referred to as *uncomfortable users* and are slightly anxious because of a lack of information about computers.

Computer anxiety is a relatively young trait compared with other types of anxiety or neuroses that psychologists have studied for more than 100 years. Marcoulides (1985) presented a paper on the Computer Anxiety Scale (CAS) and since then has taken advantage of the opportunity to investigate how computer anxiety manifests itself, whether it appears in all populations that use computer technology, and whether the experience of computer anxiety changes as a population becomes more familiar with using computers.

Marcoulides, Stocker, and Marcoulides (2004) have now translated the CAS into Chinese and German, and their research shows that computer anxiety and its manifestations have remained the same as years have progressed. The CAS developed prior to 1985 continued to be appropriate more than 15 years later. Marcoulides and colleagues conclude that computer anxiety in one population is much like computer anxiety in another population and that, although many rapid changes and advances have occurred in computer technology, the basic structure of computer anxiety has not changed.

Fortunately, computer anxiety can be overcome, and a number of training programs are available to help individuals become more familiar with computers and alleviate their anxiety.

To experience a computer anxiety test, go to www.psych.uncc.edu/pagoolka/ComputerAnxiety-intro.html.

SOURCE: Adapted from Marcoulides, G. A., Stocker, Y., & Marcoulides, L. D. (2004). Examining the psychological impact of computer technology: An updated cross-cultural study. *Educational and Psychological Measurement, 64,* 311–318.

scores for each interpretation, the computer is not able to inform the test taker that he or she is at the high or low end of the grouping. Therefore, unless tempered by human judgment and discretion, computer-based test interpretations provide more general interpretations that a test taker is more likely to misperceive.

Testing Strategies

Over the years, students and instructors have learned strategies that may improve test scores on standardized scholastic tests such as the SAT and the Graduate Record Examination (GRE). For instance, savvy test takers know to complete questions when they know the answers, skip questions that they find difficult, and return to the difficult questions after completing all of the questions to which they know the answers. This strategy works well on paper-and-pencil multiple-choice questions; however, it will not work on most computerized tests. On many computerized tests, the test takers must complete the question on the computer screen before they can continue. After the test takers move on to the next screen, they cannot return to the previous one. Some computerized tests do allow test takers to skip questions, mark questions to re-review, and return to unanswered questions at a later time. An example of such a test is the Professional in Human Resources exam, a computer-administered certification exam that measures an individual's knowledge of the technical and operational aspects of human resources. The Senior Professional in Human Resources (SPHR) and the Global Professional in Human Resources (GPHR) are also computer-administered certification exams. The SPHR measures knowledge of strategic human resources and policy issues, and the GPHR measures knowledge needed to be a viable global human resources professional.

There are successful strategies for taking computerized tests—particularly adaptive tests—that we address in the next section of this chapter.

INTERIM SUMMARY 4.1
COMPUTERIZED TESTING

- Computers now facilitate and enhance all phases of the testing process.
- Computers make it easier to construct valid classroom tests by storing test banks and test development software.
- Computerized administration allows test users to administer more sophisticated assessments such as adaptive testing and video-based scenarios.
- Test users can purchase computerized scoring programs for immediate scoring and interpretation or can ask test takers to respond directly on the test publisher's website.

- Advantages of computerized testing include greater efficiency, convenient scheduling, individual administration of standardized tests, and a decrease in administration and scoring errors.
- Some disadvantages of computerized testing may be the presence of computer anxiety, generalized test interpretations, and changing test strategies.

Computerized Adaptive Testing

In **computerized adaptive testing (CAT)**, all test takers start with the same set of questions—usually those of moderate difficulty. As the test progresses, the computer software chooses and presents each test taker with harder or easier questions depending on how well the test taker answered previous questions. According to test developers, these types of tests provide a fuller profile of a person in a shorter amount of time and the test taker does not need to spend time on questions that are too easy or too difficult. Therefore, a test that once took four or five hours may take only two or three hours using the CAT model.

The concept of adaptive testing dates back to the beginning of the 20th century, when Binet developed the Binet IQ test that was later published as the Stanford–Binet IQ Test (Binet & Simon, 1905). Weiss (2004) relates the adaptive testing method to judging an athletic competition, pointing out that it would not be practical to measure athletes' hurdle-jumping ability by having them repeatedly jump over a succession of two-foot hurdles—similar to answering a succession of multiple-choice questions:

> Rather, a series of hurdles of increasingly high levels is set up, and the athlete tries to clear each until she or he is no longer able to do so. Then, to determine a more precise indication of the level that the participant can clear, a set of hurdles that vary in a relatively narrow range around the level at which the individual began to miss is constructed. In this way, the task is "adapted" to the individual's performance in order to obtain precise estimates of each athlete's ability. (p. 71)

Adaptive testing for standardized tests remained unfeasible for most of the 20th century until the advent of computerized testing allowed adaptive testing to be used in nationwide testing situations. CAT allowed psychologists to redesign important tests, including the national nursing licensure exam, the GRE, the Armed Services Vocational Aptitude Battery, and achievement tests in local areas such as Portland, Oregon (Weiss, 2004).

CAT software begins the test with one to three questions of moderate difficulty. It then selects the subsequent test questions based on the test taker's skill level, which was determined by the answers to the beginning questions. The software continues to present questions until it affirms the test taker's skill level—at which time the test ends. In addition, the computer houses the large bank of questions required by adaptive testing, and the CAT software scores the exam. Most paper-and-pencil exams yield scores based on the number of correct responses; however, a new technology for judging test questions, *item response theory*, provides more accurate scoring than do conventional tests. For Your Information Box 4.2 presents helpful tips on how to take adaptive tests such as the GRE, the Graduate Management Admissions Test, and the Test of English as a Foreign Language.

CAT has many applications. For instance, beginning in the early 21st century, researchers presented convincing evidence that **computerized adaptive rating scales (CARS)** might help managers rate their employees more accurately than do two more popular types of rating scales (for example, Borman et al., 2001). In the CARS study, raters were presented with a pair of behavioral

FYI

FOR YOUR INFORMATION BOX 4.2

Tips for Taking Computerized Adaptive Tests

Are computerized adaptive tests more difficult than traditional standardized tests? What should a student know before taking an adaptive test? How can a student practice for an adaptive test? The Tree Foundation (n.d.), which offers preparation courses for foreign students who wish to study in the United Kingdom or the United States, has several suggestions that might help students in preparing to take adaptive tests.

First, the Tree Foundation (n.d.) suggests that students learn how adaptive tests are scored. The foundation emphasizes that an adaptive test does not give the same weight or importance to each question when determining the final score. Questions at the beginning of the test count more than those at the end of the test. Not only are the beginning questions worth more, but they also determine whether the subsequent questions will be more or less difficult. Later questions verify whether the test taker performs at the skill level that the earlier questions identified, and they contribute less to the final score. Therefore, the Tree Foundation suggests that test takers spend more time and effort doing their best on the beginning questions before they begin focusing on the middle questions.

Testing experts at Educational Testing Service (ETS) have a different outlook. They suggest that students who worry too much about the first few questions might hurt their scores. Test takers should pay close attention to the first 10 questions, but they also should pay close attention to the subsequent 10 questions. In truth, they say, test takers should concentrate on each question on the test. Placing too much emphasis on the beginning questions might cause excess anxiety that can reduce test takers' concentration (Guernsey, 2000).

According to the Tree Foundation (n.d.), the ending questions do not count as much, and test takers can use the time left in the testing session to finish the test even if they need to guess. Test takers do need to finish the test, and therefore the Tree Foundation advises them to make intelligent guesses on the last questions. Both the Tree Foundation and ETS agree that the best strategy is "Pace yourself, but don't hurry!"

Second, the Tree Foundation (n.d.) warns test takers to be cautious. Successful test takers are those who are particularly careful to answer the beginning questions accurately. The test may contain **experimental questions**—questions that do not count toward the final score. (Tests contain experimental questions because test developers must continue to develop new questions. The best way of finding out whether a question measures accurately is to try it out on current test takers.) Because some questions may be experimental questions, the Tree Foundation advises test takers not to worry about questions that are too difficult or too easy. In other words, "Focus on doing your best!"

Finally, test takers may be glad to know that obtaining an average score is relatively easy. Making a high score, however, can be quite difficult because testing companies continually add scores to their databases as soon as they score each test. Because the majority of test takers will score close to the mean, those who do exceptionally well must score better than 95% of all those who have taken the test. (Chapter 5 explains the statistics behind this statement.) The Tree Foundation (n.d.) advises test takers against taking a computerized adaptive test without proper preparation. Guessing on the beginning questions might actually cause the testing software to punish the test takers by awarding easier and easier questions. In other words, "Be prepared!"

The best strategy for doing well on a computerized adaptive test comes down to three simple rules:

- Pace yourself and do not hurry.
- Focus on doing your best.
- Be prepared.

SOURCE: Adapted from Tree Foundation. (n.d.). *CAT: Computer adaptive tests.* Retrieved June 19, 2010, from http://www.treefoundation.gr/cat.htm

statements (for example, "This employee arrives on time each day" and "This employee often arrives at work late") and were asked to choose the one that best described the employee they observed in a group of videotaped role-plays. As in CAT, the computer software selected behavioral statements based on the rater's previous responses. The outcomes of the study showed that the CARS format provided more reliable and valid ratings than did graphic rating scales or behaviorally anchored rating scales.

Web-Based Assessment

Expanding educational assessments and the rapid expansion of computer and Internet technologies have produced an increase in online assessment tools. These assessments range from informal classroom assessment, such as pretests, tests, worksheets, and class evaluations, to formal standardized tests (Doe, 2005).

Enterprise services are online standardized tests offered by companies for large numbers of test takers at multiple sites. For example, ETS, which publishes educational tests such as the SAT and the GRE, provides an enterprise service.

Companies that provide server space, web design, and maintenance provide **hosted services.** Blackboard is an example of a hosted service. Blackboard provides, among other things, a shell that instructors and students can use for sharing instructional materials (chat rooms and postings), posting grades, and conducting online assessments.

Other companies offer various **nonhosted services,** providing products that run on local area networks or private websites. Instructors use nonhosted products to construct unique websites for instructional and assessment purposes. Examples of nonhosted services include MyGradeBook, Quia Web, Examview Test Generator, Digital Teacher, and Questionmark Perception.

Web-based testing takes place under two conditions: proctored and unproctored. A **proctor** is a person similar to a test administrator who supervises the testing location; for instance, most proctored testing takes place in computer labs. Unproctored tests are those that test takers complete at a time and location of their own choice, such as their homes, businesses, or a public computer station.

Web-based assessment adds to the advantages of computerized testing. In addition to immediate scoring and reporting, web-based assessment allows test takers' data to be added immediately to a database of testing scores. This type of assessment greatly facilitates administration of standardized tests as well as informal classroom assessment. For example, instructors can administer pretests or study questions from the web as part of class activities. Web-based assessment can also enhance learning, particularly self-paced learning, when students can self-assess their level of achievement.

Ployhart and colleagues (2003) point to the increasing decisions by large employers to convert their paper-and-pencil employment tests to web-based tests, resulting in greater benefits in efficiency and cost savings. On the Web Box 4.1 describes the online testing center managed by the Society for Human Resources Management.

ON THE WEB BOX 4.1

Online Testing at the Society for Human Resources Management

www.shrm.org/TemplatesTools/AssessmentResources/SHRMTestingCenter/

 As the world's largest association devoted to human resources management, the Society for Human Resources Management (SHRM) provides HR professionals with essential information and resources, one of which is an online testing center. This testing center provides SHRM members who are qualified testing professionals with electronic access to more than 400 valid and reliable tests, from over 50 publishers, in areas such as personality and skills assessment, coaching and leadership, mechanical and technical skills, information technology skills, pre-employment screening, and career exploration. This testing center allows qualified testing professionals to purchase individual tests, administer the tests online, and receive electronic reports.

To learn more about online assessment through the SHRM, go to www.shrm.org/TemplatesTools/AssessmentResources/SHRMTestingCenter/. Click on FAQ to learn specific details from the point of view of the test purchaser or user.

SOURCE: Adapted from the Society for Human Resources Management. (2010b). *SHRM testing center: Online testing solutions.* Retrieved June 19, 2010, from http://www.shrm.org/TemplatesTools/AssessmentResources/SHRMTestingCenter

Administering Surveys Online

Survey research firms are companies that specialize in the construction, administration, and analysis of survey data for marketing, political opinion surveys, organizational satisfaction surveys, and so on also make good use of web-based assessment technology. The Council of American Survey Research Organizations (2009a) highlights the following three basic methods for conducting online surveys.

E-mail Surveys

Using e-mail to distribute and return surveys is often the fastest and simplest of the three methods. Although these surveys are easy to develop, they lack the flexibility needed for longer surveys and the administrator's data retrieval options are limited. E-mail surveys are perfect for internal organizational surveys or for any audience for which e-mail addresses are available.

HTML Surveys

Accessed via an Internet service provider (for example, Comcast, America Online) and completed online, these offer the flexibility to create more complicated surveys with skip patterns (for example, "If *yes*, then skip to the next section"), automatic data retrieval, better graphics, and sound. Typically, respondents for these surveys receive an e-mail asking them to go to a website to complete the surveys.

Interactive Surveys

Respondents usually download a software application that contains the survey and complete the survey on their own computers at a time and location convenient for them. This method offers the greatest flexibility for making the survey interesting and appealing, and the application automatically saves and transmits the survey data to the administrator. (Chapter 10 includes a detailed discussion of survey development.)

Finally, web-based assessment can be particularly appealing to researchers who often have trouble recruiting research participants. Research areas that have relied on web-based assessment include autism spectrum disorders (Skuse et al., 2004) and dietary and physical activity behaviors of middle school students (Horowitz, Shilts, & Townsend, 2004).

New Challenges

On the other hand, web-based testing presents new challenges for test developers and test users. Potosky and Bobko (2004) point out several problems that arise as a consequence of conducting testing on the web.

Issues With Timed Tests

Although computer software can track or control the time a respondent takes to answer questions, **virtual time**—the time the computer records—might not be equal to the actual time passed during test administration. Only a few items can be presented on one screen, and screens or web pages take time to load or appear before respondents can read or respond to them. The current solution to this problem is to have the timer add back the average number of seconds it takes for the screens within a test to load. In addition, when test takers can see the timer, they are likely to be distracted.

Test Taker Strategies

The strategies that test takers adopt can vary widely. On a paper-and-pencil test, strategies such as skipping and marking questions are useful. Such strategies, however, may be inefficient or impossible on a computer- or web-based test. Some of these tests might not allow test takers to return to a previous screen, and others that do allow returning to a previous screen become inefficient when test takers must wait for screens to change. When all test takers must answer questions in the same order, the test's ability to distinguish among test takers on the skills being measured improves. However, comparing paper-and-pencil administration with computer administration becomes more difficult.

Identification and Monitoring of Test Takers

Although it is possible for test takers to complete tests whenever and wherever they choose, most web-based tests are administered in a computer lab with an administrator present. In fact, organizations such as Prometric (n.d.) specialize in offering testing sites for the administration of web-based tests. There are several reasons for continuing to administer tests to groups in a single setting. First, a proctor must verify the identity of each test taker. Second, many tests (for example, knowledge tests) require that test takers not have access to information in the form of books or notes while they are taking the test. Third, test takers may be tempted to collaborate with others when they are not monitored. In other words, test takers may still be motivated to cheat. Ko and Cheng (2004) describe a system for overcoming these challenges that uses a camera at the client computer to record the test taker's face and posture at random intervals during the test. Cameras such as those used in banks and stores also could provide surveillance of the testing lab. Such systems can store the images to verify the test takers' identities and movement during the test.

Test Design

Test developers have known for some time that the format used in paper-and-pencil tests (the test taker instructions, the type of questions, and the method of response) can influence test takers and bias their scores. The same is true of computer- and web-based tests. Although there is little published research on designing online tests, Potosky and Bobko (2004) suggest that consideration of the font size and number of questions on each screen and the potential effects of color, graphics, and other enhancements are critical.

Equivalence With Paper-and-Pencil Tests

Some researchers have raised concerns about whether a computerized or web-based test yields scores similar to those yielded by paper-and-pencil tests (Ployhart et al., 2003; Potosky & Bobko, 2004; Salgado & Moscoso, 2003; Vispoel et al., 2001). However, studies suggest that both forms provide equivalent results. In a study of web-based and paper-and-pencil versions of the Career Key, an interest inventory (Buchan, DeAngelis, & Levinson 2005) found that both versions yielded comparable results. In a study of student driving behaviors, Usdan, Schumacher, and Bernhardt (2004) found that web-based assessment of drinking and driving among a sample of college students yielded results similar to those of a retroactive method of documenting behaviors. This issue is not likely to extend far into the future because newer tests may be developed in a computer- or web-based format only. Potosky and Bobko conclude that although gaining complete equivalence between paper-and-pencil tests and computer-based tests might be difficult, online testing may ultimately improve the quality of psychological tests.

INTERIM SUMMARY 4.2
WEB-BASED ASSESSMENT

- The rapid expansion of computer and Internet technologies has produced an increase in online assessment tools.
- Companies offer enterprise services, that is, online standardized tests for large numbers of test takers at multiple sites.
- Companies provide hosted services in the form of server space, web design, and maintenance.
- Nonhosted services provide products that run on local area networks or private websites.
- Web-based testing takes place under two conditions: proctored and unproctored.

- Web-based assessment greatly facilitates administration of standardized tests as well as informal classroom assessment; however, it presents challenges as well.
- Web-based testing presents several new challenges to test developers and test users, such as issues with timed tests, new test taker strategies, identifying and monitoring test takers, designing unbiased tests, and establishing equivalence with paper-and-pencil tests.

Implications for the Future

The effects and consequences of computerized and web-based testing continue to be recognized by educators, clinicians, psychologists, human resources professionals, and legislators. As the technology of CAT and online testing becomes better understood and more available, test developers and users will continue to find better ways to present tests that are realistic and tailored to the individual.

E-learning

Bill Eggers (2005), a leading expert on government reform, notes how the "digital revolution" is improving government services, producing innovative solutions, and offering ordinary individuals access to information never available to them previously. For example, he notes that **e-learning**—curricula that allow students to learn at their own pace using web-based lessons—and web-based assessment should be integral aspects of education in the future.

The old-fashioned method of assessment was to administer exams quarterly or at the end of a semester. You are probably familiar with such exams as midterms and finals. Until recently, assessment was too time-consuming for instructors to develop reliable and valid tests and to administer them weekly or daily. Now e-learning curricula include short web-based tests that use adaptive testing methodology. Instructors can rely on the tests to be accurate and valid, and students can use the tests to gauge their progress. When a student cannot provide the correct answers on such a test, he or she does not need to deal with feelings of failure or loss of self-esteem. Instead, the student can tackle the information or skill again by using a different approach.

Likewise, in an e-learning curriculum, students are free to excel in some areas while receiving remedial help in another area. An e-learning curriculum with adaptive testing units can be individualized for each student. Eggers (2005) suggests that computerized adaptive tests could eventually replace grades because they offer more accurate information, including identification of gaps in students' knowledge.

Program Assessment

You probably think of the tests you take in school or college as evaluations of your performance only. However, there is another side to that coin. The tests you take as students also reflect the performance of your teachers and your schools or colleges. Assuming that all students perform as well as they can on standardized tests, those tests also provide evaluations of the teachers, administrators, and curricula of the students' school. When standardized tests are administered statewide or nationwide, schools and their curricula can be compared with each other. Currently, the benefit of such comparisons is the ability of the public to understand how well the educational system is doing its job. For example, Florida, Texas, and Colorado use standardized tests to assign a score or grade to each school. According to Eggers (2005), only 12% of the students at Bessemer Elementary School, in Pueblo, Colorado, met state literacy requirements before their school's test score was published online along with those of other elementary schools. After the scores were published, 74%

of the students met the literacy standards. We can only speculate on how the school and its students increased their scores sixfold; however, it seems clear that the catalyst for change was posting the scores on the Internet.

As the technology becomes available to more public schools, we can expect adaptive, web-based testing to provide more accurate and detailed information to schools across the nation. We can expect schools, colleges, and universities in turn to improve the performance of individual students as well as the educational system as a whole.

Clinical Assessment

We tend to think of clinical assessment as being a one-on-one, face-to-face process. The web, however, has provided easier access to many mental health care issues. For instance, **employee assistance programs (EAPs)**—programs provided by employers as an employee benefit to help employees with problems not related to the workplace—can provide many services to their clients via websites protected with encryption software and secure connections that give some assurance of confidentiality. The digital revolution has increased EAP growth by making more services available at continually decreasing costs. For instance, follow-up for clients treated for substance abuse can be conducted using online group meetings. Specialized assessment websites can also provide follow-up by asking clients to respond online to a number of prompts and questions about their recovery process and experiences (Derr, 2005).

Certification Programs

"We're seeing certifications crop up in new areas, like with elevator technicians," observes Mitch Rubin, president of ExamBuilder, a provider of web-based testing software (quoted in Ellis, 2004, p. 43). As the number of certification programs increases, organizations and government agencies are likely to find that web-based CAT is more accurate and efficient than paper-and-pencil exams. For organizations, assessing employees' job skills, knowledge, and abilities might not always lead to training. The availability of web-based assessments allows employees to demonstrate what they know and can do, and individualized training may be offered only to employees who need it.

As you can see, computerized tests and web-based assessments are increasing in their usefulness and efficiency. They are no longer expensive, time-consuming gimmicks. We expect that computer-based tests, adaptive test formats, and web-based assessment are likely to become as commonplace in the future as cell phones and text messages are today.

INTERIM SUMMARY 4.3
IMPLICATIONS FOR THE FUTURE

- Test developers and users will continue to find better ways to present tests that are realistic and tailored to the individual.
- E-learning and web-based assessment are likely to be integral aspects of education in the future.
- We can expect adaptive, web-based testing to provide more accurate and detailed information about student learning to schools across the nation.

- The web will provide better access to many mental health care services such as employee assistance programs.
- As the number of certification programs increases, organizations and government agencies are likely to find that web-based CAT is more accurate and efficient than paper-and-pencil exams.

Chapter Summary

Computers have become a familiar tool in the psychological testing industry. They now facilitate and enhance all phases of the testing process. Computers have made it easier to construct better classroom tests by providing instructors with access to test banks, large databases of questions. Now test users can administer many types of assessments on computers. In addition, computerized administration allows test developers to use more sophisticated assessment types such as adaptive tests.

Advantages of computerized testing include efficient testing, more convenient testing times, administration at home or in other comfortable locations, improved standardization of administration, more opportunities for testing people with physical and mental challenges, fewer errors in scoring, inclusion of sound, and the accommodation of technologically advanced testing formats such as CAT. One disadvantage is increased difficulty for those who have computer anxiety.

The concept of adaptive testing dates to the early 20th century; however, computer technology has made CAT a familiar testing tool for students and job applicants today. CAT software begins the test with one to three questions of moderate difficulty. It then selects the subsequent test questions based on the test taker's skill level, which was detected in previous questions, until the test taker's skill level is affirmed. Web-based assessment has also expanded testing opportunities such as informal classroom assessment, formal standardized tests, pre-employment testing, and performance appraisal in organizations. In addition, survey research firms make use of gathering information via the web. Some issues with web-based tests include problems in timing tests, test taker strategies, monitoring test takers, and designing tests appropriate for responding online.

The effects and consequences of computerized and web-based testing are just beginning to be recognized by educators, clinicians, psychologists, human resources professionals, and legislators. E-learning, program assessment, clinical assessment, and testing for certification programs represent some current uses of web-based assessment that we expect will continue to facilitate testing in the future.

Engaging in the Learning Process

KEY CONCEPTS

After completing your study of this chapter, you should be able to define each of the following terms. These terms are bolded in the text of this chapter and defined in the Glossary.

- adaptive testing
- computerized adaptive rating scales (CARS)
- computerized adaptive testing (CAT)
- e-learning
- employee assistance programs (EAPs)
- enterprise services
- experimental question
- hosted services
- nonhosted services
- proctor

- survey research firms
- test bank
- virtual time

LEARNING ACTIVITIES

The following are some learning activities you can engage in to support the learning objectives for this chapter.

Learning Objectivesd	Study Tips and Learning Activities
After completing your study of this chapter, you should be able to do the following:	The following study tips will help you meet these learning objectives:
Describe how computers have enhanced the development, administration, and scoring of psychological tests.	• Computers are used in three broad areas of the psychological testing process: development, administration, and scoring and interpretation. Read the examples of these in your textbook.
Discuss the advantages of computerized testing.	• Review the advantages of using computers in your book. Make a list of the bullet points, and explain in your own words what is meant by each one.
Explain the differences between adaptive testing and traditional testing.	• Make a list of various test characteristics, including method of administration, length of time to complete the test, selection of questions, and method of scoring. Explain each characteristic for traditional testing and adaptive testing.
Discuss the advantages and disadvantages of administering tests using the web.	• Go to the web, and search for a test you can take online. As you take the test, make notes about what you like and dislike about web-based testing.
Discuss the implications of web-based technology for testing in the future.	• Make a list of technologies that are currently possible but impractical. How does the technology of computerized tests, CAT, and web-based assessment compare with the other technologies on your list?

PRACTICE QUESTIONS

The following are some practice questions to assess your understanding of the material presented in this chapter.

Multiple Choice

Choose the one best answer to each question.

1. Ursula took a test on a computer. She was told that the computer would choose questions from a large test bank matched to her skill level. What kind of test did she take?
   a. Adaptive test
   b. Achievement test
   c. Skills test
   d. Performance test

2. Adaptive tests
   a. are not as psychometrically sound as paper-and-pencil tests.
   b. provide a fuller profile in less amount of time than traditional tests.
   c. may present too many questions that are either too difficult or too easy.
   d. provide the same questions in the same order for each test taker.

3. Which one of the following
   is TRUE about computerized tests?
   a. The test taker must understand computers
      to take them.
   b. They are time-consuming
      for the test taker.
   c. They make standardized
      administration easier.
   d. They can increase scoring errors.

4. Which one of the following is TRUE about
   computerized tests?
   a. Men have an advantage
      over women because they
      are more experienced
      with computers.
   b. Computer-based test
      administration often compromises
      the psychometric quality of tests.
   c. Computer-based tests do not
      allow test takers to use the same
      strategies they use when
      responding to paper-and-pencil tests.
   d. Computer-based tests are not as fair as
      traditional tests.

5. A database containing a large
   number of multiple-choice,
   true/false, and short-answer
   questions on topics in a textbook is
   a. an adaptive test.
   b. a test bank.
   c. a computerized test.
   d. a classroom test.

6. Research studies comparing
   test scores on two types of test
   administration, computerized
   and paper-and-pencil, found that
   a. the resulting test scores were similar.
   b. the administration times
      were the same.
   c. students preferred paper-and-pencil tests.
   d. instructors preferred paper-and-pencil
      tests.

7. Which one of the following tests
   was not practical until computerized
   testing became possible?
   a. Standardized tests
   b. Pre-employment tests
   c. Surveys
   d. Adaptive tests

8. Whether administering or scoring tests,
   computers save test users
   a. from administering inappropriate tests.
   b. from using tests inappropriately.
   c. the cost of shipping answer sheets.
   d. the hassle of handling a database.

9. Which one of the following is
   an issue unique to web-based testing?
   a. Test takers are tempted to cheat.
   b. Timing a test becomes complicated.
   c. Web-based testing discriminates against
      some groups.
   d. The selection of test questions becomes
      difficult.

10. Adaptive testing would be impractical without
    a. standardized tests.
    b. paper-and-pencil administration.
    c. psychometric theory.
    d. powerful computers.

11. Traditionally, standardized testing was a
    lengthy process
    a. that relied on the postal service.
    b. because test takers cheated.
    c. although test takers received their scores
       immediately.
    d. that often was inappropriate.

12. E-learning refers to
    a. curricula that allow students to learn at
       their own pace using web-based lessons.
    b. web-based assessment of students.
    c. one source of software for web-based
       assessment.
    d. programs that teach educators how to use
       web-based assessment.

13. The old-fashioned method of assessment was to
    a. replicate paper-and-pencil tests on the
       computer.
    b. administer exams quarterly or at the end
       of a semester.
    c. give schools scores or grades and compare
       them.
    d. ask children to respond to essay questions.

14. The tests we take as students also reflect
    a. how educated our parents are.
    b. how much effort we put into studying.
    c. the environment of our classrooms.
    d. on the performance of our teachers,
       schools, and colleges.

15. Employee assistance programs
    a. can provide services to their clients using a secure website.
    b. provide a website that employees can use for assessment.
    c. provide health and life insurance for employees.
    d. help employees who need training in job skills.

16. One solution to the problems of administering web-based assessments without a proctor is to use
    a. informed consents.
    b. photocopies of drivers' licenses.
    c. honesty pledges.
    d. video cameras.

17. Which one of the following methods for administering online surveys is the fastest and simplest?
    a. E-mail surveys
    b. HTML surveys
    c. AOL or Comcast surveys
    d. Interactive surveys

Short Answer/Essay

Read each of the following, and consider your response carefully based on the information presented in this chapter. Write your answer to each question in two or three paragraphs.

1. Describe how computers have enhanced the development, administration, and scoring of psychological tests.
2. What are the advantages and disadvantages of computerized testing? Give an example of each.
3. Explain the differences between adaptive testing and traditional testing. Give an example of each.
4. Why might we want to administer a test using online? What might be some disadvantages?
5. What is the purpose of the Society for Human Resources Management's Testing Center? How do testing professionals in organizations use the Testing Center? Give examples.
6. Explain how the technology of web-based testing is likely to influence the fields of education, mental health, and industry. Give examples.

ANSWER KEYS

Multiple Choice

1. a	2. b	3. c	4. c
5. b	6. a	7. d	8. c
9. b	10. d	11. a	12. a
13. b	14. d	15. a	16. d
17. a			

Short Answer/Essay

Refer to your textbook for answers. If you are unsure of an answer and cannot generate the answer after reviewing your book, ask your professor for clarification.

SECTION II

PSYCHOMETRIC PRINCIPLES

Overview of Section II

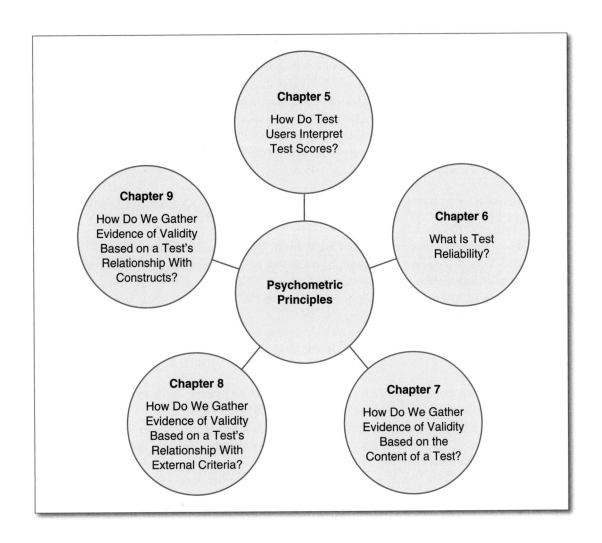

CHAPTER 5: HOW DO TEST USERS INTERPRET TEST SCORES?

In Chapter 5, we focus on increasing your understanding of the procedures used to interpret test scores. Because these procedures depend on the type of data that a test produces, we begin with a discussion of the four levels of measurement of psychological test data. We then discuss frequency distributions, measures of central tendency, measures of variability, and measures of relationship. After discussing how to convert raw scores into more meaningful units (for example, z scores, T scores), we discuss the role of norms in interpreting test scores.

CHAPTER 6: WHAT IS TEST RELIABILITY?

In Chapter 6, we describe three methods of estimating a test's reliability: test–retest or stability over time, internal consistency or homogeneity of the test questions, and scorer reliability or agreement. We discuss how to calculate an index of reliability called the *reliability coefficient*, an index of error called the *standard error of measurement*, and an index of agreement called *Cohen's kappa*. Finally, we discuss factors that increase and decrease reliability of test scores.

CHAPTER 7: HOW DO WE GATHER EVIDENCE OF VALIDITY BASED ON THE CONTENT OF A TEST?

In Chapter 7, we introduce you to the different types of evidence that is used to evaluate whether a proposed interpretation of a test score is valid. We discuss how validity is discussed in the *Standards for Educational and Psychological Testing* (American Educational Research Association, American Psychological Association, & National Council on Measurement in Education, 1999). We begin with a brief discussion of validity as defined by the *Standards*. We focus most of our attention on evidence of validity based on an evaluation of the content of the test. We end with an overview of other types of evidence of validity of a test, such as evidence based on the relationship of the test scores to other variables.

CHAPTER 8: HOW DO WE GATHER EVIDENCE OF VALIDITY BASED ON A TEST'S RELATIONSHIPS WITH EXTERNAL CRITERIA?

In Chapter 8, we describe the processes psychologists use to ensure that tests perform properly when they are used for making predictions and decisions. We begin by discussing the concept of validity evidence based on a test's relationships to other variables, specifically external criteria. We also discuss the importance of selecting a valid criterion measure, how to evaluate validity coefficients, and the statistical processes that provide evidence that a test can be used for making predictions.

CHAPTER 9: HOW DO WE GATHER EVIDENCE OF VALIDITY BASED ON A TEST'S RELATIONSHIP WITH CONSTRUCTS?

In Chapter 9, we define and illustrate the terms *psychological construct, theory,* and *nomological network*. Because establishing evidence of construct validity involves accumulating and relating all of the psychometric information known about a test, we show how familiar concepts, such as reliability, evidence of validity based on test content, and evidence of validity based on a test's relationships with other variables, are linked together. In addition, we discuss how convergent evidence of validity and discriminant evidence of validity are two other factors used for establishing validity based on a test's relationships with other variables. Finally, we describe experimental methods used to establish evidence of construct validity for a test, including two procedures: confirmatory factor analysis and exploratory factor analysis.

How Do Test Users Interpret Test Scores?

CHAPTER 5: HOW DO TEST USERS INTERPRET TEXT SCORES?

After completing your study of this chapter, you should be able to do the following:

- Describe and identify the different levels of measurement.
- Summarize test scores using frequency distributions.
- Describe the characteristics of the normal curve as well as skewed, peaked, and bimodal distributions.
- Describe the purpose and calculate measures of central tendency, measures of variability, and measures of relationship.
- Convert raw test scores into more meaningful units.
- Describe norm-based interpretation and the different types of norms.

"My professor wrote all our midterm exam scores on the whiteboard. She asked us to review the scores and then describe to her how the class performed as a whole and how each of us performed in comparison to the rest of the class. Besides saying that everyone did 'okay' and calculating the average exam score, none of us had much to say. Our professor then spent the entire class period helping us understand the different ways to describe a group of scores and compare one score to a group of scores. I didn't know there were so many ways to describe the results of a test."

"For a class assignment, I had to select a psychological test and critique it. As I was searching through the test manual for my chosen test, I noticed that in addition to what they call raw scores, some tests report their scores in T scores and z scores. What are these?"

"I recently received my SAT results. According to the results, nationally I scored in the 70th percentile, whereas in my state I scored in the 78th percentile. What do those numbers mean?"

f your friend told you she correctly answered 20 problems on her math midterm, correctly identified 18 of the organisms on her biology exam, or correctly answered 67 questions on her psychology exam, what would you think about her performance? Although your friend's attitude would probably give you a clue about how well (or poorly) she did, her raw scores (20 problems, 18 organisms, 67 questions) would actually tell you little about her performance. To properly understand and interpret raw scores, you need additional information.

In this chapter, our goal is to increase your understanding of the procedures used to interpret test scores. Because these procedures depend on the type of data that a test produces, we begin with a discussion of the four levels of measurement of psychological test data. We then discuss frequency distributions, measures of central tendency, measures of variability, and measures of relationship. After discussing how to convert raw scores into more meaningful units (for example, z scores, T scores), we discuss the role of norms in interpreting test scores.

Levels of Measurement

In Chapter 1, we explained that not all psychological tests are true measurement instruments. We said that a psychological test is a true measurement instrument when numbers are assigned to the results of the test according to rules. The numbers that we assign are used to measure attributes, traits, or characteristics of individuals. The claims we can make about the results of psychological tests depend on the properties of these numbers or what we call a test's level of measurement. For example, with the appropriate level of measurement (that is, an interval or ratio level of measurement), the results of a psychological test allow us to say that Johnny is twice as intelligent as Susan. However, if the level of measurement does not allow for this type of explanation, we may only be able to say that Johnny's intelligence is simply different from Susan's intelligence.

Most measurement experts think in terms of four **levels of measurement** based on the mathematical operations that can be performed with the data at each level (Stevens, 1946, 1951, 1961). These four levels are nominal, ordinal, equal interval, and ratio. As you will see, as we move from one level of measurement to the next, we are able to perform more mathematical operations (addition, subtraction, multiplication, and division) that allow us to make more and different claims regarding test results.

Nominal Scales

The most basic level of measurement is the **nominal scale.** With nominal scales, numbers are assigned to represent groups or categories of information. Numbers in this scale serve as labels that identify data because they are not intended for use in calculations. Nominal scales are generally used for demographic data such as grouping people based on their gender, race, or place of residence. For example, we can assign a 0 to women and a 1 to men, or we can assign a 0 to Caucasians, a 1 to Hispanics, a 2 to African Americans, and so on. Although a researcher may assign a 0 to women and a 1 to men, these numbers do not represent quantitative values; in other words, men are not worth more than women because the number assigned to them is higher or vice versa. Instead, the numbers simply give the categories a numerical label. Another example is the number marked on a football, basketball, or baseball player's uniform. Again, such numbers are labels used for identification. They do not imply that one player is superior to another.

In psychological testing, nominal scales are very important. For example, a psychologist may use the results of an intelligence test (or a battery of tests) to classify an individual as "average" or "gifted." Average individuals could be assigned a label of 1, and gifted individuals a label of 2. Similarly, a personality test may be used to determine whether an individual has a psychological disorder. We may assign each psychological disorder a number, for example, manic depressive = 1, bipolar disorder = 2, and so on.

Because nominal scales yield only **categorical data**—data grouped according to a common property—there are few ways to describe or manipulate the data they yield. Usually, researchers report nominal data in terms of the number of occurrences in each category. For example, a psychologist might report how many individuals he assigned a 1 (average) and a 2 (gifted) or how many individuals he diagnosed as manic depressive (1) or bipolar (2).

Ordinal Scales

Ordinal scales are the second level of measurement. Ordinal scales have all of the qualities of nominal scales, but also the numbers are assigned to order or rank individuals or objects on the construct being measured. If a teacher asks children to line up in order of their height, placing the shortest child first and the tallest child last, the teacher can then assign numbers based on the children's height. The shortest child may be assigned a 1, the next shortest child a 2, and so on. If there are 20 children, the tallest child would be assigned a 20. In this case, the teacher has created an ordinal scale based on the children's height. An ordinal scale indicates an individual's or object's value based on its relationship to others in the group. If another child—smaller than the others—joins the group, that child will be labeled 1 and the number assigned to each of the other children would change in relationship to the new child.

There are a number of practical uses for ordinal scales. Car dealerships often rank their salespeople based on the number of cars they sell each month. High schools and colleges rank students by grade point average (GPA), yielding a measure of class standing. Publications such as *U.S. News & World Report* and *Financial Times* rank colleges and universities. For example, in 2007, *U.S. News & World Report* ranked Rollins College number 1 out of 121 southern master's-level universities. Results of a *Financial Times* survey indicated that the University of Phoenix online MBA programs were ranked number 1 of 40 distance learning MBA programs in 2008 (Financial Times, 2009).

There are two important points to remember about ordinal scales. First, the number or rank has meaning only within the group being compared and provides no information about the group as a whole. For instance, the top student in your class may have a GPA of 3.98, but next year another student may receive the top ranking with a GPA of only 3.75. The ranks are assigned based on the comparison group and have little meaning outside the group, and they do not indicate which group performed better as a whole.

Second, an ordinal scale gives no information about how closely two individuals or objects are related. The student with the highest GPA (ranked first) may be only a little better or a lot better than the student with the next-highest GPA (ranked second). If the top student has a GPA of 3.98, the student ranked next will be second whether his or her GPA is 3.97 or 3.50 so long as the student's GPA is higher than the GPAs of the rest of the students.

Age equivalents, grade equivalents, and percentile scores (which we discuss later in this chapter) all represent ordinal scales. In fact, most psychological scales produce ordinal data. However, because we cannot add, subtract, multiply, or divide ordinal scores (nor can we compute means or standard deviations, which we talk about later in this chapter), ordinal scales are limited in their usefulness to psychologists. Therefore, some test developers make the assumption that these instruments produce equal interval data.

Equal Interval Scales

Equal interval scales are the next level of measurement. These scales have all of the qualities of the previous scales, but also their raw scores are calculated with the assumption that each number represents a point that is an equal distance from the points adjacent to it. For instance, an increase of 1 degree on a temperature scale represents the same amount of increase in heat at any point on the scale. A good example of what is often assumed to be an equal interval scale is a Likert-type scale. For example, assume that a test required you to indicate the extent to which you agreed with a number of statements where 1 = *strongly disagree,* 2 = *disagree,* 3 = *somewhat agree,* 4 = *agree,* and 5 = *strongly agree.* Professionals and researchers (as well as test takers) often assume that each point on the Likert-type rating scale represents an equal distance or amount of the construct being measured (McCall, 2001; Trochim, 2001), that is, we assume that everyone responding has the same understanding of what *somewhat agree* and *agree* represent as well as the distance between the two. Not all professionals agree that Likert-type scales are interval; many believe they are ordinal scales.

The advantage of an equal interval scale is that means and standard deviations can be calculated for these scores. These statistics allow comparison of the performance of one group with the performance of another group, or the score of one individual with the score of another individual, on the same test. These statistics also are used to calculate test norms and standard scores.

A drawback of the equal interval scale (and of the previous two scales) is that it does not have a point that indicates an absolute absence of the attribute being measured. For example, temperature scales (both Fahrenheit and Celsius) have a point that is labeled 0 (zero), but that point does not represent a total absence of heat. In other words, the zero point on an equal interval scale is arbitrary and does not represent the point at which the attribute being measured does not exist.

When we think about psychological constructs, this property makes sense. Although we can measure an individual's level of anxiety, intelligence, or mechanical aptitude, it is difficult to establish the point at which an individual totally lacks anxiety, intelligence, or mechanical aptitude. The equal interval scale allows comparison of groups and individuals, even though the point at which the attribute is totally absent cannot be specified. In a joking manner, we sometimes tell our students that a 0% score on an exam does not really mean that they have no knowledge of the subject matter; rather, the exam simply did not sample the knowledge they do have. This makes our students feel better for perhaps a minute!

Ratio Scales

Ratio scales are the fourth level of measurement. Ratio scales have all of the qualities of the previous scales, but also there is a point that represents an absolute absence of the property being measured, and that point is called zero. Most measurement scales used in everyday life for physical measurements are ratio scales. For instance, stepping on your bathroom scale gives a measure of your weight in pounds. You might weigh 150 pounds, and your roommate might weigh 165 pounds. If each of you gains 1 pound, you have gained the same amount. When nothing is on the scale, it registers 0 (zero)—an absence of any weight. Because there is a true zero point, ratio scales also allow ratio comparisons. For example, we can say that a person who weighs 160 pounds is twice as heavy as a person who weighs 80 pounds.

Although most measures of psychological constructs do not meet the requirements of a ratio scale, those that use common measures of time or distance do qualify as ratio measures. For instance, the time required to complete a task or the distance between two individuals might be used to infer attributes such as performance or preference, respectively.

Why is it important for you to understand the differences in the levels of measurement? The answer is simple: The level of measurement informs you about the statistical operations you can perform and what you can and cannot say about test scores. For example, let us say that three of your best friends score 75, 50, and 25 on a test that measures introversion. Because this test uses an ordinal scale, all we can determine from the scores is who is more or less introverted. (In fact, we cannot even say that unless we know whether a high or low score indicates the presence of introversion.) We can say that Corrine (who scored 75) is more introverted than Jean (who scored 50) when a high score indicates a high level of introversion. We cannot say that Jean (who scored 50) is twice as introverted as John (who scored 25). We cannot compare ordinal scores using multiples because ordinal scales do not have a true zero point that indicates an absence of introversion. We can compare using multiples only with a ratio level of measurement.

Table 5.1 provides an overview of the four levels of measurement. We introduce and explain many of the statistical procedures referenced in this table throughout the remainder of this chapter.

Table 5.1 Levels of Measurement

Level of Measurement	Definition	Example	Some Appropriate Statistics
Nominal	Numbers represent labels or categories of data. Numbers have no quantitative value.	Numbers on basketball players' uniforms	Frequency, mode
Ordinal	Numbers rank or order people or objects based on the attribute being measured. Distances or values between numbers vary. Numbers have meaning only within the group.	Rankings given to basketball players before the national draft	Frequency, mode, median, percentile
Equal interval	Points on the scale are an equal distance apart. This scale does not contain an absolute zero point (number that indicates the complete absence of the attribute).	Measures of basketball players' "desire to win"	Frequency, mean, mode, median, standard deviation, correlation, t test, analysis of variance
Ratio	Points on the scale are an equal distance apart. There is an absolute zero point.	Players' height and game scores	Frequency, mean, mode, median, standard deviation, correlation, proportions, t tests, analysis of variance

---

INTERIM SUMMARY 5.1
LEVELS OF MEASUREMENT

- The claims we can make about the results of psychological tests depend on the properties of these numbers or what we call a test's level of measurement.
- Test scores can be classified into one of four levels of measurement: nominal, ordinal, equal interval, or ratio.
- With nominal scales, we assign numbers to represent categories.

- With ordinal scales, we assign numbers to order or rank things.
- With equal interval scales, we assign numbers to order things and we are able to determine the distance between two numbers.
- With ratio scales, we assign numbers to order things, we are able to determine the distance between two numbers, and there is a true zero point.

Procedures for Interpreting Test Scores

Raw scores are the most basic scores calculated from a psychological test. They tell very little about how an individual has performed on a test, how an individual has performed in comparison with others who took the test, or how an individual performed on one test compared with another test. Raw scores are not very useful at all without additional interpretive information.

To make sense of raw scores, test users rely on a number of techniques. For example, test users often arrange groups of raw scores from the same test into frequency distributions, or they calculate descriptive statistics such as measures of central tendency, variability, or relationship. Frequency distributions provide test users with a picture of a group of scores, and descriptive statistics provide test users with quantitative values representing the average test score and how much distance lies between scores. Descriptive statistics also provide information on whether individuals' scores on one test relate to their scores on another test. Test users also convert raw scores into more informative standard scores so that they can make comparisons between test scores and compare converted scores with those from what we call a norm group—a previously tested group of individuals. (We talk more about norm groups later in this chapter.)

Over the years, test developers have worked hard to improve the reliability and validity of tests. Unfortunately, many test users still do not understand how to properly interpret test scores. When tests are used or interpreted improperly, people are likely to make the wrong decisions about themselves and others. Some historical examples, from Lyman (1998), can help you understand what can happen when test scores are not properly interpreted:

- A college freshman, told that she had "average ability," withdrew from college. Her counselor had not added "when compared with other students at her college where standards are exceptionally high." The freshman reasoned that if she had only average ability compared with people in general, she must be very unintelligent when compared with college students. Rather than face the situation, she dropped out of college. (p. 2; there may have been other reasons too, but this seemed to be the primary one)

- "When am I going to start failing?" a student once asked me. On being questioned, he told me this story: "My high school teacher told me that I had an IQ of only 88. She said that I might be able to get into college because I was an All-State football player but that I'd be certain to flunk out—with an IQ like that!" I pointed out to Don that he had been doing well in my course. I discovered that he had earned a B+ average during his first 2 years at our university. I reminded Don that the proof of a pudding lies in its eating—and that the proof of scholastic achievement lies in earned grades, not in a single test designed to predict grades. Two years later, Don graduated with honors. (p. 2)

Although there are a variety of questions we want to ask about the use of these tests (Is there evidence of reliability and validity? Were the tests administered properly? Were the tests scored properly?), there is one question that is most important to this chapter: Were the test scores properly interpreted? In the situations Lyman (1998) describes, it seems likely that the test users may have made unacceptable errors in interpreting these students' test scores. Is it possible that if the college counselor had compared the college freshman's ability with that of college students, she may have scored "above average"? Given that he was doing so well in school, is it possible that Don's IQ might have been a percentile rank instead of a raw score (discussed later in this chapter)?

Frequency Distributions

When a group of people take a test, their scores can be summarized by using a **frequency distribution**, an orderly arrangement of a group of numbers (or test scores). Frequency distributions show the actual number (or percentage) of observations that fall into a range or category; they provide a summary and picture of group data. Although there are numerous ways to portray frequency distributions, two of the most frequently used methods are tables and histograms.

To create frequency tables and histograms, you begin with raw scores. For example, let us imagine that we have raw test scores for the 27 children in Table 5.2. To construct a frequency table, the first step is to identify the minimum and maximum test scores and arrange the test scores from highest to lowest or vice versa. The second step is to count and document the number of individuals who earned each particular score. The third step is to document this information in the form of a frequency table, as shown in Table 5.3.

Table 5.2	Raw Test Scores for 27 Children		
Child	*Test Score*	*Child*	*Test Score*
1	21	15	29
2	22	16	16
3	25	17	23
4	14	18	27
5	25	19	27
6	26	20	28
7	28	21	30
8	17	22	24
9	22	23	19
10	10	24	31
11	34	25	31
12	36	26	32
13	37	27	40
14	20		

Sometimes we create frequency tables using grouped test scores instead of individual raw scores. To do this, the first step is to create **class intervals**, which are a way to group raw scores so as to display them. Lyman (1998) suggests that when creating class intervals in frequency tables, you should aim for approximately 15 groups of scores. To determine the width of each group, and hence the number of groups, take the highest score and subtract the lowest score. Then divide this number by 15. If the calculated width is an even number, add 1 so that each interval will have a midpoint. Table 5.4 shows how to calculate the class intervals and construct the grouped frequency distribution for the raw test scores presented in Table 5.2.

In psychological testing, it is common to display these distributions graphically as a **histogram**—a bar graph used to represent frequency data in statistics. The horizontal axis represents all of the possible values

| Table 5.3 | Frequency Table of 27 Test Scores Presented in Table 5.2 | |

Score	Frequency	Percentage
40	1	3.7
39	0	0
38	0	0
37	1	3.7
36	1	3.7
35	0	0
34	1	3.7
33	0	0
32	1	3.7
31	2	7.4
30	1	3.7
29	1	3.7
28	2	7.4
27	2	7.4
26	1	3.7
25	2	7.4
24	1	3.7
23	1	3.7
22	2	7.4
21	1	3.7
20	1	3.7
19	1	3.7
18	0	0
17	1	3.7
16	1	3.7
15	0	0
14	1	3.7
13	0	0
12	0	0
11	0	0
10	1	3.7

of some variable (class intervals), and the vertical axis represents the number of people (frequency) who scored each value on the horizontal axis. It is also common to display distributions graphically as stem-and-leaf plots, which are similar to histograms. Although they look like histograms on their sides, they are constructed in a somewhat different manner. The first digit of each raw score is placed in the left "stem" column. The second digit of each number is then placed in the second "leaf" column. Figure 5.1 shows a histogram and a stem-and-leaf plot of the data presented in Tables 5.2 and 5.4.

Table 5.4   Grouped Frequency of Test Scores Presented in Table 5.2

Class Interval	Frequency
High score = 40	1. Class interval width = 40 (high score) – 10 (low score) = 30
Low score = 10	2. 30 (difference)/15 (ideal number of intervals) = 2
	3. Because 2 is an even number, we add 1 to create an interval width of 3
10–12	1
13–15	1
16–18	2
19–21	3
22–24	4
25–27	5
28–30	4
31–33	3
34–36	2
37–39	1
40–42	1

Figure 5.1   Histogram and Stem-and-Leaf Plot of Grouped Frequency Data Presented in Table 5.4

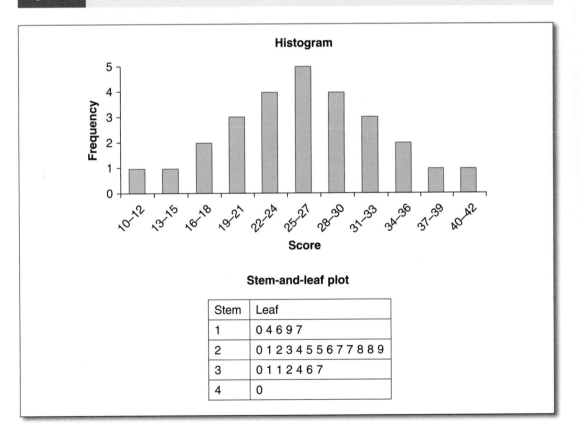

If the distribution of scores in a histogram is symmetrical (balanced on both sides), the frequency distribution might form a bell-shaped curve or what we call a **normal curve.** Distributions become more symmetrical when the sample of test scores is large because they more closely represent the entire population of scores.

The Normal Curve

When we administer a psychological test to a group of individuals, we obtain a distribution of real scores from real people. Unlike this real distribution of scores (or what we call the obtained distribution of scores), **normal probability distributions** (also referred to as normal curves) are theoretical distributions that exist in our imagination as perfect and symmetrical and actually consist of a family of distributions that have the same general bell shape—high in the middle and tapered to the ends. Figure 5.2 shows some examples of normal distributions.

| Figure 5.2 | Examples of Normal Distributions |

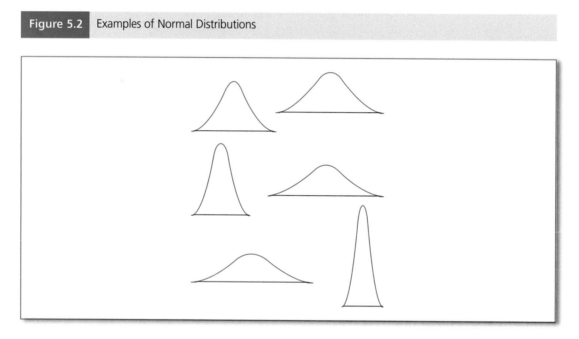

Notice how each distribution in Figure 5.2 is symmetrical, with scores more concentrated in the middle than in the tails. Although the area under each distribution is the same, the distributions differ in terms of how spread out they are or how tall or short the shape is.

The normal probability distribution has a number of characteristics that are important for the interpretation of test scores. These characteristics are displayed in the distribution pictured in Figure 5.3 and include the following:

- Most test scores cluster or fall near the middle of the distribution, forming what we refer to as the average or the central tendency. The farther to the right or left you move from the average, the fewer the number of scores there are.
- Most people will score near the middle of the distribution, making the center of the distribution the highest point.
- The curve can continue to infinity, and therefore the right and left tails of the curve will never touch the baseline.

- Approximately 34.1% of the population will score between the mean and 1 standard deviation (we explain this term later in this chapter) above the mean, and approximately 34.1% will score between the mean and 1 standard deviation below the mean. Approximately 13.6% of the population will score between 1 and 2 standard deviations above the mean, and approximately 13.6% will score between 1 and 2 standard deviations below the mean. Approximately 2.1% of the population will score between 2 and 3 standard deviations above the mean, and approximately 2.1% will score between 2 and 3 standard deviations below the mean. This curve will capture most of the scores in a population.
- The curve is convex at its highest point and changes to concave at 1 standard deviation above the mean and 1 standard deviation below the mean.

Most distributions of human traits, from height and weight to aptitudes and personality characteristics, would form a normal curve if we gathered data from the entire population. For example, although some people are as short as 4 feet and some are as tall as 6 feet 5 inches, most people are between 5 feet 2 inches and 5 feet 9 inches. Most psychological tests, when administered to large groups of individuals, approximate the normal curve.

Not all psychological measurements, however, yield normal or bell-shaped curves. Some are negatively skewed (there are many high scores). Some are positively skewed (there are many low scores). Some are peaked (most individuals have the same score). Finally, some are bimodal (there are many low scores and many high scores). For Your Information Box 5.1 provides an example of evenly distributed, skewed, peaked, and bimodal distributions using test scores from groups of children.

Figure 5.3	Normal Probability Distribution

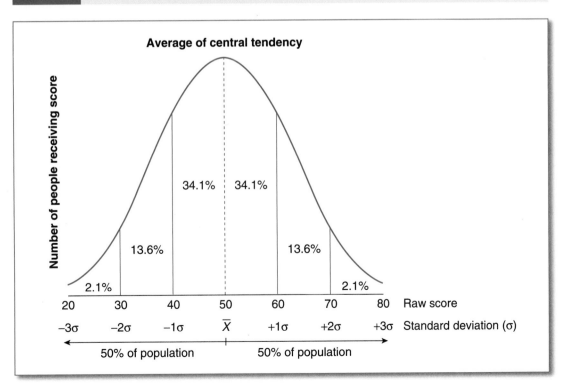

FYI

FOR YOUR INFORMATION BOX 5.1

Evenly Distributed, Skewed, Peaked, and Bimodal Distributions

Evenly Distributed Distributions

In evenly distributed distributions, most test scores cluster or fall near the middle of the distribution, forming what we refer to as the average or central tendency. The farther a point is to the right or left from the central tendency, the fewer the number of individuals represented at that point.

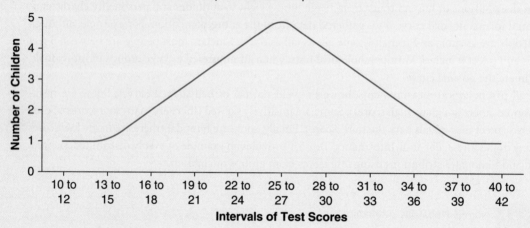

Positively Skewed Distributions

Positively skewed distributions have one high point and are skewed to the right. In positively skewed distributions, there are more low scores than high scores.

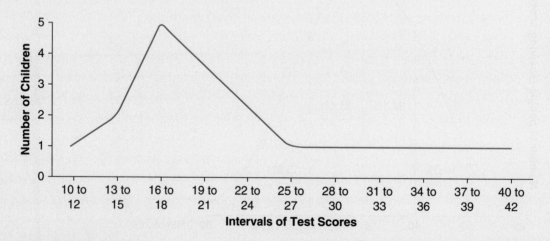

Negatively Skewed Distributions

Negatively skewed distributions have one high point and are skewed to the left. In negatively skewed distributions, there are more high scores than low scores.

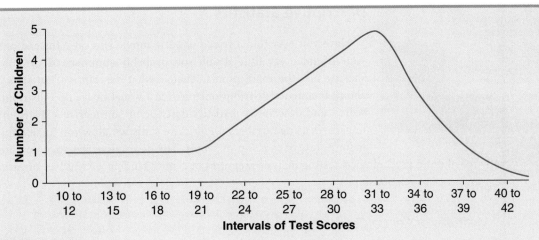

Peaked Distributions

Peaked distributions have one high point and result when many individuals score near the center of the distribution.

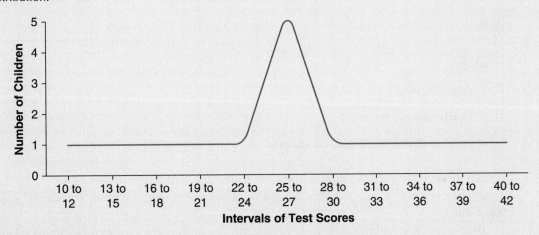

Bimodal Distributions

Bimodal distributions have two high points and result when many people score low, many people score high, and few people score in the middle.

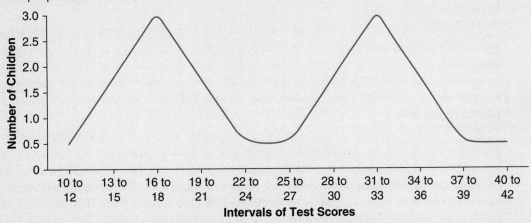

Descriptive Statistics

Have you ever told a friend about a movie you saw? Instead of telling your friend every little detail, you probably summarized the movie by sharing just the main points. That is what **descriptive statistics** are all about. Frequency distributions provide a visual image of a distribution of scores, and descriptive statistics describe or summarize a distribution of test scores using numbers. Descriptive statistics allow you to determine the main points of a group of scores. The descriptive statistics that are typically relied on in psychological testing include measures of central tendency, measures of variability, and measures of relationship.

Measures of Central Tendency

Three common **measures of central tendency** are the mean (the arithmetic average), the median, and the mode. Each tells us about the middle of a set of test scores. The **mean** (which is symbolized as $\bar{x}$ or sometimes M) is the average score in a distribution or sample. The formula for the mean is

$$\bar{x} = \Sigma x/N$$

where

Σ equals "sum of"

x equals each raw test score

N equals the total number of test scores

The mean is calculated by adding all of the scores in a distribution (x) and dividing by the total number of scores (N). You probably learned to calculate averages in elementary school; this is the same thing.

The **median** is the middle score in a distribution. The median is determined by putting all scores in a distribution in order (for example, from lowest to highest, from highest to lowest) and selecting the middle score. If there is an even number of scores, you must find the middle score by adding the two middle scores and dividing by 2. Be careful with this one; students sometimes forget to order the scores before selecting the median.

The **mode** is the most common score in a distribution. The mode is calculated by ordering the scores in a distribution and seeing which score occurs most often. There may be more than one mode or no mode at all.

For Your Information Box 5.2 provides an example of how to calculate these three measures of central tendency. As you recall, Table 5.1 shows which measures of central tendency can be calculated at each level of measurement.

What is the best measure of central tendency? It depends. Let us answer this question by looking at some examples. When Kia, the daughter of one of this textbook's authors, lost her first tooth, there was a question about how much money the Tooth Fairy should leave under her pillow. We could have collected data to help us make this decision. We could have asked a sample of parents how much money they left under their children's pillows when their children lost a tooth. Using these amounts, we could have calculated the average amount and paid Kia the mean. However, what if 2 of the 20 parents we asked had wealthy tooth fairies who paid $20 per tooth, and everyone else's tooth fairy paid between $2 and $4 per tooth? The two $20 tooth fairies would have raised the mean to a level that would have made it appear that most people paid more for a lost tooth than they really did. The point is this: The mean is the best measure of central tendency when distributions of scores are relatively symmetric. However, for skewed distributions, the central tendency can be greatly influenced by the extreme scores (in this case, the two parents who paid $20 per tooth) or what we call **outliers**—a few values that are significantly higher or lower than most of the values. When dealing with skewed distributions, the median and/or the mode would be a more informative statistic than the mean.

FYI

FOR YOUR INFORMATION BOX 5.2

Calculating Measures of Central Tendency

The following scores represent the going rate for a lost tooth according to 10 "tooth fairies."

Tooth Fairy	Going Rate	Measures of Central Tendency
1	$1.00	Mean = $1.65 (Sx/N = $16.50/10)
2	$1.25	
3	$1.00	
4	$1.25	Mode = $1.25 (1.00 1.00 1.00 1.25 1.25 1.25 1.25 1.50 2.00 5.00)
5	$1.00	
6	$1.50	
7	$5.00	Median = $1.25 [Because there is an even number of scores (10), we
8	$2.00	arrange the scores in order and add the middle two scores ($1.25 and
9	$1.25	$1.25) and divide by 2 ($1.25 + $1.25/2 = $1.25)]
10	$1.25	

If a distribution of scores is symmetric, the mean, mode, and median will be the same. As you can see in Figure 5.4, if a distribution of scores is positively skewed (where there are many low scores), the mean will be higher than the median. If the distribution is negatively skewed (where there are many high scores), the mean will be lower than the median.

Measures of Variability

Like measures of central tendency, **measures of variability** describe a set of scores in numerical form. However, measures of central tendency tell about the center of a distribution of scores, and measures of variability represent how spread out a group of scores is and provide more information about individual differences. For example, the graphs in Figure 5.5 represent the scores of 18 students on two quizzes. Although the mean of both sets of scores is approximately 6, notice that the distributions look very different; the scores in the first graph are much more spread out, and the curve is much flatter, compared with the scores in the second graph. Although students scored very similar on Quiz 2, the differences between students' scores are much greater on Quiz 1.

| Figure 5.4 | Measures of Central Tendency and Skewed Distributions |

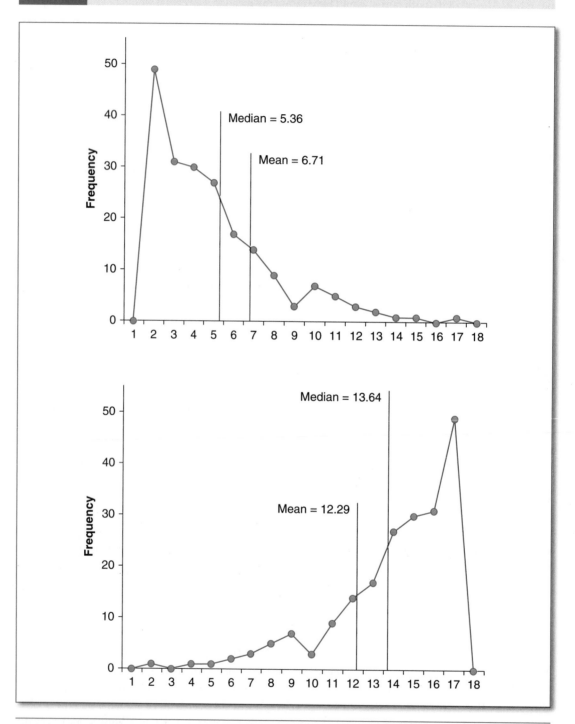

SOURCE: HyperStat Online. (n.d.). *The effect of skew on the mean and median.* Retrieved June 24, 2010, from http://davidmlane.com/hyperstat/A92403.html. Reprinted by permission of David Lane, Rice University, Houston, Texas.

| Figure 5.5 | Variability in Distributions of Test Scores |

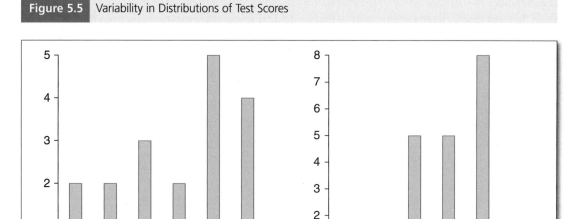

Three commonly used measures of variability are the range, variance, and standard deviation. We already introduced you to the range. Remember when we determined the class intervals for our histogram? The first thing we did was calculate the **range**—the highest score in a distribution minus the lowest score in a distribution. The range of the distribution of scores presented in For Your Information Box 5.2 would be $5.00 (highest score) − $1.00 (lowest score) = $4.00.

How does calculating the range of a distribution of scores help us? Let us say that an elementary school decides to administer a math test to all incoming second-grade students to measure their math skills. There are 150 questions on the test. When we calculate the average math test score of the students in each of the two second-grade classes, we find that each class has a mean of 100 correct answers. Does this mean that students in both second-grade classes have about the same math skills? Yes and no. Yes, all of the classes have the same mean math knowledge. But no, the individuals in each class do not necessarily all have similar math skills. Although the mean informs us about the average math knowledge of each class, it tells us nothing about how *varied* the math knowledge is within each of the classes. It is very possible that students in one of the second-grade classes scored as low as 50 and as high as 150 (a range of 100) and the other second-grade class had scores as low as 90 and as high as 110 (a range of 20). Although the mean of these two classes may have been the same, one class has a larger range and is going to require more varied math instruction than the other class.

Although the range is easy to calculate, be careful using it when a distribution of scores has outlying low and/or high scores. The low and/or high scores do not accurately represent the entire distribution of scores and may misrepresent the true range of the distribution. For example, although most of the tooth fairies in For Your Information Box 5.2 reported that the going rate for a lost tooth was between $1.00 and $1.25, one tooth fairy reported that the going rate was $5.00. A range of $4.00 may be misleading in this case.

Like the range, the variance and standard deviation tell us about the spread in a distribution of scores. However, the variance and standard deviation are more satisfactory indexes of variability than is the range.

The **variance** (s^2) tells us whether individual scores tend to be similar to or substantially different from the mean. In most cases, a large variance tells us that individual scores differ substantially from the mean, and a small variance tells us that individual scores are very similar to the mean. What is a "large" variance, and what is a "small" variance? Large and small depend on the range of the test scores. If the range of test scores is 10, then 7 would be considered a large variance and 1 would be considered a small variance. In most cases, a large variance tells us that individual scores differ substantially from the mean. In some cases, however, a large variance may be due to outliers. For example, if there are 100 scores and 99 of them are close to the mean and one is very far from the mean, there may be a large variance due to this one outlier score.

A common formula for calculating the variance of a distribution or group of test scores is

$$s^2 = \frac{\sum(x - \bar{x})^2}{N}$$

where

Σ = sum of the values

x = a raw score

$\bar{x}$ = mean of the distribution of scores

^{2} = squared

N = number of test scores

The formula for the variance requires squaring the sum of the deviations (differences) of each score from the mean. This calculation changes the unit of measurement, making it difficult to interpret the variance. Therefore, we often take the square root of the variance, which gives us what we call the **standard deviation** (S)—the most commonly used measure of variability in a distribution of test scores.

A common formula for calculating the standard deviation for a distribution of test scores[1] is

$$s = \sqrt{\frac{\sum(x - \bar{x})^2}{N}}$$

The more closely a distribution approximates the normal curve, the more likely the standard deviation will contain the same percentage of the overall distribution. This is true regardless of how similar or dissimilar test scores are in a distribution. One standard deviation above and below the mean will always contain approximately 68% (34.1% + 34.1%) of the test scores. Two standard deviations above and below the mean will always contain approximately 95% (13.6% + 34.1% + 34.1% + 13.6%) of the test scores. Approximately 99% of test scores will be included at 3 standard deviations above and below the mean (2.1% + 13.6% + 34.1% + 34.1% + 13.6% + 2.1%). Although theoretically they can go on forever, standard deviations often stop at 3 because very few scores typically fall outside of 3 standard deviations from the mean.

For Your Information Box 5.3 explains, step by step, how to calculate the standard deviation of a distribution of test scores from 11 children.

The standard deviation is an extremely useful descriptive statistic because it allows us to understand how similar or dissimilar scores are. For example, imagine that your professor administered a 100-item

FYI

FOR YOUR INFORMATION BOX 5.3

Calculating the Standard Deviation of a Distribution of Scores

Child	Raw Scores (x)	Deviation From Mean $(x - \bar{x})$	Squared Deviation $(x - \bar{x})^2$
1	20	$20 - 14 = 6$	$6 * 6 = 36$
2	18	$18 - 14 = 4$	$4 * 4 = 16$
3	15	$15 - 14 = 1$	$1 * 1 = 1$
4	15	$15 - 14 = 1$	$1 * 1 = 1$
5	14	$14 - 14 = 0$	$0 * 0 = 0$
6	14	$14 - 14 = 0$	$0 * 0 = 0$
7	14	$14 - 14 = 0$	$0 * 0 = 0$
8	13	$13 - 14 = 1$	$1 * 1 = 1$
9	13	$13 - 14 = 1$	$1 * 1 = 1$
10	10	$10 - 14 = 4$	$4 * 4 = 16$
11	8	$8 - 14 = 6$	$6 * 6 = 36$
Sum			108

Formula for Standard Deviation of a Distribution

$$s = \sqrt{\frac{\sum(x - \bar{x})^2}{N}}$$

1. List each child's raw score (x).
2. Calculate the mean ($\bar{x}$) test score of the distribution by adding all of the raw scores and dividing by the total number of test scores ($\bar{x} = \frac{154}{11} = 14$).
3. Subtract the mean from each child's raw score ($x\text{-}\bar{x}$) to determine the deviation from the mean.
4. Square (^{2}) (multiply number by itself) each deviation.
5. Sum (Σ) the squared deviations.
6. Divide the sum by the number of test scores ($\frac{108}{11} = 9.82$). This equals the variance.
7. Take the square root of the variance to determine the standard deviation ($\sqrt{9.82} = 3.1$).

multiple-choice exam to two different classes and the highest possible score on the exam was 100. Now imagine that your professor wanted to compare how well the students in both classes performed. First, your professor could calculate the mean of both distributions of scores. Let us say that the mean was calculated to be 75% of the total possible score; that is, the average score was a solid C grade. Second, your professor could calculate the standard deviation. Let us say that the standard deviation of one class was 17 and the standard deviation of the second class was 8. The standard deviation would allow your professor to understand that although the average score was the same for both classes, the scores in the first class were more varied than the scores in the second class.

Furthermore, when we know the mean and standard deviation of a distribution of scores, we can draw a picture of what the distribution of scores probably looks like. For Your Information Box 5.4 shows you how to draw a distribution of scores.

FOR YOUR INFORMATION BOX 5.4

Using the Mean and Standard Deviation to Plot a Distribution

Using the mean and standard deviation of a distribution, we can draw what the distribution most likely looks like, assuming that these statistics are calculated from a large sample and the distribution is nearly bell-shaped or normal. For example, if the mean is 14 and the standard deviation is 3.1, we can plot the distribution by doing the following:

1. Draw an x axis (horizontal axis) and place the mean (14) in the center.

2. Add the standard deviation (3.1) to the mean and place this number 1 standard deviation above the mean (14 + 3.1 = 17.1). Add the standard deviation (3.1) to this number (17.1) and place the sum 2 standard deviations above the mean (17.1 + 3.1 = 20.2). Add the standard deviation (3.1) to this number (20.2) and place the sum 3 standard deviations above the mean (20.2 + 3.1 = 23.3). Do the same to label the opposite side of the distribution, but subtract the standard deviation from the mean (14 − 3.1 = 10.9, 10.9 − 3.1 = 7.8, 7.8 − 3.1 = 4.7).

According to the characteristics of the normal distribution, approximately 34.1% of the population will score between 14 and 17.1, 34.1% will score between 14 and 10.9, and so on.

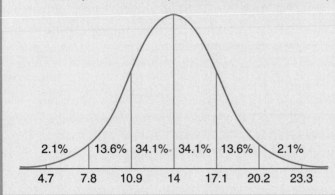

| 2.1% | 13.6% | 34.1% | 34.1% | 13.6% | 2.1% |

| 4.7 | 7.8 | 10.9 | 14 | 17.1 | 20.2 | 23.3 |

Measures of Relationship

Measures of relationship also help describe distributions of test scores. However, unlike measures of central tendency and measures of variability, you must have at least *two sets of scores* to calculate measures of relationship. The **correlation coefficient** is a statistic that is typically used to describe the relationship between two or more distributions of scores. Using a correlation coefficient, you can relate one set of scores to another to see whether the same individuals scored similarly on two different tests (for example, if they scored low on one test, did they also score low on another test?). Such a relationship is described as a positive correlation. On the other hand, if people who score high on one test are likely to score low on the other test and vice versa, the relationship is described as a negative correlation. Figure 5.6 shows two scatterplots: one of a positive correlation and one of a negative correlation.

There are various ways of computing correlations. The most common technique yields an index called the **Pearson product–moment correlation coefficient**. Represented by *r*, this coefficient measures the

Figure 5.6	Sample Positive and Negative Correlation

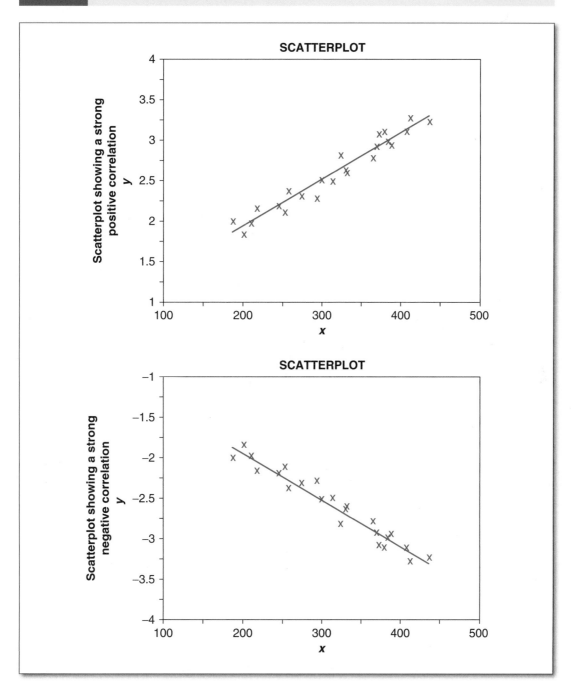

linear association between two variables, or sets of test scores, that have been measured on interval or ratio scales. The formula for the Pearson product–moment correlation coefficient is

$$r = \frac{\Sigma\,(d_x)(d_y)}{N\,(s_x)(s_y)}$$

where

r = correlation coefficient

Σ = sum of the values

d_x = deviation from the mean for the first set of scores

d_y = deviation from the mean for the second set of scores

N = number of scores

s_x = standard deviation of the first set of scores

s_y = standard deviation of the second set of scores

The correlation (r) between two distributions of scores is expressed in terms of a coefficient that can range from –1.00 to +1.00, with –1.00 indicating a perfect negative (or inverse) correlation, 0.00 indicating a complete lack of a relationship, and +1.00 indicating a perfect positive correlation. When correlating two sets of test scores, you will observe one of three types of relationships. First, there might be a positive correlation. With positive correlations, as the value of one variable (for example, the karats in a diamond) increases, the value of the other variable also increases (for example, the cost of the diamond). Second, there might be a negative correlation. With negative correlations, as the value of one variable (for example, your age) increases, the value of the other variable (for example, your visual acuity) decreases. Third, there might be no correlation, where there is no relationship at all between the variables (for example, there is no relationship between height and academic ability).

For Your Information Box 5.5 shows, step by step, how to calculate the correlation between two distributions of test scores using the Pearson product–moment correlation coefficient.

FYI

FOR YOUR INFORMATION BOX 5.5

Calculating the Correlation Between Two Distributions of Test Scores

Student	Midterm Exam Score	Final Exam Score	Midterm Deviation	Midterm Deviation Squared	Final Deviation	Final Deviation Squared	Product of Midterm and Final Deviations
	x	Y	d_x	d_x^2	d_y	d_y^2	$(d_x)(d_y)$
1	95	90	15.3	234.09	11.4	129.96	174.42
2	86	80	6.3	39.69	1.4	1.96	8.82

Student	Midterm Exam Score	Final Exam Score	Midterm Deviation	Midterm Deviation Squared	Final Deviation	Final Deviation Squared	Product of Midterm and Final Deviations
	x	Y	d_x	d_x^2	d_y	d_y^2	$(d_x)(d_y)$
3	76	66	− 3.7	13.69	−12.6	158.76	46.62
4	55	70	−24.7	610.09	−8.6	73.96	212.42
5	67	67	−12.7	161.29	−11.6	134.56	147.32
6	90	89	10.3	106.09	10.4	108.16	107.12
7	100	92	20.3	412.09	13.4	179.56	272.02
8	56	67	−23.7	561.69	−11.6	134.56	274.92
9	78	80	−1.7	2.89	1.4	1.96	−2.38
10	94	85	14.3	204.49	6.4	40.96	91.52
Total				2346.1		964.4	1332.8

1. List each student's raw score on the midterm exam and final exam.

2. Calculate the mean test score for the midterm exam and the final exam:

$$\bar{x}_x = 797/10 = 79.7 \quad \bar{x}_y = 786/10 = 78.6$$

3. Calculate the deviations (d_x and d_y) and the deviation squared (d_x^2 and d_y^2) for both exams.

4. Calculate the standard deviation for both exams:

$$s_x = \sqrt{2346.10/10} = 15.32 \qquad s_y = \sqrt{964.40/10} = 9.82$$

5. Multiply the deviations for each individual: $(d_x)(d_y)$.

6. Calculate the product moment correlation:

$$r = \frac{(d_x)(d_y)}{N\,(s_x)(s_y)} = \frac{1332.80}{10(10.35)(9.82)} = .89$$

> ### INTERIM SUMMARY 5.2
> ### PROCEDURES FOR INTERPRETING TEST SCORES
>
> - Because raw test scores tell us very little, we use descriptive statistics to describe or summarize a distribution of test scores.
> - Frequency distributions are graphs that help us understand the shape of a distribution.
> - The normal probability distribution is a theoretical distribution that helps us understand distributions of scores.
> - Measures of central tendency are numerical tools that help us locate the middle of a distribution of scores. They include the mean, mode, and median.
> - Measures of variability are numerical tools that help us understand the spread of a distribution of scores. They include the range, variance, and standard deviation.
> - Measures of relationship are numerical tools that help us understand how two sets of scores are related. The correlation coefficient is a common measure of relationship.

Standard Scores

We calculate measures of central tendency, measures of variability, and measures of relationship using raw test scores. These measures help us understand distributions of test scores. However, sometimes we convert (or transform) raw test scores into more meaningful units. Why? First, raw test scores are sometimes difficult to interpret in and of themselves. For example, if a friend told you that he earned a raw score of 19 on his midterm exam, would you say, "Great job" or "Better luck next time"? If you are like most people, you would ask your friend, "How many points were possible on the midterm exam?" This information allows you to give more meaning to your friend's score. If there were 20 points possible on the exam, you could quickly calculate that your friend earned a 95%. Now you could say, "Great job." Second, we often convert raw test scores into more meaningful units because we often have a need to compare scores. When raw test scores are expressed in different units (for example, one test score is the number correct out of 50 and the other test score is the number correct out of 75), it is difficult to make comparisons between the two tests.

These more meaningful units are called **standard scores**—universally understood units in testing that allow test users to evaluate a person's performance in reference to other persons who took the same or a similar test.

For example, if a student brought home a report that showed she had scored a 47 on her arithmetic test and a 63 on her English test, the first question we would ask her is "What kind of scores did the other students earn?" Does a 47 on her arithmetic test mean she did well? Although this raw score is concrete, it is not necessarily informative. If we knew that the mean on the arithmetic test was 40 and the mean on the English test was 60, all we would know is that the student did better than average on both tests. We would not know whether her raw score entitled her to a C+ or an A.

Transformed scores are most often used with standardized tests of aptitude, achievement, and personality and are designed to help us compare individual scores with group norms (which we talk about later in this chapter). They also help us compare one individual's score on one test with the same individual's score on another test. Using transformed scores, we can determine whether the student above scored about average, better than average, or below average in comparison with the other students in her class. We could also tell whether she did better on her arithmetic test than on her English test.

When we transform raw test scores, we create a more informative scale. A scale is a set of transformed scores that are often used to interpret a test. There are two types of transformations: linear and area. **Linear transformations** change the unit of measurement but do not change the characteristics of the raw data in any way. **Area transformations,** on the other hand, change not only the unit of measurement but also the unit of reference. Area transformations rely on the normal curve. They magnify the differences between individuals at the middle of the distribution and compress the differences between individuals at the extremes of the distribution. The most popular linear transformations include percentages, *z* scores and *T* scores, both based on the standard deviation. The most common area transformations are the percentile and the stanine.

Linear Transformations

Percentages

You are likely very familiar with **percentages.** Most of the time, your professors probably convert and report the results of your classroom exams in percentages. To calculate a percentage, you first divide a raw score by the total possible score and then multiply the answer by 100. So if you correctly answered 90 of 100 questions, your transformed percentage score would be 90% ((90/100 = .90)×100 = 90%).

Standard Deviation Units

Recall our discussion of the normal distribution. In a normal distribution, the mean is the same as the median, and therefore 50% of the scores will fall below or at the mean and 50% will fall above or at the mean. We said that if we take the mean of a distribution and add 1 standard deviation, 34% of the population will score in this range. If we add 2 standard deviations to the mean, 47% of the population will score in this range. If we add 3 standard deviations to the mean, 49% of the population will score in this range. The same is true when we subtract the standard deviation from the mean. **Standard deviation units** refer to how many standard deviations an individual score falls away from the mean. The mean always has a standard deviation unit of 0, 1 standard deviation above the mean has a standard deviation unit of 1, 2 standard deviations above the mean has a standard deviation unit of 2, and 3 standard deviations above the mean has a standard deviation of 3. Standard deviation units below the mean are represented with a negative (–) sign.

For example, if the mean of a distribution is 6 and the standard deviation is 2, then 1 standard deviation unit would represent a raw score of 8. Therefore, approximately 34% of the population will score between 6 and 8. If an individual scores a 7, her score falls within 1 standard deviation of the mean. If another individual scores a 9, his score falls between 1 and 2 standard deviations above the mean. If another individual scores a 5, her score falls within 1 standard deviation below the mean.

z Scores

z scores are very similar to standard deviation units except that they can be represented in whole numbers and decimal points. As with standard deviation units, the mean of a distribution of test scores will always have a *z* score of 0. A *z* score of 1 is always 1 standard deviation above the mean. A *z* score of –1 is always 1 standard deviation below the mean. The formula for the *z* score of a sample or distribution of scores is

$$z \text{ score} = \frac{x - \bar{x}}{s}$$

where

x = raw score

$\bar{x}$ = mean

s = standard deviation

T *Scores*

Unlike standard deviation units and *z* scores, ***T* scores** always have a mean of 50 and a standard deviation of 10. The formula for the *T* score is $T = (z \times 10) + 50$. Many test users prefer to use *T* scores over *z* scores because one half of the *z* scores in a distribution will be negative. *T* scores are always positive. *T* scores also are easier for many people to understand because people tend to think of the raw scores as if they were part of a 100-point scale.

Area Transformations

Percentiles

The mean of a normal distribution always has a percentile of 50. This means that 50% of individuals scored above the mean and 50% of individuals scored below the mean. To calculate an individual's percentile rank, you must first find the number of individuals who scored below the individual's score and the number of individuals who scored exactly the same score. You then take the number of individuals who scored below a specific raw score, add half (.5) of those who scored exactly the same raw score, and divide it by the total number of people who took the test. You then multiply this number by 100 to make the decimal a whole number. For example, let us say that an individual earned a 5 on a test for which the mean was also 5. If 100 people took the test, 50 scored below this individual, and 2 scored the same as him, his percentile rank would be

$$50 + (.5)(2) = .51 \times 100 = 51\%$$

Stanines

Although stanines are not as common as percentiles, periodically you will encounter the standard score of a stanine. Stanines are expressed in whole numbers from 1 to 9. Stanine scores of 1, 2, and 3 typically represent performance below the mean. Stanine scores of 4, 5, and 6 are generally considered to be average or close to the mean. Stanine scores of 7 and 8 are considered to be above average, and a stanine score of 9 is typically thought of as exceptional. As shown in Figure 5.7, in a normal distribution, 4% of the population

Figure 5.7   Stanines and the Normal Distribution

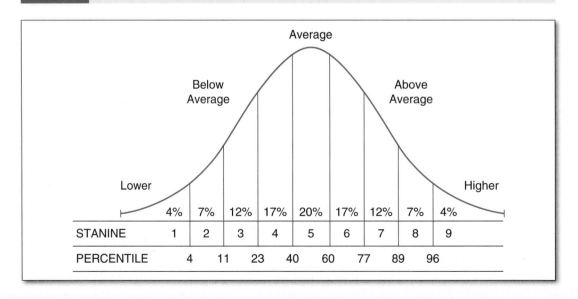

will score a stanine of 1, 7% a stanine of 2, 12% a stanine of 3, 17% a stanine of 4, 20% a stanine of 5, 17% a stanine of 6, 12% a stanine of 7, 7% a stanine of 8, and 4% a stanine of 9. For Your Information Box 5.6 provides an example of linear and area transformations.

FOR YOUR INFORMATION BOX 5.6

Linear and Area Transformations

Imagine that your class took a test of 50 questions, each worth 1 point. Given the following information (which you should now know how to calculate), we can draw a picture of what the distribution of the test scores would look like, using standard scores, assuming that the results are normally distributed:

- Number of questions = 50
- Mean = 31
- Range = 36
- Variance = 36
- Standard deviation = 6

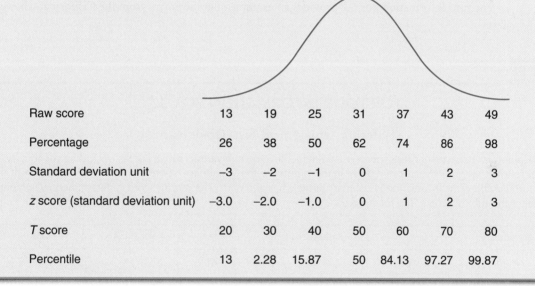

Raw score	13	19	25	31	37	43	49
Percentage	26	38	50	62	74	86	98
Standard deviation unit	−3	−2	−1	0	1	2	3
z score (standard deviation unit)	−3.0	−2.0	−1.0	0	1	2	3
T score	20	30	40	50	60	70	80
Percentile	13	2.28	15.87	50	84.13	97.27	99.87

The Role of Norms

Because few psychological tests produce ratio scale measures, we cannot say how much of an attribute, trait, or characteristic a person has. For example, we cannot say *how much* intelligence Robert has. Most test scores provide us with relative measures that allow us to conclude only that Robert is more intelligent than John, Robert scored 3 standard deviations above the mean, or Robert scored better than 75% of the people who took the test.

To help interpret test scores, we often use **norms,** which are the average scores of some identified group of individuals. These norms provide us with a standard against which we can compare individual test scores. The process of comparing an individual's test score to a norm group is referred to as **norm-based interpretation,** which helps us answer the question, "Where does a test taker stand in comparison with a group that defines the standards?" Norms are created by administering a test to a large number of individuals who are carefully selected to be representative of the population that the test is intended to serve. There are a number of different types of norms. In what follows, we consider and provide examples of three popular norms: percentile ranks, age norms, and grade norms.

Types of Norms

Age Norms and Grade Norms

Age norms and **grade norms** are also common types of norms because they allow us to determine at what age level or grade level an individual is performing. That is, they allow us to determine whether an individual's test score is similar to, below, or above the scores of others at the same age or grade level. Frequently used in educational settings, these types of norms are typically developed by administering a test to the targeted age or grade (for example, 10-year-olds or fourth graders) as well as to test takers with ages and grades immediately below and immediately above the targeted age or grade (for example, 9-year-olds or third graders and 11-year-olds or fifth graders). Although age and grade norms typically present scores for a broader age and grade than that mentioned previously, sometimes the scores that are presented in the norms are only estimates of what a younger student (for example, 8-year-old or second grader) or older student (12-year-old or sixth grader) would be likely to obtain.

For Your Information Box 5.7 provides an example of grade norms from the California Achievement Tests.

FYI

FOR YOUR INFORMATION BOX 5.7

California Achievement Tests Grade Norms

The California Achievement Tests measure student achievement in various subject areas, including vocabulary. In what follows, we provide an example of grade norms for the Vocabulary subtest from the 1970 edition of the California Achievement Tests. The Vocabulary subtest has two parts. The overall score is determined by summing together the subtest scores. The total score can range from 0 to 40.

Vocabulary Score	Grade Equivalent	Vocabulary Score	Grade Equivalent	Vocabulary Score	Grade Equivalent
0–12	0.6	29	2.6		5.1
	0.7	30–31	2.7		5.2
	0.8		2.8	39	5.3
14	0.9	32	2.9		5.4
	1.0	33	3.0		5.5
15	1.1	34	3.1		5.6
	1.2		3.2		5.7

Vocabulary Score	Grade Equivalent	Vocabulary Score	Grade Equivalent	Vocabulary Score	Grade Equivalent
16	1.3	35	3.3		5.8
17	1.4		3.4		5.9
	1.5		3.5		6.0
18	1.6	36	3.6		6.1
19	1.7		3.7		6.2
20	1.8		3.8		6.3
21	1.9		3.9	40	6.4
22	2.0	37	4.0		6.5
23–24	2.1		4.1		6.6
25	2.2		4.2		6.7
26	2.3		4.3		6.8
27	2.4		4.4		6.9
28	2.5		4.5		7.0
		38	4.6		7.1
			4.7		
			4.8		
			4.9		
			5.0		

SOURCE: Adapted from McGraw-Hill. (1970). *Examiner's manual for the California Achievement Tests, Complete Battery, Level 2, Form A*. New York: Author.

As you can see, based on these norms, the median score for children just beginning the third grade is approximately 33. What would you think if a third-grade student obtained a score of 40? Would you automatically think that this child belongs in the sixth grade? What these results mean is that this third-grade student has achieved a score that we would expect a typical sixth grader to obtain on this test. It does not mean that this third grader has the same overall achievement level as a student who is in the sixth grade. Just because this third grader obtained a score that we would expect a sixth grader to obtain does not mean that the third grader is achieving at the level of a sixth grader or that the third grader should be advanced to the sixth grade. To make a firm determination that this third grader was achieving at the level of a sixth grader, a broader assessment would be necessary. Such an assessment would need to include a number of skills tests to determine whether the third grader would be able to achieve at the sixth-grade level in other achievement areas (for example, math) and to determine whether the student would be able to cope with the social and emotional issues faced by students in higher grades.

Percentile Ranks

The **percentile rank** is a very common type of norm because it provides us with a way to rank individuals on a scale from 1% to 100%, making it relatively easy to interpret. With percentile rank norms, scores can range from the 1st percentile to the 99th percentile, with the average individual's score set at the 50th percentile. If an individual's raw score of 11 corresponds to a percentile rank of 98, we can say that the individual scored equal to or higher than 98% of the test takers in the norm group. Because percentile ranks make it easy for individuals to interpret test scores, many developers of standardized tests, particularly tests of academic achievement, provide conversion tables showing the percentile ranks in the norm group of all possible raw scores. Table 5.5 provides an example of a simple norms table for a hypothetical 11-item Technician's Aptitude and Proficiency Test. As you can see, the raw scores convert to percentile ranks, making it much easier to interpret a test taker's score meaningfully.

Table 5.5	Sample Norms Table for a Hypothetical Technician's Aptitude and Proficiency Test
Raw Score	*Percentile*
11	98
10	96
9	85
8	75
7	62
6	48
5	34
4	23
3	18
2	10
1	4
0	1

SOURCE: From Lyman, H. B. (1998). *Test scores: And what they mean* (6th ed.). Boston: Allyn & Bacon. Copyright © 1998 by Pearson Education.

 More detail about the Mini-Mental State Examination can be found in Test Spotlight 5.1 in Appendix A.

Originally developed in 1975, the Mini-Mental State Examination (MMSE) is a fairly short cognitive ability test often used to screen individuals for and estimate the severity of cognitive impairment. It is also used to measure cognitive changes over time—for example, to measure how an individual is responding to treatment. On the Web Box 5.1 provides actual normative data for the MMSE.

ON THE WEB BOX 5.1

Normative Data on the Mini-Mental State Examination

www.angelfire.com/retro/michaelpoon168/mini_mental_state_examination_normative%20data.htm

In Chapter 2, we introduced the Mini-Mental State Examination (MMSE), a 10-minute standardized test widely used in clinical settings to detect cognitive impairment in adults. The MMSE is also useful for monitoring cognitive changes over time.

The MMSE was originally published in 1975 and is currently published by PAR. The MMSE assesses orientation, immediate and short-term recall, language, and the ability to follow simple verbal and written commands. It also provides a total score that places an individual on a scale of cognitive function. For more information on the MMSE, go to the website above.

As you will learn at www.minimental.com, an individual's cognitive status is determined by comparing his or her MMSE raw score with the descriptive statistics of a norm group of test takers of similar ages and educational levels. Notice that there is a positive relationship between MMSE scores and grade, and there is an inverse relationship between MMSE scores and age. As individuals progress in their education, their MMSE scores increase. However, as individuals age, their MMSE scores decline, as shown in the following table.

Education	Age (years)												
	18–24	25–29	30–34	35–39	40–44	45–49	50–54	55–59	60–64	65–69	70–74	75–79	80–84
Fourth grade	22	25	25	23	23	23	23	22	23	22	22	21	20
Eighth grade	27	27	26	26	27	26	27	26	26	26	25	25	25
High school	29	29	29	28	28	28	28	28	28	28	27	27	25
College	29	29	29	29	29	29	29	29	29	29	28	28	27

SOURCE: From Crum, R. M., Anthony, J. J., Bassett, S. S., & Folstein, M. F., (1993). Population-based norms for the Mini-Mental State Examination by age and educational level. *Journal of the American Medical Association, 18,* 2386–2391. Reprinted by permission of the American Medical Association.

Because percentile ranks are so meaningful, many developers of standardized tests also produce test score reports that contain test percentile ranks. For Your Information Box 5.8 explains how the Florida Comprehensive Assessment Test Norm-Referenced Test reports scores using percentile ranks (and stanines).

FOR YOUR INFORMATION BOX 5.8

Florida Comprehensive Assessment Test

The Florida Comprehensive Assessment Test (FCAT) is a part of Florida's overall plan for increasing student achievement in primary and secondary schools by implementing higher standards. The FCAT consists of both criterion-referenced tests (tests that measure how well a student has learned a specific body of knowledge as defined by some criterion) and norm-referenced tests (tests that compare a student's performance against how other students in a norm group did on the test). The FCAT is administered to students in Grades 3 to 11 in Florida's public school system. In 2005, Florida administered a new version of the FCAT Norm-Referenced Tests, the Stanford Achievement Test Series–10th Edition, because the norms for the previous version were out of date. The Stanford Achievement Test Series measures academic achievement in two subjects: reading comprehension and mathematics problem solving. Developed by Harcourt Assessments, the Stanford Achievement Test Series–10th Edition was normed in spring and fall 2002.

In 2005, the daughter of one of this textbook's authors received her results from the FCAT Norm-Referenced Tests. These results are displayed in what follows. Notice how the test results are presented in various forms, including percentiles and stanines.

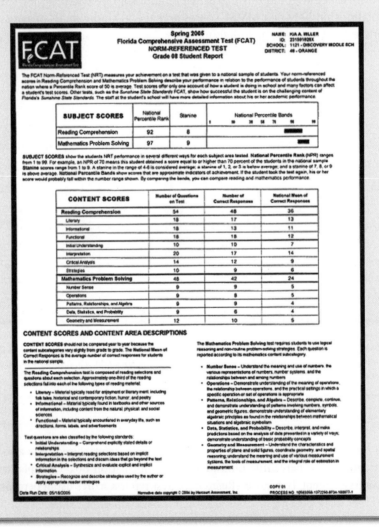

The Careful Use of Norms

As you will learn in Chapter 11, test developers often create and publish norms for more than one group. We cannot emphasize enough how important it is for test users to use the appropriate norm group when interpreting individual test scores. Using the incorrect norm group can result in very important decisions being made based on poor interpretation of test data. Consider the following example:

Alan Alexakis, a graduate assistant in philosophy at Athol University, answered 210 items correctly on the hypothetical Orange Omnibus Test (OOT) of 300 items. His raw score of 210 on the OOT means that he did as well as or better than:

- 99% of the seventh-grade pupils in the Malone Public Schools
- 92% of the Athol High School seniors
- 91% of the high school graduates in Worcester Academy
- 85% of the entering freshmen at Patricia Junior College
- 70% of the philosophy majors at Lamia College
- 55% of the graduating seniors at the University of Thessaloniki
- 40% of the graduate assistants at [the] American College of Athens
- 15% of the English professors at the University College London (Lyman, 1998, p. 82)

Although Alan's raw score on this test (210 of 300) remains the same, our interpretation of his performance will differ depending on the norm group to which we compare his test score. This is an extreme example, but it makes a point. If we compare Alan's score with scores of seventh graders, it would appear that he did very well. If we compare his score with scores of English professors, it would appear that he did poorly. The person who interprets test scores must choose the norm group that most closely resembles the test takers. The norm group chosen can have a significant impact on the interpretation of an individual's score.

Test users should also be careful to use up-to-date norms. Over time, the characteristics of populations change, and therefore their test scores change. When populations change, tests must be renormed. What was average in the past might no longer be average today. Likewise, over time, tests are modified and updated. It is not appropriate, nor fair to test takers, to compare and interpret their test scores on revised tests using norms from previous versions of tests. When tests are modified or updated, new norms must be developed, and these new norms should serve as the standard for comparison.

Test users should also be careful to look at the size of the norm group. The smaller the norm group, the greater the chance that the norm group is not representative of the entire target population. What is an adequate size for a norm group? This is a difficult question to answer. Many norm groups for educational tests contain thousands of individuals. Norm groups for research instruments are often smaller—in the hundreds.

Test users should also be careful when using age and grade norms. As we discussed in For Your Information Box 5.8, if an individual child scores at a higher age or grade level, we should not automatically assume that the child is ready to be placed with older students or in a higher grade. A broader assessment and more than one test score are necessary to determine whether a child would be able to cope with the social and emotional issues the child would face in the company of older students or students in higher grades.

INTERIM SUMMARY 5.3
STANDARD SCORES AND THE ROLE OF NORMS

- Standard scores are universally understood units of measurement in testing and allow us to evaluate how well an individual did on a test in comparison with others.
- We transform raw scores into standard scores to make comparisons.
- The most popular transformations are percentages, z scores, standard deviation units, T scores, and percentiles.
- Because most test scores provide us with relative measures, we often rely on norms—standards for interpreting scores—to describe individuals' performance.

- There are a variety of norm types, including percentile ranks, age norms, and grade norms.
- Percentile ranks tell us the percentage of the norm group that scored less than or equal to an individual.
- Age and grade norms tell us whether individuals scored below, similar to, or above their age or grade levels.
- Test users should be careful to select the appropriate norm group, ensure that the norms they use are up to date, and ensure that the size of the norm group is large enough to be representative of the target population.

Chapter Summary

Most psychological tests produce raw scores. The claims we can make using these scores depend on the scores' level of measurement. Four common levels of measurement are nominal, ordinal, equal interval, and ratio. As we move from one level of measurement to the next, we are able to perform more mathematical operations (addition, subtraction, multiplication, and division) that allow us to make more and different claims regarding test results.

To make sense of raw scores, we rely on a number of techniques. For example, we plot frequency distributions and calculate measures of central tendency, variability, and relationship. Each technique we use has a different purpose. Frequency distributions provide us with a picture of a distribution of scores. Measures of central tendency (mean, mode, and median) help us identify the center of a distribution of scores. Measures of variability (range, variance, and standard deviation) help us understand the spread of scores in a distribution. Measures of relationship (correlation coefficients) help us determine the relationship between distributions of test scores.

We also convert raw scores into standard units of measurement (for example, percentage, standard deviation unit, z score, T score, percentile) to provide more meaning to individual scores and so that we can compare individual scores with those of a previously tested group or norm group. Norms provide us with a standard against which we can compare individual test scores. There are a number of different types of norms, and test users must select and use the norm group that is most similar to the test takers. Test users should also be careful to use up-to-date norms and be sure that the norm group is representative of the target population.

Engaging in the Learning Process

KEY CONCEPTS

After completing your study of this chapter, you should be able to define each of the following terms. These terms are bolded in the text of this chapter and defined in the Glossary.

- age norms
- area transformations
- categorical data
- class intervals
- correlation coefficient
- descriptive statistics
- equal interval scales
- frequency distribution
- grade norms
- histogram
- levels of measurement
- linear transformations
- mean

- median
- measures of central tendency
- measures of relationship
- measures of variability
- mode
- nominal scales
- norm-based interpretation
- norm group
- normal curve
- normal probability distribution
- ordinal scales
- outliers

- percentages
- percentile rank
- Pearson product–moment correlation coefficient
- range
- ratio scales
- raw score
- standard deviation
- standard deviation units
- standard scores
- *T* scores
- variance
- *z* scores

LEARNING ACTIVITIES

The following are some learning activities you can engage in to support the learning objectives for this chapter.

Learning Objectives	Study Tips and Learning Activities
After completing your study of this chapter, you should be able to do the following:	*The following study tips will help you meet these learning objectives:*
Describe and identify the different levels of measurement.	• Document the different levels of measurement. For each level, write a definition, provide an example, and list some appropriate statistics.
Summarize test scores using class intervals and frequency distributions.	• Gather the shoe size and height of all students in your class. In groups or individually, summarize these two distributions of scores in a frequency table and histogram. Compare answers as a class.
Describe the characteristics of the normal curve as well as skewed, peaked, and bimodal distributions.	• Draw a variety of histograms. Indicate whether each resembles a normal curve, a positively or negatively skewed distribution, a peaked distribution, or a bimodal distribution.
Describe the purpose and calculate measures of central tendency, measures of variability, and measures of relationship.	• Read and write your answers to the following questions: 　• Why do we use measures of central tendency? What are the different measures of central tendency? 　• Why do we use measures of variability? What are the different measures of variability? What is the formula for each? 　• Why do we use measures of relationship? How do we measure relationships, and what is one formula discussed in your textbook?
Convert raw test scores to more meaningful units.	• Write down the different linear and area transformations we use to convert raw scores into more meaningful units. What is the formula for each?
Describe norm-based interpretation and the different types of norms.	• Review various test manuals. Document the following information: 　○ What norms are provided? 　○ How were these norms developed? 　○ How are these norms displayed? Be prepared to share your findings with the rest of the class.

ADDITIONAL LEARNING ACTIVITIES

1. Read each of the following situations. Then determine whether the level of measurement in each situation is nominal, ordinal, equal interval, or ratio.
   a. A professor scores a multiple-choice test by counting the number of correct answers.
   b. Eggs in the supermarket are graded as 1 = *small*, 2 = *medium*, 3 = *large,* and 4 = *jumbo.*
   c. A teacher measures the height of her first-grade students in inches.
   d. A trucking company has 10 vehicles numbered 1 through 10.
   e. An intelligence test is normed so that the average score is 100.
   f. Employees are assigned identification numbers.
   g. A local hockey team is ranked the best in the conference because it won the most games.

2. Suppose that you have magically changed places with the professor teaching this course. You have just administered the final exam. The final exam, like the midterm exam, consisted of 100 multiple-choice items (where 1 point is awarded for each correct answer). The scores your students earned on the midterm and final exams are shown below. Calculate measures of central tendency and measures of variability for each distribution of test scores. Calculate a measure of relationship between the two distributions. Be prepared to share with your classmates how students performed on each test and the relationship between the two tests.

Name	Midterm Exam	Final Exam
John	78	75
David	67	63
Kate	69	55
Zachary	63	60
Taylor	85	100
Peter	72	0
Kia	92	91
Jackie	67	75
Roger	94	90
Bill	62	65
Monique	61	60
Iara	44	55
Tonya	66	66
Amanda	87	88
Cindy	76	79
Terry	83	88
Robert	42	50
Linda	82	80

Name	Midterm Exam	Final Exam
Ruth	84	82
Tara	51	50
Kristen	69	60
Nancy	61	60
Bo	96	100
William	73	77
Sally	79	89

3. Assume that you designed a 10-item standardized test to measure college students' knowledge of psychological testing. You administer your new test to a representative group of college students who have taken a psychological testing course. You obtain the following raw scores. Create a table showing the percentage, z score, and T score for each raw score. Compare answers as a class.

Raw Score	Number of Students Who Obtained the Score
1	1
2	2
3	2
4	3
5	5
6	6
7	5
8	4
9	3
10	1

4. Imagine that you are a clinical psychologist. While conducting a comprehensive assessment of your client, Hulbert, you decide to administer various psychological tests to him. One of these tests is the Wallibee Test of Anxiety (this is not a real test). The Wallibee Test consists of 50 questions, and Hulbert answers 32 correctly. Given that the appropriate norm group has a mean of 28 and that the standard deviation of the norm group is 6, provide the following information:
    a. Assuming that the scores from the norm group are normally distributed, plot the scores (using the standard deviation) of the norm group.
    b. Calculate Hulbert's percentage, z score, and T score.

PRACTICE QUESTIONS

The following are some practice questions to assess your understanding of the material presented in this chapter.

Multiple Choice

Choose the one best answer to each question.

1. If 10 students arranged themselves from shortest to tallest and we assigned the shortest a score of 1 and the tallest a score of 10, we would be using
   a. an equal interval scale.
   b. a nominal scale.
   c. an ordinal scale.
   d. a ratio scale.

2. Most psychological tests produce which levels of measurement?
   a. Nominal and ratio
   b. Ordinal and ratio
   c. Ordinal and interval
   d. Nominal and ordinal

3. Which one of the following provides us with a visual image of a distribution of scores?
   a. Measures of variation
   b. Measures of central tendency
   c. Descriptive statistics
   d. Frequency distributions

4. What would you calculate to find out more about the middle of a distribution of scores?
   a. Levels of measurement
   b. Frequency distributions
   c. Measures of variability
   d. Measures of central tendency

5. What would you calculate if you wanted to find out whether a group of individuals who took a test performed very similar to or very different from one another?
   a. Measures of variation
   b. Measures of central tendency
   c. Descriptive statistics
   d. Frequency distributions

6. Which one of the following would be the most accurate index if a distribution of scores had outliers?
   a. Mode and median
   b. Mean and mode
   c. Mean and median
   d. Mean only

7. The correlation between two distributions of scores can range from
   a. −10.0 to +10.0.
   b. −1.0 to +1.0.
   c. 0 to 1.0.
   d. −0.5 to +0.5.

8. Which one of the following correlation coefficients would you most likely see if students' performance on a midterm exam was inversely related to their performance on a final exam?
   a. −10.0
   b. −0.6
   c. +0.2
   d. +6.0

9. What type of distribution is skewed to the left, has one high point, and has many high scores?
   a. Negatively skewed distribution
   b. Positively skewed distribution
   c. Evenly distributed distribution
   d. Peaked distribution

10. In a normal distribution, approximately what percentage of test scores will fall between 2 and 3 standard deviations above the mean?
    a. 68%
    b. 34.1%
    c. 13.6%
    d. 2.1%

11. In a normal distribution, approximately what percentage of test scores will fall between 1 standard deviation below the mean and 1 standard deviation above the mean?
    a. 95%
    b. 68%
    c. 34.1%
    d. 13.6%

12. Which one of the following standard scores always has a mean of 50 and a standard deviation of 10?
    a. *T* scores
    b. *z* scores
    c. Percentiles
    d. Standard deviation units

13. If your score on a test is calculated to be equivalent to a percentile rank of 80, we can say that
    a. you scored better than 79% of the norm group.
    b. you scored equal to or better than 80% of the norm group.
    c. you scored equal to or less than 80% of the norm group.
    d. 80% of the norm group scored higher than you.

14. If the mean of a distribution of test scores is 70 and the standard deviation is 5, what would John's z score be if he scored an 80?
    a. 0
    b. 1
    c. 2
    d. 3

15. Which one of the following standard scores changes the unit of measurement?
    a. Percentage
    b. Percentile
    c. z score
    d. T score

16. Which one of the following is FALSE about the use of norms?
    a. There is one right population that is regarded as the normative group.
    b. Test publishers often develop and publish the results of various norm groups.
    c. Test users should always be careful to use up-to-date norms.
    d. The smaller the norm group, the more likely the norm group is not representative.

Short Answer/Essay

Read each of the following, and consider your response carefully based on the information presented in this chapter. Write your answer to each question in two or three paragraphs.

1. Why is it important to understand the level of measurement of data?

2. Compare and contrast the levels of measurement. What mathematical operations can you perform for each level of measurement?

3. What is the normal probability distribution? Describe the characteristics of the normal probability distribution.

4. What procedures do we use to interpret test scores? Why do we calculate measures of central tendency, measures of variability, and measures of relationship? Give an example of each.

5. What descriptive statistics are appropriate for each level of measurement?

6. What is the purpose of transforming raw scores into standard scores? What are three commonly used standard scores, and how do you calculate each one?

7. What is norm-based interpretation? What must we be careful of when using norms?

Answer Keys

Additional Learning Activities

1.
   a. Ratio
   b. Ordinal
   c. Ratio
   d. Nominal
   e. Equal interval
   f. Nominal
   g. Ordinal

2.

Midterm Exam:

Mean = 72.12

Mode = 61, 67, 69

Median = 72

Standard deviation = 14.10

Final Exam:

Mean = 70.32

Mode = 60

Median = 75

Standard deviation = 20.70

Correlation = .66

3.

		Standard Scores	
Raw Score	Percentage	z Score	T Score
1	10	−2.18	28.21
2	20	−1.73	32.68
3	30	−1.29	37.14
4	40	−0.84	41.61
5	50	−0.39	46.07
6	60	0.05	50.54
7	70	0.50	55.00
8	80	0.95	59.46
9	90	1.39	63.93
10	100	1.84	68.39

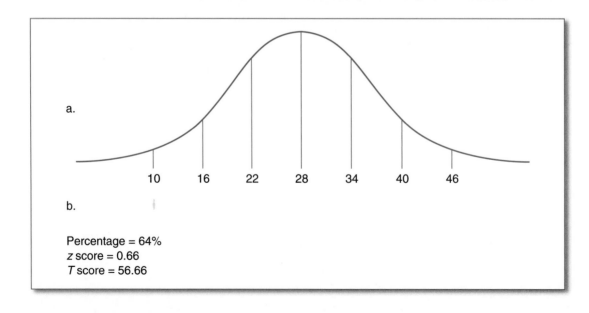

a.

10   16   22   28   34   40   46

b.

Percentage = 64%

z score = 0.66

T score = 56.66

Multiple Choice

1. c	2. c	3. d	4. d	5. a
6. a	7. b	8. b	9. a	10. c
11. b	12. a	13. b	14. c	15. b
16. a				

Short Answer/Essay

Refer to your textbook for answers. If you are unsure of an answer and cannot generate the answer after reviewing your book, ask your professor for clarification.

Note

1.   You may recall from a statistics course that sometimes the denominator of the standard deviation formula is $N - 1$. $N - 1$ is used when estimating the standard deviation of a sample drawn from a larger population. Because we are calculating the standard deviation of a known population (group of scores), we use N.

What Is Test Reliability?

CHAPTER 6: WHAT IS TEST RELIABILITY?

After completing your study of this chapter, you should be able to do the following:

- Define reliability, and describe three methods for estimating the reliability of a psychological test and its scores.
- Describe how an observed test score is made up of the *true score* and *random error*, and describe the difference between random error and systematic error.
- Calculate and interpret a reliability coefficient, including adjusting a reliability coefficient obtained using the split-half method.
- Differentiate between the KR-20 and coefficient alpha formulas, and understand how they are used to estimate internal consistency.
- Calculate the standard error of measurement, and use it to construct a confidence interval around an observed score.
- Identify four sources of test error and six factors related to these sources of error that are particularly important to consider.
- Explain the premises of generalizability theory, and describe its contribution to estimating reliability.

"My statistics instructor let me take the midterm exam a second time because I was distracted by noise in the hallway. I scored 2 points higher the second time, but she says my true score probably didn't change. What does that mean?"

"I don't understand that test. It included the same questions—only in different words—over and over."

"The county hired a woman firefighter even though she scored lower than someone else on the qualifying test. A man scored highest with a 78, and this woman only scored 77! Doesn't that mean they hired a less qualified candidate?"

"The psychology department surveyed my class on our career plans. When they reported the results of the survey, they also said our answers were unreliable. What does that mean?"

Have you ever wondered just how consistent or precise psychological test scores are? If a student retakes a test, such as the SAT, can the student expect to do better the second time without extra preparation? Are the scores of some tests more consistent than others? How do we know which tests are likely to produce more consistent scores?

If you have found yourself making statements or asking questions like those at the beginning of this chapter, or if you have ever wondered about the consistency of a psychological test or survey, the questions you raised concern reliability of responses. As you will learn in this chapter, we use the term *reliability* to describe the consistency of test scores. All test scores—just like any other measurement—contain some error. It is this error that impacts the reliability, or consistency, of test scores.

In this chapter, we describe three methods of estimating reliability of test scores: *test–retest* or stability over time, *internal consistency* or homogeneity of the test questions, and *scorer reliability* or agreement. We discuss how to calculate an index of reliability called the reliability coefficient, an index of error called the standard error of measurement, and an index of agreement called Cohen's kappa. Finally, we discuss factors that increase and decrease a test's reliability.

What Is Reliability?

As you are aware, psychological tests are measurement instruments. In this sense, they are no different from yardsticks, speedometers, or thermometers. A psychological test measures how much the test taker has of whatever skill or quality the test measures. For instance, a driving test measures how well the test taker drives a car, and a self-esteem test measures whether the test taker's self-esteem is high, low, or average when compared with the self-esteem of similar others.

The most important attribute of a measurement instrument is its **reliability.** A yardstick, for example, is a reliable measuring instrument over time because each time it measures an object (for example, a room), it gives approximately the same answer. Variations in the measurements of the room—perhaps a fraction of an inch from time to time—can be referred to as **measurement error.** Such errors are probably due to mistakes or inconsistencies of the person using the yardstick or because the smallest increment on a yardstick is often a quarter of an inch, making finer distinctions difficult. A yardstick also has **internal consistency.** The first foot on the yardstick is the same length as the second foot and third foot, and the length of every inch is uniform.

Reliability is one of the most important standards for determining how trustworthy data derived from a psychological test are. A **reliable test** is one we can trust to measure each person in approximately the same way every time it is used. A test also must be reliable if it is used to measure attributes and compare people, much as a yardstick is used to measure and compare rooms. Although a yardstick can help you understand the concept of reliability, you should keep in mind that a psychological test does not measure physical objects as a yardstick does, and therefore a psychological test cannot be expected to be as reliable as a yardstick in making a measurement.

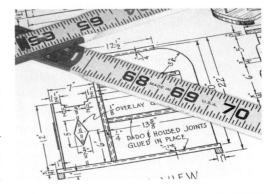

SOURCE: © PMSI Web Hosting and Design/Istockphoto.

Keep in mind that just because a test has been shown to produce reliable scores, that does not mean the test is also *valid*. In other words, evidence of reliability does not mean that the inferences that are being made from the scores on the test are correct or that it is being used properly. (We explain the concept of validity in Chapters 7, 8, and 9.)

Three Types of Reliability

If you measured a room but you were unsure whether your measurement was correct, what would you do? Most people would measure the room a second time using either the same or a different tape measure.

Psychologists use the same strategies of remeasurement to check psychological measurements. These strategies establish evidence of the reliability of test scores. Some of the methods that we will discuss require two administrations of the same (or very similar) test forms, while other methods can be accomplished in a single administration of the test. Three methods for checking reliability are (1) the test–retest method, (2) internal consistency (using split-half or coefficient alpha), and (3) scorer reliability or agreement. Each of these methods takes into account various conditions that can produce differences in test scores. Not all strategies are used for all tests. The strategy chosen to determine reliability depends on the test itself and the conditions under which the test user plans to administer the test.

Test–Retest Reliability

To estimate how reliable a test is using the **test–retest method,** a test developer gives the same test to the same group of test takers on two different occasions. The scores from the first and second administrations are then compared using correlation—a statistical technique that was discussed in Chapter 5. This method of estimating reliability allows us to examine the performance of a test over time and provides an estimate of the test's stability or precision.

The interval between the two administrations of the test may vary from a few hours up to several years. As the interval lengthens, test–retest reliability will decline because the number of opportunities for the test takers or the testing situation to change increases over time. For example, if we give a math achievement test to a student today and then again tomorrow, there probably is little chance that the student's knowledge of math will change overnight. However, if we give a student a math achievement test today and then again in two months, it is very likely that something will happen during the two months that will increase (or decrease) the student's knowledge of math. When test developers or researchers report test–retest reliability, they must also state the length of time that elapsed between the two test administrations.

Using test–retest reliability, the assumption is that the test takers have not changed between the first administration and the second administration in terms of the skill or quality measured by the test. On the other hand, changes in test takers' moods, levels of fatigue, or personal problems from one administration to another can affect their test scores. The circumstances under which the test is administered, such as the test instructions, lighting, or distractions, must be alike. Any differences in administration or in the individuals themselves will introduce error and reduce reliability.

The test developer makes the first estimates of the reliability of a test's scores. A good example of estimating reliability using the test–retest method can be seen in the initial reliability testing of the Personality Assessment Inventory (PAI). The PAI, developed by Leslie Morey, is used for clinical diagnoses, treatment planning, and screening for clinical psychopathology in adults. To initially determine the PAI's test–retest reliability, researchers administered it to two samples of individuals not in clinical

treatment. (Although the test was designed for use in a clinical setting, using a clinical sample for estimating reliability would have been difficult because changes due to a disorder or to treatment would
have confused interpretation of the results of the reliability studies.) The researchers administered the
PAI twice to 75 normal adults. The second administration followed the first by an average of 24 days. The
researchers also administered the PAI to 80 normal college students, who took the test twice with an
interval of 28 days. In each case, the researchers correlated the set of scores from the first administration
with the set of scores from the second administration. The two studies yielded similar results, showing
acceptable estimates of test–retest reliability for the PAI. (Later in this
chapter, we discuss what an "acceptable level of reliability" means).

An important limitation in using the test–retest method of estimating reliability is that the test takers may score differently (usually
higher) on the test because of **practice effects.** Practice effects occur
when test takers benefit from taking the test the first time (practice),
which enables them to solve problems more quickly and correctly
the second time. (If all test takers benefited the same amount from

 More detail about the
Personality Assessment
Inventory can be found in
Test Spotlight 6.1 in
Appendix A.

practice, it would not affect reliability; however, it is likely that some will benefit from practice more
than others will.) Therefore, the test–retest method is appropriate only when test takers are not likely
to learn something the first time they take the test that can affect their scores on the second administration or when the interval between the two administrations is long enough to prevent practice effects.
In other words, a long time between administrations can cause test takers to forget what they learned
during the first administration. However, short intervals between testing implementations may be
preferable when the test measures an attribute that may change in an individual over time due to learning or maturation, or when the possibility that changes in the testing environment that occur over time
may affect the scores.

To overcome problems such as practice effects, psychologists often give two forms of the same test—
designed to be as much alike as possible—to the same people. This strategy requires the test developer
to create two forms of the test that are referred to as **alternate forms** or **parallel forms.** Again, the sets
of scores from the two tests are compared using correlation. This method of estimating reliability provides a test of equivalence. The two forms (Form A and Form B) are administered as close in time as possible—usually on the same day. To guard against any **order effects**—changes in test scores resulting from
the order in which the tests were taken—half of the test takers may receive Form A first and the other
half may receive Form B first.

An example of the use of alternative forms in testing can be seen in the development of the Test of
Nonverbal Intelligence-4 (TONI-4). The TONI-4 is the fourth version of an intelligence test that was
designed to assess cognitive ability in populations that have language difficulties due to learning disabilities, speech problems, or other verbal problems that might result from a neurological deficit or developmental disability. The test does not require any language to be used in the administration of the test
or in the responses of the test takers. The items are carefully drawn graphics that represent problems with
four to six possible solutions. The test takers can use any mode of responding that the test administrator
can understand to indicate their answer, such as nodding, blinking, or pointing. Because this test is often
used in situations where there is a need to assess whether improvement in functioning has occurred, two
forms of the test needed to be developed—one to use as a pretest and another to use as a posttest. After
the forms were developed, the test developers assessed the alternate form reliability by giving the two
forms to the same group of subjects in the same testing session. The results demonstrated that the correlation between the test forms across all ages was .81, and the mean score difference between the two
forms was one-half of a score point. This is good evidence for alternate form reliability of the TONI-4.

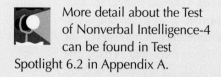

More detail about the Test of Nonverbal Intelligence-4 can be found in Test Spotlight 6.2 in Appendix A.

The greatest danger when using alternate forms is that the two forms will not be truly equivalent. Alternate forms are much easier to develop for well-defined characteristics, such as mathematical ability, than for personality traits, such as extroversion. For example, achievement tests given to students at the beginning and end of the school year are alternate forms. Although we check the reliability of alternate forms by administering them at the same time, their practical advantage is that they can be used as pre- and posttests.

Internal Consistency

What if you can give the test only once? How can you estimate the reliability? As you recall, test–retest reliability provides a measure of the test's reliability over time, and that measure can be taken only with two administrations. However, we can measure another type of reliability called internal consistency by giving the test once to one group of people. Internal consistency is a measure of how related the items (or groups of items) are to each other. Another way to think about it is whether knowledge of how a person answered one item on the test would give you information that would help you correctly predict how he or she answered another item on the test. If you can (statistically) do that across the entire test, then the items must have something in common with each other. That commonality usually is related to the fact that they are measuring a similar attribute, and therefore we say that the test is internally consistent. Table 6.1 shows two pairs of math questions. The first pair has more commonality for assessing ability to do math calculations than the second pair does.

Table 6.1	Internally Consistent vs. Inconsistent Test Questions

A. Questions with higher internal consistency for measuring math calculation skill:

Question 1:	$7 + 8 = ?$	Question 2:	$8 + 3 = ?$

B. Questions with lower internal consistency for measuring math calculation skill:

Question 1:	$4 + 5 = ?$	Question 2:	$150 \times 300 = ?$

Can you see why this is so? The problems in Pair A are very similar; both involve adding single-digit numbers. The problems in Pair B, however, test different arithmetic operations (addition and multiplication), and Pair A uses simpler numbers than Pair B does. In Pair A, test takers who can add single digits are likely to get both problems correct. However, test takers who can add single digits might not be able to multiply three-digit numbers. The problems in Pair B measure different kinds of math calculation, and therefore they are less internally consistent than the problems in Pair A, which both measure the addition of single-digit numbers. Another way to look at the issue is that if you knew that a person correctly answered Q1 in Pair A, you would have a good chance of being correct if you predicted that the person also would answer Q2 correctly. However, you probably would be less confident about your prediction about a person answering Q1 in Pair B correctly also answering Q2 correctly.

Statisticians have developed several methods for measuring the internal consistency of a test. One traditional method, the **split-half method,** is to divide the test into halves and then compare the set of individual test scores on the first half with the set of individual test scores on the second half. The two halves must be equivalent in length and content for this method to yield an accurate estimate of reliability.

The best way to divide the test is to use random assignment to place each question in one half or the other. Random assignment is likely to balance errors in the score that can result from order effects (the order in which the questions are answered), difficulty, and content. For Your Information Box 6.1 shows how a 10-question test has been divided into two 5-question tests using random assignment. The scores of the first and second halves are compared using correlation.

FYI

FOR YOUR INFORMATION BOX 6.1

Dividing the Test Into Halves Using Random Assignment

Test questions in the original test were assigned to either Split Half 1 or Split Half 2 using the method of random assignment. This procedure resulted in two tests, each one half as long as the original test.

Original Test	Split Half 1	Split Half 2
Question 1	Question 2	Question 3
Question 2	Question 1	Question 10
Question 3	Question 6	Question 4
Question 4	Question 7	Question 5
Question 5	Question 9	Question 8
Question 6		
Question 7		
Question 8		
Question 9		
Question 10		

As we explain later in this chapter, shortening a test decreases its reliability. Therefore, when using the split-half method, we must mathematically adjust the reliability coefficient to compensate for splitting the test into halves. We discuss this adjustment—using an equation called the Spearman–Brown formula—later in the chapter.

An even better way to measure internal consistency is to compare individuals' scores on all possible ways of splitting the test into halves. This method compensates for any error introduced by a lack of equivalence in the two halves. Kuder and Richardson (1937, 1939) first proposed a formula, KR-20, for calculating internal consistency of tests whose questions can be scored as either right or wrong (such as multiple-choice test items). Cronbach (1951) proposed a formula called coefficient alpha that calculates internal consistency for questions that have more than two possible responses. We discuss these formulas later in this chapter.

Estimating reliability using methods of internal consistency is appropriate only for tests that are **homogeneous**—measuring only one trait or characteristic. When tests are **heterogeneous**—measuring more than one trait or characteristic—estimates of internal consistency are likely to be lower. For example, a test for people who are applying for the job of accountant may measure knowledge of accounting principles, calculation skills, and ability to use a computer spreadsheet. Such a test is heterogeneous because it measures three distinct factors of performance for an accountant.

It is not appropriate to calculate an overall estimate of internal consistency (for example, coefficient alpha, split half) when a test is heterogeneous. Instead, the test developer should calculate and report an estimate of internal consistency for each homogeneous subtest or factor. This test for accountants should have three estimates of internal consistency: one for the subtest that measures knowledge of accounting principles, one for the subtest that measures calculation skills, and one for the subtest that measures ability to use a computer spreadsheet. In addition, Schmitt (1996) states that the test developer should report the relationships or correlations between the subtests or factors of a test. For Your Information Box 6.2 provides an example of how to present the internal consistency for a heterogeneous test.

FYI

FOR YOUR INFORMATION BOX 6.2

Reporting Internal Consistency for a Heterogeneous Test

Heterogeneous tests—those that contain multiple subtests or factors—are common. Employers often use heterogeneous tests to select employees. For instance, accountants need math skills to perform successfully, and a test for applicants for the job of accountant may cover several types of math skills. The table below contains estimates of internal reliability for three subtests.

Simulated Data for a Test for Accountants

Subtest	1	2	3
1. Accounting Skills	(.90)	.70	.51
2. Calculation Skills		(.85)	.47
3. Use of Spreadsheet			(.95)

As you can see, the subtests are listed in the first column. Each has a number and a title (for example, 1. Accounting Skills). The subtests are also in the first row by number only (for example, 1). The numbers in parentheses in the diagonal of the matrix are the coefficient alphas calculated for the subtests (for example, (.90)). Correlations between the subtests are listed above the diagonal (for example, .70). The internal consistency estimates range between .85 and .95. You can also see that Accounting Skills and Calculation Skills correlate at .70, indicating that they are quite interrelated. Although Use of Spreadsheet has positive relations with the other subtests, the relations are not as strong as they are between the other two subtests.

Later in this chapter, we discuss how to interpret reliability coefficients and decide whether the reliability for test scores is sufficient.

Furthermore, Schmitt (1996) emphasizes that the concepts of internal consistency and homogeneity are not the same. Coefficient alpha describes the extent to which questions on a test or subscale are interrelated. Homogeneity refers to whether the questions measure the same trait or dimension. It is possible for a test to contain questions that are highly interrelated, even though the questions measure two factors. This can happen when there is some third "common" factor that may be related to all the other attributes that the test measures. For instance, we described a hypothetical test for accountants that contained subtests for accounting skills, calculation skills, and use of a spreadsheet. Even though these three subtests may be considered heterogeneous dimensions, all of them may be influenced by a common factor that might be named general mathematical ability. Therefore, people who are high in this ability might do better across all three subtests than people lower in this ability. As a result, coefficient alpha might still be high even though the test measures more than one dimension. Therefore, a high coefficient alpha is not "proof" that a test measures only one skill, trait, or dimension.

The developers of the PAI also conducted studies to determine its internal consistency. Because the PAI requires test takers to provide ratings on a response scale that has five options (*false, not at all true, slightly true, mainly true,* and *very true*), they used the coefficient alpha formula. The developers administered the PAI to three samples: a sample of 1,000 persons drawn to match the U.S. Census, another sample of 1,051 college students, and a clinical sample of 1,246 persons. The coefficient alpha formula requires large numbers of respondents to estimate internal consistency because violation of assumptions underlying the formula causes coefficient alpha to overestimate or underestimate the population reliability when the number of respondents is small (Zimmerman, Zumbo, & Lalonde, 1993).

Table 6.2 shows the estimates of internal consistency for the scales and subscales of the PAI. Again, the studies yielded levels of reliability considered to be acceptable by the test developer for most of the scales and subscales of the PAI. Two scales on the test—Inconsistency and Infrequency—yielded low estimates of internal consistency. However, the test developer anticipated lower alphas because these scales measure the care used by the test taker in completing the test, and careless responding could vary during the testing period. For instance, a test taker might complete the first half of the test accurately but then become tired and complete the second half haphazardly.

Scorer Reliability

What about errors made by the person who scores the test? An individual can make mistakes in scoring that add error to test scores, particularly when the scorer must make judgments about whether an answer is right or wrong. When scoring requires making judgments, two or more persons should score the test. We then compare the judgments that the scorers make about each answer to see how much they agree. The methods we have already discussed concern whether the test itself yields consistent scores, but scorer reliability and agreement concern how consistent the judgments of the scorers are.

Some tests, such as those that require the scorer to make judgments, have complicated scoring schemes and test manuals that provide explicit instructions for making these scoring judgments. Deviation from the scoring instructions or a variation in the interpretation of the instructions introduces error into the final score. Therefore, **scorer reliability** or scorer agreement—the amount of consistency among scorers' judgments— becomes an important consideration for tests that require decisions by the administrator or scorer.

A good example of estimating reliability using scorer reliability can be seen in the Wisconsin Card Sorting Test (WCST). This test was originally designed to assess perseveration and abstract thinking, but it is currently one of the most widely used tests by clinicians and neurologists to assess executive function (cognitive abilities that control and regulate abilities and behaviors) of children and adults. Axelrod, Goldman, and Woodard (1992) conducted two studies on the reliability of scoring the WCST using adult psychiatric inpatients. In these studies, one person administered the test and others scored the test.

In the first study, three clinicians experienced in neuropsychological assessment scored the WCST data independently according to instructions given in an early edition of the test manual

Table 6.2   Estimates of Internal Consistency for the Personality Assessment Inventory

Scale	Alpha		
	Census	College	Clinic
Inconsistency (ICN)	.45	.26	.23
Infrequency (INF)	.52	.22	.40
Negative Impression (NIM)	.72	.63	.74
Positive Impression (PIM)	.71	.73	.77
Somatic Complaints (SOM)	.89	.83	.92
Anxiety (ANX)	.90	.89	.94
Anxiety-Related Disorders (ARD)	.76	.80	.86
Depression (DEP)	.87	.87	.93
Mania (MAN)	.82	.82	.82
Paranoia (PAR)	.85	.88	.89
Schizophrenia (SCZ)	.81	.82	.89
Borderline Features (BOR)	.87	.86	.91
Antisocial Features (ANT)	.84	.85	.86
Alcohol Problems (ALC)	.84	.83	.93
Drug Problems (DRG)	.74	.66	.89
Aggression (AGG)	.85	.89	.90
Suicidal Ideation (SUI)	.85	.87	.93
Stress (STR)	.76	.69	.79
Nonsupport (NON)	.72	.75	.80
Treatment Rejection (RXR)	.76	.72	.80
Dominance (DOM)	.78	.81	.82
Warmth (WRM)	.79	.80	.83
Median across 22 scales	.81	.82	.86

SOURCE: From *Personality Assessment Inventory* by L.C. Morey. Copyright © 1991. Published by Psychological Assessment Resources (PAR).

(Heaton, 1981). Their agreement was measured using a statistical procedure called intraclass correlation, a special type of correlation appropriate for comparing responses of more than two raters or of more than two sets of scores. The scores that each clinician gave each individual on three subscales correlated at .93, .92, and .88—correlations that indicated very high agreement. The studies also looked at **intrascorer reliability**—whether each clinician was consistent in the way he or she assigned scores from test to test. Again, all correlations were greater than .90.

In the second study, six novice scorers, who did not have previous experience scoring the WCST, scored 30 tests. The researchers divided the scorers into two groups. One group received only the scoring procedures in the test manual (Heaton, 1981), and the other group received supplemental scoring instructions as well as those in the manual. All scorers scored the WCST independently. The consistency level of these novices was high and was similar to the results of the first study. Although there were not significant differences between groups, those receiving the supplemental scoring material were able to score the WCST in a shorter time period. Conducting studies of scorer reliability for a test, such as those of Axelrod and colleagues (1992), ensures that the instructions for scoring are clear and unambiguous so that multiple scorers arrive at the same results.

 More detail about Wisconsin Card Sorting Test can be found in Test Spotlight 6.3 in Appendix A.

We have discussed three methods for estimating the reliability of a test: test-retest, internal consistency, and scorer reliability. Some methods require only a single administration of the test, while others require two. Again, each of these methods takes into account various conditions that could produce differences in test scores, and not all strategies are appropriate for all tests. The strategy chosen to determine reliability depends on the test itself and the conditions under which the test user plans to administer the test.

Some tests have undergone extensive reliability testing. An example of such a test is the Bayley Scales of Infant Development, a popular and interesting test for children that has extensive evidence of reliability. According to Dunst (1998), the standardization and the evidence of reliability and validity of this test far exceed generally accepted guidelines. (We discuss such guidelines later in this chapter. Of interest here is the challenge the Bayley Scales faced in gathering evidence of test–retest reliability.)

 See Test Spotlight 6.4 in Appendix A for more detail on the Bayley Scales of Infant Development.

The test developer should report the reliability method as well as the number and characteristics of the test takers in the reliability study. For some tests, such as the PAI, the WCST, and the Bayley Scales, more than one method may be appropriate. Each method provides evidence that the test is consistent under certain circumstances. Using more than one method provides strong corroborative evidence that the test is reliable.

The next section describes statistical methods for calculating estimates of test reliability. As you will see, the answer to how reliable a test's scores are may depend on how you decide to measure it. Test–retest and internal consistency are concerned with the test itself. Scorer reliability involves an examination of how consistently the person or persons scored the test. One of the causes of this inconsistency occurs when test scorers do not consistently apply the scoring rules that were provided to them. That is why test publishers may need to report multiple estimates of reliability for a test to give the test user a complete picture of the instrument.

INTERIM SUMMARY 6.1
THREE TYPES OF RELIABILITY

- The test–retest method compares the scores of the same test takers taking the same test at two different times. This method is appropriate when the test takers have not changed on the ability, trait, or attitude that the test measures. The alternate-forms method compares the scores of the same test takers on two equivalent forms.
- The internal consistency method compares the scores of test takers on two halves of the test taken at the same time (split-half method). Scores of test takers on all possible halves can be calculated using the coefficient alpha or KR-20 formula when the test questions are homogeneous.

- Scorer reliability is a method for estimating reliability or accuracy of those making judgments when scoring a test. Two types of scorer reliability are important: the comparison of judgments among scorers (interscorer) and the comparison of judgments that each scorer makes for all tests (intrascorer). We use correlation to calculate the interscorer reliability for interval data such as numerical test scores. We calculate intrascorer reliability using the formulas for calculating internal consistency.

Classical Test Theory

No measurement instrument is perfectly reliable or consistent. Many clocks are slow or fast—even if we measure their errors in nanoseconds. Unfortunately, psychologists are not able to measure psychological qualities with the same precision that engineers have for measuring speed or physicists have for measuring distance.

For instance, did you ever stop to think about the fact that when you give a test to a group of people their scores will vary, that is, they will not all obtain the same score? The obvious reason for this is that the people to whom you give the test differ in the amount of the attribute the test measures, and the variation in test scores simply reflect this fact. Now think about the situation in which you retest the same people the next day using the same test. Would each individual score exactly the same on the second testing as on the first? The answer is that they most likely wouldn't. The scores would probably be close to the scores they obtained on the first testing, but they would not be exactly the same. Some people would score higher on the second testing, while some people would score lower. But assuming that the amount of the attribute that the test measures has stayed the same in each person (after all, it's only one day later), why should the obtained test scores have changed? It turns out that according to classical test theory, any test score that a person obtains can be considered to be made up of two independent parts. The first part is a measure of the amount of the attribute that the test measures; this is known as the person's true score (T). The second part of an obtained test score consists of random errors that occur anytime a person takes a test (E). It is this random error that causes a person's test score to change from one administration of a test to the next (assuming that his or her true score hasn't changed). Because this type of error is a random event, sometimes it causes an individual's test score to go up on the second administration, and sometimes it causes it to go down. So if you could know what a person's true score was on a test, and also know the amount of random error, you could easily determine what the person's actual obtained score on the test would be. Formally, classical test theory expresses this idea by saying that any observed test score (X) is made up of two parts: a true score (T) and random error (E). Therefore,

$$X = T + E$$

True Score

The true score (T) of a test is a value that can never really be known or determined. It represents the score that would be obtained if an individual took a test an infinite number of times and then the average score across all the testings were computed. As we will discuss in a moment, random errors that may occur in any one test occasion will actually cancel themselves out over an infinite number of testing occasions. Therefore, if we could average all the scores together, the result would represent a score that no longer contained any random error. This is the true score on the test and represents the amount of the attribute the person who took the test actually possesses without any random measurement error.

One way to think about a true score is to think about choosing a member of your bowling team. You could choose a person based on watching him or her bowl a single game. But you would probably recognize that that single score could have been influenced by a lot of factors (random error) other than the person's actual bowling skill (the true score). Perhaps the person was just plain lucky that game and the score was really higher than his or her actual skill level would suggest. So perhaps you might prefer that the person bowl three games so that you could take the average score to estimate his or her true level of bowling ability. Intuitively, you may understand by asking the person to bowl multiple games that some random influences on performance might even out because sometimes these random effects will cause the observed score to be higher than the true score, and sometimes it will cause the observed score to be lower. This is the nature of random error. So you can probably see that if somehow you could get the person to bowl an infinite number of games and average all the scores, the random error would cancel itself out entirely and you would be left with a score that represents the person's true score in bowling.

Random Error

Random error is defined as the difference between a person's actual score on a test (the obtained score) and that person's true score (T). As we described above, because this source of error is random in nature, sometimes a person's obtained score will be higher than his or her true score and sometimes the obtained score will be lower than his or her true score. Unfortunately, in any single test administration, we can never know whether random error has led to an obtained score that is higher or lower than the true score. An important characteristic of this type of measurement error is that, because it is random, over an infinite number of testings the error will increase and decrease a person's score by exactly the same amount. Another way of saying this is that the mean or average of all the error scores over an infinite number of testings will be zero. That is why random error actually cancels itself out over repeated testings. Another important characteristic of measurement error is that it is normally distributed (See Chapter 5 for a discussion of normal distributions). Clearly, we can never administer a test an infinite number of times in an attempt to fully cancel out the random error component. The good news is that we don't have to. It turns out that making a test longer also reduces the influence of random error on the test score for the same reason—the random error component will be more likely to cancel itself out (although never completely). We will have more to say about this when we discuss how reliability estimations are actually computed.

Systematic Error

Systematic error is another type of error that obscures the true score. When a single source of error always increases or decreases the true score by the same amount, we call it **systematic error.** For instance, if you know that the scale in your bathroom regularly adds three pounds to anyone's weight, you can simply subtract three pounds from whatever the scale says to get your true weight. In this case, the error your scale makes is predictable and systematic. The last section of this chapter discusses how test developers and researchers can identify and reduce systematic error in test scores.

Let us look at an example of the difference between random error and systematic error proposed by Nunnally (1978). If a chemist uses a thermometer that always reads 2 degrees warmer than the actual temperature, the error that results is *systematic* and the chemist can predict the error and take it into account. If, however, the chemist is nearsighted and reads the thermometer with a different amount and direction of inaccuracy each time, the readings will be wrong and the inconsistencies will be unpredictable or *random.*

Systematic error is often difficult to identify. However, two problems we discussed earlier in this chapter—practice effects and order effects—can add systematic error as well as random error to test scores. For instance, if test takers learn the answer to a question in the first test administration (practice effect) or can derive the answer from a previous question (order effect), everyone will get the question right. Such occurrences raise test scores systematically. In such cases, the test developer can eliminate the systematic error by removing the question or replacing it with another question that will be unaffected by practice or order.

Another important distinction between random error and systematic error is that random error lowers the reliability of a test. Systematic error does not; the test is reliably inaccurate by the same amount each time! This concept will become apparent when we begin calculating reliability using correlation.

The Reliability Coefficient

We need to be as accurate as possible in describing our estimates of the reliability of test scores. Therefore, we use correlation (discussed in Chapter 5) to provide an index of the strength and direction of the linear relationship between test scores. For test–retest reliability, we correlate the scores from the first and second test administrations; in the case of alternate forms or split halves, we correlate the scores of the first test and the second test.

The symbol that stands for a correlation coefficient is *r*. To show that the correlation coefficient represents a reliability coefficient, we add two subscripts of the same letter, such as r_{xx} or r_{aa}. Often authors omit the subscripts in the narrative texts of journal articles and textbooks when the text is clear that the discussion involves reliability, and we follow that convention in this chapter. Remember that a reliability coefficient is simply a Pearson product–moment correlation coefficient applied to test scores.

Adjusting Split-Half Reliability Estimates

As we mentioned earlier, the number of questions on a test is directly related to reliability; the more questions on the test, the higher the reliability—provided that the test questions are equivalent in content and difficulty. When a test is divided into halves to calculate internal consistency, the test length is reduced by half. Therefore, researchers adjust the reliability coefficient (obtained when scores on each half are correlated) using the formula developed by Spearman and Brown. We use this formula only when adjusting reliability coefficients derived using two halves of one test. Other reliability coefficients, such as test–retest and coefficient alpha, should not be adjusted. For Your Information Box 6.3 provides the formula developed by Spearman and Brown and shows how to calculate an adjusted reliability coefficient.

FYI

FOR YOUR INFORMATION BOX 6.3

Using the Spearman–Brown Formula

The Spearman–Brown formula below represents the relationship between reliability and test length. It is used to adjust the correlation coefficient obtained when using the split-half method for estimating reliability.

$$r_{xx} = \frac{nr}{1 + (n-1)(r)}$$

where

r_{xx} = estimated reliability of the test
n = number of questions in the revised version divided by the number of questions in the original version of the test
r = calculated correlation coefficient for the two short forms of the test

Suppose that you calculated a correlation coefficient of .80 for the split halves shown in For Your Information Box 6.1. Because the whole test is twice as long as each half, n is 2. You can then follow these steps to adjust the coefficient obtained and estimate the reliability of the test.

Step 1: Substitute values of r and n into the equation.

$$r_{xx} = \frac{2(.80)}{1 + (2-1)(.80)}$$

Step 2: Complete the algebraic calculations.

$$r_{xx} = .89$$

Step 3: Our best estimate of the split-half reliability of the test is .89.

The Spearman–Brown formula is also helpful to test developers who wish to increase the reliability of a test's scores. The length of the test influences the reliability of the test; the more homogeneous questions (questions about the same issue or trait) the respondent answers, the more information the test yields about the respondent's knowledge, skill, or attitude. This increase yields more distinctive information about each respondent than fewer items would yield, and it produces more variation in test scores. Test developers who wish to increase the reliability of a test use the Spearman–Brown formula to estimate how many homogeneous test questions to add to a test to raise its reliability to the desired level.

Other Methods of Calculating Internal Consistency

As you recall, a better way to measure internal consistency is to compare individuals' scores on all possible ways of splitting the test in halves (instead of just one random split of test items into two halves). This method compensates for error introduced by any lack of equivalence in the two halves. The two formulas researchers use for estimating internal consistency are KR-20 and coefficient alpha.

Researchers use the KR-20 formula (Kuder & Richardson, 1937, 1939) for tests where the questions, such as true/false and multiple choice, can be scored as either right or wrong. (Note that although multiple-choice questions have a number of possible answers, only one answer is correct.) Researchers use the coefficient alpha formula (Cronbach, 1951) for test questions, such as ratings scales, that have more than one correct answer. Coefficient alpha may also be used for scales made up of questions with only one right answer because the formula will yield the same result as does the KR-20.

How do most researchers and test developers estimate internal consistency? Charter (2003) examined the descriptive statistics for 937 reliability coefficients for various types of tests. He found an increase over time in the use of coefficient alpha and an associated decrease in the use of the split-half method for estimating internal consistency. This change is probably due to the availability of computer software that can calculate coefficient alpha. Charter also reported that the median reliability coefficient in his study was .85. Half of the coefficients examined were above what experts recommend, and half were below what experts recommend. For Your Information Box 6.4 provides the formulas for calculating KR-20 and coefficient alpha.

FYI

FOR YOUR INFORMATION BOX 6.4

Formulas for KR-20 and Coefficient Alpha

Two formulas for estimating internal reliability are KR-20 and coefficient alpha. KR-20 is used for scales that have questions that are scored either right or wrong, such as true/false and multiple-choice questions. The formula for coefficient alpha is an expansion of the KR-20 formula and is used when test questions have a range of possible answers, such as a rating scale. Coefficient alpha may also be used for scales made up of questions with only one right answer:

$$r_{KR20} = \left(\frac{k}{k-1}\right)\left(1 - \frac{\sum pq}{\sigma^2}\right)$$

where

r_{KR20} = the Kuder-Richardson formula 20 reliability coefficient
k = number of questions on the test
p = proportion of test takers who gave the correct answer to the question
q = proportion of test takers who gave an incorrect answer to the question
σ^2 = variance of all the test scores

The formula for coefficient alpha is similar to the KR-20 formula and is used when test takers have a number of answers from which to choose their response:

$$r_\alpha = \left(\frac{k}{k-1}\right)\left(1 - \frac{\sum \sigma^2 i}{\sigma^2}\right)$$

where

r_α = coefficient alpha estimate of reliability
k = number of questions on the test
$\sigma^2 i$ = variance of the scores on one question
σ^2 = variance of all the test scores

Calculating Scorer Reliability and Agreement

We can calculate scorer reliability by correlating the judgments of one scorer with the judgments of another scorer. When there is a strong positive relationship between scorers, the scorer reliability will be high.

When scorers make judgments that result in nominal or ordinal data, such as ratings and yes/no decisions, we calculate **interrater agreement**—an index of how consistently the scorers rate or make decisions. One popular index of agreement is **Cohen's kappa** (Cohen, 1960). For Your Information Box 6.5 describes kappa and demonstrates how to calculate it.

When one scorer makes judgments, the researcher also wants assurance that the scorer makes consistent judgments across all tests. For example, when a teacher scores essay exams, we would like the teacher to judge the final essays graded in the same way that he or she judged the first essays. We refer to this concept as **intrarater agreement.** (Note that *inter* refers to between, and *intra* refers to within.) Because this is a matter of internal consistency, KR-20 or coefficient alpha would be the appropriate statistic to calculate. Table 6.3 provides an overview of the types of reliability we have discussed and the appropriate formula to use for each type.

Table 6.3   Methods of Estimating Reliability

Method	Test Administration	Formula
Test–retest reliability	Administer the same test to the same people at two points in time.	Pearson product–moment correlation
Alternate forms or parallel forms	Administer two forms of the test to the same people.	Pearson product–moment correlation
Internal consistency	Give the test in one administration, and then split the test into two halves for scoring.	Pearson product–moment correlation corrected for length by the Spearman–Brown formula
Internal consistency	Give the test in one administration, and then compare all possible split halves.	Coefficient alpha or KR-20
Interrater reliability	Give the test once, and have it scored (interval/ratio level) by two scorers or two methods.	Pearson product–moment correlation
Interrater agreement	Give a rating instrument, and have it completed by two or more judges.	Cohen's kappa
Intrarater agreement	Calculate the consistency of scores for one scorer across multiple tests.	KR-20 or coefficient alpha

FYI

FOR YOUR INFORMATION BOX 6.5

Cohen's Kappa

Cohen's kappa provides a nonparametric index for scorer agreement when the scores are nominal or ordinal data (Cohen, 1960). For example, pass/fail essay questions and rating scales on personality inventories provide categorical data that cannot be correlated. Kappa compensates and corrects interobserver agreement for the proportion of agreement that might occur by chance. Cohen developed the following formula for kappa (k):

$$\kappa = \frac{p_o - p_c}{1 - p_c}$$

where

p_o = observed proportion

p_c = expected proportion

An easier way to understand the formula is to state it using frequencies (f):

$$\kappa = \frac{f_o - f_c}{N - f_c}$$

where

f_o = observed frequency

f_c = expected frequency

N = overall total of the frequency matrix

Many researchers calculate Cohen's kappa by arranging the data in a matrix in which the first rater's judgments are arranged vertically and the second rater's judgments are arranged horizontally. For example, assume that two scorers rate nine writing samples on a scale of 1 to 3, where 1 indicates *very poor* writing skills, 2 indicates *average* writing skills, and 3 indicates *excellent* writing skills. The scores that each rater provided are shown below:

    Scorer 1: 3, 3, 2, 2, 3, 1, 2, 3, 1
    Scorer 2: 3, 2, 3, 2, 3, 2, 2, 3, 1

As you can see, Scorers 1 and 2 agreed on the first writing sample, did not agree on the second sample, did not agree on the third sample, and so on. We arrange the scores in a matrix by placing a check in the cell that agrees with the match for each writing sample. For example, the check for the first writing sample goes in the bottom right cell where *excellent* for Scorer 1 intersects with *excellent* for Scorer 2, the check for the second writing sample goes in the middle right cell where *excellent* for Scorer 1 intersects with *average* for Scorer 2, and so on:

		Scorer 1		
		Poor (1)	Average (2)	Excellent (3)
Scorer 2	Poor (1)	√		
	Average (2)	√	√√	√√
				√√√

To calculate kappa, each cell in the matrix must contain at least one agreement. Unfortunately, our N of 9 is too small. As you can see, our nine writing samples do not fill all of the cells in the matrix.

The following is another matrix containing data for 36 writing samples:

		Scorer 1			
		Poor (1)	Average (2)	Excellent (3)	Row Totals
Scorer 2	Poor (1)	9	3	1	13
	Average (2)	4	8	2	14
	Excellent (3)	2	1	6	9
	Column Totals	15	12	9	36

In this matrix for 36 writing samples, scorers 1 and 2 agreed a total of 23 times (the sum diagonal cells). The sum of the row totals (Σ rows) is 36, and the sum of the column totals (Σ columns) is 36, in agreement with the overall total of 36.

To calculate the expected frequency (f_c) for each diagonal, we use the following formula:

$$f_c = \frac{\text{Row Total} \times \text{Column Total}}{\text{Overall Total}}$$

f_c for the first cell in the diagonal = $(13 \times 15)/36 = 5.42$

f_c for the second cell in the diagonal = 4.67

f_c for the third cell in the diagonal = 2.25

Now we can calculate the sum of the expected frequencies of the diagonals (Σf_c):

$$\Sigma f_c = 5.42 + 4.67 + 2.25 = 12.34$$

When we plug the sum of the expected frequencies of the diagonals into the frequencies formula for kappa, we can calculate the value of kappa:

$$\kappa = \frac{\Sigma f_o - \Sigma f_c}{N - \Sigma f_c} = \frac{23 - 12.34}{36 - 12.34} = .45$$

In this example, kappa (k) equals .45.

Kappa ranges from −1.00 to 1.00. The higher the kappa, the stronger the agreement is among the judges or raters. The scorers of the 36 writing samples are in moderate agreement. They should discuss how they are making their judgments so that they can increase their level of agreement.

Using Computer Software to Calculate Reliability

When you begin developing or using tests, you will not want to calculate reliability by hand. All statistical software programs and many spreadsheet programs will calculate the Pearson product–moment correlation coefficient. You simply enter the test scores for the first and second administrations (or halves) and choose the correlation menu command. If you calculate the correlation coefficient to estimate split-half reliability, you will probably need to adjust the correlation coefficient by hand using the Spearman–Brown formula because most software programs do not make this correction.

Computing coefficient alpha and KR-20 is more complicated. Spreadsheet software programs usually do not calculate coefficient alpha and KR-20, but the formulas are available on the larger, better known statistical packages such as SAS and SPSS. Consult your software manual for instructions on how to enter your data and calculate internal consistency. Likewise, some statistical software programs calculate Cohen's kappa; however, you may prefer to use the matrix method demonstrated in For Your Information Box 6.5.

Interpreting Reliability Coefficients

As you recall from Chapter 5, we look at a correlation coefficient in two ways to interpret its meaning. First, we are interested in its sign—whether it is positive or negative. The sign tells us whether the two variables increase or decrease together (positive sign) or whether one variable increases as the other decreases (negative sign).

Second, we look at the number itself. As you also recall, correlation coefficients range from −1.00 (a perfect negative correlation) to +1.00 (a perfect positive correlation). Most often, the coefficient's number will fall in between. Therefore, if a test's reliability estimate is +.91, we know that its sign is positive; people who made high scores on the first administration made similarly high scores on the second, and people who made low scores on the first administration made similarly low scores on the second. Furthermore, the coefficient .91 is very close to +1.00 or perfect agreement, so the test appears to be very reliable.

Psychologists have not set a fixed value at which they regard reliability as satisfactory or unsatisfactory because the amount of reliability necessary and the amount of error that can be tolerated depend on the purpose of the test. Nunnally (1978) suggests that reliability for tests should be at least .70, and Cascio (1991), referring to employment tests, suggests that reliability should be greater than .90 when the test compares individuals. Cascio notes, however, that tests with reliabilities as low as .70 have been useful in certain situations. Schmitt (1996) notes (but does not necessarily agree with) a common presumption among many researchers that a coefficient alpha of .70 is adequate.

To better understand the amount of error in a test score, we use the reliability coefficient to calculate another statistic called the standard error of measurement.

Calculating the Standard Error of Measurement

Psychologists use the **standard error of measurement (SEM)** as an index of the amount of inconsistency or error expected in an individual's test score. In other words, the SEM is a measure of how much the individual's test score (X) is likely to differ from the individual's true test score (T). As you recall, the true test score is the theoretical score that would occur if there were no measurement errors. For Your Information Box 6.6 shows how to calculate the SEM.

FOR YOUR INFORMATION BOX 6.6

Calculating the Standard Error of Measurement

The formula for calculating the standard error of measurement is

$$SEM = \sigma\sqrt{1 - r_{xx}}$$

where

SEM = standard error of measurement

σ = standard deviation of one administration of the test scores

r_{xx} = reliability coefficient

If $\sigma = 14.327$ and $r_{xx} = .91$, you can calculate the SEM by substituting these values into the equation and completing the algebraic calculations as follows:

$$SEM = 14.327\sqrt{1 - .91}$$

$$SEM = 4.2981 \text{ or } 4.3$$

The SEM can be used to construct a confidence interval around a test score to provide a better estimate of the range in which the test taker's true score is likely to fall. This process is demonstrated in For Your Information Box 6.7.

Interpreting the Standard Error of Measurement

To understand what the SEM means, we must apply it to an individual's test score. As you now know, if an individual took a particular test two times, the scores on the first and second administrations of the test would likely be different due to random errors in measurement. If the person took the test 10 times, we would probably observe 10 similar, but not identical scores. Remember, we are assuming the person's true score has not changed across the administrations, but rather the observed differences in scores are due to random measurement error. Also recall that random error is assumed to be normally distributed. What this means is that each time a person takes a test there will be a variation between the person's actual (unknowable) true score and observed score. Because random error is normally distributed, its contribution to the observed score may vary from one test administration to another. The SEM acts as a measure of this variation. Formally, it is the standard deviation of the distribution that would be created if you could give a test an infinite number of times and calculate the error in measurement in each administration. Because of the characteristics of the normal distribution, we can assume that if the individual took the test an infinite number of times, the following would result:

- Approximately 68% of the observed test scores (X) would occur within ±1 SEM of the true score (T).
- Approximately 95% of the observed test scores (X) would occur within ±2 SEM of the true score (T).
- Approximately 99.7% of the observed test scores (X) would occur within ±3 SEM of the true score (T).

(To understand this assumption, refer to our discussion of the properties of the normal curve in Chapter 5.)

We can then use the preceding information to construct a **confidence interval**—a range of scores that we feel confident includes the true score. For Your Information Box 6.7 shows how to calculate a confidence interval for an observed score.

Confidence intervals are important because they give us a realistic estimate of how much error exists in an individual's score. We calculated the confidence interval in For Your Information Box 6.7 using the data in Table 6.4. If you look at the table, you will see that the test scores fall at 5-point intervals. Although the reliability estimate was high (+.91), the confidence intervals still overlap adjacent scores. A person who scores 75 may have the same true score as the person who scored 70. Therefore, it is possible that the person who scored 75 and the person who scored 70 have the same true score.

Using the SEM to calculate confidence intervals and overlap between adjacent confidence intervals may be less accurate for extremely high or low scores. As Embretson (1996) demonstrates, SEMs are not constant across the entire set of scores. In other words, SEMs tend to be lower for scores near the mean (or average) scores and higher for extreme scores (the highest and lowest scores).

Table 6.4 Test Scores for 10 Candidates on Two Administrations

Test Taker	First Administration	Second Administration
Adams	90	95
Butler	70	75
Chavez	50	65
Davis	100	95
Ellis	90	80
Franks	70	75
Garrison	60	65
Hart	75	80
Isaacs	75	80
Jones	85	80

FYI

FOR YOUR INFORMATION BOX 6.7

Calculating a 95% Confidence Interval

The formula for calculating a 95% confidence interval around a score is

$$95\% \ CI = X \pm 1.96(SEM)$$

where

  95% CI = the 95% confidence interval

  X = an individual's observed test score

  ± 1.96 = the 2 points on the normal curve that include 95% of the scores

  SEM = the standard error of measurement for the test

Therefore, if the observed test score is 90 and the SEM is 4.3, we can say that there is a 95% chance that this confidence interval will contain the true test score (T) which falls between (90 − 8.428) or 81.572 and (90 + 8.428) or 98.428:

$$95\% \ CI = 81.572 \ to \ 98.428$$

When reliability of the test scores is high, the SEM is low. This is due to the fact that high reliabilities imply low random measurement error. As that reliability decreases, random measurement error increases and the SEM increases. Although high reliability is always important, it is especially so when test users use test scores to distinguish among individuals.

For instance, many government agencies interview and hire people from a list that ranks candidates using scores from employment tests. The person with the highest score is ranked first, the person with the second-highest score is ranked second, and so on. Managers interview the top three people instead of simply hiring the person with the highest score. Sometimes the person who is hired has a lower score than do others on the list. Does this mean that the hired person is less qualified?

Although factors other than test scores may be taken into account for hiring, the answer to whether the candidate really had a lower test score can be found by using the SEM to calculate a 95% confidence interval around each candidate's score. Often there will be a substantial overlap of confidence intervals, suggesting that although there is a difference in observed scores, there might not be a difference in true scores of candidates.

Cohen's Kappa

As you know, individuals can make mistakes when scoring a test, adding error to the test scores. When scorers make judgments that are ratings or yes/no decisions, using nominal or ordinal data, we recommend using the scorers' decisions to calculate Cohen's kappa, an index of **interscorer agreement**, to determine how consistently the scorers rate or make decisions. See For Your Information Box 6.5.

Next we discuss how the reliability estimate—and thus the reliability of the test scores—may be increased or decreased.

INTERIM SUMMARY 6.2
CALCULATING AND INTERPRETING THE RELIABILITY COEFFICIENT

- A reliability coefficient (r_{xx}) is calculated by correlating the scores of test takers on two administrations of a test.
- A reliability coefficient is interpreted by examining its sign (positive or negative) and its proximity to 1.00. Reliability coefficients should be positive and very close to 1.00.
- The standard error of measurement provides a measure of how much an individual's score is likely to differ from his or her true score.

- Using the standard error of measurement, we can calculate a confidence interval that is likely to contain the true score.
- Cohen's kappa is a measure of agreement for use with nominal or ordinal data such as ratings and decisions. The closer kappa is to 1.00, the stronger the agreement.

Factors That Influence Reliability

Because reliability is so important to accurate measurement, we need to consider several factors that may increase or decrease the reliability of the test scores. Error that can increase or decrease individual scores, and thereby decrease reliability, comes from four sources:

- *The test itself* can generate error by being poorly designed; by containing trick questions, ambiguous questions, or poorly written questions; or by requiring a reading level higher than the reading level of the test takers. (Chapter 10 provides information on designing survey and test questions that yield a minimal amount of error.)

- *The test administration* can generate error when administrators do not follow instructions for administration in the test manual or allow disturbances to occur during the test period. For example, the test administrator might misread the instructions for the length of the test period; answer test takers' questions inappropriately; allow the room to be too hot, cold, or noisy; or display attitudes that suggest the test is too difficult or unimportant.
- *The test scoring* can generate error if it is not conducted accurately and according to the directions in the test manual. For example, scorers might make errors in judgment or in calculating test scores. Although computer scoring is likely to decrease scoring errors, it is important to enter the correct scoring scheme into the computer software.
- *Test takers* themselves also can contribute to test error. Fatigue, illness, or exposure to test questions before taking the test can change test scores. In addition, test takers who do not provide truthful and honest answers introduce error into their test scores.

Six factors related to these sources of error—test length, homogeneity of questions, test–retest interval, test administration, scoring, and cooperation of test takers—stand out as particularly important and worthy of consideration in detail. Test developers and administrators focus on these factors to increase the reliability and accuracy of the test scores.

Test Length

As a rule, adding more questions that measure the same trait or attribute can increase a test's reliability. Each question on a test serves as an observation that indicates the test taker's knowledge, skill, ability, or trait being measured. The more observations there are, the less random error will contribute to the observed scores and the more accurate the measure is likely to be.

Adding more questions to a test is similar to adding finer distinctions to a measuring tape, for example, adding indications for each sixteenth of an inch to a tape that previously had indications only for each eighth of an inch. Likewise, shortening a test by skipping or dropping questions causes the test to lose reliability. An extreme example is the test that has only one question—a most unreliable way to measure any trait or attitude.

As you recall, the Spearman–Brown formula adjusts the reliability estimate for test length. Test developers can also use the Spearman–Brown formula to estimate the number of questions to add to a test so as to increase its reliability to the desired level.

Embretson (1996) points out an important exception to this rule when using adaptive tests (for example, the computer-based version of the GRE). A short adaptive test can be more reliable than a longer version. In an adaptive test, the test taker responds to questions selected based on his or her skill or aptitude level, and therefore the SEM decreases. As a result, the test taker answers fewer questions without sacrificing reliability. This circumstance, however, does not suggest that a test made up of one question or only a few questions would be reliable.

Homogeneity

Another important exception to the rule that adding questions increases reliability is that an increase in test questions will increase reliability only when the questions added are homogeneous with those on the test. That is, to increase reliability, the test developer must add questions that measure the same attribute as the other question on the test. Heterogeneous tests can be expected to have lower reliability coefficients. As you recall, estimating reliability by calculating internal consistency is not appropriate for heterogeneous tests. If you have ever taken a test in which it seemed you were asked the same questions a number of times in slightly different ways, you have experienced a test that is homogeneous and probably very reliable.

Test–Retest Interval

The longer the interval between administrations of a test, the lower the reliability coefficient is likely to be. A long interval between test administrations provides more opportunity for test takers to change in terms of the factor being measured. Such changes cause a change in individuals' true scores. In addition, the longer time increases the possibility of error through changes in test administration, environment, or personal circumstances. A long interval may lessen practice effects; however, a better way to decrease practice effects would be to use alternate forms.

Test Administration

Proper test administration affects the reliability estimate in three ways. First, carefully following all of the instructions for administering a test ensures that all test takers experience the same testing situation each time the test is given. In other words, test takers hear the same instructions and take the test under the same physical conditions each time. Treating all test takers in the same way decreases error that arises from creating differences in the way individuals respond. Second, constancy between two administrations decreases error that arises when testing conditions differ. Third, effective testing practices (discussed in detail in Chapter 11) decrease the chance that test takers' scores will be contaminated with error due to poor testing conditions or poor test instructions.

Scoring

Even tests scored by computer are subject to incorrect scoring. Test users must be careful to use the correct scoring key, to check questions that have unusually high numbers of correct or incorrect answers for mistakes in scoring, and to exercise considerable care when scoring tests that require judgments about whether an answer is right or wrong. Frequent checks of computations—including those made by computers—also decrease the chance of scoring errors. Scorers who will make qualitative judgments when scoring tests, such as using a rating scale, must receive training together to calibrate their judgments and responses.

Cooperation of Test Takers

Some tests, such as the PAI, have a built-in method for determining whether test takers guessed, faked, cheated, or in some other way neglected to answer questions truthfully or to the best of their ability. Many times, however, it is up to the test administrator to observe and motivate respondents to cooperate with the testing process. For instance, test administrators need to be aware of individuals who complete the test in an unusually short amount of time. These individuals might have checked answers without reading the questions or skipped whole pages either deliberately or by mistake. Although respondents cannot be forced to participate honestly, their tests can be dropped from the group of tests used to calculate reliability when there are doubts about the truthfulness of their answers.

Generalizability Theory

Up to now in this chapter, we have used classical test theory to describe the processes for measuring a test's consistency or reliability. Another approach to estimating reliability is **generalizability theory** proposed by Cronbach, Gleser, Nanda, and Rajaratnam (1972). This theory concerns how well and under what conditions we can generalize an estimation of reliability of test scores from one test administration to another. In other words, the test user can predict the reliability of test scores obtained under different circumstances such as administering a test in various plant locations or school systems. Generalizability theory proposes separating sources of systematic error from random error to eliminate systematic error.

Why is the separation of systematic error and random error important? As you recall, we can assume that if we were able to record the amount of random error in each measurement, the average error would be zero and over time random error would not interfere with obtaining an accurate measurement. However, systematic error does affect the accuracy of a measurement; therefore, using generalizability theory, our goal is to eliminate systematic error.

For example, if you weigh yourself once a week in the gym, your weight will consist of your true weight and measurement error. One possible source of measurement error would be random error in the scale or in your precision in reading the scale. But another source of the measurement error could be the weight of your clothes and shoes. Another source might be the time of day when you weigh yourself; generally speaking, you will weigh less in the morning than you will later in the day. These sources of error would not be random, but would be more systematic because each time they occurred, they would have the same impact on the measurement.

Using generalizability theory, you could look for systematic or ongoing predictable error that occurs when you weigh yourself. For instance, the weight of your clothes and shoes will vary systematically depending on the weather and the time of the year. Likewise, your weight will be greater later in the day. On the other hand, variations in the measurement mechanism and your ability to read the scale accurately vary randomly. We would predict, therefore, that if you weighed yourself at the same time of day wearing the same clothes (or, better yet, none at all), you would have a more accurate measurement of your weight. When you have the most accurate measurement of your weight, you can confidently assume that changes in your weight from measurement to measurement are due to real weight gain or loss and not to measurement error.

Researchers and test developers identify systematic error in test scores by using the statistical procedure called analysis of variance (ANOVA). As you recall, we discussed four sources of error: the test itself, test administration, test scoring, and the test taker. Researchers and test developers can set up a generalizability study in which two or more sources of error (the independent variables) can be varied for the purpose of analyzing the variance of the test scores (the dependent variable) around the mean to find systematic error.

As an example, consider the situation in which 20 employees participate in three business simulations each on different occasions, all designed to measure the same set of leadership skills. The employees are all observed and scored by the same two raters. So we have the scores of each of two raters scoring 20 employees on three simulations, or 120 scores. As you would expect, these scores will not all be the same, but rather they will vary. The question becomes, why do the scores vary? Well, intuitively you probably realize that each person's score might vary because of different levels of leadership skills each person has. But is that the only reason why the scores might vary? Another component that will cause the scores to vary is that although the simulations were all designed to measure the same leaderships skills, perhaps they are not equally difficult in general. Or perhaps one of the simulations is easier for employees who happen to have a background in finance, while another of the simulations is easier for employees with a background in sales. Another possibility is that one of the raters might be systematically more lenient or stringent than the other raters across all the simulations when rating the performance of the employees. The beauty of generalizability theory is that it allows you to actually quantify each of these (and other) possible sources of variation so that you can determine whether the results you obtain are likely to generalize (thus the name) to a different set of employees evaluated by different raters on different occasions. This is conceptually different from the classical measurement of the reliability of a test because reliability measurement focuses on the amount of random measurement error and does not evaluate error that may be systematic. The actual calculations are somewhat complicated and beyond the scope of this book, but we wanted to give you an idea of another approach that can be used to evaluate the reliability of a measure.

INTERIM SUMMARY 6.3
FACTORS THAT INFLUENCE RELIABILITY

- Errors that increase or decrease individual scores and change the reliability estimate result from four sources: the test itself, test administration, test scoring, and test takers.
- Errors resulting from poor test design include trick, ambiguous, or poorly worded questions and reading levels that are too high for the test takers.
- Test administration can generate error when administrators do not follow instructions for test administration or when the testing environment is uncomfortable or distracting.
- Tests must be scored accurately and according to the instructions in the test manual.

- Test takers can contribute to test error by being fatigued or ill, by cheating, or by providing dishonest answers.
- Reliability is related to test length—the longer the test, the more reliable it is likely to be—provided that the questions on the test are homogeneous.
- Although classical test theory remains the most popular method for sorting true scores from error, generalizability theory is also useful. Generalizability theory analyzes the many causes of inconsistency error in test scores and seeks to separate sources of systematic error from random error.

Chapter Summary

Psychological tests are measurement instruments. An important attribute of a measurement instrument is its reliability or consistency. We need evidence that the test yields the same score each time a person takes the test unless the test taker has actually changed. When we know a test is reliable, we can conclude that changes in a person's score really are due to changes in that person. Also, we can compare the scores of two or more people on a reliable test.

Test developers use three methods for checking reliability. Each takes into account various conditions that could produce differences in test scores. Using the test–retest method, a test developer gives the same test to the same group of test takers on two different occasions. The scores from the first and second administrations are then correlated to obtain the reliability coefficient. The greatest danger in using the test–retest method of estimating reliability is that the test takers will score differently (usually higher) on the test because of practice effects.

To overcome practice effects and differences in individuals and the test administration from one time to the next, psychologists often give two forms of the same test—alike in every way—to the same people at the same time. This method is called alternate or parallel forms.

If a test taker can take the test only once, researchers divide the test into halves and correlate the scores on the first half with the scores on the second half. This method, called split-half reliability, includes using the Spearman–Brown formula to adjust the correlation coefficient for test length. An even better way to measure internal consistency is to compare individuals' scores on all possible ways of splitting the test into halves. The KR-20 and coefficient alpha formulas allow researchers to estimate the reliability of the test scores by correlating the answer to each test question with the answers to all of the other test questions.

The reliability of scoring is also important. Tests that require the scorer to make judgments about the test takers' answers and tests that require the scorer to observe the test takers' behavior may have error contributed by the scorer. We estimate scorer reliability by having two or more persons score the same test and then correlating their scores to see whether their judgments are consistent.

No measurement instrument is perfectly reliable or consistent. We express this idea by saying that each observed test score (X) contains two parts: a true score (T) and error (E). Two types of error appear in test scores: random error and systematic error.

To quantify a test's reliability estimate, we use a reliability coefficient, which is another name for the correlation coefficient when it estimates reliability. This statistic quantifies the estimated relationship between two forms of the test. The statistical procedure we use most often to calculate the reliability coefficient is the Pearson product–moment correlation. All statistical software programs and many spreadsheet programs will calculate the Pearson product–moment correlation. Coefficient alpha and KR-20, both of which also use correlation, are available in statistical packages only.

To interpret the meaning of the reliability coefficient, we look at its sign and the number itself. Correlation coefficients range from –1.00 (a perfect negative correlation) to +1.00 (a perfect positive correlation). Psychologists have not set a fixed value at which reliability can be interpreted as satisfactory or unsatisfactory.

Psychologists use the standard error of measurement (SEM) as an index of the amount of inconsistency or error expected in an individual's test score. We can then use the SEM to construct a confidence interval—a range of scores that most likely includes the true score. Confidence intervals provide information about whether individuals' scores are truly different. Six factors—test length, homogeneity of questions, the test–retest interval, test administration, scoring, and cooperation of test takers—are important factors that influence the reliability of the test scores.

Another approach to estimating reliability is generalizability theory, which concerns how well and under what conditions we can generalize an estimation of reliability from one test to another or on the same test given under different circumstances. Generalizability theory seeks to identify sources of systematic error that classical test theory would simply label as random error. Using analysis of variance, researchers and test developers can identify systematic error and then take measures to eliminate it, thereby increasing the overall reliability of the test.

Engaging in the Learning Process

Key Concepts

After completing your study of this chapter, you should be able to define each of the following terms. These terms are bolded in the text of this chapter and defined in the Glossary.

- alternate forms
- Cohen's kappa
- confidence interval
- correlation
- generalizability theory
- heterogeneous test
- homogeneous test
- internal consistency
- interrater agreement

- interscorer agreement
- intrarater agreement
- intrascorer reliability
- measurement error
- order effects
- parallel forms
- practice effects
- random error
- reliability

- reliable test
- scorer reliability
- split-half method
- standard error of measurement (SEM)
- systematic error
- test–retest method

LEARNING ACTIVITIES

The following are some learning activities you can engage in to support the learning objectives for this chapter.

Learning Objectives	Study Tips and Learning Activities
After completing your study of this chapter, you should be able to do the following:	*The following study tips will help you meet these learning objectives:*
Define reliability, and describe three methods for estimating the reliability of a psychological test.	• Distinguish among the three methods by writing down *who, what,* and *when* for each method.
Describe how an observed test score is made up of the true score and random error. Describe the difference between random error and systematic error.	• Weigh yourself several times on your bathroom scale. Do you get the same weight each time? If not, your scale may have random error. Now try another scale. Compare your weights on the first and second scales. Does your first scale weigh too heavy or too light? If so, your scale may have systematic error.
Calculate and interpret a reliability coefficient, including adjusting a reliability coefficient obtained using the split-half method.	• The learning activities that follow are designed to help you understand how to calculate and interpret reliability coefficients. Complete the activities. If you have questions, be sure to ask your instructor.

Differentiate between the KR-20 and coefficient alpha formulas, and describe how they are used to estimate internal consistency.	• Write a short answer in complete sentences that answers these questions:
	  ○ What kinds of questions require the KR-20 formula?
	  ○ What kinds of questions require the coefficient alpha formula?

Calculate the standard error of measurement, and use it to construct a confidence interval around an observed score.	• Weigh yourself again three times in a row. Do not adjust the scale if your weight appears to vary. Calculate the standard error of measurement of the three weights, and construct a confidence interval around your mean weight. Interpret your weight in terms of the confidence interval.
Identify the four sources of test error and six factors related to these sources of error that are particularly important to consider.	• Try to come up with your own examples for each of these. Check with a classmate and/or your instructor to see whether they agree with your examples.
Explain the premises of generalizability theory, and describe its contribution to estimating reliability.	• Review the study proposed in the section on generalizability theory. Then propose your own study for detecting systematic error in test results. Share your proposed study with your classmates or your instructor.

ADDITIONAL LEARNING ACTIVITIES

1. The following matrix shows data on a test that was administered on two occasions three weeks apart. Do the following:

   a. Calculate test–retest reliability and the standard error of measurement.
   b. Construct a 95% confidence interval around the score of Test Taker 1 on the first administration.
   c. Interpret the reliability coefficient you have calculated. Do the test scores show sufficient test–retest reliability? Do the confidence intervals of some scores overlap?

Test Taker	First Occasion	Second Occasion
1	80	82
2	70	75
3	50	45
4	60	60
5	80	78
6	65	70
7	50	50
8	55	60
9	78	80
10	78	76

2. *Estimating Reliability.* Below are the data for a test that was administered on one occasion to the same people to estimate reliability of the test scores. Answer the following questions regarding these data:

   a. What type of reliability can be estimated from these data?
   b. What is the reliability coefficient for the test when corrected using the Spearman-Brown formula?
   c. What is the standard error of measurement?
   d. What is the confidence interval that we can be 95% confident contains Tony's true score?
   e. Would you say that Tony definitely scored higher than Tina did?

| Test Taker | Scores | |
	First Half	Second Half
Tony	6	6
Meg	5	4
Chris	8	7
Sam	4	2
Tina	5	5
Ted	2	1
Abe	9	10
Ricardo	3	3

3. *Estimating Reliability Appropriately.* Following are descriptions of situations in which the researcher needs to identify one or more ways to estimate reliability. In each instance, choose one or more methods for estimating reliability, tell why you chose the method(s), and describe the steps necessary for gathering the data needed to calculate your reliability coefficient:

   a. An instructor has designed a comprehensive math exam for students entering community college. The exam contains multiple-choice questions that measure each of the following dimensions: reading formulas, carrying out math calculations, and solving word problems. The instructor can give the exam only once, but he needs to know how reliable the test scores are. What should the instructor do?

b. A researcher wants to assess attitudes about quality of work life. She wants to be sure that her instrument is reliable. Her instrument contains 20 statements that respondents rate from 1 to 5. She has designed her instrument to be homogeneous. What method(s) should she use to estimate reliability?

c. A promotion test for firefighters requires two fire chiefs to rate firefighters on their knowledge and their use and maintenance of safety equipment. How can the ratings be checked for reliability?

d. A test developer is constructing a measure of critical thinking. The instrument consists of a number of anagrams and riddles—problems for which answers are not readily apparent until solved. The test score depends on the percentage of questions the test taker solved correctly. How should the test developer estimate reliability?

4. *Explaining Various Reports of Reliability.* Julian Rotter (1966) published a monograph describing a personality construct he called *locus of control*—the extent to which a person believes that the reinforcements received in life are due to his or her own effort and ability. The monograph also contains a personality test to measure the extent of this belief in individuals. The table below contains the reliability information that Rotter published for his test. Identify the types of reliability measured and explain why the reliability coefficients differ.

Sample	Type	N	Sex	r
Ohio State University	Split half	50	M	.65
Elementary psychology students	Spearman–Brown	50	F	.79
Sample 1		100	Combined	.73
	Kuder–Richardson	50	M	.70
		50	F	.76
		100	Combined	.73
Ohio State University	Kuder–Richardson	200	M	.70
Elementary psychology students		200	F	.70
		400	Combined	.70
National stratified students	Kuder–Richardson	1,000	Combined	.69
Sample				
Purdue opinion poll			M & F approximately	
			equal Ns	

	Test–Retest Reliability			
Sample	Type	N	Sex	r
Ohio State University	1 month	30	M	.60
Elementary psychology students	Group administration	30	F	.80
		60	Combined	.72
Prisoners	1 month	28	M	.78
Colorado Reformatory				
Ohio State University	1st group administration	54	F	.61
	2nd individual administration	117	Combined	.55

PRACTICE QUESTIONS

The following are some practice questions to assess your understanding of the material presented in this chapter.

Multiple Choice

Choose the one best answer to each question.

1. When we talk about the fact that each inch on a yardstick is the same length, we are talking about the _____ of the yardstick.
   a. reliability
   b. internal consistency
   c. order effects
   d. scorer reliability

2. Which one of the following methods examines the performance of a test over time and provides an estimate of the test's stability?
   a. Test–retest reliability
   b. Split-half reliability
   c. Scorer reliability
   d. Alternate forms reliability

3. Marsha, a student teacher, wanted to check the reliability of a math test that she developed for her fourth graders. She gave the test to students on Monday morning and then again on Tuesday morning. On the first administration of her test, there was a wide variety of scores, but on the second administration, nearly all of the children made A's on the test. Marsha wondered, "Why did all the students make A's on Tuesday but not on Monday?" Which of the following do you think caused this outcome?
   a. Order effects
   b. Practice effects
   c. Measurement error
   d. Scorer error

4. Researchers administered the Personality Assessment Inventory (PAI) to two samples of individuals. First, they administered the PAI twice to 75 normal adults, with the second administration following the first by an average of 24 days. They also administered the PAI to 80 normal college students who took the test twice, with an interval of 28 days. In each case, the researchers were conducting studies to measure the PAI's
   a. internal consistency.
   b. scorer reliability.
   c. split-half reliability.
   d. test–retest reliability.

5. Jon developed a math test for fourth graders, but he was not able to give the test twice. What method can Jon use to estimate the reliability of the math test?
   a. Criterion-related
   b. Construct
   c. Internal consistency
   d. Test-retest

6. When using the split-half method, an adjustment must be made to compensate for splitting the test into halves. Which one of the following is used to make this adjustment?
   a. Coefficient alpha
   b. Pearson product–moment correlation
   c. Spearman–Brown formula
   d. KR-20

7. Which one of the following is the appropriate method for estimating reliability for tests on which the questions are homogeneous and have more than two possible responses?
   a. Coefficient alpha
   b. Pearson product–moment correlation
   c. Spearman–Brown formula
   d. KR-20

8. _____ describes the amount that questions on a test or subscale are interrelated. _____ refers to whether the questions measure the same trait or dimension.
   a. Homogeneity; Coefficient alpha
   b. Coefficient alpha; Homogeneity
   c. Heterogeneity; Coefficient alpha
   d. Homogeneity; Test–retest reliability

9. Researchers conducted two studies on the reliability of the Wisconsin Card Sorting Test (WCST) using adult psychiatric inpatients. In these studies, more than one person scored the WCST independently. What kind of reliability were the researchers interested in establishing?
   a. Test–retest reliability
   b. Scorer reliability
   c. Split-half reliability
   d. Internal consistency

10. Katie and Kathy are roommates who share the same bathroom scale. Neither Katie nor Kathy is on a special diet to lose or gain weight. Each morning they both weigh themselves. From day to day, it seems that each gains or loses two to three pounds. Some days Katie gains three pounds and Kathy loses two pounds. Other days Katie loses two pounds and Katie gains three pounds. Every day their weights are different from their weights the previous day, and they cannot distinguish a pattern. They decide to start weighing themselves on a scale at the wellness center. To their surprise, they neither gain nor lose weight from time to time when using the scale at the wellness center. Which of the following best explains this situation?

    a. Their home scale has systematic error, and the wellness center scale is more accurate.

    b. Their home scale has random error, and the wellness center scale is more accurate.

    c. The scale at the wellness center has systematic error, and their home scale is accurate.

    d. The scale at the wellness center has random error, and their home scale is accurate.

11. Test developers who wish to increase the reliability of a test use the _____ formula to estimate how many homogeneous test questions should be added to a test to raise its reliability to the desired level.

    a. coefficient alpha

    b. KR-20

    c. Spearman–Brown formula

    d. Pearson product–moment correlation

12. Which one of the following is important in interpreting individual test scores and is necessary for calculating confidence intervals?

    a. Standard error of measurement

    b. Pearson product–moment correlation

    c. Test variance

    d. Spearman–Brown formula

13. When test reliability is high, the standard error of measurement is _____. As test reliability decreases, the standard error of measurement _____.

    a. high; decreases

    b. low; decreases

    c. high; increases

    d. low; increases

14. As a rule, adding more questions that measure the same trait or attribute _____ a test's reliability.

    a. can increase

    b. can decrease

    c. can overestimate

    d. does not affect

15. What makes generalizability theory different from classical test theory?

    a. Generalizability theory focuses on identifying systematic error.

    b. Generalizability theory focuses on identifying random error.

    c. Generalizability theory focuses on identifying systematic and random error.

    d. Generalizability theory states that if a test is reliable in one setting, it is reliable in all other settings.

16. Which one of the following is associated with generalizability theory?

    a. Pearson product–moment correlation

    b. Interrater reliability

    c. Analysis of variance (ANOVA)

    d. Cohen's kappa

17. Who is most likely to apply generalizability theory?

    a. Test taker

    b. Test user

    c. Test administrator

    d. Test developer

Short Answer/Essay

Read each of the following, and consider your response carefully based on the information presented in this chapter. Write your answer to each question in two or three paragraphs.

1. What are the similarities and differences between the different methods for estimating test reliability?

2. Explain the difference between test–retest reliability and internal consistency. Give an example of each.

3. Explain the concepts of interscorer agreement and intrascorer agreement. On what types of tests are these most important?

4. What is the difference between random error and systematic error? Give an example of each.

5. What is the purpose of the Spearman–Brown formula? Give an example.

6. Describe the purpose of the KR-20 formula and the coefficient alpha formula. When should each be used?

7. What is a confidence interval? How does the confidence interval help interpret an individual's test score? Give an example.

8. Name six factors that affect a test's reliability. Explain each in terms of how it increases or decreases reliability, and give an example.

9. How is systematic error associated with generalizability theory?

Answer Keys

Additional Learning Activities

1. Calculations and answers are shown below. Evidence of test–retest reliability for this test is very good. Confidence intervals for some scores may overlap (for example, 78 and 80). This overlap should be taken into account when making decisions based on individual test scores.

Test Taker	X_1	X_2	D_1	D_1^2	D_2	D_2^2	$D_1 \times D_2$	X_1^2
1	80	82	13.4	179.56	14.4	207.36	192.96	6,400
2	70	75	3.4	11.56	7.4	54.76	25.16	4,900
3	50	45	−16.6	275.56	−22.6	510.76	375.16	2,500
4	60	60	−6.6	43.56	−7.6	57.76	50.16	3,600
5	80	78	13.4	179.56	10.4	108.16	139.36	6,400
6	65	70	−1.6	2.56	2.4	5.76	−3.84	4,225
7	50	50	−16.6	275.56	−17.6	309.76	292.16	2,500
8	55	60	−11.6	134.56	−7.6	57.76	88.16	3,025
9	78	80	11.4	129.96	12.4	153.76	141.36	6,084
10	78	76	11.4	129.96	8.4	70.56	95.76	6,084
Sum	666	676		1,362.4		1,536.4	1,396.4	45,718
Mean	66.6	67.6						
Standard deviation of X_1	11.67							
r_{xx}	0.97							
SEM	2.02							
95% confidence Interval	80 + 3.96 = 83.96 and 80 − 3.96 = 76.04							

2. *Estimating Reliability*

   a. Split half
   b. r_{xx} = .979 when corrected with Spearman-Brown formula (.96 if uncorrected)
   c. SEM = 0.76
   d. 95% CI = X ± 1.96(SEM) = X ± 1.5, so Tony's 95% CI is 12 ± 1.5 = 10.5 to 13.5. Tina's is 10 ± 1.5 = 8.5 to 11.5 (You must add the scores from the first and second halves of the test together to get the total test score for each person.)
   e. No. Tony's confidence interval and Tina's confidence overlap.

3. *Estimating Reliability Appropriately*

   a. Because the test covers several dimensions, it is heterogeneous. The instructor needs to estimate internal consistency because he can administer the test only once. The best he can do is to calculate the internal consistency of the questions that measure each concept. He can use split-half reliability, correlating the scores on two halves selected randomly and adjusting for test length using the Spearman–Brown formula, or he can use the KR-20 or coefficient alpha formula to estimate the internal consistency of all possible split halves. He will end up with three reliability coefficients—one for each section of the test.
   b. The researcher may estimate reliability using the test–retest method provided that there are no intervening developments, such as a change in company benefits, that will change employee attitudes between administrations. She cannot use alternate forms unless she develops another form—a lengthy and difficult task. She can use either form of internal consistency—split half or coefficient alpha. (Coefficient alpha is used when there are multiple responses.)
   c. This is a case for interrater reliability. The ratings given by each expert can be correlated to determine how well they agreed. Intrarater agreement can also be calculated to determine how consistently each expert assigned the ratings.
   d. Because test takers are likely to remember the answers to the problems, the test–retest method will not work. The developer can calculate internal consistency.

4. Type of reliability test appears in the second column. Coefficients differ due to sample size, sex differences, and type of reliability tested.

Multiple Choice

1. b	2. a	3. b	4. d	5. c
6. c	7. a	8. b	9. b	10. b
11. c	12. a	13. d	14. a	15. c
16. c	17. d			

Short Answer/Essay

Refer to your textbook for answers. If you are unsure of an answer and cannot generate the answer after reviewing your book, ask your professor for clarification.

How Do We Gather Evidence of Validity Based on the Content of a Test?

CHAPTER 7: HOW DO WE GATHER EVIDENCE OF VALIDITY BASED ON THE CONTENT OF A TEST?

After completing your study of this chapter, you should be able to do the following:

- Explain what validity is.
- Discuss the five sources of validity evidence described in the *Standards for Educational and Psychological Testing* (American Educational Research Association [AERA], American Psychological Association [APA], & National Council on Measurement in Education [NCME], 1999).
- Describe the general nature of validity evidence based on test content, validity evidence based on the test's relations with other variables, and how these sources of evidence suggest construct validity.
- Explain, at a general level, the appropriate use of various validation strategies.
- Describe methods for generating validity evidence based on the content of a test.
- Explain the nature and importance of face validity and why it does not provide evidence for interpreting test scores.

"I purchased an intelligence test at the bookstore. I showed it to my psychology professor, and he told me to be careful. He said that just because the test is called an intelligence test doesn't necessarily mean that it does a good job of measuring intelligence. How do you know whether a test measures what it says it measures?"

"I took the driving portion of my driver's license test yesterday. It took about an hour. I had to show the evaluator how to use the blinkers, flashers, and lights. I also had to make a right turn,

left turn, parallel park, merge into traffic, and drive in the city and on the highway. Why did they make me do so many things?"

"We have a psychology midterm exam next week. The psychology professor showed us what he called a test plan. He said that the test would cover five chapters. He said we would need to know the terms and be able to apply the principles. He also said that there would be 50 questions on the test. Why would he give us this information?"

"I applied for a secretarial job last week. As a part of the selection process, they administered a written test. The test didn't seem very professional, nor did it appear to measure anything related to a secretarial job. The test form was dirty and crumpled, the questions were confusing, and I had to answer questions that were totally unrelated to secretarial work. What is the deal?"

I f you are like many individuals, when you take a test you don't think twice about whether the test you are taking is accurate or predictive. You likely assume that the test measures what it says it measures or predicts what it says it predicts. We encourage you to not automatically make such assumptions and to remember that the title of a test actually tells us very little. A test may measure some broader, narrower, or even different attribute, trait, or characteristic than it claims or than is implied by the title. A test titled the Math Achievement Test may measure academic achievement (which is broader), achievement in geometry (which is narrower), or general intelligence (which is a different attribute altogether). Although measures of reliability tell us whether a test measures whatever it measures consistently, only measures of validity can increase our confidence that any interpretations or inferences we make from a test score are likely to be correct.

In this chapter, we introduce the different types of evidence that is used to evaluate whether a proposed interpretation of a test score is valid. We introduce you to how **validity** is discussed in the *Standards* (AERA, APA, & NCME, 1999). We begin with a brief discussion of validity as defined by the *Standards*. We focus most of our attention on evidence of validity based on an evaluation of the content of a test. Other types of evidence of test validity, such as evidence based on the relationship of the test scores to other variables (what traditionally was referred to as criterion-related validity) and the overarching concept of construct validity, are briefly covered here but are discussed in more detail in Chapters 8 and 9.

Sources of Evidence of Validity

In general, when we speak of **validity** as it relates to a test, we are asking the question, "Are the inferences I am going to draw from a person's score on a test appropriate?" Test validity is a function of how the scores are used—the inferences that will be made about the meaning of a person's test scores. This definition of test validity did not truly evolve until the late 20th century, when measurement experts began questioning the strict rules for evaluating test validity that were in common use. This questioning resulted in a complete reinterpretation of test validity when the *Standards* were published in 1999, which stated that validity refers not to a characteristic of the test, but rather to whether there is evidence supporting the interpretation of the resulting test scores for their intended purpose. In other words, we no longer refer to a test as valid, rather we discuss whether there is evidence that supports the proposed use of the resulting test scores.

Traditional Views of Validity

Prior to 1999, test developers and users evaluated a test's accuracy by speaking about content, criterion-referenced, and construct validity. The 1985 *Standards* (APA, 1985) cautioned testing experts that "the use of the category labels [of content, criterion-related, and construct validity] should not be taken to imply that there are distinct types of validity" (p. 9). Others, such as Brennan (1998), talked about traditional types of validity as being subjective, incomplete, and not equal to one another. They suggested that we remember that "although many kinds of evidence may be used, we do not have different kinds of validity. Validity involves an overall evaluation of the plausibility of the intended interpretations" (Kane, 1994, p. 136).

Here is a simple example of how this current view of validity differs from a previous view. In the past, validity was often described as an evaluation of whether the test "measures what it was designed to measure." Under this definition, a new test could be designed to measure a group of personality traits based on some well-researched theory of personality. After the test was constructed, the test developer evaluated how well the test was measuring what it had been designed to measure by comparing test takers' results on this new test with their results on a different test known to measure the same characteristics. The results on the two tests were similar, so the test developer reported that the test was valid because there was evidence to support the fact that the test was measuring what it was designed to measure.

When test developers refer to a test as being valid, test users are likely to assume that a valid test is good for measuring almost anything. Here is an example of what may happen as a result. A personnel manager finds this test, sees the claim that it is valid, and decides to use it to help select salespeople because the manager reasons that all salespeople need a personality, and more personality should be better than less personality! You can probably see the problem here. The personnel manager wants to use the test scores to make an inference about likely future sales performance of job applicants who take the test. However, such an inference would be inappropriate because the test developer or publisher cannot provide evidence that the test would be valid for predicting which test takers would be good salespeople. Although the test publisher declares that the test is a valid measure of personality traits identified and defined by a personality theorist, his or her research results do not indicate that the test scores are appropriate for identifying successful salespeople. A common misconception that persists today is that when we speak about validity, we are speaking about evaluating a characteristic of the test, implying that a particular test can be judged as being valid or invalid.

Our Current Views of Validity

Having said that the current view of validity centers around the correct interpretations that will be made from a test's scores, we do not mean to imply that investigating whether a test "measures what it is supposed to measure" is not important. In fact, a critical part of the development of any test revolves around investigating whether the concepts or characteristics that the test developer is interested in measuring via the test are actually being measured as intended. Without that evidence, test users who have a need to measure particular attributes would have no way of determining which tests to choose for their specific purposes. The important point is that a test can measure exactly what it is intended to measure and yet not be valid to use for a particular purpose.

In the past, testing experts, instructors, and psychological testing textbooks typically referred to three forms of validity: content, criterion related, and construct. The 1999 *Standards* as well as the 1985 *Standards* now view validity as a unitary or single concept. The *Standards* focus on evaluating the interpretation of test scores and "accumulating evidence to provide a sound scientific basis for the proposed score interpretations" (Goodwin & Leech, 2003, p. 3). The *Standards* describe the following five sources of evidence of validity (Goodwin & Leech, 2003):

1. *Evidence based on test content.* Previously referred to as content validity, this source of validity evidence involves logically examining and evaluating the content of a test (including the test questions, format, wording, and processes required of test takers) to determine the extent to which the content is representative of the concepts that the test is designed to measure.

2. *Evidence based on response processes.* This source of validity evidence involves observing test takers as they respond to the test and/or interviewing them when they complete the test. We use these observations and interviews to understand the mental processes that test takers use to respond. For instance, if the test was designed to measure logical reasoning, test takers should report mentally processing the test information while they solve the test problems. We would not want test takers to respond with memorized answers! If the test is scored by using trained observers or judges, this source of validity evidence also involves exploring whether those observers or judges used the criteria that were defined to document and evaluate test taker behaviors or performances.

3. *Evidence based on internal structure.* This type of evidence was previously considered part of construct validity. It focuses on whether the conceptual framework used in test development could be demonstrated using appropriate analytical techniques. For instance, if a test was designed to measure a single concept (such as anxiety), we would analyze the test results to find out how many underlying concepts account for the variations in test taker scores. (One such analysis that we will discuss later is factor analysis.) If the test was designed to measure one concept only, the analysis should show that only one concept (presumably anxiety in our example above) accounts for a majority of the information the test takers provided. If the analysis suggested that the scores were affected by more than one underlying concept or factor, then we would question whether we had evidence of validity of the test based on its underlying single concept structure.

Studies of the internal structure of the test are also used to determine whether certain items on the test are more difficult for some groups of people than for others, such as would be the case if minority test takers responded to certain items differently than nonminority test takers. This type of analysis may show whether test takers with the same ability, but belonging to different groups, have different probabilities of correctly answering a test question. For example, men and women would probably score quite differently on a test that measures knowledge of childbirth.

4. *Evidence based on relations with other variables.* Traditionally referred to as criterion-related validity and also a facet of construct validity, this source of validity evidence typically involves correlating test scores with other measures to determine whether those scores are related to other measures which we would expect them to relate. Likewise, we would want to know that the test scores are not related to other measures which we would not expect them to relate. For instance, a test designed to be used in employee selection should correlate with measures of job performance (criterion-related validity). A test of mechanical aptitude should correlate with another test of mechanical aptitude, while not correlating with a vocabulary test (construct validity).

5. *Evidence based on the consequences of testing.* Any time we make a psychological measurement, both intended and unintended consequences may occur. For example, an intended consequence of a test for personnel selection would be obtaining accurate information for hiring. However, if the test is biased, an unintended consequence might be that test scores appear to favor to one group over another. (We discuss the reasons for such an outcome in Chapter 12.) Therefore, test users need to be aware that it is important to distinguish between consequences of testing associated with the validity of the test itself (that is, whether correct inferences are being made from the interpretation of the test scores) versus other outcomes not related to the purpose for which the scores will be used.

Consider the following example: Traditionally, males have scored higher than females on standardized achievement tests. The traditional interpretation of such data was that men were smarter or more skilled than women. However, when psychologists began to examine the content of the tests, they found that many questions assumed knowledge of sports, mathematics, mechanics, and so on. These areas of information were closely allied with the male sex role, and women who were unfamiliar with sports rules or gear systems did not understand the questions..

Although the latest version of the *Standards* (AERA, APA, & NCME, 1999) no longer directly use the terms *content, construct,* and *criterion-related validity,* these terms are still widely used in professional practice. Therefore, we may from time to time use these more traditional terms in this chapter and following chapters. In our opinion, a student would not be able to interpret more than 100 years of testing literature, including case law, without a strong understanding of these terms. However, it is important to understand that in spite of the fact that multiple terms may still be used to describe approaches to gathering evidence of test validity, validity is considered to be a unitary or single concept with multiple sources of evidence available to demonstrate it. It would be incorrect to assume that one type of validity is better or more scientific than another type of validity. Ultimately, it is the combined evidence from multiple sources and research approaches that will determine whether any particular inference made about the meaning of a test score is appropriate and defensible.

Evidence Based on Test Content/Content Validity

All tests are designed to measure something, and the actual content of the test must contain items that are related to the "something" that you want to measure. The current *Standards* (AERA, APA, NCME, 1999) uses the term **construct** to indicate any concept or characteristic that a test is designed to measure. However, many testing professionals still use the term in a slightly different manner. A construct, in the more traditional usage, is an attribute, trait, or characteristic that in itself is not directly observable, but can only be inferred by looking at observable behaviors, which are believed to indicate the presence of that construct. For

See Test Spotlight 7.1 in Appendix A for more detail about the Fundamental Interpersonal Relations Orientation–Behavior.

instance, if a test was designed to measure a construct called "sales ability," you would not be able to directly observe it. Rather, you would look to observe whether a person could demonstrate some knowledge (perhaps via test questions) or other sales-specific behaviors that you believe indicate that sales ability is present.

Whether you are using the newer or traditional conception of a construct, any test must contain test items that are sampled from a broad domain of content that is believed to be related to the construct being measured. This is the essence of evidence of validity based on test content. If a midterm exam that is intended to assess your understanding of the material covered during the first half of a course does indeed contain a representative sample of the material covered during the first half of the course, the exam demonstrates evidence of validity based on test content. As another example, consider a test called the Fundamental Interpersonal Relations Orientation–Behavior. This test, which is sometimes used by organizations to help people improve their interactions with others, is designed to measure needs in three areas—inclusion, control, and affection—believed to relate to three fundamental dimensions of interpersonal relationships. Test takers are asked to respond to behavioral statements that are expected to be related to each of these needs.

Evidence Based on Relations With Other Variables/Criterion-Related Validity

Many psychological tests are developed to make predictions about future outcomes or behaviors. For example, the SAT was developed to help predict success in college. Many employment tests are designed to predict success on the job. Evidence of validity based on relations with other variables is a frequently used method of demonstrating evidence of validity. These other variables, called *criteria,* are outcomes that the test has been designed to predict (such as job performance or success in a training program). When evidence of validity is used in this fashion, it has traditionally been referred to as **criterion-related validity**—a validation method that is used to determine whether a test indeed predicts what it was designed to predict. A test has criterion-related evidence of validity when it demonstrates that its scores are systematically related to a relevant criterion. The necessary level of accuracy of the test's prediction of the criterion depends on how the prediction will be used. For example, if applicants' scores on an employment test designed to predict managers' potential correlate with scores on a valid measure of job performance (the criterion), such as a performance appraisal, the test shows evidence of criterion-related validity. Furthermore, test scores used for hiring employees would need to be considerably more accurate than scores on a career interest inventory that test takers use to make individual decisions.

As you will learn in Chapter 8, traditionally there are two types of research designs used to demonstrate criterion-related validity: predictive and concurrent. The predictive method involves administering a test to a large group of individuals (for instance, applicants for a job) and holding their scores for a pre-established period of time (often six months or more), but not actually using those scores as part of the selection process. When the time has elapsed, a measure of one or more behaviors that the test was designed to predict (the criteria) is taken. Then the test scores that were gathered at the time of hire are correlated with the scores on the criteria. A test has **predictive evidence of validity** when its scores are significantly correlated with the scores on the criteria. For example, if people who obtain high scores on an a test given to them before they are hired later also receive high scores on their performance appraisals, while people who scored lower on the test also received lower performance appraisal scores, we can say that the test shows predictive evidence of validity.

On the other hand, with **concurrent evidence of validity,** the focus is on determining whether scores on a specific test are related to a criterion collected at the same time as the test is given. For example, employers often cannot wait six months or more to get the results of a predictive study because they desire to use the test as quickly as possible as part of their selection process. So they collect criterion data from a group of current employees (often performance appraisal data) and then give those same employees the test they wish to use as part of their selection process. We refer to this as a concurrent validation approach because both the predictor data (the test scores) and the criterion data (measures of job performance) are collected close in time to one another. If the performance appraisal used as the criteria indicates that employees who are doing well on the job also tend to perform better on the test than employees who are not performing as well on the job (that is, are significantly correlated), the test has demonstrated concurrent evidence of validity.

Evidence Based on Relations With Other Variables/Construct Validity

As we said earlier, the most current *Standards* (AERA, APA, & NCME, 1999) uses the term *construct* to indicate any concept or characteristic that a test is designed to measure. We also pointed out that the traditional, slightly different view of construct is as an attribute, trait, or characteristic that in itself is not directly observable. The traditional construct can only be inferred by looking at observable behaviors. The test developer infers which observable behaviors indicate the presence of the construct. It is important to understand that many testing professionals still refer to something called **construct validity** when they talk about whether there is evidence to demonstrate that a test is measuring the underlying hypothetical (not directly observable) concept that the test was designed to measure. Some examples of constructs are concepts such as shyness, self-image, frustration, and intelligence. Evidence of construct validity is not as easy to determine as are evidence of validity based on test content and evidence of validity based on relationships with external criteria. Construct validity involves accumulating evidence that a test is based on sound psychological theory. The process of establishing construct validity for a test is a gradual accumulation of evidence that the scores on the test relate to observable behaviors in ways predicted by the theory underlying the construct. The *Standards* refer to evidence based on the internal structure of the test as well as evidence of its relation or nonrelation to other measures of similar or different constructs.

There are two basic sources of evidence for demonstrating construct validity: convergent and discriminant. **Convergent evidence of validity** shows that other or similar constructs that theoretically should be related to the construct measured by the test in question are indeed related, and **discriminant evidence of validity** shows that constructs that should not be related to the construct measured by the test in question are in fact not related. For example, assume that we designed a test to measure marital satisfaction. We would expect marital satisfaction to be related to some constructs, such as shared values, but not to others, such as intelligence. If the scores on the marital satisfaction test correlate with the scores on the PREParation for Marriage Questionnaire (PREP-M; Holman, Busby, & Larson, 1989), the test demonstrates evidence of convergent validity. (We provide more information on the PREP-M in Chapter 8.) If the scores on our marital satisfaction test do not correlate with those on the intelligence test, we have demonstrated discriminant evidence of validity. If you can show that a test demonstrates both convergent and discriminant evidence of validity, you have demonstrated strong evidence of the validity of the construct being measured.

INTERIM SUMMARY 7.1
THE DIFFERENT SOURCES OF VALIDITY EVIDENCE

- When we ask whether a test is valid, we are asking, "Are the inferences I am going to draw from a person's score on a test appropriate?"
- The *Standards* (AERA, APA, & NCME, 1999) recognize five sources of evidence of validity: evidence based on test content, evidence based on response processes, evidence based on internal structure, evidence based on relations with other variables, and evidence based on the consequences of testing.
- Traditionally, testing experts have recognized three primary types of evidence of validity: content, criterion related, and construct.
- Currently, validity is considered to be a unitary or single concept that can be demonstrated via the collection of a number of different types of evidence.

- The traditional concept of content validity is a validation strategy that involves scrutinizing the content of a test to determine whether the questions/items on it are representative of the construct being measured by the test.
- The traditional concept of criterion-related validity is a validation strategy that involves determining whether test scores are systematically related to other indicators of success or criteria. There are two methods for gathering evidence of criterion-related validity: predictive and concurrent.
- The traditional concept of construct validity is a validation strategy that involves accumulating evidence that the scores on a test relate to observable behaviors in the ways predicted by the theory underlying the test. There are two types of evidence of construct validity: convergent and discriminant.

The Appropriate Use of Various Validation Strategies

As you just learned, in order for the inferences made from a test score to be appropriate, it is important that the test measure the attribute, trait, or characteristic it was designed to measure or predict the outcome it claims to predict. Developing different types of evidence of validity helps determine whether a test measures what it says it measures or predicts what it says it predicts.

ON THE WEB BOX 7.1

Validity and the SAT

To help make admissions decisions, many colleges and universities rely on applicants' SAT scores. Because the academic rigor can vary from one high school to the next, the SAT—a standardized test—provides schools with a fair and accurate way to put students on a level playing field so as to compare one student with another. However, whether the SAT truly predicts success in college—namely, first-year college grades—is controversial.

To learn more about the validity of the SAT, visit the following websites:

Website	Major Topics
General Information:	
www.fairtest.org/facts/satvalidity.html	General discussion of the following: • What the SAT is supposed to measure • What SAT I validity studies from major colleges and universities show • How well the SAT I predicts success beyond the freshman year • How well the SAT I predicts college achievement for females, students of color, and older students • How colleges and universities should go about conducting their own validity studies • Alternatives to the SAT
Research Studies:	
http://professionals.collegeboard.com/ profdownload/Validity_of_the_SAT_for_Predicting_ First_Year_College_Grade_Point_Average.pdf	Research study exploring the predictive validity of the SAT in predicting first-year college grade point average
www.ucop.edu/news/sat/research.html	Research study presenting findings on the relative contributions of high school grade point average, SAT I scores, and SAT II scores in predicting college success for 81,722 freshmen who entered the University of California from fall 1996 through fall 1999
www.collegeboard.com/prod_downloads/sat/n ewsat_pred_val.pdf	Summary of research exploring the predictive value of the SAT Writing section
www.principalspartnership.com/SATbrief.pdf	A list of online resources exploring the validity of the SAT
www.psychologicalscience.org/pdf/ps/frey.pdf	A paper that looks at the relationship between SAT scores and general cognitive ability

If you are like most students, you might be wondering whether it is necessary to gather all the different types of evidence of validity for all tests. It is sometimes possible, but not always necessary, to do so for a single test. The appropriate strategy for gathering validity evidence often depends on the purpose of the test.

Some tests measure concrete constructs such as knowledge of psychological testing and the ability to play the piano. **Concrete attributes** are attributes that can be clearly described in terms of observable and measurable behaviors. Most people would agree that there are specific observable and measurable behaviors associated with being able to play the piano. Other tests measure abstract attributes such as personality, intelligence, creativity, and aggressiveness. **Abstract attributes** are those that are more difficult to describe in terms of behaviors because people may disagree on what these behaviors represent. For example, what does it mean to be intelligent? If your friend is a high academic achiever, does that mean she is highly intelligent? If your friend has common sense, does that mean he is intelligent? Is creativity part of intelligence?

Evidence of validity using test content is most appropriate for tests such as achievement tests that measure concrete attributes, because the job of an achievement test is to measure how well someone has mastered the content of a course or training program. To feel confident that the test measures what it is designed to measure, we can compare the content of the test with the content of the course. We do so by making sure that the questions on the test are representative of all the relevant information covered and match the instructional objectives of the course. Gathering evidence of validity based on test content is more difficult (but not necessarily less appropriate) when the attribute being measured, such as personality or intelligence, is abstract because such attributes need to be carefully defined and linked to observable behaviors. (We discuss concrete and abstract attributes and how to define them in more detail in Chapter 9.)

Evidence of validity based on relationships with other variables, criterion-related validity, is most appropriate for tests that claim to predict outcomes such as success on the job. If an employment test needs to forecast who is likely to be successful on the job, its purpose is to predict future job performance rather than to determine how well certain concepts have been mastered. Gathering this type of validity evidence is therefore appropriate for employment tests, college admissions tests, and diagnostic clinical tests.

Evidence of validity based on relationships with other variables, construct validity, is appropriate when a test measures an abstract construct such as marital satisfaction.

Although it is not always necessary to gather all evidences of validity for a single test, researchers try to gather more than one type of evidence. It is acceptable to rely on one strategy at first, but the more evidence you can gather to support the validity of a test, the better. To learn more about the evidence that has been gathered to support the validity of the SAT, see On the Web Box 7.1.

INTERIM SUMMARY 7.2
THE DIFFERENT EVIDENCE OF VALIDITY

- Although it might not be appropriate or necessary to gather all the possible evidence of validity for a single test, the more evidence you can gather to support the validity of a test, the better.
- The appropriate strategy for gathering validity evidence depends on the purpose of a test.
- Evidence based on test content (content validity) is most appropriate for tests that measure concrete attributes, such as achievement tests.

- Evidence based on the relationship with other variables (criterion-related validity) is most appropriate for tests that claim to predict outcomes.
- Evidence based on the relationship with other variables (construct validity) is most appropriate when a test measures an abstract construct.

Evidence of Validity Based on Test Content/Content Validity

As you just learned, evidence of validity based on test content is one type of evidence that can be used to demonstrate the validity of a test. This evidence of validity reflects the extent to which the questions on the test are representative of the attribute being measured. Theoretically, if a test is designed to measure a specific attribute, it demonstrates evidence of validity based on its content when the items in the test are a representative sample of the universe of items that represent the attribute's entire domain. For example, if we designed a test to measure your knowledge of the material presented in this textbook, the test would demonstrate more evidence of validity based on content if we included test items that measured your knowledge of material presented in all 15 chapters versus material presented in just 1 or 2 chapters. The entire textbook is the universe, and therefore evidence of validity of the test would be demonstrated by including test items that measure your knowledge across the entire textbook.

Although all types of evidence of validity share the common purpose of helping us make appropriate inferences from the scores on a test, the ways in which the different types of evidence are gathered differ from one another (as you will see in Chapters 8 and 9). Evidence of validity based on test content involves examining the questions or behaviors required on the test and making a judgment regarding the degree to which the test provides an adequate sample of the construct being measured. Evidence of validity based on relationships with other variables (criterion or construct validity) involves correlating the test scores to a measure of performance or another test.

Evidence of validity based on test content is important to many types of psychological tests. Here are some examples:

- A paper-and-pencil test of "attitude toward life" includes questions that adequately represent the wide-ranging situations in which people can demonstrate their attitudes toward life—in the home, on the job, and in social situations.
- An employment test intended to measure mechanics' aptitude contains test questions that represent not just one or two tasks but rather the many tasks a mechanic must perform.
- A classroom math achievement test shows evidence of validity based on test content when the proportion and type of math questions on the exam represent the proportion and type of material read and/or covered in the class.
- A computerized adaptive test shows evidence of validity based on test content when the test bank represents all possible questions regarding the attribute being measured.

How do you obtain this kind of evidence of validity? Evidence of validity based on test content is demonstrated in two ways. The first method involves performing a series of systematic steps as a test is being developed—steps to ensure that the construct being measured is clearly defined and that the items used to measure the construct are representative of the construct's domain. This method does not result in any final number (quantitative value) that represents the evidence of validity of the test; rather, it provides confidence to the test developer and user that the questions on the test are representative of a clearly defined domain.

The second method for obtaining evidence of validity based on content involves evaluating the content of a test after the test has been developed. This evaluation may be done by the test developer as part of the validation process or by others using the test. This method may result in a final number that can be used to quantify the content validity of the test.

Demonstrating Evidence of Validity Based on Test Content During Test Development

Again, the first method for obtaining evidence of validity based on the content of a test involves performing a series of systematic steps as a test is being developed. Although we discuss the process of test development in more detail in Chapter 11, here we provide a brief summary of these steps.

Defining the Testing Universe

The first step in ensuring a content-valid test is to carefully define the **testing universe**—the body of knowledge or behaviors that a test represents. This step usually involves reviewing other instruments that measure the same construct, interviewing experts who are familiar with the construct, and researching the construct by locating theoretical or empirical research on the construct. The purpose is to ensure that you clearly understand and can clearly define the construct you will be measuring. Evidence of validity based on test content requires that the test cover all major aspects of the testing universe (of the construct) in the correct proportion (Groth-Marnat, 1997).

For example, let's say you are interested in designing a test to measure the abstract attribute of self-esteem. Before writing test items, you would need to clearly understand what self-esteem is and the behaviors people demonstrate when they have high or low self-esteem. To increase your understanding, one of the first things you might do is review various theories and studies of self-esteem. You might also review other tests of self-esteem, and you might choose to interview experts in self-esteem.

On the other hand, if you were interested in developing a test to measure a more concrete attribute such as an employee's job knowledge, you should review other tests that measure the same job knowledge, training manuals, and job descriptions, and you could interview job incumbents and managers for a job analysis. (Chapter 15 explains the concept of job analysis and how it serves as content-based evidence of validity.)

Developing the Test Specifications

After the testing universe has been defined, the second step in developing a content-valid test is to develop the **test specifications**—a documented plan containing details about a test's content. Test specifications are very similar to the blueprints that are prepared prior to building a home. Although the contents of test plans vary depending on the type of test being developed, many test specifications, especially those for knowledge tests, include not only a clearly defined testing universe but also the **content areas**—the subject matter that the test will measure—and the number of questions that will be included to assess each content area.

Establishing a Test Format

Once the testing universe has been defined and the test specifications have been documented, the third step in designing a test is to decide on its format. For example, will it be a **written test,** a paper-and-pencil test in which a test taker must answer a series of questions; a computerized adaptive test; or a

practical test, which requires a test taker to actively demonstrate skills in specific situations? If it is a written test, the test developer must also decide what types of questions (multiple choice, true/false, matching, and so on) to use. (You will learn more about the different types of test questions in Chapter 11.)

For Your Information Boxes 7.1 and 7.2 provide examples of test specifications for different tests—one measuring job knowledge and the other measuring academic achievement. For Your Information Box 7.3 discusses the importance of content-based evidence of validity to competency exams.

Constructing Test Questions

After the testing universe has been defined, the test specifications have been developed, and the test format has been established, the fourth step in test development is to write the test questions or items, being careful that each question represents the content area and objective it is intended to measure. (We discuss the process of constructing test questions in more detail in Chapter 11.)

For Your Information Box 7.4 includes a discussion of assessment centers, which are used by organizations to measure employees' job skills, and how content-based evidence of validity is established for these simulations.

FYI

FOR YOUR INFORMATION BOX 7.1

Test Specification Table of a 43-Item Job Knowledge Test

When one of this textbook's authors was asked to develop a series of job knowledge tests for a local organization, she knew that one of the first things she needed to do for each test was to define the testing universe and create test specifications. Below are the test specifications for one job. As you can see, these specifications are very much like a blueprint; among other things, they contain detailed information about the testing universe, the content areas, and the number of questions. Creating these test specifications helped the author clearly understand and document the body of knowledge that the test needed to measure. It provided the foundation for the writing of test questions that sampled the testing universe representatively.

TEST PLAN FOR JOB OF UNIVERSAL PROCESSOR

Type of Test: Job Knowledge	Job: Universal Processor	Item Format: Multiple Choice	Test Length: 43 items

Testing Universe: This test is intended to measure the technical and professional expertise and knowledge required to successfully perform the role of the Universal Processor – expertise and knowledge required to accurately process cash, invoices, and policies according to company standards.

			KNOWLEDGE OF TERMS AND CONCEPTS	APPLICATION (PROCESS / PROCEDURES)
MAIL DISTRIBUTION AND HANDLING	Mail delivery and distribution methods	9% (4 Qs)	1	1
	Mail prioritization and distribution			1
	Ordering of documentation			1
CASH AND INVOICE PROCESSING	Log In and Envelope creation	40% (17 Qs)	1	1
	Cash handling		2	2
	✓ Entering checks			
	✓ Entering invoice/statement documentation		2	1
	✓ Applying payments		1	6
	Completing envelopes			1
POLICY PROCESSING	Associating policies to checks	35% (15 Qs)		2
	Entering policy information		3	10
END OF DAY PROCESSING	Individual Deposit List	16% (7 Qs)	1	3
	Tape			3
TOTAL		100%	11	32

FOR YOUR INFORMATION BOX 7.2

Test Specification Table of a 70-Item Academic Achievement Test

When test developers design academic achievement tests, they write instructional objectives and include them in the test specification tables. (The learning objectives in this textbook are the instructional objectives that appear in the test specification table for the test bank.) Below is a test specification table similar to those that this textbook's authors use to write questions for an exam intended to measure students' knowledge of reliability and validity. As you can see, the content areas are test–retest reliability, alternate forms reliability, split-half reliability, interrater reliability, evidence of validity based on content, evidence of validity based on relationships with other variables, and construct validity. The instructional objectives guide students' learning of the terms and concepts of *reliability* and *validity*. (The activities associated with each learning or instructional objective in this book help students apply the concept in the learning objective.) As you can see, the specification table indicates that the same number of questions will be asked to measure students' knowledge of each of the content areas and each of the instructional objectives.

Instructional Objectives

Content Areas	Knowledge of Terms and Concepts	Application of Concepts	Number of Questions
Test–retest reliability	5	5	10
Alternate forms reliability	5	5	10
Split-half reliability	5	5	10
Interrater reliability	5	5	10
Evidence of validity based on content	5	5	10
Evidence of validity based on relationships with other variables	5	5	10
Construct validity	5	5	10
Total questions	35	35	70

Demonstrating Evidence of Validity Based on Test Content After Test Development

Although ensuring that a test will be able to provide evidence of validity based on its content is aided by performing a series of systematic steps during test development, often test developers and others assess content validity after a test has been developed. One popular technique involves examining the extent to which experts agree on the relevance of the content of the test items (Lawshe, 1975). With this technique, experts review and rate how essential test items are to the attribute the test measures. Then a **content validity ratio** is calculated, providing a measure of agreement among the judges. Based on minimum values, questions that experts agree are essential are considered as evidence of validity, and items that experts do not agree are essential are not considered evidence of validity.

For example, to develop evidence of validity based on the content of the job knowledge test in For Your Information Box 7.1, one of this textbook's authors created and administered the content validation survey shown in Figure 7.1. Five managers who were very familiar with the job were provided with a copy of the test and asked to rate whether the knowledge measured by each test item was *essential, useful but not essential,* or *not necessary* for successful performance of the job. As shown in Figure 7.2, ratings of each panelist were documented in a spreadsheet. The content validity ratio for each question was then calculated using the following formula (Lawshe, 1975):

$$CVR_i = \frac{n_e - \frac{N}{2}}{\frac{N}{2}}$$

where

CVR_i = value for an item on the test

n = number of experts indicating that an item is *essential*

N = total number of experts in the panel

Notice how the content validity ratios can range between –1.00 and 1.00, where 0.00 means that 50% of the experts believe that an item is essential. To determine whether an item is essential, its minimum value is compared with minimum values, shown in Table 7.1, that depend on the number of experts who contributed ratings. Highlighted items did not meet the minimum value required (.99) for five raters, and therefore they were not rated as essential by enough experts to be considered evidence of validity. These items were eliminated from the test.

Content validity ratios have been used to provide the evidence of validity based on a test's content of employment tests (Ford & Wroten, 1984), measures of the work behavior of psychiatric aides (Distefano, Pryer, & Erffmeyer, 1983), mathematics achievement tests (Crocker, Llabre, & Miller, 1988), and assessment centers.

Table 7.1   Minimum Values for Lawshe's (1975) Content Validation Ratings

Number of Experts	Minimum Value
≤5	0.99
6	0.99
7	0.99
8	0.75
9	0.78
10	0.62
20	0.42
40	0.29

| Figure 7.1 | Content Validation Survey for a Test of Job Knowledge |

The purpose of this survey is to quantitatively determine the content validity of the Universal Researcher Knowledge Test. A test is considered content valid if the knowledge or skills measured in the test are critical to success on the job.

Directions: Please read each of the test items in the Universal Researcher Knowledge Test. For each item, please indicate whether the knowledge measured by the item is *essential, useful but not essential,* or *not necessary* to the performance of the job. Indicate your response by circling or bolding the appropriate number.

TEST ITEM	IS THE KNOWLEDGE MEASURED BY THIS ITEM		
	Essential	Useful but not Essential	Not Necessary
1.	1	2	3
2.	1	2	3
3.	1	2	3
4.	1	2	3
5.	1	2	3
6.	1	2	3
7.	1	2	3
8.	1	2	3
9.	1	2	3
10.	1	2	3
11.	1	2	3
12.	1	2	3
13.	1	2	3
14.	1	2	3
15.	1	2	3
16.	1	2	3
17.	1	2	3
18.	1	2	3
19.	1	2	3
20.	1	2	3
21.	1	2	3
22.	1	2	3
23.	1	2	3
24.	1	2	3
25.	1	2	3
26.	1	2	3
27.	1	2	3
28.	1	2	3
29.	1	2	3
30.	1	2	3
31.	1	2	3
32.	1	2	3

Figure 7.2 Content Validation Ratings From Validation Survey Shown in Figure 7.1

Q#	Panelist 1			Panelist 2			Panelist 3			Panelist 4			Panelist 5			Content Validity Ratio Numerator	Content Validity Ratio Denominator	CVR
	Essential	Useful	Not Necessary	Essential	Useful	Not Necessary	Essential	Useful	Not Necessary	Essential	Useful	Not Necessary	Essential	Useful	Not Necessary			
1	1			1			1			1			1			2.5	2.5	1
2	1			1			1			1			1			2.5	2.5	1
3	1					1	1				1		1			0.5	2.5	0.2
4	1			1			1			1			1			2.5	2.5	1
5	1			1			1			1			1			2.5	2.5	1
6	1				1		1			1			1			1.5	2.5	0.6
7	1			1			1			1			1			2.5	2.5	1
8	1			1			1			1			1			2.5	2.5	1
9	1			1			1			1			1			2.5	2.5	1
10	1			1			1			1			1			2.5	2.5	1
11	1			1			1			1			1			2.5	2.5	1
12	1			1			1			1			1			2.5	2.5	1
13	1				1		1			1			1			1.5	2.5	0.6
14	1			1			1			1			1			2.5	2.5	1
15		1		1			1			1			1			1.5	2.5	0.6
16	1			1			1			1			1			2.5	2.5	1
17	1			1			1			1			1			2.5	2.5	1
18	1			1			1			1				1		1.5	2.5	0.6
19	1				1		1			1			1			1.5	2.5	0.6
20	1				1		1			1			1			1.5	2.5	0.6
21	1			1			1			1			1			2.5	2.5	1
22	1			1			1			1			1			2.5	2.5	1
23	1			1			1			1			1			2.5	2.5	1
24	1			1			1			1			1			2.5	2.5	1
25	1			1			1			1			1			2.5	2.5	1
26	1			1			1			1			1			2.5	2.5	1
27	1			1			1			1			1			2.5	2.5	1
28	1			1			1			1			1			2.5	2.5	1
29	1			1			1			1			1			2.5	2.5	1
30	1			1			1			1			1			2.5	2.5	1
31	1			1			1				1		1			1.5	2.5	0.6
32	1			1			1			1			1			2.5	2.5	1

Evidence of Validity Based on Test Content Summary

Although not all tests (for example, the Minnesota Multiphasic Personality Inventory, discussed in Chapter 8) have evidence of validity based on their content, most psychological tests, particularly in educational settings, should show that evidence. When purchasing a test, users should not make any assumptions about whether the test can show evidence of validity based on its content. The purchaser has the responsibility of comparing the specifications of the purchased test with the content domain of the test. Furthermore, the test user must consider whether different aspects of the content domain are underrepresented or overrepresented in the test based on its intended use and must make adjustments accordingly.

The usefulness of evidence of validity based on the content of a test is clear in educational and organizational settings. In educational settings, this evidence plays an important role in validating educational achievement tests that assess how well a student has learned the content of a course. In organizational settings, this evidence is essential for tests used in personnel selection to establish that a test is job related. Although less clear, evidence of validity based on content has come to play more of a role in clinical and personality assessment because test developers are constantly working to define their constructs (Butcher, Graham, Williams, & Ben-Porath, 1990; Haynes, Richard, & Kubany, 1995; Millon, 1994).

FYI

FOR YOUR INFORMATION BOX 7.3

Evidence of Validity Based on Test Content and Competency Exams

Because training plays a critical role in developing employees, many organizations invest significant funds, time, and energy in developing and administering training programs. To help training directors make informed decisions about which training programs to offer or modify, organizations also invest funds, time, and energy in evaluating the effectiveness of training programs.

Although there are a variety of methods to evaluate the effectiveness of training, some organizations do so by administering competency exams at the completion of training programs (Smith & Merchant, 1990). Competency exams attempt to measure how well a person learned the knowledge and skills taught during training. These can be paper-and-pencil or web-based exams, or they can be practical "hands-on" or web-based assessments. (Paper-and-pencil exams require test takers to answer questions on paper, and practical exams require individuals to demonstrate their knowledge or display their new skills in real-life situations.)

When competency exams are developed and administered properly, they help organizations in a variety of ways. For example, they can determine the following:

- Whether employees can use the new computer software they have been trained to use
- Whether customer service representatives can provide the correct information to customers

If a competency exam suggests that students do not have the necessary knowledge or cannot demonstrate the necessary skills, organizations will often reevaluate the content and delivery of their training programs.

Like other types of tests, competency-based tests are only useful if they contain content that is appropriate for their intended purpose. Therefore, the developers of competency-based training programs must ensure that their exams can show evidence of their validity—that they measure trainees' knowledge, skills, and behaviors adequately (Smith & Merchant, 1990). To develop and administer a competency exam that will be able to demonstrate this evidence, test developers perform the following steps:

1. *Determine the learning objectives of the training program.* These objectives come from an in-depth analysis of the knowledge, skills, and abilities required for a particular job. The requirements of a job can be determined by conducting a job analysis, reviewing job descriptions, or interviewing job incumbents.

2. *Outline the content areas of the exam.* An outline ensures that relevant subject matter is neither omitted nor emphasized inappropriately on an exam.

3. *Establish the format for the exam.* Test developers must decide whether the exam will be a written exam or a practical exam and what types of items will be included on the exam (for example, multiple choice, true/false).

4. *Write the exam items.* Using the learning objectives and content areas as a guide, test developers must develop questions or problems that measure the content areas and meet the learning objectives.

The following table provides a sample outline of the content for a manufacturing orders training module competency exam.

Examination Content Outline

Content General Categories	Areas Subcategories	Weight (percentage of total score)	Question Number Written Questions (paper and pencil)	Question Number Practical Questions (work samples and simulations)
Manufacturing repair process-II		25	1, 2, 3, 4, 5	
Manufacturing repair process-II	A. Concepts B. Netting logic and application C. BOM	50	9, 10, 11, 13, 18, 19, 25, 26, 27, 6, 7, 17, 28	1, 2, 4, 3, 5, 6, 7, 11, 13, 8, 9, 10, 12, 14, 15, 16
Maintenance transactions	A. Creating an order B. Allocating material C. Releasing order	25	20, 21, 22, 23, 24, 29, 30, 31	17, 18, 21, 19, 20, 22, 23, 24, 25, 26

SOURCE: Adapted from Smith, J. E., & Merchant, S. (1990). Using competency exams for evaluating training. *Training & Development Journal, 44,* 65–71.

When the developers finish writing the exam, they reevaluate the content of the exam by asking the following questions (Smith & Merchant, 1990):

1. *Are all exam items job related?* Knowledge or skills that are not needed on the job should not be included on the competency exam.

2. *Are the knowledge and skills being tested adequately covered in the training program?*

3. *Is the exam comprehensive, and does it weight areas appropriately?*

Competency exams can provide organizations with valuable information about whether their training programs are teaching the knowledge, skills, and abilities necessary to be successful on a job. However, the usefulness of competency exams, like all psychological tests, depends on showing evidence that the tests are valid for their intended purpose.

FYI

FOR YOUR INFORMATION BOX 7.4

Establishing Evidence of Validity Based on Content of an Assessment Center

An assessment center is a method—not a place—that organizations use for assessing the extent to which individuals demonstrate skills critical to success in a job. Depending on the job, these skills might include leadership, problem solving, teamwork, decision making, planning, and organizing. Organizations use the results of assessment centers to make decisions regarding hiring, promoting, and training individuals.

A typical assessment center contains several job simulations that engage the test taker in role-play activities. Some common simulations, known as exercises, include the following:

- The in-basket exercise, where the test taker is provided with several days' worth of hypothetical incoming mail, phone messages, and memos likely to be received on the job. Directions instruct the test taker to take appropriate action on each memo and piece of mail.
- Role-play, where the test taker interacts with one or more persons (trained assessment center role-players) to solve problems encountered on the job. The test taker is typically provided some background information prior to the role-play. A typical theme might be handling a difficult employee or customer.
- Leaderless discussion group, where the test taker is placed in a small group with the goal of discussing or solving a job-related issue.

In all of these exercises, trained assessors observe and document test takers' behaviors during the simulations and make judgments regarding the test takers' demonstration of expertise on well-defined dimensions of job performance.

Although psychologists had been combining assessment methods for a number of years, a selection program used by the U.S. Office of Strategic Services (OSS) during World War II is credited with marking the beginning of the assessment center movement (Smither, 1994). The OSS, a forerunner to the Central Intelligence Agency, developed a three-day psychological screening program for potential agents that was used to predict how an individual would perform (and succeed) as a spy. What was different and remarkable about this screening program was that candidates for the job of spy were observed and evaluated on a number of behavioral simulations.

One role-play required the candidate to devise a cover story in 12 minutes that would explain why he was carrying secret government files. Three examiners then questioned the candidate relentlessly in a manner that became progressively more hostile and abusive. After the questioning ended, all candidates were told they had failed the exercise and then were directed to another office, where a friendly colleague encouraged them to discuss the exercise. When the candidates relaxed and openly discussed their interrogations, they found that they had made a fateful misjudgment: They had just confided important information—not to a friend but rather to another examiner (Smither, 1994).

After World War II, large industrial organizations began to use the assessment center method to hire managers. Gatewood and Feild (1997) cite the Management Progress Study of AT&T, begun in 1956, as the first industrial application of the method. Other early users included Michigan Bell, Sears Roebuck, and General Electric. Such programs provided information that was used for hiring and promotion decisions based on managers' performance and personality.

During the next two decades, assessment centers continued to achieve growing acceptance. One expert (Cohen, 1978) estimated that during the early 1970s the number of organizations using assessment centers had grown from 100 to 1,000. Assessment centers also took on importance in the public sector as state and local governments discovered that this method was fair and accurate for hiring police officers and firefighters.

Today, assessment centers remain a popular method for hiring, developing, and promoting employees. Many Fortune 500 and smaller emerging companies use assessment centers, primarily for management jobs, although a number of companies discontinued or streamlined their programs as part of the austerity movement of the 1980s. A major barrier to the use of assessment centers during the 1990s was the labor cost. Assessment centers require a number of professionally trained assessors and role-players. Because untrained assessors are not likely to provide accurate judgments or ratings, assessors must be professionally trained on observing, documenting, and rating behaviors.

Most assessment centers rely on a strategy of evidence of validity based on content. The "Uniform Guidelines on Employee Selection Procedures" (1978) require organizations to link tests that are used for selection with a thorough job analysis to provide evidence of the test's validity based on its content. Haymaker and Grant (1982) present a nine-step model for developing evidence of validity based on the content of assessment centers:

1. *Identification of job task domain.* Job analysts compile a list of tasks performed by job incumbents.

2. *Refinement of job task content domain.* Incumbents rate each task for its importance, frequency, and whether they learned to perform the task on the job.

3. *Identification of content domain of knowledge, skills, and abilities.* Experts determine the knowledge, skills, and abilities (KSAs) needed to perform each task.

4. *Refinement of content domain of KSAs.* Incumbents rate each KSA on its importance for successful performance of the job.

5. *Deviation and definition of assessment center dimensions.* Test developers analyze the KSA ratings to determine the dimensions on which individuals will be tested.

6. *Affirmation of assessment center dimensions.* Job experts review test dimensions for suitability.

7. *Development of assessment center exercises.* Simulations that directly reflect job tasks are written by test developers.

8. *Affirmation of the adequacy of dimension behavior sampling.* An independent panel rates each simulation on the extent to which appropriate behaviors are elicited by the exercise.

9. *Standardization and assessor training.* The preparation of a test manual containing instructions for assessors, assessor trainers, and administrators ensures that the assessment center will be properly conducted. Assessors receive training on the unique aspects of the simulations as well as rater training and calibration.

Research suggests that assessment centers provide one of the best predictors of job performance. A meta-analysis of validation studies estimates the criterion-related validity for assessment centers to be .53 for job potential and .36 for job performance (Gaugler, Rosenthal, Thornton, & Bentson, 1987). (Chapter 8 provides a thorough discussion of validity coefficients and their interpretation.) A related advantage for the assessment center method is its relative lack of sex and race bias.

The results of a validation study (Knowles & Bean, 1981) for an assessment center that the City of St. Louis used to select captains in its fire department are typical. This examination contained a written test and an assessment center. On the written test, the average score for Blacks was more than 8 points lower (statistically different at $p < .05$) than the average score for Whites; however, on the assessment center, the average score for Blacks was less than 1 point different from that of Whites (not statistically different). This study suggested that assessment centers were free of race bias, a finding that was confirmed in later studies. Likewise, assessment center scores do not show differences in the average ratings for men and women.

Face Validity

At the beginning of this chapter, we introduced you to five types of evidence that can be used to demonstrate test validity. Face validity is another term that is often used when discussing tests that has nothing to do with evaluating the constructs that are being measured by a test. Face validity answers the question, "Does it appear to the test taker that the questions on the test are related to the purpose for which the test is being given?" As such, face validity is only concerned with how test takers perceive the attractiveness and appropriateness of a test.

In spite of the fact that the concept of face validity does not have anything to do with the evaluation of test validity, it sometimes can be an important consideration in choosing a test that might be used in an applied setting. Consider the case of using a personality test as part of an employee selection system. The test might ask job applicants to indicate how well statements such as "I sympathize with others' feelings" or "I have a soft heart" describe them. Questions like this may be reflective of certain personality characteristics that have been demonstrated to be predictive of job performance on the job for which applicants are applying. But if the test takers cannot perceive the connection between the test questions and the requirements for the job, the test is said to lack face validity. This can result in the applicants not taking the test seriously or, in the worst case, viewing the hiring process as being unfair. As a result, making a decision on what kind of test to use often involves consideration of the face validity of the instrument.

Although it is helpful for a test to have face validity in circumstances like those we described, face validity is never an acceptable means of demonstrating evidence of the validity of a test. To learn more about what supporters and challengers say about face validity, see On the Web Box 7.2.

ON THE WEB BOX 7.2

Supporting and Challenging the Importance of Face Validity

www.jalt.org/test/rob_1.htm

www.jalt.org/test/new_2.htm

 Face validity has nothing to do with whether a test measures what it says it measures; rather, it is concerned with how test takers *perceive* the attractiveness and appropriateness of a test. In the past, and more so today with the introduction of new sources of evidence of validity in the *Standards* (AERA, APA, & NCME, 1999), testing experts have debated the importance and usefulness of face validity. To learn more about face validity and why some experts support the notion while others challenge it, visit the websites listed above.

INTERIM SUMMARY 7.3
EVIDENCE OF VALIDITY BASED ON TEST CONTENT

- Evidence of validity based on test content (traditionally called content validity) is the extent to which the questions on a test are representative of the construct, trait, or attribute being measured.
- Evidence of validity based on test content helps us determine how adequately a test measures what it says it measures.
- Evidence of validity based on test content differs from evidence of validity based on relationships with other variables (traditionally called criterion-related and construct validity) because it involves examining the questions on a test rather than correlating the test scores with a criterion or another test.
- One method for establishing content-based evidence of validity involves performing a series of systematic steps as a test is being developed.
- Another method for establishing content-based evidence of validity involves evaluating the content of a test after it has been developed.
- Although helpful, face validity alone—the perception of the test taker that the test questions are appropriate—is not an acceptable means for determining the validity of a test.

Chapter Summary

Because decisions are made using psychological tests, it is important that the inferences made from the scores on psychological tests are justified and that test users administer tests only for their intended purposes. The validity of a test helps us understand whether the conclusions we are going to draw from test scores are appropriate and defensible. Traditionally, testing experts have evaluated three primary measures of validity: content, criterion related, and construct. The latest revision of the *Standards* (AERA, APA, & NCME, 1999) no longer refers to these traditional types of validity; instead, the *Standards* cite five sources of evidence that a test is valid. It is usually not appropriate, or even possible, to estimate the validity of a test using all of these validation procedures. The strategy chosen to provide evidence of validity depends on the nature and purpose of the psychological test.

There are two methods for determining content-based evidence of validity of a test. The first involves performing a series of systematic steps during test development to ensure that the test samples the construct being measured representatively. The second method involves reviewing test items after the test development and determining the extent to which experts agree that test items are essential.

Although different from other evidence of validity, face validity—the perception of the test taker that the test questions are appropriate—is sometimes important to consider, especially in applied settings.

Engaging in the Learning Process

KEY CONCEPTS

After completing your study of this chapter, you should be able to define each of the following terms. These terms are bolded in the text of this chapter and defined in the Glossary.

- abstract attributes
- concrete attributes
- concurrent evidence of validity
- construct
- construct validity
- content areas
- content validity
- content validity ratio
- convergent evidence of validity
- criterion-related validity
- discriminant evidence of validity
- face validity
- instructional objectives
- practical test
- predictive evidence of validity
- test specifications
- testing universe
- validity
- written test

LEARNING ACTIVITIES

The following are some learning activities you can engage in to support the learning objectives for this chapter.

Learning Objectives	Study Tips and Learning Activities
After completing your study of this chapter, you should be able to do the following:	*The following study tips will help you meet these learning objectives:*
Explain what validity is.	Write your definition of *validity*. Search the Internet for and document various definitions of validity. Compare your definition with the definitions on the Internet and in this chapter. Be prepared to share your definitions with your classmates and to compare your definitions with theirs.
Discuss the five sources of evidence of validity described in the *Standards*.	Review the five sources of evidence of validity described in the *Standards*. Write the names of the five sources of evidence of validity. In your own words, write how evidence of each source is obtained.
Describe the general nature of the traditional terms *content validity, criterion-related validity,* and *construct validity*. How are these terms related to the terms used in the *Standards*?	Search the Internet for definitions of *content validity, criterion-related validity,* and *construct validity*. Document as least three different definitions for each form of validity. Compare these definitions with the definitions in your textbook and with the way in which the *Standards* defines validity.
Explain, at a general level, the appropriate use of various validation strategies.	Obtain a test manual. Review the manual and determine what evidence of validity is provided by the test publisher. Be prepared to discuss your findings with your class.
	Identify a standardized achievement test and a standardized personality test that interest you. Consult the *Mental Measurements Yearbook, Tests in Print,* or other testing resources, and gather as much information as you can about how evidence of the test's validity was obtained. Create a table showing the similarities and differences between the validation strategies. Be prepared to share your findings with your class.
Describe and execute the steps involved in ensuring that a test demonstrates evidence of validity based on its content.	Construct a test specification table for an exam to assess students' knowledge of the information presented in this chapter. Share your table with your class. Discuss similarities and differences in your tables. Come to a consensus on what test specifications would lead to content-based evidence of validity of an exam.
Describe the different methods for demonstrating evidence of content validity.	Imagine that you are developing a test to measure the abstract attribute of job satisfaction. Conduct Internet research to learn more about what job satisfaction is. Use what you learn to define your testing universe. Create a test specification table outlining the content areas to be included in your test. Be prepared to share your research and test specification table with your class.
Explain the nature and importance of face validity.	Review the definition of face validity. Consider two tests that you have previously taken: one that had face validity and one that did not. Write about why one test has face validity and the other does not.

PRACTICE QUESTIONS

The following are practice questions to assess your understanding of the material presented in this chapter.

Multiple Choice

Choose the one best answer to each question.

1. A valid test
   a. consistently measures whatever it measures.
   b. consistently measures multiple constructs.
   c. measures only one construct.
   d. allows one to make correct inferences about the meaning of the scores.

2. The new *Standards* recognize five sources of evidence of validity. Which of the following is one of those sources?
   a. Construct validity
   b. Criterion-related validity
   c. Test content
   d. Face validity

3. Which one of the following is NOT considered a traditional type of validity?
   a. Content
   b. Criterion related
   c. Construct
   d. Alternate forms

4. Demonstrating evidence of validity is often logical rather than statistical for
   a. face validity and validity evidence based on a test's relationships with a criterion.
   b. construct validity and validity evidence based on a test's relationships with a criterion.
   c. face validity and validity evidence based on a test's content.
   d. validity evidence based on a test's content and validity evidence based on a test's relationships with a criterion.

5. If we demonstrate that a test allows us to identify individuals who are likely to become depressed, we have demonstrated evidence of validity based on its
   a. content.
   b. relationship with a criteria.
   c. relationship with a construct.
   d. appearance to the test taker.

6. If you took an algebra test that required you to perform a representative sample of algebraic calculations, the test has evidence of
   a. validity based on its content.
   b. validity based on its relationship with a criterion.
   c. validity based on its relationship with a construct.
   d. face validity.

7. If a test developer finds that the scores on a new test of mathematical achievement correlate with the scores on another test of mathematical achievement, the test shows evidence of
   a. validity based on the test's relationship with a criteria.
   b. validity based on the test's relationship with a construct.
   c. validity based on the test's content.
   d. face validity.

8. If a test developer finds that scores on a new employment test, designed to predict success on the job, correlate with employees' performance appraisal ratings, the test shows evidence of
   a. validity based on the test's relationship with a criteria.
   b. validity based on the test's relationship with a construct.
   c. validity based on the test's content.
   d. face validity.

9. If a test measures an attribute that can be described in terms of specific behaviors, the test measures
   a. abstract attributes.
   b. nonspecific attributes.
   c. concrete attributes.
   d. specific attributes.

10. Which type of attribute is more difficult to describe in terms of behaviors?
    a. Abstract
    b. Concrete
    c. Nonspecific
    d. Specific

11. Evidence of validity based on a test's content is most appropriate for tests such as mathematical achievement tests that measure _____ and tests such as personality tests that measure _____.
    a. abstract attributes; concrete attributes
    b. concrete attributes; abstract attributes
    c. nonspecific attributes; specific attributes
    d. specific attributes; nonspecific attributes

12. Attributes than can be described in terms of specific behaviors are
    a. abstract attributes.
    b. nonspecific attributes.
    c. concrete attributes.
    d. specific attributes.

13. If test takers perceive a test as attractive, they are referencing evidence of its
    a. face validity.
    b. reliability.
    c. validity based on content.
    d. validity based on its relationship with a construct.

14. If a writing test requires the test taker to perform a representative sample of writing activities (for example, writing a poem, writing an essay, writing a term paper), there is evidence that the test has
    a. validity based on the test's relationship with a construct.
    b. validity based on the test's relationship with a criterion.
    c. face validity.
    d. validity based on the test's content.

15. The two types of approaches that can be used to demonstrate evidence of validity based on a test's relationship with criteria are
    a. proactive and retroactive.
    b. predictive and nonpredictive.
    c. content and construct.
    d. predictive and concurrent.

16. The first step to ensure that a test demonstrates evidence of validity based on its content is to
    a. develop test specifications.
    b. define the testing universe.
    c. determine the content areas.
    d. determine the instructional objectives.

17. The content validity ratio for a test item can range from what to what?
    a. −1.00 to 0
    b. 0 to 1.00
    c. −1.00 to 1.00
    d. 1.00 to 10.00

Short Answer/Essay

Read each of the following, and consider your response carefully based on the information presented in this chapter. Write your answer to each question in two or three paragraphs.

1. How are the traditional terms of content, criterion-related, and construct validity similar? How are they different? Give examples.

2. Discuss the five sources of evidence of validity described in the new *Standards*.

3. How does the 1999 treatment of validity in the *Standards* differ from the more traditional approach?

4. What does it mean when we say that validity should be viewed as a unitary concept?

5. In what situations is it appropriate to demonstrate evidence of content, criterion-related, and construct validity? When would it be appropriate to collect evidence of more than one type of validity?

6. What are the steps involved in demonstrating the evidence of validity based on the content of a test during test development? Give an example.

7. Describe how to evaluate the evidence of validity based on a test's content subsequent to its development. Give an example.

8. How does face validity compare with other forms of evidence of validity? Why is face validity important?

Answer Keys

Multiple Choice

1. d	2. c	3. d	4. c	5. b
6. a	7. b	8. a	9. c	10. a
11. b	12. c	13. a	14. d	15. d
16. b	17. c			

Short Answer/Essay

Refer to your textbook for answers. If you are unsure of an answer and cannot generate the answer after reviewing your book, ask your professor for clarification.

How Do We Gather Evidence of Validity Based on a Test's Relationships With External Criteria?

CHAPTER 8: HOW DO WE GATHER EVIDENCE OF VALIDITY BASED ON A TEST'S RELATIONSHIPS WITH EXTERNAL CRITERIA?

After completing your study of this chapter, you should be able to do the following:

- Identify evidence of validity of a test based on its relationships to external criteria (criterion-related validity), and describe two methods for obtaining this evidence.
- Read and interpret validity studies.
- Discuss how restriction of range occurs and its consequences.
- Describe the differences between evidence of validity based on test content and evidence based on relationships with other variables.
- Describe the difference between reliability and validity.
- Define and give examples of objective and subjective criteria, and explain why criteria must be reliable and valid.
- Calculate a validity coefficient and the coefficient of determination, and conduct a test of significance for the validity coefficient.
- Explain the concept of regression, calculate and interpret a linear regression formula, and interpret a multiple regression formula.

"The graduate school I'm applying to says they won't accept anyone who scores less than 1,000 on the GRE. How did they decide that 1,000 is the magic number?"

"Before we married, my fiancé and I went to a premarital counselor. She gave us a test that predicted how happy our marriage would be."

"My company uses a test for hiring salespeople to work as telemarketers. The test is designed for people selling life insurance and automobiles. Is this a good test for hiring telemarketers?"

Have you ever wondered how psychological tests really work? How can we be comfortable using an individual's answers to test questions to make decisions about hiring him for a job or admitting her to college? Can mental disorders really be diagnosed using scores on standard questionnaires? Psychologists who use tests for decision making are constantly asking these questions and others like them. When psychologists use test scores for making decisions that affect individual lives, they as well as the public want substantial evidence that the correct decisions are being made.

This chapter describes the processes that psychologists use to ensure that tests perform properly when they are used for making predictions and decisions. We begin by discussing the concept of validity evidence based on a test's relationships to other variables, specifically external criteria. As we discussed in Chapter 7, this evidence has traditionally been called criterion-related validity. We also discuss the importance of selecting a valid criterion measure, how to evaluate validity coefficients, and the statistical processes that provide evidence that a test can be used for making predictions.

What Is Evidence of Validity Based on Test-Criteria Relationships?

In Chapter 7, we introduced you to the concept of evidence of validity based on a test's relationship with other variables. We said that one method for obtaining evidence is to investigate how well the test scores correlate with observed behaviors or events. When test scores correlate with specific behaviors, attitudes, or events, we can confirm that there is evidence of validity. In other words, the test scores may be used to predict those *specific* behaviors, attitudes, or events. But as you recall from Chapter 7, we cannot use such evidence to make an overall statement that the test is valid. We also said that this evidence has traditionally been referred to as *criterion-related validity* (a term that we use occasionally in this chapter as it is still widely used by testing practitioners).

For example, when you apply for a job, you might be asked to take a test that is designed to predict how well you will perform on the job. If the job is clerical and the test really predicts how well you will perform on the job, your test score should be related to your skill in performing clerical duties such as word processing and filing. To provide evidence that the test predicts clerical performance, psychologists correlate test scores for a large number of people with another measure of their performance on clerical tasks, such as supervisor ratings. The measure of performance that we correlate with test scores is called the **criterion**. And if higher test scores are associated with higher performance ratings, then we can say that the test has demonstrated evidence of validity based on the relationship between these two variables. In more traditional usage people say that the test has demonstrated criterion-related validity.

Educators use admissions tests to forecast how successful an applicant will be in college or graduate school. The SAT and the Graduate Record Examination (GRE) are examples of admissions tests used by colleges. The criterion of success in college is often the student's first-year grade point average (GPA).

In a clinical setting, psychologists often use tests to diagnose mental disorders. In this case, the criterion is the diagnoses made by several psychologists or psychiatrists independent of the test. Researchers then correlate the diagnoses with the test scores to establish evidence of validity.

Methods for Providing Evidence of Validity Based on Test-Criteria Relationships

As you also recall from Chapter 7, there are two methods for demonstrating evidence of validity based on test-criterion relationships: predictive and concurrent. This section defines and gives examples of each method.

The Predictive Method

When it is important to show a relationship between test scores and a future behavior, researchers use the predictive method to establish evidence of validity. In this case, a large group of people take the test (the predictor), and their scores are held for a predetermined time interval. When the time interval has elapsed, researchers collect a measure of some behavior, for example, a rating or other measure of performance, on the same people (the criterion). Then researchers correlate the test scores with the criterion scores. If the test scores and the criterion scores have a strong relationship, we say the test has demonstrated **predictive evidence of validity.**

Researchers at Brigham Young University used the predictive method to demonstrate evidence of validity of the PREParation for Marriage Questionnaire (PREP-M). For Your Information Box 8.1 describes the study they conducted.

Psychologists might use the predictive method in an organizational setting to establish evidence of validity for an employment test. To do so, they administer an employment test (predictor) to candidates for a job. Researchers file test scores in a secure place, and the company *does not* use the scores for making hiring decisions. The company makes hiring decisions based on other criteria such as interviews or different tests. After a predetermined time interval, usually three to six months, supervisors evaluate the new hires on how well they perform the job (the criterion). To determine whether the test scores predict the candidates who were successful and unsuccessful, researchers correlate the test scores with the ratings of job performance. The resulting correlation coefficient is called the **validity coefficient,** a statistic used to infer the strength of the evidence of validity that the test scores might demonstrate in predicting job performance.

To get the best measure of validity, everyone who took the test would need to be hired so that all test scores could be correlated with a measure of job performance. It is desirable to get the widest range of test scores possible (including the very low ones) to understand fully how all the test scores relate to job performance.

Gathering evidence of predictive validity can present problems for some organizations because it is important that everyone who took the test is also measured on the criterion. Some organizations might

FOR YOUR INFORMATION BOX 8.1

Evidence of Validity Based on Test-Criteria Relationships
of a Premarital Assessment Instrument

In 1991, researchers at Brigham Young University (Holman, Larson, & Harmer, 1994) conducted a study to determine the evidence of validity based on test-criteria relationships of the PREParation for Marriage Questionnaire (PREP-M; Holman, Busby, & Larson, 1989). Counselors use the PREP-M with engaged couples who are participating in premarital courses or counseling. The PREP-M has 206 questions that provide information on couples' shared values, readiness for marriage, background, and home environment. The researchers contacted 103 married couples who had taken the PREP-M a year earlier as engaged couples and asked them about their marital satisfaction and stability.

The researchers predicted that those couples who had high scores on the PREP-M would express high satisfaction with their marriages. The researchers used two criteria to test their hypothesis. First, they drew questions from the Marital Comparison Level Index (Sabatelli, 1984) and the Marital Instability Scale (Booth, Johnson, & Edwards, 1983) to construct a criterion that measured each couple's level of marital satisfaction and marital stability. The questionnaire showed an internal consistency of .83. The researchers also classified each couple as either "married satisfied," "married dissatisfied," or "canceled/delayed" and as either "married stable," "married unstable," or "canceled/delayed." These classifications provided a second criterion.

The researchers correlated the couples' scores on the PREP-M with their scores on the criterion questionnaire. The husbands' scores on the PREP-M correlated at .44 ($p < .01$) with questions on marital satisfaction and at .34 ($p < .01$) with questions on marital stability. The wives' scores on the PREP-M were correlated with the same questions at .25 ($p < .01$) and .20 ($p < .05$), respectively. These correlations show that PREP-M is a moderate to strong predictor of marital satisfaction and stability—good evidence of the validity of the PREP-M. (Later in this chapter, we discuss the size of correlation coefficients needed to establish evidence of validity.)

In addition, the researchers compared the mean scores of those husbands and wives classified as married satisfied, married dissatisfied, or canceled/delayed and those classified as married stable, married unstable, or canceled/delayed. As predicted, those who were married satisfied or married stable scored higher on the PREP-M than did those in the other two respective categories. In practical terms, these analyses show that counselors can use scores on the PREP-M to make predictions about how satisfying and stable a marriage will be.

not be able to hire everyone who applies regardless of qualifications, and there are usually more applicants than available positions, so not all applicants can be hired. Also, organizations frequently will be using some other selection tool such as an interview to make hiring decisions, and typically, only people who do well on the interview will be hired. Therefore, predictive studies in organizations may only have access to the scores of a portion of the candidates for the job. Because those actually hired are likely to be the higher performers, a **restriction of range** in the distribution of test scores is created. In other words, if the test is a valid predictor of job performance and the other selections tools that are used to make a hiring decision are also valid predictors, then people with lower scores on the test will be less likely to be hired. This causes the range of test scores to be reduced or restricted to those who scored relatively higher. Because a validity study conducted on these data will not have access to the full range of test scores, the validity coefficient calculated only from this restricted group is likely to be lower than if all candidates had been hired and included in the study.

Think of it like this: The worst case of restricted range would be if everyone obtained exactly the same score on the test (similar to what would happen if you hired only those people who made a perfect score on the test). If this situation occurred, the correlation between the test scores and any other criteria would be zero. As you can see, if the test scores do not vary from person to person, high performers and lower performers would all have the same test score. We cannot distinguish high performers from low performers when everybody gets the same score, and therefore these test scores cannot be predictive of job performance. Using the full range of test scores enables you to obtain a more accurate validity coefficient, which usually will be higher than the coefficient you obtained using the restricted range of scores. Fortunately, the correlation coefficient can be statistically adjusted for restriction of range, which, when used properly, can provide a corrected estimate of the validity coefficient of the employment test in the unrestricted population.

These problems exist in educational and clinical settings as well because individuals might not be admitted to an institution or might leave during the predictive study. For Your Information Box 8.2 describes a validation study that might have failed to find evidence of validity because of a flawed design.

The Concurrent Method

The method of demonstrating **concurrent evidence of validity** based on test-criteria relationships is an alternative to the predictive method that we discussed earlier in this chapter. In the concurrent method, test administration and criterion measurement happen at approximately the same time. This method does not involve prediction. Instead, it provides information about the present and the status quo (Cascio, 1991). A study by Watson and colleagues (1996), described in For Your Information Box 8.3, is a good example of a concurrent validity study.

The concurrent method involves administering two measures, the test and a second measure of the attribute, to the same group of individuals at as close to the same point in time as possible. For example, the test might be a paper-and-pencil measure of American literature, and the second measure might be a grade in an American literature course. Usually, the first measure is the test being validated, and the criterion is another type of measure of performance such as a rating, grade, or diagnosis. It is very important that the criterion test itself be reliable and valid (we discuss this further later in this chapter). The researchers then correlate the scores on the two measures. If the scores correlate, the test scores demonstrate evidence of validity.

In organizational settings, researchers often use concurrent studies as alternatives to predictive studies because of the difficulties of using a predictive design that we discussed earlier. In this setting, the process is to administer the test to employees currently in the position for which the test is being considered as a selection tool and then to collect criterion data on the same people (such as performance appraisal data). In some cases, the criterion data are specifically designed to be used in the concurrent study, while in other cases recent, existing data are used. Then the test scores are correlated with the criterion data and the validity coefficient is calculated.

FOR YOUR INFORMATION BOX 8.2

Did Restriction of Range Decrease the Validity Coefficient?

Does a student's academic self-concept—how the student views himself or herself in the role of a student—affect the student's academic performance? Michael and Smith (1976) developed the Dimensions of Self-Concept (DOSC), a self-concept measure that emphasizes school-related activities and that has five subscales that measure level of aspiration, anxiety, academic interest and satisfaction, leadership and initiative, and identification versus alienation.

Researchers at the University of Southern California (Gribbons, Tobey, & Michael, 1995) examined the evidence of validity based on test-criteria relationships of the DOSC by correlating DOSC test scores with grade point average (GPA). They selected 176 new undergraduates from two programs for students considered at risk for academic difficulties. The students came from a variety of ethnic backgrounds, and 57% were men.

At the beginning of the semester, the researchers administered the DOSC to the students following the guidelines described in the DOSC manual (Michael, Smith, & Michael, 1989). At the end of the semester, they obtained each student's first-semester GPA from university records. When they analyzed the data for evidence of reliability and validity, the DOSC showed high internal consistency, but scores on the DOSC did not predict GPA.

Did something go wrong? One conclusion is that self-concept as measured by the DOSC is unrelated to GPA. However, if the study or the measures were somehow flawed, the predictive evidence of validity of the DOSC might have gone undetected. The researchers suggested that perhaps academic self-concept lacks stability during students' first semester. Although the internal reliability of the DOSC was established, the researchers did not measure the test–retest method reliability of the test. Therefore, this possibility cannot be ruled out. The researchers also suggested that GPA might be an unreliable criterion.

Could restriction of range have caused the validity of the DOSC to go undetected? This is a distinct possibility for two reasons. First, for this study the researchers chose only those students who were at risk for experiencing academic difficulties. Because the unrestricted population of students also contains those who are expected to succeed, the researchers might have restricted the range of both the test and the criterion. Second, the students in the study enrolled in programs to help them become successful academically. Therefore, participating in the programs might have enhanced the students' academic self-concept.

This study demonstrates two pitfalls that researchers designing predictive studies must avoid. Researchers must be careful to include in their studies participants who represent the entire possible range of performance on both the test and the criterion. In addition, they must design predictive studies so that participants are unlikely to change over the course of the study in ways that affect the abilities or traits that are being measured.

Barrett, Phillips, and Alexander (1981) compared the two methods for determining evidence of validity based on predictor-criteria relationships in an organizational setting using cognitive ability tests. They found that the two methods provide similar results.

How Validity Differs From Reliability

As you recall from Chapter 6, reliability refers to the consistency of test results and derives from two factors: reliability within the test (internal consistency) and reliability across time (test–retest reliability). The reliability coefficient provides a quantitative estimate of a test's consistency of measurement. A yardstick, for example, is a reliable or consistent measuring instrument because each

FOR YOUR INFORMATION BOX 8.3

Diagnosing Alcohol Abuse at a Veterans Affairs Medical Center

Watson and colleagues (1996) administered two self-report alcoholism measures to 118 volunteers recruited from chemical dependency or psychiatric wards at a Veterans Affairs medical center. At roughly the same time, the researchers asked the volunteers to complete the criterion measure, a computerized version of the Diagnostic Interview Schedule (C-DIS; Blouin, 1987). The C-DIS asks questions that reflect the revised third edition of the *Diagnostic and Statistical Manual of Mental Disorders* (*DSM-III-R;* American Psychiatric Association, 1987), a reference book for psychologists and psychiatrists that lists symptoms of various mental disorders. The researchers chose the C-DIS as a criterion because it has shown high test–retest reliability and good evidence of validity based on content.

Correlations of the self-report tests with the criterion, the C-DIS, were .75 for the first self-report alcoholism measure and .60 for the second self-report alcoholism measure. These data suggest that the self-report measures of alcoholism have high evidence of validity using a concurrent study and are appropriate tools for diagnosis of alcohol dependency. (Later in this chapter, we describe how to interpret validity coefficients to provide evidence of validity based on test-criteria relationships.)

time it measures an item it gives the same answer. In addition, a yardstick is an appropriate measure for measuring distance, and therefore we can say the yardstick has validity as a distance measure. On the other hand, a yardstick is not a valid measure of intelligence. There is no relation between height and intelligence, and therefore we would not use a yardstick to predict IQ. This example demonstrates the principle that reliability and validity are two separate issues. A psychological test might be reliable but not valid, as in the case of the yardstick trying to predict intelligence. Reliability is a characteristic of the test itself, and validity depends on the inferences that are going to be made from the test scores.

While reliability and validity are different concepts, there is a relationship between them when it comes to gathering evidence of validity through test-criterion relationships. Mathematically, the square root of the reliability of a test will set the upper limit of the validity coefficient of a test. So if a test has a relatively low reliability of .64, the maximum correlation that the test could have with any criteria is .8. The point is that while a test can be reliable but not valid for a particular use, a test cannot be valid for any use if the scores are very unreliable.

INTERIM SUMMARY 8.1
DEMONSTRATING EVIDENCE OF VALIDITY FROM TEST-CRITERIA RELATIONSHIPS

The two basic methods for showing relation between a test and independent events or behaviors (the criterion) are as follows:

- Predictive Method—Established by correlating test scores taken at one time with scores on a criterion measure obtained at a later date, usually months later. This method establishes that the test provides information about events in the future.
- Concurrent Method—Established by correlating test scores and criterion scores obtained at approximately the same time. This method establishes that the test can provide information about independent events or behaviors in the present.

Selecting a Criterion

A criterion is an evaluative standard that researchers use to measure outcomes such as performance, attitude, or motivation. Evidence of validity derived from test-criteria relationships provides evidence that the test relates to some behavior or event that is independent of the psychological test. As you recall from For Your Information Box 8.1, the researchers at Brigham Young University constructed two criteria—a questionnaire and classifications on marital satisfaction and marital stability—to demonstrate evidence of validity of the PREP-M.

In a business setting, employers use pre-employment tests to predict how well an applicant is likely to perform a job. In this case, supervisors' ratings of job performance can serve as a criterion that represents performance on the job. Other criteria that represent job performance include accidents on the job, attendance or absenteeism, disciplinary problems, training performance, and ratings by **peers**—other employees at the work site. None of these measures can represent job performance perfectly, but each provides information on important characteristics of job performance.

Objective and Subjective Criteria

Criteria for job performance fall into two categories: objective and subjective. An **objective criterion** is one that is observable and measurable, such as the number of accidents on the job, the number of days absent, or the number of disciplinary problems in a month. A **subjective criterion** is based on a person's judgment. Supervisor and peer ratings are examples of subjective criteria.

Table 8.1   Common Criteria

	Objective	Subjective
Educational settings		
Grade point average	X	
Withdrawal or dismissal	X	
Teacher's recommendations		X
Clinical settings		
Diagnosis		X
Behavioral observation	X	
Self-report		X
Organizational settings		
Units produced	X	
Number of errors	X	
Ratings of performance		X

Each has advantages and disadvantages. Well-defined objective criteria contain less error because they are usually tallies of observable events or outcomes. Their scope, however, is often quite narrow. For instance, dollar volume of sales is an objective criterion that might be used to measure a person's sales ability. This number is easily calculated, and there is little chance of disagreement on its numerical value. It does not, however, take into account a person's motivation or the availability of customers. On the other hand, a supervisor's ratings of a person's sales ability may provide more information on motivation, but in turn ratings are based on judgment and might be biased or based on information not related to sales ability, such as expectations about race or gender. Table 8.1 lists a number of criteria used in educational, clinical, and organizational settings.

Does the Criterion Measure What It Is Supposed to Measure?

The concept of validity evidence based on content (addressed in Chapter 7) also applies to criteria. Criteria must be representative of the events they are supposed to measure. Criterion scores have evidence of validity to the extent that they match or represent the events in question. Therefore, a criterion of sales ability must be representative of the entire testing universe of sales ability. Because there is more to selling than just having the highest dollar volume of sales, several objective criteria might be used to represent the entire testing universe of sales ability. For instance, we might add the number of sales calls made each month to measure motivation and add the size of the target population to measure customer availability.

Subjective measures such as ratings can often demonstrate better evidence of their validity based on content because the rater can provide judgments for a number of dimensions specifically associated with job performance. Rating forms are psychological measures, and we expect them to be reliable and valid, as we do for any measure. We estimate their reliability using the test–retest or internal consistency method, and we generate evidence of their validity by matching their content to the knowledge, skills, abilities, or other characteristics (such as behaviors, attitudes, personality characteristics, or other mental states) that are presumed to be present in the test takers. (Chapters 10 and 15 contain more information on various types of rating scales and their uses in organizations.)

By reporting the reliability of their criteria, researchers provide us with information on how accurate the outcome measure is. As you may have noticed, the researchers at Brigham Young University (Holman et al., 1989) who conducted the study on the predictive validity of the PREP-M reported high reliability for their questionnaire, which was their subjective criterion. Likewise, the researchers at the Veterans Affairs medical center (Watson et al., 1996) chose the computerized version of the Diagnostic Interview Schedule (C-DIS) as a criterion because it reflected the *Diagnostic and Statistical Manual of Mental Disorders* (*DSM-III-R;* American Psychiatric Association, 1987) diagnosis of alcohol dependency—an indicator that the C-DIS showed evidence of validity based on content.

Sometimes criteria do not represent all of the dimensions in the behavior, attitude, or event being measured. When this happens, the criterion has decreased evidence of validity based on its content because it has underrepresented some important characteristics. If the criterion measures more dimensions than those measured by the test, we say that **criterion contamination** is present. For instance, if one were looking at the test-criterion relationship of a test of sales aptitude, a convenient criterion might be the dollar volume of sales made over some period of time. However, if the dollar volume of sales of a new salesperson reflected both his or her own sales as well as sales that resulted from the filling of back orders sold by the former salesperson, the criterion would be considered contaminated.

As you can see, when evaluating a validation study, it is important to think about the criterion in the study as well as the predictor. When unreliable or inappropriate criteria are used for validation, the true validity coefficient might be under- or overestimated. For Your Information Box 8.4 describes the issues associated with identifying appropriate criteria to represent success in graduate school.

FYI

FOR YOUR INFORMATION BOX 8.4

Choosing a Criterion to Represent Success in Graduate School

Choosing an appropriate criterion is often difficult. For example, how do you measure success in graduate school? In 1980, two psychologists at Educational Testing Service described the "criterion problem" as an important issue in validation studies of graduate school admissions tests (Hartnett & Willingham, 1980). Grades in graduate school, they said, are often used as a criterion of success; however, grades have low consistency. Furthermore, graduate school students receive only As and Bs—causing restriction of range—and grading standards vary from professor to professor.

Whether a student graduates is certainly an important measure of success; however, this criterion also has disadvantages. Students drop out of graduate school for many reasons, some of which have nothing to do with academic success. The time students spend in graduate school has also been used as a criterion, but it has the same drawback. Students might be delayed in completing their graduate programs for reasons not related to academic achievement, such as family tragedies, illnesses, and financial problems.

Calculating and Evaluating Validity Coefficients

As you recall from Chapter 5, the correlation coefficient is a quantitative estimate of the linear relationship between two variables. In validity studies, we refer to the correlation coefficient between the test and the criterion as the validity coefficient and represent it in formulas and equations as r_{xy}. The x in the subscript refers to the test, and the y refers to the criterion. The validity coefficient represents the amount or strength of the evidence of validity based on the relationship of the test and the criterion.

Validity coefficients must be evaluated to determine whether they represent a level of validity that makes the test useful and meaningful. This section describes two methods for evaluating validity coefficients and how researchers use test-criterion relationship information to make predictions about future behavior or performance.

Tests of Significance

A validity coefficient is interpreted in much the same way as a reliability coefficient, except that our expectations for a very strong relationship are not as great. We cannot expect a validity coefficient to have as strong a relationship with another variable (test-criterion evidence of validity) as it does with itself (reliability). Therefore, we must evaluate the validity coefficient by using a test of significance and by examining the coefficient of determination.

The first question to ask about a validity coefficient is, "How likely is it that the correlation between the test and the criterion resulted from chance or sampling error?" In other words, if the test scores (for example, SAT scores) and the criterion (for example, college GPA) are completely unrelated, then their true correlation is zero. If we conducted a study to determine the relationship between these two variables and found that the correlation was .4, one question that we need to ask is, "What is the probability that our study would have yielded the obtained correlation by chance alone, even if the variables were truly unrelated?" If the probability that the correlation occurred by chance is low—less than 5 chances out of 100 ($p < .05$)—we can be reasonably sure that the test and its criterion (in this example, SAT scores and college GPA) are truly related. This process is called a **test of significance.** In statistical terms, for this example we would say that the validity coefficient is significant at the .05 level. In organizational settings, it can be challenging for validity studies to have statistically significant results at $p < .05$ because of small sample sizes and criterion contamination.

Because larger sample sizes reduce sampling error, this test of significance requires that we take into account the size of the group (N) from which we obtained our data. Appendix E can be used to determine whether a correlation is significant at varying levels of significance. To use the table in Appendix E, calculate the degrees of freedom (df) for your correlation using the formula $df = N - 2$, and then determine the probability that the correlation occurred by chance by looking across the row associated with those degrees of freedom. The correlation coefficient you are evaluating should be larger than the critical value shown in the table. You can determine the level of significance by looking at the column headings. At the level where your correlation coefficient is smaller than the value shown, the correlation can no longer be considered significantly different from zero. For Your Information Box 8.5 provides an example of this process.

When researchers or test developers report a validity coefficient, they should also report its level of significance. You might have noted that the validity coefficients of the PREP-M (reported earlier in this chapter) are followed by the statements $p < .01$ and $p < .05$. This information tells the test user that the likelihood a relationship was found by chance or as a result of sampling error was less than 5 chances out of 100 ($p < .05$) or less than 1 chance out of 100 ($p < .01$).

If the correlation between the test and the predictor is not as high as the critical value shown in the table, we can say that the chance of error associated with the test is above generally accepted levels. In such a case, we would conclude that the validity coefficient does not provide sufficient evidence of validity.

The Coefficient of Determination

Another way to evaluate the validity coefficient is to determine the amount of variance that the test and the criterion share. We can determine the amount of shared variance by squaring the validity coefficient to obtain r^2—called the **coefficient of determination.** For example, if the correlation (r) between a test and a criterion is .30, the coefficient of determination (r^2) is .09. This means that the test and the criterion have 9% of their variance in common. Larger validity coefficients represent stronger relationships with greater overlap between the test and the criterion. Therefore, if $r = .50$, then $r^2 = .25$—or 25% shared variance.

We can calculate the coefficient of determination for the correlation of husbands' scores on the PREP-M and the questionnaire on marital satisfaction and stability. By squaring the original coefficient, .44, we

FOR YOUR INFORMATION BOX 8.5

Test of Significance for a Correlation Coefficient

Here we illustrate how to determine whether a correlation coefficient is significant (evidence of a true relationship) or not significant (no relationship). Let's say that we have collected data from 20 students. We have given the students a test of verbal achievement, and we have correlated students' scores with their grades from a course on creative writing. The resulting correlation coefficient is .45.

We now go to the table of critical values for Pearson product–moment correlation coefficients in Appendix E. The table shows the degrees of freedom (*df*) and alpha (a) levels for two-tailed and one-tailed tests. Psychologists usually set their alpha level at 5 chances out of 100 ($p < .05$) using a two-tailed test, so we use that standard for our example.

Because we used the data from 20 students in our sample, we substitute 20 for *N* in the formula for degrees of freedom ($df = N - 2$). Therefore, $df = 20 - 2$ or 18. We then go to the table and find 18 in the *df* column. Finally, we locate the critical value in that row under the .05 column.

A portion of the table from Appendix E is reproduced in the table below showing the alpha level for a two-tailed test. The critical value of .4438 (bolded in the table) is the one we use to test our correlation. Because our correlation (.45) is greater than the critical value (.4438), we can infer that the probability of finding our correlation by chance is less than 5 chances out of 100. Therefore, we assume that there is a true relationship and refer to the correlation coefficient as significant. Note that if we had set our alpha level at a more stringent standard of .01 (1 chance out of 100), our correlation coefficient would have been interpreted as not significant.

Critical Values for Pearson Product–Moment Correlation Coefficients

df	.10	.05	.02	.01	.001
16	.4000	.4683	.5425	.5897	.7084
17	.3887	.4555	.5285	.5751	.6932
18	.3783	**.4438**	.5155	.5614	.6787
19	.3687	.4329	.5034	.5487	.6652
20	.3598	.4227	.4921	.5368	.6524

SOURCE: From *Statistical Tables for Biological, Agricultural and Medical Research* by R.A. Fisher and F. Yates. Copyright © 1963. Published by Pearson Education Limited.

obtain the coefficient of determination, $r^2 = .1936$. This outcome means that the predictor, the PREP-M, and the criterion, the questionnaire, shared (or had in common) approximately 19% of their variance.

Unadjusted validity coefficients rarely exceed .50. Therefore, you can see that even when a validity coefficient is statistically significant, the test can account for only a small portion of the variability in the criterion. The coefficient of determination is important to calculate and remember when using the correlation between the test and the criterion to make predictions about future behavior or performance.

How Confident Can We Be About Estimates of Validity?

Conducting one validity study that demonstrates a strong relationship between the test and the criterion is the first step in a process of validation, but it is not the final step. Studies that provide evidence of a test's validity should continue for as long as the test is being used. No matter how well designed the validation study is, elements of chance, error, and situation-specific factors that can over- or underinflate the estimate of validity are always present. Ongoing investigations of validity include cross-validation (where the results that are obtained using one sample are used to predict the results on a second, similar sample) and meta-analyses (where the results from many studies are statistically combined to provide a more error-free estimate of validity). Psychologists also inquire about whether validity estimates are stable from one situation or population to another—a question of validity generalization. (Chapters 12 and 15 address these issues in more detail.)

INTERIM SUMMARY 8.2
EVALUATING VALIDITY COEFFICIENTS

- Tests of significance establish the likelihood that a correlation observed between a test and a criterion was obtained by chance.
- The coefficient of determination describes how much variance a test and a criterion share.

- Ongoing investigations of validity include cross-validation and meta-analyses.
- Psychologists also inquire about whether validity estimates are stable from one situation or population to another—a question of validity generalization.

Using Validity Information to Make Predictions

When a relationship can be established between a test and a criterion, we can use test scores from other individuals to predict how well those individuals will perform on the criterion measure. For example, some universities use students' scores on the SAT to predict the students' success in college. Organizations use job candidates' scores on pre-employment tests that have demonstrated evidence of validity to predict those candidates' scores on the criteria of job performance.

Linear Regression

We use the statistical process called **linear regression** when we use one set of test scores (X) to predict one set of criterion scores (Y'). To do this, we construct the following linear regression equation:

$$Y' = a + bX$$

where

Y' = the predicted score on the criterion

a = the intercept

b = the slope

X = the score the individual made on the predictor test

This equation actually provides a predicted score on the criterion (Y') for each test score (X). When the Y' values are plotted, they form the linear regression line associated with the correlation between the test and the criterion.

We can calculate the **slope** (b) of the regression line—the expected change in one unit of Y for every change in X—using the following formula:

$$b = r\frac{S_Y}{S_X}$$

where

r = the correlation coefficient

Sx = the standard deviation of the distribution of X

Sy = the standard deviation of the distribution of Y

The **intercept** is the place where the regression line crosses the y-axis. The intercept (a) is calculated using the following formula:

$$a = \bar{Y} - b\bar{X}$$

where

$\bar{Y}$ = the mean of the distribution of Y

b = the slope

$\bar{X}$ = the mean of the distribution of X

For Your Information Box 8.6 shows the calculation of a linear regression equation and how it is used to predict scores on a criterion.

The process of using correlated data to make predictions is also important in clinical settings. For Your Information Box 8.7 describes how clinicians use psychological test scores to identify adolescents at risk for committing suicide.

FYI

FOR YOUR INFORMATION BOX 8.6

Making Predictions With a Linear Regression Equation

Research suggests that academic self-efficacy (ASE) and class grades are related. We have made up the following data to show how we could use the scores on an ASE test to predict a student's grade. (Note: Our fake data set is small to facilitate this illustration.)

For instance, we can ask the question, "If a student scores 65 on the ASE test, what course grade would we expect the student to receive?" We have assigned numbers to each grade to facilitate this analysis, therefore, 1 = D, 2 = C, 3 = B, and 4 = A.

Student	ASE ($\bar{X}$)	Grade ($\bar{Y}$)
1	80	3
2	62	2
3	90	4
4	40	2
5	55	2
6	85	2
7	70	4
8	75	3
9	25	1
10	50	3

Step 1: Calculate the means and standard deviations of X and Y.

$\bar{X} = 63.2$
$\bar{Y} = 2.6$
$S_x = 20.82$
$S_y = .97$

Step 2: Calculate the correlation coefficient (r_{xy}) for X and Y.

$r_{xy} = .67$

Step 3: Calculate the slope and intercept.

$b = r (S_y/S_x)$, so $b = .67(.97/20.82)$, so $b = .031$
$a = \bar{Y} - b\bar{X}$, $a = 2.6 - (.031)(63.2)$, so $a = .64$

Step 4: Calculate Y' when X = 65.

$Y' = a + bX$
$Y' = .64 + (.031)(65)$
$Y' = .64 + .2.05 = 2.59$

Step 5: Translate the number calculated for Y' back into a letter grade.

Therefore, 2.59 would be a grade of between C and B, perhaps a C+.

The best prediction we can make is that a person who scored 65 on an ASE test would be expected to earn a course grade of C+. Note that by substituting any test score for X, we will receive a corresponding prediction for a score on Y.

FYI

FOR YOUR INFORMATION BOX 8.7

Evidence of Validity of the Suicide Probability Scale Using the Predictive Method

Although the general incidence of suicide has decreased during the past two decades, the rate for people between 15 and 24 years old has tripled. Suicide is generally considered to be the second or third most common cause of death among adolescents, even though it is underreported (O'Connor, 2008).

If young people who are at risk for committing suicide or making suicide attempts can be identified, greater vigilance is likely to prevent such actions. Researchers at Father Flanagan's Boys' Home, in Boys Town, Nebraska, conducted a validity study using the predictive method for the Suicide Probability Scale (SPS) that provided encouraging results for predicting suicidal behaviors in adolescents (Larzelere, Smith, Batenhorst, & Kelly, 1996).

The SPS contains 36 questions that assess suicide risk, including thoughts about suicide, depression, and isolation. The researchers administered the SPS to 840 boys and girls when they were admitted to the Boys Town residential treatment program from 1988 through 1993. The criteria for this study were the numbers of suicide attempts, suicide verbalizations, and self-destructive behaviors recorded in the program's Daily Incident Report completed by supervisors of the group homes. (The interrater reliabilities for reports of verbalizations and reports of self-destructive behaviors were very high at .97 and .89, respectively. The researchers were unable to calculate a reliability estimate for suicide attempts because only one attempt was recorded in the reports they selected for the reliability analysis.)

(Continued)

(Continued)

After controlling for a number of confounding variables, such as gender, age, and prior attempts of suicide, the researchers determined that the total SPS score and each of its subscales differentiated ($p < .05$) between those who attempted suicide and those who did not. In other words, the mean SPS scores of those who attempted suicide were significantly higher than the mean SPS scores of those who did not attempt suicide. The mean SPS scores of those who displayed self-destructive behaviors were also significantly higher ($p < .01$) than the mean SPS scores of those who did not attempt self-destructive behaviors. Finally, the total SPS score correlated .25 ($p < .001$) with the suicide verbalization rate. Predictions made by the SPS for those at risk for attempting suicide showed that each 1-point increase in the total SPS score predicted a 2.4% greater likelihood of a subsequent suicide attempt.

The researchers suggest a cutoff score of 74 for those without prior suicide attempts and a cutoff score of 53 for those with prior suicide attempts. In other words, if an adolescent who has no previous history of suicide attempts scores above 74 on the SPS, the youth would be classified as at risk for suicide and treated accordingly. If an adolescent who has a previous history of a suicide attempt scores below 53, the youth would be classified as not at risk for suicide.

The researchers emphasize, however, that although the SPS demonstrated statistically significant validity in predicting suicide attempts, it is not a perfect predictor. A number of suicide attempts were also recorded for those with low scores, and therefore a low SPS score does not ensure that an adolescent will not attempt suicide. The SPS does, however, provide an instrument for accurately identifying adolescents at risk for committing suicide.

Multiple Regression

Complex criteria, such as job performance and success in graduate school, are often difficult to predict with a single test. In these situations, researchers use more than one test to make an accurate prediction. An expansion of the linear regression equation helps in this situation.

We use the statistical process of **multiple regression** for predicting a criterion (Y') using *more than one* set of test scores ($X_1, X_2, ... X_n$). The multiple regression equation that incorporates information from more than one predictor or test is as follows:

$$Y' = a + b_1X_1 + b_2X_2 + b_3X_3 \ldots b_nX_n$$

where

Y' = the predicted score on the criterion

a = the intercept

b = the slope of the regression line and amount of variance the predictor contributes to the equation, also known as **beta** (β)

X = the predictor

The numbers following b and X indicate the test from which the information was drawn.

In multiple regression, there is one criterion (Y), but there are several predictors (X). To describe this relationship, we use a multiple correlation (R). We can evaluate R by calculating the coefficient of multiple determination (R^2), which indicates the proportion of variance in the criterion accounted for by all of the predictors. The R can also be subjected to a test of significance to determine whether it is significantly different from zero. We can also calculate the contribution that each predictor (X) by itself contributes to the total explained variance (R^2). We must bear in mind, however, that when a predictor is first in the multiple regression equation, it is likely to explain more variance than when the predictor is last. This is the case when the predictors share variance (are correlated) with each other as well as with the criterion.

Because each combination of $a + bX$ in the preceding equation indicates the presence of a different regression line, the multiple regression equation is difficult to plot. It works in theory, however, much the same as does the linear regression equation. The value of each b (partial regression coefficient) indicates how many units Y increases for every increase in X, and therefore each b indicates the contribution that each predictor makes in determining a predicted score on the criterion (Y').

Chibnall and Detrick (2003) published a study that examined the usefulness of three personality inventories—the Minnesota Multiphasic Personality Inventory-2 (MMPI-2), the Inwald Personality Inventory (IPI; an established police officer screening test), and the Revised NEO Personality Inventory (NEO PI-R)—for predicting the performance of police officers. They administered the inventories to 79 police recruits and compared the test scores with two criteria: academic performance and physical performance. Tables 8.2 and 8.3 show the outcomes of the study for the academic performance criterion.

On the Web Box 8.1 guides you in researching the Inwald Personality Test. Can you find information on evidence of validity based on test-criteria relationships for this test?

When the researchers entered recruit class, marital status, and race first, they accounted for 20% of the prediction of academic performance. In the second step, the researchers entered the test scores from the IPI. The table shows the contribution of the inventory dimensions that contributed significantly to the prediction. Together, the three dimensions of the IPI contributed 16% of the prediction ($R^2\Delta$). In the third step, the researchers entered two dimensions of the MMPI-2, and together they accounted for 8% of the prediction. Finally, the researchers entered three dimensions of the NEO PI-R, and together they accounted for another 11% of the prediction. Altogether, the demographic characteristics and the three inventories accounted for 55% of the prediction of academic performance (R^2).

Table 8.2 Regression Model for Predicting Academic Performance ($R^2 = .55$)

| Step 1 | | Step 2 | | Step 3 | | Step 4 | |
| Demographic Variables | | IPI | | MMPI-2 | | NEO PI-R | |
Predictor	β	Predictor	β	Predictor	β	Predictor	β
Recruit class	.32	Trouble law	−.26	Depression	−.21	Assertiveness	−.40
Marital status	.27	Antisocial	−.35	Hypomania	−.27	Ideas	.20
Race	.24	Obsessiveness	.29			Depression	−.28
$R^2\Delta$	.20	$R^2\Delta$	.16	R^2D	.08	$R^2\Delta$	.11

SOURCE: Reprinted with permission from Chibnall, J. T., & Detrick, P. (2003). The NEO PI-R, Inwald Personality Inventory, and MMPI-2 in the prediction of police academy performance: A case for incremental validity. *American Journal of Criminal Justice, 27*, 233–248.

NOTE: *Step* refers to the introduction of a predictor into the regression equation for predicting academic performance. The predictors are the individual demographic characteristics or the subscales that reached significance. $R^2\Delta$ is the percentage of prediction of academic performance contributed by each predictor.

Table 8.3	Range of Variance Explained (R^2) by Each Inventory at Each Step in the Regression Models That Predict Academic Performance

Predictor	Step 1	Step 2	Step 3	Step 4
Demographics	.20	—	—	—
NEO PI-R	—	.20	.14 to .16	.11 to .16
IPI	—	.16	.00 to .05	.03 to .03
MMPI-2	—	.14	.08 to .10	.00 to .08

SOURCE: Reprinted with permission from Chibnall, J. T., & Detrick, P. (2003). The NEO PI-R, Inwald Personality Inventory, and MMPI-2 in the prediction of police academy performance: A case for incremental validity. *American Journal of Criminal Justice, 27*, 233–248.

NOTE: *Step* refers to the introduction of a predictor into the regression equation for predicting academic performance. MMPI-2 = Minnesota Multiphasic Personality Inventory-2, IPI = Inwald Personality Inventory, NEO PI-R = Revised NEO Personality Inventory.

Demographic characteristics did not contribute to the prediction of physical performance. Only the NEO PI-R predicted 20% ($R^2\Delta = .20$) of the variance for physical performance. The dimensions of the NEO PI-R that accounted for variance in the criterion were Fantasy ($\beta = .47$), Deliberation ($\beta = .26$), and Feelings ($\beta = .25$).

Two studies (Kolb, Race, & Seibert, 2000; Meyer, Woodard, & Suddick, 1994) illustrate the usefulness of multiple regression in providing evidence of validity from test-criterion relationships. Kolb and colleagues evaluated the evidence of validity of a questionnaire designed to assess the satisfaction of psychiatric inpatients. They distributed the questionnaire to inpatients in 37 psychiatric units. Their data analysis showed that all coefficient alphas for the six scales in the questionnaire were above .74. The results of a multiple regression analysis, in which the six scales were used as predictors and the overall quality-of-care ratings were used as the criterion, are displayed in Table 8.4.

Table 8.4	Power of Inpatient Psychiatric Scales to Predict Quality-of-Care Ratings

Scale	Pearson Product–Moment Correlation Coefficient	Partial R^2	R^2
Staff	.667	.422	.422
Nonclinical Services	.642	.199	.541
Program Components/Activities	.570	.026	.576
Psychiatric Care	.534	.006	.573
Medical Outcome	.445	.002	.575
Patient Education	.425	.002	.577

SOURCE: From Kolb, S. J., Race, K. E. H., & Siebert, J. H. (2000). Psychometric evaluation of an inpatient psychiatric care consumer satisfaction survey. *Journal of Behavioral Health Services and Research, 27*, 75–86. Published by Springer Science and Business Media.

NOTE: Stepwise multiple regression is based on a sample of 1,351 patients. Partial R^2 = additional variance explained at each step. The proportion of variance explained at each step is affected by the order in which these scales are entered into the model. Modifying the order of inclusion could result in proportional changes in this variance. R^2 = total variance explained at each step.

As you can see, Table 8.4 shows the correlation of each scale with the criterion in the Pearson's Product–Moment Correlation Coefficient column. The Partial R^2 column shows the increase in percentage of variance that each scale provides. The partial R^2 values will vary when the order in which the scales appear in the formula changes. The R^2 column (the coefficient of determination for R) shows the percentage of variance accounted for at each step in the formula. Using just one scale on the questionnaire accounts for 42.2% of the variance in the overall score, but using all six scales accounts for 57.7% of the variance. We would expect such an outcome because each scale provides information about a different aspect of inpatient satisfaction. Although Kolb and colleagues' (2000) report of the results of their data analysis is clear, they do not provide information on how the criterion was developed, measured, or calculated. As you know from our discussion of criterion validity, we cannot rely on the results of studies that do not provide information on the criterion measure.

ON THE WEB BOX 8.1

Conducting Research

This book contains detailed information on the revised Minnesota Multiphasic Personality Inventory-2 (see Chapter 11) and the Revised NEO Personality Inventory (see Chapter 14). Using professional databases, such as *ProQuest, Mental Measurements Yearbook, Tests in Print,* and *Education Resources Information Center (ERIC)*, research the Inwald Personality Inventory. Chapter 1 provides information on using the *Mental Measurements Yearbook* and *Tests in Print.* (Hint: Detrick, Chibnall, & Rosso, 2001, is also relevant to this exercise.)
Find the following:

- Test purpose
- Target audience
- Reliability and validity estimates

Taking into account the information you found on the Inwald Personality Inventory, would you recommend that organizations use the test for selection purposes? Back up your recommendation with the information you found.

Meyer and colleagues (1994) conducted a validity study using the predictive method of two of the Descriptive Tests of Mathematics Skills (DTMS) of the College Entrance Examination Board. The researchers' university requires elementary education majors to pass the Arithmetic Skills and Elementary Algebra Skills tests of the DTMS. The university also requires elementary education majors to take an upper-division mathematics concepts and structures course. In this study, the Arithmetic Skills and Elementary Algebra Skills tests were the predictors, and the grade received in the upper-division math course became the criterion in a study of 60 elementary education majors.

In their data analysis, Meyer and colleagues (1994) found evidence of internal consistency for the two tests: Arithmetic Skills (.72) and Elementary Algebra Skills (.77). Course grades (the criterion) correlated with Arithmetic Skills at .48 ($p < .001$) and correlated with Elementary Algebra Skills at .49 ($p < .001$).

Then the researchers used both tests in a multiple regression equation to predict course grades. They found a multiple R of .54—higher than either test predicted independently—that accounted for approximately 29% of the variance in the two tests and course grades ($R^2 = .286$). Most of the variance, however, was predicted by one test, Elementary Algebra, which accounted for 24% of the variance ($R^2 = .241$). The multiple R for Elementary Algebra alone and the R for both tests together were not significantly different.

Meyer and colleagues (1994) concluded that each test showed evidence of validity and could be used as a predictor of math performance for elementary education majors. In addition, they suggested simplifying the assessment program by using one test instead of two tests because the tests supplied redundant information about the criterion (course grades).

Ethical Issues Associated With Test Validation

Decisions based on test predictions have far-reaching consequences. Each day in the United States and other industrialized nations, individuals are hired or rejected by organizations that base their decisions on employment tests. Therefore, test users must rely on validity studies to ensure that the tests they use make accurate predictions.

Educators also use test results to admit or refuse admittance to programs based on predictions made by educational ability tests, and clinicians use tests to screen clients for residential or outpatient treatment and to admit them to specific treatment programs based on diagnoses made by tests. As you recall from Chapter 3, Michael Elmore's teacher used Michael's score on an intelligence test to decide that Michael was borderline retarded even though he was not.

The increasing diversity of the population in the United States presents questions about the suitability of tests for students, clinical clients, employees, and job seekers from various minorities. Also, as the use of psychological assessment spreads to countries whose primary languages are not English, questions arise concerning translations and norms associated with translations of standardized tests developed in the United States and Great Britain. When test takers are members of minorities, especially those who do not speak standard English as their primary language, test users must be aware of test bias and how it affects test validity. Cofresi and Gorman (2004) assert that the test users' responsibilities include testing assessment tools to ensure that they are valid for the minority population who will be the test takers. Appropriate assessments, they emphasize, should be free of questions that require a specific cultural background (for example, knowledge of sports, holidays, or foods; etiquette related to specific cultures, races, or religions). The use of test norms that were developed without inclusion of the minority being tested is likely to be inappropriate for interpreting test scores of the minority group.

With each decision, the test user is ethically and morally responsible for ascertaining that the test instrument shows acceptable evidence of reliability and validity. In some cases, such as employment decisions in which there is discrimination against protected classes, test users might be held legally liable for improper test use. Test users rely on researchers and test publishers to provide full information about tests. Test publishers have a particular responsibility to prevent test misuse by making test manuals and validity information available and accessible *before* test users purchase their tests. Publishers should also refuse to provide test materials to persons who do not have testing credentials or who are likely to misuse the tests. Finally, psychologists in general have a responsibility to increase public awareness about the importance of test reliability and validity so that the public can understand the role that tests play in decisions that affect individuals' lives.

INTERIM SUMMARY 8.3
USING VALIDITY INFORMATION AND ETHICAL ISSUES

- When a relationship can be established between a test and a criterion, the test scores can be used to predict how well individuals are likely to perform on the criterion.
- Linear regression is used to make predictions from scores from one test.
- The slope b (the expected change in one unit of Y for every change in X) and the intercept a (the point where the regression line crosses the y-axis) are important for plotting a regression line.

- Multiple regression is used to make predictions about a single criteria from two or more different tests.
- Decisions based on test scores have far-reaching consequences, and test users should have evidence of validity to be sure that the test scores and their predictions will be accurate.
- When test takers are members of minorities, especially those who do not speak standard English as their primary language, test users must be aware of test bias and how it affects test validity.

Chapter Summary

Evidence of validity based on test-criteria relations—the extent to which a test is related to independent behavior or events—is one of the major methods for obtaining evidence of test validity. The usual method for demonstrating this evidence is to correlate scores on the test with a measure of the behavior we wish to predict. This measure of independent behavior or performance is called the criterion.

Evidence of validity based on test-criteria relations depends on evidence that the scores on the test correlate significantly with an independent criterion—a standard used to measure some characteristic of an individual, such as a person's performance, attitude, or motivation. Criteria may be objective or subjective, but they must be reliable and valid. There are two methods for demonstrating evidence of validity based on test-criteria relations: predictive and concurrent.

We use correlation to describe the relationship between a psychological test and a criterion. In this case, the correlation coefficient is referred to as the validity coefficient. Psychologists interpret validity coefficients using tests of significance and the coefficient of determination.

Either a linear regression equation or a multiple regression equation can be used to predict criterion scores from test scores. Predictions of success or failure on the criterion enable test users to use test scores for making decisions about hiring.

Finally, decisions based on test predictions have far-reaching consequences. Researchers, test developers, test publishers, and test users are ethically and morally responsible for ascertaining that any psychological test used for making predictions and decisions shows acceptable evidence of reliability and validity. Their responsibility also extends to guarding against test misuse and to increasing public awareness about the important role that tests play in test takers' lives.

Engaging in the Learning Process

KEY CONCEPTS

After completing your study of this chapter, you should be able to define each of the following terms. These terms are bolded in the text of this chapter and defined in the Glossary.

- beta
- coefficient of determination
- concurrent evidence of validity (concurrent method)
- criterion
- criterion contamination

- evidence of validity based on test-criteria relationships (criterion-related validity)
- intercept
- linear regression
- multiple regression
- objective criterion
- peers

- predictive evidence of validity (predictive method)
- restriction of range
- slope
- subjective criterion
- test of significance
- validity coefficient

LEARNING ACTIVITIES

The following are some learning activities you can engage in to support the learning objectives for this chapter.

Learning Objectives	Study Tips and Learning Activities
After completing your study of this chapter, you should be able to do the following:	The following study tips will help you meet these learning objectives:
Identify validity evidence of a test based on its relationships to external criteria (criterion-related validity), and describe two methods for obtaining this evidence.	• Make a chart of the similarities and differences between predictive and concurrent methods. • Be sure to include when the criterion is measured and its purpose.
Read and interpret validity studies.	• Do Additional Learning Activities 1, 2, and 3, which follow this table.
Discuss how restriction of range occurs and its consequences.	• Review For Your Information Box 8.2. • Explain the reasons why restriction of range may have occurred in this study.
Describe the differences between evidence of validity based on test-criteria relationships and evidence of validity based on test content.	• Make a chart of the similarities and differences. • Be sure to include the method of validation and method of statistical analysis.
Describe the difference between reliability and validity.	• List the differences between reliability and validity.
Define and give examples of objective and subjective criteria, and explain why criteria must be reliable and valid.	• Study Table 8.1. • See whether you can add other examples of objective and subjective criteria to the list. • Check your additions with a classmate or your instructor. • Do Additional Learning Activity 2, which follows this table.
Calculate a validity coefficient and the coefficient of determination, and then conduct a test of significance for the validity coefficient.	• Work through the example in For Your Information Box 8.5 to see how the test of significance works. • Consider the following: Would the correlation have been significant at $p < .001$? • Do Additional Learning Activities 3, 5, and 6, which follow this table.
Explain the concept of regression, calculate and interpret a linear regression formula, and interpret a multiple regression formula.	• Use your calculator to work through the example of making a prediction with linear regression in For Your Information Box 8.6. • Write a short essay that explains the difference between linear regression and multiple regression. • Do Additional Learning Activities 3 and 4, which follow this table.

ADDITIONAL LEARNING ACTIVITIES

1. *Interpreting Validity Studies.* Read the summarized published criterion-related validation studies below. For each summary, identify the following elements:

    (1) Predictor(s)
    (2) Criterion
    (3) Evidence of validity examined
    (4) Validity coefficient and its strength
    (5) Type of reliability
    (6) Reliability of the test scores (where given)

    a. *College Students' Recent Life Experiences.* Researchers administered to 216 undergraduate students (in the same time period) the Inventory of College Students' Experiences and a measure of daily hassles. The total coefficient alpha was .92 for the inventory and .96 for the measure of daily hassles. The inventory correlated with the measure of daily hassles at .76 ($p < .001$). (Adapted from Osman, Barrios, Longnecker, & Osman, 1994)

    b. *The Pilot Personality.* Test scores for the Eysenck Personality Inventory and Cattell's 16 Personality Factor Questionnaire were obtained for male army applicants for flyer training. Forms A and B were used for each test, and the correlations between forms for the same test ranged from .39 to .85. Some of the men entered flying school several years after taking the tests. The correlations of the subscales on the two tests with training outcome (pass or fail) averaged approximately .20. (Adapted from Bartram, 1995)

    c. *Computer Aptitude and Computer Anxiety.* Researchers gave 162 students enrolled in computer courses a test that measured computer anxiety and another test that measured computer aptitude. Both tests were given at the beginning of the course. Student performance in the course was measured by the grades the students earned in the course. Computer aptitude correlated with course grade at .41 ($p < .01$) for one course and at .13 (*ns*; note that *ns* stands for "not significant") for the other course. Correlations of computer anxiety and course grade were .01 and .16 (*ns*). (Adapted from Szajna, 1994)

2. *Objective and Subjective Criteria.* A number of criteria are listed in the table below. Decide what type of criterion each is, and mark either "Objective" or "Subjective" in the Type column. Discuss the advantages and disadvantages you think might be associated with using each of the criteria.

Criterion	Type
Ratings of training success	
Letters of reference	
Completion of a work sample (pass/fail)	
Ratings based on a work sample	
Annual salary	
Number of alcoholic drinks	
Self-ratings of drug use	
Course grade	
Number of weeks in therapy	
Therapist's estimate of weekly progress	

3. *Interpreting Statistics.* The following table contains symbols that stand for statistics used in validation studies. Identify each, and explain when to use it and what it means.

R	
r^2	
R^2	
Y'	
β	
X	
p	
df	

4. *A Case for Incremental Validity.* Return to the description of the study by Chibnall and Detrick (2003) described in the section on multiple regression. Reread the information about this study, including Tables 8.3 and 8.4, and then answer the following questions:

(1) What are the predictors and criteria for this study?
(2) What did the predictors have in common?
(3) What are the strengths and weaknesses of this study?
(4) Would you feel comfortable using the predictors in this study to select men and women for admission to a police academy? Why or why not?

5. *Testing the Significance of Validity Coefficients.* Complete the table below, and then express an opinion on whether each coefficient provides sufficient evidence of criterion-related validity. Test the coefficients using a two-tailed test with $p < .05$. If the degrees of freedom are not listed in the table, use the next lowest degrees of freedom listed.

Validity Coefficient	Size of Sample	df	Critical r From Appendix E	Significant at $p < .05$?	Coefficient of Determination
.23	40				
.43	10				
.33	50				
.22	1,000				
.50	6				

6. *Calculating a Validity Coefficient.* The following simulated data were collected when an organization tested job candidates before they were hired and then evaluated them using supervisor ratings after they had worked for six months. Calculate the validity coefficient for these data. What kind of evidence of validity does it represent? Now suppose that the company had not hired those who scored 60 or below on the employment test. What would the validity coefficient be for the six employees only? Can you explain why the validity coefficient changed?

Candidate	Employment Test	Supervisor Rating (1–5)
Abel	80	2
Bartmann	98	3
Cardoza	95	5
Dixon	55	3
Everett	70	2
Friedman	75	4
Grass	50	2
Hart	55	1
Isaacs	90	2
Jensen	60	1

PRACTICE QUESTIONS

The following are some practice questions to assess your understanding of the material presented in this chapter.

Multiple Choice

Choose the one best answer to each question.

1. When a test is used to predict future performance, there must be evidence of validity
   a. based on test taker's perceptions.
   b. based on test relationship with a criteria.
   c. using the predictive method.
   d. using the concurrent method.

2. Sarah conducted a study in which she correlated students' scores on the SAT taken in high school with students' grade point averages at the end of the first year of college. Her study was designed to find evidence of validity
   a. based on test content.
   b. using the concurrent method.
   c. based on test takers' perceptions.
   d. using the predictive method.

3. In the study at Brigham Young University, the researchers correlated scores on the PREParation for Marriage Questionnaire with measures of marital satisfaction and marital stability. In this study, the measures of marital satisfaction and marital stability were
   a. predictors.
   b. tests.
   c. criteria.
   d. coefficients.

4. One problem with studies of validity using the concurrent method is that there may be
   a. no evidence of validity based on test content.
   b. no criterion measure.
   c. restriction of range.
   d. low reliability.

5. Both the predictive method and the concurrent method are ways to establish evidence of
   a. validity based on test-criteria relationships.
   b. validity based on test content.
   c. validity based on the perceptions of the test takers.
   d. both validity and reliability.

6. A major difference between the predictive method and the concurrent method is the _____ the criterion is measured.
   a. place where
   b. people to whom
   c. time when
   d. format in which

7. _____ is a characteristic of the test itself; _____ depends on how the test is used.
   a. Reliability; validity
   b. Validity; reliability
   c. Face validity; content validity
   d. Content validity; face validity

8. Sharon wanted to show evidence of validity for a test that was designed to predict reading readiness for kindergarten children. She chose as her criterion the overall score on a published standardized test of academic performance that was administered to the children after they completed first grade. What is the problem with her criterion?
   a. Low reliability
   b. Low validity
   c. Low face validity
   d. Criterion contamination

9. When we ask the question, "What is the probability that our study would have yielded the validity coefficient we are evaluating by chance alone?" we are conducting a
   a. validation study.
   b. reliability study.
   c. test of significance.
   d. linear regression.

10. Which one of the following helps us interpret a validity coefficient by telling us how much variance the predictor and the criterion share?
    a. Reliability coefficient
    b. Test of significance
    c. Content validity ratio
    d. Coefficient of determination

11. The difference between linear regression and multiple regression is the number of
    a. predictors.
    b. criteria.
    c. coefficients of determination.
    d. participants.

12. What does the linear regression formula ($Y' = a + bX$) allow us to do?
    a. Predict the value of the criterion measure associated with any test score
    b. Calculate the predictive validity of a test
    c. Provide evidence of validity based on test content
    d. Estimate the accuracy of any test score

13. When using test scores for decision making, the test user is ethically and morally responsible for ascertaining that the test shows acceptable evidence of
    a. the use of both predictive and concurrent studies.
    b. face validity and test taker acceptance.
    c. reliability and validity.
    d. reliability and face validity.

14. Who has the responsibility for preventing test misuse by making test manuals and validity information available before purchase?
    a. Test users
    b. Test takers
    c. Test publishers
    d. Test developers

15. When assessing groups that include minorities, it is preferable for the test user to
    a. always refuse to test minorities with standardized tests.
    b. not allow minority job candidates to participate in employment testing.
    c. use tests that have norms that include the minority groups being tested.
    d. warn minorities that their scores on the test may be invalid or uninterpretable.

Short Answer/Essay

Read each of the following, and consider your response carefully based on the information presented in this chapter. Write your answer to each question in two or three paragraphs.

1. What is meant by evidence of validity based on test-criteria relationships? Describe two research methods for obtaining it.

2. What is the difference between evidence of validity based on test content and evidence of validity based on test-criteria relationships? Give examples.

3. What are some challenges that organizations face when seeking to obtain predictive evidence of validity for a test?

4. Why is it important to evaluate the quality of the criterion when gathering evidence of validity of a test using the concurrent method?

5. What is the difference between reliability and validity? Give an example.

6. Discuss the difference between objective criteria and subjective criteria. Give examples of each.

7. Why do we conduct tests of significance and calculate the coefficient of determination? Explain the role of each.

8. What is the relation between correlation and linear regression? How does the process of linear regression help us make predictions?

9. Discuss ethical issues that arise when assessing test takers with diverse cultures, primary languages, races, and/or religions.

ANSWER KEYS

Additional Learning Activities

1. Interpreting Validity Studies

Exercise	(1) Predictor	(2) Criterion	(3) Validity Study Method Used	(4) Validity Coefficient	(5) Type of Reliability	(6) Reliability Coefficient
A	Inventory of college students' experiences	Measure of daily hassles	Concurrent	Strong .76 ($p < .001$)	Internal consistency, coefficient alpha	Inventory = .92; daily hassles = .96
B	Eysenck Personality Inventory and 16 Personality Factor Questionnaire	Training outcome (pass/fail)	Predictive	Very weak; average of coefficients approximately .20	Test–retest	Ranges between .39 and .85
C	Computer anxiety and computer aptitude tests	Course grades	Predictive	Computer aptitude = .41 ($p < .01$; moderate) and .13 (ns); Computer anxiety = .01 and .16 (ns)	Not given	Not given

2. Objective and Subjective Criteria

Criterion	Type
Ratings of training success	Subjective
Letters of reference	Subjective
Completion of a work sample (pass/fail)	Objective
Ratings based on a work sample	Subjective
Annual salary	Objective
Number of alcoholic drinks	Objective
Self-ratings of drug use	Subjective
Course grade	Subjective
Number of weeks in therapy	Objective
Therapist's estimate of weekly progress	Subjective

3. Interpreting Statistics

R	Multiple regression coefficient
r^2	Coefficient of determination for linear relationship
R^2	Coefficient of determination for multiple regression coefficient
Y	The number on the y axis that a linear regression coefficient predicts
β	Beta for multiple regression equation
X	Raw score
p	Probability
df	Degrees of freedom

4. A Case for Incremental Validity

The predictors in the Chibnall and Detrick (2003) study were the Minnesota Multiphasic Personality Inventory-2, the Inwald Personality Inventory, and the Revised NEO Personality Inventory, and the criteria were the academic performance of police officers. The information in the tables describes the prediction of the first criterion, namely, academic performance.

At first glance, the predictors are well-known personality tests. From the data in Table 8.3, we can tell that the predictors share variance among themselves and with the predictor. We know this because the contributions of the predictors vary depending on how they are arranged in the multiple regression equation.

The study's strength is that the researchers used well-known predictors with evidence of validity. The study's weaknesses are that the sample contained only 79 participants and that the study, as reported in this textbook, does not provide information on reliability and evidence of validity of the criteria.

However, we would be comfortable using the predictors in this study to select men and women for a police academy in the area in which the study was conducted. The study suggests that the three predictors and demographic variables account for 55% of variance of the predictors and the criterion—assuming the criterion scores are reliable.

5. Testing the Significance of Validity Coefficients

Validity	Size of Sample	df	Critical r From Appendix D	Significant at $p < .05$?	Coefficient of Determination
.23	37	35	.3246	No	.0529
.43	10	8	.6319	No	.1849
.33	52	50	.2732	Yes	.1089
.22	1,000	998	.1946	Yes	.0484
.50	6	4	.8114	No	.2500

The best evidence of validity is when the coefficient is statistically significant and also accounts for a substantial amount of shared variance. In this case, $r = .33$ for a sample of 52 provides the best evidence of criterion-related validity.

6. Calculating a Validity Coefficient

Test Taker	X	Y	D_x	D_x^2	D_y	D_y^2	$D_x \times D_y$
Abel	80	2	7.2	51.84	−0.5	0.25	−3.6
Bartmann	98	3	25.2	635.04	0.5	0.25	12.6
Cardoza	95	5	22.2	492.84	2.5	6.25	55.5
Dixon	55	3	−17.8	316.84	0.5	0.25	−8.9
Everett	70	2	−2.8	7.84	−0.5	0.25	1.4
Friedman	75	4	2.2	4.84	1.5	2.25	3.3
Grass	50	2	−22.8	519.84	−0.5	0.25	11.4
Hart	55	1	−17.8	316.84	−1.5	2.25	26.7
Isaacs	90	2	17.2	295.84	−0.5	0.25	−8.6
Jensen	60	1	−12.8	163.84	−1.5	2.25	19.2
Sum	728	25		2805.60		14.50	109.0
Mean	72.8	2.5					
Standard deviation (calculated using the formula presented in Chapter 5)	16.75	1.20					
r	.54						
Abel	80	2	−4.67	21.78	−1.00	1.00	4.67
Bartmann	98	3	13.33	177.78	0.00	0.00	0.00
Cardoza	95	5	10.33	106.78	2.00	4.00	20.67
Everett	70	2	−14.67	215.11	−1.00	1.00	14.67
Friedman	75	4	−9.67	93.44	1.00	1.00	−9.67
Isaacs	90	2	5.33	28.44	−1.00	1.00	−5.33
Sum	508	18		643.33		8	25
Mean	84.67	3.00					
Standard deviation (calculated using the formula presented in Chapter 5)	10.35	1.15					
r	.35						

The validity coefficient changed because of restriction of range.

Multiple Choice

1. c	2. d	3. c	4. c	5. a
6. c	7. a	8. d	9. c	10. d
11. a	12. a	13. c	14. c	15. c

Short Answer/Essay

Refer to your textbook for answers. If you are unsure of an answer and cannot generate the answer after reviewing your book, ask your professor for clarification.

How Do We Gather Evidence of Validity Based on a Test's Relationship With Constructs?

CHAPTER 9: HOW DO WE GATHER EVIDENCE OF VALIDITY BASED ON A TEST'S RELATIONSHIP WITH CONSTRUCTS?

After completing your study of this chapter, you should be able to do the following:

- Discuss the concept of a construct, and give examples of theoretical constructs.
- Explain how the current *Standards for Educational and Psychological Testing* (American Educational Research Association [AERA], American Psychological Association [APA], & National Council on Measurement in Education [NCME], 1999) treatment of constructs in testing differs from the more traditional usage of the term *construct validity*.
- Explain and give examples of the three steps of construct explication.
- Explain the process of establishing evidence of validity based on a test's relationship with other constructs.
- Explain how Campbell and Fiske's Multitrait–Multimethod Matrix provides evidence of validity based on a test's relationship with other constructs.
- Discuss the roles of confirmatory and exploratory factor analysis in establishing validity.

"What does it mean when a person has a dependency on alcohol? Does it mean they drink every day? Or when they drink they get very drunk? Do you have to lose your job, your house, and your family to be classified as an alcoholic?"

"My professor says that spanking can be classified as child abuse. I disagree! Child abusers are people who torture children and use them for their sexual pleasure. Discipline is something else!"

"My eight-year-old has an IQ of 130. She makes good grades, but sometimes she says and does really silly things. I thought she was supposed to be smart!"

Another chapter on validity? How many kinds of validity can there be? As you remember from Chapters 7 and 8, psychologists now think of validity as a single concept that can be demonstrated using various kinds of evidence. Evidence of validity may be drawn from a relationship of test scores with test content or from the relationship of test scores with other variables. So it is really not correct to speak of multiple types of validity, only different sources of *evidence* of validity.

So why do we need a chapter on validity based on the relationship of test scores with constructs when we already devoted a chapter to evidence of validity based on a test's relationship to other variables, specifically external criteria? To understand that, we first need to review what a construct is.

In Chapter 7 we told you that a construct is an attribute, trait, or characteristic that in itself is not directly observable, but can only be inferred by looking at observable behaviors, which are hypothesized to indicate the presence of that construct. For example, we never really observe the construct of aggression, but we do observe behaviors that would lead us to conclude that a person might be demonstrating the construct of aggression. Likewise, if a test were designed to measure the construct of aggression, it might have questions relating to the frequency and intensity of these aggressive behaviors. Then a score on this test would be interpreted as indicating the test takers' standing on this hypothetical construct called aggression. The question of validity of this test then becomes a question of whether there is evidence that this inference is valid. Traditionally, this type of evidence was referred to as an indication that the test possessed **construct validity.**

We have already discussed a number of ways in which this evidence can be collected. But because the current *Standards for Educational and Psychological Testing* (AERA, APA, & NCME, 1999) views all tests as a measure of one or more constructs, all the evidence of validity of a test is simply a demonstration that the test is measuring those constructs. So current thinking is that the traditional term *construct validity* is just another way of saying validity.

The methods previously described for gathering evidence of validity, particularly evidence of validity based on response processes and relations with other variables, are the types of evidence that were used to establish what was traditionally called construct validity. So why would we still have this chapter in our textbook? Because the ideas underlying the concept of constructs are crucially important to psychologists, even if our definitions have changed. Various tests designed to measure the same construct all ought to be measuring similar things, and we need to understand how we gather evidence for validity regardless of our terminology. Therefore, we take a more traditional approach to describing the role that psychological constructs play in testing, with the understanding that when we use the term *construct validity*, we are using it for convenience and do not mean to imply that it is a separate type of validity.

This chapter defines and illustrates the terms *psychological construct, theory,* and *nomological network.* Because establishing evidence of construct validity involves accumulating and relating all of the psychometric information known about a test, we show how familiar concepts, such as reliability, evidence of validity based on test content, and evidence of validity based on a test's relationships with other variables, are linked together. In addition, we discuss how convergent evidence of validity and discriminant evidence of validity are two other strategies used for establishing validity based on a test's relationships with other variables. This evidence focuses on the constructs that a test is designed to measure as opposed to the test's relationship to an external criterion. Finally, we discuss experimental methods used to establish evidence of construct validity for a test, including two procedures: confirmatory factor analysis and exploratory factor analysis.

Construct Validity

Prior to 1954, psychologists had gathered evidence of the validity of tests by pursuing two of the methods we discussed in Chapters 7 and 8: validity based on test content and validity based on a test's relationship to external criteria. A number of theorists, however, challenged these strategies because this evidence of validity did not link the testing instrument to an accepted theory of psychological behavior (Rogers, 1995). In 1954, the APA published recommendations that established a new method for establishing validity in which the researcher provides evidence that the testing instrument measures behavior predicted by a psychological theory. The APA (1954) called this evidence *construct validity* and defined it as the extent to which the test measures a theoretical construct. The process of establishing construct validity for a test is a gradual accumulation of evidence that the scores on the test relate to observable behaviors in the ways predicted by the underlying theory.

The process of establishing evidence of construct validity implies one important consideration pointed out by Cronbach and Meehl (1955): When test users accept evidence of construct validity, they must accept the underlying definition of the construct used in the validation process. In other words, test users accept the definition of the construct used by those who developed and validated the test.

At first glance, this consideration does not seem to be a problem. Recall, however, that definitions of a construct may vary from theorist to theorist. An example of this variation is the numerous definitions given to the construct of intelligence. Who is highly intelligent? Is it someone who always receives perfect grades? Is it someone who is highly creative and farsighted? Is it someone who is perfectly rational and logical? Is it someone who displays knowledge and skills greater than those displayed by others of the same chronological age? Is intelligence inherited? Is it a series of learned behaviors? Is it a combination of some or all of these traits? As you can see, choosing a test to measure intelligence means choosing a test that matches your definition of intelligence. Without this consideration, the test scores would be confusing or meaningless.

What Is a Construct?

Before discussing how to establish evidence of construct validity, we need to define what we mean by a theoretical or psychological construct. As you recall from Chapter 7, psychologists gain their understanding of people and other organisms by focusing their attention on concrete and abstract constructs. **Behaviors**—actions that are observable and measurable—are concrete constructs. Underlying attitudes or attributes that exist in our imaginations are abstract constructs. Intelligence, beauty, love, and self-esteem all are psychological constructs, but your instructor cannot bring a bucket of intelligence or a big box of self-esteem to class. These constructs exist in theory. We cannot observe or measure them directly. They are hypothetical.

We can, however, observe and measure the behaviors that show evidence of these constructs. Psychological theories propose the presence of constructs, such as intelligence, beauty, love, and self-esteem, and make predictions about behaviors that are related to them. By observing and measuring those behaviors, we assume that we have measured the abstract construct. As an example of this process, Murphy and Davidshofer (1994) use the theoretical construct of gravity. Before Isaac Newton, the notion of gravity did not exist. Newton theorized that apples fall to the earth because of a concept he called *gravity*. We cannot see gravity, but we see what we assume to be its result—falling apples!

As you can see from the statements at the beginning of this chapter, definitions of constructs can vary from person to person. Many times the definitions that professionals use for constructs such as alcoholism, child abuse, and intelligence differ from those used by the general population. Psychologists even disagree among themselves, so they must clearly define constructs before they can measure them. To illustrate this process in terms of testing, let's consider an abstract construct proposed by Albert Bandura, a well-known cognitive psychologist. Bandura (1977) suggests the existence of a construct he calls *self-efficacy*—a person's expectations and beliefs about his or her own competence and ability to accomplish an activity or a task. He proposes that "expectations of personal efficacy determine whether coping behavior will be initiated, how much effort will be expended, and how long it will be sustained in the face of obstacles and aversive experiences" (p. 191).

Figure 9.1 illustrates Bandura's theory of self-efficacy. People form their opinions about their own self-efficacy from their own performance accomplishments, their experience from watching others perform (vicarious experience), the messages they receive from others about their performance (verbal persuasion), and their emotional arousal. Mode of Induction in the model shows the various ways a person receives information. The test developer can use this model as a test plan for constructing an instrument that measures self-efficacy. For instance, the instrument may ask test takers questions about their experience with each source of information.

Figure 9.1	Illustration of Bandura's Theory of Self-Efficacy

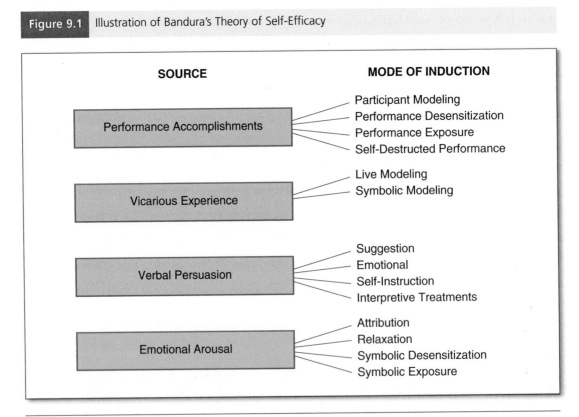

SOURCE: From Bandura, A. (1977). Self-efficacy: Toward a unifying theory of behavioral change. *Psychological Review, 84,* 191–215. Copyright © 1977 by the American Psychological Association.

Since Bandura published his self-efficacy theory, researchers have developed numerous tests that measure general self-efficacy—individuals' expectations of competency and resulting coping behaviors and extended effort in general (Lee & Bobko, 1994; Sherer et al., 1982; Tipton & Worthington, 1984). In addition to general measures, researchers have developed tests that measure self-efficacy for specific tasks such as mathematics (Pajares & Miller, 1995), computer skills (Murphy, Coover, & Owen, 1989), social interactions (Wheeler & Ladd, 1982), and career choice (Betz & Hackett, 1986), to name only a few.

Most research using tests of self-efficacy have borne out Bandura's predictions about coping behavior (Bandura, Barbaranelli, Caprara, & Pastorelli, 1996). In addition, researchers have found self-efficacy to be a good predictor of performance (Sharpley & Ridgway, 1993; Tam, 1996; Weinberg, Gould, & Jackson, 1979).

 See Test Spotlight 9.1 in Appendix A for more detail about the Mathematics Self-Efficacy Scale.

Construct Explication

Measurement of an abstract construct depends on our ability to observe and measure related behavior. Murphy and Davidshofer (1994) describe three steps for defining or explaining a psychological construct, referred to as **construct explication:**

1. Identify the behaviors that relate to the construct.

2. Identify other constructs that may be related to the construct being explained.

3. Identify behaviors related to similar constructs, and determine whether these behaviors are related to the original construct.

A construct validation study of the Self-Efficacy Scale conducted by Mark Sherer and colleagues (1982) illustrates these principles of construct explication. These researchers were interested in validating a scale that measures self-efficacy. They reviewed the research of Bandura and others and determined that positive correlations exist between therapeutic changes in behaviors and changes in self-efficacy. In other words, as an individual's self-efficacy increases, the individual's behavior in treatment is likely to improve as well (Step 1). Sherer and colleagues also noted that past performance or expectations are related to self-efficacy (Step 2). In addition, individuals who have experienced numerous successes in the past are likely to have developed high self-efficacy, as demonstrated by their persistence in pursuing goals with which they have limited experience (Step 3). Figure 9.2 provides a model of this explication process.

As theorists identify more constructs and behaviors that are interrelated, they construct what Cronbach and Meehl (1955) refer to as a **nomological network**—a method for defining a construct by illustrating its relation to as many other constructs and behaviors as possible. (Cronbach [1988] later amended his earlier vision of a nomological network, noting that actually identifying a complex model of associations for a construct had proved to be difficult in practice.) However, a listing of a particular construct's relations and nonrelations with other constructs and tests can provide a number of **hypotheses**—educated guesses or predictions—about the behaviors that people who have small or large quantities of the construct should display. For instance, based on the research on self-efficacy, we expect people with high self-efficacy to express positive attitudes regarding their own competence and to display persistence in accomplishing new and difficult tasks. Establishing evidence of construct validity, then, is the process of testing the predictions made by that model.

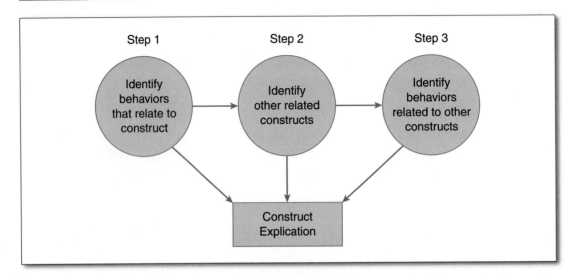

Figure 9.2 The Process of Construct Explication

Gathering Evidence of Construct Validity

To understand the process of establishing evidence of construct validity, we apply the scientific method for testing the hypotheses proposed by theories. We can divide this process into two parts: gathering theoretical evidence and gathering psychometric evidence. Figure 9.3 provides an overview of this methodology.

Gathering Theoretical Evidence

The first step in the validation process is establishing a listing of associations the construct has with other constructs. As we illustrated with the example of self-efficacy, researchers seek to find relationships with other constructs. They then review as many studies of the construct as possible to establish the construct's relation with observable and measurable behaviors. Establishing evidence of construct validity requires a thorough understanding of the construct in question, and there is no substitute for careful

| Figure 9.3 | Methodology for Establishing Construct Validity |

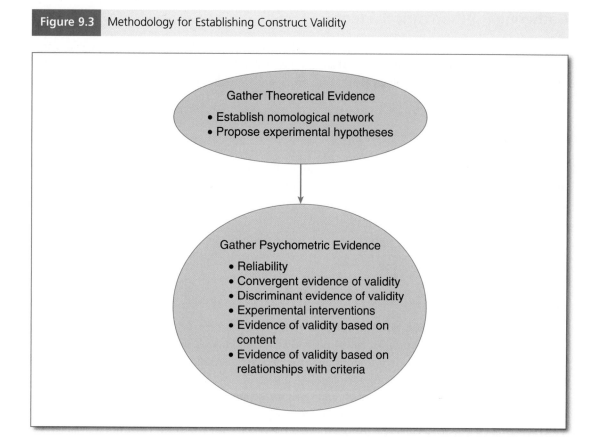

reading of all available literature—both theoretical observations and empirical studies. Researchers then develop a model of the construct that links it to other constructs and observable behaviors.

Second, researchers propose one or more experimental hypotheses using the test as an instrument for measuring the construct. If the test is a true or valid measure of the construct, scores on the test should perform in accordance with the predictions made for the construct.

Let's return to the validation of the Self-Efficacy Scale (Sherer et al., 1982) to examine how this process works. A review of theoretical and empirical studies of self-efficacy revealed that self-efficacy is linked to a number of personality characteristics: locus of control, social desirability, ego strength, interpersonal competency, and self-esteem. Sherer and colleagues hypothesized that scores on the Self-Efficacy Scale would be significantly correlated with personality tests measuring each of these constructs but that the correlation would not be strong enough to suggest that the scales were measuring exactly the same construct. Consequently, the researchers designed a study to test this hypothesis.

Note that Sherer and colleagues (1982) proposed a specific hypothesis based on the accepted definition of self-efficacy and the nomological network they constructed. According to Cronbach (1988, 1989), the preferred method for establishing evidence of construct validity is to propose a hypothesis based on the nomological network and to test it. He referred to the alternative as *dragnet empiricism*, which involves collecting evidence based on convenience rather than a specific hypothesis. Dragnet empiricism, as you probably realize, is not an acceptable way to establish evidence of construct validity.

Gathering Psychometric Evidence

As you recall, establishing evidence of construct validity for a test involves an ongoing process of gathering evidence that the scores on the test relate to observable behaviors in the ways predicted by the underlying theory and the nomological network. There are a number of ways to establish quantitative evidence to suggest that the test has construct validity.

Reliability

As you recall from Chapter 6, reliability is an essential characteristic for a psychological test. Evidence of test–retest reliability is important; otherwise, the test scores may correspond to theoretical predictions one time but might not do so again. In addition, the theory underlying psychological testing suggests that a test cannot have a stronger correlation with any other variable than it does with itself, and therefore we can use estimates of reliability to evaluate the strength of correlations with other variables that are related to the theoretical construct.

Convergent Evidence of Validity

If the test is measuring a particular construct, we expect the scores on the test to correlate strongly with scores on other tests that measure the same or similar constructs. This correlation provides us with **convergent evidence of validity.** For example, researchers have developed a number of tests to measure general self-efficacy as well as self-efficacy related to a specific task. We would expect two measures of general self-efficacy to yield strong, positive, and statistically significant correlations. They may also correlate with scores from task-specific tests, but not to as great an extent.

This concept always raises a very good question: If there is already a test that measures the construct, why develop another one? A test author might develop another test to create parallel forms, create a test for specific populations (for example, children, people who speak another language), revise the test to increase reliability and validity, reproduce the test in another format (for example, for administration by computer or in a shortened version), or develop a test that represents an altered definition of the underlying construct. In each of these cases, the original test and the new test would yield different scores, but we would expect the two sets of scores to correlate strongly.

If the test scores correlate with measures of constructs that the underlying theory says are related, we would also describe those correlations as convergent evidence of validity. For example, Bandura's (1977) theory of self-efficacy suggests that self-efficacy is related to measures of competency. Sherer and colleagues (1982) administered their measure of self-efficacy and a measure of interpersonal competency to 376 students and found a moderate correlation ($r = .45$) between the two tests. This correlation coefficient or validity coefficient describes the extent of convergent evidence of validity for their measure of general self-efficacy.

Sometimes students confuse *convergent evidence of validity* with the *concurrent method of gathering evidence of validity.* Convergent evidence of validity is gathered when a researcher reviews the literature for other tests that claim to measure constructs that are the same as, or similar to, the construct in which the researcher is interested. If the tests are given to the same group of people and there is a significant correlation between the scores, then convergent evidence of validity has been demonstrated. On the other hand, the concurrent method is a strategy for establishing validity evidence based on the correlation that the test scores have with a specific external criterion measure gathered around the same time that the test is administered. Criteria, as you recall, are objective or subjective measures of behavior, such as job performance ratings, course grades, and results of interviews.

Discriminant Evidence of Validity

Just as we would expect some tests to correlate with our new tests, there are other tests we would *not* expect to correlate with our test. When the test scores do not correlate with unrelated constructs, we can say that the test is demonstrating **discriminant evidence of validity.** For example, a test that measures skill at performing numerical calculations would not be expected to correlate with a test that measures reading comprehension. If the correlation between the numerical calculations test and a test of reading comprehension is zero (or not statistically significant), there is discriminant evidence of validity for the numerical calculations test.

Coombs and Holladay (2004), test authors researching a new test, the Workplace Aggression Tolerance Questionnaire—which assesses workplace aggression behaviors such as physical and verbal, active and passive, and direct and indirect forms of aggression—correlated the test with the Marlowe–Crowne Social Desirability Scale, which measures a person's need for being perceived favorably. They found a weak relationship ($r = -.18$, $p < .01$) between aggressive behaviors and wishing to be perceived favorably. The researchers presented this weak relationship as discriminant evidence of validity because it is not likely that aggressive persons are worried about being perceived favorably by others. (We discuss the Marlowe–Crown Social Desirability Scale in detail in Chapter 11.)

Multitrait–Multimethod Design

Campbell and Fiske (1959) cleverly combined the need to collect evidence of reliability, convergent evidence of validity, and discriminant evidence of validity into one study. They called it the **multitrait–multimethod design** for investigating construct validity. Using this approach, investigators test for "*convergence* across *different* measures . . . of the same 'thing' . . . and for *divergence* between measures . . . of related but conceptually distinct 'things'" (Cook & Campbell, 1979, p. 61). In other words, the researcher chooses two or more constructs that are unrelated in theory and two or more types of tests—such as objective, projective, and a peer rating—to measure each of the constructs. Data are collected on each participant in the study on each construct using each method. Figure 9.4 shows a multitrait–multimethod correlation matrix from Campbell and Fiske's article.

In a **correlation matrix,** the same tests and measures are listed in the horizontal and vertical headings, and correlations are in the body of the table. The correlation coefficient for two tests appears at the place where the row for one test and the column for the other test intersect. In the multitrait–multimethod correlation matrix in Figure 9.4, three methods are used for measuring each of three constructs (A, B, and C) and are listed horizontally across the top of the matrix and vertically in the first column. The reliability estimate for each measure is shown in parentheses in the diagonal. The correlation coefficients arranged diagonally between the broken-line triangles represent convergent validity coefficients—correlations between tests that measure the same construct but have different methods or formats. The triangles in solid lines are correlations of different tests that have the same format or method of measurement. These correlations provide an estimate of method bias that may be associated with the method or format of the test. This is because tests of different attributes may appear to be more related than they actually are simply because they both used the same method of

| Figure 9.4 | A Multitrait–Multimethod Correlation Matrix |

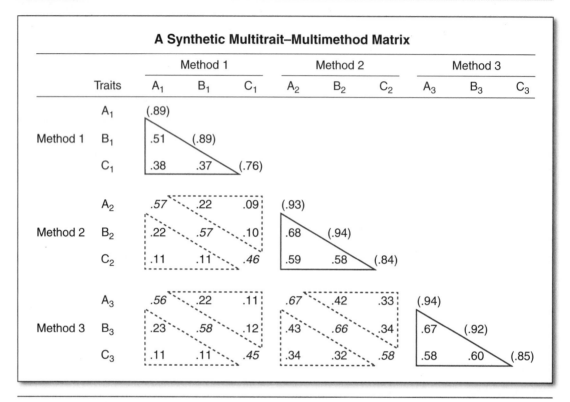

A Synthetic Multitrait–Multimethod Matrix

	Traits	Method 1			Method 2			Method 3		
		A_1	B_1	C_1	A_2	B_2	C_2	A_3	B_3	C_3
Method 1	A_1	(.89)								
	B_1	.51	(.89)							
	C_1	.38	.37	(.76)						
Method 2	A_2	.57	.22	.09	(.93)					
	B_2	.22	.57	.10	.68	(.94)				
	C_2	.11	.11	.46	.59	.58	(.84)			
Method 3	A_3	.56	.22	.11	.67	.42	.33	(.94)		
	B_3	.23	.58	.12	.43	.66	.34	.67	(.92)	
	C_3	.11	.11	.45	.34	.32	.58	.58	.60	(.85)

SOURCE: Adapted from Campbell, D. T., & Fiske, D. W. (1959). Convergent and discriminant validity by the multitrait–multimethod matrix. *Psychological Bulletin, 56,* 81–105, p. 82.

NOTE: The validity diagonals are the three sets of italicized values. The reliability diagonals are the three sets of values in parentheses. Each heterotrait–monomethod triangle is enclosed by a solid line. Each heterotrait–heteromethod triangle is enclosed by a broken line.

measurement (for example, paper and pencil) or format (for example, they both are given via the computer). The triangles shown in broken lines are estimates of discriminant validity or correlations of tests using different methods and measuring different constructs.

Following is a list of the coefficients in the multitrait–multimethod correlation matrix in Figure 9.4 along with explanations of how to interpret them.

- *Coefficients in parentheses:* We would inspect the coefficients in the diagonal in which the reliability of the test (how well the test correlates with itself) appears. If we simply correlate the test scores with themselves, the correlation coefficient would be +1.00. However, with this method the researcher inserts the reliability coefficient into the matrix.
- *Coefficients in the triangles with solid lines:* We would examine the coefficients for tests with different formats (methods) measuring the same construct because they represent convergent evidence of validity.

- *Coefficients in the triangles with broken lines.* Likewise, we would inspect the coefficients for tests with different formats measuring different constructs because they represent discriminant evidence of validity. We would expect the correlations to be weak or not statistically significant.

The correlations of tests with the same format measuring different constructs represent measures of bias associated with the format of the test. In other words, a certain format (for example, projective tests) might elicit similar responses from test takers regardless of the construct being measured. When these correlations are found to be weak or not statistically significant, we can assume there is little or no bias due to the type of test.

Experimental Interventions

Experimental interventions in which the test is used as an independent variable or a dependent variable make a substantial contribution to the argument for evidence of construct validity. If the underlying theory predicts that a course of treatment or training will increase or decrease the psychological construct, a significant difference between pretest scores and posttest scores would be evidence of construct validity for the test used to measure the construct. For example, if a clinician conducted a 12-week course of treatment intended to raise the participants' self-efficacy, she might administer Sherer and colleagues' (1982) Self-Efficacy Scale, along with other reliable and valid measures of self-efficacy, to participants at the beginning of treatment and at the end of treatment. If the other measures indicated that the treatment successfully raised individual participants' perceptions of self-efficacy and the Self-Efficacy Scale showed comparable results, we could say that the study provided evidence of construct validity for the Self-Efficacy Scale.

Another study that provides evidence of construct validity for a test would be one that verifies a prediction that group membership affects the construct. For instance, if the underlying theory predicts that one group will have higher or lower mean test scores than another group and the data yield such a result, the study provides evidence of construct validity.

For example, researchers administered the Counselor Self-Efficacy Scale (CSES) to 138 participants who were either students enrolled in graduate counseling courses or licensed professional psychologists (Melchert, Hays, Wiljanen, & Kolocek, 1996). Because Bandura's theory states that experience with a particular activity is likely to raise self-efficacy for that activity, the researchers hypothesized that those who had higher levels of training and experience would score higher on the CSES. Their data yielded four groups—first-year master's students, second-year master's students, post-master's doctoral students, and professional psychologists—who were differentiated by scores on the CSES that increased as levels of training and experience increased. These data provide evidence of construct validity for the CSES.

Evidence of Validity Based on Content

As you recall from Chapter 6, a test demonstrates evidence of validity based on its content when its questions are a representative sample of a well-defined test domain. This type of evidence is usually the appropriate approach for math, reading, or other test domains with known boundaries. Because psychological constructs exist primarily in our imaginations and are not observable, it is more difficult to define a test domain well enough to construct a test that contains a representative sample from the construct. In some cases, however, psychological constructs do lend themselves to content validation, and when evidence of validity based on content can be provided, it greatly strengthens the case for construct validity.

Cronbach (1989) distinguishes between content-based evidence and construct-based evidence of validity in this way:

> Content validation stops with a demonstration that the test conforms to a specification; however, the claim that the specification is well chosen embodies a CV [construct validity] claim. . . . Any interpretation invokes constructs if it reaches beyond the specific, local, concrete situation that was observed. (p. 151)

Bandura's (1977) construct of self-efficacy is one that lends itself to content-based evidence of validity because it specifies four sources of self-efficacy: performance accomplishments, vicarious experience, verbal persuasion, and emotional arousal. To develop a test plan for an instrument that measures self-efficacy, the test developer would stipulate that an equal number of questions would represent a connection to each source of self-efficacy (Fritzsche & McIntire, 1997). Showing that the test questions do indeed reflect the four sources of self-efficacy, however, is a matter of construct validity. Such information, in addition to evidence of reliability, convergent evidence of validity, and discriminant evidence of validity, substantially strengthens the argument that the test measures the theoretical construct and thus has construct validity.

Evidence of Validity Based on Relationships With External Criteria

Likewise, although evidence of validity based on a test's relationship with external criteria relies solely on the statistical relationship between the test and that criterion, it too can provide evidence of construct validity. If the underlying theory predicts that a psychological construct is related to observable behaviors, such as job performance or a cluster of behaviors that denote a mental disorder, evidence of that relationship adds to the evidence of construct validity as well. In other words, when an underlying theory *explains* the relation between a predictor and a criterion, there is evidence of construct validity.

There are numerous examples of this validation strategy for tests of self-efficacy. Bandura's (1977) theory predicts that persons who have high self-efficacy will perform better than persons with low self-efficacy, and many validation studies of measures of self-efficacy include evidence of validity based on this relationship as well as convergent evidence of validity and reliability. For instance, Sherer and colleagues (1982), in addition to demonstrating convergent evidence of validity for their measure of general self-efficacy, demonstrated criterion-based evidence of validity by finding significant correlations between self-efficacy scores (predictor) and current employment, number of jobs quit, and number of times fired (criteria). Because Bandura's theory predicts these relationships, evidence of criterion-related validity strengthens the argument that the instrument is construct valid.

Multiple Studies

Because gathering evidence of construct validity is an ongoing process, the argument that a test is construct valid is strengthened when the test demonstrates one or all of these characteristics in a number of studies conducted on different samples of participants by different researchers. Cross-referencing of such studies suggests that individual studies were not unduly affected by biases related to the experimenter or to special characteristics of the sample, and therefore test users can conclude that the test faithfully represents and measures the underlying construct.

INTERIM SUMMARY 9.2
GATHERING EVIDENCE OF CONSTRUCT VALIDITY

- We gather theoretical evidence by establishing a nomological network and proposing experimental hypotheses using the test to measure the construct.
- We gather psychometric evidence of construct validity by conducting empirical studies of the following:
  - *Reliability:* Test developers and researchers should provide evidence of internal consistency or homogeneity. Evidence of test–retest reliability is also appropriate.
  - *Convergent evidence of validity:* A strong correlation between the test and other tests measuring the same or similar constructs is necessary.
  - *Discriminant evidence of validity:* Lack of a correlation between the test and unrelated constructs is also valuable.
- Designing a study that yields a multitrait–multimethod matrix of data is an elegant way to demonstrate the first three of these strategies: reliability, convergent evidence of validity, and discriminant evidence of validity.
- Experimental interventions in which the test is used as an independent or dependent variable make a substantial contribution to the argument for evidence of construct validity.
- Evidence of validity based on content and relationships with external criteria, when available and appropriate, strengthens the argument for construct validity.

Factor Analysis

Over the past two decades, the introduction and availability of computer software to psychological researchers and test developers has allowed them to broaden studies of the constructs that tests are measuring by identifying the **factors**—the underlying concepts or constructs that the tests or groups of test questions are measuring. To investigate underlying aspects of constructs, researchers use a statistical technique called **factor analysis**—an advanced procedure based on the concept of correlation that helps investigators explain why two tests are correlated (Murphy & Davidshofer, 1994). For Your Information Box 9.1 provides a brief overview of the statistical procedure of factor analysis.

Confirmatory Factor Analysis

Using factor analysis, researchers and test developers consider the theory associated with a test and propose a set of underlying factors that they expect the test to contain. Then they conduct a factor analysis procedure to see whether the factors they proposed do indeed exist. Such a study is called a **confirmatory factor analysis** and provides an excellent method for obtaining evidence of construct validity.

F Y I

FOR YOUR INFORMATION BOX 9.1

Factor Analysis

Factor analysis is a statistical procedure that can be used to identify whether the pattern of responses to all the questions on a test can be more simply explained by referring to a smaller number of underlying constructs, or factors. For instance, the pattern of individual responses on a test that contains 200 arithmetic questions might be explainable based on a person's standing on four underlying constructs—addition, subtraction, multiplication, and division. Not all measures have multiple underlying factors. Some measures are referred to as unidimensional because there is only a single underlying factor that can explain most of the variance in test scores. In our arithmetic test example, it is also possible that there might be only a single factor that can explain the pattern of results on the individual questions—general mathematical ability. In other words, unidimensional constructs are homogeneous. On the other hand, other measures may be multidimensional in nature because there is more than one underlying factor that explains most of the variance in test scores. These measures are sometimes referred to as heterogeneous.

Although early researchers calculated factor analyses by hand laboriously or with the help of calculators, we can now conduct factor analyses using statistical software such as SPSS, SAS, and LISREL. The researcher enters a matrix of raw data (usually individual answers to test questions), and the software program calculates a correlation matrix of all variables or test questions. The software program then uses the correlation matrix to calculate a factor solution based on each test question's relationship to the other test questions. Factors are formed by finding groups of questions that are more correlated with each other than they are with other questions on the test. For instance, if we had a test that contained both reading and arithmetic questions, we might expect it to produce two factors—one for the verbal factor (as represented by the reading questions) and one for the mathematical factor (as represented by the arithmetic questions). This is because we would expect that each person's answers to the arithmetic questions would be more correlated with their answers to other arithmetic questions than with their answers to the reading questions. As the test questions group together, they form factors—underlying dimensions that measure the same trait or attribute. The researcher then examines which test questions group together to form each factor and uses this information to provide a name for that factor. Figure 9.5 shows a plot of a factor solution.

| Figure 9.5 | Plot of a Hypothetical Factor Solution |

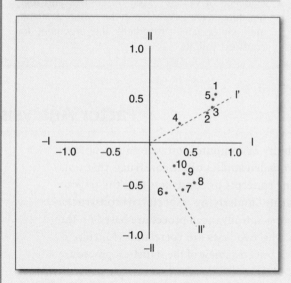

The diagram in the figure plots the outcome of a factor analysis for 10 hypothetical test questions. The diagram has a horizontal axis and a vertical axis. These axes intersect and divide the figure into four parts. The horizontal axis is labeled from –I to I. The vertical axis is labeled from –II to II. Zero is where the axes intersect. We can plot the outcome for each test question on these axes to illustrate their relation to each other.

As you can see, Questions 1 to 5 appear in the upper right quadrant, and Questions 6 to 10 appear in the lower right quadrant. We interpret the factor analysis by drawing a straight line from zero through the plots of the questions that are grouped together. Since the questions form two groups, we know that the test has two factors (represented by the two broken lines). We can identify and name factors by looking at the test questions to see what each measures.

SOURCE: From Anastasi, A., & Urbina, S. (1997). *Psychological testing* (7th ed.; pp. 190, 304). Upper Saddle River, NJ: Prentice Hall. Copyright © 1997. Reprinted by permission of Pearson Education, Inc.

There are a number of ways to calculate a factor matrix that depend on basic assumptions, such as whether the underlying factors are presumed to be independent (not correlated) or dependent (correlated). A full explanation of this procedure is beyond the intended scope of this textbook. For a more complete explanation of factor analysis, we suggest you consult a textbook on multivariate statistical techniques.

A good example of the process of confirmatory factor analysis is provided by Longshore, Turner, and Stein (1996), who tested the construct validity of a scale developed to measure self-control in a population of offenders in the criminal justice system (Grasmick, Tittle, Bursik, & Arneklev, 1993). A general theory of crime (Gottfredson & Hirschi, 1990) suggests that self-control—the degree to which a person is vulnerable to momentary temptation—is important in predicting whether a person will commit a crime. Other researchers have challenged this theory, citing a lack of empirical evidence of self-control as a stable trait. To answer these charges, Grasmick and colleagues developed a scale measuring self-control as defined by Gottfredson and Hirschi. The scale contains 23 statements about noncriminal predispositions, such as impulsiveness and risk seeking, with which test takers agree or disagree. Studies of the scale by the test developers suggest that it is reliable and valid (Grasmick et al., 1993).

To conduct their confirmatory factor analysis, Longshore and colleagues (1996) used data collected during an evaluation of a program to treat offenders. The researchers hypothesized, based on the Gottfredson and Hirschi (1990) theory and previous research conducted by the test developers (Grasmick et al., 1993), that the measure of self-control would have six underlying factors:

1. *Impulsiveness:* People with low self-control seek immediate gratification.

2. *Simple tasks:* People with low self-control prefer simple tasks and lack the diligence and tenacity needed for benefiting from more complex tasks.

3. *Risk seeking:* People with low self-control are drawn to excitement and adventure.

4. *Physical activity:* People with low self-control prefer physical activity to contemplation and conversation.

5. *Self-centeredness:* People with low self-control tend to be indifferent to the needs of others.

6. *Temper:* People with low self-control have low tolerance for frustration and are likely to handle conflict with confrontation.

Longshore and colleagues' (1996) factor analysis provided support for the hypothesis. The data yielded the predicted factors; however, the factors of impulsiveness and self-centeredness combined, resulting in five factors instead of six. Based on these data, the researchers concluded that there was good evidence of construct validity for the measure of self-control.

Exploratory Factor Analysis

Researchers also use factor analysis as a means of exploring underlying factors of psychological tests. In an **exploratory factor analysis,** researchers do not propose a formal hypothesis but instead use the procedure broadly to identify underlying components. An exploratory factor analysis does not provide the verification required to establish construct validity. Probst (2003), however, used an exploratory factor analysis in addition to a confirmatory factor analysis in the development and validity of the Job Security Index and the Job Security Satisfaction Scale.

Probst (2003) defines job security as "the perceived stability and continuance of one's job as one knows it" (p. 452) and developed two instruments to measure job security. He developed the Job Security Index to measure test takers' cognitive appraisal of their job security and the Job Security Satisfaction Scale to assess test takers' attitudes concerning their level of job security. In addition to performing a confirmatory factor analysis on the combined questions of the Job Security Index and the Job Security

Satisfaction Scale to verify that the two measures represented two distinct constructs, Probst conducted an exploratory factor analysis to investigate the total number of underlying factors for which the data could account. He found four factors that accounted for 68.7% of the variance. The first factor was made up of most of the questions from the Job Security Index. The second factor contained the negatively phrased questions from the Job Security Satisfaction Scale. The third factor contained the positively phrased questions from the Job Security Satisfaction Scale. The fourth factor, although technically appropriate for extraction, was uninterpretable.

Probst's (2003) validation study provides an excellent example of the different purposes of confirmatory factor analysis and exploratory factor analysis. Probst hypothesized that there would be two factors (two tests) in the combined test questions. This confirmatory factor analysis provided evidence of construct validity. In the exploratory factor analysis, he widened the possibilities for the number of factors and found four factors. However, as you can see, the four factors clearly represented the two tests. The first factor represented the Job Security Index, and the second and third factors represented the Job Security Satisfaction Scale. The fourth factor, which was uninterpretable, probably represented errors associated with the test scores. Probst concluded, "Future researchers are advised to apply confirmatory factor analysis to the scales to confirm their factor structures" (p. 451).

Putting It All Together

The validation study of the Brief Multidimensional Students' Life Satisfaction Scale (BMSLSS; Seligson, Huebner, & Valois, 2003) provides a real-life example of the validation concepts we have discussed in Section II. According to Seligson and colleagues, the array of "quality of life" instruments for children and adults prior to 2003 did not contain a brief multidimensional measure, and therefore they decided to develop the BMSLSS for adolescents. The BMSLSS contains 40 self-report questions, and the researchers carried out their first validation study with 221 middle school students. The students completed six measures: the Positive and Negative Affect Schedule–Children (Laurent et al., 1999), the Students' Life Satisfaction Scale (Huebner, 1991), the Multidimensional Students' Life Satisfaction Scale (Zulig, Huebner, Gilman, Patton, & Murray, 1994), the Children's Social Desirability Questionnaire (Crandall, Crandall, & Katkovsky, 1965), one rating of global life satisfaction on a 7-point scale, and the BMSLSS. The students also completed a demographic information sheet before responding to the questionnaires and rated their satisfaction with their lives on a global life satisfaction scale.

Seligson and colleagues (2003) conducted a multiple regression analysis using the global life satisfaction rating as the criterion and the five BMSLSS domains, the five importance domains, and the five interaction terms as the three predictors. All of the BMSLSS beta weights, entered first in the multiple regression procedure, were significant at $p < .01$. The beta weights for school in the importance group and the interaction group were also significant at $p < .01$.

Seligson and colleagues (2003) found evidence of convergent validity for the BMSLSS when they calculated the strength and relationship between the scores on the BMSLSS and the scores on the Multidimensional Students' Life Satisfaction Scale ($r = .66$) and the Student Life Satisfaction Scale ($r = .62$). Table 9.1 shows a multitrait–multimethod matrix contrasting the Multidimensional Students' Life Satisfaction Scale with the BMSLSS. As you can see, this matrix contrasts only two variables, each having the same five scales.

| Table 9.1 | Multitrait–Multimethod Matrix for the Brief Multidimensional Students' Life Satisfaction Scale (BMSLSS) and the Multidimensional Students' Life Satisfaction Scale (MSLSS) |

	MTMM matrix for middle school students									
	MSLSS					BMSLSS				
	A1	B1	C1	D1	E1	A2	B2	C2	D2	E2
A1										
B1	0.43									
C1	0.26	0.27								
D1	0.39	0.38	0.36							
E1	0.55	0.51	0.34	0.25						
A2	**0.55**	0.26	0.08	0.31	0.24					
B2	0.24	**0.52**	0.23	0.32	0.23	0.41				
C2	0.25	0.26	**0.53**	0.35	0.21	0.31	0.40			
D2	0.26	0.27	0.17	**0.60**	0.17	0.39	0.41	0.40		
E2	0.35	0.33	0.13	0.14	**0.47**	0.42	0.34	0.30	0.24	

SOURCE: From Seligson, J. L., Huebner, S., & Valois, R. F. (2003). Preliminary validation of the Brief Multidimensional Students' Life Satisfaction Scale (BMSLSS). *Social Indicators Research, 61*(2), 121. Published by Springer Science and Business Media.

NOTE: A = Family, B = Friends, C = School, D = Living Environment, E = Self. The numbers in bold are the validity coefficients. The heterotrait–monomethod correlations are underlined. The heterotrait–heteromethod correlations are in italics.

The note at the bottom of Table 9.1 will help you identify the tests and dimensions. The numbers in bold are the correlations that provide the convergent evidence of validity or the correlations between the same dimension on the two tests. All of theses correlations are positive and have moderate strength. The underlined numbers (heterotrait–monomethod correlations) show the intercorrelations *within* each test. The intercorrelations among dimensions for the MSLSS are shown in the top left quadrant, and the intercorrelations among dimensions for the BMSLSS are shown in the bottom right quadrant. The intercorrelations within each test provide information on how the dimensions in the test are related to each other. We would expect these correlations to be low when the test is multidimensional. The numbers in italics (heterotrait–heteromethod correlations) show the correlations of different dimensions in the two tests; these are estimates that provide discriminant evidence of validity. As you can see, the convergent coefficients are higher than the discriminant coefficients. Overall, the matrix provides strong evidence of construct validity for the BMSLSS.

In conclusion, it is important to remember Cronbach's (1989) advice about construct validation: "To call Test A valid or Test B invalid is illogical. Particular interpretations are what we validate. . . . Validation is a lengthy, even endless process" (p. 151).

Section II has discussed the basic psychometric principles associated with establishing test reliability and validity. As you can see, these research-based activities provide cumulative evidence regarding a test's usefulness and interpretation. Section III discusses the process of developing psychological tests and surveys and describes in more detail how researchers conduct validation studies.

INTERIM SUMMARY 9.3
FACTOR ANALYSIS

- Researchers use factor analysis to identify underlying variables or factors that contribute to a construct or an overall test score.
- A confirmatory factor analysis is a study in which researchers hypothesize the underlying variables and then test to see whether the variables are there.
- Confirmatory factor analyses that confirm predicted underlying variables provide evidence of construct validity.

- Exploratory factor analyses take a broad look at the test data to determine the maximum number of underlying structures.
- The validation of the Brief Multidimensional Students' Life Satisfaction Scale (Seligson et al., 2003) provides an example of how researchers carry out validation studies.

Chapter Summary

Psychologists measure behaviors (activities that are observable and measurable) and constructs (underlying attitudes or attributes that exist only in our imaginations). Although we cannot observe or measure constructs directly, we can predict behaviors that influence and measure those behaviors.

Because definitions of constructs vary from person to person, psychologists define and explain constructs carefully. Construct explication is the process of relating a construct to a psychological theory and proposing a nomological network of the constructs and behaviors to which the construct is related.

We gather theoretical evidence of construct validity by proposing the nomological network and experimental hypotheses. We then gather psychometric evidence by establishing evidence that the test is reliable and correlates with other tests measuring constructs in the nomological network (convergent evidence of validity) and by confirming that it is not correlated with constructs to which it is theoretically unrelated (discriminant evidence of validity). In addition, evidence of validity based on test content or a test's relationship with other criterion measures also bolsters the argument that we have strong evidence of validity. Finally, researchers can propose and conduct experiments using the test to measure the construct.

Confirmatory factor analysis is a method that tests theoretical predictions about underlying variables or factors that make up a construct. Although some constructs are unidimensional or homogeneous, many constructs are made up of subordinate variables. The process of confirmatory factor analysis involves proposing underlying factors and then verifying their existence using the statistical procedure of factor analysis. Exploratory factor analysis takes a broad look at test data to determine how many underlying components are possible.

The validation of the Brief Multidimensional Students' Life Satisfaction Scale provides an example of many of the validation procedures described in Section II.

Engaging in the Learning Process

KEY CONCEPTS

After completing your study of this chapter, you should be able to define each of the following terms. These terms are bolded in the text of this chapter and defined in the Glossary.

- behavior
- confirmatory factor analysis
- construct
- construct explication
- construct validity
- convergent evidence of validity
- correlation matrix

- discriminant evidence of validity
- exploratory factor analysis
- factor analysis
- factors
- hypotheses
- multitrait–multimethod design
- nomological network

LEARNING ACTIVITIES

The following are some learning activities you can engage in to support the learning objectives for this chapter.

Learning Objectives	Study Tips and Learning Activities
After completing your study of this chapter, you should be able to do the following:	The following study tips will help you meet these learning objectives:
Discuss the concept of a construct, and give examples of theoretical constructs.	• Complete Additional Learning Activity 1, which follows this table, and compare your answers with those of your classmates.
Explain and give examples of the three steps of construct explication.	• Using *Proquest* or a similar database, find a construct validity study and compare it with the study by Sherer and colleagues (1982). Make a list describing the similarities and differences between the two studies.
Explain the process of establishing evidence of validity based on a test's relationship with other constructs.	• Complete Additional Learning Activity 3, which follows this table, and compare your work with that of your classmates.
Explain how Campbell and Fiske's multitrait–multimethod matrix provides evidence of validity based on a test's relationships to other constructs.	• Make a list of each type of evidence provided by a multitrait–multimethod matrix, and describe how to locate it in the matrix. • Complete Additional Learning Activity 4, which follows this table.
Discuss the roles of confirmatory and exploratory factor analysis in establishing construct validity.	• Compare the purposes of confirmatory and exploratory factor analyses. Describe in writing their similarities and differences.

ADDITIONAL LEARNING ACTIVITIES

1. Define and propose an observable behavioral measure for each of the following constructs. Which of the following are theoretical constructs?

Artistic talent	Beauty	Cooking ability
Decisiveness	Intelligence	Temperature

2. *Defining Various Types of Evidence of Validity.* In Section II, we have discussed the different types of evidence of validity listed below in Column II. Find the definition in Column III that matches each type of evidence. Place your answer in Column I.

I	*II*	*III*
	Discriminant evidence of validity	A. The test provides a representative sample of the behaviors in the testing universe.
	Face validity	B. The test scores are related to independent behaviors, attitudes, or events.
	Evidence of validity based on test content	C. Questions on the test appear to the test taker to measure what the test is supposed to measure.
	Evidence of validity based on relationships with external criteria	D. The test demonstrates a relationship between a test and a future behavior or outcome.
	Convergent evidence of validity	E. Test scores are correlated with measures of constructs that are theoretically related to the test's construct.
	Predictive evidence of validity	F. The test is highly correlated with itself.
	Concurrent evidence of validity	G. The test is related to behaviors or events in the present.
	Reliability	H. The test is not correlated with measures of constructs with which the test has no theoretical relationship.

3. *Validating a Measure of Self-Esteem.* A psychology professor at Northwest Random College gave his Tests and Measurements class this assignment: Design a validation study for a test that measures self-esteem in preadolescents. The test contains 30 statements to which the test taker responds *true of me* or *not true of me*. In general, the statements reflect test takers' satisfaction with their academic and athletic skills, physical attractiveness, and relationships with friends and family. The elementary school across the street from the college has agreed to participate in an empirical study by administering the test to its students.
   a. What psychometric information would you like to get about the test to gather evidence of its validity?
   b. Would you need to administer to the participants measures other than the test you are validating? If so, what other measures would you like to administer?
   c. Can you gather all of the information you need in one administration? Explain why or why not.
   d. What statistical procedures will you use to analyze your data?
   e. Describe the specific types of judgments or decisions your study will allow you to make. What types of judgments or decisions will you not be able to make?
   f. Describe any follow-up studies your validation study will require.

4. *Interpreting a Multitrait–Multimethod Design.* As you recall from this chapter, Seligson and colleagues (2003) carried out a validation study of the Brief Multidimensional Students' Life Satisfaction Scale (BMSLSS). In addition to using data from students in Grades 6–8, the researchers carried out another study using 46 high school students from a different school. Table 9.2 contains the multitrait–multimethod correlation matrix from the second study. Using the information provided in Table 9.2, answer the following questions:
   a. Which figures represent convergent evidence of validity? Which pair had the greatest convergent evidence? Which pair had the least?
   b. Which figures represent discriminant evidence of validity? How do the discriminant coefficients compare with the convergent coefficients?
   c. Do these data indicate evidence of construct validity for the BMSLSS? Explain your answer.

Table 9.2	Multitrait–Multimethod Matrix for the Brief Multidimensional Students' Life Satisfaction Scale (BMSLSS) and the Multidimensional Students' Life Satisfaction Scale (MSLSS) for the Second Study

MTMM matrix for high school students										
	MSLSS					*BMSLSS*				
	A1	*B1*	*C1*	*D1*	*E1*	*A2*	*B2*	*C2*	*D2*	*E2*
A1										
B1	0.26									
C1	0.36	0.36								
D1	0.62	0.56	0.46							
E1	0.64	0.55	0.54	0.70						
A2	**0.70**	*0.34*	*0.31*	*0.56*	*0.66*					
B2	*0.32*	**0.67**	*0.31*	*0.50*	*0.57*	<u>0.52</u>				
C2	*0.23*	*0.26*	**0.63**	*0.35*	*0.37*	<u>0.28</u>	<u>0.33</u>			
D2	*0.47*	*0.33*	*0.31*	**0.61**	*0.42*	<u>0.55</u>	<u>0.25</u>	<u>0.40</u>		
E2	*0.40*	*0.44*	*0.17*	*0.46*	**0.57**	<u>0.35</u>	<u>0.61</u>	<u>0.12</u>	<u>0.20</u>	

SOURCE: From Seligson, J. L., Huebner, S., & Valois, R. F. (2003). Preliminary validation of the Brief Multidimensional Students' Life Satisfaction Scale (BMSLSS). *Social Indicators Research, 61*(2), 121. Published by Springer Science and Business Media.

NOTE: A = Family, B = Friends, C = School, D = Living Environment, E = Self. The numbers in bold are the validity coefficients. The heterotrait–monomethod correlations are underlined. The heterotrait–heteromethod correlations are in italics.

PRACTICE QUESTIONS

The following are some practice questions to assess your understanding of the material presented in this chapter.

Multiple Choice

Choose the one best answer to each question.

1. A number of theorists challenged the strategies of developing evidence of test validity based on content or relationships with other criteria because the
   a. theorists did not believe they got good results.
   b. strategies were difficult to understand and implement.
   c. strategies failed to link the testing instrument to a theory of psychological behavior.
   d. strategies were seldom used by test developers.

2. Serena investigated the relation between influence and sales in her thesis. She collected data on several objective criteria, but she also wanted to use a subjective criterion. Which should she use?
   a. Gross monthly sales
   b. Supervisor rating of sales ability
   c. Annual net sales
   d. Number of sales calls

3. For his senior thesis, Mohammed identified the behaviors that relate to self-esteem. He then identified other constructs that may be related to self-esteem. And finally he identified behaviors related to similar constructs, such as self-efficacy, and determined whether these behaviors were related to self-esteem. In his thesis, Mohammed was carrying out the process of
   a. scientific investigation.
   b. scientific experimentation.
   c. scientific explication.
   d. construct explication.

4. According to the example in your textbook, gravity is
   a. a subjective criterion.
   b. an objective criterion.
   c. a theoretical construct.
   d. a physical construct.

5. When Susan provided in her thesis a number of educated guesses or predictions about aggression, she was defining the _____ for aggression.
   a. nomological network
   b. hypotheses
   c. measurement instrument
   d. clinical interview

6. Self-efficacy is an example of
   a. a subjective criterion.
   b. an objective criterion.
   c. a theoretical construct.
   d. a physical construct.

7. Which one of the following does NOT provide evidence of construct validity?
   a. Reliability
   b. Convergent correlations
   c. Dragnet empiricism
   d. Evidence based on test content

8. The theory underlying psychological testing suggests that a test
   a. cannot have a stronger correlation with any other variable than it does with itself.
   b. cannot have a stronger correlation with itself than it does with an outside criterion.
   c. must have an equally strong correlation with a criterion as it does with itself.
   d. must have a stronger correlation with a criterion than it does with itself.

9. Which of the following is NOT provided by the multitrait–multimethod design?
   a. Reliability
   b. Predictive evidence of validity
   c. Convergent evidence of validity
   d. Discriminant evidence of validity

10. If test scores correlate with constructs that the underlying theory says are related, we would describe those correlations as providing _____ evidence of validity
    a. predictive
    b. concurrent
    c. discriminant
    d. convergent

11. Hiroshi carried out a study in which he measured self-efficacy and academic performance. He found that those who had high self-efficacy performed better than those who had low self-efficacy. Which of the following methods was he using for establishing evidence of construct validity?
    a. Multitrait–multimethod design
    b. Experimental intervention
    c. Nomological network
    d. Construct explication

12. Sherer and colleagues (1982) administered their measure of self-efficacy and a measure of interpersonal competency to 376 students and found a moderate correlation between the two tests. This correlation provides _____ evidence of validity for these researchers' measure of general self-efficacy.
    a. predictive
    b. face
    c. convergent
    d. content

13. Selena developed a math test for her thesis. She administered the math test with a test of reading ability and found that the scores on the two tests were not related. She was happy because this lack of correlation provided _____ evidence of validity for her math test.
    a. face
    b. concurrent
    c. discriminant
    d. convergent

14. For his senior thesis Ricardo proposed a set of underlying factors for the construct of altruism. He then administered a test of altruism and used an advanced statistical technique based on correlation to analyze these data. Which one of the following did he use?
    a. Confirmatory factor analysis
    b. Linear regression
    c. Multitrait–multimethod design
    d. Exploratory factor analysis

15. Yassi carried out a factor analysis in which she looked for underlying theoretical structures in her construct. Which one of the following designs did she use?
    a. Confirmatory factor analysis
    b. Linear regression
    c. Multitrait–multimethod design
    d. Exploratory factor analysis

Short Answer/Essay

Read each of the following, and consider your response carefully based on the information presented in this chapter. Write your answer to each question in two or three paragraphs.

1. What is construct validity? How is it different from reliability, evidence of validity based on content, and evidence of validity based on relationships with external criteria? Is construct validity really a different "type" of validity? Why or why not?

2. What are the steps of construct explication? What activities take place at each step?

3. What information constitutes evidence of construct validity? Explain how each type of information provides evidence of construct validity.

4. Draw a diagram of a multitrait–multimethod matrix. Explain where information on reliability, convergent evidence of validity, and discriminant evidence of validity is found.

5. Explain the concepts of a confirmatory factor analysis and an exploratory factor analysis, including their purposes and how they differ.

ANSWER KEYS

Additional Learning Activities

1. All are theoretical constructs. The behavioral measure defines the construct. Here are some examples:

Artistic talent	Beauty	Cooking ability
Ratings by expert judges; Holland's Self-Assessment Inventory also identifies "artistic" persons.	Ratings of pleasing personal appearances of people in pictures.	Ratings of dishes cooked by test takers; the Culinary Institute of America conducts a master chef certification test described by Ruhlman (2000).
Decisiveness	Intelligence	Temperature
Again, ratings made by assessors in assessment centers measure decisiveness or the ability to make a timely decision.	A number of tests are available to measure intelligence, for example, the Wechsler Adult Intelligence Scale-Revised.	Thermometers measure temperature mechanically on two scales: Fahrenheit and Celsius.

2. Defining Various Evidence of Validity

Evidence of validity based on test content	A. The test provides a representative sample of the behaviors in the testing universe.
Evidence of validity based on relationships with external criteria	B. The test scores are related to independent behaviors, attitudes, or events.
Face validity	C. Questions on the test appear to measure what the test is supposed to measure.

(Continued)

Predictive evidence of validity	D. The test demonstrates a relationship between a test and a future behavior or outcome.
Convergent evidence of validity	E. Test scores are correlated with measures of constructs that are theoretically related to the test's construct.
Reliability	F. The test is highly correlated with itself.
Concurrent evidence of validity	G. The test is related to behaviors or events in the present.
Discriminant evidence of validity	H. The test is not correlated with measures of constructs with which the test has no theoretical relationship.

3. Validating a Measure of Self-Esteem
   a. Necessary information about the test would include its test–retest reliability and KR-20 for scales that represent the four situations that the questions cover. Convergent and discriminant correlations would provide evidence of construct validity. Evidence of validity based on relationships with criteria would not be appropriate because the professor did not ask for a criterion measurement. Evidence of validity based on content would require a list of all possible questions in the domain and a test plan.
   b. Convergent evidence and discriminant evidence of validity require administering tests that measure a similar construct and a different construct.
   c. Except for evidence of test–retest reliability, all of the information can be gathered in one administration.
   d. The data can be analyzed using correlation. A multitrait–multimethod analysis would also be appropriate.
   e. The validation study can establish empirical evidence of construct validity; however, construct validity alone is not recommended for decision making.

4. Interpreting a Multitrait–Multimethod Design
   a. Convergent coefficients appear in bold. The highest is for Family (.70), and the lowest is for Self (.57).
   b. The discriminant coefficients appear in italics, and they are lower than the convergent coefficients.
   c. Yes, the data indicate evidence of construct validity for the BMSLSS because they demonstrate both convergent and discriminant evidence of validity.

Multiple Choice

1. c	2. b	3. d	4. c	5. b
6. c	7. c	8. a	9. b	10. d
11. b	12. c	13. c	14. a	15. d

Short Answer/Essay

Refer to your textbook for answers. If you are unsure of an answer and cannot generate the answer after reviewing your book, ask your professor for clarification.

SECTION III

DEVELOPING AND PILOTING SURVEYS AND PSYCHOLOGICAL TESTS

Overview of Section III

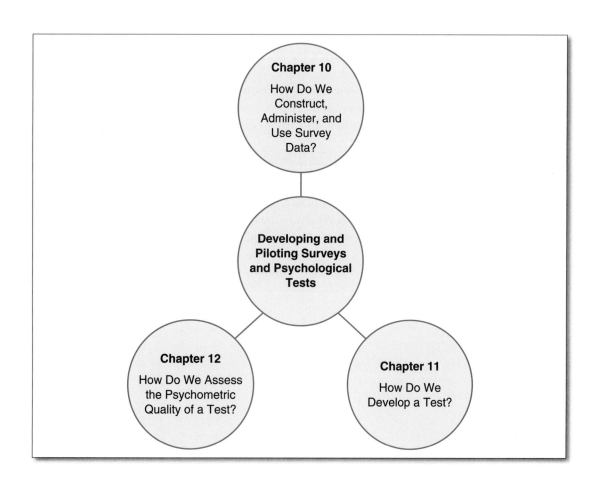

CHAPTER 10: HOW DO WE CONSTRUCT, ADMINISTER, AND USE SURVEY DATA?

In Chapter 10, we begin by defining what a survey is and discussing that surveys are popular research tools. Knowing that how we collect information affects its quality, we present an overview of the different ways to collect and acquire data. We focus on one approach, the scientific method, which is the very essence of collecting accurate survey data. After briefly reviewing the scientific method, we focus on a five-phase scientific approach to constructing, administering, and analyzing surveys. Finally, we discuss survey reliability and validity.

CHAPTER 11: HOW DO WE DEVELOP A TEST?

In Chapter 11, we discuss the steps for developing psychological tests. We look at the process of constructing a test plan, various formats for writing questions (for example, multiple choice, true/false), the strengths and weaknesses of different formats, and how test takers' perceptions and preconceived notions can influence test scores. Finally, we present guidelines on how to write test questions and discuss the importance of the instructions that accompany a test.

CHAPTER 12: HOW DO WE ASSESS THE PSYCHOMETRIC QUALITY OF A TEST?

In Chapter 12, we continue to describe the test development process by discussing piloting the test and analyzing the items in terms of their difficulty, their ability to discriminate among respondents, and their likelihood of introducing error into the test results. We also describe the process of revising the test and gathering evidence of reliability and validity. Finally, we briefly discuss the contents of the test manual.

How Do We Construct, Administer, and Use Survey Data?

CHAPTER 10: HOW DO WE CONSTRUCT, ADMINISTER, AND USE SURVEY DATA?

After completing your study of this chapter, you should be able to do the following:

- Describe the six methods for acquiring knowledge.
- Explain how the scientific method differs from other methods for acquiring information, and describe the five steps associated with the scientific method.
- Apply the five-phase scientific approach to constructing and administering surveys and analyzing their data.
- Describe survey reliability and validity and associated concepts.

"I am taking a survey research methods class. The instructor told us we needed a foundation in the scientific method before we studied surveys. She said that survey construction is both a science and an art. I wanted to learn how to construct a survey—not what science is all about. What is the deal?"

"Our human resources department was interested in finding out how employees feel about our company benefits program. They wanted to know whether employees were aware of the medical, retirement, and flexible spending plans that were available to them—and if so, whether the plans are valuable to them. They wanted this information to find out whether the existing benefits program needed to be modified to fit employees' needs. It took the human resources staff about two months to design this survey. Why did it take so long?"

"I had to complete a course evaluation survey for my research methods class. One of the questions on the survey was 'Was the teacher available and responsive to your needs?' Another question was 'How much time did you spend studying for this class?' My teacher said that these were not very good survey questions. Why not?"

n Chapter 1, we briefly discussed the similarities and differences between psychological tests and surveys. Because surveys, like psychological tests, are popular measurement instruments and important decisions are often made based on their results, we have devoted an entire chapter to increasing your understanding of how to properly design and administer surveys and analyze their data.

We begin by defining what a survey is and discussing the fact that surveys are popular research tools. Knowing that how we collect information affects its quality, we present an overview of the different ways to collect and acquire data. We focus on one approach, the scientific method, which is the very essence of collecting accurate survey data. After briefly reviewing the scientific method, we focus on a five-phase scientific approach to constructing, administering, and analyzing surveys. Finally, we discuss survey reliability and validity.

Although this chapter contains an excellent overview of surveys, we encourage those interested in constructing and administering surveys and analyzing their data to consult the additional sources mentioned throughout the chapter.

What Are Surveys?

Broadly defined, **surveys** are research tools that collect information that enable us to describe and compare people's attitudes (how they feel), knowledge (what they know), and behaviors (what they do; Fink, 2003). Surveys, like psychological tests, are used for various reasons. For example, it is not uncommon for elementary schools to administer surveys to better understand how parents feel about the implementation of a new policy (how they feel), how much parents know about the school's curriculum (what they know), or what parents do with their children to facilitate the learning process (what they do). Every four years, television news stations administer surveys (or what they call political polls) to learn how people plan to vote so that they can make predictions about who the next president of the United States will be. Organizations use surveys to measure employee satisfaction and organizational effectiveness.

The U.S. federal government conducts the Current Population Survey to determine the unemployment rate; the Consumer Expenditure Survey to determine how people spend their money; the National Health Interview Survey to collect information about people's health conditions, their use of health services, and the behaviors that affect their risk of illness; and the National Crime Victimization Survey to determine the crime rate. To learn more about one of the nation's most important surveys, the Current Population Survey, read On the Web Box 10.1.

ON THE WEB BOX 10.1

The Current Population Survey

www.bls.gov/cps/home.htm

Below are the annual unemployment rates of the civilian noninstitutional population for 2000–2008. The annual unemployment rate in 2008 was 5.8%, which is 1.2% higher than in 2007 and 0.2% lower than in 2003.

Have you ever wondered where statistics on the unemployment rate come from? The Current Population Survey (CPS) is a monthly household survey conducted by the U.S. Census Bureau for the U.S. Bureau of Labor Statistics. CPS data are gathered through personal and

2000	2001	2002	2003	2004	2005	2006	2007	2008
4.0%	4.7%	5.8%	6.0%	5.5%	5.1%	4.6%	4.6%	5.8%

telephone interviews from a sample of approximately 60,000 households. The primary purpose of the survey is to provide comprehensive data on the employment and unemployment experiences of the nation's population classified by age, sex, race, and other characteristics.

The CPS provides data that are used by lawmakers, researchers, and the general public. These data include the following:

- Employment status of the civilian noninstitutional population age 16 years or older by age, sex, race, Hispanic origin, marital status, family relationship, and Vietnam-era veteran status
- Employed persons by occupation, industry, class of worker, hours of work, full- or part-time status, and reasons for working part-time
- Employed multiple jobholders by occupation, industry, number of jobs held, and full- or part-time status of multiple jobs
- Unemployed persons by occupation, industry, class of worker of last job, duration of unemployment, reason for unemployment, and methods used to find employment
- Discouraged workers and other persons not in the labor force
- Information on weekly and hourly earnings by detailed demographic group, occupation, education, union affiliation, and full- or part-time employment status
- Special topics such as the labor force status of particular subgroups of the population, such as women maintaining families, working women with children, displaced workers, and disabled veterans

Data are also available on work experience, occupational mobility, job tenure, educational attainment, and school enrollment of workers.

SOURCE: U.S. Bureau of Labor Statistics. (n.d.). *Labor force statistics from the current population survey.* Retrieved June 4, 2010, from http://www.bls.gov/cps/home.htm

---

In 1790, one of the first known surveys was the decennial census conducted by the U.S. Census Bureau. Since that time, surveys have become very popular research tools, and millions of them are conducted each year in the United States. As a result of their popularity, according to the Council of American Survey Research Organizations (CASRO; 2009a), today there are well over 2,000 **survey research firms**—companies that specialize in the construction and administration of surveys and analysis of survey data. Some of the larger, well-known survey research firms are highlighted in On the Web Box 10.2. As with psychological tests, there are standards that guide the use of surveys; see On the Web Box 10.3 for more information on the CASRO Standards.

As with psychological tests, we use the data collected from surveys to make important decisions. For example, an elementary school may require children to wear uniforms to school if the results of a survey indicate that parents believe this would be a positive move. An organization may decide to invest significant training dollars in a management development program when survey results suggest that lack of management skill plays a significant role in organizational turnover. A network news organization may decide to broadcast who will be elected president, prior to the closing of the polls, based on the results of exit polls.

ON THE WEB BOX 10.2

Popular Survey Research Firms

www.gallup.com

www.jdpower.com

www.westat.com

www.isr.umich.edu

Thousands of survey research firms are dedicated to constructing and administering surveys and/or analyzing survey data. Although most of these firms are smaller companies that specialize in interviewing people, there are a number of full-service companies that design surveys, collect survey data, tabulate survey answers, interpret survey data, and report survey results to organizational sponsors. Some of the larger, well-known survey research firms are highlighted below.

Gallup (www.gallup.com). Established more than 70 years ago and employing many of the world's leading scientists in management, economics, psychology, and sociology, Gallup helps organizations increase customer engagement and maximize employee growth. Gallup provides measurement tools (surveys), coursework, and strategic advisory services to client organizations via the web, at Gallup University campuses, and in 40 offices around the world.

J. D. Power & Associates (www.jdpower.com). Established in 1968, J. D. Power & Associates, a business unit of the McGraw-Hill Companies, is a global marketing information firm that conducts independent surveys of customer satisfaction, product quality, and buyer behavior.

Westat (www.westat.com). Established in 1961 and employee owned, Westat is a contract research organization that provides custom research and program evaluation studies to organizations. Its surveys cover a broad range of topics, including health conditions and expenditures; academic achievement and literacy; medical treatments and outcomes; exposure assessments; program participation; employment and earnings; and respondents' knowledge, attitudes, and behaviors.

University of Michigan Institute for Social Research (www.isr.umich.edu). The Institute for Social Research (ISR) is one of the largest and oldest (more than 50 years old) academic survey and social research organizations in the world. ISR is dedicated to advancing public understanding of human behavior by directing and conducting some of the longest-running and most widely cited and used empirical research studies in the United States.

As with psychological tests, the data collected from surveys are used to make important decisions. Therefore, survey developers must pay careful attention to the design and administration of surveys and the analysis of data gathered. Unfortunately, although surveys are popular and valuable research tools, like psychological tests they are also often misunderstood or misinterpreted. Surveys, like psychological tests, are not error free, and how one approaches the design, administration, and analysis can affect how well the survey data describe what they are intended to describe.

ON THE WEB BOX 10.3

Council of American Survey Research Organizations:
Code of Standards and Ethics for Survey Research

www.casro.org/codeofstandards.cfm

 Founded in 1975 with a membership of 15 research organizations, the Council of American Survey Research Organizations (CASRO) now represents more than 250 companies and research operations in the United States and abroad. It serves as the "voice and values" of the survey research industry and provides benchmarks of ethical standards for research and development of surveys. Its specific purpose is to:

- promote a rigorous code of conduct that enhances the image of survey research and protects the public's rights and privacy,
- advocate our industry's effective self-regulation when legislators propose bills that threaten legitimate survey research,
- champion legitimate research companies and marginalize disreputable research "pretenders" who threaten to tarnish the industry's reputation and alienate respondents. (CASRO, 2009b)

To guide research standards and ethics, CASRO has assembled and published a Code of Standards and Ethics for Survey Research, which includes agreed-on guidelines of ethical conduct for survey research organizations. The code describes in detail the responsibilities of survey research organizations to respondents, clients, and outside contractors in reporting study results. It serves as a living document, meaning that it will be revised as necessary when circumstances arise and change in the world of survey research.

SOURCE: Council of American Survey Research Organizations. (2009a). *Surveys and you.* Retrieved May 24, 2010, from http://www.casro .org/survandyou.cfm

Knowledge Acquisition and the Scientific Method

Every day we are bombarded with information. At the breakfast table, we might read a newspaper article describing a miracle cure for a common disease or an article claiming that the unemployment rate has increased. Later in the day, we might watch a television commentary suggesting that television viewing increases teenage violence and that attending preschool improves children's intelligence. On our way home from work or school, we might drop by the drugstore, where a pharmacist might tell us that a certain brand of aspirin is more effective than another brand for alleviating headaches.

Usually we take this information for granted and use it to make decisions about ourselves and others. For example, we might decide that our children will watch very little television or that we will change the brand of aspirin we use. Unfortunately, some of the information we hear and learn about is misleading and, if taken as fact, could result in poorly informed decisions.

Knowledge Acquisition

Before making decisions that are based on what we hear or see, we must verify that the information is accurate. To do this, we must look at how the information was obtained. How did the pharmacist come to the conclusion that one brand of aspirin is more effective than another brand? How did the radio talk show host come to the conclusion that watching television increases teenage violence?

According to Helmstadter (1970), and as summarized in Table 10.1, we obtain knowledge in at least six ways: through tenacity, intuition, authority, rationalism, empiricism, and the scientific method.

The Scientific Method

Although Helmstadter's (1970) first five methods help us gather information, they are not the best means for gathering *accurate* information. The sixth, the **scientific method**—a process for generating a body of knowledge (Marczyk, DeMatteo, & Festinger, 2005)—often allows us to obtain more accurate information through systematic and objective observations. While there is some disagreement among

| **Table 10.1** | Helmstadter's Six Methods for Acquiring Knowledge |

Method	*Definition*
Tenacity	We acquire information based on superstition or habit, leading us to continue believing something we have always believed. For example, we come to believe that walking under a ladder will bring us bad luck.
Intuition	We acquire information without any reasoning or inferring. For example, we come to believe that one brand of aspirin is more effective than another brand just because we believe it is so.
Authority	We acquire information from a highly respected source. For example, we come to believe that one brand of aspirin is better than another brand because a pharmacist tells us so.
Rationalism	We acquire information through reasoning. For example, we come to believe that one brand of aspirin reduces headaches more effectively than another brand because the first brand includes ingredients that are similar to another medicine we use that really works for us.
Empiricism	We acquire information through personal experience. For example, we come to believe that one brand of aspirin reduces headaches more effectively because we have used it and it works for us.
Scientific method	We acquire information by testing ideas and beliefs according to a specific testing procedure that can be observed objectively. This method is without personal beliefs, perceptions, biases, values, attitudes, and emotions. For example, we come to believe that one brand of aspirin is more effective at reducing headaches than another brand because systematic research has accumulated evidence of its effectiveness.

SOURCE: Helmstadter, G. C. (1970). *Research concepts in human behavior.* New York: Appleton-Century-Crofts.

researchers regarding the exact elements of the scientific method, many researchers speak of five steps associated with it:

1. Identifying a problem or an issue and forming a hypothesis

2. Designing a study to explore the problem or issue and test the hypothesis

3. Conducting the study

4. Analyzing and interpreting the data

5. Communicating the research results

The scientific method involves several ways of collecting information, which can be categorized as experimental research techniques and descriptive or correlation-based research techniques. In general, **experimental research techniques** help us determine cause and effect, and **descriptive research techniques** help us describe a situation or a phenomenon. Most surveys are descriptive—used to describe, or even compare, a situation or phenomenon; for example, a class evaluation survey might indicate that your Tests and Measurements professor was an effective professor or even that this professor appeared to be more effective than your Cognitive Psychology professor. Surveys are not commonly used for determining cause and effect; for example, survey data cannot establish that having Professor Miller teach your tests and measurements class will cause you to learn more than having Professor Lovler teach the same class! A true experiment (in which there is a control group and an experimental group and participants are randomly assigned to these groups) must be set up to establish cause and effect. In some cases, however, surveys can be used as data collection instruments within an experimental technique.

INTERIM SUMMARY 10.1
SURVEYS, KNOWLEDGE ACQUISITION, AND THE SCIENTIFIC METHOD

- Surveys are research tools that collect information that enables us to describe and compare people's attitudes, knowledge, and behaviors.
- To determine whether information is accurate, we must look at how the information was obtained.
- According to Helmstadter (1970), there are six methods for obtaining information: tenacity, intuition, authority, rationalism, empiricism, and the scientific method.
- Information obtained using the scientific method is more accurate and reliable than information obtained in other ways.
- The scientific method is a process or method for generating a body of knowledge.
- This process includes identifying a problem or an issue and forming a hypothesis, designing a study to explore the problem or issue and the hypothesis, conducting the study, analyzing and interpreting the results, and communicating the research results.
- The scientific method can be followed using both experimental and descriptive research techniques.
- Descriptive research techniques often involve the use of surveys—research tools that collect information to facilitate the description and comparison of people's attitudes, knowledge, and behaviors.
- Surveys can be used as data collection instruments in true experiments—where there is a control group and an experimental group and participants are randomly assigned to these groups.

The Survey Research Method

Many people believe that constructing a survey is a simple procedure. To demonstrate, we constructed the course evaluation survey in For Your Information Box 10.1 in five minutes. It looks okay, doesn't it? In fact, it is not very good at all. It has several weaknesses. First, we did not take the time to think through the objective(s) or purpose of the survey. Second, we did not take the time to carefully construct the survey questions, and we did not pretest the survey to determine whether students would understand the questions as we intended. Third, we did not take the time to carefully format the survey—including instructions and professional formatting—to make it easy to complete and score. This is not a complete list of the weaknesses of this survey, but we have made our point. Although this survey may, at first glance, appear to be a good one, it is probably not very reliable or valid. We hope that no one would want to make any decisions (for example, promotion of a faculty member, elimination of a course) based on the results of this survey.

Constructing a good survey, and demonstrating evidence of reliability and validity, takes time. It is as much a science as it is an art. Surveys are a science because science is a process—and good surveys

---

FYI

FOR YOUR INFORMATION BOX 10.1

Quickly Developed Course Evaluation Survey

1. How did you hear about this course?

    ____ Another student
    ____ College catalog
    ____ Faculty member

2. Did the professor show preferential treatment to certain students?

    ____ Yes
    ____ No

3. What treatment did you observe? _____

4. Please give your overall opinion of the course.

	Excellent	Okay	Mediocre	Poor
Course organization	____	____	____	____
Course content	____	____	____	____
Clarity of presentation	____	____	____	____
Audiovisual aids	____	____	____	____
Syllabus materials	____	____	____	____

5. Overall, did you enjoy and would you recommend this course to other students?

    ____ Yes
    ____ No

follow a scientific process (method). Survey research is an art because knowing how much rigor to put into the design and writing good questions takes years of practice.

For Your Information Box 10.2 includes a much better course evaluation survey. By the end of this chapter, you should be able to determine what makes this one better than the survey in For Your Information Box 10.1.

FYI

FOR YOUR INFORMATION BOX 10.2

Better Course Evaluation Survey

The purpose of this survey is to gather your feedback on the success of the course. Please take a few moments to answer the following questions to the best of your ability. Your comments are essential for the planning of future courses.

1. How did you hear about this course? (*Please select one of the following.*)

    ____ Another student
    ____ College catalog
    ____ Faculty member
    ____ Other (please specify) _____

2. Did the professor show preferential treatment to certain students?

    ____ Yes
    ____ No (skip to Question 4)

3. What preferential treatment did you observe? _____

4. Please rate each of the following as *being excellent, good, fair,* or *poor.* (*Please make a check mark on the appropriate line.*)

	Excellent	Good	Fair	Poor
Course organization	____	____	____	____
Course content	____	____	____	____
Clarity of presentation	____	____	____	____
Audiovisual aids	____	____	____	____
Syllabus materials	____	____	____	____

5. Overall, did you enjoy this course?

    ____ Yes
    ____ No

6. Would you recommend this course to other students?

    ____ Yes
    ____ No

The Scientific Method of Survey Design

Experienced **survey researchers**—people who design and conduct surveys and analyze their results—generally would tell you the same things about what makes a good survey. First, they would probably tell you that good surveys share the following characteristics:

- Have specific and measurable objectives
- Contain straightforward questions that can be understood similarly by most people
- Have been pretested to ensure that there are no unclear questions or incorrect skip patterns
- Have been administered to an adequate sample of respondents so that the results are reflective of the population of interest
- Include the appropriate analysis to obtain the objectives
- Include an accurate reporting of results (both verbal and written)
- Have evidence of reliability and validity

Second, experienced survey researchers would probably tell you that using a scientific approach to survey research increases the chances that a survey will have these features. A scientific approach to surveys involves five general phases that correspond to the five steps of the scientific method. Table 10.2 shows those five steps, the corresponding steps of survey design, and the competencies a survey researcher needs to be able to perform each step.

Table 10.2   A Scientific Approach to Survey Design

Step in the Scientific Method	Corresponding Step for Designing Surveys	Competencies of the Survey Researcher
1. Identify a problem and form a hypothesis	Presurvey issues	• Know how to conduct a literature review • Know how to gather people who are knowledgeable about the survey topic • Know how to conduct focus groups
2. Design a study to explore the problem and test the hypothesis	Construct the survey	• Know the different types of surveys • Know the different types of survey questions • Know how to write effective survey questions • Know how to assemble questions into a survey instrument • Know the various methods for pretesting surveys • Know how to interpret data to revise and finalize the survey
3. Conduct the study	Administer the survey	• Know the methods for sampling respondents • Understand the logistics of administering various surveys
4. Analyze the research data	Analyze the survey data	• Know how to code survey data • Know how to enter survey data into a database • Know the methods for analyzing survey data
5. Communicate the research findings	Communicate the findings of the survey	• Know how to write a report • Know how to prepare presentation materials • Know how to present information to a group

SOURCE: From Fink, A. (2003). *The survey handbook* (2nd ed.). Thousand Oaks, CA: Sage. Copyright © 1995 by Sage Publications. Reprinted by permission of Sage Publications.

Third, experienced survey researchers would probably tell you to choose a level of detail appropriate for the purpose of the survey project. Regardless of the purpose of a survey, it is important to identify the objectives of the survey carefully, construct the survey carefully, enter and analyze survey data carefully, and present the findings clearly. However, because the scientific approach to survey research requires detailed planning, is complex and time-consuming, and can be expensive, the amount of energy and time you spend on each of these phases may vary depending on the objectives of the survey. For example, designing and administering a class evaluation survey is less complex and therefore requires less planning, time, and money, than designing and administering the **decennial census survey**—a survey that is administered by the U.S. Census Bureau every 10 years, primarily to determine the population of the United States.

Preparing for the Survey

The first phase in developing a survey involves identifying the objectives of the survey, defining the objectives operationally, and constructing a plan for completing the survey.

Identifying the Objectives

The first step in preparing the survey is to define the **survey objectives**—the purpose of the survey and what the survey will measure. For example, one survey's objective may be to determine why there is a high degree of turnover in an organization. Another survey's objective may be to assess public opinion regarding a new product or service. The objective of a third survey may be to determine whether students thought a college course was beneficial.

Where do the objectives come from? They come from a particular need, from literature reviews, and from experts. For example, suppose that your college's administrators decide that they need to know whether their courses are fulfilling students' needs. They may ask the college's institutional research office to design a course evaluation survey to be administered in each class at the end of the semester. There is an obvious need here, and the exact objectives of the survey would come from discussions with college administrators, faculty, and students.

Survey objectives can also come from **literature reviews**—systematic examinations of published and unpublished reports on a topic. By reviewing the literature on a specific topic, survey researchers find out what is known about the topic. They then use this information to identify important aspects of a topic or gaps in knowledge about the topic. The survey objectives can also come from **experts**—individuals who are knowledgeable about the survey topic or who will be affected by the survey's outcomes. By talking to experts, you can take an idea about a survey (for example, I just want to design a class evaluation survey) and define exactly what information the survey should collect—its specific objectives (for example, determine whether faculty are treating some students preferentially, determine whether faculty are meeting students' needs, determine whether faculty are presenting information in an organized manner). For a class evaluation survey, your experts might be faculty, college administrators, or students.

Defining the Objectives Operationally

After identifying the objective(s) of the survey, the next step is to define the objective(s) operationally and determine how many questions are needed to gather the information to meet the objective(s). For Your Information Box 10.3 lists the objectives, the operational definitions for each objective, and the number of questions used to measure each objective of a class evaluation survey designed by students in the Survey Research Methods course taught by one of this textbook's authors. The objectives are listed separately in the left-hand column. The **operational definitions**—specific behaviors that represent the purpose—are listed in the second column for each objective. The numbers of questions used to measure the objectives are in the third column. Note how similar this table is to the test specification table for ensuring the content validity of a psychological test (discussed in Chapter 7).

FOR YOUR INFORMATION BOX 10.3

Operational Definitions for a Class Evaluation Survey

As part of a survey research methods course, one of this textbook's authors required students to develop a college-level course evaluation survey. Discussions with subject matter experts (faculty, administrators, and students), reviews of course evaluations used by other colleges, and a literature review helped students clearly define the survey objectives. After defining these objectives, students operationally defined each one and determined how many questions would be developed to measure each objective. The objectives, operational definitions, and numbers of questions are shown below:

Objective	Operational Definition	Number of Questions
To measure student opinions of course format and learning materials	• Did the course use relevant reading material and contribute to students' intellectual growth? • Did exams assess the information presented in class?	5
To measure the instructor's organization	• Was the instructor prepared for class and organized? • Did the instructor make learning objectives clear?	5
To measure the instructor's knowledge of subject matter	• Was the instructor knowledgeable about the material? • Did the instructor show enthusiasm for the material?	5
To determine the overall effectiveness of the course	• Was the instructor effective overall? • Was the course a good course?	5

Constructing a Plan

The next step is to construct a plan for completing the survey. Such a plan includes a list of all the phases and steps necessary to complete the survey; an estimate of the costs associated with the survey's development and administration, and analysis of the survey data; and a timeline for completing each phase of the survey.

Constructing the Survey

The second phase in developing a survey involves selecting the type of survey to be constructed, writing survey questions, preparing the survey instrument, and pretesting the survey.

Selecting the Type of Survey

Before starting from scratch, developers find that it is always a good idea to search for an existing survey that meets the survey's objectives. They find existing surveys by conducting literature reviews and speaking with subject matter experts.

If an appropriate survey does not exist, developers must design their own survey, first deciding what type of survey to develop. Surveys take many forms. **Self-administered surveys** are those that individuals complete themselves. These include **mail surveys** (mailed to respondents with instructions for respondents to complete and return them) and **individually administered surveys** (administered by a facilitator in person for respondents to complete in the presence of the facilitator). At one time or another, you have probably received a survey in the mail. Likewise, you have probably been stopped in a shopping mall and asked to complete a survey. These are examples of mail and individually administered surveys, respectively.

Personal interviews are surveys that involve direct contact between the survey researcher and the respondents in person or by phone. Personal interviews include **face-to-face surveys,** in which an interviewer asks a series of questions in respondents' homes, a public place, or the researcher's office. These also include **telephone surveys,** in which an interviewer calls respondents and asks them questions over the phone. You have probably been stopped at one time or another and asked a few questions about a product. Likewise, you may have been contacted on the phone and asked to indicate whether you like, have heard enough of, or dislike various music segments. These are examples of face-to-face and telephone surveys, respectively. For both, interviewers can read survey questions from a paper-and-pencil form or a laptop. We are even beginning to see instances in which computers dial and ask survey questions over the telephone by themselves!

Writing Survey Questions

After selecting the type of survey, researchers write survey questions that match the survey's objectives. Just as there are different types of surveys, there are also various types of survey questions. These are some of the most popular:

- Open-ended
- Closed-ended
- Yes/No questions
- Fill in the blank
- Implied no choice
- Single-item choice
- Enfolded
- Free choice
- Multiple choice
- Ranking
- Rating
- Guttman format
- Likert and other intensity scale formats
- Semantic differential
- Paired comparisons and constant referent comparisons

The type of questions chosen depends on the kind of information needed. For Your Information Box 10.4 provides examples of various types of survey questions.

FYI

FOR YOUR INFORMATION BOX 10.4

Examples of Survey Questions

Different types of survey questions serve different purposes, and each has strengths and weaknesses. Below are some examples of the types of survey questions. Although it is an older reference, the U.S. General Accounting Office's (1993) *Developing and Using Questionnaires* is a very valuable resource for not only planning and using surveys, but also understanding the strengths and weaknesses of different survey question types.

Open-Ended

Last year you were a member of student government. Please comment on your experience.

_____

Closed-Ended

Did you attend last week's biology study group?

_____ Yes   _____ No

Fill in the Blank

How many brothers and sisters do you have? _____

Row Format

Please indicate how many hours per week you study for each of the following courses.

Course	Hours	Course	Hours
Psychology	_____	Calculus	_____
Biology	_____	Art history	_____

Column Format

For each of the courses listed below, identify how many hours you study per week and how many pages you read for the course per week.

Course	Hours per week you study	Pages per week you read
Psychology	_____	_____
Biology	_____	_____
Calculus	_____	_____
Art history	_____	_____

Implied No Choice

Why didn't you pass your psychology exam?

_____ I did not study.

_____ I did not feel well.

_____ I don't know.

Did your professor review the following materials before your exam?

	Yes	No
Test–retest reliability	_____	_____
Alternate forms reliability	_____	_____
Split-half reliability	_____	_____
Content validity	_____	_____
Criterion-related validity	_____	_____
Construct validity	_____	_____

Single-Item Choice

There are two methods that can be used to evaluate your understanding of course material. One method is to give you an in-class exam, and the other method is to have you write a term paper. The question is, which method do you prefer?

_____ In-class exam

_____ Term paper

Free Choice

If the psychology department started a Psychology Club, would you attend the meetings?

_____ Yes   _____ Probably not

_____ Probably   _____ No

_____ Uncertain

Multiple Choice

Which of the following statements best explains why you decided to transfer to another college/university? (*Select one only.*)

_____ I could not afford the tuition.

_____ I did not like the other students.

_____ I did not like the faculty.

_____ Other (describe) _____

Ranking

Students select colleges for various reasons. Consider each of the following items that may influence a student's decision to apply to a specific college. Rank order each of the items from most important (1) to least important (5).

Cost	_____	Faculty	_____
Location	_____	Clubs/organizations	_____
Majors	_____		

Rating

How organized was your professor?

_____ Very organized

_____ Somewhat organized

_____ Marginally organized

_____ Not organized at all

(Continued)

(Continued)

Likert-Type Format

Being able to approach your professors is a major advantage of attending a small college. Please indicate the extent to which you agree or disagree with the following statements about your professors.

	Strongly agree	*Agree*	*Neither agree nor disagree*	*Disagree*	*Strongly disagree*
Has set office hours					
Is approachable					

Semantic Differential

Please circle the number representing the demeanor of your professor.

Happy 1   2   3   4   5   6   7   **Grumpy**

No matter the type of questions, writing survey questions is not an easy task due to the complex cognitive processes a test taker goes through to answer a survey question. See For Your Information Box 10.5 for an explanation of the cognitive aspects of answering questions.

FYI

FOR YOUR INFORMATION BOX 10.5

Cognitive Aspect of Answering Questions

Answering survey questions is a complex cognitive task (Cannell, Miller, & Oksenberg, 1981; Groves, 1989; Kahn & Cannell, 1957; Miller, Mullin, & Herrmann, 1990; Tourangeau, 1984). Research suggests that when people answer survey questions, they go through at least four stages:

Comprehension   →   Retrieval   →   Judgment   →   Response Communication

First, they must comprehend the question. Second, they must retrieve the answer to the question. Third, they must judge the appropriate answer to the question. Fourth, they must communicate the answer.

Comprehension

When the respondents are asked a question, they must first understand each word in the question and what the entire question is asking. To comprehend or understand a survey question, respondents must have a long enough attention span to pay attention to the question, a certain level of language ability so that they can understand the vocabulary and the entire question, and the appropriate general knowledge so that they can understand certain concepts contained in the question.

Retrieval

Once the respondents understand the meaning of the question, they must search their memories for the appropriate answer. When answer choices are presented to respondents, they must recognize the most appropriate answer. When answer choices are not presented to respondents, they must search their memories in a more thorough fashion for the correct answer. When the appropriate cues or hints are available, respondents will probably find the answer. When inappropriate cues are available, respondents will take bits and pieces of the information and reconstruct an answer to fit what is most likely to be the answer.

Judgment

After the respondents have retrieved an answer from memory, they must judge or decide whether the information meets the objectives of the question. For example, if the question asks respondents to recall events from a specific time period, they will judge whether the events occurred during the appropriate time frame (that is, if the question asks for their expenditures over the past three months, they will judge whether their answer includes *all* of their expenditures over the past *three* months).

Response Communication

Once the respondents have comprehended the question, searched for and found an answer, and judged an answer for its appropriateness, they must communicate the answer to the question. If a question involves response choices, respondents must match their answer to the available choices. If the question requires that respondents articulate a response, they must construct an understandable response. However, before they communicate their response, respondents will evaluate whether the answer to the question meets their own personal motives and objectives. If respondents believe that their answer is threatening or not socially desirable, they may choose not to provide the correct answer. In other words, they may refuse to answer or may provide a "fake" answer.

Although less common, **structured record reviews,** which are forms that guide data collection from existing records (for example, using a form to collect information from personnel files), and **structured observations,** which are forms that guide an observer in collecting behavioral information (for example, using a form to document the play behaviors of children on the playground), are also considered to be surveys.

Each type of survey has advantages and disadvantages. The type that is appropriate depends on the objectives of the research and the target audience. For further information about the advantages and disadvantages of different types of surveys, read the U.S. General Accounting Office's (1993) *Developing and Using Questionnaires.*

Survey developers must pay careful attention to writing understandable, readable, and appealing survey questions because there are many chances for error in understanding a question, formulating an answer, and providing a response (Fowler, 2002). To facilitate the question-answering process and increase the likelihood of obtaining accurate information, survey developers make sure their survey questions have the characteristics described in the following subsections.

Survey questions should be purposeful and straightforward. The relationship between what the question is asking and the objectives of the survey should be clear. In fact, the survey researcher should begin with an explanation of the purpose of a group of questions. This helps the survey respondent focus on the appropriate issue(s). For example, given the second and third objectives of the class evaluation survey presented in For Your Information Box 10.3, the following statements and questions would be purposeful:

Now we would like to ask you about the instructor. Please indicate whether you strongly agree (SA), agree (A), neither agree nor disagree (N), disagree (D), or strongly disagree (SD) with each of the following statements by placing a circle around the number that best represents your response.

The instructor . . .	SA	A	N	D	SD
• presented material in an organized fashion	5	4	3	2	1
• seemed well prepared for class	5	4	3	2	1
• explained assignments clearly	5	4	3	2	1
• allowed ample time for completion of assignments	5	4	3	2	1
• kept students informed about their progress/grades in the course	5	4	3	2	1
• was available outside of class time	5	4	3	2	1
• had a thorough knowledge of course content	5	4	3	2	1
• showed enthusiasm for the subject	5	4	3	2	1
• utilized teaching methods that were well suited for the course	5	4	3	2	1

Survey questions should be unambiguous. All survey questions should be concrete and should clearly define the context of the question. Questions should not contain jargon or acronyms unless all respondents to a particular survey are familiar with the jargon and acronyms.

Unacceptable

Do you go out often?
_____ Yes
_____ No

Better Alternative

Which of the following best describes how often you have gone out to dinner during the past three months? (*Please select one*)

_____ Not at all

_____ 1–2 times

_____ 3–4 times

_____ 5 or more times

The question above and to the left is unacceptable because it does not clearly define what information the survey developer is seeking. Is the survey developer asking whether you go *outside* often, to *the movies* often, or *what*? The question to the right makes the exact meaning clearer.

Survey questions should be written in correct syntax. That is, all survey questions should be complete sentences with an orderly arrangement of words.

Unacceptable

School attended? _____

Better Alternative

Where did you attend graduate school? _____

Survey questions should use appropriate rating scales and response options. Many questions ask respondents to rate their attitudes about something on a rating scale. The rating scale should always match the type of information being requested. Look at the following question from a local hotel satisfaction survey. Do you see a problem?

How satisfied were you with the overall quality of the services you received?

- Excellent   • Very Good   • Average   • Below Average   • Poor

The rating scale does not match the type of information the question is seeking. In other words, the rating scale describes "quality of services," although the question asks about the customer's level of satisfaction. A better alternative would be the following:

How satisfied were you with the overall quality of the services you received?

- Extremely satisfied   • Very satisfied   • Somewhat satisfied
- Not very satisfied   • Not satisfied at all

For Your Information Box 10.6 displays the types of rating scales identified by Censeo Corporation, a leading human resources consulting firm specializing in the design and delivery of assessments using state-of-the-art technology.

FYI

FOR YOUR INFORMATION BOX 10.6

Different Types of Rating Scales

Industrial-organizational psychologists have researched the pros and cons of alternative response scales for many years, but there is no consensus on the "one best scale." What works best depends on the purpose of the survey and on the types of items included. However, there is consensus on the basic criteria for what constitutes a good response scale:

- The scale is simple and easy to understand.
- To the extent possible, raters have a common understanding about what the scale means—they interpret the scale in a similar fashion.
- The words used to define the levels are clearly ordered (for example, it may not be clear which is higher—*excellent* or *outstanding*).
- The scale is suitable for the types of items in the survey (for example, a scale in which one of the levels is *always* may or may not be appropriate, depending on the types of items).
- The scale leads to variance in ratings (competencies and participants are not all rated the same; there is a good spread in ratings).
- The scale is aligned with the main purpose of feedback (for example, different scales would be appropriate when the purpose is developmental versus evaluating performance against expectations/requirements).

Three other general conclusions can be drawn from the research:

1. Increasing the number of rating levels will, up to a point, lead to a greater spread in ratings (which is desirable). In most situations, having at least five levels is preferable. However, scales with more than seven levels can lead to more error being introduced.

2. The labels or anchor terms tend to confuse raters when there are more than six levels and each level is labeled.

3. In many cases, regardless of the themes or number of levels used, raters tend to inflate ratings, and there is less variance in scores than one would desire.

(Continued)

(Continued)

Listed below are the general types of response scales, based on the main theme or aspect on which the ratings are made:

- *Simple qualitative*: How would you rate the person in this area? (for example, from *Poor* to *Excellent*)
- *Extent*: To what extent does the statement describe the person? (for example, from *Very little extent* to *Very great extent*)
- *Frequency*: How often does the person demonstrate effective use of the behavior/skill? (for example, from *Almost never* to *Almost always*)
- *Developmental* (strength/development need): How would you rate the person's capabilities in this area? (for example, from *Significant development need* to *Exemplary—a role model*)
- *Comparison with others*: Compared to others with whom I have worked, this person is _____ in this area (for example, from *Significantly below average* to *Best I've ever worked with*)
- *Performance*: How would you rate his or her performance in this area? (for example, from *Does not meet expectations* to *Far exceeds expectations*) Note that this theme would make sense for performance appraisal purposes, but probably not for development purposes where peers and subordinates also provide ratings.

It is possible to construct a response scale that has more than one theme. For example, an anchor point of *Best I've ever worked with* combines the qualitative and comparison themes. However, unless this is carefully done, there is a danger of the response scale becoming too complex and thereby confusing.

As a final comment on general types of response scales, it is important that each level in a scale relate to the same theme(s). It is not appropriate, for example, that some levels of a scale relate to frequency and other levels relate to capability (developmental). This is a common failing of many "home-grown" response scales.

Anchor Points

Response scales vary in terms of two main factors—the number of levels (5-point, 6-point, etc.), and the theme or themes captured by the anchor terms and scale definitions. There are obviously a very large number of possible scales. Normally, each level in the scale has a descriptive anchor when there are four or fewer levels, but all the levels do not necessarily have to be anchored when there are five or more levels. The example below shows Censeo's standard scale for established surveys:

5—Exceptional strength

4–

3—Competent

2–

1—Weak

The theme for the 5-point scale above is developmental, and only three of the levels are anchored. It is highly questionable whether adding anchors for the second and fourth levels, using intermediate terms, would lead to more accurate and valid ratings. Raters implicitly form a mental image of the scale and its meaning, and are able to easily understand that a rating of 4 is halfway between *Competent* and *Exceptional strength*.

The response scale below is an example of a 5-point frequency scale in which only three points are anchored:

Never		Sometimes		Always
1	2	3	4	5

There are many different types of response scales, including the following:

Qualitative Scales

4—Excellent	5—Outstanding	6—Extraordinary
3—Good	4—Very good	5—Superior
2—Fair	3—Good	4—Very good
1—Poor	2—Fair	3—Good
	1—Poor	2—Fair
		1—Poor

Extent Scales

4—Exactly descriptive	5—Very great extent	6—Completely true description
3—Very descriptive	4—Great extent	5—Largely true
2—Somewhat descriptive	3—Some extent	4—Somewhat true
1—Not descriptive	2—Little extent	3—Somewhat false
	1—Very little extent	2—Largely false
		1—Completely false description

Frequency Scales

4—Almost always	5—Almost always	6—100% of the time
3—Usually	4—Most of the time	5—90+% of the time
2—Sometimes	3—Often	4—80+% of the time
1—Seldom	2—Sometimes	3—70+% of the time
	1—Seldom	2—60+% of the time
		1—Less than 60% of the time

Developmental Scales

4—Towering strength	5—Exemplary, best possible	6—No room for improvement
3—Strength	4—Real strength	5—Significant strength
2—Competent	3—Fully competent	4—Strength
1—Development need	2—Development need	3—Competent
	1—Weakness	2—Development need
		1—Significant development need

Comparison Scales

4—One of the very best	5—Far above average	6—Top 5%
3—Better than most	4—Above average	5—80–95th percentile
2—Better than some	3—Average	4—50–80th percentile
1—Not as good as most	2—Below average	3—20–50th percentile
	1—Far below average	2—5–20th percentile
		1—Bottom 5%

Performance Scales

4—Commendable	5—Far above requirements	6—Exceeds all standards
3—Exceeds	4—Above requirements	5—Exceeds most, meets others
2—Meets	3—Meets requirements	4—Meets most, exceeds others
1—Does not meet	2—Below requirements	3—Meets all
	1—Far below requirements	2—Meets most, below on some
		1—Below on many standards

Survey questions should include the appropriate categorical alternatives. When you are asking a question for which you have no idea of the possible responses, you should leave the question open-ended. If you do provide alternatives, the question should include an inclusive list of response alternatives or an "other" category. For example, if you are interested in finding out whether students enjoyed their psychology class, it would not be appropriate to allow them to respond only *Yes, extremely* or *No, not at all*.

Unacceptable	*Better Alternative*
Did you enjoy your introductory psychology course?	Did you enjoy your introductory psychology course?
_____ Yes, extremely	_____ Yes, extremely
_____ No, not at all	_____ Yes, for the most part
	_____ No, for the most part
	_____ No, not at all

Survey questions should ask one and only one question. Be careful not to ask a **double-barreled question**—a question that is actually asking two or more questions in one. Here are two examples of double-barreled questions (really a triple-barreled question in one case) that we found in a hotel satisfaction survey:

1. Was our staff well informed, knowledgeable, and professional?

2. Were we responsive to your needs, solving any problems you may have had efficiently and to your satisfaction?

If a survey respondent says yes to either of these questions, it is impossible to tell whether the respondent is saying yes to the entire question or to only part of it. The same is true when a survey respondent says no to either of these questions. It would have been more appropriate to ask one or more of the following questions:

Was our staff well informed?	_____ Yes _____ No
Was our staff knowledgeable?	_____ Yes _____ No
Was our staff professional?	_____ Yes _____ No
Was our staff responsive to your needs?	_____ Yes _____ No
Did our staff efficiently solve any problems you may have had?	_____ Yes _____ No
Did our staff solve any problems you may have had to your satisfaction?	_____ Yes _____ No

Survey questions should be at a comfortable reading level. Survey developers try to write questions that are easy to read (low readability level) so that respondents will be more likely to understand and interpret questions appropriately. Microsoft Word and similar software will calculate the reading level of any passage you write.

Preparing the Survey Instrument

Once the survey developer has written the questions, he or she must put them together into a package. The goal is to catch survey respondents' attention and motivate respondents to complete the survey so as to reduce the errors associated with incomplete surveys. Figure 10.1 displays the course evaluation survey developed by a Research Methods class taught by one of this textbook's authors. This survey highlights each of the items discussed subsequently.

Title and seal. The front page of the survey should always have a title in large font centered on the top of the page so that it stands out from the survey questions. The title should indicate what the questionnaire is about (for example, Course Evaluation Survey). Many times, survey researchers also identify the target audience (for example, Survey of Employees Regarding Child Care Arrangements). When possible, the first page should also include a seal or a company logo to lend more credibility.

Appeal and instructions. The front page should include an appeal to the respondent and instructions on how to complete the survey. The instructions should do the following both concisely and courteously:

1. State the purpose of the survey.

2. Explain who is sponsoring or conducting the survey.

3. Explain why it is important for respondents to complete the survey to the best of their ability.

4. Explain how to complete the form.

5. Assure respondents that their answers are confidential and will be reported in group format only.

6. Thank respondents for their cooperation. (U.S. General Accounting Office, 1993)

When the survey is a mail survey, the instructions should also include information about how to return it. If a professional administers the survey, he or she should read these instructions to respondents.

Headings and subheadings. The survey should include headings and subheadings to help guide respondents through the survey. These should be short phrases that tell respondents what each part of the survey is about and should stand out from the survey questions.

Transitions. Survey respondents should be introduced to each new section with a topic heading that informs them about the next section of the survey. The transition should also include any specific instructions about how to answer the questions when the type of question changes.

Response instructions. Survey developers should provide response instructions that tell respondents how to answer appropriately or that lead them to another part of the questionnaire. Response instructions should be short directions, often in parentheses and italics. For example, some response forms that will be scanned electronically require that respondents complete the forms with a pencil.

Figure 10.1   A Course Evaluation Survey Developed by Students

COURSE EVALUATION SURVEY

_____   _____   _____   _____   _____
COURSE NAME   COURSE #   TERM   YEAR   INSTRUCTOR NAME

At the conclusion of each course, the Hamilton Holt School of Rollins College administers a course evaluation survey to all students. Responses to this survey are used by the instructor to refine and improve the course, and by Rollins administration to evaluate instructor performance as well as make decisions about tenure, promotions, and other personnel issues.

Rollins College Hamilton Holt School would like your feedback on the course and the effectiveness of the instructor. It is very important that you complete the entire survey. Your name will not be associated with your response.

PART I—COURSE

First, we would like to ask you about the course. Please indicate whether you strongly agree (SA), agree (A), neither agree nor disagree (N), disagree (D), or strongly disagree (SD) with each of the following statements by placing a circle around the number that best represents your response.

The course . . .	SA	A	N	D	SD
• contributed to my intellectual growth	5	4	3	2	1
• was useful to my work/career	5	4	3	2	1
• used a current text	5	4	3	2	1
• included helpful text readings	5	4	3	2	1
• exams tested my understanding of the material	5	4	3	2	1

PART II—INSTRUCTOR

Now we would like to ask you about the instructor. Please indicate whether you strongly agree (SA), agree (A), neither agree nor disagree (N), disagree (D), or strongly disagree (SD) with each of the following statements by placing a circle around the number that best represents your response.

The instructor . . .	SA	A	N	D	SD
• presented material in an organized fashion	5	4	3	2	1
• seemed well prepared for class	5	4	3	2	1
• explained assignments clearly	5	4	3	2	1
• allowed ample time for completion of assignments	5	4	3	2	1
• kept students informed about their progress/grades in the course	5	4	3	2	1
• was available outside of class time	5	4	3	2	1
• had a thorough knowledge of course content	5	4	3	2	1
• showed enthusiasm for the subject	5	4	3	2	1
• utilized teaching methods that were well suited for the course	5	4	3	2	1

Since the instructors are very interested in identifying ways in which to improve the content of each course and their effectiveness as instructors, please comment below for those statements listed above that you have circled a 2 or below.

_____

Next, please comment on each of the following questions. Your opinion counts, so please be candid with your response!

1. Overall, why was the instructor effective or ineffective?

_____

2. Overall, why would you classify this as a good course or a poor course?

_____

3. Overall, on a scale of 1 to 10 (with 10 being the highest), I would rate this course:

_____

4. Add any other comments.

_____

THANK YOU FOR YOUR FEEDBACK

_____

Bold typeface. Survey researchers often use bold typeface to emphasize key points in directions or questions.

Justification of response spaces. A common practice is to justify the response spaces (for example, a line, a checkbox) to the left of response choices and columns to the right.

Shading. When there are spaces on the survey that you want respondents to leave blank, it is a good idea to use shading in these spaces to prevent respondents from writing in them. You might also separate rows of text on a horizontal layout to guide respondents across a page of text.

White space. Survey designers should also make sure that there is adequate white (blank) space on the survey. A crowded survey does not look inviting and is often difficult to complete. For instance, designers leave margins of at least one inch and ample space between questions and sections of the survey. Some designers are tempted to try to fit the entire survey on one sheet of paper. Although surveys should be printed on as few pages as possible, the designer must balance the need for white space with the need to conserve paper and printing costs.

Printing. Surveys fewer than three pages in length are usually printed on two sides of a sheet of paper. When it is necessary for the survey to be longer, pages should be stapled in the upper left corner. Extremely long surveys may be spiral bound or printed in a booklet format.

Font. Survey designers should use an attractive, businesslike, and readable font and should make sure the overall format is organized and inviting. This makes the survey look professional and easier to complete—and, in turn, makes respondents pay more attention to the survey, decreasing survey completion time and respondents' effort.

Pretesting the Survey

The third task in the survey construction phase is to pretest the survey. **Pretesting** allows you to

1. Identify sources of **nonsampling measurement errors**—errors associated with the design and administration of the survey,

2. Examine the effectiveness of revisions to a question or an entire survey,

3. Examine the effect of alternative versions of a question or survey,

4. Assess the final version of a survey for respondent understanding, time to complete, and ease of completion,

5. Obtain data from the survey and make changes to the format that might make data entry or analysis more efficient.

The methods may differ for pretesting surveys. The method the survey developer chooses depends on the objectives of the pretest and the available resources such as time, funds, and staff. Some pretesting methods are more appropriate for the preliminary stages of survey development. For example, the following methods are useful for providing survey designers with knowledge of respondent understanding of survey concepts and wording (qualitative analysis).

One-on-one interviews
- *Concurrent "think-aloud" interviews:* Respondents describe their thoughts as they think about and answer the survey questions.
- *Retrospective "think-aloud" interviews:* Typically one-on-one interviews during which the interviewer asks respondents how they went about generating their answers after they complete the survey.
- *Paraphrasing:* The interviewer asks respondents to repeat questions in their own words.
- *Confidence ratings:* After answering survey questions, respondents rate how confident they are that their responses are correct.

Respondent focus groups. A **focus group** brings together people who are similar to the target respondents in order to discuss issues related to the survey. Usually, each person in the group completes the survey, and then the respondents discuss the survey experience with the test developer or a trained facilitator. Some pretesting methodologies evaluate the drafted survey under conditions that mimic the actual survey process. These methodologies help researchers identify problems, such as respondent fatigue, distraction, hostility, and lack of motivation, that are difficult to identify using other pretesting methods.

Behavior coding of respondent/interviewer interactions. Behavior coding involves coding the interchange between an interviewer and a survey respondent to provide a systematic technique for identifying problems with questions. Behavior coding helps identify the types and frequencies of interviewer behaviors (for example, the interviewer reads question exactly as written, the interviewer reads question with a major change in meaning) and respondent behaviors (for example, the respondent provides an adequate response, the respondent asks for clarification) that can comprise the reliability and validity of a survey. Behavior coding is most useful for personal interviews; however, the technique can be modified for other types of surveys. Behavior coding is a popular pretesting technique for government surveys.

Interviewer and respondent debriefings. This method involves asking interviewers or respondents questions following a **field test**—an administration of the survey to a large representative group of individuals to determine any problems with administration, item interpretation, and so on. (We discuss the field or pilot test in more detail in Chapter 12.)

Split-sample tests. This method involves field-testing two or more versions of a question, sets of questions, or surveys. The objective is to determine which version of the question, set of questions, or survey provides the most accurate results.

Item nonresponse. This method involves distributing the survey and then calculating the **item nonresponse rate**—how often an item or question was not answered.

It is very important that a survey be pretested to ensure that the questions are appropriate for the target population. Most survey questions need to be revised multiple times before they are finalized. Before moving on to the survey administration phase, the survey should meet the following criteria:

- The questions reflect the purpose of the survey.
- There is no technical language or jargon (unless you are sure that it will be understood universally).
- There are no long and complex questions that may be difficult to understand.
- The meanings of all key terms are explained.
- There are no double-barreled questions.
- Adequate, explicit, and inclusive alternatives are presented for multiple-choice questions.
- The survey vocabulary is appropriate for all respondents.
- There are no misspelled words or grammatical errors.
- The survey has a title and headings.
- The survey includes instructions.
- The survey layout includes adequate white space.
- The type on the survey is large enough to be read comfortably.
- There are introductory and transition statements between questions.
- The directions for answering are clear.
- The style of the items is not too monotonous.
- The survey format flows well.
- The survey items are numbered correctly.
- The skip patterns are easy to follow.
- The survey is not too long.
- The survey is easy to read and is attractive.

Fink (2003) suggests that survey researchers ask the questions presented in For Your Information Box 10.7 when pretesting surveys. These questions are categorized by the type of survey being used.

FOR YOUR INFORMATION BOX 10.7

Questions to Ask When Pretesting Surveys

Mail and Other Self-Administered Surveys

- Are instructions for completing the survey clearly written?
- Are the questions easy to understand?
- Do respondents know how to indicate their answers (for example, circle or mark the response, use a special pencil, use the space bar)?
- Are the response choices mutually exclusive (not double-barreled)?
- Are the response choices exhaustive?
- Do respondents understand what to do with completed questionnaires (for example, return them by mail in a self-addressed envelope, fax them)?
- Do respondents understand when to return the completed survey?
- If it is a computer-assisted survey, can respondents use the software commands correctly?
- If it is a computer-assisted survey, do respondents know how to change (or "correct") their answers?
- If an incentive is given for completing the survey, do respondents understand how to obtain it (for example, it will automatically be sent on receipt of the completed survey, it is included with the questionnaire)?
- Is privacy respected and protected?
- Do respondents have any suggestions regarding the addition or deletion of questions, the clarification of instructions, or improvements in format?

Telephone Interviews

- Do interviewers understand how to ask questions and present options for responses?
- Do interviewers know how to get in-depth information, when appropriate, by probing respondents' brief answers?
- Do interviewers know how to record information?
- Do interviewers know how to keep the interview to the time limit?
- Do interviewers know how to return completed interviews?
- Are interviewers able to select the sample using the instructions?
- Can interviewers use the phone logs readily to record the number of times and when potential respondents were contacted?
- Do interviewers understand the questions?
- Do interviewees understand how to answer the questions (for example, pick the top two, rate items according to whether they agree or disagree)?
- Do interviewees agree that privacy has been protected and respected?

In-Person Interviews

- Do interviewers understand how to ask questions and present options for responses?
- Do interviewers know how to get in-depth information, when appropriate, by probing respondents' brief answers?
- Do interviewers know how to record information?
- Do interviewers know how to keep the interview to the time limit?
- Do interviewers know how to return completed interviews?
- Do interviewees understand the questions?
- Do interviewees understand how to answer the questions (for example, pick the top two, rate items according to whether they agree or disagree)?
- Do interviewees agree that privacy has been protected and respected?

Administering the Survey

The third phase in developing a survey requires administering the survey to the target population. This phase involves three steps: selecting the appropriate respondents, determining the sample size, and distributing the survey.

Selecting the Appropriate Respondents

Although the survey might be administered to the entire **population**—all members of the target audience—it is more typical to administer the survey to a representative subset of the population, known as a **sample.** The decision often depends on the survey's purpose, the cost of administering the survey, and the availability of respondents.

If you were interested in designing a class evaluation survey to measure the success of a particular class, your population would be all of the members of the class. Because it would be easy to do, you would probably choose to administer the survey to the entire population (all class members). However, if you were interested in designing a survey to determine how high school seniors feel about the usefulness of the SAT as a college admissions test, your population would be all high school seniors who have completed the SAT and plan to attend college. Because it would be very expensive and infeasible to distribute your survey to all high school seniors who have completed the SAT, you would probably sample all high school seniors who have completed the SAT and who plan to attend college.

A good sample would be a representative group of the population of high school seniors. If the sample is not representative, it is difficult to generalize the survey results to the entire population—that is, to say that the results would be the same if we had given the survey to the entire population. The goal is to find a sampling method that gives everyone—or nearly everyone—in your population an equal chance of being selected and to end up with a sample that is truly representative of the population (Fowler, 1993). There are various methods for selecting a sample. Most can be classified into two categories: probability sampling and nonprobability sampling.

Probability sampling. Probability sampling is a type of sampling that uses statistics to ensure that a sample is representative of a population. Simple random sampling, stratified random sampling, and cluster sampling are examples of probability sampling methods.

With **simple random sampling,** every member of a population has an equal chance of being chosen as a member of the sample. To select a random sample, many people use a table of random numbers. Using this technique, a researcher assigns consecutive numbers to each individual in the population. Then, using a table of random numbers (found in the appendixes of many statistics books), the researcher reads the numbers in any direction. When he reaches a number that matches one of the assigned numbers, the individual corresponding to that number becomes a member of the sample. Of course, researchers could also write the names of individuals on pieces of paper, throw them into a hat, and select individuals to be included in their sample by randomly pulling pieces of paper out of the hat!

Because each member of a population has an equal chance of being selected, we often presume that a simple random sample will be representative of the characteristics of a population. Unfortunately, simple random sampling does not ensure that the sample will include adequate proportions of individuals with certain characteristics. For example, if a particular population is 75% female and 25% male, simple random sampling will not guarantee the same proportion of females to males in the sample.

A variation of simple random sampling is **systematic sampling,** in which every *n*th (for example, every fifth) person in a population is chosen as a member of the sample. To sample systematically, the researcher assigns consecutive numbers to each individual in the population and then selects every nth person to become a member of the sample. This technique has the same weakness as random sampling; it might not have the same proportion of individuals as the population, and if the list is arranged alphabetically, not everyone will have an equal chance of being chosen.

Unlike simple random sampling, with **stratified random sampling** a population is divided into subgroups or *strata* (for example, gender, age, socioeconomic status). A random sample is selected from each stratum. The strata should be based on some evidence that they are related to the issue or problem the survey addresses. For example, if you are interested in exploring how high school seniors feel about the value of the SAT for predicting college success, your population would include all high school seniors. You may wish to stratify your sample by gender because the SAT seems to be a better predictor for females.

Cluster sampling is used when it is not feasible to list all of the individuals who belong to a particular population and is a method often used with surveys that have large target populations. With cluster sampling, clusters (for example, regions of the country, states, high schools) are selected and participants are selected from each cluster. For Your Information Box 10.8 includes an example of cluster sampling.

FYI

FOR YOUR INFORMATION BOX 10.8

An Example of Cluster Sampling

Population

Cluster 1	*Cluster 2*	*Cluster 3*	*Cluster 4*
(NW)	(SW)	(NE)	(SE)
(Urban)(Rural)	(Urban)(Rural)	(Urban)(Rural)	(Urban)(Rural)
(HS1)(HS2)(HS1)(HS2)	(HS1)(HS2)(HS1)(HS2)	(HS1)(HS2)(HS1)(HS2)	(HS1)(HS2)(HS1)(HS2)
High school seniors	High school seniors	High school seniors	High school seniors

Let us say you were interested in surveying high school seniors. You could divide the population of high school seniors into four initial clusters, namely, the regions of the country where they attend high school: Northwest, Southwest, Northeast, and Southeast. Then you would divide the high schools in each of these regions into those that are in urban settings and those that are in rural settings. You could then randomly select two high schools from each rural setting and two high schools from each urban setting and administer your survey to each student in the randomly selected high schools or randomly select students in each of these high schools.

Nonprobability sampling. Nonprobability sampling is a type of sampling in which not everyone has an equal chance of being selected from the population. Nonprobability sampling methods are often used because they are convenient and less expensive than probability sampling. One method of nonprobability sampling is convenience sampling. With **convenience sampling,** the survey researcher uses any available group of participants to represent the population. For example, if your population of interest is high school seniors, you might choose to use the high school seniors at a local high school as your participants. Table 10.3 includes a summary of different types of samples, how they are drawn, and some strengths and weaknesses of each.

Table 10.3	Types of Samples

Type of Sample	How to Draw	Strengths	Weaknesses
Simple random	There are different ways to draw a random sample. For example: • Every participant can be assigned a number and a predetermined number of participants can be drawn from a hat. • Every participant can be listed on a piece of paper and a table of random numbers, or a statistical software program, can be used to select a predetermined number of participants.	• Every case in the population has an equal chance of being selected • Results in an unbiased, representative sample of the population studied.	• Can be time consuming. • It is not always practical/feasible to randomly select individuals from the population.
Stratified random	• Members of the population are classified into strata/categories (e.g., gender, age, region of country), and then a random sampling technique is used to select participants from within the strata in the same proportion as they exist in the population being studied.	• Participants will be representative of the population.	• It is not always practical to randomly select individuals from the population. • Can be time consuming because the categories/strata must be identified and calculated.
Cluster	• Instead of randomly sampling participants, the researcher uses naturally occurring groupings of participants (e.g., participants in Classroom 1 and participants in Classroom 2).	• Can be used when it is not practical to randomly select individual participants. • It is easy to obtain participants.	• Subjects in the naturally occurring groupings may not be equivalent, making it hard to interpret study results.
Convenience	• The researcher uses whatever participants are available, for example, volunteers.	• It is easy to obtain participants.	• Participants are likely not representative of the entire population. • The results likely cannot be generalized to the population.

Determining the Sample Size

The **sample size** refers to the number of people needed to represent the target population accurately. How many people constitute a good sample size? This is not an easy question because there are various factors that must be considered when deciding how many people to include in a sample. One thing to consider is the **homogeneity of the population**—how similar the people in your population are to one another. The more similar the members of the population, the smaller the sample that is necessary. The more dissimilar the members of the population, the larger the sample that is necessary to have this variation represented in the sample. Remember that the fewer the people chosen to participate in a survey (the smaller the sample), the more error the survey results are likely to include. This error is referred to as **sampling error**—a statistic that reflects how much error can be attributed to the lack of representation of the target population by the sample of respondents chosen.

There are various references that include statistical calculations that researchers use to estimate a sample size (for example, see Howell, 1995). For an online resource for calculating survey sample sizes, see On the Web Box 10.4.

ON THE WEB BOX 10.4

Calculating Sample Size

www.surveysystem.com/sscalc.htm

How many people must you sample to represent the entire population accurately? There are various print materials available to help researchers estimate a sample size, and there are also online resources. For example, Creative Research Systems (2007–2010) offers, as a public service, an online sample size calculator. This easy-to-use calculator can help you determine how many people you need to survey to get results that reflect the attitude or knowledge of your target population. This calculator also allows you to find out how precise your results are when you have already sampled a population.

Some surveys are administered to an entire population, and others are administered to a representative sample or a random sample of the population. As you probably have noted, representative samples and random samples are different. A representative sample is chosen so that the demographics of the sample match the demographic characteristics of the population. On the other hand, a random sample contains simply those individuals who were chosen using a random numbers table or by drawing names out of a hat. One of the assumptions we must make when using the Creative Research Systems online sample size calculator is that the sample we choose will be a random sample. Representative samples and convenience samples require far more responses than a simple random sample.

Another thing to remember when estimating sample size is that not everyone who receives a survey will complete and return it. Therefore, when deciding how many surveys to send, the researcher must first estimate the expected response. The expected response rate will be the number the calculator gives you, not the number of surveys to distribute. If you have already administered a survey and wish to know if the number that responded is sufficient, you can put in the number of received responses and calculate how confident you can be that the responses represent the responses you would have received if you had surveyed the entire population.

To use this calculator to determine a sample size, you will need to know the confidence interval and confidence level you are willing to accept. As you learned in Chapter 6, the confidence interval is the range of scores that we feel confident includes the true score. For example, if we have a confidence interval of 5 and 50% of our sample picks a particular answer, we can be certain that if we had asked the question of the entire population, somewhere between 45% (50 − 5) and 55% (50 + 5) would have selected that answer.

On the other hand, the confidence level is how certain we can be that the true percentage of the population who would pick an answer lies within the confidence level. For example, if our confidence level is 95%, this means that we can be 95% sure. By combining the confidence interval and the confidence level, we can say, for example, that we are 95% certain that the true percentage of the population who answered positively is between 45% and 55%.

When we are willing to accept wider confidence intervals, we can be more certain that the entire population would be within our range. For example, if we asked 500 Florida teenagers to name their favorite fast-food restaurant and 60% named the same one, we could be very certain that between 40% and 80% of all Florida teenagers actually do prefer this fast-food restaurant, but we cannot be so sure that between 59% and 61% of the teenagers prefer this one.

If you know the size of the population, you will want to enter it as well. On the other hand, if the population is unknown or is very large, you can leave it blank. Remember, random samples can be taken only from finite populations, that is, samples for which every individual can be identified and therefore have an equal chance of being chosen.

Here is an example of how the sample size calculator works. If we indicate that we are willing to accept a 99% confidence level, with a confidence interval of 5, and we know we have a population size of 1,000, the calculator estimates that we would need a random sample of 400. Note that if we leave the population blank, the required sample size increases to 666.

If we estimate that only half of those who receive the survey will complete and return it—a response rate of 50%—then we will need to administer or mail twice as many as we need, or 800.

Many people would say, "If I must administer 800 surveys for a population of 1,000, why not administer them to all 1,000?" However, as the size of the population grows, the proportion of the sample in relation to the population decreases. You can test this assertion by calculating the random sample size needed for a population of 10,000.

One way to decrease the size of the sample needed is to settle for a larger confidence level. For example, if we are willing to accept a confidence level of 95%, we would need a random sample of only 278 respondents. With an expected response rate of 50%, we would need to administer only 556 surveys, and that number would provide considerable savings of administration and analysis costs when compared to surveying the entire population.

For more information on calculating sample sizes, or to use the online sample size calculator, go to www.surveysystem.com/sscalc.htm.

Determine Sample Size

Confidence Level: ☐ 95% ◉ 99%

Confidence Interval: 5

Population: 1000

Calculate   Clear

Sample size needed: 400

Determine Sample Size

Confidence Level: ◉ 95% ☐ 99%

Confidence Interval: 5

Population: 1000

Calculate   Clear

Sample size needed: 278

SOURCE: Reprinted by permission of Creative Research Systems.

Distributing the Survey

The last step is to distribute the survey. How we distribute the survey depends on the type of survey (for example, mail survey, face-to-face interview, telephone survey). The survey user who is conducting an individually administered or face-to-face survey must decide when, where, and how people will meet with the survey researcher. The survey user who is conducting a telephone survey must decide who will make the phone calls, how the participants will be selected, and when the participants will be called. For mail surveys, the survey user must decide when, how, and to whom he or she will mail the surveys. Dillman's (1978) *Mail and Telephone Surveys: The Total Survey Design Method* is an older, yet excellent reference for conducting mail and telephone surveys. Fink's (2002) *The Survey Kit* is another excellent reference for conducting all types of surveys.

Special materials (for example, special paper on which to print the survey, envelopes for mail surveys, pencils for self-administered surveys, telephones for telephone surveys) might be required. Finally, self-administered surveys must be assembled (stapling papers together and stuffing and addressing envelopes) so that they are ready for respondents to complete.

Coding, Entering, and Analyzing Survey Data

The fourth phase of survey development involves coding and entering the survey data into the computer software for analysis. This process includes coding the survey questions, entering the data into a spreadsheet program, verifying that the data are entered correctly, and conducting the statistical analysis.

Coding the Survey Questions

The answers to all survey questions must be coded before they can be entered into a computer program. Although coding answers to closed-ended survey questions is relatively simple, coding answers to open-ended questions can be difficult. With closed-ended questions, survey researchers typically assign a code or numerical value to each of the response choices. For example, let us say the question was, "Why didn't you pass your psychology exam?" (*Select one of the following.*)

_____ I did not study

_____ I did not feel well

_____ I don't know

_____ Other

The first response option may be coded as a 1, the second as a 2, the third as a 3, and the fourth as a 4. Thus, each person's response would get a 1, 2, 3, or 4. Sometimes researchers use A, B, C, D, and so on instead of numbers, depending on the level of measurement of the question. Note that these are categorical data; therefore, statistical analyses are limited to calculating frequency of responses and percentage of responses.

If the respondent were allowed to choose more than one answer to a question (for example, "*Please select all that apply*"), the data analyst would code the corresponding number to the response options chosen by the respondent. When respondents choose more than one answer to a question, it is often necessary to record the answers to the question as if it were two questions. For more information on coding survey items, see Fink (2003).

Coding becomes more difficult for open-ended questions. Usually the first step is to take all of the answers to a particular open-ended question and sort them based on a criterion. For example, imagine the following survey item: "Last year you were a member of student government. Please comment on your experience." You might sort by positive and negative experiences (the criterion), or you might sort by the contents of the answers (another criterion; Edwards & Thomas, 1993). All open-ended questions need to be coded before they can be entered into the computer program.

Entering and Verifying the Data

Survey researchers usually use statistical software packages, such as SPSS, SAS, and Excel, to record and analyze responses. As the responses are entered into the computer program, the researcher constructs a **database**—a matrix in the form of a spreadsheet that shows the responses given by each participant (row) and for each question (column) in the survey. After entering the data and before starting the data analysis, the researcher verifies that the data have been entered correctly. For instance, if your survey questions have four possible responses numbered 1 to 4, you or the software can check to be sure that there is no datum less than 1 or greater than 4. If such a number is found, it is an entry error and can be corrected.

Conducting the Statistical Analysis

Usually survey developers plan the data analysis at the time of the survey's construction. Having a data analysis plan ensures that the data gathered will be appropriate for meeting the survey's objectives. (Recall our discussion of nominal, ordinal, interval, and ratio data in Chapter 5.) The actual analysis is usually a matter of pointing the mouse and clicking a button.

One statistic important for all surveys is the **response rate**—the number of individuals who responded to the survey divided by the total number of individuals to whom the survey was sent. Response rates tend to vary depending on the type of survey. For instance, one-on-one interviews can be expected to have higher response rates than mail surveys.

Survey researchers also calculate and report the reliability (internal consistency) of each of the dimensions on the survey. For example, earlier in this chapter we said that one objective of the course evaluation survey was to measure student opinions of course format. The reliability coefficient (KR-20 or coefficient alpha) shows how strongly the items in the survey that were intended to measure one objective are related (Edwards & Thomas, 1993).

The data analysis also includes calculating the sampling error. Used with means and standard deviations, sampling error tells us how accurately the data reflect what the results would have been if the researchers had surveyed the entire population. Many survey researchers believe that if the results of a survey come within 5 percentage points of what the results would have been if the entire population had been surveyed, the survey has done a good job. For more information on computing sampling errors for surveys, read Fowler (1988).

Next the researcher conducts **univariate analyses**—computation of statistics that summarize individual question responses. Univariate analyses include frequency counts, percentages, means, modes, and medians. Frequency counts are tallies of how many participants chose each of the response options for a question. Percentages are calculated by taking the number of individuals who chose a particular response and dividing that number by the total number of people who responded to the question. For questions that yield interval-level data, such as ratings from 1 to 10, the researcher may wish to calculate the mean, median, or mode. (We discussed these concepts in detail in Chapter 5.)

The survey objectives may require the researcher to compare the responses given by two or more sub-groups of respondents or the responses to two or more questions by all respondents. Such an analysis requires bivariate or multivariate analysis. **Bivariate analyses** provide information on two variables or groups, and **multivariate analyses** provide information on three or more variables or groups. These analyses may include calculating correlation coefficients, cross-tabulations, chi-square comparisons, *t* tests, or analyses of variance. (Some of these statistical tests are beyond the scope of this textbook; however, you will find them explained in most introductory statistics textbooks.) The technique the researcher chooses depends on the objectives of the survey and the level of measurement provided by the survey.

Presenting the Findings

The fifth and final phase involves reporting the survey results to those who commissioned the survey's development and sometimes to the public at large. Whether the report is written or oral, its effectiveness and usefulness depend on how well it is prepared and how well it addresses the questions and general knowledge of its audience (Fink, 2003). For instance, reports that contain numerous tables and statistical jargon will be useful for statisticians, but the general public needs a simpler version in everyday words.

Outlining a Report

In general, a survey report includes a description of the survey's objectives, details about survey construction and administration, and the survey findings. To ensure that each of these areas is covered in the report, the researcher prepares an outline of the information similar to the one shown in Figure 10.2.

Ordering and Determining the Contents of a Presentation

The general headings of the presentation outline provide a summary of the report and can serve as a structure for presenting the survey results. The focus of the presentation and the amount of detail provided should be adjusted to reflect the needs of the audience. For example, if you are presenting to researchers, they might be interested in knowing more about the size of the sample, the response rate, and the methods of analysis than would a general audience that might be more interested in the results and implications of the survey.

Using Slides and Handouts

Professionals use learning aids, such as slides and handouts, to keep the attention of the audience and to increase the audience's understanding of the results. You can use these learning aids to

Figure 10.2	Survey Report Outline

1. Survey Objectives—Class Evaluation Survey

   - To measure student opinions of course format and learning materials
   - To measure the instructor's organization and knowledge of the subject matter
   - To determine the overall effectiveness of the course

2. Survey Methods

   - Performed literature review
   - Communicated with subject matter experts

     —Dean of the faculty
     —Faculty

   - Identified survey objectives
   - Operationally defined survey objectives
   - Wrote survey questions
   - Prepared survey instrument
   - Pilot-tested survey
   - Revised and finalized survey
   - Administered survey

3. Survey Findings

   - 80% reported that the reading material was relevant.
   - 90% reported that exams assessed information presented in class.
   - 90% reported that the instructor was prepared for class.
   - 85% reported that the instructor was organized.
   - 90% reported that the instructor made course objectives clear.
   - 100% reported that the instructor was knowledgeable of the material.
   - 80% reported that the course was effective.
   - 90% reported that this was a good course.

4. Implications

   - Students liked the course.
   - Students thought the instructor was organized and knowledgeable.
   - Students thought the course was effective.

SOURCE: From Fink, A. (2003). *The survey handbook* (2nd ed.). Thousand Oaks, CA: Sage. Copyright © 2003 by Sage Publications. Reprinted by permission of Sage Publications, Inc.

display your presentation outline; major points related to each section of the outline; and charts, tables, and graphs. Typically this information is prepared on a transparency, on a slide, or in a PowerPoint (or some other software) presentation. You can also make copies of the information to provide to the audience as handouts, which help the audience follow the presentation and make notes only as needed.

INTERIM SUMMARY 10.2
THE SURVEY RESEARCH METHOD

- Surveys are one of various research methods you can use to collect information.
- Constructing a reliable and valid survey takes time, and it is as much a science as it is an art.
- Using a scientific approach to survey research will increase the reliability and validity of a survey.
- A scientific approach to surveys involves five general phases: identifying survey objectives and forming a hypothesis, constructing the survey, administering the survey, entering and analyzing the data, and presenting the findings.
- During the first phase, researchers identify the survey objectives, operationally define the objectives, and construct a plan for completing the survey.
- During the second phase, researchers select the type of survey, write the survey questions, prepare the survey for distribution, and pretest the survey.
- During the third phase, researchers select the appropriate respondents, determine the sample size, and distribute the survey.
- During the fourth phase, researchers code the survey questions, enter and verify the data, and conduct the analyses.
- During the fifth phase, researchers prepare and present an oral or written report.

Survey Reliability and Validity

Only well-developed and well-administered surveys provide information about attitudes, behaviors, and knowledge that we can feel confident about using. Psychometrics (which we discussed previously in Section II) allows us to determine when a survey is good. What is a good survey? Like a good psychological test, a good survey measures what it says it is measuring consistently and accurately. If a survey does not measure what it is intended to measure consistently and accurately, then it will not collect accurate information. Without accurate information, we tend to make poor decisions.

An unreliable survey cannot be valid because with inconsistent data you cannot have accurate findings (Fink, 2003). However, a reliable survey can be invalid; it can give you similar information each time you use it, but not information that is related to the purpose of the survey.

Survey Reliability

In survey research, we often speak of two types of errors: random errors and measurement errors. **Random errors** are those that are unpredictable, and **measurement errors** are those that are associated with how a survey performs in a particular population. As you recall from Chapter 6, reliability is a statistical measure that tells you how good an instrument is at obtaining similar results each time it is used. A reliable survey is one that gives you similar information each time you use it. A reliable survey is as free as possible from measurement error caused by poorly worded questions, ambiguous terms, inappropriate reading level, unclear directions, and incorrect skip patterns—to name a few.

As with psychological tests, there are various ways for gathering evidence of the reliability of a survey: test–retest, alternate forms, and split-half reliability. Test–retest and split half are the most common (discussed in detail in Chapter 6). You can increase a survey's reliability by writing multiple items for each dimension, determining whether other organizational members would assign an item to the same dimension for which it was written, and grouping all items from a single dimension together.

Survey Validity

As you recall from Chapters 7, 8, and 9, when we speak of test validity, we are asking the question "Are the inferences I am going to draw from a person's score on a test appropriate?" Validity refers to whether there is evidence to support the interpretation of the test scores. In survey research, when speaking of validity, we often refer to the degree to which the survey reflects or assesses the concept that a researcher is attempting to measure. If a survey is designed to measure students' satisfaction with course content, it should measure only students' satisfaction with course content—not students' satisfaction with their grades!

In survey research, we speak of both internal and external validity. Various methods exist for demonstrating evidence of internal validity. In survey research, we typically assess evidence of validity using four methods discussed in previous chapters: content, criterion-related, construct, and face validity. We are also concerned with external validity, or the extent to which the survey results obtained from a sample are generalizable to a larger population.

INTERIM SUMMARY 10.3
SURVEY RELIABILITY AND VALIDITY

- Good surveys are reliable and valid.
- A reliable survey is free of measurement error and provides you with similar information each time you use it.
- As with psychological tests, we can determine the reliability of a survey using a number of methods, including test–retest, alternate forms, and split-half reliability.

- A valid survey is one that measures what it claims to measure.
- As with psychological tests, we can determine the validity of a survey using a number of methods, including content, criterion-related, construct, and face validity.

Chapter Summary

We acquire information in many different ways. When we acquire information using the scientific method, we can feel more confident that the information is accurate than when we acquire it using other methods. The scientific method is a process of collecting information that involves five steps: identifying the issues and forming a hypothesis, designing the study, conducting the study, analyzing the results, and communicating the results.

Survey researchers use a variety of research techniques when following the scientific method to acquire knowledge. One technique is the survey—a measurement instrument that helps us collect information about people's attitudes, behaviors, and knowledge. The scientific approach to survey development involves five phases: identifying the survey objectives, constructing the survey, administering the survey, entering and analyzing the data, and presenting the findings. During the first phase, the researcher identifies the objectives of the survey, defines the objectives operationally, and constructs a plan for completing the survey. During the second phase, the researcher selects the type of survey to conduct, writes survey questions, prepares the survey, and pretests the survey. During the third phase, the researcher administers the survey. During the fourth phase, the researcher develops coding schemes for entering the data into a computer program, verifies the data, and analyzes the data. During the fifth phase, the researcher presents the results orally or in written format to the survey user. As with psychological tests, it is very important that surveys be reliable and valid.

Engaging in the Learning Process

KEY CONCEPTS

After completing your study of this chapter, you should be able to define each of the following terms. These terms are bolded in the text of this chapter and defined in the Glossary.

- bivariate analyses
- cluster sampling
- convenience sampling
- database
- decennial census survey
- descriptive research techniques
- double-barreled question
- experimental research techniques
- experts
- face-to-face surveys
- field test
- focus group
- homogeneity of the population
- individually administered surveys
- item nonresponse rate
- literature reviews
- mail surveys
- measurement errors
- multivariate analyses
- nonprobability sampling
- nonsampling measurement errors
- operational definition

- personal interviews
- population
- pretesting
- probability sampling
- random error
- response rate
- sample
- sample size
- sampling error
- scientific method
- self-administered surveys
- simple random sampling
- stratified random sampling
- structured observations
- structured record reviews
- survey objectives
- survey research firms
- survey researcher
- surveys
- systematic sampling
- telephone surveys
- univariate analysis

LEARNING ACTIVITIES

The following are some learning activities you can engage in to support the learning objectives for this chapter.

Learning Objectives	Study Tips and Learning Activities
After completing your study of this chapter, you should be able to do the following:	*The following study tips will help you meet these learning objectives:*
Describe the different ways we acquire knowledge.	• Review Helmstadter's (1970) six categories for how we acquire information. Write down information you have obtained in these different ways.
Explain how the scientific method differs from other methods for acquiring information, and describe the five steps associated with the scientific method.	• Think of the scientific method as a process. Write down the five steps associated with this process.
Apply the five-phase scientific approach to constructing, administering, and analyzing surveys.	• Review Table 10.2. Write down the five steps associated with the scientific method and the corresponding steps for designing surveys. • Brainstorm a purpose statement for a survey. Operationalize your purpose statement.

Learning Objectives	Study Tips and Learning Activities
	• Find an existing survey (for example, your college's course evaluation survey, a hotel customer satisfaction survey, a survey used by a faculty member as part of his or her research). What are the survey's strengths? What are its weaknesses?
Describe survey reliability and validity and associated concepts.	• Think back to Chapters 6–9. Write down the different forms of reliability and validity. Consider how you would gather evidence of the reliability and validity of a survey. Give examples.

ADDITIONAL LEARNING ACTIVITIES

1. Read the following anecdote from the beginning of this chapter and document what is wrong with the two questions in it:

   • "I had to complete a course evaluation survey for my research methods class. One of the questions on my survey was, 'Was the teacher available and responsive to your needs?' Another question was, 'How much time did you spend studying for this class?' My teacher said that these were not very good survey questions. Why not?"

2. Name the type of sampling used in the following examples:

   • Your psychology professor constructs a survey to measure college students' attitudes toward the Greek community on your college campus. The professor gets a list of all students from the registrar's office. He divides the students into freshmen, sophomores, juniors, and seniors. He then divides them into males and females. He randomly samples students from each of these groups.

   • Your sociology professor constructs a survey to measure females' attitudes toward all-male schools. The professor administers the survey to all of the students in her classes.

   • The U.S. Census Bureau constructs a supplement to the decennial census. The decennial census is a census of all people in the United States. The Census Bureau takes all people who responded to the most recent decennial census and uses a computer to select 5,000 to take the supplemental survey.

PRACTICE QUESTIONS

The following are some practice questions to assess your understanding of the material presented in this chapter.

Multiple Choice

Choose the one best answer to each question.

1. Psychological tests focus on _____ outcomes, and surveys focus on _____ outcomes.
   a. individual; group
   b. group: individual
   c. individual; individual
   d. group; group

2. The results of psychological tests are usually reported _____, and the results of surveys are often reported _____.
   a. as an overall score; as an overall score
   b. as an overall score; at the question level
   c. at the question level; as an overall score
   d. at the question level; at the question level

3. Surveys are research tools that collect information to describe and compare what?
   a. People's attitudes
   b. People's attitudes and knowledge
   c. People's attitudes, knowledge, and behaviors
   d. People's attitudes, knowledge, behaviors, and motives

4. If we asked parents to complete a survey to find out how they feel about their children wearing school uniforms, we would be asking them about their
   a. knowledge.
   b. attitude(s).
   c. behavior(s).
   d. motive(s).

5. If we come to believe that Friday the 13th is an unlucky day because of a superstition, we have acquired this information through
   a. intuition.
   b. authority.
   c. tenacity.
   d. rationalism.

6. According to Helmstadter (1970), which one of the following methods of acquiring information is the best for gathering accurate information?
   a. Intuition
   b. Tenacity
   c. Authority
   d. Scientific method

7. How many steps are associated with the scientific method?
   a. Three
   b. Five
   c. Seven
   d. Nine

8. Which one of the following statements is FALSE about surveys?
   a. Constructing surveys is as much a science as it is an art.
   b. In most cases, surveys are experimental research techniques.
   c. Surveys are used to collect important information from individuals.
   d. Surveys gather information about attitudes, knowledge, and behaviors.

9. When constructing a survey, the developer must have knowledge of all EXCEPT which one of the following?
   a. Different types of surveys
   b. Different types of survey questions
   c. How to conduct focus groups
   d. How to assemble questions into a survey instrument

10. Research suggests that when people answer survey questions they go through what stages?
    a. Comprehension, retrieval, and response communication
    b. Comprehension, retrieval, judgment, and response communication
    c. Comprehension, judgment, and response communication
    d. Comprehension, judgment, retrieval, and response communication

11. Which one of the following would you NOT recommend when assembling a survey?
    a. Use shading to prevent respondents from writing in specific sections, to separate text, and to guide respondents across a page.
    b. Ensure that there is adequate white space on the survey so that it looks inviting and is easy to complete.
    c. Print surveys on one side of the paper so that respondents can use the other side for taking notes.
    d. Spiral bind extremely long surveys.

12. Nonsampling errors are errors associated with the
    a. sampling of the individuals included in the survey.
    b. design and administration of the survey.
    c. quality of the survey questions.
    d. administration of the survey.

13. Which one of the following is NOT a purpose for pretesting a survey?
    a. Identifying sources of sampling measurement errors
    b. Examining the effectiveness of question revisions
    c. Indicating the effect of alternative versions of a question or survey
    d. Assessing the final version of a survey for ease of completion

14. With simple random sampling,
    a. every member of a population has an equal chance of being chosen.
    b. every nth (for example, every fifth) person in a population is chosen.
    c. a population is divided into subgroups or strata.
    d. clusters are selected and participants are selected from each cluster.

15. When should you use cluster sampling?
    a. When the population is very small
    b. When it is not feasible to list all individuals who belong to a population
    c. When it is impossible to select a random sample from the population
    d. When the population is very homogeneous

16. Which one of the following is FALSE about sample size?
    a. The sample size should be equal to or greater than 30% of the population size.
    b. The sample size can be calculated by knowing the confidence interval and level.
    c. The more dissimilar the members of the population, the larger the sample.
    d. The smaller the sample size, the more error the survey results are likely to include.

17. Computations of statistics that summarize individual question responses are called
    a. descriptive statistics.
    b. frequency distributions.
    c. univariate analyses.
    d. bivariate analyses.

18. Univariate analyses include all of the following EXCEPT
    a. frequency counts.
    b. percentages.
    c. means, modes, and medians.
    d. correlations.

19. Bivariate analyses include all of the following EXCEPT
    a. correlation coefficients.
    b. cross-tabulations.
    c. chi-square comparisons.
    d. percentages.

Short Answer/Essay

Read each of the following, and consider your response carefully based on the information presented in this chapter. Write your answer to each question in two or three paragraphs.

1. Describe the similarities and differences between surveys and psychological tests. Give examples.

2. Compare and contrast the methods for acquiring knowledge according to Helmstadter (1970). Give an example of each.

3. How does the scientific method differ from other methods of acquiring knowledge? What steps do we follow when using the scientific method? Describe each step.

4. Describe and give an example of each of the five phases of the scientific approach to constructing, administering, and analyzing surveys.

5. List four different types of survey questions. Give an example of each.

6. Explain why it is important for a survey to be both reliable and valid. Include definitions of reliability and validity as they apply to surveys, and provide an example of each.

ANSWER KEYS

Additional Learning Activities

1. Both of these course evaluation questions have difficulties. The first question ("Was the teacher available and responsive to your needs?") is actually asking more than one question—what we refer to as a double-barreled question. If a survey respondent replied yes to this question, it would be impossible to tell whether the respondent was saying yes to the teacher being available, responsive, or to both. The same difficulty would exist if the survey respondent replied no to this question. It would have been more appropriate to break this question into two questions such as "Was the teacher available?" and "Was the teacher responsive to your needs?" Although at first glance the second question ("How much time did you spend studying for this class?") might seem like a clear and concise question, it does not clearly define the context or unit of analysis. Is the survey developer interested in how much time students spent studying per day, per week, or over the course of the entire semester? And is the survey developer interested in the number of hours or number of days? A better question would be "On average, how many hours did you spend per week studying for this class?"

2. Each of the three examples uses a different type of sampling. The first uses stratified random sampling, where a population is divided into subgroups (or strata) and a random sample is selected from each stratum. The second example uses convenience sampling, where any available group of participants is used to represent the population. The third example uses simple random sampling, where every member of a population has an equal chance of being chosen as a member of the sample.

Multiple Choice

1. a	2. b	3. c	4. b	5. c
6. d	7. b	8. b	9. c	10. b
11. c	12. b	13. a	14. a	15. b
16. a	17. c	18. d	19. d	

Short Answer/Essay

Refer to your textbook for answers. If you are unsure of an answer and cannot generate the answer after reviewing your book, ask your professor for clarification.

How Do We Develop a Test?

CHAPTER 11: HOW DO WE DEVELOP A TEST?

After completing your study of this chapter, you should be able to do the following:

- Describe how to define the test domain, the target audience, and the purpose of the test.
- Develop a test plan, including defining the construct or constructs the test measures, choosing the test format, and specifying how to score the test.
- Differentiate between objective and subjective test questions, and describe the strengths and weaknesses of each.
- Describe the important issues in writing instructions for the test administrator and the test taker.

"Some of my professors use a test bank supplied by the publisher of our textbook to make up their tests. I don't think that's right since those questions are much harder than the questions that professors make up themselves."

"I made up a self-esteem test and gave it to my friends. All my friends had high scores, so I know they all have high self-esteem."

"My supervisor at work has a test she put together herself that she gives to everyone who applies for a job. She won't hire anyone who doesn't pass the test. When I looked at the test, I could tell right away what the right answers were even though I don't know anything about the job!"

Why Develop a New Test?

As you learned in Chapter 1, thousands of psychological tests are available from commercial marketers, test publishers, and research journals. Although you learned about many of these test publishers and research journals in Chapter 1, that discussion was limited to U.S. publishers and journals. On the Web Box 11.1 provides information and web addresses for test developers in South Africa, India, Korea, Malaysia, and Great Britain. Whether published in the United States or overseas, there are plenty of psychological tests from which the user can choose.

ON THE WEB BOX 11.1

Test Development Around the World

Because we wrote this textbook in the United States, most of our examples of psychological testing come from American journals and newspapers. However, psychologists, educators, and organizations develop and use psychological tests around the world. This box introduces you to websites on test development in South Africa, India, Korea, Malaysia, and Great Britain. These are only a few examples of the many test developers and consultants around the world.

In South Africa, the Human Sciences Research Council (HSRC; www.hsrc.ac.za) supports applied social scientific research projects and coordinates research that is large scale, collaborative, policy relevant, user driven, and public sector oriented. One research project of the HSRC is developing and classifying early childhood development and conducting continuing surveys about HIV.

SOURCE: Human Sciences Research Council. (n.d.). Retrieved June 13, 2010, from http://www.hsrc.ac.za

In India, the Social Sciences division of the Indian Statistical Institute (www.isical.ac.in/~psy) funds research and training on test development. For example, in March 2010 the Psychology Research Institute of the Indian Statistical Institute held a workshop on reliability in psychological research. Visit this site to find a list of tests that the division has funded and information on ongoing projects.

SOURCE: Indian Statistical Institute. (n.d.). *Psychology research unit.* Retrieved June 13, 2010, from http://www.isical.ac.in/~psy

In South Korea, the Korea Institute for Curriculum and Evaluation (KICE; www.kice.re.kr/en/functions/curriculum.jsp) conducts research on educational curriculum and evaluation. KICE also promotes and strengthens educational tests using scientific development and implementation. KICE oversees research, development, and implementation of the College Scholastic Ability Test, including scoring and results analysis of the test.

SOURCE: Korea Institute for Curriculum and Evaluation. (n.d.). Retrieved June 10, 2010, from http://www.kice.re.kr/en/functions/curriculum.jsp

In Malaysia, McPhee Andrewartha (www.mcpheeandrewartha.com.au) is a consulting firm and counseling and consulting management/psychology group. They provide products and services in vocational assessment, human resources evaluation, early assessment of schoolchildren, and employee attitude surveys.

SOURCE: McPhee Andrewartha. (n.d.). Retrieved June 13, 2010, from http://www.mcpheeandrewartha.com.au/

In Great Britain, The Psychometrics Centre at the University of Cambridge (www.psychometrics.sps.cam.ac.uk) strives to promote excellence in psychological, occupational, clinical, and educational assessment. The focus is on four core areas: research, training, services to industry, and developing new tests.

SOURCE: University of Cambridge, Psychometrics Centre. (2008). *Psychometrics Centre.* Retrieved June 13, 2010, from http://www.psychometrics.sps.cam.ac.uk

As we discussed in Section II, test validity depends on the suitability of a test for a particular audience of test takers, adequate sampling of behaviors from a specific test domain, and the purpose for which test scores are used. Therefore, researchers develop new tests to meet the needs of a special group of test takers, to sample behaviors from a newly defined test domain, or to improve the accuracy of test scores for their intended purpose. For instance, an achievement test may be needed for a special population of individuals with a disability that affects how they perceive or answer the test questions. A new theory may suggest fresh definitions of constructs and require a new test to assess them. Finally, a better-defined test domain may generate test scores that predict a critical criterion more accurately.

In Chapter 10, we discussed the scientific method of survey design. In this chapter and Chapter 12, we discuss the steps for developing psychological tests. The scientific method discussed in Chapter 10 also applies to developing and validating psychological tests. This chapter looks at the process of constructing a test plan, various formats for writing questions (for example, multiple choice, true/false) along with their strengths and weaknesses, and how test takers' perceptions and preconceived notions can influence test scores. Finally, we present guidelines on how to write test questions and discuss the importance of the instructions that accompany a test.

You will find many similarities between developing a scientific survey and developing a psychological test. Both rely on the scientific method, behavior observation, data collection, and analysis. Both require conducting a study to determine the validity of the results.

We have divided the test development process into 10 steps. Figure 11.1 provides a flowchart depicting this process. This chapter discusses the first four steps:

1. Defining the testing universe, audience, and purpose.

2. Developing a test plan.

3. Composing the test items.

4. Writing the administration instructions.

Chapter 12 covers the last six steps:

5. Conducting the pilot test.

6. Conducting the item analysis.

7. Revising the test.

8. Validating the test.

9. Developing the norms.

10. Compiling the test manual.

Defining the Testing Universe, Audience, and Purpose

The first step in test development is to define the testing universe, the target audience, and the purpose of the test. As you recall from Chapter 7, the testing universe is the body of knowledge or behaviors that the test represents, the target audience is the group of individuals who will take the

Figure 11.1   Flowchart of the Test Development Process

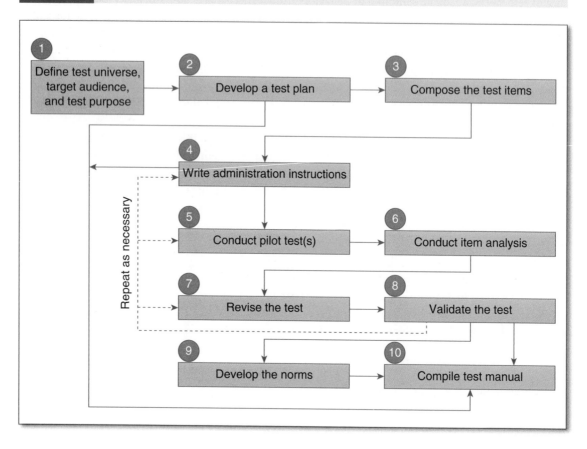

test, and the purpose of the test is the information that the test will provide to the test user. This stage provides the foundation for all other development activities, so it is important to put ample time and thought into these important issues. You may find a review of Chapter 7 helpful before you continue reading.

Defining the Testing Universe

To define the testing universe, the developer prepares a working definition of the construct that the test will measure. If the test is going to measure an abstract construct, the developer conducts a thorough review of the psychological literature to locate studies that explain the construct and any current tests that measure the construct. As discussed in Chapters 7 and 9, we need to define constructs operationally in terms of behaviors that are associated with the construct.

Defining the Target Audience

When defining the target audience, the developer makes a list of the characteristics of the persons who will take the test—particularly those characteristics that affect how test takers will respond to the test questions. For instance, in many cases we cannot just develop a test for "children"; instead, we must indicate the characteristics of the children, such as age and reading level. A test for sixth graders will differ considerably from a test for first graders, preschoolers, or infants.

Developers must also consider what reading level is appropriate for the target audience. Obviously, young children would not be expected to read a psychological test. They usually require one-on-one administration. As you recall, the Bayley Scales are appropriate for testing very young children (Bayley, 1993). Some adults also might not have sufficient reading skills to read test questions and instructions. For example, adults for whom English is a second language or who have a reading disability will also require one-on-one test administration.

Another consideration is whether the individuals in the target audience have any disabilities or characteristics that would require a special test administration or interpretation. As you recall from Chapter 3, individuals with sensory, motor, or cognitive impairments may require modifications to the testing process. For example, these test takers may require special equipment, such as an electronic amplification apparatus, or a reader or writer to assist them in completing the test.

Finally, developers must consider whether test takers will be motivated to answer the test questions honestly. Sometimes test takers may want to provide false answers to achieve high or low scores on a test. For instance, a dishonest person may wish to "pass" an honesty test, or a mentally ill person may wish to achieve a healthy diagnosis. Researchers have designed special test formats, which we discuss later in this chapter, for such persons who desire to "fake" a test.

Defining the Test Purpose

The purpose includes not only what the test will measure—for instance, self-esteem—but also how the test users will use the test scores. Will the scores be used to compare test takers (normative approach), or will they be used to indicate achievement (criterion approach)?

An example of the normative approach to test interpretation is an employment test in which the applicant who achieves the highest score will receive the job offer (you recall from Chapter 2 that this can be a comparative decision). In this case, the individual's actual score is not as important as the individual's score in relation to the scores of others who also took the test. You might be interested to know that the normative approach is used to determine who wins the gold medal in each Olympic event. The athlete does not need to perform better than athletes did during past years to win the gold medal. The athlete simply needs to perform better than the athletes who competed that year.

An example of the criterion approach is the way we interpret achievement test results. In this approach, the individual must achieve a certain score to qualify as passing or excellent (recall from Chapter 2 that this is an absolute decision). A good example of this is how we often classify student performance using the letter grades A to F. Students who achieve a test score that qualifies as an A will receive that letter grade.

Many or all students may achieve A's, or many or all students may achieve F's. The interpretation of the test score does not depend on the performance of others. (Chapter 13 discusses the normative and criterion approaches in more detail.)

Another question when determining the test purpose is whether the scores will be used cumulatively to test a theory (for instance, identify a correlation between intelligence and another variable) or individually to provide information about the individual (for instance, his or her IQ). In the former case, the purpose of the test is to deliver a distribution of scores. In the latter case, the accuracy of the individual scores is most important. In other words, when test users employ a large number of test scores to establish a statistical relationship, the accuracy of each score is not as important as when test users' interest is in the score of each individual. Therefore, a shorter test, perhaps with lower reliability, may be sufficient when using many test scores, and a longer, highly reliable test will be necessary when the focus of interest is on individual scores.

Information about the testing universe, target audience, and test purpose provides the basis for making other decisions about the test. For instance, information about the intended test takers and how test scores will be used determines whether the test can be administered to groups, individuals, or both. Special populations may require special types of administration, and characteristics of the test takers, such as reading level, determine whether the construct can be measured in a group setting using a paper-and-pencil format or whether the test should be administered orally in a one-on-one setting.

Developing a Test Plan

Just as survey development requires writing a plan that operationalizes the survey objectives, test development requires writing a test plan. As you recall from Chapter 7, the test plan specifies the characteristics of the test, including an operational definition of the construct and the content to be measured (the testing universe), the format for the questions, and the administration and scoring of the test. Let us consider each part of the test plan in more detail.

Defining the Construct and the Content to Be Measured

After reviewing the literature about the construct and any available tests, the test developer is ready to write a concise definition of the construct. Such a definition includes operationalizing the construct in terms of observable and measurable behaviors. The definition also provides boundaries for the test domain by specifying what content should be tested and excluding content that is not appropriate for testing.

The test plans for clinical tests are based on carefully researched constructs. For example, For Your Information Box 11.1 contains operational definitions of the constructs measured by the College Adjustment Scales (Anton & Reed, 1991), a test designed to measure common developmental and psychological problems experienced by college students.

In organizations, test developers base their test plan on a job analysis that defines the knowledge, skills, abilities, and other characteristics (KSAOs) required to perform a job successfully. These KSAOs are the constructs that the test measures. The job analysis also describes the tasks performed on the job. These tasks are the observable and measurable behaviors associated with each KSAO. (Chapter 15 discusses job analysis in more detail.)

In educational settings, the curricula (for instance, assigned readings, handouts, lectures) provide the basis for developing a test plan. As you recall, Chapter 7 described test plans and their relation to evidence of validity based on the content of the test.

In addition to defining and operationalizing the construct, the test plan specifies the approximate number of questions needed to sample the test domain. Should the test developer write 5 questions or 50 questions to measure each construct? This decision affects the reliability of the test and depends in part on the test format that the test developer chooses.

Choosing the Test Format

The test format refers to the type of questions that the test will contain. Most test developers prefer to use one type of format throughout the test to facilitate the administration and scoring. Sometimes test inventories or batteries that measure several different constructs use different formats in each section. In such cases, it is important to provide administration instructions for each section and to administer each section separately.

Test formats provide two elements: a stimulus to which the test taker responds and a mechanism for response. For instance, a multiple-choice question may provide a question (stimulus) followed by four or five possible answers (mechanisms for response). A multiple-choice format is also an objective test format because it has one response that is designated as "correct" or that provides evidence of a specific construct. In other words, the test taker receives credit for choosing only one correct response. Other types of

FYI

FOR YOUR INFORMATION BOX 11.1

Constructs Measured by the College Adjustment Scales

Anxiety

Definition: A measure of clinical anxiety focusing on common affective, cognitive, and physiological symptoms.

Behaviors:

High anxiety is indicated by muscle tension, increased vigilance and scanning of the environment, rapid and shallow respiration, and excessive concerns and worries about real or expected life events that may be experienced as intrusive and unwanted thoughts.

Depression

Definition: A measure of clinical depression focusing on common affective, cognitive, and physiological symptoms.

Behaviors:

Depression is indicated by easy or chronic fatigue, lost interest or pleasure in normally enjoyable activities, feelings of sadness and hopelessness, and social withdrawal or isolation from friends and peers.

Suicidal Ideation

Definition: A measure of the extent of recent ideation (ideas) reflecting suicide, including hopelessness and resignation.

Behaviors:

Suicidal ideation is indicated by reports of thinking about suicide or behaviors associated with suicide attempts, including formulating a suicide plan.

Substance Abuse

Definition: A measure of disruption in interpersonal, social, academic, and vocational function as a result of substance use and abuse.

Behaviors:

Substance abuse is indicated by difficulty in interpersonal, social, academic, and vocational functioning as a result of substance abuse or by reporting guilt or shame about substance use, including embarrassment about behaviors displayed while abusing drugs or alcohol.

Self-Esteem Problems

Definition: A measure of global self-esteem that taps negative self-evaluations and dissatisfaction with personal achievement.

Behaviors:

Self-esteem problems are indicated by self-criticism and dissatisfaction with perceived skills, abilities, or achievement in comparison with peers, including seeing oneself as unassertive, excessively sensitive to criticism from others, and/or physically or sexually unattractive.

Interpersonal Problems

Definition: A measure of the extent of problems in relating to others in the campus environment.

Behaviors:

Interpersonal problems are indicated by difficulty in relating to others, including excessive dependence or increased vulnerability and/or a distrustful, argumentative style of relating to others.

Family Problems

Definition: A measure of difficulties experienced in relationships with family members.

Behaviors:

Family problems are indicated by difficulty in achieving emotional separation from family and learning to live independently, including worry or concern over problems occurring in a conflicted or tumultuous family.

Academic Problems

Definition: A measure of the extent of problems related to academic performance.

Behaviors:

Academic problems are indicated by poor study skills, inefficient use of time, poor concentration ability, and/or test anxiety.

Career Problems

Definition: A measure of the extent of problems related to career choice.

Behaviors:

Career problems are indicated by difficulty in setting career goals and making decisions that are important for career goal attainment, including anxiety or worry about selecting an academic major or future career.

objective test formats include true/false questions and fill-in-the-blank questions. Most test developers prefer objective test formats because the scorer does not need to make any judgment to determine the correct response. Objective test formats also are easily related to the test plan and the construct designated for measurement. These attributes facilitate documentation of the test's reliability and validity.

Subjective test formats, on the other hand, do not have a single response that is designated as "correct." Interpretation of the response as correct or providing evidence of a specific construct is left to the judgment of the person who scores or interprets the test taker's response. **Projective tests,** such as the Rorschach Inkblot Test and the Thematic Apperception Test (described in detail in Chapter 14), are subjective test formats because the stimuli for these tests are ambiguous pictures. As you learned in previous chapters, the test taker provides a story or an explanation (mechanism for response), which the scorer judges to be appropriate or inappropriate. Other examples of subjective test formats are open-ended or essay questions and the traditional employment interview. In each of these, the test taker or interviewee responds with any answer he or she considers appropriate. Documenting the reliability and validity of tests based on a subjective test format is more difficult than doing so based on an objective test format. For this reason, many test developers prefer objective test formats. We discuss these formats in more detail later in this chapter.

Administering and Scoring the Test

After choosing a test format (objective or subjective) and the appropriate type of question (for example, true/false, multiple choice, open-ended), the test developer needs to specify how to administer and score the test. This information is an important part of the test plan that will influence the format and content of the test items. For example, will the test be administered in writing, orally, or by computer? How much time will test takers have to complete the test? Will the test be administered to groups or individuals? Will the test be scored by a test publisher, the test administrator, or the test takers? Finally, what type of data is the test expected to yield? In other words, will the test scores provide the information required by the purpose of the test?

The **cumulative model of scoring** is probably the most common method for determining an individual's final test score. The cumulative model assumes that the more the test taker responds in a particular fashion (with either "correct" answers or ones that are consistent with a particular attribute), the more the test taker exhibits the attribute being measured. To score a test using the cumulative model, the test taker receives 1 point for each correct answer, and the total number of correct answers becomes the test score. Assuming that the test questions are comparable, the cumulative model of scoring can yield interval-level data. In any case, psychologists traditionally assume that such tests produce interval-level data that can then be interpreted using the norming procedures described in Chapter 5.

The **categorical model of scoring** is used to place test takers in a particular group or class. For instance, the test taker must display a pattern of responses that indicates a clinical diagnosis of a certain psychological disorder or the attributes that make up a behavioral trait. The categorical model typically yields nominal data because it places test takers in categories.

The **ipsative model of scoring** differs from the cumulative and categorical models because this type of format requires the test taker to choose among the constructs that the test measures. The forced-choice format yields ipsative data when the statements in an item represent different constructs. In another ipsative model, scorers can compare the test taker's scores on various scales within the inventory to arrive at a profile. This relative standing on various traits then provides information on the test taker's overall performance or attributes. Test users should not compare individual test scores for decision making because the ipsative model assumes that individuals themselves are unique and incomparable.

Meade (2004) provides psychometric and statistical evidence that the ipsative method can yield quite different results from those of the cumulative method for individuals. He compared forced-choice ipsative data with normative data collected from job applicants in an organizational setting. Meade found that the job applicants shown as suitable for hiring by the ipsative method were different from those identified as suitable for hiring by the normative method. He suggests that the decision process that respondents must use to select an item as "most like me" or "least like me" is unknown and inherently alters the psychometric properties of forced-choice items. Meade asserts that using the forced-choice format in employment testing is inappropriate.

The cumulative model can be combined with either the categorical model or the ipsative model. For instance, scale scores are usually obtained using the cumulative method, and then the categorical model is applied to obtain an overall interpretation or diagnosis of the individual test taker's performance.

Developing the Test Itself

After completing the test plan, the test developer is ready to begin writing the test questions and instructions. Because composing the actual testing stimuli is an important and time-consuming activity, we devote the remainder of this chapter to the art of writing the test itself. Again, you will find many similarities between writing survey questions and writing test questions.

Before we discuss writing test questions, you should know that after writing the initial test questions, the test developer conducts a **pilot test**—a scientific evaluation of the test's performance—followed by revisions to determine the final form that the test will take. The test developer then follows up the pilot test with other studies that provide the necessary data for validation and norming. Conducting the pilot test and analyzing its data are integral parts of the test development process. (We address them in detail in Chapter 12.)

INTERIM SUMMARY 11.1
STEPS IN TEST CONSTRUCTION

- The first step in test development involves defining the testing universe, the target audience, and the purpose of the test.
- The next step is to write a test plan that includes the construct(s) definition, the testing universe, the test format, the administration method, and the scoring method.
- After a review of the literature, the test developer writes a concise definition of the test construct or constructs and operationalizes each construct in terms of observable and measurable behaviors.
- The test developer chooses an objective or subjective format and the type of test question to be used (for example, multiple choice, true/false, open-ended, essay).

- Next the test developer specifies how the test will be administered and scored. Three models for scoring are the cumulative model, the categorical model, and the ipsative model. The scoring model determines the type of data (nominal, ordinal, or interval) that the test will yield.
- After completing the test plan, the test developer is ready to begin writing the actual test questions and administration instructions.
- After writing the test, the developer conducts a pilot test followed by other studies that provide the necessary data for validation and norming.

Composing the Test Items

As you can see, test developers have much to do before they begin to write the test itself. Careful definition and review of the constructs, however, makes development much easier and yields more questions that are successful. Many decisions, such as method of administration, are considered and resolved while developing the test plan. Therefore, the test plan becomes the blueprint for proceeding with development. Imagine what it would be like to build a home without a blueprint. Without a detailed blueprint, the home builders would have no clear understanding of what they were building. The same is true for test development.

Throughout this textbook, we have referred to the *stimulus* to which the test taker responds as a *test question*. In reality, test questions are not always questions. Stimuli are frequently presented on tests in the form of statements, pictures, or incomplete sentences as well as other less common forms. Therefore, psychologists and test developers refer to these stimuli or test questions as **test items,** and we refer to them as such for the remainder of this chapter and Chapter 12.

Test developers choose the item format based on information in the test plan, such as the target audience, method of administration, and requirements for scoring. Following is a discussion of some standard item formats, including strengths or weaknesses that may cause test developers to choose or reject them as appropriate formats in various situations. Recall that Chapter 10 provided a list of various types of survey questions. Types of test items include those in Chapter 10 as well as a few more types such as projective item formats. We consider item formats in terms of whether they are objective or subjective.

Objective Items

Multiple Choice

The item format used most often is **multiple choice.** Because this format is familiar, many people use it for personality inventories, pre-employment tests, standardized tests, and classroom tests. The multiple-choice format consists of a question or partial sentence, called a **stem,** followed by a number of responses (usually four or five), of which only one is correct. The incorrect responses are called **distracters** and are designed to appear correct to someone who does not know the correct answer.

When writing a multiple-choice item, it is important that the developer clearly differentiate the correct response from the distracters. Distracters that are "almost right" can be tricky and confusing to the respondent. Such items rarely yield accurate assessment information. On the other hand, the distracters must be realistic enough to appeal to the uninformed test taker. In no case should funny or unrealistic distracters be included; they decrease the accuracy of the assessment.

Multiple-choice items are popular because having one right answer eliminates confusion or controversy in scoring a correct response. Scoring is also easily accomplished either by a nonprofessional or electronically (for example, by a computer). One problem, however, is that test takers who do not know the correct answer may obtain credit by guessing. A test taker who does not know the correct answer for a multiple-choice item with four responses has a 1 in 4 (25%) chance of guessing the correct answer. These odds can be decreased if the test taker can eliminate one or two of the distracters, yielding a 1 in 3 (33%) or 1 in 2 (50%) chance of guessing the correct answer. This disadvantage is offset by presenting a large number of items. For instance, although an uninformed test taker may have a 1 in 4 chance of guessing the correct answer on one item, those odds are significantly increased by increasing the number of items. The odds of an uninformed test taker correctly guessing the correct response (when there are four responses) to each of 10 multiple-choice questions are 1 in 1,048,576! See For Your Information Box 11.2 for an example of a multiple-choice question.

True/False

The stem of a **true/false** item asks, "Is this statement TRUE or FALSE?" If a test contains only true/false items, the instructions contain the stem and direct the test takers to mark each statement as true or false. Again, test takers can gain some advantage by guessing, and the odds of guessing correctly on one item are 50% (1 in 2). The Hogan Personality Inventory, discussed in Chapter 15, uses the true/false format. This format converts to a multiple-choice format by presenting four or five statements, from which the test taker chooses the one statement that is true or false. For Your Information Box 11.2 shows two examples of true/false items.

Forced Choice

The **forced choice** format is similar to the multiple-choice format; however, test developers typically use forced-choice items for personality and attitude tests rather than for knowledge tests. This format requires the test taker to choose one of two or more words or phrases that appear unrelated but are equally acceptable. The stem of the forced-choice question (often included in the test instructions) may ask the respondent, "Which of each pair is most descriptive of you?" Although the words or phrases appear to be unrelated, the test developer must have empirical evidence that the responses yield significantly different responses from different types of people. In other words, people with similar personality traits usually prefer one response to the other.

FYI

FOR YOUR INFORMATION BOX 11.2

Examples of Objective Item Formats

Multiple Choice

Which one of the following levels of measurement involves ranking from lowest to highest?

   a. Nominal
   b. Ordinal
   c. Equal interval
   d. Ratio

True/False

Indicate whether the following statements are true or false by placing a T for true or an F for false in the space to the left of the statement:

   1. _____ Proportions can be calculated only from data obtained using a ratio scale.
   2. _____ Equal-interval scales do not have a true zero point.

Forced Choice

Place an X in the space to the left of the word in each pair that best describes your personality:

   1. _____ Sunny   2. _____ Outgoing
        _____ Friendly   _____ Loyal

Researchers during World War II designed forced-choice items to yield ratings with less bias (Berkshire & Highland, 1953). This format subsequently became popular, making it more difficult to "fake" a test. This format would be appropriate to use when the potential test takers are likely to answer dishonestly. For Your Information Box 11.2 shows two examples of forced-choice items. One version of the Myers–Briggs Personality Inventory, discussed in Chapter 1, has a section of forced-choice questions.

The strength of the forced-choice format is that the items are more difficult for respondents to guess or fake. Because the paired words or phrases appear to have little in common, the test taker cannot guess what the best response should be. On the other hand, the forced-choice format has little face validity, that is, no apparent connection with the stated purpose of the test. As you recall from Chapter 7, lack of face validity may produce poor responses from test takers. Making a number of decisions between or among apparently unrelated words or phrases can become distressing, and test takers who want to answer honestly and accurately often become frustrated with forced-choice questions.

Subjective Items

Some test users prefer subjective items to objective items. Although objective items are easy to score and interpret, they also rely on cues provided by the test. Subjective items, on the other hand, give the test taker fewer cues and open wider areas for response.

Essay questions, similar to open-ended survey questions, are popular subjective items in educational settings. Such questions are usually general in scope and require lengthy written responses by test takers. Essays provide a freedom of response that facilitates assessing higher cognitive behaviors such as analysis, synthesis, and evaluation (Hopkins & Antes, 1979). Because the responses that essays generate may vary in terms of breadth and depth of topic, the scorer must make a judgment regarding whether the response is correct. Often the scorer awards points based on how closely the test taker's response matches a predetermined correct response.

Many students prefer essay questions because this format allows them to focus on demonstrating what they have learned rather than limiting them to answering specific questions. Others point out, however, that writing skills, ranging from readability of handwriting to graceful phrasing, may influence scorer judgments. Unless writing skills are part of the testing universe, such considerations may lead to inaccurate judgments and so to inaccurate test scores.

In organizational settings, the traditional subjective test is the employment interview. **Interview questions,** like essay questions, are general in scope. In this case, the interviewer decides what is a "good" or "poor" answer. Again, the interviewee has a wide range of responses; however, as with the essay, the interview format introduces many opportunities for causing inaccurate judgments.

As you recall from Chapter 1, test developers in the early 20th century developed a number of **projective techniques** for diagnosing mental disorders. This subjective format uses a highly ambiguous stimulus to elicit an unstructured response from the test taker. In other words, the test taker "projects" his or her perspective and perceptions onto a neutral stimulus. Such tests contain a variety of projective stimuli, including pictures and both written and spoken words. Test takers may respond verbally or by drawing pictures. Interpretation of children's play also can be categorized as a projective technique (Krall, 1986). (Chapter 14 describes projective techniques in more detail.)

Another subjective format often used in attitude and personality scales is the **sentence completion** format, which presents an incomplete sentence such as "I feel happiest when I am _____." The respondents then complete the sentence in any way that makes sense to them. One person might say, "I feel happiest when I am *playing the piano.*" Another might respond, "I feel happiest when I am *studying for an important exam.*" The person scoring the test will then compare the test taker's responses with responses supplied by the test developer to award points or identify a trait or type.

For Your Information Box 11.3 shows an example of each of these subjective item formats.

FOR YOUR INFORMATION BOX 11.3

Examples of Subjective Item Formats

Essay

Compare and contrast the four levels of measurement, and give an example of each.

Interview

Please tell me about a time that you were in disagreement with your colleagues. What was the disagreement about, what did you do, and what was the outcome?

Projective Technique

What do you see when you look at this picture?

Sentence Completion

I am at my best when _____.

By their nature, subjective tests are at risk for introducing judgment error into test scores. Therefore, evidence of interrater reliability is of particular importance for subjective tests. Test developers can reduce scoring errors by providing clear and specific scoring keys that illustrate how various types of responses should be scored. Test users can increase the reliability of scoring essays, interviews, and projective tests by providing training for scorers and using two scorers who make independent evaluations. If not carefully constructed, both objective and subjective test item formats are likely to introduce error into test scores.

Response Bias

Another source of error in test scores comes from test takers. Researchers have found that some people have response sets (also known as response styles) for choosing answers to test items. Response sets are patterns of responding that result in false or misleading information. These sources of error limit the accuracy and usefulness of test scores, so test developers need to consider the possible effects of response bias when they develop a test. Social desirability, acquiescence, random responding, and faking are response sets that test developers have researched a great deal. Others, such as poor handwriting, not reading instructions, and inattention to detail, also pose problems for test scorers.

Social Desirability

One problem for test developers is the tendency of some test takers to provide or choose answers that are socially acceptable or that present themselves in a favorable light. This response is called **social desirability.** Research suggests that many people have a desire to make a favorable impression. Crowne and Marlowe (1960, 1964) developed a social desirability scale to assess the extent to which individuals tend to respond in a socially desirable fashion. For Your Information Box 11.4 contains information on identifying test takers who are likely to have the social desirability response set.

FYI

FOR YOUR INFORMATION BOX 11.4

Identifying the Social Desirability Response Set

In 1960, Douglas Crowne, at Ohio State University, and David Marlowe, at the University of Kentucky's College of Medicine, published an article in the *Journal of Consulting Psychology* describing a new scale they had developed to identify persons who have a high need for presenting themselves in a favorable light. In 1964, they published *The Approval Motive: Studies in Evaluative Dependence,* which details the development of the Marlowe–Crowne Social Desirability Scale. They describe the items in the scale as being "behaviors which are culturally sanctioned and approved but which are improbable of occurrence" (Crowne & Marlowe, 1960, p. 350).

The scale soon became widely used by test developers who wished to identify tests and test items that suggested responses that would appeal to persons who wished to show themselves in a favorable light. The scale, still used in research today, became the accepted operationalization of the social desirability response set.

As you can see from the sample items below, the test provides statements that are very socially acceptable. Those statements, however, are not ones that many people could sincerely attribute as true of themselves. The scale format is true/false, and Crowne and Marlowe provide a key to show which answer (shown in parentheses) a person with a high need for approval is likely to provide.

Sample Items

- Before voting, I thoroughly investigate the qualifications of all the candidates. (T)
- I never hesitate to go out of my way to help someone in trouble. (T)
- On occasion, I have had doubts about my ability to succeed in life. (F)
- I sometimes feel resentful when I don't get my way. (F)

SOURCE: From Crowne, D., & Marlowe, D. (1960). A new scale of social desirability independent of social psychopathology. *Journal of Consulting Psychology, 24,* 349–354. Copyright © 1960 by the American Psychological Association.

When writing test items, it is important to consider social desirability. For instance, developers try to balance the social desirability of the correct response and the distracters in multiple-choice questions. When using the forced-choice format, developers can pair responses based on their desirability. When social desirability is likely to cause error, test developers may conduct a study to determine how socially desirable each proposed response is to a sample of people who resemble the test's target audience. The developers then discard responses that correlate strongly with a social desirability scale.

Acquiescence

Another response set familiar to test developers is **acquiescence,** the tendency to agree with any ideas or behaviors presented. For instance, someone who labels each statement on a true/false test as true would be demonstrating a response set of acquiescence. Javeline (1999) points out how an acquiescence response set may have a cultural basis as well as being an individual inclination. According to Javeline, the inclination to agree is most prevalent in societies that value deference and politeness. If such a bias is not taken into account, conclusions drawn from attitude surveys, such as public opinion polls, may be interpreted incorrectly. For this reason, test and survey developers should balance items for which the correct response would be positive with an equal number of items for which the correct response would be negative. For Your Information Box 11.5 illustrates this strategy and describes how balancing positive and negative items affects cumulative scoring.

FYI

FOR YOUR INFORMATION BOX 11.5

Using Reverse Scoring to Balance Positive and Negative Items

Some test takers are inclined to give mostly positive responses to questions regardless of the questions' content. The test developer tries to offset the effects of this response set, known as acquiescence, by balancing positive statements with negative statements. Because scoring is usually a cumulative estimate of how much the test taker exhibits or agrees with the test's construct, it then becomes necessary to reverse the responses to negative items.

For example, a test assessing a student's attitude toward studying may ask the test taker to respond using the following 5-point scale:

1 = rarely true
2 = sometimes true
3 = neither true nor false
4 = very often true
5 = almost always true

High responses (4 or 5) to positive statements, such as "I enjoy memorizing vocabulary words," would reflect a positive attitude toward studying. However, high responses to negative items, such as "When I sit down to study, I get depressed," would indicate the opposite—a negative attitude toward studying. Therefore, the test scorer reverses the response numbers of negative items. A response of 5 to a negative item would be changed to 1, a response of 4 would be changed to 2. A neutral response of 3 would remain the same.

After reversing the responses on the negative items, the test scorer then uses the cumulative model of scoring in which the numbers indicated for each response are added to arrive at the overall score.

Random Responding and Faking

Sometimes test takers are unwilling or unable to respond to test items accurately. In this case, they may engage in **random responding**—responding to items in a random fashion by marking answers without reading or considering them. This response set is likely to occur when test takers lack the necessary skills (such as reading) to take the test, do not wish to be evaluated, or lack the attention span necessary to complete the task.

Earlier in this chapter, we discussed **faking,** which refers to the inclination of some test takers to try to answer items in a way that will cause a desired outcome or diagnosis. For instance, a test taker completing a personality test for a prospective employer may try to answer items in a way that makes him or her appear to be friendly and cooperative (faking good). On the other hand, a test taker who has been charged with a serious crime may wish to appear to be mentally disturbed (faking bad). As you recall, one way to prevent faking is to use a forced-choice format for the test items.

Rather than prevention, some test developers include special items in the test to detect which test takers are giving dishonest answers. These items are scored separately from the test, and test developers refer to them as *faking scales* or *validity scales*. A high score on a faking scale identifies test takers who are uncooperative, responding randomly, or faking. The items on a faking scale usually have nothing to do with the test construct and have obvious responses for most of the population. In other words, they will be either true or false for nearly everyone in the target audience. Test takers who respond dishonestly are likely to answer differently from most people on a number of these items, thereby tipping off the scorer that they were not cooperating.

Although these scales are useful for detecting uncooperative test takers, many cooperative test takers may resent tests that ask questions about personal feelings and activities that have no relation to the purpose of the test. For instance, job applicants may interpret employment tests that ask personal questions as unfair. As you recall from Chapter 7, face validity—what the test appears to measure—is not essential for a test to be valid, but it can enhance the test taker's willingness to cooperate with the testing process.

Writing Effective Items

As you can see, researchers and test developers have thought a lot about how to write test items that will elicit accurate and honest information. Most developers consider item writing to be an art that depends on originality and creativity as well as a science that uses research about how test takers respond to various types of items for constructing reliable items. In Chapter 10, we discussed how to write effective survey questions, and those guidelines also apply to writing effective test items.

After writing the test items, the developer should administer them as a test, with appropriate instructions for the test administrator and test taker, to a sample of the target audience. This pilot test provides objective data to help determine whether the items yield the desired information. (We discuss the pilot test in detail in Chapter 12.)

Experienced item writers know that not all of the items they write will end up being good test items—that is, items that measure the construct as expected. Test takers will misinterpret some items. Some items will be too easy or too difficult, and men and women may answer a few items differently. Therefore, developers follow a general rule of thumb: "Write twice as many items as you expect to use in the final test." By writing twice as many items as needed, the developers will be able to discard poor items and use only those items that yield useful information. (In Chapter 12, we also discuss how to choose the best test items using a process called *item analysis*.)

Although there is no set of rules that guarantees that items will perform as expected, we can pass along some suggestions from the test development literature.

- *Identify item topics by consulting the test plan.* In this way, the test developer maximizes the relation between the test plan and the test itself, thereby increasing content validity.

- *Be sure that each item is based on an important learning objective or topic.* Structure the item around one central idea or problem. Do not test for trivial or peripheral information or skills.

- *Write items that assess information or skills drawn only from the testing universe.* This guideline is important for education and training programs. If the test's purpose is to measure how much the test taker learned in a training class, the test developer needs to write items from the course material. Such items should ask questions that respondents are unlikely to be able to answer from general knowledge.

- *Write each item in a clear and direct manner.* Precise words and simple sentence structure, as well as correct grammar and punctuation, enable the item writer to describe the problem or ask the intended question.

- *Use vocabulary and language appropriate for the target audience.* According to Doak, Doak, and Root (1996), the average adult in the United States cannot read above an eighth-grade reading level, and 40% of people over 65 years of age read below a fifth-grade reading level. Therefore, the developer should research the reading level of the target audience and create appropriate items. Items intended for the general population should be appropriate for an eighth-grade reading level or lower. Other test populations may require a lower reading level or a form of administration that does not require the test taker to read either the items or the instructions.

- *Avoid using slang or colloquial language.* In today's multicultural society, test takers will come from diverse backgrounds. The test author should use standard English and avoid figures of speech or frames of reference that may be unfamiliar to segments of the population. A test item that requires knowledge of customs associated with holidays (for example, foods associated with a traditional Thanksgiving meal) or sports (for example, tailgating) may be confusing to test takers not familiar with such customs.

- *Make all items independent.* Developers need to check all items to be sure that cues for the correct response to one item are not found elsewhere in the test.

- *Ask someone else—preferably a subject matter expert—to review items in order to reduce unintended ambiguity and inaccuracies.* This step ensures that the test items convey clear information and questions. Questions that have multiple interpretations should be revised or discarded.

Multiple-Choice and True/False Items

The following are some specific guidelines for writing multiple-choice and true/false questions.

- *Avoid using negative stems and responses.* Instead of asking "Which of the following is NOT true?" it is better to ask "Which of the following is FALSE?" Likewise, a response that reads "Confidentiality means that individuals are assured that all personal information they disclose will be kept private" is preferable to a negatively worded response such as "Individuals that are NOT assured that all personal information they disclose will be kept private are NOT assured of confidentiality."

- *Make all responses similar in detail and length.* The tendency to make the correct response more detailed can be avoided by making sure that all responses are similar in detail and length.

- *Make sure the item has only one answer that is definitely correct or "best."* To ensure that there is only one correct answer, construct an answer key that contains a brief rationale for the correct answer for each item.

- *Avoid determining words such as "always" and "never."* Instead, use "sometimes" and "often" as qualifiers. You might have noticed that the items on the Marlowe–Crowne Social Desirability Scale in For Your Information Box 11.4 often include "always" or "never," and therefore the probability that a test taker could truthfully agree is very low.

- *Avoid overlapping responses.* For instance, quantitative responses such as "10 to 20" and "20 to 30" overlap and leave the test taker who wishes to answer "20" confused about how to respond.

- *Avoid using inclusive distracters.* "All of the above," "None of the above," and "Both a and c" are called inclusive distracters. This type of response usually makes items very easy or difficult. If you choose to use them, be sure to balance the number of times they appear as the correct or incorrect response.

- *Use random assignment to position the correct response.* Research suggests that test takers often assign the correct response to "b" or "c." Random assignment of the correct response ensures uniformity of response probability and decreases test takers' ability to guess the correct response.

Essay and Interview Questions

The following tips provide some guidance in developing and scoring effective essay and interview questions.

- *Use essay items appropriately.* As mentioned earlier in this chapter, essays are most effective for assessing higher-order skills such as analysis, synthesis, and evaluation. If the developer wishes to measure simple recall, an objective format may be more efficient.

- *Consider time necessary for response.* Frame instructions and items in a way that lets the test taker know the expected length of response. In this way, the developer can provide the appropriate number of essay questions for the time allotted for testing. Remember that some individuals will take longer to complete the test than others will because of variations in writing skills. Ample time should be allotted for all test takers to respond to their satisfaction.

- *Prepare an answer key.* The key for open-ended essays and interviews should outline the expected correct response. In addition, it should list other possible responses along with scores based on the appropriateness of the responses. For example, a response that matches the desired response may receive full credit, and other responses that contain unrelated information may receive partial credit. Remember that in subjective testing, it is possible for a test taker to submit an unexpected solution or response that is as correct as, or even better than, the expected response.

- *Score essays anonymously.* Replacing the test taker's name or other identifiers with a number decreases the possibility of bias associated with the scorer's personal knowledge of the respondent or the respondent's characteristics such as sex, race, and age.

- *Use multiple independent scorers.* Using two or more scorers who read essays or conduct interviews provides an opportunity to detect and decrease bias as well as to create scorer reliability.

A Comparison of Objective and Subjective Formats

In this section, we draw from the work of Kryspin and Feldhusen (1974) to summarize the strengths and weaknesses associated with objective and subjective item formats. First, we consider how thoroughly the test developer can sample the test domain. Second, we look at ease of construction. Third, we consider the process of scoring. Finally, we look at how the test taker uses response sets.

Sampling

Objective formats with structured responses, such as multiple-choice and true/false items, provide many opportunities to sample the testing universe. Because test takers expend less time and effort to answer these items, the test developer can cover a wider array of topics, thereby increasing content validity. With subjective formats, such as essay and interview questions, the test developer is limited to the number of questions or topics to which the test taker can respond in one session. When the testing universe covers a wide range of topics, content validity usually suffers for the test using subjective formats.

Construction

Objective items, especially multiple-choice items, require extensive thought and development time because the test developer needs to balance responses in terms of content depth, length,  and appeal to the test taker. Novice test developers are quick to note that supplying three or four distracters that resemble the correct response is not an easy task. On the other hand, subjective tests require fewer items and those items are easier to construct and revise. Furthermore, some measurement experts suggest that essay and interview questions are better suited for testing higher-order skills such as creativity and organization.

Scoring

Scoring of objective items is simple and can be done by an aide or computer with a high degree of reliability and accuracy. Scoring subjective items, however, requires time-consuming judgments by an expert. Essay and interview scoring is most reliable and accurate when there are two independent scorers who have been trained to avoid biased judgments. Scoring keys are important for subjective items. They are, however, more difficult to construct because they need to address as many likely responses as possible.

Response Sets

Test takers have the option of guessing the correct responses on objective tests. They also may choose socially desirable responses or acquiesce to positive statements. For subjective items, such as essays, respondents may bluff or pad answers with superfluous or excessive information. Scorers might be influenced by irrelevant factors such as poor verbal or writing skills.

As you can see, each format has advantages and drawbacks. Objective items require more time and thought during the development phase. When objective questions are developed properly, they have high evidence of validity based on their content and provide reliable and accurate scores. On the other hand, subjective items, such as essays and interviews, may be more appropriate for assessing higher-order skills. In addition, subjective items require less time to develop. This advantage, however, is offset by the time and expertise required to score or interpret subjective responses and their greater susceptibility to scorer bias.

INTERIM SUMMARY 11.2
COMPOSING TEST ITEMS

- The test developer chooses the item format based on information in the test plan, such as the target audience, method of administration, and requirements for scoring.
- Objective formats include multiple-choice, true/false, and forced-choice items.
- Subjective formats include essay and interview questions.
- Projective tests are another type of subjective format that uses a highly ambiguous stimulus to elicit an unstructured response from the test taker. Projective stimuli include pictures and written or spoken words. Test takers may respond verbally or by drawing pictures.
- Some test takers display response sets—patterns of responding that result in false or misleading information—such as social desirability, acquiescence, random responding, and faking.
- Although there is no set of rules that guarantees that items will perform as expected, the test development literature contains a number of suggestions for writing successful items.
- Objective items provide ample sampling of the testing universe, but they are more time-consuming to develop. Scoring of objective items is easier and likely to be more accurate and reliable.
- Subjective items are easier to construct and revise. Some experts suggest that essay and interview questions are better suited for testing higher-order skills such as creativity and organization. Scoring of subjective items is more difficult, requiring independent scoring by two experts to increase reliability and accuracy.

Writing the Administration Instructions

Although the test items make up the bulk of the new test, they are meaningless without specific instructions on how to administer and score the test. The test developer needs to write three sets of instructions: one for the person administering the test, another for the person taking the test, and a third for the person scoring the test and interpreting its results.

Administrator Instructions

Administrator instructions should cover the following:

- Whether the test should be administered in a group and/or individually
- Specific requirements for the test administration location, such as privacy; quiet; and comfortable chairs, tables, or desks
- Required equipment such as No. 2 pencils, a computer with a CD-ROM drive, and/or Internet access
- Time limitations or the approximate time for completing the test when there are no time limits
- A script for the administrator to read to test takers, including answers to questions that test takers are likely to ask
- Credentials or training required for the test administrator

The last point is very important. Not just anyone can administer a test appropriately. Some tests, such as interviews, essays, and projective tests, require that the test administrator satisfactorily complete training on administering the test. In the case of interviews, for instance, the test publisher or the test user should provide training for the administrator on how to ask the interview questions and record the interviewee's replies. Some tests, such as projective tests, may require that the administrator has completed certain graduate courses in psychological testing.

The **testing environment**—the circumstances under which the test is administered—can affect how test takers respond. A standardized testing environment, as you recall, decreases variation or error in the test scores. Specific and concise instructions for administering the test help ensure that it will be administered properly under standardized conditions. For Your Information Box 11.6 provides an example of instructions for a test administrator.

FOR YOUR INFORMATION BOX 11.6

Example of Administrator Instructions

Testing Materials

Assemble a numbered testing booklet, answer sheet, and two No. 2 pencils for each person scheduled to take the test. Test takers cannot use any aids, such as calculators and dictionaries, while taking the test.

Testing Location

The testing room must be well lit with temperature control set at approximately 72°. Each test taker should sit alone at a table approximately 3 feet wide and 2 feet deep. All test takers must face the front of the room, where the administrator's desk is located. The administrator will ask test takers to turn off all cell phones and pagers and to place them on their tables.

Testing Time

The test takers will have 60 minutes to read and respond to the test items. Test takers who complete the test in less than 60 minutes should remain in their seats until the 60-minute time period is over and the administrator has collected the testing materials. Test takers who do not complete the test in the 60-minute time period must lay down their pencils and close their test booklets when asked to do so.

Frequently Asked Questions

(Q) When will I find out my test results?

(A) In three weeks, the testing company will send your results to you in the mail.

(Q) Can I use my own pen or pencil?

(A) Please use the pencils provided to ensure that your test can be machine scored.

(Q) May I leave the room during the test?

(A) If you leave the room during the testing period, your test will not be scored. Does anyone need to leave the room before we begin?

Instructions for the Test Taker

The test administrator usually delivers instructions for the test taker orally by reading a prepared script written by the test developer. Instructions also appear in writing at the beginning of the test or test booklet. The test taker needs to know where to respond (on an answer sheet or in the test booklet) and how to respond (blackening the appropriate space on an answer sheet or circling the correct multiple-choice answer). Each type of item (for example, multiple choice, essay) should be preceded by specific directions for responding. (Chapter 4 discussed research on providing test taker instructions for computer-based tests.)

Instructions for the test takers often encourage them to provide accurate and honest answers. The instructions may also provide a context for answering, such as "Think of your current work situation when replying to the following questions." Test instructions need to be simple, concise, and written at a low reading level. Complicated methods for responding are likely to lead to confused test takers and an increased probability of response errors. For Your Information Box 11.7 provides an example of instructions for test takers.

FYI

FOR YOUR INFORMATION BOX 11.7

Example of Test Taker Instructions

1. This testing booklet contains 100 multiple-choice questions. Please do *not* write your name or make any marks in the test booklet.

2. Write your name on Line 1 of the blue answer sheet. Begin with your last name, followed by your given name.

3. Write the number of your test booklet on Line 2 of your answer sheet. You will find the testing booklet number in the top-right corner of the booklet cover.

4. Read each of the following multiple-choice questions carefully. Decide which response alternative (a, b, c, d, or e) is the *best* answer. Indicate your response by completely blackening the appropriate circle on the answer sheet.

5. You have 60 minutes to complete this test. If you complete the test in less than 60 minutes, please place your answer sheet inside your closed testing booklet. Please remain seated at your table until the testing period expires and the administrator collects your testing booklet. Please sit quietly so that other test takers will not be distracted. If you have not completed the test when the administrator indicates that the testing period has expired, please place your answer sheet inside your closed testing booklet and wait for the administrator to collect your testing booklet and answer sheet.

Scoring Instructions

Finally, the test is not complete without scoring instructions. The scoring instructions and test key ensure that each person who scores the test will follow the same process. The scoring instructions must also explain how the test scores relate to the construct the test measures. For instance, what does a high score mean, and what does a low score mean? Remember that low scores indicate high performance on some tests, so the developer should not assume that the test taker or test user automatically will know what the score indicates.

INTERIM SUMMARY 11.3
WRITING THE ADMINISTRATION INSTRUCTIONS

- The instructions for the test administrator should cover group or individual administration; specific requirements for the location, required equipment, time limitations, or approximate time for completion of the test; the script for the administrator to read to test takers; and required training for the test administrator.
- The instructions for the test takers need to be simple, concise, and written at a low reading level.

Complicated instructions for responding are likely to lead to confused test takers and an increased probability of response errors.
- The scoring instructions and test key ensure that each person who scores the test will follow the same process. The scoring instructions should explain how the test scores relate to the construct that the test measures.

Chapter Summary

This chapter discussed the initial steps for developing psychological tests. The first step in test development is defining the testing universe, the target audience, and the purpose of the test. This stage provides the foundation for all other development activities. After a review of the literature, the test developer writes a concise definition of the construct, operationalizing the construct in terms of observable and measurable behaviors. The next step is to write a test plan that specifies the characteristics of the test, including a definition of the construct, the content to be measured (the testing universe), the format for the questions, and instructions for administering and scoring.

The cumulative model of scoring—which assumes that the more the test taker responds in a particular fashion, the more the test taker exhibits the attribute being measured—is probably the most common method for determining an individual's final test score. The categorical model and the ipsative model are other scoring methods.

After completing the test plan, the test developer begins writing the test questions and instructions. The questions, which test developers call *items*, can be in an objective format (multiple choice, true/false, and forced choice) or a subjective format (essays and interviews). Projective tests are another type of subjective format that uses ambiguous stimuli (words or pictures) to elicit responses from the test taker.

Some people have response sets—patterns of responding that result in false or misleading information—such as social desirability, acquiescence, random responding, and faking that cause test scores to contain error. Therefore, test developers need to be aware of these types of responses and guard against them. Although there is no set of rules that guarantees that items will perform as expected, the test development literature contains a number of suggestions for writing successful items.

Objective items provide ample sampling of the testing universe, but they are more time-consuming to develop. Scoring of objective items is easier and likely to be more accurate and reliable. Subjective items are easier to construct and revise. Some experts suggest that essay and interview questions are better suited for testing higher-order skills such as creativity and organization. Scoring of subjective items is more difficult, requiring independent scoring by two experts to increase reliability and accuracy.

Although the test items make up the bulk of the new test, they are meaningless without specific instructions on how to administer and score the test. The test developer should write three sets of instructions: one for the administrator, another for the test taker, and a third for the person who scores and interprets the test results.

After writing the test items, the test developer conducts a pilot test to determine the final form the test will take. The test developer then follows up the pilot test with other studies that provide the necessary data for validation and norming. Conducting the pilot test and analyzing its data are an integral part of the test development process. (We address them in detail in Chapter 12.)

Engaging in the Learning Process

KEY CONCEPTS

After completing your study of this chapter, you should be able to define each of the following terms. These terms are bolded in the text of this chapter and defined in the Glossary.

- acquiescence
- categorical model of scoring
- cumulative model of scoring
- distracters
- essay questions
- faking
- forced choice
- interview questions
- ipsative model of scoring
- multiple choice

- objective test format
- pilot test
- projective techniques
- projective tests
- random responding
- response sets
- sentence completion
- social desirability

- stem
- subjective test format
- test bank
- test format
- test item
- test plan
- testing environment
- true/false

LEARNING ACTIVITIES

The following are some learning activities you can engage in to support the learning objectives for this chapter.

Learning Objectives	Study Tips and Learning Activities
After completing your study of this chapter, you should be able to do the following:	*The following study tips will help you meet these learning objectives:*
Describe how to define the test domain, the target audience, and the purpose of the test.	• Using a source such as the *Mental Measurements Yearbook* database, look at the various tests that measure intelligence. How many different target audiences do you find? How does the target audience affect the characteristics of the test?
Develop a test plan, including defining the construct or constructs that the test measures, choosing the test format, and specifying how to score the test.	• Test plans in educational settings are based on the material presented for students to learn. Now that you have read and studied this chapter, use it to develop a test plan for a multiple-choice and essay test to measure the information learned from this chapter.
Differentiate between objective and subjective test questions, and describe the strengths and weaknesses of each.	• Try writing multiple-choice questions for this chapter, and then write essay questions that measure the same material. Make notes on how the question format affects your ability to measure the construct.
Describe the important issues in writing instructions for the test administrator and the test taker.	• Make a list of types of information that should be covered in the instructions for the test administrator. Make another list of the types of information that should be covered in the instructions for the test taker. Compare your lists with those of a classmate.

ADDITIONAL LEARNING ACTIVITIES

In addition to the study tips presented with each learning objective, here are more activities that you can carry out alone or in a group.

1. Read the description of an item format in Column A. Then write the name of the format in Column B.

Column A	Column B
Format Description	Format Name
A subjective format traditionally used by organizations for hiring employees	
An objective format that gives the respondent a 50% chance of guessing the correct answer	
An objective format developed during World War II to prevent bias in performance ratings	
A subjective format used by educational institutions to elicit detailed information from students on a test	
The most familiar objective format	
A subjective format used in early personality tests that relies on the test taker's imagination to provide an answer	

2. Choose a chapter from a textbook other than this one—perhaps one you are using in another class—and develop a test plan from its content. Then write objective and subjective test questions for the chapter. (This is not only a good way to practice test development but also an excellent way to study for an exam.) Exchange your test with a classmate who has done the same, and take each other's test. Finally, compare the tests and discuss their strengths and weaknesses.

3. Which question format(s) do you like best? Is there one format by which you prefer to be tested? Are there other formats that you do not like? Write a short essay on why you prefer one test format and dislike another. Compare your essay with the essays of your classmates.

4. Form a group of three or four students, and then as a group develop your own college adjustment scale. Construct your own measure of college adjustment using the constructs, definitions, and behaviors for the College Adjustment Scales described in For Your Information Box 11.1. Develop a test plan, define your target audience, compose test items, and write test instructions. Compare your test with the tests of other groups in your class.

PRACTICE QUESTIONS

The following are some practice questions to assess your understanding of the material presented in this chapter.

Multiple Choice

Choose the one best answer to each question.

1. What is the first step in developing a new test?
   a. Developing a test plan
   b. Examining the suitability of the test format
   c. Adequately sampling behaviors from a specific test domain
   d. Defining the testing universe, audience, and purpose

2. Making a list of the characteristics of persons who will take a test is which part of the test development process?
   a. Defining the purpose
   b. Defining the target audience
   c. Defining the test universe
   d. Developing the test plan

3. A job analysis provides the basis for a test plan in
   a. organizations.
   b. clinical settings.
   c. educational settings.
   d. No Child Left Behind.

4. We call the type of questions that a test contains the
   a. construct explication.
   b. construct operationalization.
   c. behavioral definition.
   d. test format.

5. Which one of the following is an objective test format?
   a. Multiple choice
   b. Sentence completion
   c. Interview
   d. Essay

6. Which one of the following models assumes that the more the test taker responds in a particular fashion, the more the test taker exhibits the attribute being measured?
   a. Categorical model of scoring
   b. Ipsative model of scoring
   c. Cumulative model of scoring
   d. Validity model of scoring

7. In a test Alice developed, the test user assigned a diagnosis to the test taker based on the test taker's score. Which one of the following models of scoring was she using?
   a. Categorical
   b. Cumulative
   c. Ipsative
   d. Validity

8. A(n) _____ question has a stem followed by a number of distracters.
   a. forced-choice
   b. true/false
   c. essay
   d. multiple-choice

9. For which one of the following formats is scoring easiest?
   a. Essay
   b. Interview
   c. Multiple choice
   d. Sentence completion

10. Eric developed a test that instructed test takers to choose one of two words that appeared to be unrelated but equally acceptable. Which one of the following formats was he using?
    a. Multiple choice
    b. Forced choice
    c. Sentence completion
    d. True/false

11. What is the traditional subjective test used in organizations?
    a. Essay
    b. Multiple choice
    c. Interview
    d. Projective drawing

12. Felicia was concerned that the target audience for her test would be more likely to choose the most acceptable answer instead of the truest answer. She was concerned about
    a. acquiescence.
    b. social desirability.
    c. faking.
    d. projection.

13. Test developers use reverse scoring to offset the effects of
    a. social desirability.
    b. acquiescence.
    c. faking.
    d. random responding.

14. Random responding is most likely to occur when test takers
    a. lack the necessary skills to take a test or do not wish to be evaluated.
    b. wish to make themselves appear favorably to the test user.
    c. wish to make themselves appear mentally ill or incompetent.
    d. have the tendency to agree with any ideas or behaviors presented.

15. A rule of thumb for test developers is to write _____ items as called for by the test plan.
    a. three times as many
    b. two and one half times as many
    c. two times as many
    d. the same amount of

16. The suggestion in your book to "make all test items independent" means to
    a. be sure that all items are independent of the test universe.
    b. make all items heterogeneous.
    c. make sure that information in one item does not give away the answer to another item.
    d. ensure that all items are reliable and valid.

17. "Behaviors which are culturally sanctioned and approved but which are improbable of occurrence" is the definition of
    a. social desirability.
    b. items on the Marlowe–Crowne Social Desirability Scale.
    c. response sets.
    d. acquiescence.

18. What instrument do test developers use to identify test responses that appeal to people who wish to show themselves in a favorable light?
    a. College Adjustment Scales
    b. Computer-adapted test
    c. Marlowe–Crowne Social Desirability Scale
    d. The multiple-choice test

Short Answer/Essay

Read each of the following, and consider your response carefully based on the information presented in this chapter. Write your answer to each question in two or three paragraphs.

1. Identify the first four steps of developing a test, and tell what activities are involved in each step.

2. Explain why it is important to follow the test development process. What do you risk by not following the test development steps?

3. Discuss the benefits and drawbacks of using an objective test format. Give three examples of objective test formats.

4. Discuss the benefits and drawbacks of using a subjective test format. Give three examples of subjective test formats.

5. Describe the multiple-choice format. What are its advantages and disadvantages? Include a discussion of scoring a multiple-choice test.

6. Describe the essay format. What are its advantages and disadvantages? Include a discussion of scoring an essay test.

7. Describe three models for scoring tests. What is the best format?

ANSWER KEYS

Additional Learning Activities

Column A	Column B
Format Description	*Format Name*
A subjective format traditionally used by organizations for hiring employees	Traditional interview
An objective format that gives the respondent a 50% chance of guessing the correct answer	True/false
An objective format developed during World War II to prevent bias in performance ratings	Forced choice
A subjective format used by educational institutions to elicit detailed information from students on a test	Essay
The most familiar objective format	Multiple choice
A subjective format used in early personality tests that relies on the test taker's imagination to provide an answer	Projective technique

Multiple Choice

1. d	2. b	3. a	4. d
5. a	6. c	7. a	8. d
9. c	10. b	11. c	12. b
13. b	14. a	15. c	16. c
17. b	18. c		

Short Answer/Essay

Refer to your textbook for answers. If you are unsure of an answer and cannot generate the answer after reviewing your book, ask your professor for clarification.

How Do We Assess the Psychometric Quality of a Test?

CHAPTER 12: HOW DO WE ASSESS THE PSYCHOMETRIC QUALITY OF A TEST?

After completing your study of this chapter, you should be able to do the following:

- Explain the importance of conducting a pilot test.
- Describe how a pilot test should be set up, and specify the types of information that should be collected.
- Describe the collection, analyses, and interpretation of data for an item analysis, including item difficulty, item discrimination, interitem correlations, item–criterion correlations, item bias, and item characteristic curves.
- Describe the collection and interpretation of data for a qualitative item analysis.
- Identify and explain the criteria for retaining and dropping items to revise a test.
- Describe the processes of validation and cross-validation.
- Explain the concepts of differential validity, single-group validity, and unfair test discrimination.
- Explain the purpose of a cut score, and describe two methods for identifying a cut score.
- Explain what information should be included in a test manual and why.

"Last week I participated in a study of a new self-esteem test. The test administrator asked us to take the test anonymously. She said she could not be sure the test was a true measure of our self-esteem, so she couldn't tell us our scores. Why can't she tell us our self-esteem scores?"

"I have a copy of a test on organizational values that I took at work. I wanted to give it as a demonstration in class. My instructor objected because he said we could not interpret the test scores without the test manual. What's so important about having a test manual?"

"I created a test on math skills to find out which students need tutoring. When I showed it to my supervisor, she asked about the 'cut score.' What's a cut score?"

"My son's class took a standardized math test. There were a number of questions that were answered correctly by more girls than boys. I suggested to the teacher that the test might be biased against boys. She said that comparing the percentage of each group who answered questions correctly is not a good measure of bias. Why not?"

I n Chapter 11, we described the process for designing a test, developing the test's items, and writing the instructions for the test administrator, test takers, and test scorer. In this chapter, we continue describing the test development process by discussing piloting the test and analyzing the items in terms of their difficulty, their ability to discriminate among respondents, and their likelihood of introducing error into the test results. We also describe the process of revising the test and gathering evidence of reliability and validity. Finally, we discuss briefly the contents of the test manual. You may wish to refer to Figure 11.1 to familiarize yourself with the overall process of test development.

Conducting the Pilot Test

When developers design a new test, they cannot assume that the test will perform as expected. Just as engineers who have designed a new airplane conduct flight tests to find out how well the plane flies, test developers conduct studies to determine how well a new test performs. The **pilot test** is a scientific investigation of evidence that suggests that the test scores are reliable and valid for their specified purpose. The pilot-testing process involves administering the test to a sample of the test's target audience and analyzing the data obtained from the pilot test. The test developers then revise the test to fix any problems with the test's performance. It would be unsafe to carry passengers on a new airplane that has not been tested for performance and safety. Likewise, it is improper to rely on the results of a

psychological test that has not been studied to ensure that its data are valid and reliable—that is, that the results are consistent and that the inferences that are going to be made from the scores on the test are appropriate.

As we saw in Chapter 11, new psychological tests are developed from a test plan—similar to an airplane's blueprints. To the extent that the test matches the test plan, we can say that it has demonstrated evidence of validity based on content. However, there are a number of important issues beyond this evidence that the test developer should investigate to ensure that the test scores are accurate and meaningful. For example, are the test items too difficult or too easy? Do the test items differentiate among individuals; in other words, do the test scores vary, or does everyone get approximately the same score? Are the test takers who receive high scores on the test those that possess the greatest amount of the skill or construct being measured? Are any of the items more difficult for a certain group of respondents such as women or minorities? In addition, developers want to know whether the test instructions for the administrator and respondent are clear and easy to follow. Is the length of time allotted for administering the test adequate? Do respondents react to the test favorably and cooperatively? Finally, can the test user rely on the test scores to provide the information described in the test's purpose? Just as engineers rely on flight tests to provide evidence of a new plane's safety and performance to specifications, test developers rely on their pilot tests to provide evidence that their new test will produce scores that will be useful for decision making without harming test users or respondents.

Setting Up the Pilot Test

Because the purpose of the pilot test is to study how well the test performs, it is important that the test be given in a situation that matches as closely as possible the actual circumstances in which the test will be used. Therefore, for the pilot test, developers choose a sample of people who resemble or are a part of the test's target audience.

For example, if the test is designed to diagnose emotional disabilities in adolescents, the participants for the pilot study should be adolescents. Part of the sample should be adolescents who have been determined to have emotional disabilities. The others should be adolescents who have been determined not to have emotional disabilities. In addition, it would be important to ensure that each of those groups contains both males and females from various economic and ethnic backgrounds. The sample should be large enough to provide the power to conduct statistical tests to compare responses of each group. For example, developers need to compare the responses of males with emotional disabilities with those of females with emotional disabilities.

Likewise, the test setting of the pilot test should mirror the planned test setting. If school psychologists will use the test, the pilot test should be conducted in a school setting using school psychologists as administrators. Conducting the pilot test in more than one school would be preferable because error introduced by one school's situation can be identified or offset by other schools.

In setting up pilot studies, developers follow the *Standards for Educational and Psychological Testing* (American Educational Research Association [AERA], American Psychological Association [APA], & National Council on Measurement in Education [NCME], 1999) discussed in Chapter 3. This means that test takers (and their parents or guardians, where appropriate) understand that they are participating in a research study and that the test scores will be used for research purposes only. Developers observe strict rules of confidentiality and publish only aggregate results of the pilot study.

Conducting the Pilot Study

The depth and breadth of the pilot study usually depend on the size and complexity of the target audience. For instance, tests designed for use in a single company or college program require less extensive studies than do tests designed for large audiences such as students applying for graduate school in the United States and adults seeking jobs as managers. In either case, however, it is important that the test administrators adhere strictly to the test procedures outlined in their test instructions.

In addition, pilot studies often require gathering extra data such as a criterion measure and the length of time needed to complete the test. Developers may use questionnaires or interviews that gather information from respondents about the test. For example, developers may want to know, "Did you readily understand the test instructions?" "Were there any questions you did not understand?" "Did you object to the content of any questions?" and "Do you believe the test assessed your skills fairly?" Information on respondents' reactions and thoughts about the test can help developers understand why some questions yielded more useful data than others. This information makes the process of revising the test easier.

Most pilot studies go well and yield useful data that guide developers in making necessary revisions. However, some pilot tests simply might not work. For instance, administrators may ignore test instructions, respondents may complete answer sheets incorrectly, or respondents may exhibit hostility toward the test or the test administrator. In such cases, it is important to recognize the problems with the test administration, make all necessary revisions before continuing, and conduct a new pilot test that yields appropriate results.

Analyzing the Results

The pilot test provides an opportunity to gather both quantitative and qualitative data about the test. The developers use statistical procedures to analyze the test responses for information regarding each item's difficulty, ability to discriminate among individuals, and likelihood of introducing bias or error. In addition, developers can estimate internal consistency. When data on an external criterion—such as performance or diagnoses—have been collected, developers may also gather preliminary information about how well the test scores correlate with the external criterion scores. This quantitative information is then reviewed with the qualitative information, such as test takers' reactions, to make revisions that enhance the performance of the test.

In the next section, we discuss how developers evaluate the performance of each test item—a process called **item analysis.**

Conducting Quantitative Item Analysis

Each item in a test is a building block that contributes to the test's outcome or final score. Therefore, developers examine the performance of each item to identify those items that perform well, to revise those that could perform better, and to eliminate those that do not yield the desired information. The major portion of such a study involves **quantitative item analysis**—statistical analyses of the responses test takers gave to individual items. As you recall from Chapter 11, developers usually write twice the number of items they expect to use in the final test. Therefore, they can choose the very best items from the many they have written.

Item Difficulty

The purpose of norm-referenced tests (described in Chapter 5) is to compare the test scores of various individuals. Therefore, it is important for there to be variability in individuals' test scores. Items that everyone gets "right" or everyone gets "wrong" provide no basis for comparison and yield similar test scores for all test takers. Therefore, developers analyze each test item for its difficulty. We define **item difficulty** as the percentage of test takers who respond correctly. We calculate each item's difficulty or p value (percentage value) by dividing the number of persons who answered correctly by the total number of persons who responded to the question. (Note that *p* stands for percentage as well as probability. In Chapter 8, we discussed tests of significance in which *p* stands for probability of occurring by chance.) When test developers write items, they can only guess at how difficult each item will be. The pilot test provides the data for judging item difficulty.

Items with difficulty levels or *p* values of .5 yield distributions of test scores with the most variation. Because difficulty levels can be expected to vary, most developers seek a range of difficulty levels among all items that averages approximately .5. They discard or rewrite items with extreme *p* values, usually defined as 0 to .2 (too difficult) and .9 to 1 (too easy).

The concept of item difficulty makes intuitive sense for knowledge and skills tests where there is one right answer. Difficulty levels can also be calculated, however, for tests of personality and attitudes. In these tests, no one answer is "correct." Yet the test developer still needs assurance that items are not likely to be answered in the same direction or with the same answer by everyone. The answer that indicates the presence of a construct or an attitude is labeled as correct for the purpose of the item analysis.

The *p* value of the item difficulty provides an accurate indication of how difficult the item was for the test takers in the pilot study. However, the *p* value does not provide information on the usefulness of the item in measuring the test's construct. Those who have more of the attribute being measured are more likely to respond correctly to the item, but this is not always the case. Sometimes an item may be more difficult for those who have a high degree of the test attribute than for those who have little of the test attribute—a situation that would call for revising or discarding the item.

One other thing to keep in mind when interpreting the difficulty of the items on a test is that a high or low *p* value can result from two different conditions. For instance, if the *p* value was very high it could mean that the item was legitimately too easy, or it could mean that the group selected for the pilot test possessed an especially high level of knowledge, skill, or ability in the construct being measured. That is why it is important to carefully review the characteristics of the population participating in the pilot tests and to attempt to select a population that varies as much as possible in ability level. Later in this chapter we discuss another approach to analyzing test items, called item response theory (IRT). This method uses a complex mathematical process to calculate statistics on test items that are independent of the of the skill level of the population being tested.

Item Discrimination

Because inferences regarding the meaning of high test scores versus low test scores are going to be made by the users of a test, it is important to obtain a measure of how well each item separates those test takers who demonstrate a high degree of skill, knowledge, attitude, or personality characteristic from those who demonstrate little of the same skill, knowledge, attitude, or personality characteristic. If a test is well constructed, each item on it (or on the subtest if the test is designed to measure multiple concepts) should be a measure of the concept of interest. If this is the case, there should be a statistical relationship between how an individual answers a particular item and his or her overall score on the test. For instance, in a test where each item has one correct answer (such as a test of knowledge), people who answer a particular question correctly should score statistically higher on the overall test than people who answer the same question incorrectly. One of the ways that test developers evaluate this is by calculating a **discrimination index,** which compares the performance of those who obtained very high test scores (the Upper Group [*U*]) with the performance of those who obtained very low test scores (the Lower Group [*L*]) on each item. Calculating the percentage of test takers in each group who responded correctly and then obtaining the difference (*D*) between the two percentages creates the discrimination index. The formulas look like this:

$$U = \frac{\text{Number in Upper Group who responded correctly}}{\text{Total number in Upper Group}} \times 100$$

$$L = \frac{\text{Number in Lower Group who responded correctly}}{\text{Total number in Lower Group}} \times 100$$

$$D = U - L$$

The Upper Group and Lower Group are formed by ranking the final test scores from lowest to highest and then taking the upper third and the lower third to use in the analysis. Murphy and Davidshofer (2005) suggest that any percentage from 25% to 35% may be used to form the extreme groups, with little difference in the resulting discrimination index.

After calculating a D value for each item, test developers look for items that have high positive numbers. Negative numbers indicate that those who scored low on the test overall responded to the item correctly and that those who scored high on the test responded incorrectly. Low positive numbers suggest that nearly as many people who had low scores responded correctly as did those who had high scores. Each of these situations indicates that the item is not discriminating between high scorers and low scorers. Therefore, test developers discard or rewrite items that have low or negative D values. Later in this chapter we discuss a second index of an item's ability to discriminate high scorers from low scorers when we cover item-total correlations.

Interitem Correlations

Another important step in the item analysis is the construction of an **interitem correlation matrix,** which displays the correlation of each item with every other item. Usually each item has been coded as a dichotomous variable—correct (1) or incorrect (0). Therefore, the interitem correlation matrix will be made up of **phi coefficients,** which are the result of correlating two dichotomous (having only two values) variables. These coefficients are interpreted much like Pearson product–moment correlation coefficients. Table 12.1 shows an interitem correlation matrix displaying the correlation of six items with each other. (Chapter 9 explained how to read a correlation matrix.) As you can see, Item 1 correlates fairly well with the other five items. Item 3 correlates less well with the other items.

The interitem correlation matrix provides important information for increasing the test's internal consistency. Ideally, each item should be correlated with every other item measuring the same construct and

Table 12.1   Interitem Correlation Matrix for Pilot Test

Item	1	2	3	4	5	6
1	—	.61	.39	.36	.74	.73
2		—	.11	.55	.14	.08
3			—	.03	.01	.19
4				—	.32	.43
5					—	.72
6						—

should not be correlated with items measuring a different construct. In practice, interitem correlations tend to be relatively small in size, often in the .15 to .20 range, except for those items that are simple restatements of one another. As you recall from Chapter 6, one method for increasing a test's reliability is to increase the number of items measuring the same construct. In revising the test, however, the developer faces another problem: Which items can the developer drop without reducing the test's reliability?

The answer is that items that are not correlated with other items measuring the same construct can be (and should be) dropped to increase internal consistency. An item that does not correlate with other items (developed to measure the same construct) is probably measuring a different construct from that being measured by the other items. This is not always apparent when writing or reading the items because the item may be interpreted differently by the target audience.

As you recall from Chapter 6, a test's overall internal consistency is calculated using the KR-20 formula for dichotomous items (items coded right or wrong) or the coefficient alpha formula for items that have multiple options for answers. The test developer uses the data from the pilot test to calculate an overall estimate of internal consistency, and then the developer consults the interitem correlation matrix to see which items should be dropped or revised to increase the test's overall internal consistency.

Item–Total Correlations

Another way to assess the contribution of a single item to overall test consistency as well as assess the item's ability to discriminate high-scoring individuals from lower-scoring individuals is to calculate the item–total correlation. This is a measure of the strength and direction of the relation between the way test takers responded to one item and the way they responded to all of the items as a whole. We calculate the item–total correlation using the Pearson product–moment correlation formula discussed in Chapter 5. (If the test items measure several constructs or dimensions, the analyst should compare the item only to the total number of other items that measure the same thing.) In the case of multiple-choice or other objective formats, the answers for the item are dichotomous. Analysts usually code correct answers as 1 and incorrect answers as 0. Technically, the correlation of a dichotomous item with a continuous total score results in a statistic called the point biserial correlation coefficient; however, the calculation using the Pearson product–moment correlation formula or the correlation procedure on statistical software will provide the same correct answer. Items that have little or no correlation with the total item score may measure a different construct from that being measured by the other items.

More commonly, however, testing practitioners use item–total correlations as an alternative to the discrimination index discussed earlier. When items on a test are all measuring a similar construct, it is reasonable to assume that, on average, individuals who answer a particular question correctly will obtain a higher total score on the test than will individuals who answer the question incorrectly. Because of this, item-total correlations are usually reviewed as part of the process of item analysis. Test developers want to retain those items that strongly differentiate high-scoring individuals from lower-scoring individuals. This is indicated by a positive item-total correlation. In the worst case, however, the item–total correlation coefficient can be negative. This would mean that people who answered a question correctly actually did worse on the test than people who got the question wrong. Such an occurrence is often indicative of a question that has been poorly worded and is confusing the more capable test takers. It could also indicate a question where the wrong answer was keyed as being correct. Questions with negative item–total correlations should be either reworked or removed from the test as they will reduce the test's reliability. The item–total correlation coefficient provides one number that is easy to interpret and use to make decisions about retaining or discarding an item based on how much the item contributes to the internal consistency of the test and how well it discriminates high scorers from lower scorers.

Item–Criterion Correlations

Some developers also correlate item responses with a criterion measure such as a measure of job performance for pre-employment tests or a diagnostic measure for clinical tests. Because the responses to the item are usually dichotomous (correct or incorrect), the resulting correlation coefficients are likely to be low and unlikely to reach statistical significance. However, the item–criterion correlation can be used as a guide for determining whether the item contributes to prediction of the criterion. For instance, items that correlate strongly with the criterion would be helpful in predicting the criterion.

Some tests are designed so that test scores can be used to sort individuals into two or more categories based on their scores on the criterion measure. These tests are referred to as **empirically based tests** because the decision to place an individual in a category is based solely on the quantitative relationship between the predictor (test score) and the criterion (possible categories). One advantage of an empirically based test is that the test questions are not required to reflect the test's purpose, and therefore test takers have difficulty in faking responses. Questions that have no apparent relation to the criterion are referred to as **subtle questions.** However, although empirically based tests can lead to optimal correlations with criteria, they are susceptible to bias derived from sample-specific characteristics.

 Test Spotlight 12.1 in Appendix A describes the development of the Minnesota Multiphasic Personality Inventory and some research it has stimulated.

The Minnesota Multiphasic Personality Inventory (MMPI), a widely used personality inventory, is an example of an empirically based test. The original developers of the MMPI, Starke Hathaway and John McKinley, wanted to develop a paper-and-pencil test that would distinguish between normal individuals and those with a psychological disorder. They developed the MMPI-1 using data from a sample of White adults in Minnesota. The MMPI-2, the revised version, was improved by using data from a more diverse sample representative of the U.S. population.

The Item Characteristic Curve

During recent years, test developers have begun to rely on the concepts of **item response theory (IRT)** for item analysis. One of the reasons for this is that IRT can provide estimates of the ability of test takers that is independent of the difficulty of the items presented as well as estimates of item difficulty and discrimination that are independent of the ability of the test takers. This theory relates the performance of each item to a statistical estimate of the test taker's ability on the construct being measured. A fundamental aspect of IRT is the use of **item characteristic curves (ICCs).** An ICC is the line that results when we graph the probability of answering an item correctly with the level of ability on the construct being measured. The ICC provides a picture of the item's difficulty and how well it discriminates high performers from low performers.

Figures 12.1 and 12.2 show ICCs for hypothetical items that measure verbal ability. In Figure 12.1, test takers with high ability have a higher probability of answering the item correctly than do test takers with low ability. In Figure 12.2, test takers with high ability have only a slightly higher probability of answering the question correctly. We can conclude that the item with the greater slope provides better discrimination between high performers (those presumed to have higher ability in reading comprehension) and low performers (those presumed to have lower ability in reading comprehension).

Figure 12.1	Item Characteristic Curve Showing That Test Takers With High Ability Have a High Probability of Answering Correctly

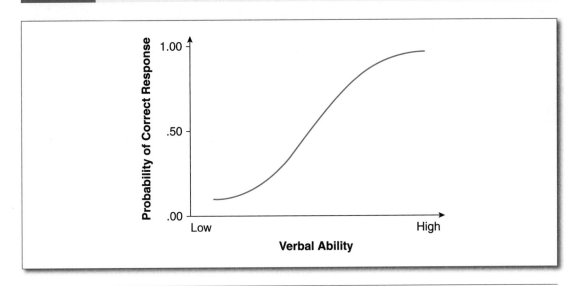

SOURCE: From Murphy, K. R., & Davidshofer, C. O. (2005). *Psychological testing: Principles and applications* (6th ed., pp. 214, 215, 223). Copyright © 2005. Published by Pearson Education Inc., Upper Saddle River, NJ.

Figure 12.2	Item Characteristic Curve Showing That Test Takers With High Ability Have Only a Slightly Higher Probability of Answering Correctly

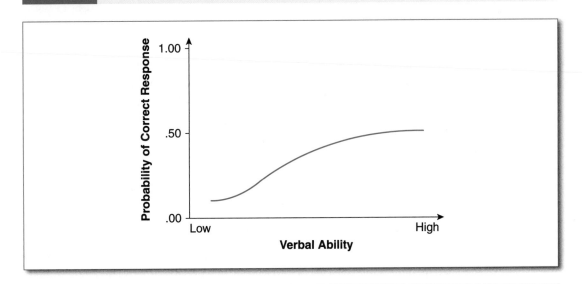

SOURCE: From Murphy, K. R., & Davidshofer, C. O. (2005). *Psychological testing: Principles and applications* (6th ed., pp. 214, 215, 223). Copyright © 2005. Published by Pearson Education Inc., Upper Saddle River, NJ.

We can determine the difficulty of an item on the ICC by locating the point at which the curve indicates a probability of .5 (a 50–50 chance) of answering correctly. The higher the ability level associated with this point, the more difficult the question. Figure 12.3 shows three ICCs plotted for three different items. Item 1 is easier because less ability is associated with having a 50–50 chance of answering correctly. Items 2 and 3, which have different slopes, both intersect at the same point for having a 50–50 chance of answering correctly. Therefore, these items have the same difficulty level, and both are more difficult than Item 1.

| Figure 12.3 | Hypothetical Item Characteristic Curves for Three Items |

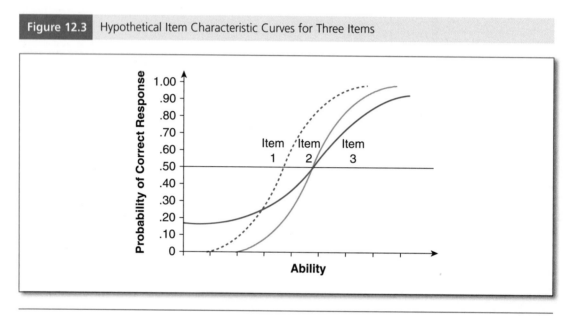

SOURCE: From Anastasi, A., & Urbina, S. (1997). Psychological testing (7th ed., pp. 190, 304). Copyright © 1997. Published by Pearson Education Inc., Upper Saddle River, NJ.

IRT is also important in computerized adaptive testing (CAT). As you recall from Chapter 4, in computerized adaptive tests, all test takers start with the same set of questions. The CAT software then chooses items for individuals based on their level of ability determined from their previous responses. ICCs play a major role in analyzing and scoring test takers' responses. For multiple-choice questions, the CAT software uses a maximum likelihood estimation that weights each item by its difficulty, discrimination, and pseudo-guessing parameter. The pseudo-guessing parameter estimates the probability that the test taker with a low ability level will respond correctly simply by guessing. Using IRT and the maximum likelihood parameters, the final test score represents the test taker's entire pattern of responses. According to Weiss (2004), using this method yields more distinctions among the test takers than does simply adding the number of correct answers. Counting correct answers on a 10-item test provides 11 scores (0–10). Using IRT theory and CAT software on the same 10-item test yields 210 (or 1,024) distinctions.

You may be wondering why IRT is not used for all test item analyses. One of the answers is that very large sample sizes are required for stable IRT analyses. According to Nunnally & Bernstein (1994) unless the scale you are analyzing is very short, a good IRT analysis requires a minimum sample size of 200 individuals, and could require as many as 500. In many applied settings, there are an insufficient number of subjects available to perform an item analysis using IRT. The development of ICCs relies on complex methodology and sophisticated computer programming beyond the scope and objectives of this textbook. However, an ability to interpret ICCs can enable test developers and test users to better understand test development data and documentation.

Item Bias

Test developers are interested in analyzing responses to individual test items to identify bias that results from various sources so as to correct or delete items that contain systematic error. One important area of analysis is item difficulty. Test items should be of equal difficulty for all groups. Researchers have proposed a number of methods for investigating **item bias**—when an item is easier for one group than for another group. These methods range from comparing scores or passing rates of various groups to comparing group performance in terms of an external criterion (Murphy & Davidshofer, 2005).

The preferred method by researchers, such as Lim and Drasgow (1990), involves the computation of item characteristics by group (for instance, men and women) and using the ICCs to make decisions about item bias. By plotting the curves on a graph, differences in difficulty and discrimination can be detected readily. Figure 12.4 shows ICCs for men and women on one test item. As you can see, the item discriminates between high and low performers better for women than for men. The item is also more difficult for men. Such an item should be discarded from a test.

For Your Information Box 12.1 illustrates the advantages of using IRT to detect bias in its discussion of the Golden Rule Insurance Company lawsuit, and For Your Information Box 12.2 discusses bias associated with **acculturation**—the degree to which an immigrant or a minority member has adapted to a country's mainstream culture.

Figure 12.4   Item Characteristic Curves for Men and Women on One Test Item

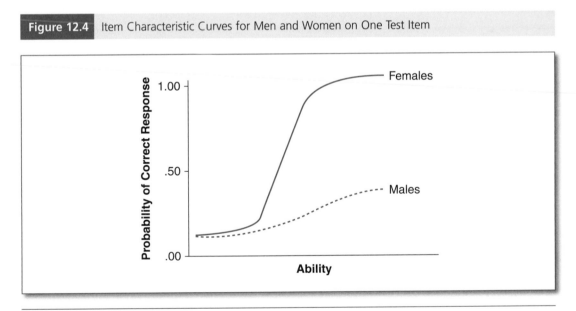

SOURCE: From Murphy, K. R., & Davidshofer, C. O. (2005). *Psychological testing: Principles and applications* (6th ed., pp. 214, 215, 223). Copyright © 2005. Published by Pearson Education Inc., Upper Saddle River, NJ.

FOR YOUR INFORMATION BOX 12.1

The Golden Rule Case

During the early 1980s, the Golden Rule Insurance Company sued the Illinois Department of Insurance and Educational Testing Service (ETS), asserting that two insurance licensing exams developed by ETS for the state of Illinois were biased against Black test takers. The basis for their claim was that the percentage of correct responses from Whites was greater than the percentage of correct responses from Blacks on a number of items. The statistic to which the suit referred was the p value that indicates level of difficulty. This difference in difficulty level for Whites and Blacks resulted in a larger number of Whites than Blacks passing the test and obtaining their licenses. The case was settled out of court with the stipulation that ETS would develop subsequent exams using items for which the proportions of correct responses for all test takers are at least .40. Furthermore, the settlement stipulated that items in which the difference between proportions correct for Whites and Blacks exceeded .15 would not be used.

A number of testing experts suggested that there was a problem with the Golden Rule settlement. They noted that comparing item difficulty levels in the form of p values failed to take into consideration the level of ability of test takers. In other words, was the failure to give the correct answer because the item was poorly written or simply because the test taker did not know how to answer the question correctly?

As researchers noted in a symposium at an American Psychological Association (APA) annual meeting (Bond, 1987; Faggen, 1987; Linn & Drasgow, 1987) and in an official statement by the APA, item response theory (IRT) provides a better way to detect items that are more difficult for one group than for another group. As you recall, item characteristic curves (ICCs) associate item difficulty with test takers' ability. Comparing ICCs provides a better way to evaluate item difficulty because it takes test taker ability into account. Furthermore, Rodney Lim, in his master's thesis, demonstrated this principle empirically by using both methods to evaluate item responses from a simulated data set (Lim & Drasgow, 1990). He found that the Golden Rule procedure identified 90% of the items as biased, in contrast to the IRT method, which found that approximately 25% of the items were biased when ability was taken into account.

FOR YOUR INFORMATION BOX 12.2

The Role of Acculturation Assessment

When we conduct a quantitative item analysis, our purpose is to identify sources of error that may be introduced into final test scores by the test itself, its scoring scheme, administration, or interpretation. Therefore, we examine test responses to determine whether an item is easier for one group than for another group, and we examine responses to ensure that an item distinguishes among test takers only on the construct being measured.

Until recently, those test developers who analyzed items for cultural bias did so by including minority members in the norming sample and following up using item characteristic curves (ICCs) or qualitative measures to identify biased items. At that point, the discovery of cultural bias usually led to editing or deleting biased items. Although this methodology is good, it is not sufficient for identifying culture bias in a very diverse population. The populations of the United States and Europe in the 21st century will be truly multicultural in the sense that many individuals will have behaviors and traditions associated with two or more cultures. Furthermore, one individual might have varying degrees of acculturation in two or more cultures. For example, one young person living in a bicultural family, such as Mexican American or Chinese American, may have embraced one culture more than has another person from a similar bicultural family. Conducting item analyses for every minority group with members acculturated to various degrees in a diverse population is likely to become cumbersome and potentially ineffective.

Two researchers from The Netherlands (Van de Vijver & Phalet, 2004) have proposed taking a different approach to dealing with item and test bias associated with the degree to which test takers understand and conform to mainstream culture. They have proposed administering a test that measures the degree to which each test taker belongs to the mainstream culture and then using those test scores to adjust raw scores for error in the test score caused by lack of acculturation. Current measures of acculturation are usually short surveys (about 20 items) that examine test takers' sense of belonging to one or more groups and their attitudes toward those groups.

According to Van de Vijver and Phalet (2004), three types of cultural bias arise in tests:

1. *Construct bias* arises when items do not have the same meaning from culture to culture or subculture. For example, the behaviors associated with being a good daughter or son (filial piety) are different in various cultures.

2. *Method bias* arises when the mechanics of the test work differently for various cultural groups. For example, individuals schooled in North America and Europe may be more familiar with using an electronic scan sheet or a computerized test than may others who are used to writing essays or verbally answering questions asked by the test administrator or an examiner.

3. *Differential item functioning* arises when test takers from different cultures have the same ability level on the test construct, but the item or test yields very different scores for the two cultures. For example, a history test that contains a large proportion of questions on the history and geography of the original 13 colonies of the United States might favor test takers from New England over test takers from California and Mexico—even though both groups are equally familiar with American history overall.

SOURCE: Adapted from Van de Vijver, F. J. R., & Phalet, K. (2004). Assessment in multicultural groups: The role of acculturation. *Applied Psychology: An International Review, 53,* 215–236.

Conducting Qualitative Item Analysis

In addition to conducting a quantitative analysis of test takers' responses, test developers often ask test takers to complete a questionnaire about how they viewed the test itself and how they answered the test questions. Such questionnaires enable developers to conduct a **qualitative analysis.** Test developers might also use individual or group discussions with test takers for understanding how test takers perceived the test and how changes in the test content or administration instructions would improve the accuracy of the test results. Finally, test developers can also ask a panel of experts—people knowledgeable about the test's content or about testing in general—to review the test and provide their opinions on possible sources of error or bias.

Questionnaires for Test Takers

Cohen, Swerdlik, and Phillips (1996) provide a comprehensive list of questions for test takers, shown in Table 12.2. Some or all of these topics can be addressed in an open-ended survey, or the test developers may wish to construct Likert rating scales (discussed in Chapter 10) to make responding easier for the pilot test participants. The open-ended format yields more information; however, the participants might not have enough time to answer a lengthy questionnaire. If Likert scales are used, discussion groups with a sample of participants can focus on portions of the test that are targeted for revision. For instance, test takers may find the test length to be appropriate; however, they may express concerns about face validity. Therefore, discussion would focus on face validity, not test length.

Table 12.2	Potential Areas of Exploration by Means of Qualitative Item Analysis

This table lists sample topics and questions of possible interest to test users. The questions could be raised either orally or in writing shortly after a test's administration. Additionally, depending on the objectives of the test user, the questions could be placed into other formats, such as true/false or multiple choice. Depending on the specific questions to be asked and the number of test takers being sampled, the test user may wish to guarantee the anonymity of the respondents.

Topic	Sample Question
Cultural Sensitivity	Did you feel that any item or aspect of this test was discriminatory with respect to any group of people? If so, why?
Face Validity	Did the test appear to measure what you expected it would measure? If not, what about this test was contrary to your expectations?
Test Administrator	Did the presence of the test administrator affect your performance on this test in any way? If so, how?
Test Environment	Did any conditions in the room affect your performance on this test in any way? If so, how?
Test Fairness	Do you think the test was a fair test of what it sought to measure? Why or why not?
Test Language	Were there any instructions or other written aspects of the test that you had difficulty understanding?
Test Length	How did you feel about the length of the test with respect to (a) the time it took to complete and (b) the number of items?
Test Taker's Guessing	Did you guess on any of the test items? About what percentage of the items would you estimate you guessed on? Did you employ any particular strategy for guessing, or was it basically random guessing?
Test Taker's Integrity	Do you think that there was any cheating during this test? If so, please describe the methods you think may have been used.
Test Taker's Mental/Physical State Upon Entry	How would you describe your mental state going into this test? Do you think that your mental state in any way affected the test outcome? If so, how? How would you describe your physical state going into this test? Do you think that your physical state in any way affected the test outcome? If so, how?
Test Taker's Mental/Physical State During the Test	How would you describe your mental state as you took this test? Do you think that your mental state in any way affected the test outcome? If so, how? How would you describe your physical state as you took this test? Do you think that your physical state in any way affected the test outcome? If so, how?
Test Taker's Overall Impressions	How would you describe your overall impression of this test? What suggestions would you offer the test developer for improvement?
Test Taker's Preferences	Was there any part of the test that you found entertaining or otherwise rewarding? What specifically did you like or dislike about the test? Was there any part of the test that you found anxiety provoking, condescending, or otherwise upsetting? If so, why?
Test Taker's Preparation	How did you prepare for this test? If you were going to advise others as to how to prepare for it, what would you tell them?

SOURCE: From Cohen, R. J., Swerdlik, M. E., & Phillips, S. M. (1996). *Psychological testing and assessment: An introduction to tests and measurement* (3rd ed.). Mountain View, CA: Mayfield. Reproduced with the permission of the McGraw-Hill Companies.

Expert Panels

Test developers also find the information provided by experts to be helpful in understanding and improving test results. One group of experts would be people who are knowledgeable about the test's constructs. For example, if the test measures job skills such as financial planning or systems analysis, people who perform these jobs well can be recruited to review the test and provide their opinions on the test's content.

Another area of expertise is psychological measurement. Review by another test developer who has not been involved in the development process can provide a fresh look at issues of test length, administration instructions, and other issues not related to test content.

INTERIM SUMMARY 12.1
PILOT TEST AND ITEM ANALYSIS

- The pilot test provides a thorough examination of how the new test works and the results that it yields.
- After the test has been administered to a sample of participants, the test developers review and analyze the pilot test data.
- Quantitative item analysis examines how well each test item performs.
- The difficulty of each item is calculated by finding the percentage of test takers who responded to the item correctly. Most developers seek a range of difficulty levels that average roughly .5.
- Test developers also create a discrimination index, which compares the performance of those who made very high test scores on each item with the performance of those who made very low test scores on each item.

- Average interitem correlation and item–total correlation provide information for increasing the test's internal consistency. Each item should be correlated with every other item measuring the same construct.
- In item response theory, the performance of each item is related to the test taker's ability on the construct being measured. The resulting item characteristic curve is a graph of the probability of answering an item correctly given a certain level of ability. It combines item difficulty and discrimination.
- Item bias refers to whether an item is easier for one group than for another group. Item characteristic curves provide information on item bias by comparing group scores.
- Test developers use questionnaires and expert panels for a qualitative analysis of the test items.

Revising the Test

Revision of the test is a major part of the test development process. Test developers write more items than are needed. They use the quantitative and qualitative analyses of the test to choose those items that together provide the most information about the construct being measured. Because the instructions for test takers and test administrators are an essential part of the test, the information provided by test takers and experts provides a basis for revising the instructions in a way that facilitates the process of test administration.

Choosing the Final Items

Choosing the items that make up the final test requires the test developer to weigh each item's evidence of validity, item difficulty and discrimination, interitem correlation (a measure of reliability), and bias. Issues such as test length and face validity must also be considered.

Many test developers find that constructing a matrix makes choosing the best items easier. Table 12.3 lists each item, followed by its performance in terms of internal consistency (item–total correlation), validity (item–criterion correlation), difficulty discrimination, and bias. The test developer's job is to choose the best-performing items, taking care that each area of content is represented in the proportion required by the test plan. In addition to the matrix, developers can review the ICCs to make visual comparisons of items.

As you recall, positive interitem correlation coefficients and item–total correlations suggest that the item is measuring the same construct as are other items—evidence of internal reliability. The best items will have higher positive correlation coefficients. They will also be close to .5 in difficulty with discrimination indexes that are positive and high. Items that have evidence of bias are not acceptable unless they can be rewritten to relieve that problem. (Such rewrites may require further testing to ensure that bias no longer exists.) It is unusual for all items to meet all of the criteria for a "good" item, and therefore the test developer has the complicated job of weighing the merits of each item and choosing a set of final items that work well together to provide accurate test results for all participants.

As you can see from the data in Table 12.3, the items represented have varying merits. Item 1 has appropriate difficulty and is not biased; however, both its discrimination index and item–total correlation are negative, suggesting that poor performers were more likely to get this item right and good performers were more likely to get it wrong. Also, this item is not correlated with a criterion. Item 2, on the other hand, has a good item–total correlation and shows no bias, but it is very difficult, with only 20% of the test takers correctly answering it. Item 3 has the best data of the items measuring translation (T). Its item–total correlation is high, its difficulty level is close to .5, its discrimination index is high and positive, and it shows no evidence of bias. Therefore, Item 3 would be a better choice than Item 1 or 2.

Now you can see why the test developer must write many more items for a test than are required. Each item must be judged as acceptable on a number of criteria to be chosen for inclusion in the test. Of the

Table 12.3 Item Statistics Matrix for Items From a Hypothetical Reading Comprehension Test

Item Number	Content Area [a]	Item–Total Correlation	Item–Criterion Correlation	Difficulty (p)	Discrimination (D)	Bias
1	T	−.20	.00	.50	−10	No
2	T	.35	.00	.20	35	No
3	T	.40	.08	.60	36	No
4	I	.80	.12	.65	40	No
5	I	.25	.01	.50	15	Yes
6	I	−.05	−.02	.50	−35	No
7	E	.56	.25	.49	30	No
8	E	.84	.20	.70	48	No
9	E	.03	−.05	.90	−20	Yes

a. The test plan calls for items that measure translation (T), interpretation (I), and extrapolation (E).

remaining items, which ones would you choose to include in the final test? If you chose Items 4, 7, and 8, you agree with the authors of this textbook.

When test developers have written an ample number of test items, the task of compiling the final test is simply a matter of choosing the correct number of "good" items that meet the requirements of the test plan. When test items must be rewritten to increase or decrease difficulty or discrimination or to avoid bias, those items should be piloted again to be sure that the changes made produced the desired results. Extensive changes or rewrites signal the need for another pilot test.

Revising the Test Instructions

No matter how well the final items work together, the test cannot produce accurate results unless the instructions for test takers and test administrators are concise and understandable. Clear and comprehensive directions ensure that the test will be administered in the same way for all participants and under circumstances that are advantageous for test taking. Likewise, directions for test takers help prevent test takers from giving useless responses. The qualitative information obtained from test takers and administrators provides a useful guide for revising instructions to promote maximum performance.

Instructions to the test administrator should provide guidance on topics such as choosing the testing room (a quiet place where interruptions are unlikely), answering questions (clarify instructions, but do not elaborate or provide help), equipment or supplies needed (No. 2 pencils), and test length (a specified time period or unlimited time). The instructions may include a section on answering frequently asked questions—information obtained during the pilot test.

Instructions to test takers should include directions for responding (for example, "Darken the box next to the answer you have chosen with a No. 2 pencil"), instructions on guessing (whether or not guessing is penalized), and special instructions (for example, "Think of how you interact with people at work when answering these questions"). Often tests include sample questions that test takers complete with the test administrator to be sure that directions for responding are clearly understood. (Chapter 11 discussed test and survey instructions in more detail.)

INTERIM SUMMARY 12.2
REVISING THE TEST

- Test items are dropped based on their consistency, difficulty, discrimination, and bias until a final form of the test is reached.
- If enough items were piloted, no items will be rewritten. Items that are rewritten must be piloted to be sure that they now meet criteria for retention in the test.

- Other test components, such as the instructions, should be revised based on the results of a qualitative analysis in the form of questionnaires or interviews with test takers, subject matter experts, and testing experts.

Validating the Test

When the final test has been compiled, it is time to move to the next stage of test development—conducting the validation study. Chapters 7, 8, and 9 described the various types of evidence that demonstrate validity in detail. Therefore, this section in the chapter simply provides an overview of designing the validation study.

The first part of the validation process—establishing validity based on test content—is carried out as the test is developed. Evidence that the test measures one or more constructs (construct validity) and has the ability to predict an outside criterion such as performance (evidence of validity based on relationships with an external criterion) must be gathered during another round of data collection.

Standards for setting up the validation study are similar to those suggested for designing the pilot study. The validation study should take place in one or more situations that match the actual circumstances in which the test will be used. Using more than one test site will provide evidence that the results are **generalizable,** meaning the test can be expected to produce similar results even though it has been administered in different locations. Likewise, developers choose as test takers a sample of people who resemble or are part of the test's target audience. The sample should be large enough to provide the power to conduct the desired statistical tests. The test developers continue to follow the *Standards for Educational and Psychological Testing* (AERA, APA, & NCME, 1999) by observing strict rules of confidentiality and by affirming their intentions to publish only aggregate results of the validation study. Again, as in the pilot study, the scores resulting from the administration of the test should not be used for decision making or evaluation of individuals. The sole purpose of the validation study is to affirm the test's ability to yield meaningful results.

Test developers collect data on the test's reliability, its correlation with any appropriate outside criteria such as performance evaluations, and its correlation with other measures of the test's construct. In addition, the developers collect data on the demographic characteristics of the test takers (for example, sex, race, age). (Chapters 6, 7, 8, and 9 provided guidelines for evaluating the test results for acceptable levels of reliability and validity.) Test developers also conduct another item analysis similar to that conducted in the pilot study to affirm that each item is performing as expected. Minor changes in the test, such as dropping items that do not contribute to prediction of an outside criterion and further clarifying test instructions, may be made at this time.

Cross-Validation

If the final revision yields scores with sufficient evidence of reliability and validity, the test developers conduct a final analysis called **cross-validation** for tests that rely on criterion-related validity to make predictions. The process of cross-validation involves a final round of test administration to another sample of test takers representative of the target audience. Because of chance factors that contribute to random error, this second administration can be expected to yield lower correlations with criterion measures. In other words, the validity coefficient will be lower than the one found in the original validation study. This decrease in correlation with an outside criterion—referred to as *shrinkage*—is largest when sample size for the initial validation study is small. However, attention to prediction of the criterion in the pilot study and initial validation study can reduce shrinkage during cross-validation (Cascio, 1991).

Shrinkage in the validity coefficient is so predictable that researchers have developed formulas to predict the amount of shrinkage that can be expected (Cattin, 1980; Wherry, 1931). When resources are not available to carry out a cross-validation study, estimation of shrinkage statistically is acceptable or even preferred (Cascio, 1991).

Differential Validity

Sometimes tests have different validity coefficients for different groups. For example, a test may be a better predictor for women than for men or for Blacks than for Whites. Tests can also produce different slopes or different intercepts for different subgroups. When a test yields significantly different validity coefficients for subgroups, we say it has **differential validity.** When a test is valid for one group but not for another group (for instance, valid for Whites but not for Blacks), it has **single-group validity.**

The differential validity of standardized college admissions tests for women and minorities (Elliott & Strenta, 1988; Grant & Sleeter, 1986; Linn, 1990; Strenta & Elliott, 1987) is an example of this phenomenon. According to Young (1994), research on standardized college admissions tests has consistently yielded higher validity coefficients for women than for men and higher validity coefficients for White students than for minority students. Young decided to verify these findings in a replication study using 3,703 college freshmen who subsequently earned undergraduate degrees within five years.

Young (1994) computed prediction equations for the total sample and for women and men as subgroups using multiple regression analysis. (Chapter 8 explained the purpose and interpretation of multiple regression.) Three measures—SAT verbal score (SATV), SAT mathematical score (SATM), and high school rank in class (HS)—were the predictors. Cumulative grade point average (GPA) at graduation was the criterion. Table 12.4 shows the resulting multiple regression equations for men and women.

As you can see from Table 12.4, the validity coefficients (multiple R values) and the equations themselves are different for men and women. Young (1994) reports that his findings are typical of what is reported in institutional studies. In Young's study, men generally scored higher on both sections of the SAT than did women who earned higher grades in high school. In general, women also scored higher on the criterion measure (college GPA). The predictors also showed differential validity for Whites and minorities, although the sample of Whites was much larger than any of the minority samples.

What accounts for this difference in validity for men and women? Young (1994) suggests that differences in course selection between men and women may partially account for the underprediction of women's grades by the single validity coefficient. In other words, courses and departments with higher average grades are likely to have a higher proportion of women enrolled. Others might disagree with Young's suggestion.

What is the practical significance of differential validity? If a single validity coefficient and regression line is used to establish cutoff scores to select applicants for admissions, the equation will overpredict the number of men and underpredict the number of women who will be successful in college. On the other hand, as Cascio (1991) points out, establishing different scores for admissions by subgroup is likely to be viewed with suspicion and perceived as unfair.

Table 12.4	Multiple Regression Equations for Total Sample and Subgroups by Sex From Young's Differential Validity Study	
Group	*Multiple Regression Formula*	*Multiple R*
Total	GPA = 1.4856 + .0014 x SATV + .0002 x SATM + .0084 x HS	.41
Women	GPA = 1.4258 + .0015 x SATV + .0003 x SATM + .0075 x HS	.44
Men	GPA = 1.5426 + .0012 x SATV + .0003 x SATM + .0075 x HS	.38

SOURCE: From Young, J. W. (1994). Differential prediction of college grades by gender and by ethnicity: A replication study. *Educational and Psychological Measurement, 54,* 1022–1029. Reprinted with permission of Sage Publications, Inc.

Defining Unfair Discrimination

When psychological tests are used to compare individuals, their purpose is to discriminate or illuminate the differences among individuals. That discrimination, however, should be the result of individual differences on the trait or characteristic being measured. When group membership changes or contaminates test scores, test bias exists and members of some groups might be treated unfairly as a result.

Guion (1966) states that employment tests discriminate unfairly "when persons with equal probabilities of success on the job have unequal probabilities of being hired for the job" (p. 26). In other words, performance on both the predictor and the criterion must be taken into consideration. Cascio (1991) states that

> a selection measure cannot be said to discriminate unfairly if inferior predictor performance by some group also is associated with inferior job performance by the same group. . . . A selection measure is unfairly discriminatory only when some specified group performs less well than a comparison group on the measure, but performs just as well as the comparison group on the job for which the selection measure is a predictor. (p. 179)

Based on empirical investigations, researchers generally agree that differential validity is not a widespread phenomenon. The only statistic for which there is consistent evidence of difference is the intercept of regression lines when they are calculated separately for Whites and minorities (Bartlett, Bobko, Mosier, & Hannan, 1978; Cleary, Humphreys, Kendrick, & Wesman, 1975; Gael, Grant, & Richie, 1975; Hartigan & Wigdor, 1989; Linn, 1982). When differential prediction takes place, the result is usually a slight overprediction of minority group performance. In other words, tests may predict that minorities will do better on the job than they actually do (Cascio, 1991). (Chapter 11 discussed ways to address the problem of bias when developing a test.)

Testing for Validity Equivalence

When a test is updated or revised in a different format (for example, from paper-and-pencil to a computerized test), test users need to know whether the forms are comparable in terms of validity. According to Ghiselli (1964), four conditions must be met to claim that two forms of the same test are comparable:

1. The tests must yield identical scores.

2. The tests should yield the same distribution of scores (equivalent means and standard deviations).

3. The individual rank-ordering of scores should be identical.

4. The scores from each test must correlate equally well with external criteria. (cited in Rojdev, Nelson, Hart, & Fercho, 1994, p. 362)

Rojdev and colleagues (1994) conducted a study to examine Ghiselli's (1964) fourth condition; they compared the evidence of validity based on relationships with other variables of the MMPI-1 and the MMPI-2, looking for evidence of equal relationships between the tests and an external criterion. They correlated test scores of 137 undergraduate students on the MMPI-1, the MMPI-2, and the Symptom Checklist-90–Revised (SCL-90-R; Derogatis, Rickels, & Rock, 1976) on eight dimensions.

Table 12.5 compares the validity coefficients of the MMPI-1 and MMPI-2 using the dimensions of the SCL-90-R as the outside criterion. As you can see, the validity coefficients for the SCL-90-R and the MMPI-1 all reached statistical significance. Only two validity coefficients of the MMPI-2 (Hypochondriasis and Social Introversion) reached significance. The researchers then conducted a z test for the significance of difference between independent correlations and found only one dimension (Psychasthenia) of the MMPI-1 and MMPI-2 to be significantly different. Although the MMPI-2 dimensions do not correlate as well with the SCL-90-R as do the MMPI-1 correlations, Rojdev and colleagues concluded that the MMPI-1 and MMPI-2 were equivalent. Because of all the differences between the correlations with the SCL-90-R on all dimensions, only the correlation of the MMPI-1 Psychasthenia scale with the SCL-90-R Obsessive–Compulsive scale was significantly different.

In summary, test developers administer the test items a number of times to ensure that the test is effectively measuring the construct as intended. First, test developers pilot the test and revise test items and instructions. They compile the test from items that perform effectively and then re-administer it to new participants to obtain data on reliability and validity. Finally, they cross-validate the test by administering

| **Table 12.5** | Validity Equivalence of the MMPI-1 and MMPI-2 With an Outside Criterion |

MMPI-1 and MMPI-2 Dimension	SCL-90-R Dimension	Validity Coefficient for MMPI-1 and SCL-90-R	Validity Coefficient for MMPI-2 and SCL-90-R	z Score for Validity Coefficient	Probability of Difference Occurring by Chance
Hypochondriasis	Somatization[a]	.51**	.42**	.65	.27
Depression	Depression	.33**	.16	1.01	.16
Conversion Hysteria	Somatization[a]	.38**	.22	.92	.18
Paranoia	Paranoid Ideation	.36**	.12	1.35	.05
Psychasthenia[a]	Obsessive–Compulsive	.52**	.20	2.02	.02*
Psychasthenia[a]	Anxiety	.46**	.25	1.31	.10
Schizophrenia	Psychoticism	.40**	.11	1.59	.05
Social Introversion	Interpersonal Sensitivity	.33**	.28*	.03	.38

SOURCE: Adapted from Rojdev, R., Nelson, W. M., III, Hart, K. M., & Fercho, M. C. (1994). Criterion-related validity and stability: Equivalence of the MMPI and the MMPI-2. *Journal of Clinical Psychology, 50*, 361–367. Published by John Wiley & Sons, Inc.

NOTE: SCL-90-R = Symptom Checklist-90–Revised.

a. These scales are matched to more than one scale on the other test.
*p < .05.
**p < .01.

it again to different test takers, or they adjust the validity coefficients obtained in the initial validation study for shrinkage. Validation studies also check for evidence of differential validity.

Validation of a test is an ongoing process. Responsible test developers and publishers monitor the test by continuing to collect information about how it is performing. They also invite others to collect data on the test and to publish the results of their analyses. Sometimes over the course of time, tests may become outdated or flaws may be identified. In this case, publishers often choose to revise the test—using the procedures outlined in this chapter—to increase the test's effectiveness. Educational tests, such as the Graduate Record Examination (GRE) and SAT, have been revised a number of times. Likewise, clinical tests, such as the MMPI and the California Personality Inventory, have been revised to increase their effectiveness.

Developing Norms and Identifying Cut Scores

Both norms and **cut scores**—decision points for dividing test scores into pass/fail groupings—provide information that assists the test user in interpreting test results. Not all tests have published norms or cut scores. The development of norms and cut scores depends on the purpose of the test and how widely it is used.

Developing Norms

As you recall from Chapter 5, norms—distributions of test scores—are one aid for interpreting an individual's test score. Comparing an individual's score with the test norms, such as the mean and standard deviation, provides information about whether the person's score is high or low. For instance, if Roberto scores 70 on the final exam, we would like to know the mean and standard deviation of that exam. If Roberto scores 70 on an exam that has a mean of 80 and a standard deviation of 10, we can interpret his score as low. If Roberto scores 70 on an exam that has a mean of 60 and a standard deviation of 5, he has done very well.

The purpose of test norms is to provide a reference point or structure for understanding one person's score. Ideally, the test norms would contain a test score for each person in the target audience or the population for which the test has been developed. Such a case, however, is rarely possible. Instead, test developers must rely on constructing norms from a sample of the target audience.

The next best situation would be for test developers to obtain a random sample of the target audience. As you know, the larger and more representative the sample is of the population, the less error is associated with its measurement. Again, this is rarely possible. Random sampling requires that each member of the population have an equal chance of being selected. To obtain a true random sample, researchers must have a list of all members of the population—an unlikely circumstance for tests with large target audiences.

Therefore, test developers rely on administering the test to people in the target audience in various locations, usually constructing a large database from which various statistics can be computed to be used as norms. Test developers may start with data obtained during the validation process and then supplement those scores with new data as the test begins to be used. Although it is not appropriate to use test scores obtained during the validation process for making decisions about individuals, it is appropriate to use these scores as a basis for calculating norms. Likewise, scores from tests administered for use by individuals can be added to the database used for calculating norms. As the size of the database grows, the statistics used for norms will become more stable or unchanging. At this point, test developers can publish the norms with some confidence that the sample in the database is representative of the test's target audience.

Larger databases also allow **subgroup norms**—statistics that describe subgroups of the target audience—to be developed for demographic characteristics, such as race, sex, and age, or for locations, such as regions and states. Again, a large sample is needed for each subgroup so that the statistics it yields will be stable or unchanging as new scores are added.

The test norms—means, standard deviations, percentile rankings, and so on—are published in the test manual. When there are indications that norms are changing due to changes in the target audience or the test environment, publishers should publish new norms. This has been the case with the SAT published by Educational Testing Service.

Identifying Cut Scores

When tests are used for making decisions (for example, whether to hire an individual, whether to recommend a person for clinical treatment), test developers and test users often identify a cut score—the score at which the decision changes. For example, an employer may decide that the minimum score needed for hiring is 60 on a test that yields possible scores of 0 to 100. Those who score at least 60 will be eligible for hire, and those who score less than 60 will be ineligible for hire. Therefore, we would refer to 60 on this particular test as the cut score. Not all tests have cut scores, and sometimes it is appropriate for the test user (for example, an employer), rather than the test developer, to set the cut score.

Setting cut scores is a difficult process that has legal, professional, and psychometric implications beyond the scope of this textbook (Cascio, Alexander, & Barrett, 1988). In the News Box 12.1 provides an example of the difficulty involved in setting the cut score for the Regents Math A exam in New York in 2005.

There are generally two approaches to setting cut scores. One approach used for employment tests as well as tests used for professional licensure or certification involves a panel of expert judges who provide an opinion or rating about the number of test items that a *minimally qualified* person is likely to answer correctly. The concept of a minimally qualified person may seem strange to you. Why would we want to set a cut score at such a seemingly low level? The answer is that a minimally qualified person is an individual who is able to perform his or her job at a level that is considered to be satisfactory. When test scores are used for decision making, it would not be appropriate to exclude from consideration individuals who can perform the tasks required by their job or profession at a satisfactory level. Therefore, test developers can use this information to arrive at a cut score that represents the lowest score that is still considered to be acceptable.

The other general approach is more empirical and uses the correlation between the test and an outside criterion to predict the test score that a person who performs at a minimum level of acceptability is likely to make. For example, if the validation study correlates test scores with supervisor ratings (5 = *excellent*, 4 = *very good*, 3 = *good*, 2 = *fair*, 1 = *unacceptable*), we can use a regression formula to predict the score that persons rated 2 (fair) are likely to make. This score then becomes the cut score.

Often the expert panel approach and the empirical approach are combined. Experts identify a minimum level of test and criterion performance, and then the consequences of using the cut score are tested empirically. Cut scores on employment tests are also affected by external variables such as the labor market.

IN THE NEWS

Box 12.1   What's in a Cut Score?

"No student's future should depend on instruments of such questionable validity," wrote Jeanne Heifetz (2003, p. A10), a Brooklyn resident, to the editor of *The New York Times.* Heifetz was complaining about the Regents Math A exam administered by the New York State Education Department (NYSED). Students in New York have been taking the Regents exams voluntarily for decades. Recently, as part of an eight-year effort to strengthen education, NYSED began requiring all students to pass five exams, including math, to graduate (Arenson, 2003c).

In 2003, the public began questioning the testing system, and there were charges that NYSED established a passing score for the Regents physics test in a manner that violated the *Standards for Educational and Psychological Testing* (American Educational Research Association, American Psychological Association, & National Council on Measurement in Education, 1999). (See Chapter 3 for information on the *Standards.*) In addition, something went wrong with the Regents Math A exam. Two-thirds of the students who took the exam failed it, and Black and Hispanic students passed the exam at lower rates than did White and Asian students (Arenson, 2003a). As a result, the Board of Regents ordered a review of the exam and a change in the scoring criteria. In other words, the Regents ordered NYSED to rescore the tests (Saulny, 2005).

The Regents also appointed a math standards committee to analyze what went wrong. After reviewing the exam, the committee reported that the effort that year to establish rigorous standards for math had failed. It also reported that the state had not provided teachers with adequate information about what to teach. Finally, the committee found that the exam was poorly pilot-tested and that it lacked evidence of validity based on content; in other words, the exam focused too much on some areas and not enough on others (Arenson, 2003c).

After rescoring the test, NYSED predicted that thousands who had failed the test the first time would pass under the new scoring system. For example, it predicted that nearly two-thirds of the 10th graders who took the exam would pass—approximately twice the proportion of those who had failed the exam originally (Arenson, 2003b).

The next year, however, a new scoring system and cut scores also raised concerns and complaints from the public. This time, the exam was too easy. The test contained more multiple-choice questions and fewer open-ended questions, and the cut score in 2004 for high school graduation was 28 of a possible 84 points. One professional pointed out that the cut score required answering only one-third of the test items correctly. He and other educators pointed out that the cut score had been set too low. One assistant high school principal suggested that teachers and parents should be pleased with the new scoring scheme because so many students passed the exam (Gootman, 2004)!

Cut scores are also used with some educational and clinical tests. For example, many graduate programs use a score on the GRE of 1,000 as the minimum score acceptable for admission, and clinical tests suggest diagnoses based on cut scores.

A major problem with setting cut scores is that test scores are not perfectly reliable. Any test score has error inherent in it. As you recall from Chapter 6, the standard error of measurement is an indicator of how much error exists in an individual's test score. It is quite possible that a person who scores only a few points below the cut score might score above the cut score if that person took the test again. The difference in the two scores would be due to test error, not to the person's performance. For this reason, Anastasi and Urbina (1997) suggest that the cut score should be a band of scores rather than a single score. Using this method, the cut score of 60 proposed in our first example might be expanded to a 5-point band, 58 to 62. The standard error of measurement provides the information necessary for establishing the width of that band.

Compiling the Test Manual

As we have pointed out in previous chapters, the test manual is an important part of the test itself. The manual provides the rationale for constructing the test, a history of the development process, and the results of the validation studies. In addition, the manual describes the appropriate target audience and instructions for administering and scoring the test. Finally, the manual contains norms and information on interpreting individual scores.

For Your Information Box 12.3 shows the table of contents for the test manual for the Wisconsin Card Sorting Test (Heaton, Chelune, Talley, Kay, & Curtiss, 1993) discussed in Chapter 6. As you can see, the manual provides important information for administering the test and interpreting the results. A review of the manual provides the test user with information about the test's reliability and validity as well as the limitations of its use and measurement accuracy.

FYI

FOR YOUR INFORMATION BOX 12.3

Table of Contents for the Wisconsin Card Sorting Test (WCST)

Table of Contents

(Continued)

(Continued)

SOURCE: From Heaton, R. K., Chelune, G. J., Talley, J. L., Kay, G. G., Curtiss, G. (1993). *Wisconsin Card Sorting Test manual*: Revised and Expanded. Odessa, FL: Psychological Assessment Resources. Copyright © 1993. Published by Psychological Assessment Resources.

Although we have left the discussion of the test manual to the end of our discussion of test development, we must emphasize that writing the test manual is an ongoing process that begins with the conception of the test. This process continues throughout development as a source of documentation for each phase of test construction. After the processes of piloting, revising, and validating the test are complete, test developers compile the information they have accumulated into a readable format. This compilation of information then is published as the test manual.

> ### INTERIM SUMMARY 12.3
> ### VALIDATION, NORMS, CUT SCORES, AND TEST MANUAL
>
> - Standards for designing the validation study are similar to those for designing the pilot study, including using a representative sample of the target audience that is large enough to conduct the desired statistical tests.
> - The test developers should follow the *Standards for Educational and Psychological Testing* (AERA, APA, & NCME, 1999). Using more than one test site will provide evidence that the results generalize from site to site.
> - The scores resulting from the validation study should not be used for decision making or evaluation of individuals.
> - When the test user will make predictions from test results, a cross-validation study is important. Test developers expect the resulting validity coefficient to be lower, and the difference between the coefficients in the validation study and those in the cross-validation study is called *shrinkage*.
> - Differential validity results when tests have different validity coefficients for different groups. Single-group validity means that a test is valid only for a specific group.
> - Norms and cut scores can be developed from the validation data to provide test users with information for interpreting test scores.
> - Cut scores can be determined empirically, using the correlation between the test and an outside criterion, or by a panel of expert judges.
> - Finally, the developers compile the test manual, which has been in the process of development along with the test. The test manual includes the answer key, instructions for the administrator and test user, information on test development, validation and cross-validation, norms, and cut scores.

Chapter Summary

The pilot test is a scientific investigation of the new test's reliability and validity for its specified purpose. Because the purpose of the pilot test is to study how well the test performs, it is important that the test is given in a situation that matches the actual circumstances in which the test will be used. Therefore, developers choose a sample of test takers who resemble or are part of the test's target audience. When the test is given, it is important that the test administrators adhere strictly to the test procedures outlined in their test instructions. In addition, test developers or administrators may use questionnaires or interviews that gather extra information about the respondents or the test.

Each item in a test is a building block that contributes to the test's outcome or final score. Therefore, developers examine the performance of each item to identify those items that perform well, revise those that could perform better, and eliminate those that do not yield the desired information. Developers analyze each item for its difficulty (the percentage of test takers who respond correctly), discrimination (how well it separates those who show a high degree of the construct from those who show little of the construct), correlation with other items (for reliability) and with an outside criterion (for evidence of validity), and bias (whether it is easier for one group than for another group). Item characteristic curves provide pictures of each item's difficulty and discrimination. They also can provide information about whether an item is biased against a subgroup of test takers. Test developers might also use individual or group discussions with test takers or experts to gather qualitative information about how to revise the test to improve its accuracy.

After the test has been revised, developers conduct the validation study by administering the test to another sample of people. Standards for the validation study are similar to those for designing the pilot study. The validation study provides data on the test's reliability, its correlation with any appropriate outside criteria such as performance evaluations (evidence of validity), and its correlation with other measures of the test's construct (evidence of the construct that the test measures). If the validation study provides sufficient evidence of reliability and validity, the test developers conduct a final analysis called cross-validation—a final round of test administration to yet another sample of test takers. This second administration can be expected to yield lower validity coefficients. When resources are not available to carry out a cross-validation study, statistical estimation of the decrease in the validity coefficients is acceptable.

After validation is complete, test developers can develop norms (distributions of test scores used for interpreting an individual's test score) and cut scores (decision points for dividing test scores into pass/fail groupings). Their development depends on the purpose of the test and how widely it is used.

At the end of the validation process, the test manual is assembled and finalized. Contents of the manual include the rationale for constructing the test, a history of the development process, the results of the validation studies, a description of the appropriate target audience, instructions for administering and scoring the test, and information on interpreting individual scores.

Engaging in the Learning Process

KEY CONCEPTS

After completing your study of this chapter, you should be able to define each of the following terms. These terms are bolded in the text of this chapter and defined in the Glossary.

- acculturation
- cross-validation
- cut scores
- differential validity
- discrimination index
- empirically based tests
- generalizable
- interitem correlation matrix
- item analysis
- item bias

- item characteristic curve (ICC)
- item difficulty
- item response theory (IRT)
- phi coefficient
- pilot test
- qualitative analysis
- quantitative item analysis
- single-group validity
- subgroup norms
- subtle questions

LEARNING ACTIVITIES

The following are some learning activities you can engage in to support the learning objectives for this chapter.

Learning Objectives	Study Tips and Learning Activities
After completing your study of this chapter, you should be able to do the following:	*The following study tips will help you meet these learning objectives:*
Explain the importance of conducting a pilot test.	• Make a list of problems that could arise if a clinical practitioner, a human resources department, or a college (choose one) used a new test without carrying out a pilot test and validity studies. Compare your list with that of a classmate.
Describe how a pilot test should be set up, and specify the types of information that should be collected.	• Set up conditions for pilot testing one of the tests that you developed as an activity for Chapter 11.
Describe the collection, analyses, and interpretation of data for an item analysis, including item difficulty, item discrimination, interitem correlations, item–criterion correlations, item bias, and item characteristic curves.	• Reread the section titled "Conducting Quantitative Item Analysis," and make a chart that shows each statistic used in an item analysis, its definition, and its sign and formula where appropriate (for example, p = items correct/total items).
Describe the collection and interpretation of data for a qualitative item analysis.	• Review Table 12.3. Are there other questions you would add to this list? Which areas would you want to explore in a focus group? Which would you ask in a paper-and-pencil test?
Identify and explain the criteria for retaining and dropping items to revise a test.	• Review Table 12.4. Carefully analyze the information on each item. Do you agree with the authors about which items work best? If not, discuss the criteria for choosing items with a classmate or your instructor.
Describe the processes of validation and cross-validation.	• Make a chart that shows the similarities and differences among the pilot test, the validation study, and the cross-validation study.
Explain the concepts of differential validity, single-group validity, and unfair test discrimination.	• Using a search engine such as Google, research the concepts of differential validity, single-group validity, and unfair test discrimination. See whether the information you find corroborates the information in this textbook.
Explain the purpose of a cut score, and describe two methods for identifying a cut score.	• Make a chart of the advantages and disadvantages of having a cut score for a classroom test, an employment test, and a clinical diagnostic test.
Explain what information should be included in a test manual and why.	• Review For Your Information Box 12.3. Write an essay that explains why each type of information in the test manual is important. Share your essay with a classmate or your instructor.

ADDITIONAL LEARNING ACTIVITIES

In addition to the study tips presented with each learning objective, here are more activities that you can carry out alone or in a group.

1. The following data are from a pilot study for a math test. Interpret the data, and decide which items you would retain to make a 10-item test. Note that all questions are intended to be homogeneous, and analyses for bias showed none of the items as biased.

Item Number	Average Interitem Correlation	Difficulty	Discrimination Index
1	.40	.90	10
2	.38	.50	60
3	.05	.50	19
4	.30	.48	−2
5	.50	.50	50
6	.01	.98	0
7	.60	.60	48
8	.00	.10	10
9	.55	.49	40
10	.30	.61	−5
11	.44	.51	80
12	−.10	.66	7
13	.40	.55	75
14	.77	.43	−10
15	.71	.71	60
16	.33	.56	40
17	.00	.2	15
18	.22	.35	60
19	.55	.43	70
20	.04	.40	16

2. The following are the raw data for 10 questions from the pilot study for another math test. Calculate the difficulty and discrimination index for each item. Score the test using the cumulative method. Contrast the top third with the bottom third for the discrimination index. Correct answers are marked 1, and incorrect answers are marked 0.

Test	Item 1	Item 2	Item 3	Item 4	Item 5	Item 6	Item 7	Item 8	Item 9	Item 10	Score
1	1	1	0	1	1	0	1	1	0	1	
2	0	0	0	1	0	0	0	0	1	1	
3	0	0	1	1	0	0	1	1	0	1	
4	0	0	0	0	0	0	1	0	0	1	
5	1	1	0	1	0	0	1	1	1	1	
6	1	1	1	1	1	1	1	1	1	1	
7	1	0	1	1	0	1	0	1	0	1	
8	1	1	1	1	1	1	1	1	0	1	

Test	Item 1	Item 2	Item 3	Item 4	Item 5	Item 6	Item 7	Item 8	Item 9	Item 10	Score
9	0	1	1	1	1	1	1	1	1	1	
10	0	0	0	1	0	1	1	1	1	1	
11	0	0	0	1	0	0	0	0	0	0	
12	0	1	1	1	1	1	1	1	1	1	
13	1	1	1	1	1	1	1	1	1	1	
14	0	1	0	1	0	1	1	1	1	1	
15	1	1	1	1	0	1	0	1	1	1	
16	0	1	0	1	0	0	0	0	0	0	
17	0	0	0	0	0	0	0	0	0	0	
18	1	1	1	0	0	1	1	1	0	0	
p											
D											

3. *Design a Pilot Test.* Following are descriptions of three situations in which a test has been developed. Read each situation, and then design a pilot test. Answer the following questions about each pilot test:

   a. Who will take the test?
   b. What information will you gather, and how will you gather it?
   c. What should the testing environment be like?
   d. Who should administer the test?
   e. Do you foresee any problems that need to be investigated during the pilot test?

   Situation 1. The admissions office at your college has developed a test for incoming students. The purpose of the test is to identify students who may have difficulty in adapting to campus life at your college. The college accepts students of both traditional and nontraditional ages with varying cultural and socioeconomic backgrounds. The 50-item test has a multiple-choice format that can be scored using an electronic scan system. The admissions office plans to include the test in its application package and will ask prospective students to return the test with their applications.

   Situation 2. Dr. Query has a local clinical practice for individuals who show signs of depression. She has noticed that some of her clients do better when they participate in group interventions, and others make more progress when she sees them individually. She has developed a 20-minute intake interview that can be conducted by a graduate assistant or caseworker in her office. The purpose of the interview is to identify the type of treatment (group or individual) that is likely to work best for each client.

   Situation 3. AAAA Accounting prepares individual and corporate tax returns. The company has developed a test to measure knowledge of federal income tax law that it wants to use to hire tax preparers. The test has 400 items, 100 of which require calculations. The test will be administered in the company's offices when prospective employees apply to be tax preparers.

4. *Which Statistic Should I Use?* This chapter described a number of statistics that are used for quantitative item analysis. The table below contains a research question in Column A. In Column B, write in the appropriate statistic(s) that answer(s) the research question. Note: More than one statistic may answer some questions.

A Research Question	B Appropriate Statistic
1. Does this item measure the same construct as other items?	
2. Is this item easier for men than for women?	
3. Does this item provide information that helps predict a criterion?	
4. How difficult is this item?	
5. If I drop this item from the test, will it increase or decrease internal reliability?	
6. How did the people who did well on this test do on this item?	
7. Is this item of sufficient difficulty, and does it discriminate between high and low performers on the test?	
8. Is this test biased against a minority group?	
9. How well does the answer on this item correlate with the individual's overall test score?	

5. *What's the Difference?* This chapter describes three data collection studies: the pilot test, the validation study, and the cross-validation study. What are the differences among these studies? What are the similarities? Address issues such as the following: Who are the test takers? What is done with the data? What decisions might be made with the data?

6. *What Went Wrong With the Regents Math A Exam?* Carefully review In the News Box 12.1, which describes the testing problems that faced the New York State Education Department after it administered the Regents Math A exam to high school students. Do you think the problem was with the test itself, the cut score, or both? Would conducting a validation study have averted some of these problems? If so, how?

PRACTICE QUESTIONS

The following are some practice questions to assess your understanding of the material presented in this chapter.

Multiple Choice

Choose the one best answer to each question.

1. Marie designed a self-esteem test for preschool children. Her instructions to the administrator required that the test questions be read orally. The children were instructed to circle the face (variations of a face smiling or frowning) that indicated their answers. Because she could not find any preschoolers to use in her pilot study, she administered the test to fifth graders instead. What is wrong with what Marie did?

   a. Preschoolers' self-esteem cannot be measured.
   b. Tests should not be administered orally to preschoolers.
   c. The test takers in her pilot study were not the same as her target audience.
   d. Nothing was wrong with what Marie did.

2. When Isaac conducted an item analysis of the data from his pilot study, he first calculated for each item the percentage of test takers who got the item right. In this analysis, he was measuring
   a. item difficulty.
   b. item discrimination.
   c. item reliability.
   d. item bias.

3. Items for which the *p* value falls in the range of .90 to 1.00 are usually considered
   a. too difficult.
   b. about right.
   c. too easy.
   d. too biased.

4. When analyzing the data from her pilot study, Lucretia compared the performance on each item of those who achieved very high test scores with the performance on each item of those who achieved very low test scores. She was calculating
   a. item difficulty.
   b. item discrimination.
   c. item reliability.
   d. item bias.

5. Items for which the *D* value is negative
   a. do not discriminate among test takers.
   b. are too easy for test takers.
   c. are too difficult for test takers.
   d. are biased against low performers.

6. The interitem correlation matrix provides important information for
   a. identifying items that are too easy.
   b. identifying items that are too difficult.
   c. identifying items that do not discriminate among test takers.
   d. increasing the test's internal consistency.

7. _____ contrasts the probability of answering an item correctly with the level of ability on the construct being measured.
   a. The *p* value
   b. The *D* value
   c. The item characteristic curve (ICC)
   d. The interitem correlation matrix

8. The preferred method for determining item bias is to use the
   a. item discrimination index.
   b. item characteristic curve (ICC).
   c. item difficulty level.
   d. interitem correlation matrix.

9. Which of the following would be the most appropriate person to put on an expert panel for conducting a qualitative analysis of a school test?
   a. A parent of a child who was tested in the pilot study
   b. An expert on the constructs being measured
   c. A member of the school board
   d. An outside objective party who has no knowledge of the test

10. Which of the following items would be best to drop from a test?
    a. $p = .4$, $D = 9$
    b. $p = .5$, $D = 7$
    c. $p = .6$, $D = 5$
    d. $p = .9$, $D = -1$

11. Which of the following does NOT need to be included in the test manual?
    a. The test itself
    b. Evidence of reliability
    c. Evidence of validity
    d. A description of the target audience

12. Validity coefficients resulting from the cross-validation study are expected to be _____ the validity coefficients resulting from the original validation study.
    a. lower than
    b. the same as
    c. higher than
    d. of no relation to

13. When Erica conducted the validation study for her test, she found that the validity coefficient for "men only" was not statistically significant; however, the validity coefficient for "women only" was statistically significant. These results suggest that the test has
    a. discriminant evidence of validity.
    b. single-group validity.
    c. differential validity.
    d. no evidence of validity.

14. Statistics that describe subgroups of the target audience are called
    a. norms.
    b. subgroup norms.
    c. differential norms.
    d. in-group norms.

15. When tests are used for making decisions, test users often identify _____ as the score at which the decision changes.
    a. a norm
    b. the standard error of measurement
    c. the cut score
    d. the maximum score

16. Which one of the following coefficients is the result of correlating two dichotomous (having only two values) variables?
    a. Validity coefficient
    b. Reliability coefficient
    c. Phi coefficient
    d. Correlation matrix

17. The strength and direction of the relationship between the way test takers responded to an item and the way they responded to all of the items as a whole is described by the
    a. item–total correlation coefficient.
    b. phi coefficient.
    c. item–criterion correlation coefficient.
    d. reliability coefficient.

18. Researchers (Rojdev, Nelson, Hart, & Fercho, 1994) concluded that the Minnesota Multiphasic Personality Inventory-1 (MMPI-1) and MMPI-2
    a. measure different constructs.
    b. have significantly different validity coefficients.
    c. have significantly different reliability estimates.
    d. are equivalent.

Short Answer/Essay

Read each of the following, and consider your response carefully based on the information presented in this chapter. Write your answer to each question in two or three paragraphs.

1. What is the purpose of a pilot test? When and how should one be conducted?

2. What are the implications of not conducting a pilot test?

3. If you were going to conduct a quantitative item analysis, what statistics would you calculate and why?

4. What is the purpose of a qualitative item analysis? How and when is one conducted?

5. Discuss the process of revising the test after the pilot study. What process would you use to determine the final test?

6. Discuss the process of validation and cross-validation. What are the outcomes of the validation study?

7. When does a test discriminate unfairly? Include discussions of differential validity and single-group validity.

8. What is a cut score? When is it necessary for a test to have a cut score? What are two methods for determining a cut score?

9. What is the purpose of a test manual? What information should the test manual contain?

ANSWER KEYS

Additional Learning Activities

1. Items recommended to retain for a 10-item test are indicated by boldface.

Item Number	Average Interitem Correlation	Difficulty	Discrimination Index
1	.40	.90	10
2	**.38**	**.50**	**60**
3	.05	.50	19
4	.30	.48	−2
5	**.50**	**.50**	**50**
6	.01	.98	0
7	**.60**	**.60**	**48**
8	.00	.10	10
9	**.55**	**.49**	**40**
10	.30	.61	−5
11	**.44**	**.51**	**80**
12	−.10	.66	7
13	**.40**	**.55**	**75**
14	.77	.43	−10
15	**.71**	**.71**	**60**
16	**.33**	**.56**	**40**
17	.00	.2	15
18	**.22**	**.35**	**60**
19	**.55**	**.43**	**70**
20	.04	.40	16

2. Here are the calculations for the cumulative score for each test taker, item difficulty, and discrimination index.

Test Taker	Item 1	Item 2	Item 3	Item 4	Item 5	Item 6	Item 7	Item 8	Item 9	Item 10	Score
1	1	1	0	1	1	0	1	1	0	1	**7**
2	0	0	0	1	0	0	0	0	1	1	**3**
3	0	0	1	1	0	0	1	1	0	1	**5**
4	0	0	0	0	0	0	1	0	0	1	**2**
5	1	1	0	1	0	0	1	1	1	1	**7**
6	1	1	1	1	1	1	1	1	1	1	**10**

(Continued)

(Continued)

Test Taker	Item 1	Item 2	Item 3	Item 4	Item 5	Item 6	Item 7	Item 8	Item 9	Item 10	Score
7	1	0	1	1	0	1	0	1	0	1	**6**
8	1	1	1	1	1	1	1	1	0	1	**9**
9	0	1	1	1	1	1	1	1	1	1	**9**
10	0	0	0	1	0	1	1	1	1	1	**6**
11	0	0	0	1	0	0	0	0	0	0	**1**
12	0	1	1	1	1	1	1	1	1	1	**9**
13	1	1	1	1	1	1	1	1	1	1	**10**
14	0	1	0	1	0	1	1	1	1	1	**7**
15	1	1	1	1	0	1	0	1	1	1	**8**
16	0	1	0	1	0	0	0	0	0	0	**2**
17	0	0	0	0	0	0	0	0	0	0	**0**
18	1	1	1	0	0	1	1	1	0	0	**6**
P	.44	.61	.50	.83	.33	.56	.67	.72	.50	.78	
D	67	83	83	33	83	100	50	83	67	50	

Multiple Choice

1. c	2. a	3. c	4. b	5. a
6. d	7. c	8. b	9. b	10. d
11. a	12. a	13. b	14. b	15. c
16. c	17. a	18. d		

Short Answer/Essay

Refer to your textbook for answers. If you are unsure of an answer and cannot generate the answer after reviewing your book, ask your professor for clarification.

SECTION IV

USING TESTS IN DIFFERENT SETTINGS

Overview of Section IV

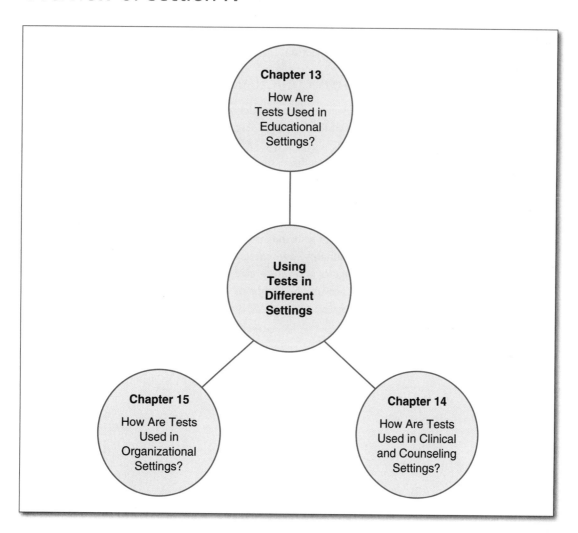

CHAPTER 13: HOW ARE TESTS USED IN EDUCATIONAL SETTINGS?

In Chapter 13, we begin with an overview of the types of decisions that are made in education based on the results of psychological tests. We discuss educators as test users and provide a few examples of situations in which educators did not use tests properly. Following a detailed discussion of exactly how tests are used in the classroom, we highlight how tests are used in educational settings to make selection and placement decisions, counseling and guidance decisions, and curriculum/administrative policy decisions. We end with a discussion of norm- and criterion-referenced tests and authentic assessment in educational settings.

CHAPTER 14: HOW ARE TESTS USED IN CLINICAL AND COUNSELING SETTINGS?

In Chapter 14, we begin with an overview of three models clinicians and counselors use in psychological testing. We discuss the types of tests used for diagnosis and intervention, including clinical interviews and various projective techniques. After discussing neuropsychology and neuropsychological tests, we conclude with a discussion of specialized tests for clinical disorders.

CHAPTER 15: HOW ARE TESTS USED IN ORGANIZATIONAL SETTINGS?

In Chapter 15, we begin with a brief history of the role psychological assessment has played in organizations. We examine various types of tests that are used for hiring employees, such as interviews and tests of performance, personality, and integrity. We consider legal constraints on employment testing legislated by Congress and interpreted by the executive branch and the federal court system. Finally, we describe how organizations use psychological assessment to evaluate employee performance.

CHAPTER 13

How Are Tests Used in Educational Settings?

CHAPTER 13: HOW ARE TESTS USED IN EDUCATIONAL SETTINGS?

After completing your study of this chapter, you should be able to do the following:

- Describe the types of decisions educators make based on the results of psychological tests.
- Explain why educators are test users and why they need to follow the test user guidelines discussed in Chapter 3.
- Describe how teachers use psychological tests in the classroom before, during, and after instruction.
- Describe how psychological tests can benefit student motivation, retention and transfer of learning, self-assessment, and instructional effectiveness.
- Describe how educational institutions use tests to make selection and placement decisions, counseling and guidance decisions, program and curriculum decisions, and administrative policy decisions.
- Explain the differences between norm-referenced and criterion-referenced tests.
- Describe authentic assessment and the perceived advantages and disadvantages of authentic assessment.

"I asked my teacher why she always identifies and discusses the instructional objectives of a specific unit of instruction before she begins teaching. She said that she needs the objectives to guide her teaching and to determine what material should be included on classroom exams. She also mentioned the objectives should help me understand what I should know or be able to do at the end of the unit. I always wondered how teachers choose what to put on the exams."

"This year in school, I had to take a number of tests, but only a few of them were used to make grading decisions. Why do teachers make us take all of these tests? How else are the results of these tests used?"

"One of my elementary school teachers once told me that she did not believe that tests can by themselves accurately measure a student's understanding of material. What other options do teachers have for measuring student learning and achievement?"

If you are like many students, prior to reading this textbook you probably believed that the primary purposes of psychological tests were to determine when someone is psychologically disturbed and to measure someone's intelligence. By now you should realize that psychological testing is much broader than personality and intelligence testing and that psychological tests are used for more than diagnosing psychological disorders and measuring intelligence.

The first three sections of the text focused on the foundations of psychological testing, and in this fourth and final section we discuss how tests are used in three settings: educational, clinical, and organizational. In this chapter, we focus on how individuals use psychological tests in educational settings. We begin with an overview of the types of decisions made in education based on the results of psychological tests. We discuss educators as test users and provide a few examples of situations in which educators did not use tests properly. Following a detailed discussion of exactly how teachers use tests in the classroom, we highlight how tests are used in educational settings to make selection and placement decisions, counseling and guidance decisions, and curriculum and administrative policy decisions. We end with a discussion of norm- and criterion-referenced tests and authentic assessment in educational settings.

Decision Making in the Educational Setting

Every day, educators make important individual, school, district, and state decisions based on the results of psychological tests. According to the most recent *Standards for Educational and Psychological Testing* (American Educational Research Association [AERA], American Psychological Association [APA], & National Council on Measurement in Education [NCME], 1999), educational administrators and teachers use test results to provide information about individual performance and about the status, progress, or accomplishment of schools, school districts, and states. At the individual student level, tests are used to "(a) evaluate a student's overall achievement and growth in a content domain, (b) diagnose student strengths and weaknesses in and across content domains, (c) plan educational interventions and to design individualized instructional plans, (d) place students in appropriate educational programs, (e) select applicants into programs with limited enrollment, and (f) certify individual achievement or qualification" (p. 137). At the group level, tests are used to "(a) judge and monitor the quality of educational programs for all or for particular subsets of individuals, and (b) infer the success of policies and interventions that have been selected for evaluation" (p. 137).

On the other hand, others classify tests used in educational settings into different categories. For example, Thorndike, Cunningham, Thorndike, and Hagen (1991) classify tests used in education by the type of decision the results are used for: instructional, grading, diagnostic, selection, placement, counseling and guidance, program and curriculum, and administrative policy. The first three types of decisions—instructional, grading, and diagnostic—are made most frequently by classroom teachers using tests that they developed and sometimes standardized tests. The next five types of decisions—selection, placement, counseling and guidance, program and curriculum, and administrative policy—are typically developed by testing specialists, educational administrators, or committees and are often based on standardized tests of aptitude or achievement. Table 13.1 summarizes the different types of decisions.

| Table 13.1 | Types of Decisions Made by Educational Institutions Based on Psychological Tests |

Type of Decision	Individuals Who Typically Make This Decision	Type of Test Typically Used to Make This Decision	Example
Instructional	Classroom teacher	Teacher made	Teachers use the results of tests to determine the pace of their courses (for example, should they slow down, speed up, continue their teaching pace, or skip a topic altogether?).
Grading	Classroom teacher	Teacher made	Teachers use the results of tests to assign grades to students (for example, teachers administer quizzes, midterm exams, and final exams).
Diagnostic	Classroom teacher	Teacher made	Teachers use the results of tests to understand students' learning difficulties (for example, a test may reveal that Zachary can write a complete sentence but only a simple sentence).
Selection	Specialist or administrator at the school level	Standardized	Specialists or administrators use the results of tests, such as the SAT, to make admissions decisions and select individuals for special programs (for example, gifted and remedial programs).
Placement	Specialist or administrator at the school level	Standardized	Specialists or administrators use tests to place individuals into the proper level of a course (for example, colleges and universities may use test scores to determine the math course in which individuals should be placed).
Counseling and Guidance	Specialist or administrator at the school or district level	Standardized	Specialists or administrators use test scores to help students select majors and careers that match the students' strengths and interests.
Program and Curriculum	Specialist or administrator at the district level	Standardized	Specialists or administrators use test scores to determine the success of a program or curriculum (for example, are students who go through the new curriculum learning more than students who go through the old curriculum?) and to determine whether a program or curriculum should be implemented or dropped.
Administrative Policy	Specialist or administrator at the district, state, or national level	Standardized	Specialists or administrators use the results of tests to determine where money should be spent and what programs should be implemented to improve the achievement scores of a school, district, state, or nation (for example, No Child Left Behind programs often divert funds to schools where students earn low scores on standardized tests).

SOURCE: Adapted from Thorndike, R. M., Cunningham, G., Thorndike, R. L., & Hagen, E. (1991). *Measurement and evaluation in psychology and education.* New York: Macmillan.

Educators as Test Users

As you can see, a variety of individuals—from classroom teachers to district-level administrators—use psychological tests in educational settings to make a wide range of important decisions. Further, many tests serve more than one purpose; a test may be used by a teacher to monitor student achievement and by a school or district to evaluate the quality of educational programs at the school. Since the No Child Left Behind Act, which we introduced in Chapter 1 and discuss in more detail later in this chapter, became law in 2002, the role of psychological tests in educational settings has increased (National Education Association, 2002–2010).

In Chapter 3, we defined a test user as anyone who participates in purchasing, administering, interpreting, or using the results of a psychological test. Because teachers, specialists, and administrators create, administer, score, and use the results of psychological tests, they are test users. As test users, all educators and educational administrators who participate in any part of the testing process should be properly trained on the appropriate use of psychological tests. When educators who use psychological tests are not properly informed and trained, the results can include embarrassment of the educator, improper grade assignment, improper placement, and inappropriate administrative decisions, among other things.

The following two dialogues demonstrate what can happen when educators are not properly trained on the proper use of psychological tests. The first dialogue occurs between one of the authors of *Educational Testing and Measurement: Classroom Application and Practice* (Kubiszyn & Borich, 2007) and a classroom teacher. The second dialogue, from the same book, occurs between "Ms. Wilson" (a sixth-grade teacher) and some of her colleagues at school.

Dialogue 1

Teacher: Hi, I'm Jeff's second-grade teacher. What can I do for you so early in the year?

Author: Jeff says he's in the low reading group, and I am curious about why he is. Could you explain that to me?

Teacher: Oh, don't worry—we don't label kids at this school. I think that would be a terrible injustice.

Author: I see, but could you explain why Jeff is in the "Walkers" instead of the "Runners"?

Teacher: Oh, those are just names, that's all.

Author: Are both groups at the same level in reading?

Teacher: They're both at the first-grade level, yes.

Author: I'm beginning to catch on. Are they reading in the same-level books in the same reading series?

Teacher: Of course not! Some children are further along than others—that's all—but the kids don't know.

Author: Let me guess—the "Runners" are further ahead?

Teacher: Yes, they're in Book 9.

Author: And the "Walkers" are in . . .

Teacher: Book 5. But they are grouped for instructional purposes. I have twenty-five students, you know!

Author: I'm confused. Jeff's reading scores on the California Achievement Test last May were above the ninetieth percentile.

Teacher: [chuckles to herself] I can understand your confusion. Those test scores are so hard to understand. Why, even we professionals can't understand them.

Author: A score at the ninetieth percentile means the score was higher than the score of 90 percent of the students who took the test all across the country.

Teacher: Oh, really? It is very complicated. As I said, even professional educators don't understand testing.

Author: Some do, Mrs. B.

Dialogue 2

Ms. Wilson: I know you all feel we've covered a tremendous amount this year. Well, you're right. We have. And now it's time to find out how much you've learned. It's important for you to know how well you're doing in each subject so you can work harder in the areas where you might need improvement. It's also nice to know in what areas you might be smarter than almost everyone else. So, next week, I want you to be ready to take tests over all the material we have covered so far. [A few students groan in unison.] Remember, this will be your chance to show me how smart you are. I want you to get plenty of sleep Sunday night so you'll be fresh and alert Monday. [As the bell rings, Ms. Wilson shouts over the commotion of students leaving the classroom.] Don't forget, I'll be collecting homework on Monday! [As Ms. Wilson collapses into her chair, Ms. Palmer, an experienced teacher, walks in.]

Ms. Palmer: Glad this grading period is just about over. Next week will be a nice break, don't you think? Just reviewing and giving tests. It'll sure be nice to have this weekend free without any preparations to worry about.

Ms. Wilson: You mean you won't be making up tests this weekend?

Ms. Palmer: No. I have tests from the last three years that I've been refining and improving. With only a few modifications, they'll do fine.

Ms. Wilson: You're awfully lucky. I'm afraid I haven't had a chance to even think about how I'm going to test these kids. All these subjects to make tests for, and then all the scoring and grading to do by next Friday. I think I'm going to have an awful weekend.

Ms. Palmer: Will you be giving criterion-referenced or norm-referenced tests?

Ms. Wilson: Umm . . . well . . . I don't know. I remember hearing those terms in a tests and measurements class I once took, but I guess I just haven't had time to worry about those things until now. I suppose I'm going to have to get my old textbook out tonight and do some reviewing. Gosh! I hope I can find it.

Ms. Palmer: Well, if you use norm-referenced tests, there are some available in Ms. Cartwright's office. You know, she's the counselor who is always so helpful with discipline problems. In fact, she has a whole file full of tests.

Ms. Wilson: Will you be using norm-referenced tests next week?

Ms. Palmer: Not really. For these mid-semester grades, I like to make my tests very specific to what I've been teaching. At this point in the year, it seems to provide better feedback to the kids and parents—especially the parents. Anyway, the parents aren't really interested in where their kid scores in relation to other students until later in the semester, when I've covered more content and the kids have had a chance to get their feet on the ground.

Ms. Wilson: You mean these norm-referenced tests don't cover specifically what you've taught?

Ms. Palmer: [trying to be tactful] Well, no. Not exactly. I guess you have forgotten a few things since you took that tests and measurements course.

Ms. Wilson: I guess so.

Ms. Palmer: Why don't you make a test blueprint and compare it to some of the items in Ms. Cartwright's test file?

Ms. Wilson: A test what print?

Ms. Palmer: A test blueprint. You know, where you take the objectives from your lesson plans and construct a table that shows the content you've been teaching and the level of complexity—knowledge, comprehension, applications—that you're shooting for. Then see how Ms. Cartwright's tests match the test blueprint.

Ms. Wilson: But what if I didn't write down all my objectives? I had objectives, of course, but I just didn't write them down all the time, or when I did, I usually didn't keep them for long. You know what I mean? [no comment from Ms. Palmer] And I don't think I wrote them so they included levels of complexity according to the taxonomy-of-objectives thing I think you're referring to.

Ms. Palmer: But I'm afraid that without objectives, you won't know if the items on Ms. Cartwright's tests match what you've taught. Would you believe that last year a teacher in this school flunked half his class using a test that didn't match what he taught? Boy, what a stir that caused.

Ms. Wilson [looking worried] I guess I'll have to start from scratch, then. It looks like a very long weekend.

Ms. Palmer: Of course, you might consider giving some essay items.

Ms. Wilson: You mean long answer, not multiple choice, questions?

Ms. Palmer: Yes, but you'll have to consider the time it will take to develop a scoring guide for each question and the time you'll spend grading all those answers. And then, of course, only some of your objectives may be suited to an essay format.

Ms. Wilson: [trying to sort out all of what Ms. Palmer just said without sounding too stupid] By scoring guide, do you mean the right answer?

Ms. Palmer:	Well, not quite. As you know, essay items can have more than one right answer. So, first you will have to identify all the different elements that make an answer right and then decide how to assign points to each of these elements, depending on what percentage of the right answer they represent.
Ms. Wilson:	How do you decide that?
Ms. Palmer:	[trying to be polite and being evasive for the sake of politeness] Well . . . very carefully.
Ms. Wilson:	I see. [long pause] Well, maybe my old tests and measurements book will have something on that.
Ms. Palmer:	I'm sure it will.
Ms. Wilson:	Sounds as though I have my work cut out for me. I guess I'll just have to organize my time and start to work as soon as I get home. [Ms. Palmer and Ms. Wilson leave the classroom and meet Mr. Smith, another teacher.]
Mr. Smith:	You won't believe the meeting I just had with Johnny Haringer's parents!
Ms. Palmer and Ms. Wilson:	What happened?
Mr. Smith:	Well, they came to see me after Johnny missed an A by two points on one of my weekly math tests. It was the first time that he had missed an A the entire semester.
Ms. Wilson:	Were they mad?
Mr. Smith:	They were at first. But I stayed calm and explained very carefully why two points on the test really should make a difference between an A and a B.
Ms. Wilson:	What kinds of things did you tell them?
Mr. Smith:	Well, luckily I keep student data from past years for all my tests. This allows me to calculate reliability and validity coefficients for my tests using one of the PCs in the math lab. I simply explained to Johnny's parents, in everyday commonsense language, what reliability and validity of a test meant and then gave them some statistical data to support my case. I also explained the care and deliberation I put into the construction of my tests—you know, all the steps you go through in writing test items and then checking their content validity and doing qualitative and quantitative item analyses. I think they got the idea of just how much work it takes to construct a good test.
Ms. Wilson:	And?
Mr. Smith:	And after that they calmed down and were very responsive to my explanation. They even commented that they hadn't realized the science of statistics could be so helpful in determining the reliability and validity of a test. They even commended me for being so systematic and careful. Can you believe that?
Ms. Wilson:	Umm . . . reliability and validity? Do you mean we have to know the reliability and validity for every test we use?

Mr. Smith:	Ever since that lawsuit by the parents of some kid over at Central for unfair testing, the school board has made every teacher individually responsible for using reliable and valid tests. [Looking surprised, Ms. Wilson turns to Ms. Palmer and Ms. Palmer slowly and painfully nods to indicate her agreement with what Mr. Smith has been saying.]
Ms. Wilson:	Boy! I don't think I could explain reliability and validity that well—at least not to parents—and I know I wouldn't have the slightest idea of how to calculate them.
Mr. Smith:	Well, I guess we won't have any preparations to worry about this weekend. Nothing but review and testing next week. You have a nice weekend.
Ms. Palmer:	Well, it may not be all that bad. You've got that tests and measurements text at home, and next quarter, who knows? You may have time to plan for all this ahead of time.
Ms. Wilson	[being purposely negative] That's if I don't have to explain reliability and validity to some irate kid's parents, construct a test blueprint, learn the difference between norm-referenced and criterion-referenced tests, make a scoring key for an essay test, and of course compute some test item statistics I probably can't even pronounce!

SOURCE: Both dialogues are from Kubiszyn, T., & Borich, G. (2007). *Educational testing and measurement: Classroom application and practice* (8th ed.). Reprinted with permission of John Wiley & Sons, Inc.

Discussion of Dialogues 1 and 2

The teacher in the first dialogue obviously did not understand how to interpret test scores and therefore made an inappropriate decision about the reading group in which she placed Jeff. What's the problem? By placing Jeff in a lower-level reading group, the teacher was not challenging Jeff appropriately.

Ms. Wilson, in the second dialogue, did not know very much at all about psychological testing. Perhaps most important, she did not know that a test should be constructed or selected based on the objectives of a specific unit of instruction. Without this knowledge, we can guarantee that Ms. Wilson's tests would not be content valid and thus would not measure how well her students learned the material she taught. How would you feel if your classroom grade was based on your performance on tests that did not measure what you had been learning in class?

INTERIM SUMMARY 13.1
DECISION MAKING IN THE EDUCATIONAL SETTING AND EDUCATORS AS TEST USERS

- Psychological tests play an important role in educational settings, and their role will likely continue to increase.
- Educational administrators and teachers use test results to provide information about individual performance and about the status, progress, or accomplishment of schools, school districts, and states.
- Teachers, testing specialists, and educational administrators use psychological tests to make a variety of important decisions.
- Teachers use psychological tests to make instructional, grading, and diagnostic decisions.

- Testing specialists and educational administrators use psychological tests to make selection, placement, counseling and guidance, program and curriculum, and administrative policy decisions.
- As test users, teachers, testing specialists, and educational administrators should be properly trained on the appropriate use of psychological tests.
- Educators without proper testing knowledge can make improper decisions that can cause them embarrassment and deny educational opportunities to some students.

Psychological Test Use in Educational Settings

In this section, we discuss in more detail the specific uses of psychological tests in educational settings. Although we focus most of our attention on how psychological tests are used by teachers in the classroom to make instructional, grading, and diagnostic decisions, we also highlight how specialists and administrators use psychological tests to make selection and placement decisions; how specialists use tests to help students make decisions about their futures and careers; and how specialists, administrators, and committees use tests to make program, curriculum, and administrative policy decisions.

Tests Used for Making Decisions in the Classroom

Teachers must make a variety of decisions in the classroom. Teachers must decide whether students are ready to learn new material, and if so, they must determine how much of the new material students already know. Teachers must decide what information students are learning and what information they are having difficulty learning. Teachers must also decide what grades students have earned. Teachers often use tests, combined with other assessment methods, to help them make these and other types of decisions.

Teachers make some of these decisions at the beginning of instruction and other decisions during or at the end of instruction. Teachers often use tests to answer questions they have—the answers to which will allow the teachers to both evaluate and improve student learning (Gronlund & Waugh, 2008). Some of the questions teachers may ask during different phases of the instructional process are presented in Table 13.2.

Table 13.2 Decision Making in the Classroom: The Questions Teachers Ask

Beginning of Instruction	During Instruction	End of Instruction
What knowledge, skills, and abilities do students already possess?	What knowledge, skills, and abilities are students learning?	What knowledge, skills, and abilities have students mastered?
What learning outcomes have students already mastered?	Where do students need help?	What grade should be assigned to each student?

SOURCE: From Gronlund, N. E. (1998). *Assessment of student achievement* (6th ed.). Boston: Allyn & Bacon. Copyright © 1998 by Pearson Education.

Decisions Made at the Beginning of Instruction

At the beginning of a course or before a new unit of instruction, teachers will often use psychological tests as **placement assessments,** which are used to determine the extent to which students possess the knowledge, skills, and abilities necessary to understand new material and how much of the material to be taught students already know.

For example, as a teacher, one of this textbook's authors may decide to give the students in her research methods course a test to measure their understanding of statistics before proceeding to the last section of the course, which covers data analysis techniques. She may use this information to determine whether she needs to begin her discussion of data analysis techniques by focusing on basic data analysis skills or whether she can go right into advanced data analysis skills. She might also use this information to break the class into two groups; those students who have the appropriate statistical knowledge will be taught more advanced data analysis techniques, and those who lack statistical knowledge will be taught more basic data analysis techniques. She might also administer a test to measure how much her students already know about advanced statistical techniques. If students have mastered some of the material, she may modify her teaching plans or place students into different levels of advanced instruction.

Decisions Made During Instruction

Periodically throughout the school year, teachers may use psychological tests as **formative assessments.** These help teachers determine what information students are and are not learning during the instructional process so that the teacher can identify where students need help and decide whether it is appropriate to move to the next unit of instruction. Teachers can use this information to adjust the pace of their teaching and the material they are covering. For example, in a tests and measurements course, we may choose to administer a test at the end of every unit of instruction to determine what students have and have not learned. If a number of students do poorly on a particular test item or group of items, we may choose to spend more time reviewing the material. If only a few students do poorly on a test item, we may choose to work with those students individually and assign them additional reading or problems.

If a student continues to experience problems with some material, teachers may suggest evaluating the student's learning abilities using a more thorough **diagnostic assessment**—an in-depth evaluation of an individual. Diagnostic assessments often include psychological tests that consist of many very similar items. For example, a teacher may administer a diagnostic test to a student who is having difficulties adding numbers. In the test, one group of test items may require the test taker to add two numbers that do not require any carrying (for example, $3 + 5$). Another set may require the test taker to add items requiring minimal carrying (for example, $5 + 6$), and another group of test items may require more carrying (for example, $56 + 84$). These slight differences allow the teacher to determine the exact difficulty the learner is experiencing.

Often, clinical or educational psychologists conduct diagnostic testing because tests designed for use by teachers might not be thorough enough to detect some learning difficulties. Educational and clinical psychologists are specifically trained to conduct the evaluation and diagnostic testing necessary to identify specific learning difficulties.

Decisions Made at the End of Instruction

At the end of the year, teachers typically use tests as **summative assessments,** which help them determine what students do and do not know (to gauge student learning) and are typically used to assign earned grades. For example, a teacher may administer a final exam to students in an introductory psychology class to determine whether students learned the material the teacher intended them to learn and to determine what grades students will earn. Or a teacher may administer a standardized test of achievement at the end of the school year to determine how students' knowledge compares with the knowledge of other students or whether students have achieved important benchmarks (learning targets or objectives).

Sometimes students confuse formative and summative assessment. Teachers use tests as both formative and summative assessments. However, when used as a formative assessment, the test is used to direct future instruction—to provide the teacher with information about what information students have already mastered and where the teacher should spend his or her time teaching. When used as a summative assessment, the test is often used as a final evaluation—for example, to determine what grade to assign to students. Garrison and Ehringhaus (2007) provide a good example, using the road portion of the driving test you likely took to receive your driver's license:

What if, before getting your driver's license, you received a grade every time you sat behind the wheel to practice driving? What if your final grade for the driving test was the average of all of the grades you received while practicing? Because of the initial low grades you received during the process of learning to drive, your final grade would not accurately reflect your ability to drive a car. In the beginning of learning to drive, how confident or motivated to learn would you feel? Would any of the grades you received provide you with guidance on what you needed to do next to improve your driving skills? Your final driving test, or summative assessment, would be the accountability measure that establishes whether or not you have the driving skills necessary for a driver's license—not a reflection of all the driving practice that leads to it. The same holds true for classroom instruction, learning, and assessment. (para. 7)

Additional Ways Assessment Can Benefit the Instructional Process

Psychological tests can benefit the instructional process in other ways. For example, tests can be used to help motivate students and help students understand their strengths and weaknesses. Tests can be used to help students retain and transfer what they have learned to new problems, issues, and situations. Tests can also be used to help teachers evaluate the effectiveness of their teaching methods. Table 13.3 includes some examples of how tests can benefit the instructional process. Tests can also help students and teachers understand learning styles. See On the Web Box 13.1 for more information on assessing learning styles.

Table 13.3 Additional Ways Assessment Can Benefit the Instructional Process

Student Motivation	Tests are great tools for motivating students. Tests contain items to measure student learning. When a student takes a test, the student can see what knowledge, skills, or abilities he or she is expected to learn. After taking a test, a student typically receives the test back with test items marked correct or incorrect. A student can use what he or she is expected to learn, as well as what he or she did indeed learn, to target future study efforts.
Retention and Transfer of Learning	Tests can help students retain information and apply retained information to day-to-day activities. Tests expose students to information repeatedly and require students to practice demonstration of knowledge. Repeated exposure to information and practice can facilitate the retention of information. Also, often tests contain application test items—that is, they require learners to apply learned information to real-world situations. Exposure to such information can help learners understand how what they are learning can be applied to different situations.
Student Self-Assessment	Tests can promote self-awareness. Test results provide students with objective information about what they know (their strengths) and what they must still learn (what they do not know, or their development areas). Students can use their strengths and development areas to make decisions about themselves, such as whether to continue studying a specific content area.
Instructional Effectiveness	Tests results can help teachers understand the effectiveness of their teaching methods. If many students perform poorly on a test (or on a particular section of a test) this may indicate that they were not yet ready to learn the material or the teaching methods were ineffective. While there may be other reasons for poor performance (for example, poorly written test items), teachers may want to consider modifying learning outcomes or changing their instructional methods.

ON THE WEB BOX 13.1

Assessing Learning Styles

Your learning style refers to the way you learn best. Students can benefit from understanding their learning style. Because your learning style guides the way you learn, understanding it should help you study more effectively using techniques that will improve the chances that what you study you will understand and retain. Teachers can also benefit from understanding student learning styles. Because these guide the way students learn, teachers can adjust their teaching styles to better facilitate the learning styles of students.

Many tests are available to help students understand their learning style. Many of the tests assess different types of learning styles. For example, some tests measure learning style as visual, auditory, kinesthetic, or tactile. Others measure learning style using the Jungian dimensions of introversion/extroversion, intuition/sensation, thinking/feeling, and judging/perceiving. Many of these tests are available for free online. Some of the most frequently referenced online learning style tests, and what they measure, are listed below.

Test	Description	Website
Memletics Learning Styles Questionnaire	Measures preferred learning styles based on seven styles: visual, aural, verbal, physical, logical, social, and solitary	www.learning-styles-online.com/inventory/questions.asp?cookieset=y
Paragon Learning Style Inventory	Measures preferred learning style and cognitive preference based on the four Jungian dimensions: introversion/extroversion, intuition/sensation, thinking/feeling, and judging/perceiving	www.oswego.edu/plsi/
Index of Learning Styles	Measures preferred learning style based on four dimensions: active/reflective, sensing/intuitive, visual/verbal, and sequential/global	www4.ncsu.edu/unity/lockers/users/f/felder/public/ILSpage.html
Learning Styles Self-Assessment	Measures preferred learning style based on four styles: visual, auditory, kinesthetic, and tactile	www.ldpride.net/learning_style.html
Personal Learning Styles Inventory	Measures preferred learning style based on three preferences: visual, auditory, and kinesthetic	www.howtolearn.com/lsinventory_student.html

Tests Used for Selection and Placement Decisions

Some educational institutions offer admission only to select individuals (for example, magnet schools, some private secondary schools, colleges and universities, graduate and professional schools). Likewise, some educational institutions offer special programs for students once they begin attending those institutions (for example, gifted learning programs, English as a second language programs, honors degree programs). Some institutions even offer students the opportunity to enroll in different levels of a course (for example, Math 101 instead of Math 100, German 200 instead of German 100). Administrators and testing specialists are often responsible for deciding who will be selected for admittance to educational institutions and who will be selected for and benefit from specific programs or classes within educational institutions. Teachers often create their own tests to make decisions in the classroom, and administrators and testing specialists often use standardized tests of achievement, aptitude, and intelligence to make such selection and placement decisions in educational settings.

Tests Used for Selection Decisions

Educational institutions have numerous requirements for admissions and use various criteria when reviewing applications to make admissions decisions. See On the Web Box 13.2 for the role of tests in the admissions process for a highly competitive institution of higher education: the University of California, Los Angeles.

ON THE WEB BOX 13.2

Role of Tests in the Admission Process at the University of California, Los Angeles

www.admissions.ucla.edu/prospect/adm_fr/frsel.htm

Educational institutions have numerous requirements for admission, and their administrators evaluate applications and make admission decisions using various criteria. For example, the University of California, Los Angeles (UCLA), one of the most sought-after universities in the nation with more than 55,000 freshman applications each year, evaluates applicants both academically and personally using various unweighted criteria: college-preparatory academic achievement (number, rigor, and grades in courses), personal qualities (for example, leadership, character), likely contributions to the intellectual and cultural vitality of the campus, performance on standardized tests (for example, SAT, ACT), achievement in academic enrichment programs, other evidence of achievement (for example, performing arts, athletics), the opportunities afforded to candidates, and challenges faced by the applicant (Luther, 2009).

While UCLA uses standardized tests scores as part of the selection process, they do not require a minimum test score to be considered for admission. Trained readers use test scores as one part of the admissions decision and look for a demonstrable relationship to curriculum and to Academic Senate statements of competencies expected of entering college students.

To learn more about UCLA's requirements for admission and the role that test scores play in the admission process, go to www.admissions.ucla.edu/prospect/adm_fr/frsel.htm. To learn more about how UCLA's requirements and admissions standards compare with a variety of public and private institutions of higher education, including military academies, visit the websites in the following table.

Institution of Higher Education	Admission Website
University of Washington	http://admit.washington.edu/Apply/Freshman/ReviewProcess
University of North Carolina at Chapel Hill	www.unc.edu/admissions/
Rollins College	www.rollins.edu/internet/admissions/index.html
Harvard University	www.admissions.college.harvard.edu/index.html
U.S. Military Academy	http://admissions.usma.edu/
U.S. Naval Academy	www.usna.edu/admissions/

More detail about the Graduate Record Examination can be found in Test Spotlight 13.1 in Appendix A.

As a part of the application process, many educational institutions (for example, some private secondary schools, most colleges and universities, most graduate and professional schools) require students to submit standardized test scores. At the very least, colleges and universities typically require undergraduate applicants to submit their scores on the SAT or the ACT (previously referred to as the American College Test). For a comparison of the SAT and ACT, see For Your Information Box 13.1. Graduate non-business schools often require students to submit their scores on the Graduate Record Examination (GRE). The GRE measures verbal reasoning, quantitative reasoning, critical thinking, and analytical writing skills not directly related to any specific field of study.

Professional schools typically require students to submit their scores on the following:

- Medical College Admissions Test (MCAT; for application to medical school)
- Law School Admissions Test (LSAT; for application to law school)
- Dental Admissions Test (DAT; for application to dental school)
- Graduate Management Admissions Test (GMAT; for application to business school)
- Optometry Admissions Test (OAT; for application to optometry school)
- Pharmacy College Admissions Test (PCAT; for admission to pharmacy school)
- Veterinary Admissions Test (VAT; for admission to veterinary medicine school)

FYI

FOR YOUR INFORMATION BOX 13.1

Differences Between the SAT and the ACT

Sample SAT Item	*Sample ACT Item*
A special lottery is to be held to select the student who will live in the only deluxe room in a dormitory. There are 100 seniors, 150 juniors, and 200 sophomores who applied. Each senior's name is placed in the lottery 3 times; each junior's name, 2 times; and each sophomore's name, 1 time. What is the probability that a senior's name will be chosen?	A rock group gets 30% of the money from sales of its newest compact disc. That 30% is split equally among the 5 group members. If the disc generates $1,000,000 in sales, how much does one group member receive?
A. 1/8 B. 2/9 C. 3/7 D. 3/8* E. 1/2	A. $30,000 B. $50,000 C. $60,000* D. $200,000 E. $300,000

In the past, colleges and universities stipulated which college admissions test they would accept (usually the SAT or the ACT). Colleges and universities on the West Coast and East Coast, as well as those in the Northeast, typically required the SAT. Colleges and universities in the Midwest typically required the ACT. Today, most colleges and universities will accept either test. Given this information, it makes sense that college-bound high school students take both the SAT and ACT and submit the test on which they scored best. However, for various reasons, it is not always possible for all college-bound students to take both tests. At a minimum, college-bound students should realize that although these tests measure some of the same skills (see the similar sample questions below), they also measure different skills. Therefore, the test they choose can dramatically affect their chances for admission to a college or university. Depending on their skills, students may perform better on the SAT than on the ACT or vice versa.

The SAT	The ACT
• Aptitude test that tests reasoning and verbal abilities	• Content-based achievement test that measures what students have learned in school
• Consists of three sections: Verbal, Mathematics, and a required Writing Test	• Consists of five sections: English, Mathematics, Reading, Science, and an optional Writing Test
• Does not include science reasoning	• Includes a science reasoning test
• Math makes up 50% of score	• Math makes up 25% of score
• Math section does not include trigonometry	• Math section includes trigonometry
• Measures more vocabulary	• Tests less vocabulary
• Does not test English grammar	• Tests English grammar
• Is not entirely multiple choice	• Is entirely multiple choice
• Points are deducted for wrong answers (has a guessing penalty)	• Scored based on number of questions correctly answered (does not have a guessing penalty)
• Policy is to send all scores to universities and colleges	• Students can decide what scores to send to universities and colleges

SOURCE: Adapted from "What is the difference between the SAT and the ACT?" Published by ACT Publications.

Portfolios

Although art professionals, such as musicians, artists, photographers, writers, and models, have long used portfolios to display samples of their work, the use of portfolios in the educational setting is relatively new. It was not until the 1990s that portfolios became popular assessment tools in education. Today, many educators use **portfolios,** or collections of an individual's work, to highlight student learning and assess student performance, which may be difficult to assess with standardized testing.

Because portfolios include a collection of work, they can tell a story about a student. Portfolios may include observations of a student's behavior (for example, observing a student forming a sculpture), the results of specific projects (for example, research reports, scrapbooks), other items selected by the individual that reflect what he or she has learned (for example, photographs, sculptures, videotapes, reports, models, narratives, musical scores), as well as other information.

Because a growing number of educators believe a single test is not a good measure of an individual's ability or knowledge, admissions offices are now assessing portfolios for information on making admissions decisions. The use of portfolios in college admissions is reforming how admissions offices evaluate candidates. For example, in 2007 Rollins College administrators announced that students applying for admission beginning with the fall of 2008 did not have to submit ACT or SAT test scores. According to David Erdman, dean of admissions for Rollins's College of Arts and Sciences,

> it is too easy to be distracted by low test scores that are not accurate predictors of a student's college academic potential. . . .We want to take a more holistic approach and believe that a candidate's academic record, level of challenge in course work, talents, interests, and potential to contribute to the Rollins and local community should be as important, if not more important, than test scores. (Rollins College, 2007, para. 2)

Rollins College administrators recognize that not all students perform well on standardized tests and that students have other intelligences besides those assessed on standardized tests of aptitude and achievement. Therefore, instead of standardized test scores, Rollins applicants may submit supplemental materials: (a) a graded paper from a core academic course in the senior year, and (b) a portfolio showcasing their strengths, talents, or interests. Sometimes these portfolios consist of theatrical performances and musical scores, sometimes they consist of slides of photography and sculptures, and sometimes they consist of scrapbooks of community service involvement. However, although Rollins allows students to submit portfolios instead of standardized test scores for admissions consideration, applicants who submit only portfolios and a writing sample are not yet eligible for academic merit scholarships.

Despite their increasing popularity and numerous advantages, portfolios are subjective assessment tools, making them time-consuming to implement, maintain, and evaluate. As with any evaluation (for example, a teacher-made test, a standardized test, an essay), portfolios must be constructed using test specifications and standards (AERA, APA, & NCME, 1999). If they are constructed using test specifications and standards, educators will have more confidence that the portfolios measure what they are intended to measure and will be better able to compare portfolio scores.

Established, objective criteria for portfolio evaluation also must exist (AERA, APA, & NCME, 1999). The criteria should address what type of performances educators are willing to accept as evidence that a student displays the intended learning outcomes and that the student displays work that truly shows his or her ability. Educators can use the criteria to prepare rating scales or scoring rules for evaluating the portfolio. Without written guidelines and evaluator training, the portfolio will likely lack demonstrated reliability and validity.

Tests Used for Placement Decisions

To qualify for placement in a program (for example, gifted program, remedial program, English as a second language program), most educational institutions require students to take standardized tests. In many cases, the results of an achievement, aptitude, or intelligence test are used, along with other evaluative information, to determine whether an individual would benefit from the program. For example, educators may use the results of an achievement test, along with general classroom performance, to place a student in a gifted or honors program.

Some educational institutions also require students to take placement tests before enrolling in certain courses. For example, college educators may use the results of a standardized test of math achievement, along with a student's performance in high school math courses, to place the student in the appropriate college-level math course.

Many tests used to make placement decisions are what we call **high-stakes tests**. When student test performance significantly impacts educational paths or choices, a test is said to have high stakes (AERA, APA, & NCME, 1999). High-stakes testing also involves test scores being used to determine whether a student is retained in a grade level, is promoted to the next grade level, or graduates.

 See Test Spotlight 13.2 in Appendix A for more detail about the Self-Directed Search.

Tests Used for Counseling and Guidance Decisions

Have you ever asked yourself one or more of the following questions: Should I go to college? What should I major in? What career should I pursue? Psychological tests can play a major role in helping answer these questions. Along with other evaluative information, career counselors use the results of psychological tests to help individuals understand their interests, strengths, abilities, and preferences and to translate this information into career guidance decisions. One commonly used test is the Self-Directed Search (SDS). Developed by John Holland, the SDS measures interests and abilities, which are matched to the interests and abilities of individuals who are both satisfied and successful in the career. See On the Web Box 13.3 for a list of tests commonly used to provide career counseling and guidance to individuals.

ON THE WEB BOX 13.3

Tests Used for Counseling and Guidance Decisions

For many years, people have been using psychological tests to understand vocational interests and make career guidance decisions. The use of tests for this purpose probably began in 1915, when James Miner developed a questionnaire to help students make vocational choices. However, the first authentic vocational test was developed 12 years later by E. K. Strong. In 1927, Strong developed the first version of his Strong Vocational Interest Blank. After another 12 years, G. F. Kuder developed the first version of his Kuder Preference Record. Now in the 21st century, a variety of measures of vocational interest are available. Below are some of the most popular tests, along with the publishers' websites, for measuring vocational interest.

Test	Website
Campbell Interest and Skill Survey	www.pearsonassessments.com/tests/ciss.htm
Career Assessment Inventory	www.pearsonassessments.com/tests/cai_e.htm
Jackson Vocational Interest Survey	www.sigmaassessmentsystems.com/assessments/jvis.asp
Kuder Assessments	www.kuder.com/solutions/kuder-assessments.html
Self-Directed Search	www.self-directed-search.com/
SIGI^3	www.valparint.com/
Strong Interest Inventory	www.cpp.com/products/strong/index.asp

Tests Used for Program, Curriculum, and Administrative Policy Decisions

Educational administrators are responsible for maintaining and improving the quality of our educational system. Of course, administrators must have a way of assessing the quality of the educational system and a way of assessing what would improve the quality of the system. As you would expect, educational administrators use the results of psychological tests, along with other evaluative information, to evaluate and modify educational systems. For example, two schools may use two different math curricula, and district administrators might want to know which curriculum fosters greater student learning. At the end of the school year, district administrators may decide to administer math achievement tests to the students in each curriculum to determine which curriculum is benefiting students the most.

Administrators may use the results of the test, along with other information, to determine which curriculum should be implemented or dropped. Likewise, district, state, and national educational administrators may use the results of psychological tests and other information to determine where money should be spent (for example, they may decide to give money to a school to buy more books because its students' reading scores are low) or what program should be implemented (for example, they may decide to start a gifted program because a number of students scored in the 99th percentile on intelligence tests). In the News Box 13.1 describes another important way that boards of education and school superintendents use test scores.

IN THE NEWS

Box 13.1   Paying Teachers for Student Test Performance

Should teacher's be paid and should their job security be based on how students perform on standardized tests? A 2010 article in the Florida *Sun Sentinel* and *Orlando Sentinel* reported that Florida's legislature is lobbying for a controversial bill to remove the tenure and advanced degree based pay system and replace it with a pay system based on student test performance. The bill includes the requirement that assessments be developed for all subjects not measured by current state assessments or by Advanced Placement or International Baccalaureate tests. The bill is controversial primarily because standardized test scores are viewed by many as an unfair representation of what students have learned and teacher performance. Further, the standardized tests used, often a single test, are thought by some to not be sophisticated enough to make such important decisions. Beginning in 2014, passing the bill would mean student test scores and teacher performance reviews would be used to determine teacher's job security and salaries. Moving the bill forward, in March 2010 Florida's Senate passed the plan, 6 to 2, which will completely change the way teachers are evaluated and paid.

SOURCE: Adapted from Hafenbrack, J. (2010, March 10). Bill would tie teacher pay to performance, student test scores. *Sun Sentinel.* Retrieved from http://articles.sun-sentinel.com/2010-03-10/news/fl-teacher-merit-pay-20100310_1_broward-teachers-union-teacher-tenure-weed-out-bad-teachers

SOURCE: Adapted from Hafenbrack, J. (2010, March 10). Florida Senate OKs merit pay, tougher graduation rules. Orlando Sentinel. Retrieved from http://articles.orlandosentinel.com/2010-03-24/news/os-education-reforms-senate-03-25-2010-20100324_1_merit-pay-plan-rank-and-file-teachers-public-school

At the beginning of this textbook, we introduced you to the No Child Left Behind Act of 2001 (NCLB), signed into law in 2002 by President George W. Bush. NCLB focuses on improving the performance of America's primary and secondary schools. See For Your Information Box 13.2 for more information on the role that psychological tests have played in one state, Florida, in assessing the extent to which children and schools measure up to state standards. See In The News Box 13.2 for a discussion of the February 2010 decision of the Central Falls, Rhode Island, school board to fire all the teachers and staff in a chronically underperforming school.

IN THE NEWS

Box 13.2   All Teachers and Staff Fired in a Chronically Underperforming School

In February 2010, all teachers and staff were fired from an underperforming high school in Central Falls, Rhode Island (Jordan, 2010). The firing occurred immediately after a rally where the Central Falls School Board of Trustees voted in favor of firing 93 employees, including the principal, three assistant principals, the school psychologist, and 74 classroom teachers as well as reading specialists, guidance counselors, and physical education teachers. While the decision was supported by state and local education officials and U.S. Secretary of Education Arne Duncan for having the courage to stand up for children, the president of the Rhode Island AFL-CIO and a representative from the American Federation of Teachers claimed the firing was wrong and they would continuing fighting for justice.

According to federal and state education officials, "they must take painful and dramatic steps to transform the nation's lowest-performing schools" (Jordan, 2010, para. 10). However, representatives from the teacher unions share that the steps "undermine hard-won protections in their contracts" (para. 10).

According to Duncan, "students only have one chance for an education . . . and when schools continue to struggle we have a collective obligation to take action" (Jordan, 2010, para. 11). New regulation requires states to fix the lowest 5% of chronically poor-performing and low-graduation rate schools. States have four options:

1. Close the school

2. Have the school be managed by a charter or school-management organization

3. Effect other transformations, including increasing the length of the school day

4. Engage in turnaround by firing the entire teaching staff, with a rehire of no more than 50%

Central Falls High School has a 48% graduation rate, and students have very low test scores. In January 2010, State Education Commissioner Deborah Gist identified six schools in Rhode Island and told districts they had until March 17 to move on one of the four options.

After teachers and union leaders were unable to agree on a method of transformation, Superintendent Frances Gallo reported her loss in confidence about the possibility of transformation and moved forward with a recommendation of a turnaround.

What's your position?

For more information, go to www.projo.com/news/content/central_falls_trustees_vote_02-24-10_EOHI83C_v59.3c21342.html

SOURCE: Jordan, J. D. (2010, February 24). Every Central Falls teacher fired, labor outraged. *The Providence Journal*. Retrieved July 1, 2010, from http://www.projo.com/news/content/central_falls_trustees_vote_02-24-10_EOHI83C_v59.3c21342.html

As a part of Florida's overall plan to raise standards and improve student achievement, the state administers the Florida Comprehensive Assessment Test (FCAT) in Grades 3–11. A criterion-referenced test, the FCAT measures student progress toward meeting the Sunshine State Standards benchmarks in mathematics, reading, science, and writing (Florida Department of Education, 2009).

Results of the FCAT are used to assign grades to schools, to determine which students will be promoted to the next grade level, and to determine which students will receive high school diplomas or certificates of completion.

Each year, after administration of the FCAT, Florida schools earn a grade of A, B, C, D, or F. As you can see in Figure 13.1, school grades are based on the percentage of students in the school who meet higher standards and the percentage of students in the school who make learning gains. Financial incentives are offered to schools that meet specific criteria. In terms of promotion to the next grade level, students in third grade must earn an FCAT reading score of Level 2 or higher (on a scale of 1–5) to be promoted to the fourth grade. Individual school districts set the FCAT score required to pass to the next grade level. To graduate from high school with a standard diploma, seniors must pass the reading and math sections of the 10th-grade FCAT. Students who do not earn passing scores in the 10th grade may retake the reading and/or math portions of the FCAT in October, March, or June of their 11th- and 12th-grade school years.

Figure 13.1 | Florida Comprehensive Assessment Test Grades

Grading Florida Public Schools
2007-08

School grades for 2007-08 utilize a point system. Schools are awarded one point for each percent of students who score *high on the FCAT and/or make annual learning gains.*

FLORIDA DEPARTMENT OF EDUCATION
DR. ERIC J. SMITH, COMMISSIONER

Scoring High on the FCAT

The Florida Comprehensive Assessment Test (FCAT) is the primary measure of students' achievement of the Sunshine State Standards. Student scores are classified into five achievement levels, with 1 being the lowest and 5 being the highest.

⇒ Schools earn one point for each percent of students who score in achievement levels 3, 4, or 5 in **reading**, one point for each percent of students who score 3, 4, or 5 in **mathematics**, and one point for each percent of students who score 3, 4, or 5 in **science**. If a school has fewer than 30 students with science scores, the district average for science will be used.

⇒ The **writing** exam is scored by at least two readers on a scale of 1 to 6. Schools earn one point for each percent of students scoring 3.5 or above. If a school has fewer than 30 students with writing scores, the district average for writing will be used.

Making Annual Learning Gains

Since FCAT **reading and mathematics** exams are given in grades 3 – 10, it is possible to monitor how much students learn from one year to the next.

⇒ Schools earn one point for each percent of students who make learning gains in **reading** and one point for each percent of students who make learning gains in **mathematics**. Students can demonstrate learning gains in any one of three ways:
1. Improve achievement levels from 1-2, 2-3, 3-4, or 4-5; **or**
2. Maintain within the relatively high levels of 3, 4, or 5; **or**
3. Demonstrate more than one year's growth within achievement levels 1 or 2 (does not include retained students).

⇒ Special attention is given to the reading and mathematics gains of students in the lowest 25%[1] in levels 1, 2, or 3 in each school. Schools earn one point for each percent of the lowest performing students who make learning gains from the previous year in **reading** and **mathematics**. It takes at least *50%* in both **reading** and **mathematics** to make "adequate progress" for this group. Schools that fall short of 50% can still meet the requirement if they show annual improvement in this percentage.

[1] For schools with fewer than 30 students in the lowest 25%, the 30 lowest performing students will be substituted.

SCHOOL GRADING SCALE

A	**B**	**C**	**D**	**F**
• 525 points or more • Meet adequate progress of lowest students in reading and mathematics • Test at least 95% of eligible students	• 495-524 points • Meet adequate progress of lowest students in reading and mathematics within two years • Test at least 90% of	• 435-494 points • Meet adequate progress of lowest students in reading and mathematics within two years • Test at least 90% of eligible students	• 395-434 points • Test at least 90% of eligible students	• Fewer than 395 points OR • Less than 90% of eligible students tested

Which students are included in school grade calculations? As in previous years, only standard curriculum students (including Speech impaired, gifted, hospital/home bound, and English Language Learner students (ELL) with more than two years in an English Speakers of other Languages (ESOL) program) enrolled in the same school in both October and February are included in the components for scoring high on the FCAT. All students, including Students with Disabilities (SWD) and ELL students, are included in the learning gains components of the school grade calculation.

What happens if the lowest students in the school do not make "adequate progress" in reading and mathematics? Schools that do not make adequate progress with their lowest students in reading and mathematics must develop a School Improvement Plan component that addresses this need. If a school, otherwise graded "A", does not demonstrate adequate progress in the current year, the final grade will be reduced by one letter grade. If a school, otherwise graded "B" or "C", does not demonstrate adequate progress in either the current or prior year, the final grade will be reduced by one letter grade.

SOURCE: Copyright © Florida Department of Education.

FOR YOUR INFORMATION BOX 13.2

Florida's Response to the No Child Left Behind Act

With more than 2.7 million members, the National Education Association (NEA) is a professional organization committed to advancing the cause of public education—from preschool through university graduate education. In support of the NEA's pledge to guarantee every child an opportunity to succeed in U.S. public schools, in 1965 the Elementary and Secondary Education Act (ESEA) was signed into law by President Lyndon B. Johnson to provide guidance and federal assistance to K–12 schools. Nearly 40 years later, in January 2002, President George W. Bush reauthorized ESEA when he signed the No Child Left Behind Act of 2001 (NCLB). As introduced in Chapter 1 of this book, NCLB's objective is to bring high-quality education to all students nationwide and includes four basic education reform principles: more accountability for results, expanded local control and flexibility, expanded parental options, and emphasis on what teaching methods work best based on scientific research.

To promote accountability, NCLB has a goal that every child will meet state-defined education standards by the end of the 2013–2014 school year. To ensure they meet this goal, all states have defined yearly achievement benchmarks, or minimum levels of improvement, in student performance to measure student progress. To ensure that no child is overlooked, NCLB requires states to explore student achievement data for several subgroups of students. School districts or schools that do not meet yearly achievement benchmarks for two years in a row overall, or for any one subgroup, are found to be "in need of improvement" and must develop and implement an improvement plan based on scientific research (U.S. Department of Education, 2004). They must also offer students the option of transferring to a public or charter school in the district that has made adequate yearly progress. Schools that do not make adequate yearly progress for three years in a row must remain on the improvement plan, must continue to offer students the option of attending another school, and must provide state- and parent-approved supplemental educational services (for example, tutoring, remedial classes) to students from low-income families. For schools that do not make adequate yearly progress for four years in a row, in addition to the above, the school district must take corrective action such as replacing staff or implementing a new curriculum. If a school does not make adequate yearly progress for five years in a row, it must take more severe action such as restructuring and opening as a charter school, replacing all staff, or turning over operations to a private company that has demonstrated the ability to improve student test performance.

As mandated by NCLB, by the 2005–2006 school year, every state was to have implemented a process for measuring whether students were making adequate yearly progress in each of Grades 3–8, and once in Grades 10–12. By the 2008–2009 school year, states also had to have implemented a process for measuring student progress in science on three separate occasions—at least once in Grades 3–5, in Grades 6–9, and in Grades 10–12. States may also require school districts to evaluate students in other areas, such as writing skills, history, and geography, but this requirement is not mandated by NCLB.

Psychological tests play a major role in (a) assessing the extent to which children are meeting state benchmarks in reading, language arts, math, and science; (b) assessing student and school progress over time; (c) providing teachers with information on what students do and do not know and on what teachers can do to improve their teaching; and (d) providing educational administrators with the information they need to evaluate curriculum choices.

Florida has responded to the increased accountability requirements of NCLB by implementing the Florida Comprehensive Assessment Test (FCAT). The FCAT is not one test; rather, it is multiple criterion- and norm-referenced tests. Administered in Grades 3 through 11, the criterion-referenced tests are used to measure the extent to which students can demonstrate the skills and competencies defined by Sunshine State Standards in math (Grades 3–10), reading (Grades 3–10), science (Grades 5, 8, and 10), and writing (Grades 4, 8, and 10). Also administered in Grades 3–11, the norm-referenced tests are used to compare Florida student performance in reading and math with national norms (Florida Department of Education, 2005). Student achievement on the FCAT is used to report educational status and annual progress for students, schools, districts, and the state as a whole.

(Continued)

(Continued)

The following tables show Sunshine State Standards for reading and math. The achievement level scores are used to measure student achievement, and the developmental scale scores are used to measure the progress students are making.

Achievement Level Scores

Achievement levels for each subject area and at each grade level are reported on a scale of 1 (lowest) to 5 (highest) and describe the success a student has attained on the Sunshine State Standards (SSS) tested on the FCAT. The five levels (defined by cut scores on a 100–500 scale) were adopted by the State Board of Education. There are no scale scores lower than 100. Level 1 performance was designated by the Commissioner of Education to be low enough to question the student's academic progress. The state average score was about 300 when the test was first administered in 1998. Since then, the average score has fluctuated as students have been tested. The levels do not indicate passing scores.

The table below lists achievement levels for FCAT SSS Reading, Mathematics, and Science scores along with the scale score ranges associated with each achievement level and grade.

FCAT Reading Achievement Scale Scores					
Grade	Level 1	Level 2	Level 3	Level 4	Level 5
3	100–258	259–283	284–331	332–393	394–500
4	100–274	275–298	299–338	339–385	386–500
5	100–255	256–285	286–330	331–383	384–500
6	100–264	265–295	296–338	339–386	387–500
7	100–266	267–299	300–343	344–388	389–500
8	100–270	271–309	310–349	350–393	394–500
9	100–284	285–321	322–353	354–381	382–500
10	100–286	287–326	327–354	355–371	372–500

FCAT Mathematics Achievement Scale Scores					
Grade	Level 1	Level 2	Level 3	Level 4	Level 5
3	100–252	253–293	294–345	346–397	398–500
4	100–259	260–297	298–346	347–393	394–500
5	100–287	288–325	326–354	355–394	395–500
6	100–282	283–314	315–353	354–390	391–500
7	100–274	275–305	306–343	344–378	379–500
8	100–279	280–309	310–346	347–370	371–500
9	100–260	261–295	296–331	332–366	367–500
10	100–286	287–314	315–339	340–374	375–500

FCAT Science Achievement Scale Scores					
Grade	**Level 1**	**Level 2**	**Level 3**	**Level 4**	**Level 5**
5	100–272	273–322	323–376	377–416	417–500
8	100–269	270–324	325–386	387–431	432–500
11	100–278	279–323	324–379	380–424	425–500

Developmental Scale Scores

A different measurement, called a developmental scale score (DSS), is needed to understand whether a student has "gained" in achievement. For the individual student reports (started in 2002), student scores are linked to the score scale of 100–500 and converted to scores on the developmental scales. The FCAT developmental scores range from 0 to about 3,000 across Grades 3–10 and link two years of student FCAT data that track student progress over time. By using FCAT developmental scores, parents and educators can assess changes in scores across years and monitor a student's academic progress from one grade to the next. Each year, the student's scores should increase according to his or her increased achievement.

In comparing student gains across grade levels, subject areas, and school years, it is important to consider the following limitations of the developmental scale:

- Developmental scores are available to students in Grades 3–10 who have two years of FCAT data.
- Developmental score scales typically show larger increases (more student growth) at the lower grade levels and less student growth at the higher levels.
- Student FCAT data reflect only one year of FCAT "growth" information, which should be considered within the total contest of each student's annual academic record of achievement.
- Some students may show no growth based on their two years of FCAT scores.

The following table lists the FCAT developmental scale scores for each achievement level.

FCAT Reading Developmental Scale Scores					
Grade	**Level 1**	**Level 2**	**Level 3**	**Level 4**	**Level 5**
3	86–1045	1046–1197	1198–1488	1489–1865	1866–2514
4	295–1314	1315–1455	1456–1689	1690–1964	1965–2638
5	474–1341	1342–1509	1510–1761	1762–2058	2059–2713
6	539–1449	1450–1621	1622–1859	1860–2125	2126–2758
7	671–1541	1542–1714	1715–1944	1945–2180	2181–2767
8	886–1695	1696–1881	1882–2072	2073–2281	2282–2790
9	772–1771	1772–1971	1972–2145	2146–2297	2298–2943
10	844–1851	1852–2067	2068–2218	2219–2310	2311–3008

(Continued)

(Continued)

	FCAT Mathematics Developmental Scale Scores				
Grade	**Level 1**	**Level 2**	**Level 3**	**Level 4**	**Level 5**
3	375–1078	1079–1268	1269–1508	1509–1749	1750–2225
4	581–1276	1277–1443	1444–1657	1658–1862	1863–2330
5	569–1451	1452–1631	1632–1768	1769–1956	1957–2456
6	770–1553	1554–1691	1692–1859	1860–2018	2019–2492
7	958–1660	1661–1785	1786–1938	1939–2079	2080–2572
8	1025–1732	1733–1850	1851–1997	1998–2091	2092–2605
9	1238–1781	1782–1900	1901–2022	2023–2141	2142–2596
10	1068–1831	1832–1946	1947–2049	2050–2192	2193–2709

SOURCE: Florida Department of Education. (2008). *FCAT achievement levels*. Retrieved July 5, 2010, from http://fcat.fldoe .org/mediapacket/2008/pdf/08pressPacketGR4_10_page2.pdf. Copyright © Florida Department of Education. Reprinted with permission.

INTERIM SUMMARY 13.2
PSYCHOLOGICAL TEST USE IN EDUCATIONAL SETTINGS

- Teachers use psychological tests as placement assessments, formative assessments, diagnostic assessments, and summative assessments.
- As placement assessments, teachers use tests to determine whether students have the skills or knowledge necessary to understand new material and to determine how much information students already know about new material.
- As formative assessments, teachers use tests to determine what information students are and are not learning.
- As diagnostic assessments, teachers use tests to assess students' learning abilities.
- As summative assessments, teachers use tests to determine whether students have achieved what teachers intended them to achieve and to assign grades.
- Tests can also help motivate students, help students retain and apply information, and help students understand themselves.

- Tests can also help teachers understand the effectiveness of their teaching methods.
- Administrators and testing specialists often use standardized tests of achievement, aptitude, and intelligence to help make selection and placement decisions.
- Although they have been around for many years, portfolios are becoming a more popular alternative for making admissions decisions and evaluating performance and potential.
- Career counselors and other testing professionals use psychological tests, along with other information, to help students understand their interests, strengths, abilities, and preferences and to translate this information into career guidance decisions.
- Educational administrators use psychological tests to make program, curriculum, and administrative policy decisions.

Norm-Referenced, Criterion-Referenced, and Authentic Assessment of Achievement

Norm-Referenced Tests

Throughout this chapter, we have discussed how tests are used in educational settings, providing you with examples of tests along the way. All of these tests can be classified as either norm-referenced or criterion-referenced tests. **Norm-referenced tests** are standardized tests in which one test taker's score is compared with the scores of a group of test takers who took the test previously. As you recall from Chapter 5, the comparison group is called the *norm group*. Norm-referenced tests allow us to determine how well an individual's achievement compares with the achievement of others and to distinguish between high and low achievers. You may remember taking a test and then receiving your results in terms of a percentile such as the 85th percentile. Such score interpretations typically are provided for norm-referenced tests.

Educators use norm-referenced tests to compare students' performance with the performance of other students. With norm-referenced tests, we can compare a student's performance with the performance of his or her classmates or with the performance of students in general. We can compare the performance of students at one school with the performance of students at other schools. We can make statements such as "Zachary scored better than 60% of his third-grade classmates on the math achievement test" and "Students at XYZ High School performed better than 70% of schools in the south on their SAT." In Chapter 5, we discussed one such norm-referenced test: the Stanford Achievement Test.

Some educators believe that using norm-referenced tests to measure student achievement can be harmful to the educational process. They state that because teachers and other educators know the material that norm-referenced tests measure, instead of teaching the subject matter, they do whatever it takes to improve their students' chances of scoring well—"teaching to the test" and teaching test-taking skills. For a list of some commercially available, national norm-referenced tests used by educational institutions, see On the Web Box 13.4.

ON THE WEB BOX 13.4

Common National Norm-Referenced Tests Used by Educational Institutions

Test	Website
SAT	http://sat.collegeboard.com/
ACT	www.act.org/aap/
GRE	www.ets.org/gre/
Stanford Achievement Test	http://psychcorp.pearsonassessments.com/haiweb/cultures/en-us/productdetail.htm?pid=SAT10C
Iowa Tests of Basic Skills	www.education.uiowa.edu/itp/itbs/

Criterion-Referenced Tests

On the other hand, **criterion-referenced tests** are tests that compare a test taker's scores with an objectively stated standard of achievement such as the learning objectives for this chapter. With criterion-referenced tests, an individual's performance is based on how well he or she has learned a specific body of knowledge or skills or on how well the individual performs compared with some predetermined standard of performance.

Criterion-referenced tests allow us to make statements such as "Zachary has learned 50% of the material he needs to know to demonstrate proficiency in third-grade mathematics" and "Zachary still needs to work on his multiplication." Many teacher-made classroom tests are criterion-referenced tests.

Many educators believe that criterion-referenced tests are more useful to students and teachers than are norm-referenced tests, because instead of comparing a student's performance with the performance of other students, criterion-referenced tests help identify how much material a student has learned and what the student must still learn. Furthermore, using criterion-referenced tests makes it possible for every student to achieve the criteria necessary for earning an A. As you know, on norm-referenced tests most test takers are likely to earn the "average" score—no matter how well they perform. For a comparison of the traditional differences between norm- and criterion-referenced tests, see Table 13.4.

Table 13.4 A Comparison of Norm-Referenced and Criterion-Referenced Tests

	Norm-Referenced Tests	*Criterion-Referenced Tests*
What is the purpose of the test?	To determine how well an individual's achievement compares with the achievement of others and to distinguish between high and low achievers	To determine whether an individual has learned a specific body of knowledge or can demonstrate specific skills as identified in a predetermined standard of performance
What does the test measure?	Broad knowledge and skills that come from academic textbooks and teacher syllabi and that are based on the judgments of curriculum subject matter experts	Narrow knowledge and skills taught in a specific educational curriculum or unit of instruction, as defined by specific instructional objectives
What are the characteristics of the test items?	Test items are constructed to distinguish between high and low performers. Knowledge and skills typically are tested by one to four items that vary in level of difficulty.	Test items are constructed to match the most critical learning objectives or outcomes. Knowledge and skills typically are tested by multiple items, of similar level of difficulty, to obtain an adequate sample of individual performance and to minimize the effect of guessing.
How are the scores interpreted?	An individual's raw score is calculated and then compared with the scores of others (the appropriate norm group). Raw scores are transformed and reported in more meaningful units such as percentiles or grade equivalents.	An individual's raw score is calculated and then compared with the total possible score on the test. Raw scores are then transformed and reported in more meaningful units such as percentages.

SOURCE: Adapted from Popham, J. W. (1975). *Educational evaluation.* Englewood Cliffs, NJ: Prentice Hall.

Authentic Assessment

Although they are efficient and typically easy to score, some individuals criticize norm- and criterion-referenced tests because they measure understanding rather than application, are too structured, and often contain only true/false or multiple-choice questions. Some contend that the focus must be changed from measuring understanding to measuring application—or students' ability to apply the knowledge and skills they gain to performing real-world tasks and solving real-world problems. Authentic assessment does this. The focus of **authentic assessment** is on assessing a student's ability to perform real-world tasks by applying the knowledge and skills he or she has learned. Proponents of authentic assessment believe students acquire their knowledge to perform a task or produce a product—and assessment should focus on evaluating student ability to perform the task or produce the product. Authentic assessment relies on more than one measure of performance, is criterion referenced, and relies on human judgment.

Traditional and authentic assessments are grounded in different reasoning and practice (Mueller, 2010). If you examine the mission statement of most schools, you will likely find discussion of developing students into productive citizens. While there is often significant overlap in the mission of schools, you will often find two different perspectives on assessment: traditional and authentic.

Traditional assessment includes using standardized criterion- and norm-referenced tests and teacher-created tests. With the traditional assessment model, curriculum drives assessment. Assessments to measure knowledge and skills are developed and administered to measure the extent to which students acquire the knowledge and skills of the curriculum. Here is the rationale: From the traditional assessment perspective, to be productive citizens, students must demonstrate certain knowledge and skills. Curriculum is created and teachers in schools deliver curriculum to teach students the knowledge and skills. To determine whether students have gained the required knowledge and skills, schools must measure gained knowledge and skills using traditional assessment techniques—or tests.

On the other hand, with the authentic assessment model, assessment drives the curriculum. Educational administrators and classroom teachers identify the tasks students must perform to demonstrate mastery of knowledge and skills. To teach students to perform the tasks, and to ensure that students have the essential knowledge and skills to perform the task, administrators and teachers develop curriculum. Here is the rationale: From the authentic assessment perspective, to be a productive citizen, students must be able to perform real-world, meaningful tasks. The objective of school is to develop students' ability to perform the tasks they will face in the real world. To determine whether students can perform the tasks, teachers must ask students to perform tasks that replicate real-world challenges.

For example, one of this textbook's authors used to teach children to do gymnastics. Instead of asking gymnasts to complete a traditional test to measure their knowledge of gymnastics and their ability to perform key skills, the author required the gymnasts to perform tasks essential to being a successful gymnast (for example, demonstrating balance, doing forward and backward rolls). The same can be done for academic subjects. For example, we can teach students to not just understand the concepts associated with an academic subject, such as mathematics and statistics, but to *do* mathematics and statistics (Mueller, 2010). We can assess student performance by having them perform tasks in which math and statistics are required in the real world—such as trying to predict the winner of an election and calculating the margin of error—or calculating the probability of winning the lottery, or determining where traffic lights should be installed based on the percentage of accidents at intersections.

Both traditional and authentic assessments have defining attributes. Table 13.5 includes Mueller's (2010) elaboration of these attributes. Traditional assessments tend to fall more toward the left of the continuum, while authentic assessments fall more toward the right end.

Table 13.5	Defining Attributes of Traditional and Authentic Assessment

Traditional Assessments	*Authentic Assessments*
Selecting a response ⟵⟶	Performing a task
On traditional assessments, students are typically given several choices (for example, a, b, c, or d; true or false; which of these match with those) and asked to select the right answer. In contrast, authentic assessments ask students to demonstrate understanding by performing a more complex task usually representative of more meaningful application.	
Contrived ⟵⟶	Real-life
It is not very often in life outside of school that we are asked to select from four alternatives to indicate our proficiency at something. Tests offer these contrived means of assessment to increase the number of times you can be asked to demonstrate proficiency in a short period of time. More commonly in life, as in authentic assessments, we are asked to demonstrate proficiency by doing something.	
Recall/recognition ⟵⟶	Construction/application
Well-designed traditional assessments (i.e., tests and quizzes) can effectively determine whether students have acquired a body of knowledge. Thus, tests can serve as a nice complement to authentic assessments in a teacher's assessment portfolio. Furthermore, we are often asked to recall or recognize facts, ideas, and propositions in life, so tests are somewhat authentic in that sense. However, the demonstration of recall and recognition on tests is typically much less revealing about what we really know and can do than when we are asked to construct a product or performance out of facts, ideas, and propositions. Authentic assessments often ask students to analyze, synthesize, and apply what they have learned in a substantial manner, and students create new meaning in the process as well.	
Teacher-structured ⟵⟶	Student-structured
When completing a traditional assessment, what a student can and will demonstrate has been carefully structured by the person(s) who developed the test. A student's attention will understandably be focused on and limited to what is on the test. In contrast, authentic assessments allow more student choice and construction in determining what is presented as evidence of proficiency. Even when students cannot choose their own topics or formats, there are usually multiple acceptable routes toward constructing a product or performance. Obviously, assessments more carefully controlled by the teacher offer advantages and disadvantages. Similarly, more student-structured tasks have strengths and weaknesses that must be considered when choosing and designing an assessment.	
Indirect evidence ⟵⟶	Direct evidence
Even if a multiple-choice question asks a student to analyze facts or apply them to a new situation, rather than just recall the facts, and the student selects the correct answer, what do we now know about that student? Did the student get lucky and pick the right answer? What thinking led the student to pick that answer? We really do not know. At best, we can make some inferences about what the student might know and be able to do with that knowledge. The evidence is very indirect, particularly for claims of meaningful application in complex, real-world situations. Authentic assessments, on the other hand, offer more direct evidence of application and construction of knowledge. For example, putting a golf student on the golf course to play provides much more direct evidence of proficiency than giving the student a written test. Can a student effectively critique the arguments someone else has presented (an important skill often required in the real world)? Asking a student to write a critique should provide more direct evidence of that skill than asking the student a series of multiple-choice, analytical questions about a passage, although both assessments may be useful.	

SOURCE: Mueller, J. (2010). *What is authentic assessment?* Retrieved June 7, 2010, from http://jonathan.mueller.faculty.noctrl.edu/toolbox/whatisit.htm

Traditional and authentic assessments also differ with respect to the acceptability of teaching to the test. By *teaching to the test,* we are typically talking about the test preparation practices of teachers and the courses students enroll in to prepare for standardized tests (for example, the SAT). Test preparation practices include such things as drilling on test content (not on curricular content that is not assessed or covered by the test) and providing students with outdated test items from high-stakes standardized tests (Popham, 2000).

Most articles we read include discussion of how teaching to the test is bad. With the traditional assessment model, teaching to the test is indeed discouraged; however, under the authentic assessment model, teaching to the test is encouraged. As discussed in previous chapters, when designing tests, we typically representatively sample knowledge and skills in order to measure a specific content area. With traditional assessment, if teachers only drill students on the sample of knowledge and skills measured by the test, then test performance will likely not be reflective of student knowledge and skill in the entire content area. Therefore, teachers are discouraged to teach to the test.

However, with authentic assessment, students learn how to perform real-world tasks. From the observational learning theory literature, we know that when individuals see examples of how to perform a task well, they will more quickly and more effectively perform the task. Further, if you inform students of the knowledge and skills required to effectively perform the task, this really will not impact their ability to apply the knowledge and skills in the real world. Unlike traditional assessment, with authentic assessment there is usually not a right or wrong answer; rather, we are able or not able to perform a task. Therefore, teachers are encouraged to teach to the test; they are encouraged to show learners what good performance looks like and clarify the knowledge and skills required to perform well.

For many of the reasons discussed above, during the early 1990s authentic assessment in educational settings increased in popularity (Wiggins, 1993). Today, authentic assessment plays a significant role in assessing student performance. In the classroom, authentic assessment typically requires students to perform tasks and create portfolios. For example, to measure a student's knowledge of validity, a teacher may require the student to give an oral report on the validity of a particular test or to design some tests of validity. To measure a student's level of mathematics knowledge, a teacher may require the student to keep a notebook with the solutions to math problems or to answer open-ended math problems. To measure a student's understanding of the plot of a story, a teacher may require the student to create a diorama. In industrial organizational psychology, we call these assessments *work samples.*

Some educators claim that authentic assessment is a more fair and accurate measure of student achievement. Other educators criticize authentic assessment because the reliability and validity of authentic assessment are unknown (Terwilliger, 1996) and because authentic assessment is impractical for school systems that need to perform large-scale testing. Obviously, more research is necessary to determine which type of testing is best for measuring student achievement and ability.

Gronlund (1998) agrees that if you want to know whether a student can write, you should require the student to write something. This will help you determine whether the student can perform the task. Gronlund feels that an emphasis on such a type of assessment would improve the assessment of learning outcomes, but he posits that other types of tests should not be forgotten because they too play an important role. The fact is that knowledge is a critical component of much of what we do. To be good writers, we must have a good knowledge of vocabulary, grammar, and spelling. However, a writing sample does not always evaluate this knowledge effectively because it is easy to hide inabilities in an open-ended task. When we write, we are apt to use only words we know, to write only sentences we know how to punctuate, and to include only words we are confident we can spell.

INTERIM SUMMARY 13.3
NORM-REFERENCED, CRITERION-REFERENCED, AND
AUTHENTIC ASSESSMENT OF ACHIEVEMENT

- Most psychological tests used in educational settings can be classified as norm-referenced or criterion-referenced tests.
- Educators use norm-referenced tests to compare student performance with the performance of other students.
- Educators use criterion-referenced tests to compare student performance with an objectively stated standard of achievement such as being able to multiply numbers.

- Some individuals believe that norm- and criterion-referenced tests are too focused on measuring understanding of knowledge and skills, and instead promote the use of authentic assessment.
- Authentic assessment focuses on assessing a student's ability to apply in real-world settings the knowledge and skills he or she has learned.

Chapter Summary

During the instructional process, teachers use psychological tests as placement assessments (to determine whether students are ready to learn new material and to determine how much of the material they already know), formative assessments (to determine what information students are and are not learning), diagnostic assessments (to determine students' learning difficulties more accurately), and summative assessments (to determine what students have learned and to assign grades accordingly). In the classroom, psychological tests can also help motivate students, help students retain and transfer what they have learned, help students understand their strengths and weaknesses, and provide teachers with information regarding the effectiveness of their teaching methods.

Administrators and testing specialists use psychological tests to make selection and placement decisions. Unlike those used in the classroom, selection and placement decisions are typically made using standardized tests of achievement, aptitude, and intelligence. Some private secondary schools, and most undergraduate and graduate colleges and universities, require applicants to submit standardized test scores as a part of the admissions application. Commonly known standardized tests used in the undergraduate admissions process include the SAT and ACT. Some of the most popular standardized tests used in the graduate admissions process include the GRE, MCAT, LSAT, DAT, GMAT, OAT, PCAT, and VAT. Specialists and administrators use scores from these tests, along with other information, to make admissions decisions. It is also common for educational institutions to use these and other standardized test scores to place students into programs once they have been admitted to the institutions.

Career counselors use the results of psychological tests, along with other information, to help individuals explore their interests, abilities, and preferences and to consider career options that align with these.

Educational administrators also use psychological tests to maintain and improve the quality of educational systems. They may use the results of tests to select the best curriculum for a school and to determine where funds should be directed.

Many different psychological tests are used in educational settings, and each can be classified as either a norm-referenced test or a criterion-referenced test. Norm-referenced tests allow us to compare an individual's performance with the performance of a previously tested group of individuals in order to determine how well the individual performed relative to a particular norm group. The Stanford Achievement Test and all of the undergraduate and graduate tests mentioned previously are norm-referenced tests.

Criterion-referenced tests allow us to compare an individual's score with an objectively stated standard of achievement in order to determine the extent to which the individual has obtained desired knowledge and/or skills. Most teacher-made classroom tests are criterion-referenced tests.

Some educators believe that norm- and criterion-referenced tests do not measure what is important in real life. Instead, they support increased use of authentic assessment. Authentic assessment involves evaluating a student's ability to apply information to real-world settings using more than one measure of performance. When teachers require students to perform tasks and create portfolios, they are using authentic assessment techniques.

Engaging in the Learning Process

KEY CONCEPTS

After completing your study of this chapter, you should be able to define each of the following terms. These terms are bolded in the text of this chapter and defined in the Glossary.

- administrative policy decisions
- authentic assessment
- counseling and guidance decisions
- criterion-referenced tests
- diagnostic assessment
- diagnostic decisions
- formative assessment
- grading decisions
- high-stakes tests

- instructional decisions
- norm-referenced tests
- placement assessment
- placement decisions
- portfolio
- program and curriculum decisions
- selection decisions
- summative assessment

LEARNING ACTIVITIES

The following are some learning activities you can engage in to support the learning objectives for this chapter.

Learning Objectives	Study Tips and Learning Activities
After completing your study of this chapter, you should be able to do the following:	The following study tips will help you meet these learning objectives:
Describe the types of decisions educators make based on the results of psychological tests.	• Review the section titled Decision Making in the Educational Setting. Draw a table with two columns and eight rows. Label the columns Type of Decision and Type of Professional. Document the eight types of decisions made by educators in the first column, and indicate what type of professional typically makes each decision in the second column.

Describe how psychological tests are used by teachers in the classroom, before instruction, during instruction, and after instruction.	• Review the section titled Appropriate Use of Psychological Tests in Chapter 3. Now consider and write your answers to the following questions:
	  ○ What is a test user?
	  ○ What are the responsibilities of test users?
	  ○ What might be the result if an educator who uses tests is not properly informed and trained about the proper use of tests?

(Continued)

(Continued)

Learning Objectives	Study Tips and Learning Activities
Describe how educational institutions use tests to make selection and placement decisions, counseling and guidance decisions, program and curriculum decisions, and administrative policy decisions.	• Call and speak to one of your college or university's undergraduate and graduate admissions counselors. Ask the counselor what tests he or she uses to make admissions decisions and how he or she uses the tests as a part of the selection process. • Make an appointment with a college career counselor. Ask the counselor to share with you how he or she uses tests to help students explore potential career opportunities. Ask whether you can experience the process. • Call the Department of Education in your state or your county school board and see whether you can find out how it has used the results of tests administered in the school systems in your county to make program, curriculum, or administrative policy decisions. • Call the Department of Education in your state. Ask to speak to someone who can tell you more about how the results of tests are used to make administrative policy decisions. See whether you can find out how the education system has used the results of tests administered in the school systems in your state to make program, curriculum, or administrative policy decisions.
Explain why educators are test users and why they need to follow the test user guidelines discussed in Chapter 3.	• Write down your definitions of norm-referenced and criterion-referenced tests. Then search the Internet to find at least five norm-referenced tests and five criterion-referenced tests. Document the name and purpose of each test. Be prepared to share your findings with your class.
Describe authentic assessment and the perceived advantages and disadvantages of authentic assessment.	• Contact one of your college or university's admissions counselors. Ask the counselor whether the school requires that applicants submit test scores. If not, ask whether the school allows applicants to submit portfolios in lieu of test scores. If so, ask the counselor to share the criteria for submission and evaluation of portfolios.

PRACTICE QUESTIONS

The following are some practice questions to assess your understanding of the material presented in this chapter.

Multiple Choice

Choose the one best answer to each question.

1. Which one of the following types of decisions is frequently made by teachers using teacher-made tests?
   a. Placement
   b. Diagnostic
   c. Counseling
   d. Curriculum

2. If teachers use psychological tests to determine whether students have the knowledge necessary to learn new material, they are using the tests as a
   a. diagnostic assessment.
   b. formative assessment.
   c. placement assessment.
   d. summative assessment.

3. Teachers use _____ assessments to answer the question, "On which learning tasks are the students progressing satisfactorily?"
   a. diagnostic
   b. formative
   c. placement
   d. summative

4. Teachers use _____ assessment to answer the question, "Which students have mastered the learning tasks to such a degree that they should proceed to the next course or unit of instruction?"
   a. diagnostic
   b. formative
   c. placement
   d. summative

5. What was the first vocational test developed in 1927 by E. K. Strong?
    a. Graduate Record Examination (GRE)
    b. Kuder Preference Record (KPR)
    c. Strong Vocational Interest Blank (SVIB)
    d. Jackson Vocational Interest Survey (JVIS)

6. Periodically throughout a school year, teachers may use psychological tests as _____ assessments.
    a. summative
    b. formative
    c. placement
    d. diagnostic

7. If a teacher suspects a student may be having learning difficulties, the teacher may suggest that the student's learning abilities be evaluated using a _____ assessment.
    a. summative
    b. formative
    c. placement
    d. diagnostic

8. Which one of the following is FALSE about the SAT?
    a. The SAT consists of three sections.
    b. The SAT has a guessing penalty.
    c. The SAT is an achievement test.
    d. Math makes up 50% of the score.

9. Which one of the following is FALSE about the ACT?
    a. The ACT has questions on trigonometry.
    b. The ACT measures science reasoning.
    c. The ACT is an achievement test.
    d. Math questions make up 50% of the test.

10. Tests that involve comparing an individual's test score with an objectively stated standard of achievement are called
    a. authentic assessments.
    b. standardized tests.
    c. norm-referenced tests.
    d. criterion-referenced tests.

11. If you had to provide three examples of a norm-referenced test, which one of the following would you NOT provide?
    a. ACT
    b. SAT
    c. Stanford Achievement Test
    d. Authentic assessment

12. Which one of the following is TRUE about authentic assessment?
    a. Authentic assessment is most valuable for measuring application of learning.
    b. Authentic assessment is a norm-referenced test.
    c. Authentic assessment is more reliable than criterion-referenced and norm-referenced tests.
    d. Authentic assessment often includes more than one measure of performance.

Short Answer/Essay

Read each of the following, and consider your response carefully based on the information presented in this chapter. Write your answer to each question in two or three paragraphs.

1. Describe the types of decisions educators make based on the results of psychological tests. Provide an example of each.

2. How do educators use test scores to make curriculum and administrative policy decisions? Provide examples.

3. Explain why educators are test users and why they need to follow the test user guidelines discussed in Chapter 3. Give examples.

4. Compare and contrast how psychological tests are used by teachers in the classroom before instruction, during instruction, and after instruction. Give examples of each.

5. Provide some examples of how psychological tests can benefit student motivation, retention and transfer of learning, self-assessment, and instructional effectiveness.

6. Describe how tests are used by educational institutions to make selection and placement decisions. Include a discussion of some of the most common tests used for selection.

7. Describe how tests are used by educational institutions to make counseling and guidance decisions.

8. What are the similarities and differences between the ACT and the SAT? If you have well-developed math skills and an extensive vocabulary, on which test (the ACT or the SAT) might you perform better? Why?

9. What are the similarities and differences between norm-referenced and criterion-referenced tests? Provide an example of each.

10. Why would someone want to or choose to use authentic assessment? What are the perceived advantages and disadvantages of authentic assessment?

ANSWER KEYS

Multiple Choice

1. b	2. c	3. b	4. d	5. c
6. b	7. d	8. c	9. d	10. d
11. d	12. a			

Short Answer/Essay

Refer to your textbook for answers. If you are unsure of an answer and cannot generate the answer after reviewing your book, ask your professor for clarification.

CHAPTER 14

How Are Tests Used in Clinical and Counseling Settings?

After completing your study of this chapter, you should be able to do the following:

- Identify and explain three models of psychological assessment that clinicians and counselors use.
- Explain the concept of clinical diagnosis, and describe how the clinical interview and structured personality tests are used to make diagnoses.
- Describe three types of projective techniques and how practitioners use them for diagnosis and treatment.
- Describe the field of neuropsychology, and explain how neuropsychologists use electrophysiological techniques, neurobehavioral assessments, and temperament or personality measures to diagnose and treat clients of various ages.
- Describe how practitioners use paper-and-pencil tests to diagnose and treat depression, anxiety, anger, and attention deficit hyperactivity disorder.

"*My cousin was in a car accident, and later she was examined by a neuropsychologist. Does that mean she has brain damage?*"

"*How do psychologists evaluate infants and children?*"

"*My professor has suggested neuropsychological testing as an up-and-coming specialty in the field of psychology. What type of tests do neuropsychologists use?*"

"*The school psychologist tested my son by asking him to draw a house, a tree, and a person. He concluded that my son has emotional problems. Is this an appropriate way to diagnose children?*"

n Chapter 1, we discussed the difference between psychological testing and assessment. As you learned, although both are methods for collecting information, assessment is much broader than psychological testing; psychological tests are only one tool in the assessment process. In other words, psychological testing has to do with the instrumentation part of assessment—using psychometric tools for information gathering. For example, a clinical psychologist may conduct a psychological assessment of a patient and, as a part of this assessment, may administer a psychological test such as the Minnesota Multiphasic Personality Inventory-2 (MMPI-2).

More detail about the Minnesota Multiphasic Personality Inventory can be found in Test Spotlight 12.1 in Appendix A.

Defined more specifically, **clinical assessment** includes a broad set of information-gathering and interpretive skills used by the professional counselor-therapist to determine a person's state of mental health or make a diagnosis. For many years counselors and therapists have recognized the value of clinical assessment. According to one clinical practitioner, "without clinical assessment, the counselor therapist is reduced to being no more (and no less) than a social helper" (Woody, 1972, p. 1). Clinical assessment allows counselors and therapists to provide a complete picture of a client and to understand and lessen human suffering (Barlow & Durand, 2009).

In this chapter, we focus on how psychological tests are used in clinical and counseling settings for diagnosing and intervening with clients. We begin with an overview of three models that clinicians and counselors typically use in psychological testing. We discuss the types of tests used for diagnosis and intervention, including clinical interviews, structured personality tests, and various projective techniques. After discussing neuropsychology and neuropsychological tests, we conclude with a discussion of specialized tests for clinical disorders.

Models of Psychological Assessment

Major changes are taking place in the field of mental health and psychological assessment. Managed care is playing a larger role in shaping the diagnosis and treatment of individuals than ever before in the history of clinical psychology and counseling. One of the basic tenets of managed care is the demand for greater accountability. An influence of managed care is the reluctance to provide for long-term psychological interventions or counseling. According to this outlook, clients should develop a new perspective and acquire behaviors or coping skills that enable effective problem solving during a short-term program. Unfortunately, such interventions are not always successful (Butcher, 1997).

For many years, practitioners and managed care providers have disagreed about the role of psychological assessment. As early as 1997, practitioners noted a decrease in the clinical use of psychological testing because managed care organizations are reluctant to pay for extensive assessment (Finn & Tonsager, 1997). Many practitioners see this as unfortunate, given that the primary tool the clinician or counselor can use to prevent or counterbalance problems in short-term interventions is the use of psychological assessment to obtain a clear picture of the client's diagnosis, personal attributes, and amenity to treatment.

Psychological assessment has a long history in the field of mental health. Its roles have varied as approaches to the treatment and prevention of mental disorders have changed and evolved. Practitioners generally use three models of clinical assessment: the information-gathering model, the therapeutic model, and the differential treatment model. These three models, along with some classic examples of each, are described below.

The Information-Gathering Model

When a practitioner uses assessment primarily as a way to gather information to make a diagnosis and facilitate communication, the practitioner is using the information-gathering model of assessment. In this model, tests provide a standardized comparison with similar people and allow the assessor to make predictions about the client's behavior outside the assessment setting. In addition, test results provide a baseline that the clinician or counselor can use to identify disorders and design an individualized treatment program. For Your Information Box 14.1 provides an example of the information-gathering model using the case study of "Mrs. M" (Haynes, Leisen, & Blaine, 1997), who suffered from recurrent headaches and sleep problems.

FYI

FOR YOUR INFORMATION BOX 14.1

The Case of Mrs. M

Mrs. M was 35 years old, married, and the mother of a 12-year-old son. A neurologist referred Mrs. M to a behavioral practitioner because she was experiencing frequent headaches and problems in sleeping. The neurologist referred Mrs. M for behavioral therapy instead of medication because Mrs. M was 28 weeks pregnant.

The practitioner gathered information regarding Mrs. M's problem during two assessment sessions. During the first session, the practitioner interviewed Mrs. M to determine the range of her concerns. In that interview, Mrs. M reported that she and her husband were having frequent arguments, usually about disciplining their son. Mrs. M was also given a semistructured interview regarding her headaches and sleep problems. She reported that over the past three years her headaches had become more frequent and more severe. At the time of her first session, every day she was experiencing severe headaches that lasted two to four hours. She also reported that her husband was more helpful and attentive when she had a headache and she feared his helpfulness would lessen if her headaches improved. She recalled that her sleep problems started about the same time as her headaches. Her symptoms included needing roughly an hour to fall asleep, and her sleep was fragmented and shallow, with frequent awakenings.

Between the first and second assessment sessions, Mrs. M was asked to quantify her behavior problems by rating her headaches each hour on a 5-point scale (0 = *no headache*, 5 = *very severe headache*). She also kept a sleep diary in which she recorded time taken to fall asleep, number of nightly awakenings, amount of sleep lost, and time of waking in the morning. Mr. and Mrs. M also completed the Dyadic Adjustment Scale (Spanier, 1976) to assess marital adjustment, the Spouse Verbal Problem Checklist (Carter & Thomas, 1973) to assess satisfaction with communication, and a marital attitudes questionnaire.

Based on information gathered during the first assessment session, Mrs. M's marital relationship was identified as an important concern and possibly linked to her headaches and sleep problems. Therefore, both Mr. and Mrs. M completed assessments during the second session.

The data gathered by Mrs. M on her headaches and sleep agreed with what she reported in her interview. She had experienced no headache-free hours during the previous week, and her sleep was interrupted two to five times nightly. Scores on the Marital Satisfaction Questionnaire placed Mr. M within the satisfied range. Mrs. M indicated dissatisfaction with the marital relationship. Scores on the Spouse Verbal Problem Checklist indicated that both Mr. and Mrs. M perceived communication problems, although their explanations of the problems were different.

Because depression is often associated with chronic pain and sleep disturbance, Mr. and Mrs. M completed the Beck Depression Inventory (Beck, Steer, & Garbin, 1988). Mr. M's score was well within the nondepressed range. Mrs. M's score indicated mild depression, but her responses showed her depression to be related to pain rather than mood or cognitive concerns.

(Continued)

(Continued)

During this session, Mr. M was also given an unstructured interview to determine his perceptions of marital difficulties, and both Mr. and Mrs. M were given a semistructured interview regarding behaviors and methods to improve the relationship. The couple was also asked to discuss a topic that caused arguments at home for 10 minutes. This discussion was audiotaped, and two assessors independently rated the couple's interactions using the Marital Interaction Coding System (Weiss & Heyman, 1990). This behavioral assessment indicated high rates of positive and negative statements by Mrs. M, mostly negative statements by Mr. M, and low rates of problem solving by both.

Based on the data gathered during the two assessment sessions and at home by Mrs. M, the practitioner concluded that Mrs. M's headaches and sleep disturbance were probably caused by distress with her marital relationship. Furthermore, the data indicated that general communication problems, rather than child management issues, were contributing to her marital distress.

In cases like those of Mrs. M, psychological assessment in the form of interviews and objective tests provides important information such as underlying problems and contextual issues. This information allows the practitioner to design an intervention or a treatment program that addresses the root causes of behavioral problems instead of symptomatic issues.

SOURCE: Adapted from Haynes, S. N., Leisen, M. B., & Blaine, D. D. (1997). Design of individualized behavioral treatment programs using functional analytic clinical case models. *Psychological Assessment, 9,* 334–348.

Treatment programs that involve behavioral interventions, such as desensitization and establishing schedules of reinforcement, usually differ among clients even though the clients have the same behavior problems. Psychological assessment provides an important tool for designing such behavioral interventions. The case of Mrs. M shows how clinical tests provide diagnostic information for the practitioner. Using assessment for diagnosis is an example of the information-gathering model of assessment.

The Therapeutic Model

In the **therapeutic model** of assessment, the goal is to provide new experiences and new information that clients can use to make changes in their lives. The practitioner uses the assessment information to encourage self-discovery and growth. The process of assessment and the resulting dialogue that it guides become an intervention for positive change. This model evolved during the humanistic movement of the 1950s and 1960s. Although some humanists strongly objected to testing and considered psychological assessment to be dehumanizing, others believed that assessment, when used properly, provides a valuable tool for facilitating growth and insight.

For Your Information Box 14.2 shows how test results can be used as part of an intervention based on the therapeutic model. It relates the case study of "Mrs. P," who was suffering from postpartum depression.

The Differential Treatment Model

Finally, clinicians use psychological tests to conduct research and evaluate program outcomes. Tests can provide definitive answers as to whether clients as a group have responded positively to a particular therapy or intervention. Using assessment for research purposes is the **differential treatment model** of assessment, which requires tests that have evidence of high reliability and validity related to the research purpose.

One example of the differential treatment model is a study that compared the marriage satisfaction of 75 Mexican American couples and 66 non-Hispanic White American couples (Negy &

FYI

FOR YOUR INFORMATION BOX 14.2

The Case of Mrs. P

Mrs. P was 32 years old and hospitalized for postpartum depression following the birth of her second child. She had many fears and phobias, particularly of dirt and contamination that she could not control. She acted help-less and inadequate. For instance, she often burned food when she cooked.

Mrs. P's history revealed that she had been born prematurely and there had been a question of whether she would survive. Psychological tests at the time of her admission showed clear signs of organic brain damage that had not been detected before. During her lifetime, Mrs. P had developed an attitude of helplessness and inade-quacy, and she required the support of others for most tasks.

When the test results were given to Mrs. P, she was told that she had a number of strengths as well as certain limitations. In other words, it was clear that she had the ability to do certain things she was not doing. Her ther-apist told her she would be expected to begin doing the things she could do.

Mrs. P resisted the therapist's interpretation and maintained that the tests were inaccurate. The therapist, how-ever, constantly pointed out what she was doing and, using the test results, supported Mrs. P's efforts to become more self-sufficient.

A remarkable change took place. Mrs. P began to entertain friends and accept responsibilities that she would have avoided previously.

SOURCE: Adapted from Shore, M. F. (1972). Psychological testing. In R. H. Woody & J. D. Woody (Eds.), *Clinical assessment in counseling and psychotherapy*. Englewood Cliffs, NJ: Prentice Hall.

Snyder, 1997). All couples lived in the same geographic region of the southwestern United States. The researchers' analyses suggested somewhat higher levels of relationship distress for the Mexican American couples when compared with those for the non-Hispanic couples. However, these group differences disappeared when demographic variables, such as education, were controlled. This comparison allowed researchers to draw conclusions about the effects of acculturation on the marriage satisfaction of Mexican American couples.

The differential treatment model also applies to pretest–posttest research designs in which a group of clients is given a psychological test before and after an intervention to determine whether the intervention was successful in changing behavior or attitudes. For instance, Boy Scouts and Girl Scouts completed the Personal Attribute Inventory for Children (Parish, Ohlsen, & Parish, 1978), a measure of attitudes toward handicaps and persons who have them. The researchers assigned the scouts to five experimental groups and a control group. The scouts in the experimental groups interacted socially with a child with a disability one hour per week. The control group had no contact with children with disabilities. After six weeks, all scouts again completed the Personal Attribute Inventory. The five experimental groups showed an increase in favorable attitudes toward people with disabilities when compared with the atti-tudes of the control group (Newberry & Parish, 1987).

Roles of the Clinician and the Counselor

Traditionally, clinical psychologists and counselors have approached the assessment of clients from dif-ferent perspectives. Many counselors believe that the primary difference between counseling and clinical psychology or psychiatry is that counselors provide services for people with normal developmental prob-lems such as marital, career, and school adjustment problems (Hohenshil, 1996). Clinical psychologists and psychiatrists (medical doctors who specialize in mental illness) treat people who exhibit abnormal behavior, mental disorders, or emotional disabilities.

However, these roles are often blurred or overlapping, and as a result the distinctions between clinical psychology and counseling psychology are fading (Norcross, 2000). According to Norcross,

> graduates of doctoral-level clinical and counseling psychology programs are generally eligible for the same professional benefits, such as psychology licensure, independent practice, and insurance reimbursement. The American Psychological Association (APA) ceased distinguishing many years ago between clinical and counseling psychology internships: there is one list of accredited internships for both clinical and counseling psychology students. Both types of programs prepare doctoral-level psychologists who provide health care services and, judging from various studies of their respective professional activities, there are only a few meaningful differences between them. (para. 3)

Both counselors and clinicians use psychological testing to obtain information necessary for providing services to clients. It appears counselors are more apt to subscribe to the therapeutic model. V. L. Campbell (1990) states that the "major focus of test use in counseling is the test taker, who 'is viewed as the primary user of the test results'" (p. 1). In contrast, clinical psychologists may be predisposed to use the information-gathering model. In this model, the clinician is the primary user of the test results, which provide the basis for identifying a diagnosis and designing an intervention.

The next section describes how clinical psychologists and counselors use psychological tests to make diagnoses and carry out interventions.

INTERIM SUMMARY 14.1
MODELS OF CLINICAL ASSESSMENT

- The information-gathering model represents the use of standardized tests to make diagnoses.
- The therapeutic model uses tests as an intervention that provides new information for the client to use for self-discovery and growth.
- The differential treatment model represents the use of tests for conducting research or evaluating program outcomes.

- The roles of counselors and clinical psychologists differ, but they also overlap.
- Counselors primarily provide services for people with normal developmental problems, and clinical psychologists and psychiatrists generally treat people with abnormal behavior, mental disorders, or emotional disabilities.

Tests Used for Diagnosis and Intervention

Diagnosis refers to the process of determining when an individual's problem meets the criteria for a psychological disorder (Durand & Barlow, 2006). The process of arriving at a diagnosis is often called screening. As you can see from the case of Mrs. M (For Your Information Box 14.1), diagnosis may result in identifying a group of symptoms and relating them to a classification system such as one of those listed in the fourth edition of the *Diagnostic and Statistical Manual of Mental Disorders* (*DSM-IV-TR*; American Psychiatric Association, 2000). For Your Information Box 14.3 introduces the *DSM-IV-TR* and includes a brief overview of its use by mental health care professionals. Alternatively, a diagnosis may be an informal statement of a client's needs. For instance, a career counselor may draw the conclusion from assessment information that a client is having difficulty in making career decisions because she has little knowledge of her own aptitudes and values.

FOR YOUR INFORMATION BOX 14.3

The *DSM-IV-TR*

Have you ever heard terms such as *mental retardation, learning disorder, delirium,* and *dementia* and wondered exactly what they mean? What does it mean when a clinician diagnoses a person as schizophrenic or depressed? Is there really such a thing as a sexual identity disorder or a personality disorder?

Cataloging and classifying the numerous mental disorders that clinicians and researchers have documented is a necessary and perhaps overwhelming task. In fact, ever since physicians began to diagnose disorders of the psyche or mind, there have been schemes to catalog and define them.

A first attempt in recent history to identify and track mental disorders was made in the U.S. census of 1840, which recorded the frequency of "idiocy/insanity." In the 1880 census, mental illness was distinguished by seven classifications: mania, melancholia, monomania, paresis, dementia, dipsomania, and epilepsy. During the following years, the U.S. Census Bureau and the U.S. Army, in collaboration with the organization now known as the American Psychiatric Association, attempted to construct a classification system for identifying mental disorders. These classification systems were used mainly for diagnosing patients in mental hospitals.

In 1952, the American Psychiatric Association Committee on Nomenclature and Statistics published the first comprehensive manual of mental disorders, titled *Diagnostic and Statistical Manual: Mental Disorders,* designed to provide explicit definitions for clinical diagnoses. Since then, this manual has undergone three complete revisions. It now provides definitions based on the most recent research in the field of clinical psychology and psychiatry. The current *DSM-IV-TR,* published in 2000, is the result of extensive research by 13 work groups sponsored by the American Psychiatric Association. The work groups used a three-stage process to identify and classify mental disorders. First, they researched published literature. Second, they reanalyzed already-collected sets of data. Finally, they conducted field trials sponsored by organizations such as the National Institute of Mental Health and the National Institute on Drug Abuse.

The *DSM-IV-TR* classifies mental disorders into 17 aggregate categories, each of which has a number of subcategories. These subcategories contain specific disorders that are defined by diagnostic features or symptoms as well as behavioral criteria for identifying the disorders. For instance, depression is listed under the aggregate heading of mood disorders. The subcategory of depressive disorders includes major depressive disorder (single episode and recurrent), dysthymic disorder (early onset/late onset and with atypical features), and depressive disorder not otherwise specified. The manual provides specific information on symptoms and associated features; specific gender, age, and culture features; and specific diagnostic criteria for each disorder. The manual also gives each disorder a unique classification or code number.

The *DSM-IV-TR* was developed for use by persons trained and experienced in clinical diagnosis. These persons may work in clinical, educational, or research settings. The manual's introduction clearly states that the classification system is meant to serve as guidelines for informed clinical judgment. This diagnostic system is not to be applied in mechanical or strict fashion by untrained persons. The manual and its classification system provide significant resources for professionals who diagnose and develop treatment plans for individuals. They also serve as a basis for constructing criterion measures that can be used to establish validity for psychological tests used in clinical settings.

SOURCE: Adapted from American Psychiatric Association. (2000). *Diagnostic and statistical manual of mental disorders* (4th ed., text rev.). Washington, DC: Author.

Whether the assessor's goal is to treat a mental disorder or to improve the client's quality of life, the diagnosis leads to the design or selection of an intervention technique or treatment plan to alleviate unwanted behaviors or symptoms or to solve the client's problem.

The Clinical Interview

Most practitioners use the **clinical interview** as a primary tool for gathering information about the client (Durand & Barlow, 2006). The clinical interview involves a discussion between the client and the assessor—often a clinical psychologist or counselor—during which the assessor observes the client and gathers information about the client's past behavior, attitudes, emotions, and life history (Durand & Barlow, 2006). A **structured clinical interview** has a predetermined set of questions for the client to answer. The assessor might then assign numbers or scores to the answers based on their content. The assessor uses these scores to arrive at a diagnosis. An unstructured or **nondirective clinical interview,** on the other hand, has few, if any, predetermined questions (Durand & Barlow, 2006). Instead, the assessor's questions are more likely to be determined by the client's responses.

The **semistructured interview** provides a compromise between the structured interview and the nondirective interview. The semistructured interview contains a list of predetermined, carefully phrased, and tested questions (Durand & Barlow, 2006). However, the format also allows the assessor to ask some open-ended questions and follow-up questions to clarify the interviewee's responses.

The strength of the nondirective interview, according to Geertsma (1972), is its flexibility that permits the interviewer to respond to the client's responses and behavior. The assumption in using the traditional interview is that the client will directly, or indirectly, present the information that is relevant or necessary for diagnosis. The risk with this approach, as pointed out by Murphy and Davidshofer (1994) and others, is that the interviewer may have preconceived notions that influence the direction or outcome of the interview. For instance, **hypothesis confirmation bias** (Darley & Fazio, 1980) suggests that decision makers form hypotheses about the behavior of others, such as the client, and then search for and elicit information to confirm their hypotheses. Another source of bias is **self-fulfilling prophecy,** a well-documented phenomenon in which the researcher's or interviewer's expectations influence the behavior of respondents and lead them to meet the interviewer's expectations.

Cofresi and Gorman (2004) point out a third source of bias: **ethnocentrism**. This refers to the inclination to believe that one's culture is superior to other cultures and to use it as a frame of reference for judging people from other cultures. Although mental disorders are defined by a particular set of behaviors, clinicians assessing behaviors in clients from other cultures must be aware that some behaviors that might be abnormal in mainstream culture are normal or required elsewhere. Cofresi and Gorman provide this example:

Latino children are reared to show respect by looking at the floor while an elder or authority figure is speaking. A culturally unaware clinician may erroneously conclude from the consequent poor eye contact that the child is depressed or has poor interpersonal skills. (p. 104)

The nondirective interview can be divided into three parts: the initial, middle, and termination phases (Houck & Hansen, 1972). During the initial phase, the interviewer greets the client and establishes rapport. Next, the interviewer focuses on the client's perception of his or her problem and the set of attitudes and emotions that the client advocates and displays. The interviewer gathers observational data by noting facial expressions, eye contact, posture, activity (for example, nervous mannerisms), grooming, and level of responsiveness. Finally, the initial stage includes establishing expectations and goals for the interview, other assessment activities, and the eventual course of treatment.

The middle phase of the nondirective interview focuses on gathering a detailed social and medical history that includes demographic data (for example, occupation, marital status). The interviewer can also observe the client's coping behaviors (for example, changes in voice tone or posture) because the interview itself is likely to cause some stress and anxiety. During this phase, the interviewer may begin to formulate a hypothesis regarding a diagnosis, make observations, and gather information to support or refute the hypothesis. Finally, the interviewer makes a **prognosis**—an estimation of the length of treatment and the likelihood of a successful outcome. The hypothesis and prognosis are for the assessor's use and are not necessarily shared with the client.

During the termination phase, the interviewer may inquire whether the client has any questions, and after answering all questions, the interviewer briefly summarizes the interview. It is important that the interviewer and client maintain rapport and that the interviewer conveys concern and understanding. Further assessment or treatment activities, where appropriate, should be explained briefly and scheduled before ending the interview.

Research on the validity of the nondirective clinical interview (Murphy & Davidshofer, 1994; Wiggins, 1973) suggests that the interview may be more useful in a therapeutic sense than for assessment. For more than 50 years, researchers have debated the accuracy of making diagnoses using the unstructured interview (called the *clinical method*) compared with using structured psychological tests (called the *statistical method*). In 1954, Meehl published the results of his examination of 20 studies that compared clinical and statistical predictions (Meehl, 1954). His conclusion was that statistical methods were as accurate as, and often more accurate than, clinical methods. Subsequent research (Dawes & Corrigan, 1974; Goldberg, 1970; Wiggins, 1973) supports Meehl's conclusions.

Today, many clinicians are choosing to use semistructured interviews. According to Durand and Barlow (2006), more structured interviews may rob "the interview of spontaneous quality of two people talking about a problem. Also, if applied too rigidly, this type of interview may inhibit the patient from volunteering useful information that is not directly relevant to the questions being asked" (p. 79).

Structured Personality Tests

Over the years, psychologists have developed many self-report paper-and-pencil tests to provide a more objective assessment of general personality characteristics. Perhaps the most widely used instrument of this kind is the MMPI. Originally published by Hathaway and McKinley in 1943, the test underwent revisions during the 1980s. The revised version, the MMPI-2, was published in 1989. The MMPI-2 contains 10 basic clinical scales (see Chapter 12) that cover a range of personality traits or predispositions. A large number of content scales that measure specific disorders and dispositions have also been published. Interpreting the MMPI requires specialized training and knowledge. Many practitioners use computerized scoring systems that construct profiles and provide basic interpretations by comparing the individual's score with the test norms. Currently, practitioners in most hospitals and mental health

More detail about the Minnesota Multiphasic Inventory can be found in Test Spotlight Box 12.1 in Appendix A.

Test Spotlight 14.1 in Appendix A provides more detail about the California Psychological Inventory.

In Appendix A, see Test Spotlight 1.3 for more detail about the NEO Personality Inventory and Test Spotlight 14.2 for information about the 16 Personality Factor Questionnaire.

settings in the United States use the MMPI-2 as a screening and diagnostic tool. The MMPI and MMPI-2 have also been widely used in research on normal and abnormal personalities.

Another personality test that is closely related to the MMPI is the California Psychological Inventory (CPI). Gough, the original developer of the CPI, studied with Hathaway (a developer of the MMPI) at the University of Minnesota. Gough, however, developed the CPI to assess normal individuals. The revised CPI assesses 20 dimensions of interpersonal behavior. The results of a number of studies suggest that the dimensions of the CPI relate closely to the five-factor model of personality dimensions (discussed in more detail in Chapter 15), and the CPI may be interpreted in terms of the five-factor theory of personality (Bolton, 1992). The CPI is a popular instrument for research on personality, but trained clinicians and counselors also use it for therapeutic and diagnostic purposes.

The NEO Personality Inventory–Revised (Costa & McCrae, 1992) was designed specifically to measure the personality dimensions of the five-factor theory: neuroticism, extraversion, openness to experience, agreeableness, and conscientiousness. The name of the test comes from the first three factors: N (neuroticism), E (extraversion), and O (openness to experience). Like the CPI, the NEO assesses normal personality traits and, as such, provides an excellent tool for research on personality and behavior. In addition, this test may be appropriate for use by trained clinicians for therapeutic and diagnostic purposes.

Finally, the 16 Personality Factor Questionnaire (16PF) is another test that measures normal personality. Cattell designed this test during the 1940s as part of his attempt to identify and measure the fundamental building blocks of personality. The 16PF is widely used today for research and counseling.

INTERIM SUMMARY 14.2
DIAGNOSING USING THE INTERVIEW AND STRUCTURED PERSONALITY TESTS

- A diagnosis refers to the process of determining when an individual's problem meets the criteria for a psychological disorder.
- The clinical interview in which the practitioner observes and gathers information about the client is a primary diagnostic tool.
- There are three types of interviews: (a) the structured clinical interview that has a predetermined set of questions and yields a score, (b) the nondirective clinical interview in which the practitioner's questions follow up on the client's report of symptoms or problems, and (c) the semistructured interview in which some questions are predetermined, but the practitioner also asks

follow-up questions based on the client's responses.
- The practitioner who uses the nondirective approach risks three sources of bias: hypothesis confirmation bias, self-fulfilling prophecy, and ethnocentrism.
- The nondirective interview may be more useful as an intervention (the therapeutic model) than for diagnosis.
- Today, many clinicians are choosing to use semistructured interviews.
- Practitioners also use standardized personality tests, such as the MMPI-2, the NEO Personality Inventory, the CPI, and the 16PF, to make diagnoses.

Projective Techniques

As discussed in previous chapters, projective tests require test takers to respond to unstructured or ambiguous stimuli such as incomplete sentences, inkblots, and abstract pictures. In a more general sense, **projective techniques** require test takers to give meaning to ambiguous stimuli. Often the response requirements are relatively unclear so as to encourage test takers to create responses that describe the thoughts and emotions they are experiencing. This section includes a discussion of three types of projective techniques: projective storytelling, projective drawing, and sentence completion.

The idea of projective testing is based on a concept from early Freudian theory. According to psychoanalytic theory, **projection** is a defense mechanism that relieves anxiety by allowing a person to attribute thoughts or emotions to external events or individuals. Later theorists (Rabin, 1986) suggested that projection is a normal cognitive operation rather than a defense mechanism. In either case, the theoretical concept underlying projective testing assumes that individuals attribute their own thoughts and emotions to others in their environment.

Projective Storytelling

The Rorschach Inkblot Test and the Thematic Apperception Test (TAT) are two common examples of **projective storytelling**—tests that require respondents to tell a story. Swiss psychiatrist Hermann Rorschach developed the Rorschach during the four years prior to the publication of *Psychodiagnostik* (Rorschach, 1921). The test requires test takers to view inkblots and describe to the test examiner

 More detail about the Rorschach Inkblot Test can be found in Test Spotlight 3.1 in Appendix A.

the objects or people that they think the inkblots resemble. For Your Information Box 14.4 describes the Rorschach Inkblot Test and its scoring schemes.

FYI

FOR YOUR INFORMATION BOX 14.4

The Rorschach Inkblot Projective Technique

The Rorschach Inkblot Test is a projective personality test that involves showing ambiguous stimuli (inkblots) to an individual and asking the individual to respond with what he or she sees. Psychiatrists and clinical psychologists learn to administer and interpret this test in their doctoral training programs. The inkblots are sold without a test manual or administration, scoring, and interpretation instructions. Instead, numerous manuals and handbooks are available (for example, Exner, 1976; Exner & Weiner, 1982; Piotrowski, 1957). Each contains different systems for administering, scoring, and interpreting the Rorschach Inkblot Test. Figure 14.1 shows a sample inkblot.

In 1921, Herman Rorschach designed his inkblot test on the projective hypothesis, which assumes that when people attempt to understand ambiguous stimuli, their interpretations of the stimuli reflect their personal qualities or characteristics—their needs, feelings, anxieties, inner conflicts, experiences, and thought processes. Kaplan and Saccuzzo (1997) provide a good example of this rationale. When a scared little boy looks into a dark room, sees a huge shadow, and interprets the shadow as a monster, he is projecting his fear onto the shadow. The shadow is neither good nor bad. What the child sees is a reflection of the inner workings of his mind.

(Continued)

(Continued)

Figure 14.1	A Sample Inkblot From the Rorschach Inkblot Test

The Rorschach test consists of 10 cards with symmetrical inkblots. Rorschach created these inkblots by dripping ink onto a white piece of paper and then folding the paper. This procedure provided unique, bilaterally symmetrical pictures on a white background. Although Rorschach experimented with thousands of inkblots, he eventually narrowed the set to 10.

Inkblots were used to understand individuals long before the development of the Rorschach test. During the late 19th century, Alfred Binet suggested that inkblots might be useful in assessing personality. Later, Guy Whipple (1910) published the first set of inkblots. Nonetheless, Rorschach is widely known for developing and publicizing the use of inkblots for identifying psychological disorders.

In 1921, after 10 years of research, Rorschach published his book *Psychodiagnostik,* which provided the rationale for the Rorschach Inkblot Test. Rorschach, however, had a number of critics—particularly in the United States. American psychologists conducted validation studies on various scoring systems for the test, and they repeatedly found no evidence of reliability or validity. This lack of scientific verification led them to believe that the test was scientifically unsound.

Nevertheless, the Rorschach Inkblot Test became popular over the years, and some clinicians continue to administer it. This popularity is often attributed to the writings and research of individuals such as Samuel J. Beck, Marguerite Hertz, Bruno Klopfer, and Zygmunt Piotrowski (Exner, 1976). Each developed a different system for administering, scoring, and interpreting the results of the Rorschach test, and they developed a wide following of psychiatrists and clinical psychologists.

In an enlightening article titled "The Rorschach Inkblot Test, Fortune Tellers, and Cold Reading," Wood, Nezworski, Lilienfeld, and Garb (2003) attempt to explain what many considered to be the "miracle" of the Rorschach test. They suggest that the Rorschach experts knowingly or—more likely—unknowingly used several techniques used by fortune tellers, such as reading palms, tarot cards, tea leaves, or a crystal ball. These techniques included ambiguous statements or statements that could apply to anyone, followed by affirmation and information from the client, and ending in gaining the client's trust and willingness to affirm further interpretations by the clinician. Wood and colleagues state,

> The Rorschach . . . tends to mislabel most normal people as "sick." In addition, the test cannot detect most psychological disorders (with the exception of schizophrenia and related conditions marked by thinking disturbances), nor does it do an adequate job of detecting most personality traits. (p. 29)

One study analyzed 530 statistics from nine articles published during the 1970s and did find an overall internal reliability coefficient of .83 (Parker, 1983); however, this study contrasts with numerous studies that have found opposite results.

The Rorschach remains a popular psychological test even though its psychometric properties remain weak or nonexistent. Proponents of the test suggest that the low reliability and validity may be attributed to the lack of a universally accepted method for administering and scoring the Rorschach. There are a variety of "test manuals" available. Some of these include directions for lengthy introductions and explanations about how to respond to the stimuli, and others include very few explanations. Some have very lenient scoring rules, and others have rules that are more stringent. Researchers such as Wood and colleagues (2003) continue to object to using the Rorschach Inkblot Test as a measure of personality or as a diagnostic test.

American psychologists Henry A. Murray and C. D. Morgan developed the TAT. This personality test requires test takers to look at pictures and tell stories about each picture. The TAT was originally developed as a tool for therapy (the therapeutic model of assessment) rather than for diagnosis. Although a number of scoring schemes are available for the TAT, none appears to be psychometrically sound enough to warrant the test's use for diagnosis (Worchel & Dupree, 1990). Nonetheless, the TAT remains a popular instrument for training and clinical practice.

| Figure 14.2 | Boy Taking TAT Test |

Projective Drawing

Another projective technique is **projective drawing,** in which the assessor directs the test takers to draw their own pictures. Projective drawing is one of the oldest methods of assessment. Florence Goodenough (1926) first used this approach to evaluate children's intelligence. Later theorists and practitioners recognized that emotional factors were also represented in clients' drawings (Hammer, 1975).

Two well-known projective drawing methods are the House–Tree–Person and Draw-A-Person techniques. These methods, as their names imply, require the test taker to make drawings of houses, trees, or persons. In this case, the "tests" are the stimuli or instructions, and the methods and scoring schemes for interpreting the drawings provide quantitative scores that researchers use to analyze for evidence of reliability and validity. For Your Information Box 14.5 describes in more detail the administration and interpretation of the Draw-A-Person technique.

FOR YOUR INFORMATION BOX 14.5

The Draw-A-Person Projective Technique

The Draw-A-Person technique is a traditional projective test whose antecedents date to the psychoanalytic schools of Freud and Jung. Currently, this technique is a popular choice among counselors who work with victimized children, and several authors have suggested scoring schemes that relate to emotional and sexual violence (for example, Van Hutton, 1994; Wohl & Kaufman, 1995).

The assessor gives the test taker a blank paper, usually 8½ by 11 inches, and a soft pencil. The assessor asks the participant, "Will you please draw a person?" In response to questions about which person or what kind of person or drawing, the assessor says, "Draw whatever you like in any way you like." The assessor also assures the participant that artistic talent is not important and is not part of the exercise.

After the first drawing is completed, the assessor asks the participant to draw a person whose sex is opposite that of the first person drawn. For instance, the assessor may say, "This is a male figure [or man]; now please draw a female [or woman]." Figure 14.3 shows an example of the sorts of drawings that might be produced by the participant.

There are various methods for interpreting and scoring the resulting drawings. These scoring schemes, not the test itself, provide the quantitative data that allow researchers to look for evidence of reliability and validity. Studies appropriately assess interscorer reliability as well as evidence of construct validity.

Van Hutton (1994) reports rigorous development of her scoring system for the Draw-A-Person test that included conducting a pilot test similar to the pilot tests described in Chapter 12. She reported high interscorer reliability (> .90) for three scales in her scheme and .70 for the other scale. She also found evidence of discriminant validity because the scorers were able to use the scores on one scale to successfully separate test takers into two categories: normal children and sexually abused children. The remaining scales, however, were not predictive of any criteria (Dowd, 1998).

Ter Laak, de Goede, Aleva, and van Rijswijk (2005) conducted a study of the Draw-A-Person test and examined the reliability and validity of the Goodenough–Harris scoring instructions. These three counselors with some training conducted the Draw-A-Person test with 115 children ages 7 to 9. The researchers concluded that counting details and establishing developmental level could be done with acceptable interscorer reliability; however, interscorer reliability coefficients for social and emotional development as well as personality were insufficient. Ter Laak and colleagues concluded that clinicians need better scoring schemes with evidence of reliability and validity to make effective use of the Draw-A-Person test.

| Figure 14.3 | The Draw-A-Person Projective Technique |

SOURCE: From Hammer, E. F. (1975). *The clinical application of projective drawings* (4th ed.). Springfield, IL: Charles C Thomas. Copyright © 1975. Courtesy of Charles C Thomas Publisher, Ltd.

Sentence Completion

A third type of projective assessment is **sentence completion.** Like projective drawing, sentence completion techniques date to the 1920s. This technique, however, grew out of another psychoanalytic concept: word association. In sentence completion tests, the assessor administers partial sentences, verbally or on paper, and asks the test taker to respond by completing each sentence.

Research suggests that sentence completion tests are one of the main techniques used by school psychologists to assess children's personalities (Goh & Fuller, 1983). Haak (1990) describes how sentence completion tests may be used to evaluate school-age children for problems such as intellectual difficulties, attention deficit disorder, stress, depression, anxiety, thought disturbance, and defensiveness. She admits, however, that there is little research to support the psychometric soundness of these tests.

The Controversy About Projective Techniques

Most proponents of projective techniques concede that a major weakness of projective tests is a lack of evidence of traditional psychometric soundness, such as reliability and validity. Numerous scoring schemes have been devised to overcome these psychometric deficiencies, but many psychologists still doubt the validity of projective techniques. Practitioners who use these techniques contend that they provide richer and more personal data than do structured personality tests. The value of projective tests may therefore be in their usefulness as an intervention rather than as diagnostic or research instruments.

Sometimes the results of a routine administration of a battery of psychological tests, such as intelligence or personality tests, can signal that abnormal responses may be related to physiological dysfunction. In that case, the clinician conducts a more in-depth neuropsychological assessment.

On the Web Box 14.1 provides web addresses where you can learn more about a number of widely used diagnostic and personality tests.

ON THE WEB BOX 14.1

Personality Tests Used for Diagnosis and Intervention

 Clinicians and counselors use a variety of standardized and projective personality tests for diagnosis and intervention. The table below lists websites where you can learn more about these tests.

Test	Website
Minnesota Multiphasic Personality Inventory-2	www.pearsonassessments.com/tests/mmpi_2.htm
California Psychological Inventory	www.cpp.com/products/cpi/index.asp
NEO Personality Inventory–Revised	www4.parinc.com/products/product.aspx?ProductID=NEO-PI-R
16 Personality Factor Questionnaire	www.pearsonassessments.com/tests/sixtpf_5.htm
Thematic Apperception Test	www.pearsonassessments.com/HAIWEB/Cultures/en-us/Productdetail.htm?Pid=015-4019-046&Mode=summary
Rorschach Inkblot Test	www.pearsonassessments.com/HAIWEB/Cultures/en-us/Productdetail.htm?Pid=P43007&Mode=summary
House–Tree–Person	www4.parinc.com/products/product.aspx?ProductID=HTP-DAP

INTERIM SUMMARY 14.3
PROJECTIVE TECHNIQUES

- Projective techniques ask test takers to give meaning to ambiguous stimuli.
- Projective storytelling requires test takers to tell a story about some visual stimuli such as pictures.
- In projective drawing, test takers draw and interpret their own pictures.
- In sentence completion tests, the assessor administers partial sentences, verbally or on paper, and asks test takers to respond by completing each sentence.
- A major weakness of most projective tests is a lack of evidence of traditional psychometric soundness, such as reliability and validity. Therefore, the value of projective tests may be in their usefulness as interventions rather than as diagnostic or research instruments.

Neuropsychological Tests

Neuropsychology is a special branch of psychology that concentrates on the relation between how the brain functions and the behavior it produces. This field is of growing importance in assessing and treating clients with abnormal behavior as well as clients with neurological or brain damage. Neuropsychological assessment requires specialized training and is usually conducted by psychologists or psychiatrists rather than by counselors or mental health workers. For Your Information Box 14.6 provides an overview of the problems and disorders that can be explored using neuropsychological tests.

Two neuropsychological tests that you will recognize are the Wechsler Adult Intelligence Scale III (WAIS-III) and the Wisconsin Card Sorting Test (WCST), both of which were developed prior to World War II and have since become popular in detecting brain dysfunction.

 In Appendix A, see Test Spotlight 1.1 for more detail about the Wechsler Adult Intelligence Scale and Test Spotlight 6.3 for more detail about the Wisconsin Card Sorting Test.

As you recall, the WAIS-III requires test takers to define words, repeat lists of digits, explain what is missing from pictures, and arrange blocks to duplicate geometric card designs. The purpose of the WAIS-III is to measure an adult's intelligence capacity, and it is one of the most frequently taught IQ tests in psychology graduate schools (Czubaj, 1996).

First published in 1939 as the Wechsler–Bellevue Intelligence Scale, the WAIS-III incorporates verbal and performance scores into one intelligence score. Wechsler's definition of intelligence, now more than 50 years old, is still regarded as well expressed because it emphasizes the ability to act with a purpose in mind, to think in a logical manner, and to interact with the current environment. Although the WAIS-III does not encompass recent concepts such as emotional intelligence, it does address an individual's capacity for common sense (Rogers, 2001).

For Your Information Box 14.7 gives Camilla Czubaj's (1996) account of her neuropsychological assessment using the WAIS-R, a prior version of the WAIS-III. Czubaj, now a clinician and researcher, draws attention to problems that should be avoided when conducting a neuropsychological assessment.

As you recall from Chapter 6, the WCST requires the test taker to sort 64 cards according to various categories presented as stimuli. Although the purpose of this test is to assess perseveration and abstract thinking, many practitioners consider it to be a measure of executive function because of its reported sensitivity to frontal lobe dysfunction. The WCST is used to assess functions such as strategic planning,

FOR YOUR INFORMATION BOX 14.6

Areas of Neuropsychological Assessment

The field of neuropsychology developed from research conducted during the early 1940s on brain damage in adults. The medical field considers neuropsychological tests to be one of the most important means of detecting and evaluating traumatic brain injury. Contusions to the head, skull fractures, or skull lacerations can cause traumatic brain injury, as can accidents in which a person might undergo a sudden jerk to the head. A person does not need to suffer a concussion to experience traumatic brain injury (Czubaj, 1996).

Neuropsychological tests can help doctors determine the areas of the brain that may be damaged, the severity of impairment, and the prognosis for recovery or long-term adjustment. Neurological tests can also establish a baseline for the monitoring of recovery. For example, many professional sport teams require players to undergo neuropsychological evaluation to evaluate their cognitive abilities prior to participating in games where they may incur head injuries. Medical doctors and neuropsychologists use generalizations when identifying brain injury with cognitive deficits, including the following:

1. Left temporal lobe injury [to] verbal learning, memory, auditory attention and discrimination, along with language impediments.

2. Right temporal lobe damage can result in vision–spatial perception [impairment].

3. Frontal lobe injury damages numerous cognitive and neurobehavioral abilities. (Czubaj, 1996, p. 273)

Although many people still associate the use of neuropsychological tests with brain dysfunction, the scope of neuropsychological assessment has widened to include identification of a variety of disorders and abnormalities. Following is a list of applications for neuropsychological testing taken from the *Handbook of Neuropsychological Assessment* (Puente & McCaffrey, 1992):

- Identification and localization of brain lesions and related behaviors
- Assessment of the development or decline of brain function across the life span
- Assessment of competence and evaluation for disability in forensic settings
- Evaluation of students for learning disabilities and related academic problems
- Assessment for schizophrenia and mood disorders
- Health status assessment for persons with numerous general medical disorders or exposure to toxic substances
- Research on basic brain–behavior relationships
- Monitoring of the effects of drugs or experimental treatment procedures during clinical trials
- Investigation of the neurobiological roots of genetic disorders
- Assessment of the influence of medication, fatigue, or toxic substances on employee performance in industrial settings
- Supplement to traditional aptitude and achievement tests in educational settings

SOURCES: Adapted from Czubaj, C. A. (1996). The Wechsler Adult Intelligence Scale–Revised, revisited. *Education, 117,* 271–273. Reprinted by permission of the author.

organized searching, using environmental feedback to shift cognitive sets, directing behavior toward achieving a goal, and modulating impulsive responding (PAR, 2010e).

The field of neuropsychology covers a wide range of behaviors and testing, and a number of tests, such as the WAIS-III, overlap with other fields of assessment. Covering the widely used assessments by neuropsychologists is beyond the scope of this textbook. Instead, we look at categories of techniques and a few tests that represent each category.

FOR YOUR INFORMATION BOX 14.7

A Personal Account of a Neuropsychological Assessment

Knowing the importance of the assessment specialist's skills, I sought out the most renowned licensed psychologist in the state to perform my own neuropsychological evaluation. The test duration was approximately four and one half hours long. This is an enormous amount of time for one to maintain infinite attention and acute concentration. The assessment began with an assessment of grooming as well as punctuality for the appointment. Background information pertaining to my medical history, family history, and childhood was recorded along with my previous schooling and social life. The battery of tests attempts to assess a wide variety of higher and lower cerebral functional areas of the brain. There was the Full Scale IQ, Memory Scale, Verbal and Performance IQ. The Ammons QT measured the receptive vocabulary ability. The tests seemed endless and concluded with the Finger Tapping Test.

During the tests, I found periods of loss of concentration. Two lengthy successive paragraphs were read to me; the tests required me to reiterate these paragraphs with as much detail as possible. Mental arithmetic, word associations, block design, picture sequencing, spatial relationships, and visual acuity. . . . I found ambiguity in several visual perception identification [problems]. The assessment specialist "threw these out." There were two personality tests given to me. In order to save time, I was given these to complete during my lunch break. My lunch break offered me no time to recover from the incessant barrage of tests; I found numerous questions on these personality assessments to be "double loaded." "I like to gamble for small stakes," was one question in particular. If I didn't answer this question, it could be inferred I like to gamble for large stakes. I also question the semantics of the word "gamble." Changing one's occupation or relocation of one's residence could be a form of gambling. Feeling completely mentally exhausted, my motor skills were assessed prior to the closure of my neuropsychological evaluation. My long fingernails compromised speed with the placement of tiny pegs in the pegboard holes during the Purdue Pegboard Test. The Finger Tapping Test required me to press a lever on a board for a period of time, alternating with my right and then left index finger had my right hand in a fist with only my index finger extended. I found my finger begin to waiver and cramp by the end of the time frame. For the remaining five more time frames, I left my fingers extended, pressing down on the board with the tips of my fingers while my index finger pressed the lever in rapid succession. The difference in the placement of my remaining fingers created more support to my index fingers, increasing the amount of tappings significantly.

The report of my neuropsychological evaluation notated every lapse of concentration I had. My speech was even assessed to its fluency, grammar, comprehension, and relevancy. It was even notated that I wore jewelry in my assessment on grooming. It was reported I was alert, oriented to time, place, person, and situation. The effort I put forth and my pleasantness were also included in the test results. My auditory, visual, and manual dexterity were also assessed. My IQ assessments fared well. My personality testing was interpreted with a different dimension due to the fact I had deleted numerous "double-loaded" questions.

SOURCE: From C. A. Czubaj (1996). The Wechsler Adult Intelligence Scale–Revised, revisited. *Education, 117,* 271–273. Reprinted by permission of the author.

Electrophysiological Techniques

Neuropsychologists use electrophysiological techniques, such as electroencephalography, and neuroimaging methods, such as positron emission tomography (PET) and magnetic resonance imaging (MRI). Two major electrophysiological methods for investigating brain function are the **electroencephalogram (EEG)**, a continuous written record of brainwave activity, and **event-related potential (ERP)**, a record of the brain's electrical response to the occurrence of a specific event. Researchers have used individual differences in EEG and ERP indexes to predict psychological traits, cognitive function and dysfunction, and psychopathology (Boomsma, Anokhin, & de Geus, 1997). Neuroimaging involves making pictures of brain functions such as blood flow (PET records changes in brain blood flow) and magnetic fields (MRI provides a three-dimensional picture of brain tissue). Researchers have also shown a relation between neuroimaging techniques and behavior.

For Your Information Box 14.8 includes a discussion of research using electrophysiological assessment to investigate the possibility that conditions such as alcoholism might be inherited.

FYI

FOR YOUR INFORMATION BOX 14.8

Genetic Components of Electrophysiological Behavior

Investigation of a relationship between electrical activity in the brain and underlying inherited traits date to the 1930s. Recent advances in mapping human chromosomes and genes, however, have provided evidence that behavioral potentials, such as increased risk for alcoholism, may be traced to specific genes and transmitted in families, much like eye color and blood groups.

For example, individual electroencephalogram (EEG) differences caused by alcohol appear to be controlled at the genetic level. Results of several studies suggest that genes located on Chromosomes 2 and 6 may influence brain activity in the frontal, executive, and sensory-processing areas. These genes in turn have been shown to influence brain activity (low P300 amplitude) that has been linked to increased risk for alcoholism. These studies concur with pharmacological studies that suggest an association with dopamine, which is a neurotransmitter.

In addition, twin and family studies have provided evidence of greater consistency of spontaneous electrical activity in the brain for conditions such as sleep, resting wakefulness, sensory stimulation, and performance of various tasks for those sharing the same genes. Studies by some researchers (Bouchard, Lykken, McGue, Segal, & Tellegen, 1990; Stassen, Lykken, Propping, & Bomben, 1988) suggest that differences in EEG activity among individuals are determined mostly by genetic factors.

Researchers have also linked event-related potentials (ERPs) to individuals' genetic makeup, although to a lesser degree than that for EEGs. Some of this variability may be due to the variety of tasks used to evoke ERPs. For instance, elementary stimuli, such as light flashes, evoke more consistent responses attributable to a genetic influence than do ERP responses to tasks requiring language skills.

These studies represent only the start of programs of research designed to understand how genes influence electric activity in the brain. Plans for future research include linking specific genes to the brain areas where they are expressed.

SOURCE: From Boomsma, D., Anokhin, A., & de Geus, E. (1997). Genetics of electrophysiology: Linking genes, brain, and behavior. *Current Directions in Psychological Science, 6,* 106–110.

Developmental Applications

When assessing brain and neurological functioning, it is important for assessors to consider their clients' behavior in the context of their developmental period. In other words, the brain and nervous system of a child are different from the brain and nervous system of an adult. Although neuropsychologists should possess a strong knowledge of development issues and tests appropriate for children, approximately two-thirds routinely assess children and adolescents without acquiring the necessary expertise. Until recently, many inaccurate assumptions have been made about brain–behavior relationships in children based on research conducted on adults. Fortunately, research on brain–behavior relationships in children has begun to dispel some of these assumptions (Cohen, Branch, Willis, Weyandt, & Hynd, 1992).

Neonatal and Early Childhood

Neurological disorders that can occur prior to birth include spina bifida (abnormal development of neural tube), intrauterine growth retardation often caused by a small or insufficient placenta, anoxia (total reduction of oxygen), and hypoxia (partial reduction of oxygen). Assessment of neurological deficits for neonates and young children can be divided into four functional areas: biochemical, electrophysiological, neurobehavioral, and social–emotional functioning (Emory, Savoie, Ballard, Eppler, & O'Dell, 1992).

Biochemical assessment refers to analysis of blood gases to determine the concentration of oxygen and carbon dioxide at the tissue level. **Electrophysiological assessment** is the monitoring of vital

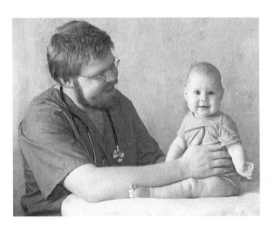

signs such as heart rate and spontaneous electrical activity of the brain. Many hospitals monitor fetal heart rate during delivery to determine fetal well-being. The clinical neuropsychologist usually does not conduct these tests. When a medical practitioner provides this information to the clinical psychologist, it is valuable information for making a psychological diagnosis.

Most neuropsychologists use diagnostic methods in the area of **neurobehavioral assessment.** Traditionally, practitioners elicit various reflexes, such as the Moro, Babinski, and tonic neck reflex, to assess the functioning and maturity of the infant's central nervous system. In addition to reflexive screening exams, psychologists rely heavily on observations of infants' and children's behaviors to assess developmental progress. Well-known batteries include developmental screening tests such as the Gesell Developmental Schedules (Knobloch, Stevens, & Malone, 1980), the Bayley Scales of Infant Development (Bayley, 1993), and the Denver Developmental Screening Test (Frankenburg, Dodds, Fandal, Kazuk, & Cohrs, 1975). For Your Information Box 14.9 provides more information on these three tests.

Social–emotional functioning includes tests that measure temperament or personality. In addition, practitioners use intelligence tests, academic achievement tests, language assessment, visual and tactile perception evaluations, and assessment of sustained attention (ability to remain aroused and vigilant over time) and selective attention (ability to focus on key aspects of the environment; Cohen et al., 1992). M. J. Cohen and colleagues point out that the child neuropsychologist must be proficient in qualitative analysis of observational data as well as in test administration and interpretation.

Attention Deficit Hyperactivity Disorder

Another important assessment for children, usually initiated by parents and teachers, is for **attention deficit hyperactivity disorder (ADHD).** Often characterized by excessive hyperactivity and impulsiveness or daydreaming and distraction, this appears to be a neural disorder that typically interferes with academic performance. Tseng, Henderson, Chow, and Yao (2004) found a significant difference between children with ADHD and those without ADHD in fine and gross motor skills, impulse control, and attention.

FYI

FOR YOUR INFORMATION BOX 14.9

Common Developmental Screening Tests

Gesell Developmental Schedules

The Gesell Developmental Schedules (Knobloch, Stevens, & Malone, 1980) represent a refinement of early attempts to construct a taxonomy of normal development. The first Gesell schedules, published in 1940, represented the results of longitudinal studies conducted by Arnold Gesell and his colleagues at Yale University (Ames, 1989). The assessor using the Gesell schedules observes and records a child's responses to predetermined toys and other stimuli. Information provided by a parent or caregiver then supplements the observational data to determine neurological defects or behavioral abnormalities (Anastasi & Urbina, 1997).

Bayley Scales of Infant Development

The Bayley Scales of Infant Development–second edition (Bayley, 1993) use a methodology similar to that of the Gesell schedules; however, the Bayley Scales are generally considered to be better constructed and accompanied by more evidence of reliability and validity. The battery is composed of three scales: the Mental Scale (perception, memory, problem solving, verbal communication, and abstract thinking), the Motor Scale (gross motor ability), and the Behavior Rating Scale (emotional and social behavior, attention span, persistence, and goal orientation). Like the Gesell schedules, the Behavior Rating Scale relies on information provided by the child's caregiver. Norms for this battery are based on 1,700 children representing ages from 1 to 42 months and representative of the U.S. population in terms of race/ethnicity, geographic regions, and parental education level. Nancy Bayley designed the battery to assess developmental status rather than to predict subsequent ability levels. Although more research is needed, the battery is helpful in early detection of sensory or neurological defects, emotional disturbances, and environmental deficits (Anastasi & Urbina, 1997). (Chapter 6 provided more information on the Bayley Scales and their psychometric properties.)

Denver Developmental Screening Test

The Denver Developmental Screening Test (Frankenburg, Dodds, Fandal, Kazuk, & Cohrs, 1975) is another norm-referenced battery designed specifically for early identification of developmental or behavioral problems. The target audience for this battery is children from birth to six years of age. Unlike the Bayley Scales, the Denver Developmental Screening Test requires no special training for the administrator and takes only a short interval of time—approximately 20 minutes—to administer. This test measures four developmental areas: personal–social development, fine motor development, language development, and gross motor development. The test contains 105 items that are administered according to the child's chronological age. The authors of the test report evidence of test–retest reliability, content validity, and construct validity.

According to Edwards and colleagues (2005), one of the most frequent mental health referrals for children is ADHD, and mental health care professionals consider a variety of assessment methods when diagnosing ADHD. A survey of pediatricians and primary care physicians (Wasserman et al., 1999, as cited in Edwards et al., 2005) provided some insight into doctors' assessment of ADHD in children. The respondents reported using five procedures to assess attentional and hyperactive problems (see Table 14.1). Edwards and colleagues inferred from the results that pediatricians and primary care physicians rely mostly on information from the home setting and observations to diagnose ADHD.

| Table 14.1 | Five Procedures Used by Clinicians to Diagnose Attention Deficit Hyperactivity Disorder |

Diagnostic Method	Percentage of Use Reported
Parent interview	87.1
Child interview	66.6
School reports	53.5
Observations	47.3
Standardized assessment tools such as behavior checklists	36.9

SOURCE: From Edwards, M. C., Schulz, E. G., Chelonis, J., Gardner, E., Philyaw, A., & Young, J. (2005). Estimates of the validity and utility of unstructured clinical observations of children in the assessment of ADHD. *Clinical Pediatrics, 44,* 49–56. Reprinted with permission from Sage Publications, Inc.

Adulthood and Aging

Neuropsychologists must take into account the normal changes in brain function that result from aging, which can exaggerate the psychological impact of medical conditions. A number of physiological changes in the brain that result from aging have been documented. These include decreases in the weight and volume of the brain, decreases in certain neurotransmitters, decreases in dominant EEG frequency, and changes in brain metabolism. Therefore, practitioners need to pay close attention to the age of the norm group when comparing individual scores with test norms. Research comparing test results for older adults with test results for younger adults reports larger standard deviations (more variation) in scores for older adults than in scores for younger adults (La Rue, 1992).

Two disorders that increase with aging are Alzheimer's disease and depression. Clients are diagnosed as having dementia of the Alzheimer type (DAT) based on specified behaviors and laboratory results. Depression often cannot be clearly identified until the condition passes. Scores on depression rating scales are often higher for older individuals because older respondents endorse more physical symptoms. Older clients may also experience cognitive deficits due to aging rather than to depression.

Psychopathological Applications

According to Puente and McCaffrey (1992), three major areas of psychopathological disorders—anxiety, depression, and schizophrenia—have been researched extensively by neuropsychologists.

Anxiety

A number of mental health conditions can be grouped under the general classification of anxiety disorders. The *DSM-IV-TR* (American Psychiatric Association, 2000) lists numerous conditions characterized by unrealistic or excessive anxiety and worry, such as generalized anxiety disorder, obsessive–compulsive disorder, panic disorder, and posttraumatic stress disorder. Researchers have identified specific associations between the emotion of anxiety and particular brain structures and neurotransmitter systems (Charney, Heninger, & Breier, 1984; Horel, Keating, & Misantone, 1975; LeDoux, Thompson, Iadelcola, Tucker, & Reis, 1983). Orsillo and McCaffrey (1992) indicate that involvement of the temporal lobe area is reported consistently. Neurological assessment procedures used by researchers include electrophysiological recordings, such as PET, computerized transaxial tomography (CT; a three-dimensional depiction of the brain), ERP, and the EEG (Orsillo & McCaffrey, 1992). These measures can be supplemented by psychological tests such as those for intelligence, auditory learning, temporal orientation, memory, and visual retention.

Depression

Recent research suggests that depression, which usually affects neurologically impaired individuals at some time during their illness, can have a significant impact on neuropsychological test performance (Miller, 1975; Newman & Sweet, 1986). Newman and Sweet suggest that these effects on test performance can be extreme or subtle. They cluster into three major areas of impairment: psychomotor speed, motivation and attention, and memory and learning. Failure to consider the effects of depression on neuropsychological tests can lead to misdiagnosis of a client's condition, resulting in inappropriate treatment.

Schizophrenia

Although once classified as a disorder without an identifiable neurological basis, researchers have now linked schizophrenia to evidence of abnormal brain functioning (Walker, Lucas, & Lewine, 1992). A number of studies have compared individuals diagnosed as schizophrenic with individuals who have known brain damage. Two neuropsychological test batteries used to study the performance of schizophrenics are the Halstead–Reitan Neurological Battery and the Luria–Nebraska Neurological Battery.

Researchers have also used PET and regional cerebral blood flow (RCBF) analysis to search for an organic basis for schizophrenia. One finding has been a reduction in frontal lobe activity in the brain in clients diagnosed as schizophrenic (Weinberger & Berman, 1988; Weinberger, Berman, & Zec, 1986).

INTERIM SUMMARY 14.4
NEUROPSYCHOLOGICAL TESTS

- Neuropsychology is a branch of psychology that focuses on the relation between brain functions and behavior.
- Neuropsychologists use electrophysiological techniques, such as the electroencephalogram (EEG), a continuous written record of brainwave activity, and event-related potential (ERP), a record of the brain's electrical response to the occurrence of a specific event.
- Developmental applications involve assessments that determine whether the client is developing normally.
- Two developmental tests for infants are biochemical assessment, which is an analysis of blood gases to determine the concentration of oxygen and carbon dioxide at the tissue level, and electrophysiological assessment, which involves monitoring vital signs such as heart rate and spontaneous electrical activity of the brain.

- Neuropsychologists conduct neurobehavioral assessments such as eliciting various reflexes to assess the functioning and maturity of the infant's central nervous system.
- Neuropsychologists use tests that measure temperament and personality, as well as intelligence, academic achievement, language, perception, and attention tests, to assess social–emotional functioning in children.
- When treating the elderly, neuropsychologists take into account the normal changes in brain function that result from aging, including the fact that aging can exaggerate the psychological impact of medical conditions.
- Three major areas of psychopathological disorders—anxiety, depression, and schizophrenia—have been researched extensively by neuropsychologists.

Specialized Tests for Clinical Disorders

Psychologists also use traditional tests to identify mental disorders such as anger, anxiety, and depression. Because thousands of specialized tests are available from publishers, a comprehensive discussion of clinical tests is beyond the scope of this textbook. Several commonly used tests are discussed here to illustrate the role that traditional tests play in clinical diagnosis. These tests differ from general personality inventories, such as the MMPI-2 and the NEO Personality Inventory–Revised, because they focus on a narrow band of traits or behaviors.

Single-Construct Tests

The Beck Depression Inventory (revised in 1996) is one of the best examples of a widely used self-report test that measures a single construct. Beck and his associates developed the original inventory in 1961. Since that time, the test has been revised and has been cited in more than 3,000 studies (Waller, 1995b). The Beck Depression Inventory is used to assess the severity of depression in adults and adolescents as well as to screen normal populations.

 Test Spotlight 14.3 in Appendix A describes the Beck Depression Inventory in more detail.

Because a number of studies have found high correlations (.40–.70) between depression and anxiety (Waller, 1995a), the development of the Beck Anxiety Inventory was a logical extension of Beck's research. This test is designed to measure characteristics of anxiety that may or may not occur with those of depression. Both tests are the products of extensive research and careful psychometric development.

Identification of Construct Duration

Charles Spielberger and his associates at the University of South Florida added another dimension to the measurement of mental constructs. Their long-term research on anxiety, anger, and curiosity included the concept of trait duration. They asked the question, "Is the attribute a temporary **state** or an ongoing part of a person's personality and therefore a **trait**?" Two well-known tests that came out of this research are the State–Trait Anger Expression Inventory-2 (STAXI-2) and the State–Trait Anxiety Inventory (STAI). The STAI attempts to distinguish between a temporary condition of anxiety—perhaps brought on by situational circumstances—and a long-standing quality of anxiety that has become a part of the person's personality. Likewise, the STAXI-2 assesses temporary anger (state anger) and angry temperament and angry reaction (trait anger).

Test Spotlight 14.4 in Appendix A describes the State–Trait Anger Expression Inventory-2 in more detail.

Observational Scales

Some clients, such as children, are not able to complete self-report measures about themselves. Therefore, trained professionals or family members can use observational scales to carry out an assessment. Typically, the assessor observes predetermined behaviors and then rates the behaviors on a Likert-type scale.

The Attention Deficit Disorders Evaluation Scale (ADDES) is a good example of a test that relies on observation of the client. The ADDES is used to assess children for attention deficit disorder as defined in the *DSM-IV-TR*. The test measures three constructs: inattention, impulsiveness, and hyperactivity. Any person who has extended contact with the child may complete the scale by rating how often each behavior occurs (0 = *does not engage in the behavior*, 1 = *week*, 2 = *day*, 3 = *an hour*). Scores are interpreted by comparing them with norms obtained by assessing thousands of individuals from 4 to 20 years of age.

The tests cited in this section were developed over a period of years using the rigorous methodology for test development described in Chapters 10 and 11. Each has demonstrated high levels of reliability and construct validity. Not all clinical tests available from test publishers or scholarly journals demonstrate psychometric soundness. It is important that the clinical practitioner or counselor use caution to select tests that meet accepted standards of psychometric soundness.

In summary, psychological tests and assessments are important tools used by clinical psychologists, counselors, and other professionals. Their primary role is one of information gathering to facilitate diagnosis; however, they are also used as part of the intervention process and for research. Psychologists, counselors, and other professionals who use tests for these purposes should receive specialized training in the general principles of psychological testing as well as specific training for interpreting each instrument.

INTERIM SUMMARY 14.5
SPECIALIZED TESTS FOR CLINICAL DISORDERS

- Psychologists also use traditional paper-and-pencil tests to identify mental disorders such as anger, anxiety, and depression.
- The Beck Depression Inventory and the Beck Anxiety Inventory are examples of tests that assess a single construct or disorder.

- Another dimension of measurement is the assessment of whether an attribute is temporary (state) or an ongoing part of the personality (trait).
- When clients, such as children, cannot complete self-report measures, trained professionals use observational scales to rate observed behaviors.

Chapter Summary

Clinical assessment includes a broad set of information-gathering and interpretive skills used by the professional counselor-therapist. There are three models of clinical assessment. The information-gathering model represents the use of standardized tests to make diagnoses. The therapeutic model uses tests as an intervention that provides new information for the client to use for self-discovery and growth. The differential treatment model represents the use of tests for conducting research or evaluating program outcomes. Counselors primarily provide services for individuals with normal developmental problems, and clinical psychologists and psychiatrists generally treat individuals with abnormal behaviors, mental disorders, or emotional disabilities.

Diagnosis is the identification of the client's problem or disorder. Screening is the process of arriving at a diagnosis. Diagnosis leads to the design or selection of an intervention to alleviate unwanted behaviors or symptoms or to solve the client's problem.

Most practitioners use the clinical interview as a primary tool for gathering information about the client. The clinical interview involves a discussion between the client and the assessor in which the assessor observes the client and gathers information. The structured clinical interview has a predetermined set of questions. The unstructured or nondirective clinical interview, on the other hand, has few predetermined questions; instead, the assessor's questions are more likely to be determined by the client's responses. The semistructured interview provides a compromise between the structured interview and the nondirective interview.

Research on the validity of the nondirective clinical interview suggests that it may be more useful in a therapeutic sense than for assessment. The practitioner who uses the nondirective approach risks three major sources of bias: hypothesis confirmation bias, self-fulfilling prophecy, and ethnocentrism. Practitioners also use standardized personality tests, such as the MMPI-2, the NEO Personality Inventory, and the 16PF, to make diagnoses.

Projective techniques ask test takers to give meaning to ambiguous stimuli. Projective storytelling requires test takers to tell a story about some visual stimuli such as pictures. In projective drawing, test takers draw and interpret their own pictures. In sentence completion tests, the assessor administers partial sentences, verbally or on paper, and asks test takers to respond by completing each sentence. A major weakness of most projective tests is a lack of evidence of traditional psychometric soundness, such as reliability and validity. Therefore, the value of projective tests may be in their usefulness as an intervention rather than as diagnostic or research instruments.

Neuropsychology is a special branch of psychology that concentrates on the relation between how the brain functions and the behavior it produces. Neuropsychologists use electrophysiological techniques, such as the EEG, a continuous written record of brainwave activity, and the ERP, a record of the brain's electrical response to the occurrence of a specific event, as well as traditional psychological tests.

Most neuropsychological testing falls into two categories: diagnosing brain damage and screening for developmental deficiencies. Two developmental tests for infants are biochemical assessment, which is the analysis of blood gases to determine the concentration of oxygen and carbon dioxide at the tissue level, and electrophysiological assessment, which is the monitoring of vital signs such as heart rate and spontaneous electrical activity of the brain. Neuropsychologists also conduct neurobehavioral assessments such as eliciting various reflexes to assess the functioning and maturity of the infant's central nervous system. Finally, neuropsychologists use tests that measure temperament and personality, as well as intelligence, academic achievement, language, perception, and attention tests, to assess social–emotional functioning in children. When treating the elderly, neuropsychologists take into account the normal changes in brain function that result from aging, including the fact that aging can exaggerate the psychological impact of medical conditions.

Psychologists also use traditional tests to identify mental disorders such as anger, anxiety, and depression. These tests differ from general personality inventories, such as the MMPI and the NEO Personality Inventory, because they focus on a narrow band of traits or behaviors. The Beck Depression Inventory and the Beck Anxiety Inventory are examples of tests that assess a single construct or disorder. Another dimension of measurement is the assessment of whether an attribute is temporary (state) or an ongoing part of the personality (trait). When clients, such as children, cannot complete self-report measures, trained professionals use observational scales to rate observed behaviors.

Engaging in the Learning Process

KEY CONCEPTS

After completing your study of this chapter, you should be able to define each of the following terms. These terms are bolded in the text of this chapter and defined in the Glossary.

- attention deficit hyperactivity disorder (ADHD)
- biochemical assessment
- clinical assessment
- clinical interview
- diagnosis
- differential treatment model
- electroencephalogram (EEG)
- electrophysiological assessment
- ethnocentrism
- event-related potential (ERP)
- hypothesis confirmation bias
- information-gathering model
- neurobehavioral assessment
- neuropsychology
- nondirective clinical interview

- prognosis
- projection
- projective drawing
- projective hypothesis
- projective storytelling
- projective techniques
- screening
- self-fulfilling prophecy
- semistructured interview
- sentence completion
- social–emotional functioning
- state
- structured clinical interview
- therapeutic model
- trait

LEARNING ACTIVITIES

The following are some learning activities you can engage in to support the learning objectives for this chapter.

Learning Objectives	Study Tips and Learning Activities
After completing your study of this chapter, you should be able to do the following:	The following study tips will help you meet these learning objectives:
Identify and explain three models of psychological assessment that clinicians and counselors use.	• Write an example or a case study for each of the models. Share this with your classmates or your instructor.
Explain the concept of clinical diagnosis, and describe how the clinical interview and structured personality tests are used to make diagnoses.	• Interview a counselor or clinical psychologist (includes instructors) about how he or she makes a clinical diagnosis. Share the results of your interview with your class or instructor.
Describe three types of projective techniques and how practitioners use them for diagnosis and treatment.	• Using the *Mental Measurements Yearbook, Tests in Print,* or an Internet search engine, find more examples of projective techniques. Share the projective tests you found with your classmates or instructor.
Describe the field of neuropsychology, and explain how neuropsychologists use electrophysiological techniques, neurobehavioral assessments, and temperament or personality measures to diagnose and treat clients of various ages.	• Interview a practicing neuropsychologist or an instructor whose specialty is neuropsychology. Ask whether he or she uses the techniques described in this chapter, and if so, ask how. Does your interviewee use other techniques not described in this chapter? Share your results with your classmates or instructor.
Describe how practitioners use single-construct tests to diagnose and treat depression, anxiety, anger, and attention deficit hyperactivity disorder.	• Using the *Mental Measurements Yearbook, Tests in Print,* or *ProQuest,* find other tests that measure depression, anxiety, anger, and attention deficit hyperactivity disorder.

ADDITIONAL LEARNING ACTIVITIES

1. For each of the following tests, list the type of test, its purpose, and what type of evidence there is for reliability and validity.

Test	Type of Test	Test Purpose	Type of Reliability	Type of Validity
Beck Depression Inventory-II				
State–Trait Anger Expression Inventory-2 (STAXI-2)				
California Personality Inventory (CPI)				
16 Personality Factor Questionnaire (16PF)				

2. What type of clinician is MOST LIKELY to use the following tests?

Test	Type of Clinician
Bayley Scales of Infant Development	
Wisconsin Card Sorting Test (WCST)	
Minnesota Multiphasic Personality Inventory (MMPI)	
Draw-A-Person	

PRACTICE QUESTIONS

The following are some practice questions to assess your understanding of the material presented in this chapter.

Multiple Choice

Choose the one best answer to each question.

1. Dr. Adair gives a nondirective interview and the Minnesota Multiphasic Personality Inventory-2 (MMPI-2) to each of her clients before making a diagnosis. Which model of clinical assessment is she using?
   a. Information-gathering model
   b. Therapeutic model
   c. Differential treatment model
   d. Nondirective model

2. Dr. Hodges uses the MMPI-2 in his research on schizophrenics. Which model of clinical assessment is he using?
   a. Information-gathering model
   b. Therapeutic model
   c. Differential treatment model
   d. Nondirective model

3. Dr. Jones uses projective drawings to give her clients a better understanding of their unconscious wishes. Which model of clinical assessment is she using?
   a. Information-gathering model
   b. Therapeutic model
   c. Differential treatment model
   d. Nondirective model

4. Counselors are more apt to subscribe to the
   a. information-gathering model.
   b. therapeutic model.
   c. differential treatment model.
   d. nondirective model.

5. Marsha Thompson is a licensed mental health counselor who asks her clients a list of predetermined questions on their first visits. When necessary, she follows up with questions or adds questions to the list. Which one of the following is she using?
   a. Nondirective clinical interview
   b. Structured interview
   c. Traditional interview
   d. Semistructured interview

6. Which one of the following does the practitioner risk when using a traditional clinical interview?
   a. Hypothesis confirmation bias
   b. Disconfirmation error
   c. Social desirability
   d. Hypothesis disconfirmation bias

7. Bob Dorado conducts clinical interviews. When he is gathering a detailed social and medical history of the client, which phase of the interview is he conducting?
   a. Introductory phase
   b. Initial phase
   c. Middle phase
   d. Termination phase

8. Which of the following contains 10 clinical scales that cover a range of personality traits or predispositions?
   a. California Psychological Inventory (CPI)
   b. NEO Personality Inventory
   c. Minnesota Multiphasic Personality Inventory (MMPI)
   d. 16 Personality Factor Questionnaire (16PF)

9. The Thematic Apperception Test (TAT) belongs to which one of the following categories of tests?
   a. Paper-and-pencil test
   b. Projective storytelling
   c. Projective drawing
   d. Sentence completion

10. Charles Monroe is a school psychologist. One of the techniques he uses is to ask children to draw a person. Which type of assessment is he using?
    a. Personality assessment
    b. Projective storytelling
    c. Projective drawing
    d. Traditional interview

11. Practitioners who use _____ contend that they provide richer and more personal data than _____.
    a. structured personality tests; projective techniques
    b. projective techniques; nondirective clinical interviews
    c. structured interviews; nondirective clinical interviews
    d. projective techniques; structured personality tests

12. Dr. Easton uses a continuous written record of brainwave activity and a record of the brain's electrical response to a specific event when examining clients for brain damage. Which type of assessment is she using?
    a. Electrophysiological
    b. Biochemical
    c. Neonatal
    d. Neurobehavioral

13. Decreased weight and volume of the brain, decreases in certain neurotransmitters, decreases in dominant electroencephalogram (EEG) frequency, and changes in brain metabolism all have been documented as physiological changes in the brain that result from
    a. schizophrenia.
    b. depression.
    c. aging.
    d. anxiety.

14. Which one of the following areas has been researched extensively by neuropsychologists?
    a. Psychotherapy
    b. Confirmatory hypothesis bias
    c. Schizophrenia
    d. Self-esteem and self-efficacy

15. The Beck Depression Inventory and the Beck Anxiety Inventory are examples of
    a. tests that measure construct duration.
    b. single-construct tests.
    c. general personality inventories.
    d. projective techniques.

16. Which one of the following tests measures normal personality traits?
    a. Minnesota Multiphasic Personality Inventory-2 (MMPI-2)
    b. California Personality Inventory, third edition (CPI)
    c. NEO Personality Inventory–Revised
    d. Bayley Scales of Infant Development, third edition

17. Clinical interviewers should avoid posing questions that reflect
    a. acculturation.
    b. multicultural issues.
    c. diagnostic hypotheses.
    d. ethnocentrism.

18. Which one of the following tests is used to measure injury or trauma to the brain?
    a. Minnesota Multiphasic Personality Inventory-2 (MMPI-2)
    b. Beck Depression Inventory
    c. Wisconsin Card Sorting Test (WCST)
    d. Bayley Scales of Infant Development, third edition

19. A good example of a test that relies on observation of the client is the
    a. Attention Deficit Disorders Evaluation Scale (ADDES).
    b. Wisconsin Card Sorting Test (WCST).
    c. 16 Personality Factor Questionnaire (16PF).
    d. Beck Anxiety Inventory.

Short Answer/Essay

Read each of the following, and consider your response carefully based on the information presented in this chapter. Write your answer to each question in two or three paragraphs.

1. What are the three models of psychological assessment used by clinicians and counselors?

2. What are the similarities and differences among the three models of assessment? Include who is most likely to use each.

3. What is clinical diagnosis?

4. Explain how the clinical interview is used in diagnosis. Give examples.

5. Name the three types of clinical interviews, and explain their similarities and differences.

6. Explain how the structured personality tests are used to make diagnoses. Give examples.

7. What is the theory behind projective testing? How does it work? Give examples of three kinds of projective tests.

8. Describe the types of tests that neuropsychologists use. Give examples of various types of tests.

9. How do practitioners use paper-and-pencil tests to diagnose and treat disorders?

10. What is a single-construct test? Give examples of two types of single-construct tests.

11. How can test developers avoid cultural bias in the tests they develop? Describe three processes for identifying and correcting cultural bias in test items.

ANSWER KEYS

Additional Learning activities

1.

Test	Type of Test	Test Purpose	Type of Reliability	Type of Validity
Beck Depression Inventory-II	Single-construct test	To assess depressive symptoms	Test–retest and Cronbach's alpha (internal consistency)	Construct and convergent validity
State–Trait Anger Expression Inventory-2 (STAXI-2)	Single personality test	To measure the experience, expression, and control of anger for adolescents and adults	Cronbach's alpha	Construct validity provided by factor analysis
California Personality Inventory (CPI)	Structured personality test	To assess personality characteristics and to predict what the test taker will say and do in specific contexts	Cronbach's alpha and test–retest	Construct and convergent validity
16 Personality Factor Questionnaire (16PF)	Structured personality test	To measure normal personality traits in people age 16 years or older	Cronbach's alpha and test–retest	Construct and concurrent validity

2.

Test	Type of Clinician
Bayley Scales of Infant Development	Child psychologist
Wisconsin Card Sorting Test (WCST)	Neurologist
Minnesota Multiphasic Personality Inventory (MMPI)	Clinical psychologist

Multiple Choice

1. a	2. c	3. b	4. b
5. d	6. a	7. b	8. a
9. b	10. c	11. d	12. a
13. c	14. c	15. b	16. b
17. d	18. c	19. a	

Short Answer/Essay

Refer to your textbook for answers. If you are unsure of an answer and cannot generate the answer after reviewing your book, ask your professor for clarification.

CHAPTER 15

How Are Tests Used In Organizational Settings?

After completing your study of this chapter, you should be able to do the following:

- Discuss the history of employment testing in the United States during the 20th century.
- Report the strengths and weaknesses of the traditional interview and the structured interview for assessing job candidates.
- Describe the characteristics of a performance test, and discuss two types of performance tests used by organizations.
- Describe the five-factor model of personality, and name two tests that are based on this model.
- Discuss two types of integrity tests, and describe the criticism these tests have received.
- Discuss performance appraisal instruments, give examples of three types of rating scales, and describe four types of rating errors.

"When I applied for a job, the company had two people interview me. The interviewers asked very similar questions about the same topics. Isn't one interview enough?"

"The company I interviewed with also asked me to complete a written test. What was that for?"

"Where I work, they do random drug tests. One time I tested positive because I took some cough syrup the night before. I really resent being treated like a criminal!"

"It's performance appraisal time again. My future depends on these ratings, and I'm not convinced they really show what a good worker I am."

Business and government have a long history of using psychological tests for hiring, performance evaluation, and research. In this chapter, we focus on how psychological tests are used in organizations. We begin with a brief history of the role psychological assessment has played in organizations. We examine various types of tests that employers use for hiring and evaluating employees, such as interviews and tests of performance, personality, and integrity. We consider legal constraints on employment testing legislated by Congress and interpreted by the executive branch and the federal court system. Finally, we describe how organizations use psychological assessment to evaluate employee performance.

A Short History of Employment Testing

Chapter 1 provided information about the history of psychological testing in general. As the United States moved into the 20th century, the idea that businesses could use scientific principles, including psychological assessment, to increase productivity became popular. Psychologists such as Walter Dill Scott, Hugo Münsterberg, and Walter Bingham began studying psychological principles and applying them to the world of work. Both Scott and Münsterberg proposed methods for validating employment tests prior to World War I (Katzell & Austin, 1992).

The Scientific Selection of Salesmen

In 1915, Scott published "The Scientific Selection of Salesmen," in which he proposed that employers use group tests for personnel selection. These tests evaluated constructs such as "native intellectual ability" and were part of a scientific selection system to assess "character" and "manner." Scott's (1915) evaluation system inspired interest and debate among academic psychologists, who questioned the scientific legitimacy of such systems, but this controversy did not deter Scott from continuing to pursue his goal of developing tests for business use.

Scott's influence among applied psychologists increased as America moved into World War I. Scott proposed to both the military and the academic community that it was possible to design tests to determine fitness for military jobs such as artilleryman and pilot. Political infighting among psychologists who were advising the military, however, resulted in Scott's withdrawal from the group that developed the U.S. Army's Alpha test (Von Mayrhauser, 1987), which was an early type of intelligence test used with recruits who could read. Scott went on to consult with private industry, and his influence in the field of employment testing had a lasting effect. For instance, his salesmen selection system years later provided the basis for a system for selecting life insurance salespeople developed by the Life Insurance Agency Management Association (Katzell & Austin, 1992).

The Legacy of World War I

Various proposals from psychologists led to the development of the U.S. Army's Alpha and Beta tests during World War I. As you recall from Chapter 2, the misuse of these intelligence tests began a controversy about intelligence tests that survives today.

Following World War I, psychologists continued investigating the advantages of employment testing. They also began studying methods for measuring job performance, and they proposed methods for placing workers in various industrial jobs based on their skills and qualifications. For example, Millicent Pond studied the selection and placement of apprentice metal workers (Pond, 1927). Others attempted to use interest inventories (questionnaires that assess a worker's attitudes and interests) to differentiate among occupational groups (Katzell & Austin, 1992). The Strong–Campbell Interest Inventory (first published as the Strong Vocational Interest Blank) originated from this early work and is still in use today.

Two consulting firms that specialized in using tests in organizations emerged during this time. Scott and his colleagues, who developed a number of instruments that included mental ability tests and performance tests for various trades, founded one consulting firm. The other was the Psychological Corporation, organized by J. McKeen Cattell, an organization that continues today under the name Harcourt Assessment as a unit of Pearson, a major publisher.

Testing From World War II to the Present

Psychologists and psychological testing again played a key role during World War II. Bingham, who served as chief psychologist of the War Department, supervised the development of the Army General Classification Test used to place U.S. Army recruits. The Office of Strategic Services explored the assessment center method (featured in Chapter 7). Psychologists also developed new methods for rating personnel and measuring morale and attitudes (Katzell & Austin, 1992).

The use of tests by organizations expanded greatly during the latter half of the 20th century. Large companies and organizations, including the federal government, began using psychological tests for selection, placement, attitude assessment, performance appraisal, and consumer surveys. In addition, the beginning of the civil rights movement in the United States drew attention to issues of test validity and fairness. When Congress passed Title VII of the Civil Rights Act in 1964, it stimulated great interest in fair employment practices, and psychological testing experts eventually played a strong role in developing the federal government's "Uniform Guidelines on Employee Selection Procedures" (1978), introduced in Chapter 2.

Today organizations use psychological tests in a variety of areas. For example, they use the results of tests to make hiring decisions and rating scales to evaluate employees' performance. Organizational surveys are a major source of information about employee attitudes, skills, and motivation. Marketing research involves surveying consumers' attitudes and assessing their behavior. In addition, individuals often use interest inventories to choose or change their career goals.

On the Web Box 15.1 provides web addresses for several large consulting firms that specialize in selecting, developing, and administering tests for organizations.

ON THE WEB BOX 15.1

Human Resources Consulting Firms

 Human resources consulting firms often guide organizations in selecting, developing, and administering paper-and-pencil and Internet-based tests to help the organizations select, develop, and retain their talent. Although many consulting firms are small, several well-known ones serve large businesses, organizations, and government agencies. Visit the following websites to learn more about the well-known consulting firms:

- Wilson Learning Corporation: http://wilsonlearning.com
- Development Dimensions International: www.ddiworld.com
- Mercer: www.mercerhr.com
- Centerpoint for Leaders: www.centerpointforleaders.org
- Drake Inglesi Milardo: www.dimihr.com
- PDI Ninth House: www.personneldecisions.com
- Censeo: www.censeocorp.com
- Center for Creative Leadership: www.ccl.org

When you visit these sites, click on the links to find descriptions of the firms' products and services. On some you will find case studies, career information, and employment opportunities.

INTERIM SUMMARY 15.1
HISTORY OF EMPLOYMENT TESTING

- In 1915, Walter Dill Scott published "The Scientific Selection of Salesmen," in which he proposed that employers use group tests for personnel selection.
- Proposals from psychologists led to the development of the U.S. Army's Alpha and Beta tests during World War I.
- Following World War I, psychologists continued investigating employment testing and began studying methods for measuring job performance and placing workers in jobs based on their skills and qualifications.
- Two consulting firms that specialized in using tests in organizations emerged. One was founded by

Scott, and the other was the Psychological Corporation (now called Harcourt Assessment), organized by J. McKeen Cattell.
- Use of tests by organizations expanded greatly during the latter half of the 20th century.
- Title VII of the Civil Rights Act of 1964 stimulated interest in fair employment practices, and psychologists played a strong role in developing the federal government's "Uniform Guidelines on Employee Selection Procedures" (1978).
- Today organizations use various types of psychological tests to meet their business needs.

Pre-employment Testing

Psychological assessment provides the basis for hiring employees in most organizations. The most popular method of assessment is the employment interview. Organizations sometimes supplement interviewing with one or more psychological tests that measure performance, skills, abilities, or personality characteristics. During the past decade, drug and integrity testing—not polygraphs (lie detectors)—have also become acceptable methods for screening out candidates who may have undesirable behaviors or attitudes.

In the News Box 15.1 describes four myths that business executives cite as their reasons for not using pre-employment testing.

IN THE NEWS

Box 15.1   Four Myths About Pre-employment Testing

Unfortunately, some organizations—both large and small—avoid using reliable and valid tests for hiring. Here are four myths they often cite as their reasons for relying on unstructured interviews and tests that have not been validated.

Myth 1: The organization will be sued

Organizations are always at risk of being sued; however, using reliable and valid selection tools can increase productivity and retention. In the event that a suit is brought against an employer, the first line of defense is to demonstrate that the test was a valid predictor of job performance and consistent with business necessity. There are also many types of employment tests that research has shown do not discriminate against people who belong to a protected class (such as race, gender, and age).

Myth 2: Pre-employment tests cost too much

Published employment tests with documentation of reliability and validity can be expensive to purchase and administer. Purchase costs may range from $25 to $200 per individual. However, most researchers and human resources professionals agree that the cost of a bad hiring decision is much greater. Hiring an unsuitable person results in lower productivity, lost opportunities, an unfilled position, coaching or training costs, and possibly the cost of hiring a replacement. Every dollar an employer invests in testing has a substantial return on investment in reduced absenteeism, improved productivity, lower turnover, safer working environments, reduced insurance premiums, and decreased employer liability.

Myth 3: Pre-employment testing is too time-consuming

Some tests, such as structured interviews, do indeed take time from several people in the organization as well as the time of the applicant. However, new tests and testing formats are now available that can be administered efficiently and accurately and can be scored in as little as 30 minutes. Some are administered using a computer (see Chapter 4), and applicants can even take some tests prior to applying for a job.

Testing systems that provide interpretive reports that can be shared with supervisors and others in the organization save time in the decision-making process. Employers might find that a reliable and valid testing system actually expedites the hiring process.

Of course, the more important the job, the more important it is to choose the right candidate. For executive positions, some organizations use a one- or two-day assessment center process. Given the costs of making bad hiring decisions, these organizations still find this process beneficial and time-saving.

Myth 4: Pre-employment testing does not work

In spite of some 100 years of scientific research on selection tests, some executives may still find the process of testing to be counterintuitive. These executives often believe that they can spot a good or unsuitable job candidate in a brief interview. Fortunately, both the research literature and professional publications report on the benefits of using a reliable and valid testing system for screening job applicants. In addition, most test publishers and human resources consultants will conduct a validity study within the organization that can provide quantitative evidence that the test works and that the benefits of using the test outweigh the costs.

SOURCE: Adapted with permission from Poskey, M. (2005). Myths of psychological testing for candidate selection. *Recruiter Magazine Online*. Retrieved June 19, 2010, from http://www.recruiter.com/magazineonline/120702_feature_pm_022803_2.cfm

The Employment Interview

The employment interview is the most popular method of pre-employment assessment used by organizations. Types of interviews vary from the **traditional interview,** in which the interviewer pursues different areas of inquiry with each job candidate, to highly **structured interviews,** which are standardized with the same questions asked of each job candidate. We focus on the ends of this continuum, keeping in mind that employers often use interviews that have varying amounts of flexibility and structure.

Traditional Interview

Few managers are willing to risk hiring an employee they have not met. The traditional, unstructured interview serves the "getting to know you" function; however, research shows that it falls far short of being a reliable or valid predictor of job performance. The unstructured interview's shortcomings were apparent in 1915 to Scott, who reported disagreement among managers interviewing potential salesmen (Cascio, 1991). Current research provides little evidence that the traditional, unstructured interview is either reliable or valid. For instance, a meta-analysis (that is, a synthesis of research results from different yet similar studies) of interviews used to predict supervisory ratings yielded a validity coefficient of .14 (Hunter & Hunter, 1984).

Researchers have found traditional interviews to be plagued with bias associated with the sex, age, race, and physical attractiveness of the interviewee (Arvey, 1979). Some researchers have argued that such bias is associated more with the competence of the interviewer than with the method itself (Dreher, Ash, & Hancock, 1988). These researchers suggest that increasing interviewers' awareness of their own perceptual bias may increase the validity of the interview. To increase the validity of the interview, Cascio (1991) suggests that all interviewer training include role-playing, training with minorities, and a planned feedback system to inform interviewers about which candidates succeed and which candidates fail.

Structured Interview

Many shortcomings of the traditional interview, including its low reliability and validity, can be overcome by structuring the interview and the interviewing procedure. In the structured interview, the interviewer has a preplanned interview and a quantitative scoring scheme. Each candidate receives the same questions in the same order. The interviewer then rates the candidate's answers on an anchored rating scale. Interviewers undergo training on question delivery, note taking, and rating. Such training standardizes the treatment candidates receive as well as the ratings and resulting interview scores. Such

standardization increases interrater reliability, internal consistency, and validity.

Structured behavioral interviews, which focus on past behaviors rather than attitudes or opinions, also provide better predictions of job performance. Questions that ask candidates to provide specific accounts of the behaviors they have used in the past (for example, planning a project, accomplishing a goal) provide information that is more accurate for interviewers to rate. Some behavioral interviews ask candidates to describe past performance, and others ask candidates to describe how they would go about doing something in the organization, such as develop a marketing plan or training course. Behavioral interviews usually require the interviewer to rate the value of the interviewee's answer using a behaviorally anchored rating scale.

Table 15.1 provides a sample of a structured behavioral interview question intended to assess an applicant's ability to create innovative solutions to business challenges, probing questions that the interviewer may choose to ask to elicit more information, and behavioral standards that provide benchmarks for rating each interviewee's answers.

Table 15.1	Sample Question From a Behavioral Interview

Question: One of the most common management tasks is creating innovative solutions to business problems. Please tell me a time when you were responsible for developing an innovative solution to a specific business problem.	
Probing Questions	*Behavioral Standards*
✓ In what way was the solution you developed innovative?	1. Suggests standard conventional alternatives and does not pursue innovative opportunities
✓ What alternative approaches did you consider, if any?	2. Suggests conventional alternatives but is open to innovative opportunities after probing
✓ How was your solution more or less innovative than the alternatives and the prior approaches?	3. Looks for innovative approaches but only if their success is relatively certain
✓ What were the relative benefits and risks of your approach compared with those of the other approaches?	4. Proposes innovative approaches but does not consider risks as well as benefits
	5. Actively proposes innovative solutions knowing the calculated risks and benefits

Evidence of validity based on content for the structured interview is established by developing questions using a job analysis or detailed job description. For Your Information Box 15.1 describes the process of job analysis.

Using a content strategy, the interview is valid to the extent that it covers important job functions and duties without including information about individual characteristics that are unrelated to job performance. As we discuss later in this chapter, evidence that the interview is job related is especially important in the event that an employer is sued because of claims that the selection system disadvantaged one group of applicants over another.

Research suggests that the interview will continue as a primary method of assessing job candidates. Unfortunately, many companies continue to use traditional interviews instead of structured interviews. Di Milia (2004) reports that human resources professionals in Australia strongly support using structured interviews conducted by two or three interviewers.

Interviews do serve useful purposes other than prediction of job performance. For instance, interviewers can provide candidates with useful information regarding the organization and can set expectations

---

FYI

FOR YOUR INFORMATION BOX 15.1

Job Analysis

"What do you do?" is a common question asked at parties or social gatherings. For organizations, it is an important question that has many implications for managing people. Even if you know a person well, you may have only a general idea of what his or her job requires. Organizations require specific information about the activities of employees so as to make important decisions about hiring, training, and evaluating employees.

Job analysis is a systematic assessment method for answering the "What do you do?" question in organizations. There are a number of ways to conduct job analysis, all of which provide a systematic and detailed procedure for documenting the activities of the job. A typical job analysis provides information on the following job factors:

- *Functions*: A group of activities that allow the job incumbent to accomplish one of the primary objectives of the job. Examples include analyzing financial data, coordinating interdepartmental communications, and supervising employees.
- *Tasks*: Actions taken by the job incumbent that accomplish a job function. Examples include estimating sales revenue to prepare a budget and monitoring customer service representatives to ensure high standards of courtesy.
- *Knowledge*: A body of related information that the worker needs to know to perform job tasks. Examples include knowledge of company policies regarding budget procedures and knowledge of the company's products and services.
- *Skills*: A group of observable and measurable behaviors acquired through training that the worker needs to perform a variety of job tasks. Examples include skill in planning and prioritizing work activities and skill in listening to others.
- *Abilities*: A physical or mental competency based on innate characteristics (generally not trained) that the worker needs to perform job tasks. Examples include the ability to stand for extended periods and the ability to lift up to 50 pounds.
- *Other characteristics*: Interests or personality traits that the worker needs to perform in or cope with the job environment. Examples include the willingness to work night shifts, conscientiousness, and honesty.

Most job analysis methods involve interviewing incumbents (persons currently in the job) and their supervisors and verifying that information by administering a job analysis questionnaire. The questionnaire asks incumbents and supervisors to rate job tasks on their importance and how often they are performed. Tasks that are identified as important and frequently performed become *critical tasks*. The critical tasks are then analyzed to determine the knowledge, skills, abilities, and other characteristics that the job incumbent needs to be successful in performing them. Table 15.2 shows a portion of a job analysis questionnaire. Table 15.3 shows the results of the same questionnaire completed by four raters.

Job analysis is an important prerequisite to employment testing because psychologists and the court system recognize it as a method for providing evidence of validity based on content. For example, a job analysis for "real estate salesperson" may specify a need for knowledge of local zoning laws, interpersonal skills, an ability to climb several flights of stairs, and a willingness to work on Sundays. Therefore, when assessing job applicants for real estate salesperson, the organization should choose assessment methods that yield information on those factors. Other factors, such as a college degree, might seem appealing, but unless they are specified in the job analysis, they would not be appropriate job requirements.

SOURCE: Adapted from McIntire, S. A., Bucklan, M. A., & Scott, D. R. (1995). *The job analysis kit*. Odessa, FL: Psychological Assessment Resources.

Table 15.2	Sample Portion of a Job Analysis Survey

PART I: Please read and rate each task statement using the scales below.												
Task Importance *The extent to which performance of the task is important to successful performance of the job*						*Task Frequency* *The frequency with which the task is performed*						
This task is . . . 0. Not applicable/not performed 1. Not important to successful job performance 2. Somewhat important to successful job performance 3. Important to successful job performance 4. Very important to successful job performance 5. Extremely important to successful job performance						Generally, this task is performed: 0. Not applicable/not performed 1. Less than once per month 2. 1–3 times per month 3. 1 time per week 4. 2–3 times per week 5. Daily or very frequently						
INVENTORY AND FILE MANAGEMENT												
1. Log on to network to access available necessary files	0	1	2	3	4	5	0	1	2	3	4	5
2. Compare available files with certification priority list to determine which files to schedule for download, copy, or batch	0	1	2	3	4	5	0	1	2	3	4	5
3. Schedule download time for applications	0	1	2	3	4	5	0	1	2	3	4	5
4. Check files to confirm previous day's downloads	0	1	2	3	4	5	0	1	2	3	4	5
DATA ENTRY												
5. Log on to network to access legal documents and prepare for data entry	0	1	2	3	4	5	0	1	2	3	4	5
6. Review source material to determine pertinent information for data entry	0	1	2	3	4	5	0	1	2	3	4	5
7. Enter data from source materials in applications according to company guidelines	0	1	2	3	4	5	0	1	2	3	4	5
8. Update transfer report to track workflow on certification documents	0	1	2	3	4	5	0	1	2	3	4	5

about what the job will entail. When candidates have realistic expectations, they are likely to remain on the job longer than will candidates who did not receive legitimate information about the job (J. W. Jones & Youngblood, 1993; Meglino, DeNisi, Youngblood, & Williams, 1988). In addition, the interview provides an opportunity to begin building positive relationships that will help new employees adjust and will prevent negative perceptions among those who are not selected for hire.

Table 15.3 Sample Portion of the Survey Results for the Items Shown in Table 15.2

Function	Item	Importance						Frequency						Mean Criticality
		Rater 1	Rater 2	Rater 3	Rater 4	Standard Deviation	Mean Importance	Rater 1	Rater 2	Rater 3	Rater 4	Standard Deviation	Mean Frequency	
Inventory and File Management														
	1.0	2.0	1.0	1.0	0.0	0.8	1.0	1.0	1.0	0.0	0.0	0.6	0.5	0.8
	2.0	2.0	1.0	1.0	0.0	0.8	1.0	1.0	1.0	0.0	0.0	0.6	0.5	0.8
	3.0	2.0	1.0	1.0	0.0	0.8	1.0	1.0	1.0	0.0	0.0	0.6	0.5	0.8
	4.0	2.0	1.0	1.0	0.0	0.8	1.0	1.0	1.0	0.0	0.0	0.6	0.5	0.8
Data Entry														
	5.0	3.0	4.0	3.0	4.0	0.6	3.5	5.0	5.0	5.0	5.0	0.0	5.0	4.3
	6.0	4.0	3.0	5.0	5.0	1.0	4.3	5.0	5.0	5.0	5.0	0.0	5.0	4.6
	7.0	4.0	4.0	5.0	5.0	0.6	4.5	5.0	5.0	5.0	5.0	0.0	5.0	4.8
	8.0	3.0	1.0	5.0	5.0	1.9	3.5	4.0		5.0	5.0	0.6	3.5	3.5

NOTE: The standard deviation is a measure of agreement among the raters. A low standard deviation indicates high agreement, and a high standard deviation indicates disagreement among the raters. Mean criticality is calculated by summing the mean importance and the mean frequency and then dividing by 2. Thus, the tasks that are rated most important and most frequent will be the most critical ones.

Performance Tests

This category of tests includes a broad range of assessments that require the test taker to perform one or more job tasks. For instance, **assessment centers** (described in detail in Chapter 7) are large-scale simulations of the job that require candidates to solve typical job problems by role-playing or to demonstrate proficiency at job functions such as making presentations and fulfilling administrative duties. **Work samples** are smaller-scale assessments in which candidates complete a job-related task such as building a sawhorse or designing a doghouse. A driving test is a performance test that organizations often use to assess people applying for jobs as heavy equipment operators or bus drivers.

Psychologists often categorize performance tests as either high or low fidelity. **High-fidelity tests** replicate job settings as realistically as possible. In a high-fidelity assessment, test takers use the same equipment that is used on the job and complete actual job tasks. For instance, pilots are often trained and assessed on sophisticated flight simulators that not only simulate flight but also re-create typical emergencies. Such high-fidelity tests allow job candidates to perform in realistic situations; however, they remove the risk of unsafe or poor performance. In other words, if the job applicant does not fly the plane well, the resulting crash is simulated, not real!

Low-fidelity tests, on the other hand, simulate the task using a written, verbal, or visual description. The test taker may respond by answering an open-ended or multiple-choice question. Some interview questions serve as low-fidelity performance tests. For example, **behavioral interview** questions ask respondents to describe a situation and give detailed information about how they performed in that situation. As you might imagine, answers to low-fidelity tests provide less accurate and useful information than does performance on high-fidelity tests. Low-fidelity tests, however, are less expensive to design and implement.

Performance tests generally yield high validity coefficients when they are designed as miniature reproductions of the job itself. A meta-analysis by Hunter and Hunter (1984) found an average validity of .54 for performance tests predicting job performance criteria. Validation studies of assessment centers have shown comparable results (Gaugler, Rosenthal, Thornton, & Bentson, 1987). Because performance tests are developed using actual job tasks and activities, they also demonstrate a high degree of evidence for validity based on their content as well as face validity.

Personality Inventories

Personality inventories measure enduring constructs usually referred to as **personality traits.** Traits such as conscientiousness, extraversion, and agreeableness are seen by personality theorists as constructs that predispose persons to behavior in certain ways. Personality theorists also suggest that the strength of various traits varies from person to person. Therefore, we might expect a person who has a high degree of extraversion to be more outgoing and energetic in a social situation than a person with a low degree of extraversion.

Cattell began conducting studies on personality assessment during the 1940s that culminated in 1949 with the publication of the 16 Personality Factor Questionnaire (16PF). Cattell's test, which stimulated the development of a number of tests and is itself in its fifth edition, defines the adult personality in terms of 16 normal personality factors. Researchers have found relationships between some factors on the 16PF and absenteeism and turnover. The 16PF has also been used to predict tenure, safety, and job performance (Krug & Johns, 1990).

More detail about the 16 Personality Factor Questionnaire can be found in Test Spotlight 14.2 in Appendix A.

The psychological literature contains numerous personality theories and as many or more personality tests. One widely accepted personality theory is the **five-factor model,** which proposes that there are five central personality dimensions: extroversion (also called surgency), emotional stability, agreeableness, conscientiousness, and openness to experience. For Your Information Box 15.2 provides a brief description of this theory and its five core dimensions.

FYI

FOR YOUR INFORMATION BOX 15.2

The Five-Factor Theory of Personality

The five-factor theory of personality arose from the work of Warren Norman, who obtained a large number of personality ratings and used factor analysis to determine the underlying constructs of personality (Liebert & Spiegler, 1994). (Chapter 9 provided an overview of the statistical procedure of factor analysis.) From the personality ratings, Norman extracted five factors that he named *surgency, emotional stability, agreeableness, conscientiousness,* and *culture.* Subsequent research has generally confirmed Norman's early findings of five factors, including evidence that the same factors exist in German, Portuguese, Hebrew, Chinese, Korean, and Japanese languages.

Robert McCrae and Paul Costa later made significant contributions to the five-factor theory by demonstrating a variety of applications and developing three personality inventories—the original NEO Personality Inventory (NEO PI; discussed in Chapter 1), the current NEO Personality Inventory–Revised (NEO PI-R), and the shorter NEO Five Factor Inventory (NEO-FFI)—that assess personality using the five-factor model. McCrae and Costa defined each factor as a continuum:

- Neuroticism/Stability
- Extraversion/Introversion
- Openness
- Agreeableness/Antagonism
- Conscientiousness/Undirectedness

SOURCES: Liebert, R. M., & Spiegler, M. D. (1994). *Personality strategies and issues* (7th ed.). Pacific Grove, CA: Brooks/Cole; and McCrae, R. R., & Costa, P. T., Jr. (1997). Personality trait structure as a human universal. *American Psychologist, 52,* 509–516.

Test Spotlight 15.1 in Appendix A describes the Hogan Personality Inventory (HPI; Hogan & Hogan, 1992), which is partially derived from the five-factor model and is widely used for organizational testing and decision making. A link to a sample report that might be used when the HPI is used for employee selection is included in that test spotlight.

Traditionally, personnel psychologists discouraged using personality tests as employment tests because research seemed to show the relationship between personality and job performance to be minimal at best,

and nonexistent in many cases. For instance, Hunter and Hunter's (1984) meta-analysis suggests that personality tests are among the poorest predictors of job performance. Recently, however, personnel psychologists have begun to look more favorably on personality tests that reflect the five-factor model (Gatewood & Feild, 1997; Heneman, Heneman, & Judge, 1997). One meta-analysis, by Barrick

 More detail about the Hogan Personality Inventory can be found in Spotlight 15.1 in Appendix A.

and Mount (1991), suggests that *conscientiousness* serves as a valid predictor of job performance for all occupational groups studied using three types of criteria. *Extraversion* and *emotional stability* appear to be valid predictors of job performance for some, but not all, occupations. Gatewood and Feild posit that "specific personality dimensions appear to be related to specific jobs and criteria" (p. 601).

More recent reviews have suggested that personality measures can be quite valuable in organizational decision making. Ones, Dilchert, Viswesvaran, and Judge (2007) state that the "Big Five personality variables as a set predict important organizational behaviors (e.g., job performance, leadership and even work attitudes and motivation)" (p. 1010). They report moderate to strong relationships ranging from .20 to .50.

Integrity Testing

Economic pressures for businesses to become more efficient and competitive have contributed to a growing concern with employee theft and other issues related to the honesty and integrity of workers. According to the 2002 Retail Security Survey conducted by the University of Florida, employees are responsible for 48.5% of retail theft, costing retailers $15 billion annually (Horan, 2003). Fitzgerald (2003) calls dishonest employees "the enemy within" (p. G7), and she notes that in Canada retail employees are responsible for 33% of theft, just short of the 38% by customers, according to the Retail Council of Canada. Writing in *Forbes,* Schoenberger (2004) has this to say about data theft by employees: "Integrity, not ability or the fear of getting caught, is all that separates a conscientious employee from a thief" (p. 82).

Horan (2003), writing in *Chain Store Age,* suggests that employers customize alarm systems to catch employees leaving the store with store merchandise. However, according to Fitzgerald (2003), the first line of defense is prevention, and employers need to "hire smart" by asking the right questions of applicants. Assessments for integrity fall into two general categories: physiological measures and paper-and-pencil tests.

Polygraph Testing

The **polygraph**—or lie detector test—is the best-known physiological measure associated with evaluating how truthfully an individual responds to questioning. The process was invented by William Marston, who created Wonder Woman, an early comic book character who elicited the truth from criminals with her magic lasso (Lilienfeld, 1993). A trained polygraph administrator interprets physiological data recorded by a polygraph machine. The machine generates a number of graphs of physiological responses such as skin resistance, pulse or heart rate, and respiration.

The theory behind the use of the polygraph suggests that when an individual gives an untruthful response, he or she exhibits increases in skin resistance, pulse or heart rate, and respiration. To evaluate honesty, the administrator asks a set of predetermined questions that establishes a physiological baseline for truthful responses. Then the administrator asks other questions regarding topics such as employee theft. When an individual's physiological response increases above the baseline, the administrator may judge that the test taker did not answer the questions truthfully.

There are two problems with this theory. First, an individual's physiological responses may increase for a number of reasons, such as general discomfort and nervousness. Second, some individuals can control their physiological responses better than other individuals can. Lilienfeld (1993) concludes that there is no scientific evidence that a specific "lie response" exists and suggests that polygraph users are making the "Othello error"—taking signs of distress as proof of unfaithfulness or dishonesty.

Gatewood and Feild (1997) state that the major drawback to using polygraphs for selection is that they generate a high rate of **false positives**—mistakenly classifying innocent test takers as guilty. In addition, polygraphs may also misclassify a large number of guilty individuals as innocent (Lilienfeld, 1993). Ruscio (2005) points out two myths regarding polygraph testing. The first is that the polygraph process is a scientific and objective way to learn whether a person is lying or telling the truth. The second is that polygraph testing is infallible and contains no error. Ruscio concludes that organizations need to find other processes to replace or supplement polygraph testing.

The Employee Polygraph Protection Act of 1988, which forbids the use of the polygraph as an employment test, was passed by Congress in recognition of the stigma associated with incorrectly labeling applicants as untruthful and causing them to be rejected for employment. Although some employers (for example, those that provide security services, government agencies) are exempted from the 1988 federal law, the poor predictive validity of polygraphs makes their usefulness for any situation highly suspect. For Your Information Box 15.3 describes the ambivalent attitude the U.S. Congress and the executive branch have demonstrated regarding scientific studies of the polygraph.

FYI

FOR YOUR INFORMATION BOX 15.3

Science or Voodoo?

In 1988, when the Employee Polygraph Protection Act became law, Peter Persaud was pleased with its constraints on polygraph testing for selection. Earlier that year, Persaud had been denied a job as vice president at a bank in Miami because he had failed two polygraph tests. Furthermore, Persaud stated, he was angered by the examiner who persistently asked questions about stealing and kickbacks and who expressed disbelief when Persaud told her that he had no credit card debt and that he owned two houses without mortgages (Karr, 1988). At the time, many in science and government believed that the ban on polygraph testing, which did not apply to federal agencies, did not go far enough.

In March 2001, after the arrest of Russian spy Robert Hanssen, Federal Bureau of Investigation (FBI) Director Louis Freeh decided to increase polygraph testing of bureau workers with access to intelligence information ("FBI Director Freeh Orders Stepped-Up Polygraph Tests," 2001). In spite of scientific studies that pointed out problems with the validity of polygraph testing, the FBI was using polygraphs to screen FBI agents for hiring. Aldrich Ames, arrested two years later and convicted of spying while working for the Central Intelligence Agency (CIA), might have been apprehended sooner if the agency had not relied on polygraph testing to clear Ames from suspicion. The arrests of Hanssen and Ames humiliated and discredited the FBI, the CIA, and the broader intelligence community.

In August 2001, the senators from New Mexico introduced a bill to limit polygraph testing of personnel at the U.S. Department of Energy (DOE) nuclear weapons facilities. The bill directed the DOE to exempt more employees from polygraph testing and to consult the National Academy of Sciences (NAS) research on polygraph testing at the DOE in order to establish a permanent testing program. The reason for the bill was the imposition by Congress of polygraph testing at Los Alamos National Laboratory and other sites as an extra security measure. Scientists and other personnel at the facilities blamed the polygraph for a decline in morale and difficulty in recruiting and retaining qualified employees ("Sen. Pete Domenici Introduced a Bill," 2001).

Two years later, after the completion of the NAS report, the DOE ignored the academy's research that recommended against using polygraphs for security screening. Instead, the DOE issued a statement maintaining that it did not believe the polygraph accuracy issues raised by the NAS warranted abandoning use of the polygraph as a screening tool (Frazier, 2003). Donald Kennedy (2003), writing in *Science,* stated that the DOE has otherwise relied on scientific knowledge and principles to carry out its responsibilities. For instance, the agency started the Human Genome Project, supports alternative energy research, and administers programs in biomedical research, science, and technology. Finally, the department continually pledged to use the best science when carrying out its responsibilities. Kennedy believed that the polygraph ruling reflected bad science.

By the end of the year, the DOE changed its earlier stance and recommended a decrease in testing of approximately 75%. One scientist at Lawrence Livermore National Laboratory stated the polygraph was still a *voodoo test* (Frazier, 2003).

Paper-and-Pencil Integrity Tests

As an alternative to physiological tests for screening applicants, a number of publishers now offer paper-and-pencil tests. These fall into two categories: overt tests and personality-oriented tests. Overt tests ask test takers to provide information about their past behavior (for example, "How many times have you borrowed cash from an employer without permission?") or to respond to hypothetical situations (for example, "Is it okay to make personal phone calls from work?"). Personality-oriented tests purport to measure characteristics that are predictive of honest behavior and positive organizational citizenship using items that relate to the Big Five personality factors. Although both types yield similar results, the differences between overt and personality-oriented tests relate to the underlying constructs measured by the tests. Overt tests correlate with honesty and supervision attitudes, and personality-oriented tests correlate with self/impulse control, home life/upbringing, risk taking/thrill seeking, diligence, and emotional stability (Wanek, Sackett, & Ones, 2003).

Paper-and-pencil integrity tests have been the subject of much research and debate among psychologists. A meta-analysis of validation studies of integrity tests yielded encouraging results (Ones, Viswesvaran, & Schmidt, 1993). First, although prediction of documented thefts was low (.13), integrity tests predicted counterproductive behaviors much better (.29 vs. .39). Second, there was evidence that these validities generalized across situations. Finally, in addition to predicting counterproductive behaviors, the meta-analysis showed that integrity tests correlated with supervisory ratings of job performance at .41.

Critics rightly point out, however, that studies available for Ones and colleagues' (1993) meta-analysis were conducted by the test publishers themselves—not by independent researchers—and that such studies often contained serious methodological flaws (Camara & Schneider, 1994, 1995; Lilienfeld, 1993). Other researchers have expressed concerns that integrity tests may systematically misclassify some honest individuals as dishonest and that most paper-and-pencil integrity tests are highly susceptible to faking (Lilienfeld, Alliger, & Mitchell, 1995).

An interesting study reported by Lilienfeld (1993) tested 41 monks and nuns—assumed to excel in the trait of honesty—using a well-known honesty test. The monks and nuns scored lower (more dishonest) than did a group of college students and a group of incarcerated criminals! Lilienfeld concludes that honesty tests, designed as an alternative to the polygraph, suffer from the same deficiencies as does the lie detector.

The use and understanding of paper-and-pencil honesty tests has grown; however, researchers continue to investigate their use as pre-employment tests, including their lack of adverse impact and their use as predictors of organizational outcomes (Wanek et al., 2003).

 Test Spotlight 15.2 in Appendix A describes the Wonderlic Basic Skills Test, a cognitive test used by organizations.

Cognitive Tests

Cognitive tests are assessments that measure the test taker's mental capabilities, such as general mental ability tests, intelligence tests, and academic skills tests. Most cognitive tests have been developed for use in educational or clinical settings. When a job analysis indicates that cognitive skills are important for high performance, cognitive tests are useful for inclusion in a pre-employment assessment. Hunter and Hunter (1984) found that the validity of cognitive tests for pre-employment screening were the most accurate for "thinking" jobs ($r = .53$) such as manager and salesperson.

Barrett, Polomsky, and McDaniel (1999) conducted a meta-analysis of the validity of written tests used in the selection and training of firefighters. Cognitive tests showed high validity (.42) with job performance criteria and even higher validity for predicting training criteria.

Legal Constraints

When Congress passed the Civil Rights Act of 1964, one of the specific areas addressed was hiring by organizations. As discussed in Chapter 2, Title VII of the Civil Rights Act covered employment practices, including psychological testing that resulted in discrimination against minorities and women. Following passage of the Civil Rights Act, various federal agencies in the executive branch as well as the federal courts began to issue guidelines and case law that sought to define the steps organizations should take to comply with the requirements of Title VII. The proliferation of guidelines and case law resulted in the federal government's publication of the "Uniform Guidelines on Employee Selection Procedures" (1978). Note that Congress did not pass the Uniform Guidelines, and therefore they are not federal law. However, they do suggest procedures for organizations to follow that enhance the fairness and legal defensibility of their employment practices. The Uniform Guidelines were compiled with the help of psychologists and present what can be referred to as "best practices" when using psychological tests in organizations. On the Web Box 15.2 directs you to the Uniform Guidelines on the web. While the Civil Rights Act is usually viewed as one legal mechanism for protected groups such as women and minorities to challenge a selection procedure, it also has been used to challenge "reverse discrimination," a situation in which a majority group feels that it has been harmed because of an allegation that less qualified minority candidates were chosen for jobs. See In The News Box 15.2 for an unusual example of a reverse discrimination case that the Supreme Court recently decided.

According to federal case law, any process that is used to make a hiring decision is defined as a test. Therefore, the Uniform Guidelines apply to all employment screening devices—including application blanks (forms), reference checks, letters of reference, and even employment interviews. The Uniform Guidelines and federal case law suggest that all employment tests should be job related and based on a job analysis. Employers should use only tests for which there is evidence of validity for the scores. Organizations should maintain records regarding the race, sex, and ethnic group membership of the applicant pool and the final group of persons hired for the job. When a test results in adverse impact—exclusion of a disproportionate number of persons in a group protected by federal law, referred to as a **protected class**—the employer should find an alternative method for assessing job candidates. Since the publication of the Uniform Guidelines, industrial/organizational psychologists have been conducting research to find testing instruments that not only have significant evidence of validity but also yield results that do not discriminate against a protected class.

One issue that frequently arises in organizations that wish to use a pre-employment test for selecting employees is demonstrating that the test is valid for use in that organization. You may remember from Chapter 7 that validity is not a function of the test itself, but rather whether there is evidence to support the interpretation of the test scores. Also, you will remember that one piece of evidence of validity for a pre-employment test would be data that show that people who score higher on the test do better on the job. You have learned that there are a couple of ways in which this evidence can be gathered (predictive method and concurrent method). In practice, however, data gathering and validation studies may be seen as too expensive and time-consuming for an organization to undertake. For example, hiring new employees is often an immediate business need, and conducting validity research can be time-consuming. Second, to develop some types of validity evidence, such as evidence

---

ON THE WEB BOX 15.2

Uniform Guidelines on Employee Selection Procedures

www.dol.gov/dol/allcfr/title_41/part_60-3/toc.htm

 The U.S. Department of Labor website contains the complete Uniform Guidelines on Employee Selection Procedures as they appeared in the *Federal Register* in 1978. Although the Uniform Guidelines are more than 25 years old, they still apply to organizations today.

The Uniform Guidelines contain 18 sections, as shown below. As you can see, they refer directly to the issues of psychological testing discussed in this textbook. Consequently, psychological testing in organizations, unlike psychological testing in other settings, is regulated by the federal government.

Section	Title
60-3.1	Statement of purpose
60-3.2	Scope
60-3.3	Discrimination defined: Relationship between use of selection procedures and discrimination
60-3.4	Information on impact
60-3.5	General standards for validity studies
60-3.6	Use of selection procedures which have not been validated
60-3.7	Use of other validity studies
60-3.8	Cooperative studies
60-3.9	No assumption of validity
60-3.10	Employment agencies and employment services
60-3.11	Disparate treatment
60-3.12	Retesting of applicants
60-3.13	Affirmative action
60-3.14	Technical standards for validity studies
60-3.15	Documentation of impact and validity evidence
60-3.16	Definitions
60-3.17	Policy statement on affirmative action (see section 13B)
60-3.18	Citations

SOURCE: U.S. Department of Labor. (n.d.). *Uniform guidelines on employee selection procedures.* Retrieved June 8, 2010, from www.dol.gov/dol/allcfr/title_41/part_60-3/toc.htm

IN THE NEWS

Box 15.2   Supreme Court Decides a Reverse Discrimination Case— Ricci v. DeStefano

On July 1, 2009, the Supreme Court handed down a decision in a case brought by a group of firefighters, 18 White and 1 Hispanic, that centered around the examination that the City of New Haven, Connecticut, used for making promotional decisions to the rank of Lieutenant and Captain. In 2003, the city had used a professionally designed multiple-choice test along with an oral examination to make promotional decisions. The multiple-choice exam comprised 60% of the final score, while the oral examination comprised 40%. After receiving the test scores, the city realized that no African American firefighters and only one Hispanic firefighter would be promoted if the city used the test scores to make the promotion decisions. Because the results disproportionately favored the White candidates, the city feared that it would face an adverse-impact lawsuit from the minority candidates if it went forward with the promotions. As a result, the city decided to discard the test scores and not promote anyone. The White firefighters who had passed the test, and would have been eligible for promotion had the test been used, filed a suit of their own against the city. They claimed they had been intentionally discriminated against based on their race because they had been denied promotion even though they scored higher on the test.

The Supreme Court, in a 5-to-4 decision, ruled that the City of New Haven had wrongly denied the White firefighters their promotions. The lead opinion, written by Justice Kennedy, said that the city's fear of an adverse impact lawsuit was not a sufficient reason to discard the results of a test unless there was a "strong basis in evidence" that the city would suffer liability as a result of such a lawsuit, and that no such basis was warranted in this case.

You may be wondering why there would be any question of the city's potential liability had the minority firefighters brought an adverse impact claim given the results of the test. The answer lies in an amendment to Title VII of the 1964 Civil Rights Act passed by Congress in 1991. The law provides that when a test disproportionately disadvantages one group over another, a defense against this claim is to demonstrate that the test was job related (valid), consistent with business necessity, and that there was no equally valid but less discriminatory alternative available. However, during the litigation, the City of New Haven did not claim or provide evidence that they believed that the results should be discarded due to flaws in the design of the test or that the test was not a valid predictor of on-the-job performance.

On the other hand, justices who dissented from the majority were concerned with the fact that nearly 60% of the population of New Haven belonged to a racial minority. If the city used test scores to make promotional decisions, minorities in the future would not be properly represented in the leadership of the fire department, just as they were not represented in the past when there was intentional discrimination.

This case underlines two different views on what is important when tests are used for individual decision making. One view focuses on the validity of the tests—are they job related and equally predictive of future performance for all demographic groups who take the test. The other view focuses on a social policy issue of fairness, concerned with whether there is equality for all groups regarding the outcomes of testing. Clearly, it is important to remember the differences in the two views expressed by the Supreme Court. A test that demonstrates evidence of validity may not be considered fair by everyone, and a test that is considered fair by some may not necessarily be valid. The concepts associated with test validity are centered around scientific issues; the concepts associated with fairness are centered around issues of social policy. What do you think the court should have decided in this case?

based on relationships with criteria, a large number of participants (more than 30) must be available for testing in order to be confident of the results. For an employer who has only a few employees in a particular job, it may be impossible to conduct that type of study.

One of the ways that organizations can deal with this issue is via something referred to as the generalization of validity evidence. There are a number of strategies that can be useful when it becomes necessary to make a case that evidence of validity will generalize from one situation to another. One common strategy for this is **transportability**. Transportability occurs when a case is made that because a test has been shown to be valid for a particular use, it can be presumed to also be valid for another, similar use (Society for Industrial and Organizational Psychology, 2003). The need for this strategy can occur when a test that has been validated for selection of employees into one job is proposed to select employees into a different but similar job.

For instance, suppose a test developer has created a test to hire retail salespeople. While the test was being developed, it was shown to be a valid predictor of sales performance of retail clothing salespeople, household goods salespeople, and giftware salespeople. Now, suppose the owner of a small number of flower shops is looking for a test to help her select her salespeople. It is not likely that she would be in a position to conduct her own local validity study for the reasons cited above. However, the test she is interested in was validated on a group of jobs very similar to the one for which she is hiring. She may be able to presume that the test would be valid for her use as well without actually conducting her own study.

Whether it is appropriate to rely on the concept of transportability when deciding whether to use a test in a different setting or for a different job other than the one for which it was validated is a subjective judgment. There are at least two criteria that should be present before deciding that the validity evidence for a test will generalize. First, a validity study that demonstrates evidence of validity for the original use of the test should have been conducted. Second, there must be evidence that there is a strong similarity between the content and requirements of the job for which the test was originally validated and the new job. For instance, if the test in our example above was proposed for selection of business-to-business telephone equipment salespeople, the transportability argument would be much less compelling because of the large differences between the necessary skill sets of retail salespeople and business-to-business salespeople. Therefore, even if prior research has shown the test to be a valid predictor of success in a retail sales position, it may not be a predictor of success in a business-to-business sales position and it should not be used without a local validation study.

Here is an example of how one of the authors of this book used a transportability strategy to generalize the validity of an assessment center for use with a different company than the one for which it was originally developed. (See Chapter 7 for a discussion of assessment centers.) This assessment center was originally developed and validated for the selection of sales managers for a large telecommunications company. The psychologists who designed the assessment center gathered evidence of its validity by first performing a job analysis of the sales manager's job to identify the knowledge, skills, and abilities (KSAs) necessary to successfully perform the job in this company. Then the psychologists designed the assessment center simulations so that sales managers would be able to demonstrate those KSAs by performing tasks that were similar to those they would actually perform on the job. You may recognize this to be a content-based approach to establishing evidence of validity. (See Chapter 7 for more detail).

After this assessment center was developed and validated, a different telecommunications organization wanted to use the same assessment center to select its sales managers. Because the business need was immediate and the company was only filling a small number of positions, it was not practical to conduct a full validity study to establish evidence of validity specifically for this company. Therefore, the psychologists decided to use a transportability strategy to provide the necessary evidence of validity. To accomplish this, they asked a group of subject matter experts from this company who were very familiar with the requirements of the job to evaluate how closely the KSAs measured in the assessment center matched the KSAs necessary to perform the duties required of their sales managers. Then these experts were asked to determine how closely the simulated tasks contained in the assessment center matched the types of tasks that their sales managers actually performed on the job. The ratings provided by these experts were analyzed to ensure that all the KSAs and tasks contained in the assessment center were relevant to the job performance of the sales managers. The experts' ratings indicated that there was a strong correspondence between what was measured in the assessment center and the requirements of their sales managers' job. Therefore, the psychologists concluded that there was sufficient evidence that the validity of the assessment center could be transported (i.e., would generalize) for the selection of sales managers in the new company.

INTERIM SUMMARY 15.2
PRE-EMPLOYMENT TESTING

- Psychological assessment provides the basis for hiring employees in most organizations.
- The most popular method of assessment is the employment interview.
- Types of interviews vary from the traditional interview, in which the interviewer pursues different areas of inquiry with each job candidate, to highly structured interviews that are standardized with the same questions asked of each job candidate.
- Many shortcomings of the traditional interview, including its low reliability and low validity, can be overcome by structuring the interview and the interviewing procedure.
- Performance tests require the test taker to perform one or more job tasks.
- Personality inventories measure stable and enduring constructs, such as conscientiousness, extraversion, and agreeableness, that may influence individuals to perform certain behaviors.

- One widely accepted personality theory is the five-factor model that proposes five central personality dimensions.
- Integrity tests that predict an employee's predisposal to be dishonest fall into two general categories: physiological measures and paper-and-pencil tests.
- When a job analysis indicates that cognitive skills are important for high performance, cognitive tests are useful for inclusion in a pre-employment assessment.
- The Uniform Guidelines on Employee Selection Procedures suggest procedures for organizations to follow that enhance the fairness and legal defensibility of their employment practices.
- When it is not practical to conduct a local validity study, organizations sometimes rely on a validity transportability approach to demonstrate that a test validated for one job would be appropriate for another similar one.

Performance Appraisal

Most organizations carry out formal evaluations of employees' job performance, called performance appraisal. Usually, each employee's supervisor or manager completes a performance appraisal form that requires assigning numerical values to employees' performance. These performance appraisals qualify legally as tests. Performance appraisals should be a part of an organization's overall business strategy. As such, they often act as organizational interventions and information-gathering procedures.

Addressing the various types of performance appraisal systems is beyond the scope of this textbook; however, in this section we do discuss several psychometric methods that underlie the performance appraisal process.

Ranking Employees

One in five Fortune 500 companies uses **forced ranking** as a method of performance appraisal (Johnson, 2004). As you recall from Chapter 5, when managers rank people, they compare the performance of one employee with that of other employees. To rank employees, the supervisor must decide who is the "best" employee, the "next best" employee, and so on based on predetermined dimensions or criteria.

Another method for performance appraisal is **forced distribution,** which requires the supervisor to assign a certain number of employees to each performance category, such as "poor," "below average," "average," "above average," and "outstanding," so that the appraisals are distributed in a way that resembles a normal curve. Using this method, no matter how well each person performs, some employees will always be ranked as "outstanding" and some will always be ranked as "poor."

The idea that a company must identify and reward top performers with bonuses and development opportunities and must train or dismiss its lowest performers leads to the use of forced ranking and forced distribution. Ranking individuals does prevent a manager from assigning all people to one category—for example, assigning all individuals to the "exceeds expectations" category. On the other hand, ranking employees may result in identifying workers who are performing satisfactorily as "poor" when compared with their peers. Forced ranking and forced distribution are controversial methods of assessing employee performance. Many management consultants advise against them because they may force the supervisor to place an employee into a category that does not accurately describe his or her performance.

Rating Employees

For annual or semiannual performance assessment, most organizations prefer to rate employee performance using a scale that specifies job dimensions or job behaviors. The traditional method for assessing employees is to ask supervisors or managers to rate employee performance. The rating scales are similar to those used in surveys discussed in Chapter 10.

As you can see, Figure 15.1 shows **graphic rating scales** that provide visual indicators to help the manager rate employees. Guided by the numbers or words—called **anchors**—the rater chooses the category that best represents the employee's performance on the specified dimension. Any type of rating format can be used with any rating dimension.

Behaviorally anchored rating scales (BARS) are another rating method that uses on-the-job behaviors as anchors for rating scales that represent job dimensions. Using BARS, such as the sample item in Figure 15.2, the rater chooses the rating category by reading the behaviors and placing a mark on the scale that is most representative of the employee's performance on that dimension. Research on the

Figure 15.1 Examples of Graphic Rating Scales

EXAMPLE A: Check the box that describes the employee on each dimension.

		1	2	3	4	5	
Performance	Low				✓		High
Efficiency	Low			✓			High

EXAMPLE B: Rate the employee's performance.

	Outstanding	Above Average	Average	Below Average	Poor
Performance		✓			
Efficiency			✓		

EXAMPLE C: Choose the example that is most descriptive of the employee.

	Consistently error free	Usually error free	Requires follow-up to correct errors	Frequent errors with time-consuming corrections
Accuracy		✓		

	Submissions are always on time	Submissions are most often on time	Submissions are sometimes on time	Submissions are rarely on time
Timeliness of submissions		✓		

EXAMPLE D: Choose the face that reminds you of the employee.

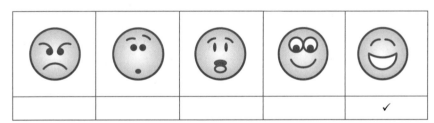

EXAMPLE E: Check all items that apply to the employee.

Courteous	✓		Hard worker	✓
Attentive	✓		Unorganized	
Uninterested			Creative	✓
Inquiring			Shy	

Figure 15.2 Example of a Behaviorally Anchored Rating Scale

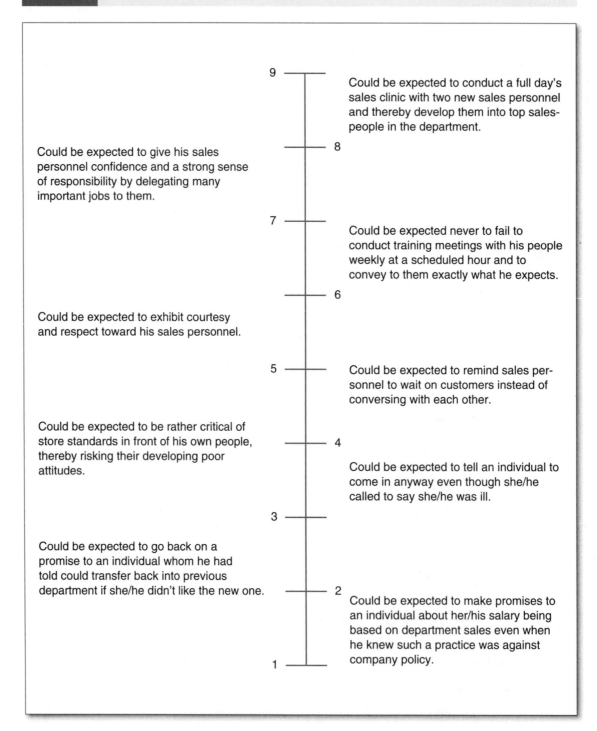

SOURCE: From *Journal of Applied Psychology, 57,* 15–22. Copyright © 1973 by the American Psychological Association.

BARS method suggests that these scales provide more accurate ratings of employee behavior than do traditionally anchored rating scales. However, they are difficult and time-consuming to develop and require concentrated rater training due to their complexity.

Raters can also evaluate performance by rating how frequently the employee performs important behaviors on the job. This method, known as the **behavioral checklist,** is illustrated in Figure 15.3. The checklist can be developed directly from the frequency ratings of the job analysis survey.

| Figure 15.3 | Two Dimensions From a Behavioral Checklist |

TOPIC (APPROPRIATE, INFORMATIVE)

Behavior Shown	Almost Never	A Few Times	Some-times	Many Times	Almost Always
Gave examples from organizations					
Referred to sources when making assertions					
Wandered from the topic					
Demonstrated enthusiasm for topic					
Provided information in a clear and logical order					
Demonstrated knowledge and understanding of the topic					
Defined terms and jargon					

PUBLIC SPEAKING SKILLS

Behavior Shown	Almost Never	A Few Times	Some-times	Many Times	Almost Always
Spoke clearly and audibly					
Connected sentences with "uh," "um," etc.					
Spoke too rapidly for audience understanding					
Spoke in a monotone voice					
Read from notes					
Used distracting gestures					
Used vulgar or politically incorrect language or phrases					

Rating Errors

Ratings of job performance involve making subjective decisions about how to quantify job performance. As you recall, measurement that involves making subjective judgments often contains error. Industrial psychologists have identified a number of systematic rating errors that occur when raters judge employee performance.

- **Leniency errors** result when raters give all employees better ratings than they deserve, and **severity errors** result when raters give all employees worse ratings than they deserve.
- **Central tendency errors** result when raters use only the middle of the rating scale and ignore the highest and lowest scale categories.
- A **halo effect** occurs when raters let their judgment on one dimension influence judgments on other dimensions. For instance, an employee who receives a low rating on "quality of work" may also be rated low on "quantity of work" even though the employee actually meets the performance standards for quantity output.

To avoid inaccurate ratings, organizations should provide rater training for all persons conducting performance appraisals. Because research on rater training (Fay & Latham, 1982) suggests that such training programs usually have only short-term effects, it is a good idea for organizations to provide "brush-up" courses for training raters. Training objectives should include mastering observing behavior, avoiding making rating errors, and maintaining consistent standards across employees (intrarater reliability).

| **Figure 15.4** | Portion of a 360° Feedback Report |

	1 2 3 4 5 6 7 8 9 10	Agrmt	Impt	Difference
Operating in an Ethical Way				
	Avg:	9.30	9.10	0.20
	MGR:	9.00	9.00	0.00
	DRPT:	9.78	9.78	0.00
	PEER:	9.17	8.75	0.42
	CUST:	9.00	8.83	0.17
Focusing on People				
	Avg:	9.11	8.93	0.18
	MGR:	9.00	9.00	0.00
	DRPT:	9.56	9.89	−0.33
	PEER:	8.83	8.17	0.66
	CUST:	9.00	9.00	0.00
Behaving with Integrity				
	Avg:	8.83	9.00	−0.17
	MGR:	8.33	8.33	0.00
	DRPT:	9.11	9.63	−0.51
	PEER:	8.75	8.83	−0.08
	CUST:	8.83	8.83	0.00

SOURCE: Reprinted with permission of Dr. Mimi Hull & Associates.

Who Should Rate?

Traditionally, organizations have given the job of rating employee performance to the employees' supervisor or manager. During recent years, however, companies have begun to use a method of performance appraisal and developmental feedback called **360° feedback.** In this method, employees receive ratings from those they work with on a day-to-day basis, such as their managers, peers, direct reports, and customers. In addition, employees rate themselves. These ratings are aggregated, except for the self-ratings and supervisor ratings, to provide employees with information on every dimension by every rater. This method provides rich feedback for the person being rated and may be perceived by some as fairer because misperceptions or rating errors by one person can be balanced by the opinions of others. Again, careful attention should be paid to training everyone to rate the performance of others honestly. Figure 15.4 shows a portion of a report from a 360° feedback session.

INTERIM SUMMARY 15.3
PERFORMANCE APPRAISAL

- Most organizations carry out formal evaluations of employees' job performance called *performance appraisals*.
- The major types of performance appraisal systems are ranking employees or rating employees on various types of scales.
- The most popular method for rating employee performance uses the graphic rating scale.

- Two other methods are behaviorally anchored rating scales (BARS) and the behavioral checklist.
- Raters need to be trained so they do not make rating errors such as leniency, severity, central tendency, and the halo effect.
- In 360° feedback, individuals are rated by their managers, peers, subordinates, and customers as well as by themselves.

Chapter Summary

During the early 20th century, psychologists such as Walter Dill Scott, Hugo Münsterberg, and Walter Bingham began studying psychological principles and applying them to the world of work. Both Scott and Münsterberg proposed methods for validating employment tests prior to World War I. Following the war, psychologists designed tests for hiring individuals and interest inventories for predicting occupational success. Psychological tests also played a key role in World War II that provided an impetus for development of assessment centers. Since World War II, organizations have made use of psychological tests for selection and placement of new employees, evaluation of current employees, and surveying of consumers.

The employment interview is the most widely used method for pre-employment testing. Most companies use the traditional interview, although structured interviews have been shown to have greater reliability and validity. Organizations also use performance tests, such as assessment centers and work samples, to assess how well job candidates can perform job tasks. High-fidelity performance tests replicate the job setting in detail. Low-fidelity performance tests simulate job tasks using written, verbal, or visual descriptions.

Personality inventories measure stable and enduring constructs usually referred to as *personality traits*, such as conscientiousness, extraversion, and agreeableness, that predispose people to perform certain behaviors. The most popular theory among personality theorists today is the five-factor model. In the past, personnel psychologists discouraged the use of personality tests as employment tests because researchers had shown little relation between personality and job performance. Recently, because of research that has demonstrated that personality measures can be predictive of job performance, personnel psychologists have begun to look much more favorably on personality tests that reflect the five-factor model.

Organizations interested in assessing job candidates' integrity may use paper-and-pencil tests; however, Congress has forbidden using the polygraph—or lie detector—for employment testing. When a job analysis indicates that cognitive skills are important for high performance, cognitive tests are useful for inclusion in a pre-employment assessment.

When Congress passed the Civil Rights Act of 1964, one of the specific areas addressed was hiring by organizations. The Uniform Guidelines on Employee Selection Procedures (1978) and federal case law suggest that all employment tests should be job related and have evidence of validity. Organizations should maintain records regarding protected classes applying for jobs. If a test results in adverse impact, an employer can be required to show evidence of the test's validity and that there was no other equally valid test that would have had less adverse impact.

Most employers conduct performance appraisals to evaluate the performance of their employees. Most organizations ask supervisors to evaluate employee performance by either ranking or rating employees on a number of predetermined dimensions, traits, and/or behaviors. The most popular method of rating employee performance uses a graphic rating scale. Two other scales based on observing and rating behaviors are behaviorally anchored rating scales (BARS) and the behavioral checklist. Persons who rate performance should be trained to avoid ratings errors such as leniency, severity, central tendency, and the halo effect. During recent years, many companies have starting using 360° feedback in which employees compare self-ratings with ratings received from their supervisors, peers, subordinates, and customers.

Engaging in the Learning Process

KEY CONCEPTS

After completing your study of this chapter, you should be able to define each of the following terms. These terms are bolded in the text of this chapter and defined in the Glossary.

- 360° feedback
- anchors
- assessment center
- behavioral checklist
- behavioral interview
- behaviorally anchored rating scales (BARS)
- central tendency errors
- cognitive tests
- false positive
- five-factor model
- forced distribution
- forced ranking
- graphic rating scale

- halo effect
- high-fidelity test
- job analysis
- leniency errors
- low-fidelity test
- performance appraisal
- personality traits
- polygraph
- protected class
- severity errors
- structured interview
- traditional interview
- transportability
- work sample

LEARNING ACTIVITIES

The following are some learning activities you can engage in to support the learning objectives for this chapter.

Learning Objectives	Study Tips and Learning Activities
After completing your study of this chapter, you should be able to do the following:	The following study tips will help you meet these learning objectives:
Discuss the history of employment testing in the United States during the 20th century.	• Make a timeline of the events described in your textbook. Now place other events, either personal (for example, a relative's birth) or historical (for example, women earn the right to vote), on the timeline. Share with your classmates.
Report the strengths and weaknesses of the traditional interview and the structured interview for assessing job candidates.	• Make a list of strengths and weaknesses of the interviews. Why do you think the structured interview is a better predictor of job performance? Check your answer with a classmate or your instructor.
Describe the characteristics of a performance test, and discuss two types of performance tests used by organizations.	• Think about high-fidelity and low-fidelity tests. What do you think are the advantages and weakness of each? Include expense of development and administration, accuracy of results, and ease of scoring. Compare your answers with those of a classmate, or discuss with your instructor.
Describe the five-factor model of personality, and name two tests that are based on this model.	• Go online and read more about the five-factor model of personality. You will find information in books and journal articles on personality.
Discuss two types of integrity tests, and describe the criticism these tests have received.	• Make a list of why employers use integrity tests, and then make a list of problems that could arise from making decisions based on inaccurate test results.
Discuss performance appraisal instruments, give examples of three types of rating scales, and describe four types of rating errors.	• Get a copy of the form that students use to evaluate their instructors at your college or university. What type of appraisal is it? Do you have suggestions for improving the form based on information in this textbook? Share your ideas with a classmate or your instructor.

PRACTICE QUESTIONS

The following are practice questions to assess your understanding of the material presented in this chapter.

Multiple Choice

Choose the one best answer to each question.

1. Who proposed a system that evaluated constructs such as "native intellectual ability" and that assessed "character" and "manner"?
   a. Walter Dill Scott
   b. Hugo Münsterberg
   c. Walter Bingham
   d. Millicent Pond

2. Which one of the following drew attention to issues of test validity and fairness during the latter half of the 20th century in the United States?
   a. The Psychological Corporation
   b. U.S. Army Alpha and Beta tests
   c. The civil rights movement
   d. Use of assessment centers during World War II

3. Which one of the following is the MOST popular method for assessing job candidates?
   a. Assessment center
   b. Traditional employment interview
   c. Structured employment interview
   d. Performance appraisal

4. Which of the following is the LEAST accurate method of predicting job performance?
   a. Traditional employment interview
   b. Structured interview
   c. Assessment center
   d. Work sample

5. Interviews that focus on _____ rather than _____ provide better predictions of job performance.
   a. attitudes; behaviors
   b. opinions; behaviors
   c. attitudes; opinions
   d. behaviors; attitudes

6. When designing a structured interview, developers use job analysis to establish evidence of validity based on
   a. relationships with other variables.
   b. reliability.
   c. constructs.
   d. content.

7. Which one of the following is an example of a high-fidelity test?
   a. Paper-and-pencil attitude survey
   b. Flight simulator
   c. Performance appraisal
   d. Traditional interview

8. Hunter and Hunter's (1984) meta-analysis suggests that personality tests are among the poorest predictors of job performance. Which one of the following has caused psychologists to look more favorably on personality tests?
   a. The traditional interview
   b. Integrity testing
   c. The five-factor model of personality
   d. Job analysis

9. Which one of the following did the U.S. Congress forbid for use as an employment test?
   a. The polygraph
   b. Traditional interviews
   c. Assessment centers
   d. Personality tests

10. Which one of the following is most likely to make the "Othello error"—taking signs of distress as proof of unfaithfulness or dishonesty?
    a. Developers of integrity tests
    b. Employment interviewers
    c. Polygraph users
    d. Assessment center raters

11. Critics of the research on integrity tests point out that
    a. studies available were conducted by the test publishers themselves.
    b. there is no such thing as a "lie response."
    c. assessment centers are a better way of establishing honesty.
    d. they are not based on the five-factor model of personality.

12. When Lilienfeld (1993) administered integrity tests to monks and nuns, college students, and incarcerated criminals, the test results showed

   a. incarcerated criminals to be the most dishonest.
   b. college students to be the most dishonest.
   c. monks and nuns to be the most dishonest.
   d. there was no significant difference among the groups.

13. The Uniform Guidelines on Employee Selection Procedures published by the U.S. federal government in 1978

   a. forbid the use of polygraphs for employment testing.
   b. forbid the use of integrity tests for employment testing.
   c. consist of laws passed by Congress.
   d. suggest procedures for organizations to follow when testing job candidates.

14. At the BKH Construction Company, supervisors are required to rank employees so that a certain number fall into each performance category. This method of performance appraisal is known as

   a. forced distribution.
   b. forced choice.
   c. graphic rating.
   d. 360° feedback.

15. Naomi supervises several employees. When she rates their performance, however, she often lets her judgment of their conscientiousness influence her ratings of their decision-making ability and their leadership ability. Which one of the following rating errors is Naomi making?

   a. Leniency error
   b. Severity error
   c. Halo effect
   d. Central tendency error

16. Which one of the following tests shows high validity for job performance criteria and even higher validity for predicting training criteria?

   a. Personality test
   b. Cognitive test
   c. Integrity test
   d. Performance test

Short Answer/Essay

Read each of the following, and consider your response carefully based on the information presented in this chapter. Write your answer to each question in two or three paragraphs.

1. List the major events in the history of pre-employment testing described in your textbook.

2. Compare and contrast high- and low-fidelity tests. Give examples of each.

3. What are the differences between the traditional interview and the structured interview? Which do organizations use most often?

4. How might a small employer demonstrate evidence of validity for a test to select supervisors for his company that has only been validated for use in a different company?

5. How are personality tests used in organizations? Are they valid predictors of job performance?

6. What is the role of the five-factor model in personality tests?

7. Discuss various ways to assess employee honesty. What does the research reveal about the utility of employee honesty tests?

8. Describe how organizations evaluate employee performance. Discuss various types of rating scales.

9. What rating errors might individuals make when judging employee performance? What can be done to avoid the errors?

10. Compare and contrast the Hogan Personality Inventory (HPI) and the Wonderlic Basic Skills Test (WBST). What do the tests have in common? What are their differences?

Answer Keys

Multiple Choice

1. a	2. c	3. b	4. a
5. d	6. d	7. b	8. c
9. a	10. c	11. a	12. c
13. d	14. a	15. c	16. b

Short Answer/Essay

Refer to your textbook for answers. If you are unsure of an answer and cannot generate the answer after reviewing your book, ask your professor for clarification.

Appendix A

Test Spotlights

 TEST SPOTLIGHT 1.1

Wechsler Adult Intelligence Scale–
Fourth Edition (WAIS-IV)

Title	Wechsler Adult Intelligence Scale–Fourth Edition (WAIS-IV)
Author	David Wechsler
Publisher	Pearson Assessments 19500 Bulverde Road San Antonio, TX 78259–3710 www.pearsonassessments.com
Purpose	The WAIS-IV is designed to assess the intellectual ability of adults. The test measures both verbal and nonverbal skills using a battery of 10 core subtests. The subtests are based on four domains of intelligence: Verbal Comprehension, Perceptual Reasoning, Working Memory, and Processing Speed. The WAIS-IV is designed for use in educational settings for the purpose of planning and placement for older adolescents and adults. It can also be used to diagnose the extent to which neurological and psychiatric disorders may affect mental functioning. The test is individually administered. It takes approximately 70 minutes to administer the test for the Full Scale IQ (FSIQ) and four index scores. Test materials include two stimulus books, two response booklets, a record form, and the administration manual. The test can be scored by hand or by using the WAIS-IV Scoring Assistant software.
Versions	The original version of the WAIS was published in 1939. At that time, it was known as the Wechsler–Bellevue Intelligence scale. The test was designed to incorporate verbal and performance scores into a composite intelligence scale. The revisions the WAIS-IV include updated norms, an extended age range (16–90 years), an expanded FSIQ range, improved floors and ceilings to obtain a more accurate measure at each extreme, improved subtest and composite reliability, shortened testing time, and revised instructions.

(Continued)

(Continued)

	The WAIS–IV also removed four subtests (Object Assembly, Picture Arrangement, Coding Recall, and Coding Copy) from the previous version (WAIS-III). Three new subtests (Visual Puzzles, Figure Weights, and Cancellations) were added. Twelve subtests (Similarities, Vocabulary, Information, Comprehension, Block Design, Matrix Reasoning, Picture Completion, Digit Span, Arithmetic, Letter-Number Sequencing, Symbol Search, and Coding) were revised with new items and revised scoring.
Scales	The WAIS-IV has four main scales that make up the FSIQ, and each main scale has several subtests: • Verbal Comprehension Scale (VIQ), contains four subtests: Similarities, Vocabulary, Information, and Comprehension. • Perceptual Reasoning Scale (PIQ), contains five subtests: Block Design, Matrix Reasoning, Visual Puzzles, Picture Completion, and Figure Weights. • Working Memory Scale (WMI), contains three subtests: Digit Span, Arithmetic, and Letter-Number Sequencing. • Processing Speed Scale, contains three subtests: Symbol Search, Coding, and Cancellation.
Report	Multiple sample reports are available at http://psychcorp.pearsonassessments.com/HAIWEB/Cultures/en-us/Productdetail.htm?Pid=015-8980-808&Mode=summary.
Reliability and Validity	Both the individual scale reliability estimates and the full test reliability estimates are quite high, ranging from .90 (for the PSI scale) and .96 for the VIQ scale. The reliability estimate for the FSIQ is .98. These reliability estimates are the same as or higher than the WAIS-III. Evidence of construct validity was provided by the correlations between the WAIS-IV and the WAIS-III, both on the individual scales and the full test. The correlations were quite high in all cases. For the VIQ scale it is .89, for the PIQ scale .83, for the WMI scale .89, and for the PSI scale and FSIQ .94.
Sources	Spies, R. A., Carlson, J. F., & Geisinger, K. F. (Eds.). *The eighteenth mental measurements yearbook.* Lincoln, NE: Buros Institute of Mental Measurements. Pearson Education. (2009). Wechsler Adult Intelligence Scale–Fourth Edition (WAIS-IV). Retrieved June 30, 2010, from http://psychcorp.pearsonassessments.com/HAIWEB/Cultures/en-us/Productdetail.htm?Pid=015-8980-808&Mode=summary

TEST SPOTLIGHT 1.2

Stanford-Binet Intelligence Scales–Fifth Edition (SB5)

Gale H. Roid

Title	Stanford-Binet Intelligence Scales (SB5)
Author	Gale H. Roid
Publisher	Riverside Publishing 425 Spring Lake Drive Itasca, IL 60143–2079 www.riverpub.com
Purpose	The SB5 was designed to assess intelligence and cognitive abilities in children and adults ages 2–85 plus. The SB5 is most commonly used to diagnosis learning disabilities and exceptionalities in children, adolescents, and adults. The test measures five factors of cognitive ability: fluid reasoning, knowledge, quantitative reasoning, visual-spatial processing, and working memory. The Full Scale IQ is individually administered through 10 subtests, five nonverbal (Nonverbal Knowledge, Nonverbal Quantitative Reasoning, Nonverbal Visual Spatial Processing, Nonverbal Working Memory, and Nonverbal Fluid Reasoning), and five verbal (Verbal Fluid Reasoning, Verbal Quantitative Reasoning, Verbal Visual Spatial Reasoning, Verbal Working Memory, and Verbal Knowledge). At the start of the test, the administrator gives two routing subtests (one for Nonverbal Fluid Reasoning, one for Verbal Knowledge). These identify the starting level (from 1 to 6) for the remaining tests. The scales have varying administration times that range from 15 to 75 minutes. Individual items on the scale are not generally timed. The Full Scale IQ takes 45–75 minutes to administer. The Verbal and Nonverbal IQ scales can be administered in 30 minutes. There is also an Abbreviated Battery IQ consisting only of the two routing subtests. The Abbreviated IQ takes 15–20 minutes to administer. Numerous scores can be produced from the test data, including composite scores, subtest scaled scores, percentile ranking, confidence intervals, age equivalents, and change-sensitive scores. The tests can be scored by hand or by computer using the SB5 Scoring Pro program.
Versions	The original version of the test was published in 1916. Since then, it has gone through five revisions. The most recent version, SB5, was published in 2003 and is an update to the fourth edition, published in 1986.
Scales	The scales include the Full Scale IQ, two domain scores (Nonverbal IQ and Verbal IQ), and five Factor Indexes (Fluid Reasoning, Knowledge, Quantitative Reasoning, Visual Spatial Processing, and Working Memory).

(Continued)

(Continued)

Report	There is an extended score report and a shorter, narrative summary report. However, sample reports do not appear to be available online.
Reliability and Validity	Reliability was calculated through various methods such as test–retest reliability, interscorer agreement, and the split-half method. Mean reliability coefficients for Nonverbal subtests are between .85 and .89. Mean reliability coefficients for Verbal subtest are between .84 and .89. Mean reliability coefficients for the Full Scale IQ is .98, for Nonverbal IQ .95, for Verbal IQ .96, and for the abbreviated battery IQ .91.
	Average reliability coefficients for the Factor Index scores were: Fluid Reasoning .90, Knowledge .92, Quantitative Reasoning .92, Visual Spatial Processing .92, and Working Memory .91.
	The SB5 technical manual (cited in the *Mental Measurements Yearbook*) presents a study comparing the SB5 to the SB4. The study found that the correlation between the Full Scale scores was .90. Construct validity was also examined through comparison of the SB5 and the Wechsler Adult Intelligence Scales III and the correlation found was .82.
Sources	Kush, J. C. (2005). Review of the Stanford-Binet Intelligence Scales: Fifth Edition. In R. S. Spies & B. S. Plake (Eds.), *The sixteenth mental measurements yearbook*. Lincoln, NE: Buros Institute of Mental Measurements.
	Riverside Publishing. (n.d.). *Stanford-Binet Intelligence Scales (SB5) Fifth Edition*. Retrieved November 7, 2009, from http://www.riverpub.com/products/sb5/index.html

TEST SPOTLIGHT 1.3

NEO Personality Inventory (NEO PI-R)

Robert R. McCrae

Title	NEO Personality Inventory (NEO PI-R)
Author	Paul T. Costa Jr. and Robert R. McCrae
Publisher	PAR 16204 North Florida Avenue Lutz, FL 33549 www4.parinc.com
Purpose	The NEO PI-R is used to assess normal personality in adults ages 17 and up. It measures the Big Five factors of personality (referred to as *domains*): Extraversion, Agreeableness, Conscientiousness, Neuroticism, and Openness to Experience. The NEO PI-R provides a summary of an individual's emotional, interpersonal, experiential, attitudinal, and motivational styles. The NEO PI-R is used in a variety of fields, including clinical psychology, psychiatry, behavioral medicine, counseling, industrial/organizational psychology, and education and personality research. The NEO PI-R is self-administered and takes approximately 40 minutes to complete. It contains 240 items and three validity-check items designed to identify whether a respondent is honestly and accurately completing the inventory. Each item is rated on a 5-point scale. The NEO PI-R can be administered via pencil and paper, or it can be administered and scored electronically with the NEO Software System. The NEO PI-R contains two parallel versions. There is a self-report (Form S) and an observer report (form R), which is written in the third person and can be used as a supplement to the self-report.
Versions	In addition to the NEO PR-I, there is a shortened form of the NEO Personality Inventory, the NEO-FFI, which has 60 items and provides scores on the five domain scales only. There is also a previous version of the inventory, the NEO PI, as well as a version that eliminates the Neuroticism Scale, the NEO 4, designed to be used in career and personnel counseling where differences in an individual's anxiety and depression are generally less relevant. As part of the update from the NEO PI to the NEO PI-R, six trait scales were added to each of the Agreeableness and Conscientiousness domains. Updates were also made to some items, and a few items were replaced with new items.
Scales	The scales include the following five domains and six traits that define each domain: • Neuroticism (Anxiety, Angry Hostility, Depression, Self-Consciousness, Impulsiveness, Vulnerability) • Extraversion (Warmth, Gregariousness, Assertiveness, Activity, Excitement-Seeking, Positive Emotions)

(Continued)

	• Openness (Fantasy, Aesthetics, Feelings, Actions, Ideas, Values) • Agreeableness (Trust, Straight-Forwardness, Altruism, Compliance, Modesty, Tender-Mindedness) • Conscientiousness (Competence, Order, Dutifulness, Achievement Striving, Self-Discipline, Deliberation)
Report	A complete sample report can be found at www4.parinc.com/Products/Product.aspx? ProductID=NEOSS-3V.
Reliability and Validity	In terms of reliability, internal consistency coefficients range from .86 to .95 for the domain scales on both Form R and Form S. Internal consistency coefficients for the facet scales range from .56 to .90 for both Form R and Form S. In terms of validity, evidence exists that groups of individuals who differ on test construct also differ in group mean scores in theoretically predictable ways. For example, psychotherapy patients tend to score high on neuroticism and drug abusers tend to score low on agreeableness and conscientiousness. Further evidence of validity comes from comparing NEO PI-R scores to scores on other personality inventories.
Sources	Botwin, M. (1995). Review of the revised NEO Personality Inventory. In J. C. Conoley & J. C. Impara (Eds.), *The twelfth mental measurements yearbook.* Lincoln, NE: Buros Institute of Mental Measurements. PAR. (2010a). *NEO Personality Inventory-Revised (NEO PI-R).* Retrieved June 9, 2010, from http://www4.parinc.com/products/product.aspx?Productid=NEO-PI-R

TEST SPOTLIGHT 1.4

Myers-Briggs Type Indicator (MBTI)

Katherine Cook Briggs   Isabel Briggs Myers

Title	Myers–Briggs Type Indicator (MBTI)
Author	Katherine Cook Briggs and Isabel Briggs Myers
Publisher	CPP 3803 East Bayshore Road Palo Alto, CA 94303 www.cpp-db.com
Purpose	The MBTI is a personality test that helps individuals understand their personality preferences. The MBTI was developed in 1943 by Katherine Briggs and her daughter, Isabel Briggs Myers, and was based on the psychological-type framework of Carl Jung and on their belief that understanding differences in personality preferences can help individuals interact with others more effectively. After extensive reading of Jung's theories and an intense study of people, Briggs and Briggs Myers determined that people differ in four primary ways. They referred to these differences as preferences and likened them to how we favor one of our hands over the other. Although every individual uses both hands, most individuals have a preference for, or favor, using one hand over the other. The results of the MBTI provide individuals with insights into their own personality preferences and can serve as a catalyst for improving relationships with others. The MBTI is often used for team development, conflict management, leadership and coaching, and career exploration. The MBTI is most appropriate for adults and students age 14 years or older. Caution should be taken when using the MBTI with younger children because research suggests that types are less developed with younger children and individuals who are less mature. Available in paper-and-pencil format and online, the self-administered MBTI requires individuals to respond to forced-choice questions. It is available in approximately 30 languages and takes 15–25 minutes to complete.
Versions	Various versions of the MBTI are available. • Form M, referred to as the standard form since 1998, is written at the seventh-grade reading level and consists of 93 items. Developed for individuals age 14 years or older, Form M includes one booklet containing the 93 items, an answer sheet, and interpretive information. Simple scoring instructions are also included. In addition, there is a self-scorable version that is ideal for use in workshop settings where there is limited time available for scoring. • Form Q consists of 144 items (93 items from Form M plus 51 additional items). This version extends the personality preferences to include explanations of why individuals of similar type may behave differently. Each preference is further expanded. • Form G, which was the standard form until 1998, consists of 126 items. It can be hand-scored by using templates. In addition, there is a 94-item self-scorable version that is ideal for use in workshop settings where there is limited time for scoring.

(Continued)

(Continued)

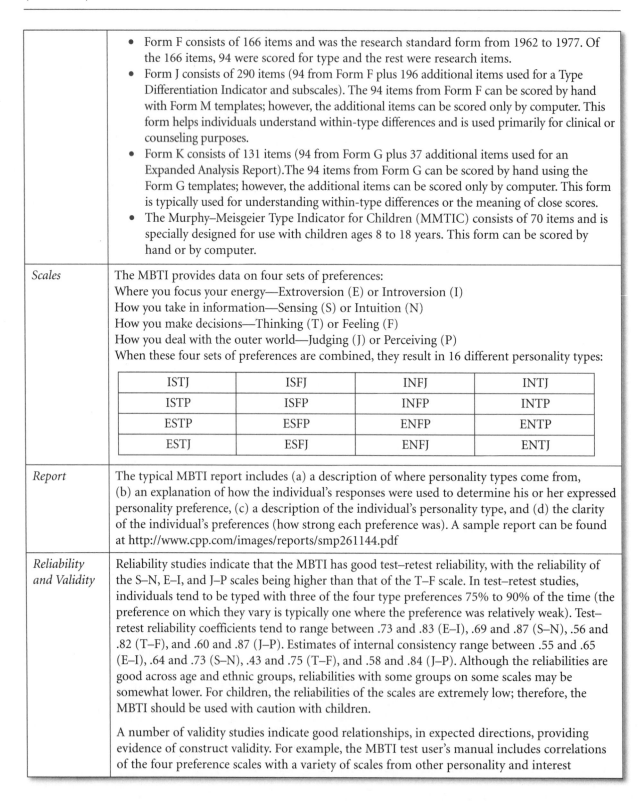

	• Form F consists of 166 items and was the research standard form from 1962 to 1977. Of the 166 items, 94 were scored for type and the rest were research items. • Form J consists of 290 items (94 from Form F plus 196 additional items used for a Type Differentiation Indicator and subscales). The 94 items from Form F can be scored by hand with Form M templates; however, the additional items can be scored only by computer. This form helps individuals understand within-type differences and is used primarily for clinical or counseling purposes. • Form K consists of 131 items (94 from Form G plus 37 additional items used for an Expanded Analysis Report).The 94 items from Form G can be scored by hand using the Form G templates; however, the additional items can be scored only by computer. This form is typically used for understanding within-type differences or the meaning of close scores. • The Murphy–Meisgeier Type Indicator for Children (MMTIC) consists of 70 items and is specially designed for use with children ages 8 to 18 years. This form can be scored by hand or by computer.
Scales	The MBTI provides data on four sets of preferences: Where you focus your energy—Extroversion (E) or Introversion (I) How you take in information—Sensing (S) or Intuition (N) How you make decisions—Thinking (T) or Feeling (F) How you deal with the outer world—Judging (J) or Perceiving (P) When these four sets of preferences are combined, they result in 16 different personality types: |ISTJ|ISFJ|INFJ|INTJ
---	---	---	---
ISTP	ISFP	INFP	INTP
ESTP	ESFP	ENFP	ENTP
ESTJ	ESFJ	ENFJ	ENTJ	
Report	The typical MBTI report includes (a) a description of where personality types come from, (b) an explanation of how the individual's responses were used to determine his or her expressed personality preference, (c) a description of the individual's personality type, and (d) the clarity of the individual's preferences (how strong each preference was). A sample report can be found at http://www.cpp.com/images/reports/smp261144.pdf
Reliability and Validity	Reliability studies indicate that the MBTI has good test–retest reliability, with the reliability of the S–N, E–I, and J–P scales being higher than that of the T–F scale. In test–retest studies, individuals tend to be typed with three of the four type preferences 75% to 90% of the time (the preference on which they vary is typically one where the preference was relatively weak). Test–retest reliability coefficients tend to range between .73 and .83 (E–I), .69 and .87 (S–N), .56 and .82 (T–F), and .60 and .87 (J–P). Estimates of internal consistency range between .55 and .65 (E–I), .64 and .73 (S–N), .43 and .75 (T–F), and .58 and .84 (J–P). Although the reliabilities are good across age and ethnic groups, reliabilities with some groups on some scales may be somewhat lower. For children, the reliabilities of the scales are extremely low; therefore, the MBTI should be used with caution with children. A number of validity studies indicate good relationships, in expected directions, providing evidence of construct validity. For example, the MBTI test user's manual includes correlations of the four preference scales with a variety of scales from other personality and interest

	instruments, including the 16 Personality Factors, Million Index of Personality Styles, California Psychological Inventory, NEO Personality Inventory, Fundamental Interpersonal Relations Orientation–Behavior, Adjective Checklist, Strong Interest Inventory, Skills Factors Inventory, Skills Confidence Inventory, Salience Inventory, Values Scale, Work Environment Scale, Maslach Burnout Inventory, Coping Resources Inventory, and State–Trait Anxiety Inventory. Although numerous validity coefficients are reported in the manual, correlation coefficients for the four scales range between .66 and .76 (E–I), .34 and .71 (S–N), .23 and .78 (T–F), and .39 and .73 (J–P). No evidence exists in the literature that the MBTI correlates with measures of job performance; therefore, the MBTI is not appropriate for job screening, placement, or selection without an independent criterion-related validation study using a large sample of applicants or employees.
Sources	Center for Applications of Psychological Type. (n.d.). *The forms of the MBTI instrument.* Retrieved October 15, 2009, from http://www.capt.org/mbti-assessment/mbti-forms.htm
	Martin, C. (n.d.). *The sixteen types at a glance.* Retrieved June 29, 2010, from http://www.capt.org/the_mbti_instrument/type_descriptions.cfm
	Consulting Psychologists Press. (2009, March). *Myers–Briggs Type Indicator interpretive report: Report prepared for Jane Sample.* Retrieved October 15, 2009, from http://www.cpp.com/images/reports/smp261144.pdf
	Myers, I. B. (1998). *Introduction to type* (6th ed.). Palo Alto, CA: Consulting Psychologists Press.
	Myers, I. B., McCaulley, M. H., Quenk, N. L., & Hammer, A. L. (1998). *MBTI manual: A guide to the development and use of the Myers–Briggs Type Indicator* (3rd ed.). Palo Alto, CA: Consulting Psychologists Press.

TEST SPOTLIGHT 2.1

SAT

Title	SAT
Author	College Board
Publisher	Educational Testing Service Rosedale Road Princeton, NJ 08541 www.ets.org
Purpose	Taken by more than two million high school juniors and seniors a year and used by most American colleges as a part of the admissions process, the SAT is a college entrance exam believed by many to be the most independent, objective, and standardized measure available for predicting success in college—more specifically, for predicting first-year college grades. The SAT, which previously was referred to as the Scholastic Aptitude Test, was developed in 1926 by Carl Campbell Brigham for the College Entrance Examination Board. At that time, people believed that the test measured an individual's aptitude or innate intelligence. Over time, primarily in response to awareness that individuals can improve SAT scores through preparation (an unlikely outcome if the test truly measured aptitude), the board revised the Scholastic Aptitude Test, added a writing sample, and called it the Scholastic Assessment Test. Today the College Board states that "SAT" no longer stands for anything; the SAT is just the SAT. It is administered in the United States, Puerto Rico, and the U.S. territories seven times a year, and six times a year overseas. Students can register online to take the SAT and receive their reports online.
Versions	The SAT consists of the SAT Reasoning Test and the SAT Subject Tests. • The SAT Reasoning Test measures the critical thinking skills students need for academic success in college. The Reasoning Test is a timed test (3 hours and 45 minutes) that measures the critical thinking, reasoning, and writing knowledge and skills that students have developed over time. • The SAT Subject Tests measure mastery of content in different subject areas. The SAT Subject Tests fall into five general categories: English (literature), history (U.S. History and World History), mathematics (Mathematics Level 1 and Mathematics Level 2), science (Biology, Chemistry, and Physics), and languages (Chinese with Listening, French, French with Listening, German, German with Listening, Spanish, Spanish with Listening, Modern Hebrew, Italian, Latin, Japanese with Listening, and Korean with Listening). Each SAT Subject Test is a timed (1 hour) multiple-choice test. (Although some of the tests have unique formats. For example, for some of the language tests, students must bring a CD player with them to the testing center.)
Scales	The SAT Reasoning Test consists of three sections: critical reading, mathematics, and writing. Each section is scored on a scale of 200–800 (with two writing subscores for multiple-choice questions and the essay).

Report	The SAT Reasoning Test score report includes (a) the individual's raw score and a 200- to 800-point scaled score for the critical reading, math, and writing sections; (b) a 0- to 12-point essay subscore; (c) information about the individual's responses, such as questions they answered correctly and incorrectly; (d) a percentile rank representing how the individual scored in comparison with other test takers at the state and national levels; and (e) a copy of the individual's essay. The report also includes detailed information about the characteristics of the colleges to which the test taker requested that score reports be sent (for example, type of school, size of school, diversity of freshman class, high school preparation requirements, freshman admission statistics and admission criteria, admissions/financial aid application deadlines). Although all students who take the SAT will receive their SAT score reports in the mail, score reports are also available online and are free to every student who takes the SAT. The online service contains a number of features to help students interpret their SAT scores.
Reliability and Validity	Most reliability studies show that the SAT is a reliable test. Internal consistency studies show reliability coefficients exceeding .90, suggesting that items measure a similar content area. Test–retest studies generally show reliability coefficients ranging between .87 and .93, suggesting that individuals tend to earn similar scores on repeated occasions.
	Researchers have conducted many studies on the validity of the SAT. In terms of content validity, over the years careful attention has been paid to reviewing SAT content to ensure that it does not become out of date, reflects appropriate and up-to-date subject matter, and contains vocabulary consistent with that used in college-level study. High school and college administrators have also spent considerable time in reviewing and modifying/removing SAT items that may be viewed as offensive due to cultural bias, sexist language, and so on.
	For decades, the College Board and other researchers have been examining the relationship among SAT scores, college grades, and other measures of success (for example, grade point average, attrition, teacher ratings, awards/honors).
	Although research suggests that the SAT does not equally predict the college success of males and females, traditional students and nontraditional students, or racial/cultural subgroups, many criterion-related validity studies indicate that SAT scores correlate with college grades and other tests used in the admissions process. One of the strongest correlations of the SAT with high school grades and freshman college grades exists for traditional White students (vs. nontraditional students who return to school later in life). SAT scores also show an acceptable correlation with a combination of high school grades. SAT scores are also the strongest predictor of freshman grades. Most validity studies suggest that SAT scores, when combined with high school records, are predictive of college freshman grades, with uncorrected validity coefficients ranging between .35 and .42 (and with corrected validity coefficients somewhat higher).
	In 2005, the College Board introduced a revised SAT, which not only includes an additional section in writing, but reflected minor changes in content to the verbal and mathematics section. In 2008, the College Board released new information regarding evidence of validity for the 2005 updated version of the SAT. Since the SAT is intended to measure student potential for success in college, many consider the most critical form of validity to be evidence of the test's predictive validity, that is, the extent to which the SAT is a good predictor of college performance.

(Continued)

	Across the United States, 726 colleges and universities provided first-year performance data from the fall 2006 entering class. The results show that the changes made to the SAT did not substantially change how predictive the test is of first-year college performance. SAT scores were correlated 0.35 (0.53 adjusted) with first-year grade point average (FYGPA). SAT Writing scores were most highly correlated (0.33, 0.51 adjusted) with FYGPA.
	To read more about the validity of the SAT, go to http://professionals.collegeboard.com/profdownload/Validity_of_the_SAT_for_Predicting_First_Year_College_Grade_Point_Average.pdf
Sources	Elert, G. (2005). The SAT: Aptitude or demographics? *E-World.* Retrieved October 15, 2009, from http://hypertextbook.com/eworld/sat.shtml
	Kobrin, J. L., Patterson, B. F., Shaw, E. J., Mattern, K. D., & Barbuti, S. M. (2008). *Validity of the SAT for predicting first-year college grade point average.* Retrieved June 29, 2010, from http://professionals.collegeboard.com/profdownload/Validity_of_the_SAT_for_Predicting_First_Year_College_Grade_Point_Average.pdf
	National Center for Fair and Open Testing. (2001). *The SAT: Questions and answers.* Retrieved October 15, 2009, from http://www.fairtest.org/facts/satfact.htm

TEST SPOTLIGHT 3.1

Rorschach Inkblot Test

Hermann Rorschach

Title	Rorschach Inkblot Test
Author	Hermann Rorschach
Publisher	Hogrefe Publishing P.O. Box 2487 Kirkland WA 98083 www.hogrefe.com
Purpose	The Rorschach Inkblot Test is used to measure personality structure and dynamics in adults, adolescents, and children. It is used in the diagnosis and treatment of a variety of psychological problems and psychiatric disorders. The test is administered by showing respondents 10 plates, each with a different inkblot. Each inkblot is designed to be symmetrical and has a mixture of colors (i.e. black and white; black, white, and red; and pastels). The first phase of the test is the free association phase. Respondents view the inkblots one at a time and are asked to describe what they think each blot might be. After test takers have responded to all 10 inkblots, the administrator starts an inquiry phase. Respondents discuss their responses and provide insights about why they responded in a particular manner to each inkblot.
Versions	The original test was published in 1921. Since then, multiple revisions have been made to the scoring and interpretation guide; however, the test still uses the 10 inkblots that Rorschach originally designed.
Scales	The test is scored based on the responses to the 10 inkblots. The responses are scored by coding different aspects of the inkblot. The scores look at whether various aspects of the inkblot, such as location, shape, and color, influenced the response in some way. There is controversy around the scoring. Initially, scores were interpreted differently among users. In 1974, Exner developed the Comprehensive System to address the inconsistency issues with scoring. There is a computerized scoring system based on the Comprehensive System, the Rorschach Interpretation Assistance Program that clinicians can use to help them score and interpret the test results.
Report	The Rorschach Interpretation Assistance Program produces two reports, a simplified Client Report and a more detailed Interpretive Report that provides clinicians with assistance in scoring and interpretation. A sample Interpretive Report is available at www4.parinc.com/products/product.aspx?Productid=RIAP5.

(Continued)

(Continued)

| Report | Following is a sample of the client report: |

Rorschach Interpretation Assistance Program™
Client Report

by

Irving B. Weiner, PhD
and
PAR Staff

Client Information

Name: Mr. C.
Test Date: 04/25/2003

The following report is based on the responses you gave to the Rorschach Inkblot Method and should be discussed with the clinician who examined you. The report describes how you appear to pay attention to your surroundings, think about your experiences, express your feelings, manage your stress, think about yourself, and relate to other people. These descriptions are based on Rorschach findings among people in general who give responses similar to yours. The descriptions do not necessarily apply in every respect to each individual person. For this reason, some of the statements in the report may describe you more accurately than others. In addition, the report may identify some aspects of yourself that have previously escaped your notice or of which you have not been fully aware. Discussing these Rorschach results with your clinician, particularly with regard to understanding them in the context of your past and present life circumstances, will help you get the maximum benefit from the information provided by the test.

You gave enough responses to provide reliable information and to support sound conclusions about yourself.

You appear to be capable of thinking about things in a flexible manner. This flexibility allows you to consider changing your opinions and your point of view. You tend to keep your mind open to new information and to previously unfamiliar ideas.

You appear to have serious difficulties in your ability to think logically. This means that you may have more problems than most people with coming to reasonable conclusions about the relationships between events and keeping track of the ideas that go through your head. You seem particularly prone to forming strange ideas when you are thinking about what people are like and how they behave.

Your responses indicate a serious impairment of your ability to form accurate impressions of yourself and to clearly see the actions and intentions of others. You are likely to have considerable difficulty with correctly anticipating the consequences of your actions and with recognizing what is appropriate behavior in various kinds of situations.

You appear to devote a lot of energy to staying alert to what is going on around you, as if situations can become dangerous or threatening if you fail to keep a close eye on them. Your excessive concern with paying attention to your environment may be accompanied by suspiciousness and mistrust that may interfere with your daily activities and result in strained relationships with other people.

Your manner of responding to this test suggests that you are inclined to examine situations very thoroughly, perhaps taking in more information than is really necessary for solving problems or arriving at decisions. As a result, you are likely to function well in situations that call for being very careful, provided that you have enough time to work at your preferred pace. On the other hand, having to work under time pressure may make you anxious or cause you to feel dissatisfied with what you have accomplished. You may also

Report

have occasional difficulty with making decisions because you feel that you do not have enough information on which to base the choices you need to make.

You appear to be somewhat inconsistent in the way you make decisions and solve problems. Sometimes you deal with situations by thinking about them and other times by taking action. Both methods can work, but it appears to be hard for you to choose whether to be primarily a thinker or primarily a doer. Therefore, your behavior may be unpredictable, and both you and the people close to you may find it difficult to anticipate how you are likely to behave.

The test findings suggest that you are far more capable than most people of managing the stresses in your life without becoming unduly upset by them. You are the kind of person who feels satisfied with his/her life and sees little need to change the way he/she is. You appear to be a psychologically stable person with a well above average capacity to tolerate frustration. There are also indications that you are far more capable than most people of controlling your behavior and avoiding emotional outbursts and impulsive actions. In crisis situations, you are probably able to remain calmer and keep a clearer head than most people around you. However, along with not letting things bother you, you may tend to ignore or minimize the implications of events that you should pay attention to and be concerned about. Your lack of sensitivity in this regard may prevent you from dealing effectively with people and situations.

You appear to be much less willing than most people to become involved in emotional situations. Because of feeling uncomfortable in social interactions, particularly when strong feelings are being expressed, and because of reluctance to exchange feelings with other people, you may be at risk for becoming emotionally and socially withdrawn.

You are showing some problems with experiencing and expressing emotions in which you are exerting considerably less control over your feelings than most adults. Your test responses suggest that you are an emotionally intense and excitable person who prefers to express your feelings rather than to hold them in. Your characteristic tendency to let your feelings flow freely is likely, at times, to result in emotional displays that interfere with your relationships with others.

You appear to be paying less attention to yourself than most people, which often results from having a poor opinion of oneself. Your test responses suggest that you tend to compare yourself unfavorably to other people. You may suffer from low self-esteem and lack self-confidence because of this tendency.

Your test responses suggest that you are more likely than most people to worry about aspects of yourself or your behavior that you view as undesirable. Your self-awareness should help you to recognize how you can have your needs met and how your behavior affects other people. At the same time, you may be inclined to be self-critical and to feel dissatisfied with yourself.

You seem to have a good ability to model yourself after people you know well. This ability should have helped you to develop a clear and stable sense of the kind of person you really are.

You seem to be highly alert to possible sources of threat to your safety and security. You also appear to be concerned about whether other people can be trusted to have your best interests at heart. To protect yourself, you may be more inclined than most people to avoid close relationships, preserve your privacy, and keep your thoughts and feelings to yourself.

You appear to be somewhat limited in your ability to form attachments to other people. This does not necessarily mean that you avoid people, but that your personal relationships tend to be emotionally distant and detached rather than close and intimate.

Your test responses suggest that you are as interested in other people as most adults. Your interest in being around people and paying attention to what they say and do is a personality strength that ordinarily contributes to good social adjustment. However, there also are indications in your test responses that you tend to feel somewhat inadequate or uncomfortable in social situations.

Your test responses indicate that you are capable of approaching other people in a spirit of cooperation, but that you are more frequently inclined to relate to those around you in an assertive or aggressive manner.

End of Report

(Continued)

(Continued)

Reliability and Validity	There are arguments for and against the Comprehensive System's average interrater reliability. According to the *Mental Measurements Yearbook*, interrater reliability has been calculated at .86 by Meyer (1997); however, this has been disputed by other researchers, such as Wood, Nezworksi, and Stejskal (1997), who indicate that various calculation errors contributed to that reliability. In either case, interrater reliability does not reflect on the test score; it reflects on the similarity and training of those who scored the tests.
	There are fewer disputes over the test–retest reliability of the Rorschach. Test–retest reliability is .70 at one- and three-year intervals, based on information presented in the *Mental Measurements Yearbook* obtained from Exner's (1974) studies.
	There are proponents for and critics against the validity of Rorschach. Proponents such as Hiller, Rosenthal, Bornstein, Berry, and Brunell-Neulib (1999) indicate that meta-analyses show a mean effect size of .26 on the Rorshach, compared to a mean effect size of .37 for the Minnesota Multiphasic Personality Inventory, both acceptable for a personality test.
	Critics question the validity of the test saying that inadequacies in the scoring system, the purpose to which the test results are applied, and the subjective nature of the test make it difficult to determine validity.
Sources	Exner, J. E. (1974). *The Rorschach: A comprehensive system (Vol. 1)*. New York: John Wiley & Sons.
	Hess, A. K., Zachar, P., & Kramer, J. (2001). Review of the Rorschach. In B. S. Plake & J. C. Impara (Eds.), *The fourteenth mental measurement yearbook*. Lincoln, NE: Buros Institute of Mental Measurements.
	Hiller, J. B., Rosenthal, R., Bornstein, R. F., Berry, D. T. R., & Brunell-Neulib, S. (1999). A comparative meta-analysis of Rorschach and MMPI validity. *Psychological Assessments, 11*, 278–296.
	Meyer, G. J. (1997). Thinking clearly about reliability: More critical corrections regarding the Rorschach Comprehensive System. *Psychological Assessment, 9*, 495–498.
	PAR. (2010c). *Rorschach Interpretation Assistance Program: Version 5 (RIAP5)*. Retrieved June 9, 2010, from http://www4.parinc.com/products/product.aspx?Productid=RIAP5
	Wood, J. M., Nezworski, M. T., & Stejskal, W. J. (1997). The reliability of the comprehensive system for the Rorschach: A comment on Meyer. *Psychological Assessment, 9*, 490–494.

TEST SPOTLIGHT 4.1

Computer Anxiety Scale (COMPAS)

Title	Computer Anxiety Scale (COMPAS)
Author	E. R. Oetting
Publisher	Rocky Mountain Behavioral Science Institute P.O. Box 1066 Fort Collins, CO 80522 www.rmbsi.com
Purpose	The COMPAS was published in 1983 to be used by researchers for measuring anxiety related to interacting with computers or having computers present in a test taker's environment. The COMPAS measures a wide variety of computer-related anxieties. The test is a self-report, paper-and-pencil measure where the test taker is presented with a situation and asked to rate the statement using a 5-point semantic differential rating scale. Each end of the scale contains bipolar adjectives (e.g., 1 = *relaxed*, 5 = *nervous*).
Versions	There are two versions of the test available, a Short Form (10 items) and a Long Form (48 items).
Scales	The COMPAS has seven subscales, each representing different actions a person can have with a computer: Hand Calculator, Trust, General Attitude, Data Entry, Word Processing, Business Operations, and Computer Science. The first two scales (Hand Calculator and Trust) are not scored. They are included in the test because they measure specific anxieties that may be important in training, but are not directly related to computer anxiety. The following are the five scored scales: • General Attitude—measures anxiety related to thinking of computers, hearing the word computer, seeing more computers emerging in the workplace, and feelings toward computers. • Data Entry—measures anxiety related to using, performing tasks, learning about, and correcting data entries on spreadsheets. • Word Processing–measures anxiety related to correcting, using word-processing tools, entering text, and taking a word-processing class. • Business Operations—measures anxiety related to making a budget, record keeping, figuring profits and losses, and trying new ideas. • Computer Science–measures anxiety related to interpreting a computer printout, knowing language about computers, discussing computers with others, and taking a course in computer applications.
Report	The COMPAS user's manual contains a profile sheet for plotting the subscale and overall computer anxiety levels of the test taker. The profile shows interpretive statements beside several of the scale values.

(Continued)

(Continued)

	Overall computer anxiety scores range from 40 to 200. The higher the score, the more computer anxiety. Oetting (1985) classified computer anxiety levels into five categories: 40–79 relaxed and confident 80–104 generally relaxed and comfortable 105–129 some mild anxiety present 130–149 anxious and tense 150–200 very anxious Subscale scores range from 4 to 20. The higher the score, the more anxiety. Oetting classified anxiety on the subscales into five categories: 4–8 very relaxed and confident 9–10 generally relaxed and comfortable 11–12 some mild anxiety present 13–14 anxious and tense 15–20 very anxious A sample report does not appear to be available online.
Reliability and Validity	Reliability and validity studies indicate that the COMPAS demonstrates evidence of reliability and validity. When administered to 435 entering freshman at Colorado State University, internal consistency (measured by Cronbach's alpha) was high, ranging from .88 for the Short Form to .96 for the Long Form. Internal. The consistency of the subscales ranged from .71 to .87. Parallel forms reliability estimates ranged from .94 to .96. Evidence of validity is based on test content gathered by having a panel of experts who reviewed the test items assess whether the items were appropriate and indeed related to anxiety. Experts agreed that questions on the Hand Calculator and Trust subscales were not direct measures of computer anxiety. When test scores were correlated with other measures of anxiety, validity coefficients ranged from .19 (with term paper anxiety) to .40 (with math test anxiety) to .48 (with science test anxiety) to .70 with another measure of computer anxiety. The average intercorrelation of the seven subscales is about .50 (they range from .07 to .71).
Sources	Kleinmuntz, B. (1989). Review of the Computer Anxiety Scale. In J. C. Conoley & J. J. Kramer (Eds.), *The tenth mental measurements yearbook*. Lincoln, NE: Buros Institute of Mental Measurements. Martin, B. L. (1998). *Computer anxiety levels of Virginia Cooperative Extension field personnel*. Unpublished doctoral dissertation, Virginia Polytechnic Institute and State University, Blacksburg. Oetting, E. R. (1985). Oetting's computer anxiety scale. In J. V. Mitchell, Jr. (Ed.), *The ninth mental measurements yearbook*. Lincoln, NE: Buros Institute of Mental Measurements.

TEST SPOTLIGHT 5.1

Mini-Mental State Examination, 2nd Edition (MMSE-2)

Marshal Folstein

Title	Mini-Mental State Examination, 2nd Edition (MMSE-2)
Author	Marshal Folstein, Susan Folstein, and Paul R. McHugh
Publisher	PAR 16204 North Florida Avenue Lutz, FL 33549 www4.parinc.com
Purpose	Originally developed in 1975, the MMSE is a cognitive ability test used by many clinicians to systematically and quickly assess cognitive status. Clinicians use the MMSE to screen for cognitive impairment, determine the severity of cognitive impairment, monitor changes in impairment over time, and document response to treatment. The MMSE is one of the most commonly used tests for complaints of memory problems or when there is reason to believe that an individual has a cognitive impairment such as dementia. The MMSE is most effectively used with older, community-dwelling, hospitalized, and institutionalized adults.
Versions and Scales	The MMSE-2 improves on the original by standardizing its administration and altering some of the original MMSE items. The MMSE-2 demonstrates high equivalency with the original MMSE, allowing test users to switch from the original MMSE to the MMSE-2:SV without compromising longitudinal data and without any change in the normal range of scores. An even briefer version, the new MMSE-2: Brief Version (MMSE-2:BV), is designed for rapid assessment in a variety of settings. The MMSE-2: Expanded Version (MMSE-2:EV), a slightly longer version, is more sensitive to subcortical dementia and to changes associated with aging. It is sufficiently difficult that it does not have a ceiling effect. Equivalent, alternate forms (Blue and Red) of each MMSE-2 version have been developed to decrease the possibility of practice effects that can occur over serial examinations. A Pocket Norms Guide provides norms for all versions of the MMSE-2. All versions of the MMSE-2 are brief, requiring 5 to 20 minutes, depending on the version. • Orientation to Time and Orientation to Place (10 points) • Registration and Attention/Calculation (8 points) • Recall (3 points) • Naming, Repetition, Comprehension, Reading, Writing, and Drawing (9 points)

(Continued)

(Continued)

Report	The publisher offers Mental Status Reporting Software that provides qualified professionals with the ability to organize information related to an individual's mental status and to generate a mental status report. Following are a few samples from the report. A complete sample report can be found at www4.parinc.com/Products/Product.aspx?ProductID=MMSE

Sample A. Client	Page 2
123-45-6789	07/15/2002

MMSE Results

The patient's score on the MMSE is below the cutoff score (23) that has been found to be most effective in identifying dementia in research studies. The possibility of cognitive impairment characteristic of dementia is further supported when her performance is compared to the performance of individuals of similar age and education level from the MMSE normative sample (Folstein, Folstein, & Fanjiaug, 2001).

The patient had difficulty on the MMSE in the following area(s):

Orientation to Time

Orientation to Place

Comprehension

Reading

Writing

Drawing

Sample A. Client	Page 3
123-45-6789	07/15/2002

MSRS Checklist Results

The patient is right-handed. The patient was alert and responsive. Her orientation, attention, and concentration were impaired. Appearance was consistent with her stated age. Eye contact during the evaluation was good. The patient was dressed appropriately and her grooming appeared to be adequate. Regarding her motor functioning, no apparent abnormalities were observed. No gait disturbances were noted. Some evidence of impaired vision was noted.

Some word finding difficulties in her speech were observed. Prosody was normal. No auditory comprehension difficulties were apparent. No apparent disturbances in remote memory were noted, but some impairment in both immediate and recent memory was evident. The patient's intellectual ability was estimated to be average. Executive functioning problems were evidenced by planning and organization deficits. Affect was flat. Her mood was anxious. Information about the patient's interpersonal behavior was not recorded. The patient denied having both suicidal or homicidal ideation. Her thought content was appropriate for the situation. Thought processes were disconnected and/or incoherent. No delusions were conveyed by the patient. She denied experiencing hallucinations. Judgment, reasoning, and insight were poor.

This sentence comes from a customizable item.

Comments

Additional information observed about this patient during the evaluation includes the following: None

Report

Sample A. Client
123-45-6789

Longitudinal Profile Record

Page 4
07/15/2002

	07/15/2002				
	07/30/2001	07/15/2002			
MMSE (Raw)	24	21			
MMSE (T)	32	9			
Consciousness	Alert	Alert			
Orientation	x3	Impaired			
Attention/Concentration	n.a.d.	Impaired			
Appearance	Consistent with stated age	Consistent with stated age			
Eye Contact	Good	Good			
Dress	Appropriate	Appropriate			
Grooming	Adequate	Adequate			
Motor Functioning	n.a.d.	n.a.d.			
Gait	n.a.d.	n.a.d.			
Visual Perception	Impaired vision	Impaired vision			
Speech	n.a.d.	Word finding difficulties			
Prosody	n.a.d.	n.a.d.			
Auditory Comprehension	Other	n.a.d.			
Immediate Memory	n.a.d.	Impaired			
Recent Memory	n.a.d.	Impaired			
Remote Memory	n.a.d.	n.a.d.			
Estimated Intellectual Ability	Average	Average			

NOTE: n.a.d. = No apparent disturbances; x3 = oriented to person, place, & time.

Sample A. Client
123-45-6789

Item Responses

Page 7
07/15/2002

MMSE Responses

1. 1	7. 1	13. 1	19. 3	25. 1
2. 1	8. 0	14. ?	20. 1	26. 0
3. 1	9. 1	15. ?	21. 1	27. 1
4. 1	10. 1	16. ?	22. 1	28. 1
5. 0	11. 1	17. ?	23. 1	29. 0
6. 1	12. 1	18. ?	24. ?	30. 0
				31. 0

Conc 0

MSRS Responses

1. 1	7. 1	13. 1	19. 2	25. 1
2. 1	8. 1	14. 1	20. 5	26. 7
3. 2	9. 1	15. 2	21. 5	27. 1
4. 2	10. 1	16. 2	22. 0	28. 1
5. 1	11. 6	17. 1	23. 2	29. 3
6. 1	12. 3	18. 2	24. 2	30. 3

Hx Left Hand 0

(Continued)

(Continued)

Reliability and Validity	Most research studies regarding the MMSE indicate a relatively high reliability of test scores. Many studies have gathered evidence of test–retest reliability and have documented that test–retest reliability may decline over time. Test–retest reliabilities for psychiatric and neurologic patients range from .38 to .92 with a time lapse of 24 hours to two years. Test–retest reliabilities using the Pearson correlation range from .86 to .92 with time lapses of less than one year. Many studies have also gathered evidence of interrater reliability. Interrater reliability estimates range from .69 to 1.00 depending on the sample population. Few studies examine and report internal consistency reliability estimates. One study reports an internal consistency reliability coefficient of .764. Research reveals evidence of validity based on content. For example, a study by Jones and Gallo (2000) came close to replicating the original structure of the MMSE, identifying five factors subsequently replicated by Baños and Franklin (2002). Predictive validity studies appear to provide conflicting results; some suggest that individuals whose test scores indicate cognitive impairment are later diagnosed with cognitive impairment at least 79% of the time, whereas others suggest a high false-positive rate of up to 86%. Reviewers of the instrument remind users that the MMSE relies heavily on verbal response and reading and writing. Therefore, clinicians should be cautious about interpreting MMSE results for patients with hearing and visual impairments and patients who have low English literacy or communication disorders. Patients with these characteristics may perform poorly due to factors other than cognitive ability.
Sources	Albanese, M. A. (2001). Review of the Mini Mental State Examination. In B. S. Plake, J. C. Impara, & R. A. Spies (Eds.), *The fifteenth mental measurements yearbook*. Lincoln, NE: Buros Institute of Mental Measurements. Baños, J. H., & Franklin, L. M. (2002). Factor structure of the Mini-Mental State Examination in adult psychiatric patients. *Psychological Assessment, 14,* 397–400. Jones, R. N., & Gallo, J. J. (2000). Dimensions of the Mini-Mental State Examination among community dwelling older adults. *Psychological Medicine, 30,* 605–618. Kurlowicz, L., & Wallace, M. (1998). *The Mini Mental State Examination.* Retrieved November 15, 2009, from http://www.suffolkhealthplan.com/Appendix Provider Manual/013MiniMentalState.pdf Lopez, M. N., Charter, R. A., Mostafavi, B., Nibut, L. P., & Smith, W. E. (2005). Psychometric properties of the Folstein Mini-Mental State Examination. *Assessment, 12,* 137–144. Psychological Assessment Resources. (2009). *Mini-Mental State Examination.* Retrieved June 29, 2010, from http://www.minimental.com/ Ward, S. (2001). Review of the Mini Mental State Examination. In B. S. Plake, J. C. Impara, & R. A. Spies (Eds.), *The fifteenth mental measurements yearbook*. Lincoln, NE: Buros Institute of Mental Measurements.

TEST SPOTLIGHT 6.1

Personality Assessment Inventory (PAI)

Leslie C. Morey

Title	Personality Assessment Inventory (PAI)
Author	Leslie C. Morey
Publisher	Psychological Assessment Resources 16204 North Florida Avenue Lutz, FL 33549 www4.parinc.com
Purpose	Leslie C. Morey developed the PAI as an objective alternative to the Minnesota Multiphasic Personality Inventory (MMPI) discussed in Chapter 8. The PAI is an objective personality test designed to identify a number of psychological disorders in adults (age 18 years or older) relevant to clinical diagnosis, treatment planning, and screening for psychopathology. The PAI contains 344 statements for which the test taker must choose one of four responses: false, not at all true; slightly true; mainly true; and very true. Sample statements on the PAI resemble the following: My friends are available if I need them. Much of the time I'm sad for no real reason. My relationships have been stormy. I have many brilliant ideas.
Versions	The original version (Morey, 1991) is available in paper-and-pencil format in English and Spanish. Another version, PAI Software Portfolio Version 2.2 (PAI-SP), is available on CD-ROM.
Scales	The PAI has 11 clinical scales (Somatic Complaints, Anxiety, Anxiety-Related Disorders, Depression, Mania, Paranoia, Schizophrenia, Borderline Features, Antisocial Features, Alcohol Problems, and Drug Problems), five treatment scales (Aggression, Suicidal Ideation, Stress, Nonsupport, and Treatment Rejection) that measure characteristics that affect treatment, and two interpersonal scales (Dominance and Warmth) that provide information about the test taker's relationships with others. In addition, the PAI has four validity scales (Inconsistency, Infrequency, Negative Impression, and Positive Impression) that are used to determine whether the test taker answered the questions consistently and in good faith.

(Continued)

(Continued)

Reliability and Validity	The reliability of the PAI has been estimated using internal consistency estimates. The median reliability estimate ranged from .81 to .82 to .86 for the general community sample, college student sample, and clinical sample, respectively. Test–retest reliability estimates for the clinical scales taken at either 24 or 28 days ranged from .79 to .82.
	The test manual for an earlier edition (Morey, 1991) contains a number of validity studies for the clinical and validity scales. For example, the validity scales were correlated with the L, F, and K scales of the MMPI and with the Marlowe–Crowne Social Desirability Scale to determine discriminant and convergent evidence of validity (see Chapter 9). Also, PAI scales (validity, clinical, treatment, and interpersonal) were correlated with the MMPI, the Beck Scales (see Chapter 14), the Wahler Physical Symptoms Inventory, and the Fear Survey Schedule, yielding moderate validity coefficients. The new manual contains 133 pages of validity studies, including correlations between certain PAI scales and the NEO Personality Inventory in a general community sample. Correlations were in the direction expected (e.g., PAI Anxiety scale correlated .75 with the NEO Neuroticism scale, PAI Paranoia scale correlated −.54 with the NEO Agreeableness scale).
Report	The publisher offers a Clinical Interpretive Report that provides qualified professionals with the ability to organize information related to an individual's personality. A complete sample report can be found at www4.parinc.com/Products/Product.aspx?ProductID=PAI-PRS
Sources	Cox A., Thorpe, G., & Dawson, R. (in press). Review of the Personality Assessment Inventory. In R. A. Spies, J. F. Carlson, & K. F. Geisinger (Eds.), *The eighteenth Mental Measurements Yearbook.* Lincoln, NE: Buros Institute of Mental Measurements.
	Morey, L. C. (1991). *Personality Assessment Inventory.* Odessa, FL: Psychological Assessment Resources.
	PAR. (2010f). Personality Assessment Inventory. Retrieved June 25, 2010, from http://www4.parinc.com/Products/Product.aspx?ProductID=PAI_INTERP_GDE

TEST SPOTLIGHT 6.2

Test of Nonverbal Intelligence 4 (TONI-4)

Susan K. Johnsen   Rita J. Sherbenou

Title	Test of Nonverbal Intelligence 4 (TONI-4)
Author	Brown, I., Sherbenou, R., and Johnsen, S.
Publisher	PRO-ED 8700 Shoal Creek Boulevard Austin, TX 78757–6897 www.proedinc.com
Purpose	The TONI-4 is a nonverbal intelligence test that does not require the use of language, written or verbal, for administration. The TONI-4 is designed to measure intelligence, aptitude, abstract reasoning, and problem solving. The test takers indicate their answers in any means at their disposal, such as pointing, nodding, or making any other gesture that can be properly interpreted by the test administrator. The TONI-4 is designed for individuals that have or are suspected to have communication disorders such as dyslexia, aphasia, or other learning or speech difficulties. It can also be used in populations that do not speak English and is designed so that no knowledge of U.S. culture is required. It is appropriate for a wide range of ages (6 years to 89 years, 11 months). The test taker is asked to respond to abstract figures that present a problem along with four to six possible responses. The test items do not use words, numbers, or pictures. Unlike previous versions, with the TONI-4, the examiner may give oral instructions to the test taker. The test is made up of five practice items and 45 scored items presented in order of increasing difficulty. The test continues until three out of five items are answered incorrectly.
Versions	The TONI-4 is the fourth revision of the test, with two equivalent forms (A, B), which enable the test to be used in situations where pre- and posttesting are needed. This test can be useful to evaluate student progress or treatment effectiveness.
Scales	Results are reported in a standard score format scaled to have a mean of 100 and a standard deviation of 15. Percentile ranks are also reported based on a normative sample of 2,272 participants from 31 U.S. states. The demographic characteristics of the sample are balanced in terms of age, gender, ethnicity, and other factors.
Report	This test does not generate a report because the test administrator records the participant's responses in an answer booklet. Then the administrator scores and interprets the responses by referencing the test norms.
Reliability and Validity	The average internal consistency reliability using Coefficient Alpha is .96. Test–retest reliability is estimated to be between .86 and .89 depending on the age subgroup measured. The average alternate form reliability across all age groups based on an immediate test–retest design was .81, and for a delayed design (generally two weeks) .89. Interscorer reliability was calculated to be .99.

(Continued)

(Continued)

	Evidence of construct validity is provided via correlations with other versions of the TONI. The TONI-4 correlated with three published reading measures with coefficients ranging from .55 to .74. The TONI-4 also correlated with three measures of math with coefficients ranging from .72 to .78.
Sources	Allen, E. (June 25, 2010). Personal communication.
	Strauss, E., Sherman, E. M., & Spreen, O. (2006). *A compendium of neuropsychological tests: Administration, norms and commentary* (3rd ed.). New York: Oxford University Press.

TEST SPOTLIGHT 6.3

Wisconsin Card Sorting Test (WCST)

Title	Wisconsin Card Sorting Test (WCST)
Author	Originally developed by David A. Grant and Esta A. Berg Revised and updated by Robert K. Heaton, Gordon J. Chelune, Jack L. Talley, Gary G. Kay, and Glenn Curtiss
Publisher	Psychological Assessment Resources 16204 North Florida Avenue Lutz, FL 33549 www4.parinc.com
Purpose	Originally designed to assess perseveration and abstract thinking, the WCST is increasingly being used by clinicians and neurologists as a neuropsychological instrument to measure executive functions performed by the frontal lobe of the brain (strategic planning, organized searching, utilizing environmental feedback to shift cognitive sets, directing behavior toward achieving a goal, and modulating impulsive responding). The test administrator places four stimulus cards in front of the test taker in a specific order. The administrator then gives the test taker a deck of 64 response cards. The cards include a picture of various shapes (circles, crosses, triangles, and stars), numbers (one, two, three, and four), and colors (red, yellow, blue, and green). The administrator asks the test taker to match each of the cards with one of the four stimulus cards that the test taker thinks it matches. The administrator tells the test taker whether his or her response is correct or incorrect, and the test taker proceeds through the various sorting possibilities. The administrator records the responses in a test booklet. The responses are then scored on three dimensions (correct/incorrect, ambiguous/unambiguous, and perseverative/nonperseverative). The test has no time limit, and the test taker can take as much time as is needed with the sort.
Versions	The original version was published in 1981. A revised version with updated norms was published in 1993. In addition to the paper-and-pencil version, a computer-based version of the WCST is also available.
Scales	The WCST allows clinicians and neuropsychologists to assess frontal lobe functions using five scales: strategic planning, organized searching, utilizing environmental feedback to shift cognitive sets, directing behavior toward achieving a goal, and modulating impulsive responding.

(Continued)

(Continued)

Report	Pages 1 and 2 from the Wisconsin Card Sorting Test® Computer Version 4-Research Edition (WCST:CV4™) Sample Score Report are reproduced below.

Wisconsin Card Sorting Test™: Computer Version 4 Research Edition by Robert K. Heaton, PhD, and PAR Staff
Client Information

Last Name: Examinee	Test Date: 05/14/2003
First Name: John	Test Description: (no description)
Client ID: 123456789	
BirthDate: 07/26/1956	Rapport: Good
Age: 46 years, 9 months	Cooperation: Adequate
Gender: Male	Effort: Adequate
Ethnicity: Caucasian (not of Hispanic Origin)	On Medication: No
Education: 8 years	Description of Medication:
Handedness: Right	
Occupation: (not specified)	
Examiner: Dr. Maguire	

Caveats

Use of this report requires a thorough understanding of the Wisconsin Card Sorting Test (WCST; Berg, 1948; Grant & Berg, 1948), its interpretation, and clinical applications as presented in the WCST Manual (Heaton, Chelune; Talley, Kay, & Curtiss, 1993). This report is intended for use by qualified professionals.

This report reflects a computerized administration of the WCST. It is important to recognize that normative data used in this report were developed using the standard 128-card version of the WCST (Heaton et al., 1993). While research to date has demonstrated general equivalence between computerized administration and card administration of the WCST (Artiola i Fortuny & Heaton, 1996; Hellman, Green, Kern, & Christenson, 1992), no definitive equivalence data are available for the computerized administration of this version of the WCST and, as such, normative scores must be interpreted cautiously. In order to estimate the potential effects of a computerized administration on test performance, users should be familiar with the original card version.

Users should refer to the WCST Manual (Heaton et al., 1993) for the clinical interpretation of this score report. Clinical interpretation of the WCST requires professional training and expertise in clinical psychology and/or neuropsychology. The utility and validity of the WCST as a clinical measure of cognitive ability are directly related to the professional's background and knowledge and, in particular, familiarity with the information contained in the WCST Manual.

WCST results should be interpreted within the context of a larger clinical assessment battery and relevant clinical and historical information about this client. Additionally, use of WCST scores for clinical or diagnostic decisions should not be attempted without a good understanding of brain-behavior relationships and the medical and psychological factors that affect them.

Version: 1.04 (4.00.010)

Client: John Q. Examinee   *Test Date:* 05/14/2003
Client ID: 123456789   *Page 2 of 4*

Test Results

WCST scores	Raw scores	Age & Education Demographically Corrected			U.S. Census Age-matched		
		Standard scores	T scores	%iles	Standard scores	T scores	%iles
Trials Administered	113						
Total Correct	92						
Total Errors	21	110	57	75%	97	48	42%
% Errors	19%	114	59	82%	100	50	50%
Perseverative Responses	5	> 145	> 80	> 99%	110	57	75%
% Perseverative Responses	4%	> 145	> 80	> 99%	125	67	95%
Nonperseverative Errors	16	94	46	34%	90	43	25%
% Nonperseverative Errors	14%	95	47	37%	90	43	25%
Conceptual Level Responses	87						

(Continued)

(Continued)

Report								
			Age & Education Demographically Corrected			**U.S. Census Age-matched**		
	WCST scores	**Raw**	**Standard**	**T**	**%iles**	**Standard**	**T**	**%iles**
		scores	**scores**	**scores**		**scores**	**scores**	
	% Conceptual Level Responses	77%	113	59	81%	127	68	96%
	Categories Completed	6			> 16%			> 16%
	Trials to Complete 1st Category	15			6–10%			11–16%
	Failure to Maintain Set	3			2–5%			6–10%
	Learning to Learn	−2.67			> 16%			> 16%

Reproduced by special permission of the Publisher, Psychological Assessment Resources, Inc., 16204 North Florida Avenue, Lutz, Florida 33549, from the Wisconsin Card Sorting Test by David A. Grant., PhD, and Esta A. Berg, PhD, Copyright 1981, 1993 by Psychological Assessment Resources, Inc. (PAR). Further reproduction is prohibited without permission of PAR.

Reliability and Validity	The reliability of the WCST has been estimated using the interscorer reliability method (Clark, 2001; Trevisan, 2003). Experienced clinicians showed a range of interscorer reliability between .88 and .93 and a range of intrascorer coefficients between .91 and .96. Coefficients found for novice examiners were also adequate—between .75 and .97 for both inter- and intrascorer data. Reliability has also been estimated using the internal consistency method. Internal consistency reliability using volunteers from the University of Colorado Health Sciences Center resulted in acceptable reliability scores ranging from .60 to .85.
	Numerous validity studies have demonstrated the construct validity of the WCST by comparing individual performance on the WCST with performance on other measures. Studies of adults with closed head injuries, demyelinating diseases, seizure disorders, and schizophrenia, as well as studies of children with traumatic brain injuries, seizures, learning disabilities, and attention deficit hyperactivity disorders, suggest that the WCST provides a valid method of assessing executive function in these individuals. Studies also suggest that the WCST is sensitive to frontal lesions as well as to dysfunction in other areas of the brain.
Source	Clark, E. (2001). Review of the Wisconsin Card Sorting Test, Revised and Expanded. In B. S. Plake & J. C. Impara (Eds.), *The fourteenth mental measurements yearbook*. Lincoln, NE: Buros Institute of Mental Measurements.
	Strauss, E., Sherman, E. M., & Spreen, O. (2006). *A compendium of neuropsychological tests: Administration, norms and commentary* (3rd ed.). New York: Oxford University Press.
	Trevisan, M. S. (2003). Review of the Wisconsin Card Sorting Test—64 card version. In B. S. Plake, J. C. Impara, & R. A. Spies (Eds.), *The fifteenth mental measurements yearbook*. Lincoln, NE: Buros Institute of Mental Measurements.

TEST SPOTLIGHT 6.4

Bayley Scales of Infant and Toddler Development, Third Edition (BAYLEY-III)

Nancy Bayley

Title	Bayley Scales of Infant and Toddler Development, Third Edition (BAYLEY-III)
Author	Nancy Bayley
Publisher	Pearson Assessments 19500 Bulverde Road San Antonio, TX 78259–3710 www.pearsonassessments.com
Purpose	The BAYLEY-III was designed to assess the developmental level of children between 1 month and 3½ years of age and to assess children who are developing slowly and who might benefit from cognitive intervention. The BAYLEY-III is administered to one child at a time. The child is given a variety of age-specific objects or toys, and the psychologist observes how the child uses the objects and then assigns a score based on a detailed scoring scheme provided by the test publisher. The child's score is then compared with the norms for that age group to determine developmental progress. Caregivers complete the Adaptive Behavior Assessment System—Second Edition, which assesses the child's ability to demonstrate adaptive skills when needed.
Versions	The original version of the Bayley Scales was published in 1969. The second edition became available in 1993. The third edition was published in 2006.
Scales	The BAYLEY-III consists of five scales 1. *The Cognitive Scale* assesses how the child thinks, learns, and reacts to the world. 2. *The Language Scale* measures how well the child recognizes sounds, understands spoken words, and communicates using sounds, gestures, or words. 3. *The Motor Scale* assesses how well the child can move his or her hands, fingers, and whole body to make things happen. 4. *The Social-Emotional Scale* assesses development by identifying the social-emotional milestones that are usually achieved by certain ages. 5. *The Adaptive Behavior Scale* asks caregivers to evaluate how well the child can adapt to the demands of everyday life and demonstrate those skills when needed.
Report	A Bayley Scales report is long and technical. A sample Caregiver's report (the report given to the parents, guardian, or physician) can be found at www.pearsonpsychcorp.com.au/userfiles/1440370509BayleyIII%20Infant%20Dev%20Caregiver%20SampleReport.pdf
Reliability and Validity	Coefficient alpha estimates of individual scales ranged from .86 for Fine Motor to .91 for Cognitive, Expressive Communication, and Gross Motor. The reliabilities for the Social-Emotional scales ranged from .83 to .94, while the reliabilities of the Adaptive Behavior Scales ranged from .79 to .98. Test–retest reliability estimates ranged from .77 to .94, with the higher reliability estimates not unexpectedly found for the older children.

(Continued)

(Continued)

	The BAYLEY-III manual provides evidence of validity based on content and relationship with other variables (both criteria and constructs). Confirmatory factor analysis was also performed, demonstrating that a three-factor solution (Cognitive, Language, and Motor) fit the data in the standardization sample well except in the youngest sample, in which a two-factor solution was also supported. Correlations with the Wechsler Preschool and Primary Scale of Intelligence-Third Edition and the Bayley Cognitive Scale was reported to range from .72 to .79.
Sources	Albers, C. A., & Grieve, A. J. (2007). Test review: Bayley N. (2006). Bayley scales of infant and toddler development—third edition. *Journal of Psychoeducational Assessment, 25,* 180–198. Bayley, N. (1993). *Bayley Scales of Infant Development* (2nd ed.). San Antonio, TX: Psychological Corporation. Harcourt Assessment. (2006). *Bayley III Scales of Infant Development caregiver report.* Retrieved June 29, 2010, from http://www.pearsonpsychcorp.com.au/userfiles/1440370509 BayleyIII%20Infant%20Dev%20Caregiver%20SampleReport.pdf Tobin, M., & Hoff, K. (2007). Review of the Bayley Scales of Infant and Toddler Development (3rd ed.). In K. F. Geisinger, R. A. Spies, J. F. Carlson, & B. S. Plake (Eds.), *The seventeenth mental measurements yearbook.* Lincoln, NE: Buros Institute of Mental Measurements.

TEST SPOTLIGHT 7.1

Fundamental Interpersonal Relations Orientation–Behavior™ (FIRO-B®)

Will Schutz

Title	Fundamental Interpersonal Relations Orientation–Behavior™ (FIRO-B®)
Author	Will Schutz
Publisher	CPP Inc. 1055 Joaquin Road, 2nd Floor Mountain View, CA 94043 www.cpp-com
Purpose	The FIRO-B is a personality instrument that measures an individual's interpersonal needs—more specifically, how an individual typically behaves with other people and how the individual expects others to act toward him or her. Developed during the late 1950s, the FIRO-B is based on the theory that beyond our needs for survival, food, shelter, and warmth, we all have unique interpersonal needs that strongly motivate us. These needs relate to three fundamental dimensions of interpersonal relationships: inclusion, control, and affection. The FIRO-B provides valuable insights into how an individual's need for inclusion, control, and affection can shape his or her interactions with others. The FIRO-B is used in one-on-one coaching sessions, small groups, or teams and is well suited for team building and development, individual development, management training programs, communication workshops, and relationship counseling. The results of the FIRO-B profile provide further insights into areas such as the following: How individuals "come across" to or are perceived by others and whether this is the impression they intend to create How and why conflict develops between people How people can manage their own needs as they interact with others The FIRO-B consists of 54 items that the individual is asked to respond to in the following two formats: 1. A frequency rating scale identifying how often the individual engages in the behavior described in the item: never, rarely, occasionally, often, usually 2. A selectivity rating scale eliciting how many people the individual engages in the behavior described in the item: nobody, one or two people, a few people, some people, many people, most people)

(Continued)

(Continued)

	The FIRO-B® is available in various formats, including self-scorable booklet, hand-scorable format using scoring keys, computer-scorable mail-in answer sheets used for interpretive reports, CPP, Inc. software system, and intranet and Internet online administration and scoring. In the early 1980s, Will Schutz expanded the underlying theory and updated the FIRO-B to Element B. Element B was published by The Schutz Company and now serves as the foundation for a comprehensive methodology for organizational development. For more information about Element B, go to www.thehumanelement.com/Science-Based-Approach.
Versions	Only one version has been successfully administered to individuals ages 14 to 90 years. This version can be self-scored or scored by a professional. There is no particular education level recommended so long as the examinee has vocabulary sufficient to understand the items and instructions as well as the cognitive level of functioning sufficient to understand a verbal or written interpretation of results. It is the responsibility of the user to ensure that the individual taking the test can understand and answer the items and, if the self-scorable format is used, to calculate the scores accurately.
Scales	The FIRO-B consists of six scales representing combinations of the three need areas (Inclusion, Control, and Affection) with the two behavior dimensions (Expressed and Wanted): Inclusion—This need indicates how much an individual generally includes other people in his or her life and how much attention, contact, and recognition the individual wants from others. Control—This need indicates how much influence and responsibility an individual wants and how much the individual wants others to lead and influence him or her. Affection—This need indicates how close and warm an individual is with others and how close and warm the individual wants others to be with him or her. Expressed—This dimension indicates how much an individual prefers to initiate behavior, what the individual actually does, and what is actually observed by others. Wanted—This dimension indicates how much an individual prefers others to initiate behavior toward him or her and whether the individual shows it openly or not. FIRO-B results are displayed in a 2 x 3 grid that includes the following six scales: 1. Expressed Inclusion: How often do you act in ways that encourage your participation in situations? 2. Expressed Control: How often do you act in ways that help you direct or influence situations? 3. Expressed Affection: How often do you act in ways that encourage warmth and closeness in relationships? 4. Wanted Inclusion: How much do you want to be part of others' activities? 5. Wanted Control: How much leadership and influence do you want others to assume? 6. Wanted Affection: How much warmth and closeness do you want from others?

Report	Several reports are available, including the FIRO-B® Profile, the FIRO-B® Interpretive Report for Organizations, and the Leadership Report Using the FIRO-B and MBTI®. A sample of the most basic report, the FIRO-B Profile, follows:

Other sample reports are available at www.cpp.com/samplereports/reports.asp

Prepared for JANE SAMPLE   April 17, 2008

The FIRO-B® instrument identifies how you tend to behave toward others and how you want them to behave toward you. Your FIRO-B results can help you increase your self-understanding in a number of important areas, including how you handle interpersonal relationships and your own social needs, how others perceive you, and how you see them.

The FIRO-B tool provides information about three fundamental dimensions of interpersonal needs:

INCLUSION	**CONTROL**	**AFFECTION**
is about recognition, belonging, participation, contact with others, and how you relate to groups	concerns influence, leadership, responsibility, and decision making	is about closeness, warmth, sensitivity, openness, and how you relate to others

The FIRO-B assessment also indicates your preferences in regard to two distinct aspects of each of these needs areas:

EXPRESSED BEHAVIOR	**WANTED BEHAVIOR**
• How much do you prefer to initiate the behavior? • How do you actually behave with respect to the three fundamental interpersonal needs? • What is your comfort level engaging in the behaviors associated with the three needs?	• How much do you prefer others to take the initiative? • How much do you want to be on the receiving end of those behaviors? • What is your comfort level when others direct their behaviors associated with the three needs to you?

This profile reports your results on the expressed and wanted aspects of the three interpersonal needs explored by the FIRO-B tool and includes basic interpretive information for each. As you read through this profile, please consider how the results compare with your own sense of how you interact with others. Results should not be used to make a judgment about whether any behavior or any person is good or bad. You should avoid making major decisions based on the results of only one assessment.

(Continued)

(Continued)

Report	

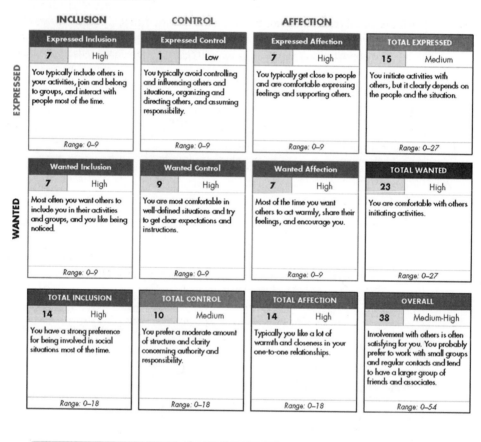

FIRO-B® Profile

JANE SAMPLE

Your FIRO-B® Results

Below are your scores for both expressed and wanted aspects of Inclusion, Control, and Affection, along with total scores for each dimension.

INCLUSION **CONTROL** **AFFECTION**

EXPRESSED

Expressed Inclusion	
7	High
You typically include others in your activities, join and belong to groups, and interact with people most of the time.	
Range: 0–9	

Expressed Control	
1	Low
You typically avoid controlling and influencing others and situations, organizing and directing others, and assuming responsibility.	
Range: 0–9	

Expressed Affection	
7	High
You typically get close to people and are comfortable expressing feelings and supporting others.	
Range: 0–9	

TOTAL EXPRESSED	
15	Medium
You initiate activities with others, but it clearly depends on the people and the situation.	
Range: 0–27	

WANTED

Wanted Inclusion	
7	High
Most often you want others to include you in their activities and groups, and you like being noticed.	
Range: 0–9	

Wanted Control	
9	High
You are most comfortable in well-defined situations and try to get clear expectations and instructions.	
Range: 0–9	

Wanted Affection	
7	High
Most of the time you want others to act warmly, share their feelings, and encourage you.	
Range: 0–9	

TOTAL WANTED	
23	High
You are comfortable with others initiating activities.	
Range: 0–27	

TOTAL INCLUSION	
14	High
You have a strong preference for being involved in social situations most of the time.	
Range: 0–18	

TOTAL CONTROL	
10	Medium
You prefer a moderate amount of structure and clarity concerning authority and responsibility.	
Range: 0–18	

TOTAL AFFECTION	
14	High
Typically you like a lot of warmth and closeness in your one-to-one relationships.	
Range: 0–18	

OVERALL	
38	Medium-High
Involvement with others is often satisfying for you. You probably prefer to work with small groups and regular contacts and tend to have a larger group of friends and associates.	
Range: 0–54	

For further information on the FIRO-B instrument and reports, refer to *Introduction to the FIRO-B® Instrument in Organizations* by Eugene Schnell and Allen Hammer, *Introduction to the FIRO-B® Instrument* by Judith Waterman and Jenny Rogers, and *Participating in Teams* by Eugene Schnell, all available from CPP, Inc.

CPP, Inc. | 800-624-1765 | www.cpp.com

Reliability and Validity	Reliability studies indicate that the FIRO-B® has good test–retest reliability over short periods of time, with correlations on the three need areas and two behavior dimensions between the two testing sessions ranging between .72 and .85 for junior high school students, between .73 and .82 for college students, and between .71 and .82 for adults. Reliability studies also indicate that the FIRO-B has acceptable ranges of internal consistency, with alpha coefficients for the six scales ranging between .85 (Wanted Affection) and .96 (Wanted Inclusion). Construct validity studies demonstrate convergent evidence and divergent evidence of validity with expected scales on the Myers–Briggs Type Indicator® assessment, the California Psychological Inventory, and the Adjective Checklist. Evidence of validity based on relationships with external criteria suggest that individuals with different FIRO-B scores clearly self-select into different occupations in ways that suggest they are doing so, at least in part, because they perceive opportunities to satisfy some of their interpersonal needs in these occupations.
Sources	Hammer, A. L., & Schnell, E. R. (2000). *FIRO-B®: Technical guide.* Mountain View, CA: CPP, Inc. Waterman, J. A., & Rogers, J. (1996). *Introduction to the FIRO-B®.* Mountain View, CA: CPP, Inc.

TEST SPOTLIGHT 9.1

Mathematics Self-Efficacy Scale (MSES)

Nancy Betz

Title	Mathematics Self-Efficacy Scale (MSES)
Author	Nancy Betz and Gail Hackett
Publisher	Mind Garden 3803 East Bayshore Road Palo Alto, CA 94303 www.mindgarden.com
Purpose	The MSES was developed to assess a person's beliefs that he or she is capable of performing math-related tasks and behaviors. The current (1993) version of the MSES contains 34 items divided into two parts: Everyday Math Tasks (18 items) and Math-Related Courses (16 items). The test taker rates each item in the test on a 10 point scale that describes his or her confidence in completing the task indicated by the question. The section on Math-Related Courses asks how confident the test taker is about being able to complete the course listed with a grade of A or B. Sample Questions: <table><tr><td>0</td><td>1</td><td>2</td><td>3</td><td>4</td><td>5</td><td>6</td><td>7</td><td>8</td><td>9</td></tr><tr><td colspan="2">No confidence at all</td><td colspan="2">Very little confidence</td><td colspan="2">Some confidence</td><td colspan="2">Much confidence</td><td colspan="2">Complete confidence</td></tr></table> Confidence Scale How much confidence do you have that you could successfully: <ul><li>Determine the amount of sales tax on a clothing purchase?</li><li>Calculate recipe quantities for a dinner for 3 when the original recipe is for 12 people?</li><li>Please rate the following college courses according to how much confidence you have that you could complete the course with a final grade of A or B:<ul><li>Economics</li><li>Calculus</li><li>Accounting</li><li>Biochemistry</li></ul></li></ul>
Versions	The original version was published in 1983. Since then, the authors have made considerable changes twice, most recently in 1993.

Reliability and Validity	For the 1983 version, internal constancy reliability estimates were given as .96 for the total scale, .92 for the Math Tasks subscale, and .96 for the Math-Related Courses subscale. Two-week test–retest reliability estimates were given as .94.
	Evidence of validity was provided based on the test's relationship with other variables. Total MSES scores were correlated with math anxiety r = .56 and confidence in doing math r = .66.
Sources	Ciechalski, J. C. (2001). Review of the Mathematics Self-Efficacy Scale. In B. S. Plake & J. C. Impara (Eds.), *The fourteenth mental measurements yearbook.* Lincoln, NE: Buros Institute of Mental Measurements.
	Smith, E. (2001). Review of the Mathematics Self-Efficacy Scale. In B. S. Plake & J. C. Impara (Eds.), *The fourteenth mental measurements yearbook.* Lincoln, NE: Buros Institute of Mental Measurements.
	Mindgarden. (2005–2009). *Mathematics Self-Efficacy Scale.* Retrieved June 10, 2010, from http://www.mindgarden.com/products/maths.htm

TEST SPOTLIGHT 12.1

Revised Minnesota Multiphasic Personality Inventory (MMPI-2)

J. C. McKinley   James N. Butcher   Starke R. Hathaway

Title	Minnesota Multiphasic Personality Inventory-2 (MMPI-2)
Author	Starke R. Hathaway, J. C. McKinley, and James N. Butcher
Publisher	The University of Minnesota Press, representing the Regents of the University of Minnesota, published the MMPI-2.
	As publisher, the University of Minnesota Press, working with its consulting board, is responsible for the substantive development of the tests, including any revisions to them. The university exclusively licenses Pearson Assessments to produce, market, and sell the MMPI test products and to offer scoring and interpretive services.
Purpose	The original MMPI—the most widely used personality test in the world—was developed during the late 1930s and published in 1943 as a tool for routine clinical assessment. Its purpose was to help clinicians assign appropriate diagnoses to persons who showed signs of mental disorders. The developers gathered a large number of questions from textbooks, personality inventories, and clinicians. They administered the questions to patients for whom diagnoses were available in hospitals and clinics in Minnesota. Then they analyzed the responses by grouping them by diagnostic category. They put in the MMPI only those questions that were answered differently by a diagnostic group (for example, schizophrenic patients). They also added three "validity" scales to detect respondents who answered questions dishonestly. When revising the MMPI, the authors added three more validity scales. (Note: Validity scales do not assess the validity of a test's scores.)
Versions	During the 1980s, a restandardization committee studied and revised the MMPI. The MMPI-2, published in 1989, was developed using a sample of persons (1,138 men and 1,461 women) randomly chosen from seven regions of the United States. The sample was designed to resemble the 1980 U.S. census in age, gender, minority status, social class, and education. (As you recall, Chapter 5 discussed the process and implications of developing norms for tests.)
Scales	The MMPI-2 contains 10 clinical scales:

1. *Hypochondriasis*—excessive or exaggerated concerns about physical health
2. *Depression*—issues of discouragement, pessimism, and hopelessness as well as excessive responsibility
3. *Conversion Hysteria*—sensory or motor disorders that have no organic basis, denial, and lack of social anxiety
4. *Psychopathic Deviation*—degree to which relatively normal individuals have a willingness to acknowledge problems, including a lack of concern for social or moral standards with a tendency for "acting out"
5. *Masculinity/Femininity*—attitudes and feelings in which men and women are thought to differ (originally a measure of homoerotic feelings)
6. *Paranoia*—interpersonal sensitivities and tendencies to misinterpret the motives and intentions of others, including self-centeredness and insecurity
7. *Psychastenia*—excessive worries, compulsive behaviors, exaggerated fears, generalized anxiety, and distress, including declarations of high moral standards, self-blame, and rigid efforts to control impulses

8. *Schizophrenia*—strange beliefs, unusual experiences, and special sensitivities related to schizophrenia

9. *Hypomania*—excessive ambition, elevated energy, extraversion, high aspirations, grandiosity, and impulsive decision making

10. *Social Introversion*—social shyness, preference for solitary pursuits, and lack of social assertiveness

The MMPI-2 contains nine validity scales, each of which contains a group of questions that provide information on the test taker's level of honesty and motivation during test administration. On the original MMPI, the Lie scale, the Infrequency scale, and the Correction scale were designed to indicate whether the respondent lied, minimized, or exaggerated difficulties; responded randomly; or demonstrated an unwillingness to cooperate. Three new validity scales were added during the test's revision. The Back-Page Infrequency scale provides a score for a test taker's diligence in completing the test, the True Response Inconsistency scale is designed to measure lack of cooperation, and the Variable Response Inconsistency scale provides a measure of the test taker's inconsistency. These scales are important for interpreting test results because, as you recall from Chapter 6, error can be added to the test score when the test taker does not answer questions truthfully or honestly.

Report

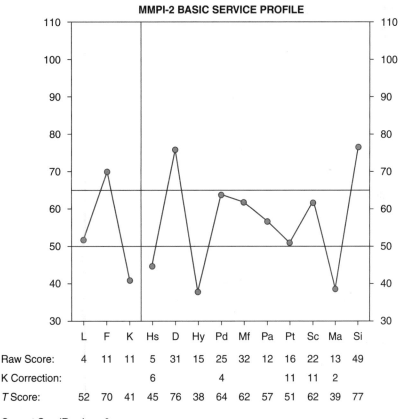

MMPI-2 BASIC SERVICE PROFILE

	L	F	K	Hs	D	Hy	Pd	Mf	Pa	Pt	Sc	Ma	Si
Raw Score:	4	11	11	5	31	15	25	32	12	16	22	13	49
K Correction:				6			4			11	11	2	
T Score:	52	70	41	45	76	38	64	62	57	51	62	39	77

Cannot Say (Raw):   0

SOURCE: Excerpted from the *MMPI®-(Minnesota Multiphasic Personality Inventory®-2) Manual for Administration, Scoring, and Interpretation, Revised Edition.* Copyright © 2001 by the Regents of the University of Minnesota Press. "MMPI" and "Minnesota Multiphasic Personality Inventory" are registered trademarks owned by the Regents of the University of Minnesota.

(Continued)

Report	
	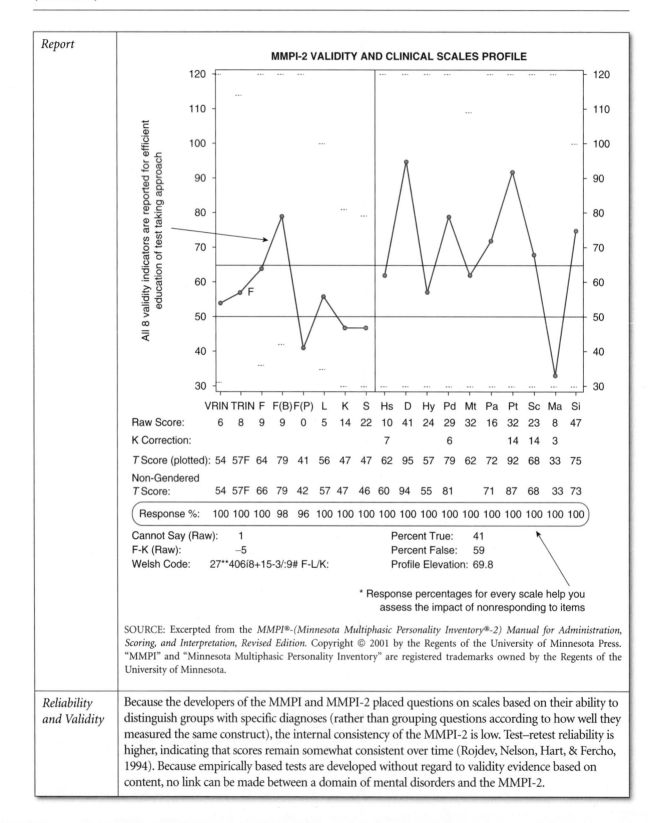

MMPI-2 VALIDITY AND CLINICAL SCALES PROFILE

All 8 validity indicators are reported for efficient education of test taking approach

	VRIN	TRIN	F	F(B)	F(P)	L	K	S	Hs	D	Hy	Pd	Mt	Pa	Pt	Sc	Ma	Si
Raw Score:	6	8	9	9	0	5	14	22	10	41	24	29	32	16	32	23	8	47
K Correction:									7			6			14	14	3	
T Score (plotted):	54	57F	64	79	41	56	47	47	62	95	57	79	62	72	92	68	33	75
Non-Gendered T Score:	54	57F	66	79	42	57	47	46	60	94	55	81		71	87	68	33	73
Response %:	100	100	100	98	96	100	100	100	100	100	100	100	100	100	100	100	100	100

Cannot Say (Raw):   1
F-K (Raw):   −5
Welsh Code: 27**406í8+15-3/:9# F-L/K:

Percent True: 41
Percent False: 59
Profile Elevation: 69.8

* Response percentages for every scale help you assess the impact of nonresponding to items

SOURCE: Excerpted from the *MMPI®-(Minnesota Multiphasic Personality Inventory®-2) Manual for Administration, Scoring, and Interpretation, Revised Edition.* Copyright © 2001 by the Regents of the University of Minnesota Press. "MMPI" and "Minnesota Multiphasic Personality Inventory" are registered trademarks owned by the Regents of the University of Minnesota.

Reliability and Validity	Because the developers of the MMPI and MMPI-2 placed questions on scales based on their ability to distinguish groups with specific diagnoses (rather than grouping questions according to how well they measured the same construct), the internal consistency of the MMPI-2 is low. Test–retest reliability is higher, indicating that scores remain somewhat consistent over time (Rojdev, Nelson, Hart, & Fercho, 1994). Because empirically based tests are developed without regard to validity evidence based on content, no link can be made between a domain of mental disorders and the MMPI-2.

Reliability and Validity	The increasing use of the MMPI stimulated a large body of research regarding its validity in various situations. Much of the research was critical, including charges regarding low validity. For example, critics noted that the norming sample for the MMPI was drawn from one region and contained mostly people of one race and ethnic background (Colligan, Osborne, Swenson, & Offord, 1983). Definitions of neurotic and psychotic conditions also changed after the MMPI was developed. For instance, in 1994, the latest revision of the *Diagnostic and Statistical Manual of Mental Disorders* discarded homosexuality, a disorder the original MMPI purportedly identified as a mental disorder. The norm group for the MMPI-2 contained 2,600 individuals, age 18 years or older, who were selected as a representative sample of the U.S. population.
	The MMPI-2, although significantly improved over the original version, still is presented as valid based on evidence of the original version. Some researchers, such as Rojdev and colleagues (1994), have reported evidence of validity. Rossi, Van den Brande, Tobac, Sloore, and Hauben (2003) have also reported convergent evidence of validity for the MMPI-2 with the Millon Clinical Multiaxial Inventory–III, a personality test designed to provide diagnostic and treatment information to clinicians in the areas of personality disorders and clinical syndromes.
Sources	Archer, R. P. (1992). Review of the Minnesota Multiphasic Personality Inventory-2. In J. J. Kramer & J. C. Conoley (Eds.), *The eleventh mental measurements yearbook.* Lincoln, NE: Buros Institute of Mental Measurements.
	Colligan, R. C., Osborne, D., Swenson, W. M., & Offord, K. P. (1983). *The MMPI: A contemporary normative study.* New York: Praeger.
	Pearson Assessments. (2009). *MMPI-2 (Minnesota Multiphasic Personality Inventory-2).* Retrieved June 10, 2010, from http://www.pearsonassessments.com/tests/mmpi_2.htm
	Rojdev, R., Nelson, W. M., III, Hart, K. J., & Fercho, M. C. (1994). Criterion-related validity and stability: Equivalence of the MMPI and the MMPI-2. *Journal of Clinical Psychology, 50,* 361–367.
	Rossi, R., Van den Brande, I., Tobac, A., Sloore, H., & Hauben, C. (2003). Convergent validity of the MCMI-III personality disorder scales and the MMPI-2 scales. *Journal of Personality Disorders, 17,* 330–340.

TEST SPOTLIGHT 13.1

Graduate Record Examination (GRE)

Title	Graduate Record Examination (GRE)
Author	Educational Testing Service (ETS)
Publisher	Educational Testing Service Rosedale Road Princeton, NJ 08541 www.ets.org
Purpose	The GRE consists of the GRE General Test and eight GRE Subject Tests that gauge undergraduate achievement in eight fields of study. The GRE General Test and Subject Tests are entrance exams used by many graduate, professional, and business programs to aid in the admissions process. Developed more than 60 years ago, the GRE General Test measures some of the reasoning skills that develop over time and that graduate school deans believe are essential to success in graduate school. The GRE General Test measures verbal reasoning, quantitative reasoning, critical thinking, and analytical writing skills. The GRE Subject Tests measure some subject matter content knowledge often emphasized in undergraduate education. The GRE General Test is offered online, year-round, at computer-based testing centers worldwide. It is offered at paper-based test centers where computer-based testing centers are not available. It takes approximately 3–3 ¾ of an hour to respond to the writing prompts and answer the 28–38 questions in each section. The GRE Subject Tests are offered three times a year at paper-based testing centers worldwide. The number of questions on each subject test varies from approximately 68 to over 200, and most are multiple choice. ETS offers practice books for each of the Subject Tests.
Versions and Scales	The GRE General Test consists of the following sections: • Verbal Reasoning—tests the ability to analyze and assess written material and synthesize information obtained from the material, to analyze relationships among parts of sentences, and to recognize the relationships between words and concepts • Quantitative Reasoning—tests the understanding of simple math concepts, knowledge of fundamental mathematical skills, and the ability to reason quantitatively and solve problems in a quantitative setting • Analytical Writing—tests critical thinking and analytical writing skills by assessing the ability to express and support complex ideas, evaluate an argument, and maintain a focused and logical discussion The GRE Subject Tests measure undergraduate achievement in eight disciplines: • Biochemistry, Cell and Molecular Biology • Biology • Chemistry • Computer Science • Literature in English • Mathematics • Physics • Psychology

	Prior to the fall of 2006, the GRE General Test was administered year-round in the United States, Canada, and various other countries. Although usually computer based, it was still offered in paper-and-pencil format, typically three times a year, in places where computer-based testing was not available. The sections of the computer-based version of the GRE (Verbal Reasoning and Quantitative Reasoning) were adaptive. That is, test takers received questions that were based on the level of ability displayed in early questions by the test takers. The adaptive versions used fewer questions than the paper-and-pencil version. With one question presented at a time, and beginning with a question of moderate difficulty, subsequent questions were based on whether test takers answered the previous question correctly or incorrectly. The test continued until test takers had received and answered the required mix of question types and question content.
	In the fall of 2006, ETS introduced a significantly revised GRE General Test. Some general changes include the following:
	• The time for the test increased from 2.5 hours to slightly more than 4 hours, with new content, a new structure, and different types of questions.
	• The test is now administered 29 times a year, instead of continuously, through the ETS global network of Internet-based centers and through Prometric, the world's largest computer-based testing network.
	• The test is no longer offered in a computer adaptive format; rather, each student who takes the test on a given day sees the same questions in the same order. Furthermore, no student sees the same questions on different dates.
	• There are experimental questions that do not count toward the final score (but will be used to select questions for future versions of the test).
	• The traditional 200- to 800-point scale for the Verbal Reasoning and Quantitative Reasoning sections were replaced with a scale that is approximately 120 to 170 points. The Analytical Writing section continues to be scored on a scale from 0 to 6.
	Some of the major changes to each section include the following:
	• *Analytical Writing*—Although 15 minutes shorter, includes more focused questions to ensure original analytical writing.
	• *Verbal Reasoning*—Places a greater emphasis on higher cognitive skills, less dependence on vocabulary, and more reading passages.
	• *Quantitative Reasoning*—Provides more real-life scenarios and data interpretation questions, fewer geometry questions, and an on-screen four-function calculator that allows test takers to calculate square roots.
	According to ETS, the new version was designed to increase the validity of the test scores; that is, to provide a more accurate measure of how qualified applicants are to do graduate-level work. The new design leverages advances in psychometric design, technology, and security measures, and it provides test score users with better information on graduate school applicants' performance.
Report	Reports are generated and sent to students who take the computerized version of the GRE approximately 10–15 days after test administration. Reports are generated and sent to students who take the paper-and-pencil version approximately 4–6 weeks after test administration. If students take the GRE more than once, their GRE score reports will show the scores they have earned on each administration over the past five years.

(Continued)

	Although the GRE score report was likely to change with the introduction of the revised test in October 2006, the 2005–2006 GRE General Test score report includes (a) a single score for the test taker's performance on the Analytical Writing section, ranging from 0 to 6, with the score typically being the average of scores from two trained readers (if the two scores differ by more than 1 point, a third reader determines the scores), and (b) a raw score (the number of questions the test taker answered correctly) and a 200- to 800-point scaled score (a score that reflects differences in difficulty between test editions) for both the Verbal Reasoning and Quantitative Reasoning sections. The GRE Subject Test score report includes an individual's raw score and a 200- to 990-point scaled score as well as subscores on a 20- to 99-point scale for the Biochemistry, Cell and Molecular Biology; Biology; and Psychology Subject Tests. To learn more about how the GRE General Test and GRE Subject Tests are scored and reported, go to www.ets.org/. The GRE test will change again in August 2011. To find out more about the changes in the test and how to prepare to take the new GRE test, go to www.ets.org/gre/revised_general/know.
Reliability and Validity	Many reliability studies show that GRE General Test and GRE Subject Test scores are reliable. For example, ETS reports the reliability coefficients for the three sections of the GRE General Test (Analytical Writing, Verbal Reasoning, and Quantitative Reasoning) to be .72, .92, and .91, respectively. The reliability coefficients for the Subject Tests range between .90 and .95, with subtest reliability coefficients ranging between .85 and .91. Similarly, research studies indicate that GRE General Test scores are valid predictors of success during the first year of graduate school; however, available samples of minority students have been very small. Correlations between GRE General Test scores and graduate first-year GPA range between .24 and .29 for Analytical Writing, .22 and .33 for Quantitative Reasoning, and .28 and .33 for Verbal Reasoning. However, when combined with undergraduate GPA, correlation coefficients across all sections range between .44 and .48, suggesting that the combination of General Test scores and undergraduate GPA is a better predictor of graduate first-year GPA. Studies of validity using the predictive method suggest that the GRE Subject Tests predict graduate first-year GPA moderately, with correlation coefficients ranging between .27 and .51. However, the combination of Subject Test scores and undergraduate GPA shows much more predictive ability, with correlation coefficients ranging between .43 and .58.
Sources	Educational Testing Service. (2005). *Interpreting your GRE scores.* Retrieved June 10, 2010, from http://www.gistguide.com/guide/gre/srinfo.pdf Educational Testing Service. (2009). *Guide to the use of scores.* Retrieved June 10, 2010, from http://ets.org/Media/Tests/GRE/pdf/gre_0910_guide.pdf Educational Testing Service. (2010). *Frequently asked questions about the GRE General Test.* Retrieved June 10, 2010, from http://ets.org/gre/general/about/faq/

TEST SPOTLIGHT 13.2

Self-Directed Search (SDS)

John L. Holland

Title	Self-Directed Search (SDS)
Author	John L. Holland
Publisher	Psychological Assessment Resources 16204 North Florida Avenue Lutz, FL 33549 www4.parinc.com
Purpose	The SDS is a career interest inventory. It can be extremely useful to individuals who might wonder what career path to follow, who want to support a tentative choice, or who want to make sure they have not overlooked obvious alternatives. The SDS can also be useful to individuals seeking a second career, returning to school, or questioning the suitability of their current job. The results of the SDS provide individuals with insights into the personality types that they are most like and occupations from the Dictionary of Occupational Titles (Coutsoukis & Information Technology Associates, 1995–2003) that map careers that reflect individuals' interests and abilities. Available online and in paper-and-pencil format in more than 25 languages, the SDS is a self-administered test that takes approximately 15–20 minutes to complete. It measures six personality types: 1. *Realistic* (R): Realistic people like jobs such as automobile mechanic, air traffic controller, surveyor, farmer, and electrician. They have mechanical and athletic abilities and like to work more with things than with people. They are described as asocial, conforming, frank, genuine, hardheaded, inflexible, materialistic, natural, normal, persistent, practical, self-effacing, thrifty, uninsightful, and uninvolved. 2. *Investigative* (I): Investigative people like jobs such as biologist, chemist, physicist, anthropologist, geologist, and medical technologist. They have mathematical and scientific ability and prefer to work alone and to solve problems. They are described as analytical, cautious, complex, critical, curious, independent, intellectual, introspective, pessimistic, precise, rational, reserved, retiring, unassuming, and unpopular. 3. *Artistic* (A): Artistic people like jobs such as composer, musician, stage director, writer, interior decorator, and actor/actress. They have artistic abilities, enjoy creating work, and have good imaginations. They are described as complicated, disorderly, emotional, expressive, idealistic, imaginative, impractical, impulsive, independent, introspective, intuitive, nonconforming, open, original, and sensitive.

(Continued)

(Continued)

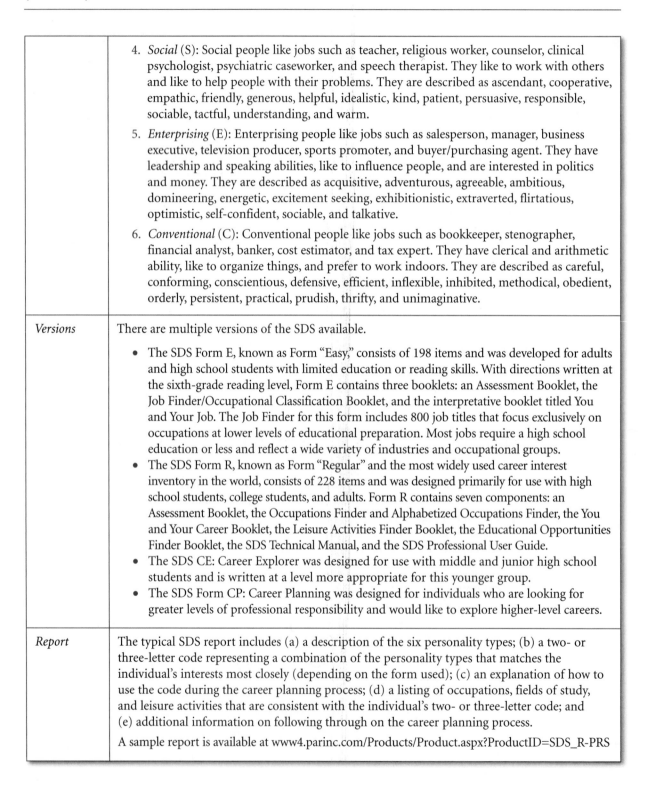

	4. *Social* (S): Social people like jobs such as teacher, religious worker, counselor, clinical psychologist, psychiatric caseworker, and speech therapist. They like to work with others and like to help people with their problems. They are described as ascendant, cooperative, empathic, friendly, generous, helpful, idealistic, kind, patient, persuasive, responsible, sociable, tactful, understanding, and warm. 5. *Enterprising* (E): Enterprising people like jobs such as salesperson, manager, business executive, television producer, sports promoter, and buyer/purchasing agent. They have leadership and speaking abilities, like to influence people, and are interested in politics and money. They are described as acquisitive, adventurous, agreeable, ambitious, domineering, energetic, excitement seeking, exhibitionistic, extraverted, flirtatious, optimistic, self-confident, sociable, and talkative. 6. *Conventional* (C): Conventional people like jobs such as bookkeeper, stenographer, financial analyst, banker, cost estimator, and tax expert. They have clerical and arithmetic ability, like to organize things, and prefer to work indoors. They are described as careful, conforming, conscientious, defensive, efficient, inflexible, inhibited, methodical, obedient, orderly, persistent, practical, prudish, thrifty, and unimaginative.
Versions	There are multiple versions of the SDS available. • The SDS Form E, known as Form "Easy," consists of 198 items and was developed for adults and high school students with limited education or reading skills. With directions written at the sixth-grade reading level, Form E contains three booklets: an Assessment Booklet, the Job Finder/Occupational Classification Booklet, and the interpretative booklet titled You and Your Job. The Job Finder for this form includes 800 job titles that focus exclusively on occupations at lower levels of educational preparation. Most jobs require a high school education or less and reflect a wide variety of industries and occupational groups. • The SDS Form R, known as Form "Regular" and the most widely used career interest inventory in the world, consists of 228 items and was designed primarily for use with high school students, college students, and adults. Form R contains seven components: an Assessment Booklet, the Occupations Finder and Alphabetized Occupations Finder, the You and Your Career Booklet, the Leisure Activities Finder Booklet, the Educational Opportunities Finder Booklet, the SDS Technical Manual, and the SDS Professional User Guide. • The SDS CE: Career Explorer was designed for use with middle and junior high school students and is written at a level more appropriate for this younger group. • The SDS Form CP: Career Planning was designed for individuals who are looking for greater levels of professional responsibility and would like to explore higher-level careers.
Report	The typical SDS report includes (a) a description of the six personality types; (b) a two- or three-letter code representing a combination of the personality types that matches the individual's interests most closely (depending on the form used); (c) an explanation of how to use the code during the career planning process; (d) a listing of occupations, fields of study, and leisure activities that are consistent with the individual's two- or three-letter code; and (e) additional information on following through on the career planning process. A sample report is available at www4.parinc.com/Products/Product.aspx?ProductID=SDS_R-PRS

Reliability and Validity	Many studies assess the reliability of the SDS scores. In general, these studies indicate that the SDS scores have good test–retest reliability. For example, Form R has demonstrated test–retest correlations for summary codes ranging between .76 and .89 over intervals from 4 to 12 weeks. Reliability studies on Form R also indicate that the SDS has acceptable ranges of internal consistency, with coefficients ranging between .72 and .92 for the various scales and between .90 and .94 for the summary scale. Form E also has demonstrated acceptable levels of internal consistency, with coefficients ranging between .94 and .96 for the summary scale and between .81 and .92 for the other scales.
	A significant number of studies have explored evidence of validity of the SDS using the concurrent method, and in general all of these have been supportive, with most validity coefficients at or above .65. According to the Mental Measurements Yearbook, one drawback of the SDS is that it does not provide predictive evidence of validity. To gather this evidence, researchers would need to follow up with individuals who took the SDS to determine how well the results of the test matched the individuals' ultimate occupational choices and job satisfaction.
Sources	Brown, M. B. (2004). Review of the Self-Directed Search (4th ed.). In J. J. Kramer & J. C. Conoley (Eds.), *The eleventh mental measurements yearbook.* Lincoln, NE: Buros Institute of Mental Measurements. Coutsoukis, P., & Information Technology Associates. (1995–2003). *Dictionary of occupational titles.* Retrieved June 10, 2010, from http://www.occupationalinfo.org/. Holland, J. L., Fritzsche, B. A., & Powell, A. B. (1996). *SDS: Technical manual.* Odessa, FL: Psychological Assessment Resources. Holland, J. L., Powell, A. B., & Fritzsche, B. A. (1994). *SDS: Professional user's guide.* Odessa, FL: Psychological Assessment Resources. Holmberg, K., Rosen, D., & Holland, J. L. (1997). *SDS: The leisure activities finder.* Odessa, FL: Psychological Assessment Resources.

TEST SPOTLIGHT 14.1

California Psychological Inventory, Third Edition (CPI)

Title	California Psychological Inventory, Third Edition (CPI)
Author	Harrison G. Gough and Pamela Bradley
Publisher	Consulting Psychologists Press 1055 Joaquin Road, 2nd Floor Mountain View, CA 94043 www.cpp.com
Purpose	The CPI is a personality inventory first designed in 1956. The third edition, CPI 434, was published in 1996. The CPI was designed for test takers, 13 years or older, to measure their social and interpersonal behaviors and to predict what they will say and do in specific contexts. The CPI 434 is a self-report test that contains 434 true-false items, nearly 40% of which were taken from the Minnesota Multiphasic Personality Inventory. The CPI 434 takes about 45 to 60 minutes to complete.
Versions	There are online and paper-and-pencil versions of the CPI, the CPI 434. (A modified and updated version of the test, the CPI 260, is often used for leadership selection and development.) There are four CPI types: • Alphas—externally oriented, norm-favoring • Betas—internally oriented, norm-favoring • Gammas—externally oriented, norm-questioning • Deltas—internally oriented, norm-questioning The CPI 434 contains 18 of the original 20 Folk Concept Scales (Dominance, Capacity for Status, Sociability, Social Presence, Self-acceptance, Independence, Empathy, Responsibility, Socialization, Self-control, Good Impression, Communality, Well-being, Tolerance, Achievement via Conformance, Achievement via Independence, Intellectual Efficiency, Psychological-mindedness, Flexibility, and Femininity/Masculinity). The Folk Scales are designed to capture cross-cultural personality themes that should be easily understood worldwide. The scales are grouped into four classes to measure (a) social expertise and interpersonal style; (b) maturity, normative orientation, and values; (c) achievement orientation; and (d) personal interest styles. There are 13 special purpose scales used to report on creative temperament, managerial potential, tough-mindedness, and a number of practical dimensions of operating style and behavior.

Report	CPI 434 results are displayed in three reports:
	• CPI 434 Profile
	• CPI 434 Narrative Report
	• CPI 434 Configural Analysis Report
	The Profile Report includes a clear and organized basic interpretation of a test taker's CPI 434 results. The report includes a gender-specific profile and a combined profile based on male/female norms. These norms can be used for employment situations when gender-neutral reporting is required. The report also includes the test taker's scores on seven special purpose scales: Creative Temperament, Managerial Potential, Work Orientation, Leadership Potential, Amicability, Tough-Mindedness, and Law Enforcement Orientation.
	To see a sample Profile Report, go to www.cpp.com/pdfs/smp210127.pdf.
	The Narrative Report includes a well-organized comprehensive interpretation of a test taker's CPI 434 results. It includes a profile of the test taker's CPI type, level, and Folk Scale results and then elaborates on that information. The report includes predictive statements about the test taker's behavior to aid in interpretation, helping test taker and administrator understand the test taker in a knowledgeable and objective manner. The report includes two scale profiles, one for the gender-specific norm group and one with combined male/female norms. These norms can be used in employment situations when gender-neutral norms are needed. The report also includes the test taker's results on several special purpose scales, including Creative Temperament, Managerial Potential, and Tough-Mindedness.
	To see a sample Narrative Report, go to www.cpp.com/pdfs/smp210128.pdf.
	The Configural Analysis Report builds on the information in the narrative report with a more complete interpretation, including two different types of interpretations (empirical analyses derived from research and speculative analyses derived from interpretations by the test author and colleagues), which are based on combinations of scales. The report is based on the author's book A Practical Guide to CPI Interpretation.
	To see a sample Configural Analysis Report, go to www.cpp.com/pdfs/smp210129.pdf.
	For more information on the CPI, see www.cpp.com/products/catalog/CPI434_2008.pdf.
Reliability and Validity	Extensive data are provided in the CPI test manual, and reliability/validity coefficients vary. The internal consistency estimates (coefficient alpha) on the 18 Folk Scales ranging from .43 to .85 (median = .76), with four scales having coefficients less than .70. The Cronbach's alphas for the 13 Specialty Scales range between .45 and .88, again with 4 scales having coefficients less than .70. The majority of test–retest reliability estimates among high school students are high (between .60 and .80 for a 1-year period). Among adults, the estimates for 1 year range between .51 and .80.
	The test's literature includes empirical evidence for the validity of the Folk Scales and the Specialty Scales. The construct validity of the Folk Scales shows moderate to strong correlations (.40–.80) between CPI scales and measures of similar constructs from well-known and well-validated personality instruments. The power of these scales to predict individual behavior in any particular situational or observational context is consistent but relatively weak.

(Continued)

Sources	CPP. (2009). *The CPI Assessments.* Retrieved November 15, 2009, from https://www.cpp.com/products/cpi/index.aspx
	CPP. (n.d.). *California Psychological Inventory: Talent.* Retrieved November 15, 2009, from https://www.cpp.com/products/catalog/CPI434_2008.pdf
	Gough, H. G. (1987). *California Psychological Inventory administrator's guide.* Palo Alto, CA: Consulting Psychologists Press.
	Hattrup, K. (2003). Review of the California Psychological Inventory, third edition. In B. S. Plake, J. C. Impara, & R. A. Spies (Eds.), *The fifteenth mental measurements yearbook.* Lincoln, NE: Buros Institute of Mental Measurements.

TEST SPOTLIGHT 14.2

16 Personality Factor Questionnaire, Fifth Edition (16PF)

Raymond B. Cattell

Title	16 Personality Factor Questionnaire, Fifth Edition (16PF)
Author	Raymond B. Cattell, Karen Cattell, Heather Cattell, Mary Russell, and Karol Darcie
Publisher	Institute for Personality and Ability Testing 1801 Woodfield Drive Savoy, IL 61874 www.ipat.com
Purpose	The 16PF is a self-report personality test designed to measure normal personality traits in people 16 years or older. Originally published in 1949, the fifth edition was published in 1993. The 16PF is based on 16 scales identified using factor analysis that are grouped into five global factors. Professionals use the 16PF in various settings, including business and clinical settings, to help make employee selection decisions, promote employee development, and understand client problems in the context of one's personality. The fifth edition includes 185 simple questions about daily behavior, interests, and opinions. It takes approximately 35–50 minutes to complete the assessment. The following are two sample true/false questions: When I find myself in a boring situation, I usually "tune out" and daydream about other things. When a bit of tact and convincing is needed to get people moving, I'm usually the one who does it.
Versions	The 16PF is available in a number of versions, including 16PF Fifth Edition Questionnaire, 16PF Adolescent Personality Questionnaire, and 16PF Couples Counseling Questionnaire. The test is available in paper-and-pencil format and online, with a number of user guides and manuals available to assist with administration and interpretation.
Scales	The 16PF has 16 scales, each of which measures one of the following: 1. Warmth 7. Social Boldness 13. Openness to Change 2. Reasoning 8. Sensitivity 14. Self-Reliance 3. Emotional Stability 9. Vigilance 15. Perfectionism 4. Dominance 10. Abstractedness 16. Tension 5. Liveliness 11. Privateness 6. Rule-Consciousness 12. Apprehensiveness

(Continued)

(Continued)

	The 16 scales are grouped into five global factors: 1. Extraversion 2. Anxiety 3. Tough-Mindedness 4. Independence 5. Self-Control The 16PF also includes three response style indices: Impression Management, Infrequency, and Acquiescence. High scores on any of these scales may serve as red flags that the test taker is not answering honestly and instead is answering in a more socially desirable way, faking, or randomly responding. This information helps those who interpret the test come to accurate conclusions.
Report	There are over 20 different reports available for the 16PF, including a Profile Report, Competency Report, Interpretive Report, Management Potential Report, Practitioner Report, Career Development Report, and Couple's Counseling Report. One of the more popular is the Basic Interpretive Report, which includes an individual's scores on each of the 16 primary factors, the 5 global factors, and the 3 response-style indexes. This report also includes (a) a narrative report for the 16 primary factors and 5 global factors; (b) predicted scores on performance, potential, and behavioral indexes; (c) vocational interests along Holland's occupational interest themes; and (d) individual item responses and raw scores.
Reliability and Validity	In terms of reliability, the test–retest reliability coefficients of the 16PF, 5th Edition, for a two-week period for the global factors range between .84 and .91. For the primary factors, test–retest reliability coefficients range between .69 and .87, and coefficient alpha values range between .64 and .85, with a mean of .74. Over 60 published studies provide evidence for the validity of the 16 personality traits measured on the 16PF. The test manual provides evidence of construct validity and validity using the concurrent method as well as the rationale for the 16PF structure. The administrator's manual cautions test users about making prognostic or predictive decisions from the results of the 16PF.
Sources	IPAT. (n.d.). *The 16PF Questionnaire*. Retrieved June 27, 2010, from http://www.ipat.com/about/16pf/Pages/default.aspx Rotto, P. C. (1995). Review of the Sixteen Personality Factor Questionnaire, Fifth Edition. In J. Conoley & J. C. Impara (Eds.), *The twelfth mental measurements yearbook*. Lincoln, NE: Buros Institute of Mental Measurements. McLellan, M. J. (1995). Review of the Sixteen Personality Factor Questionnaire, Fifth Edition. In J. Conoley & J. C. Impara (Eds.), *The twelfth mental measurements yearbook*. Lincoln, NE: Buros Institute of Mental Measurements.

TEST SPOTLIGHT 14.3

Beck Depression Inventory–II (BDI–II)

Aaron T. Beck

Title	Beck Depression Inventory–II(BDI-II)
Author	Aaron T. Beck, Robert A. Steer, and Gregory K. Brown
Publisher	Harcourt Assessment 19500 Bulverde Road San Antonio, TX 78259 www.pearsonassessments.com/pai/
Purpose	The original Beck Depression Inventory was published by Beck in 1961 to assess depressive symptoms in people 13 years or older. A revision followed in 1987. In 1996, Beck and his colleagues conducted a major study to revise the test, resulting in changes or revisions to approximately 75% of the items and realignment of the test to reflect the definition of depression published in the fourth edition of the Diagnostic and Statistical Manual of Mental Disorders (DSM-IV). Used by healthcare professionals and researchers, the BDI–II is a self-report, 21-item, multiple-choice test and takes about five minutes to complete. Each of the items includes four statements arranged in increasing severity about a particular symptom of depression. For each item, test takers select one statement that best describes how they were feeling during the past two weeks. Here is a sample item about sadness. (0) I do not feel sad. (1) I feel sad. (2) I am sad all the time and I can't snap out of it. (3) I am so sad or unhappy that I can't stand it. The test is scored by adding the ratings of each of the 21 items. The maximum total score is 63. Clinicians often use the following guidelines when interpreting the test: 0 to 13 (minimal depression) 14 to 19 (mild depression) 20 to 28 (moderate depression) 29 to 63 (severe depression)

(Continued)

(Continued)

Versions	This test is available in Arabic, Bulgarian, Chinese, English, Farsi, Finnish, French, German, Japanese, Korean, Norwegian, Portuguese, Spanish, Swedish, and Turkish in paper-and-pencil format, with computerized scoring options available.
	In addition to the BDI–II, alternate versions are available. A short version of the test exists (BDI-Short Form), as does a version for use with children ages 7–14 (Beck Depression Inventory for Youth).
Scales	The test measures a single construct, depression, and it does not have subscales. The 21 items address the following symptoms: sadness, pessimism, past failure, loss of pleasure, guilty feelings, punishment feelings, self-dislike, self-criticalness, suicidal thoughts or wishes, crying, agitation, loss of interest, indecisiveness, feelings of worthlessness, loss of energy, changes in sleeping pattern, irritability, changes in appetite, difficulty with concentration, tiredness or fatigue, and loss of interest in sex.
Report	Results are often reported in the Interpretive Report. A sample portion from the Interpretive Report is included below.
	BDI-II John Sample endorses the following statements on the BDI-II: • I feel guilty all of the time. • **I WOULD KILL MYSELF IF I HAD THE CHANCE.** • I am so restless or agitated I have to keep moving or doing something. • I am sad all the time. • As I look back on my life, I see a lot of failures. • I get very little pleasure from the things I used to enjoy. • I expect to be punished. • I am disappointed in myself. • I criticize myself for all of my faults. • I cry over every little thing. • I have lost most of my interest in other people or things. • It's hard to keep my mind on anything for very long. • I feel more discouraged about my future than I used to be. • I find it more difficult to make decisions than usual. • I don't consider myself as worthwhile or useful as I used to. • I am more irritable than usual. • I get more tired or fatigued more easily than usual. • I have as much energy as ever. • I have not experienced any change in my sleeping pattern. • I have not experienced any change in my appetite. • I have not noticed any recent change in my interest in sex.
Reliability and Validity	The reliability of the test has been established using internal consistency and test–retest methods. Internal consistency estimates range from .92 for clinical patients to .93 for nonclinical individuals (college students). Test–retest reliability has been reported to be .93.

	A primary objective of the revised BDI was to have it more closely conform to diagnostic criteria for depression in the DSM-IV. To improve the content validity of the BDI, items were reworded, deleted, and added to better align with these diagnostic criteria. Validity studies reveal correlations of .93 and .84 between the BDI-II and its previous version. The BDI-II also correlates .68 with the Beck Hopelessness Scale, (.68), .37 with the Scale for Suicide Ideation, .60 with the Beck Anxiety Inventory, .71 with the Hamilton Psychiatric Rating Scale for Depression-Revised, and .47 with the Hamilton Rating Scale for Anxiety-Revised.
Sources	Beck, A. T., & Steer, R. A. (1987). *Beck Depression Inventory manual.* San Antonio, TX: Psychological Corporation. Beck, A. T., Steer, R. A., & Garbin, M. G. (1988). Psychometric properties of the Beck Depression Inventory: Twenty-five years of evaluation. *Clinical Psychology Review, 8,* 77–100. Pearson Education. (2010). *Beck Depression Inventory–II.* Retrieved June 27, 2010, from http://www.pearsonassessments.com/HAIWEB/Cultures/en-us/Productdetail.htm?Pid=015-8018-370&Mode=summary U.S. Department of Health and Human Services. (n.d.). *Beck Depression Inventory–Second Edition (BDI-II), 1996.* Retrieved November 10, 2009, from http://www.acf.hhs.gov/programs/opre/ehs/perf_measures/reports/resources_measuring/res_meas_phic.html

TEST SPOTLIGHT 14.4

State-Trait Anger Expression Inventory-2 (STAXI-2)

Charles D. Spielberger

Title	State-Trait Anger Expression Inventory-2 (STAXI-2)
Author	Charles D. Spielberger
Publisher	Psychological Assessment Resources 16204 North Florida Avenue Lutz, FL 33549 www4.parinc.com
Purpose	The State-Trait Anger Expression Inventory was originally published in 1998 to measure the intensity of anger in adolescents (16 years old) and adults. Revised in 1999, the STAXI-2 measures the intensity of anger (State Anger) and one's disposition to experience angry feelings as a personality trait (Trait Anger). The inventory is a self-report, 57-item test. Using a 4-point scale, test takers rate themselves in terms of intensity of anger at a particular point in time and how often the anger is experienced, expressed, and controlled. The STAXI-2 is typically used for anger research and for screening and measuring outcomes of anger management programs.
Versions	The STAXI-2 now has a companion test for children and adolescents, ages 9 to 18.
Scales	The inventory consists of six scales measuring the intensity of anger and the disposition to experience angry feelings. • *State Anger:* the current intensity of angry feelings (has three subscales) • *Trait Anger:* general and ongoing expressions of anger (has two subscales) • *Anger Expression–In:* how often anger is suppressed • *Anger Expression–Out:* how often anger is expressed • *Anger Control–In:* how often the person tries to control anger within by calming down • *Anger Control–Out:* how often the person visibly seeks to control anger There are also five subscales (State Anger–Feeling, State Anger–Verbal, State Anger–Physical, Trait Anger–Temperament, and Trait Anger–Reaction) and an Anger Expression Index, an overall measure of expression and control of anger.
Report	Results are often reported in the Interpretive Report, which includes summary scores for the scales and subscales, general interpretive information for the test taker's scale and subscales, and an overview of any health or medical risks the test taker may face based on his or her inventory scores.

Report	Section 1 from the State-Trait Anger Expression Inventory-2 (STAXI-2™) Sample Interpretive Report is printed below.

Section I

This Score Summary Table presents the raw scores, percentiles, *T* scores, and score levels (low, moderate, high, very high) for each valid STAXI-2 scale and subscale. The percentile results are shown graphically on a following page; the raw scores for each of the 57 items are reported in the Item Response Summary Table.

STAXI-2 Score Summary Table

Scale/subscale	Raw score	Percentile	*T* score	Score level
State Anger				
S-Ang	22	85	58	high
S-Ang/F	7	60	48	low-moderate
S-Ang/V	10	90	66	high
S-Ang/P	5	50	40	low-moderate
Trait Anger				
T-Ang	19	65	52	moderate
T-Ang/T	5	30	42	moderate
T-Ang/R	11	80	56	high
Anger Expression and Anger Control				
AX-O	12	20	42	low
AX-I	16	55	50	moderate
AC-O	28	80	58	high
AC-I	24	50	50	moderate
AX Index	24	30	44	moderate

Note: "---" indicates a scale that is invalid due to an excessive number of missing items.

STAXI-2 Item Response Summary Table

State Anger		Trait Anger		Anger Expression and Anger Control			
Item	Response	Item	Response	Item	Response	Item	Response
1.	1	16.	2	26.	4	42.	3
2.	1	17.	1	27.	2	43.	1
3.	2	18.	1	28.	3	44.	3
4.	1	19.	3	29.	2	45.	2
5.	1	20.	3	30.	3	46.	3
6.	1	21.	1	31.	2	47.	2
7.	1	22.	2	32.	3	48.	3
8.	1	23.	2	33.	2	49.	2
9.	2	24.	1	34.	4	50.	4
10.	2	25.	3	35.	1	51.	1
11.	1			36.	3	52.	3
12.	2			37.	1	53.	2
13.	3			38.	4	54.	3
14.	1			39.	2	55.	1
15.	2			40.	3	56.	3
				41.	3	57.	2

(Continued)

(Continued)

Report	To view a complete sample report go to www4.parinc.com/Products/Product.aspx?ProductID=STAXI-2:IR.

Section III

Medical Health Issues

Several of the STAXI-2 scales have been linked to health problems, particularly coronary heart disease (CHD), including hypertension, blood pressure problems, and cardiovascular reactivity. Several studies have investigated the relationship between anger, lipid levels, platelet aggregation, and other indicators of CHD to determine whether a person's level or type of anger increases the risk of CHD when overwhelmed by anger and other emotions. The STAXI-2 scales that have been found to be most closely associated with cardiovascular and other medical or health problems are presented below together with a brief evaluation of the respondent's scores. Please note that not all of the problems are likely for all members of the same STAXI-2 groups; many studies are correlational and thus do not have clear causal links. Furthermore, many of the studies have been carried out with Caucasian males, further limiting the applicability of the results.

State Anger (*S-Ang*)

This person scored in the high or very high range on *S-Ang*. Her *S-Ang* score is more like people with hypertension than normotensives. However, it should be noted that males with addiction problems also show higher *S-Ang* scores than males without addiction problems. For both males and females, higher preoperative *S-Ang* scores have been associated with poorer postoperative outcome, and higher *S-Ang* scores before exercise are related to higher systolic blood pressure (SBP) after exercise. If any of these factors are relevant to this individual, a referral for cognitively based anger management training needs to be seriously considered before surgery or extensive exercise. No research findings are yet available for the *S-Ang* subscales.

Trait Anger (*T-Ang*)

This respondent's *T-Ang* score is in the low or moderate range. Thus, there is little chance that she will experience elevations in blood pressure, hypertension, or coronary heart disease problems as a result of being chronically angry.

However, some preliminary data on elevated *T-Ang/R* scores suggest that this person may be more prone to experience elevations in either diastolic blood pressure (DBP) or systolic blood pressure (SBP) as a function of her high anger reactivity.

Anger Expression-Out (*AX-O*)

This person's *AX-O* score is in the low or moderate range. This suggests she has no increased risk of developing hypertension or CHD problems related to the expression of anger outwardly toward other people or objects.

Anger Expression-In (*AX-I*)

AX-I is the single best predictor of blood pressure among the STAXI-2 scales and tends to be most closely associated with hypertension. There are suggestions of relationships to other CHD variables as well.

Reliability and Validity	The reliability of the STAXI-2 has been established by calculating internal consistency. Alpha coefficients ranging between .73 and .95 provide evidence of internal consistency for the scales and subscales. Lindqvist, Daderman, and Hellstrom (2003) found coefficient alphas for the scales that ranged between .64 (Anger Expression–Out) and .89 (Anger Control–In). The test manual does not provide evidence of test–retest reliability. The author reports evidence of construct validity for the scales and subscales on the State-Trait Anger Expression Inventory-2 (STAXI-2). However, most evidence of validity for this test relies on studies conducted with the original version, even though the State-Trait Anger Expression Inventory-2 (STAXI-2) is quite different from the original version. Extensive evidence exists for the validity for the original versions of inventory based on concurrent validation studies. Scores on the original inventory tend to correlate with scores on other assessment instruments, including the Multiphasic Inventory, Buss-Durkee Hostility Inventory, and the Eysenck Questionnaire.
Sources	Freeman, S. J. (2003). Review of the State-Trait Anger Expression Inventory-2. In B. S. Plake, J. C. Impara, & R. A. Spies (Eds.), *The fifteenth mental measurements yearbook*. Lincoln, NE: Buros Institute for Mental Measurements. Klecker, B. M. (2003). Review of the State-Trait Anger Expression Inventory-2. In B. S. Plake, J. C. Impara, & R. A. Spies (Eds.), *The fifteenth mental measurements yearbook*. Lincoln, NE: Buros Institute for Mental Measurements. Lindqvist, J. K., Daderman, A. M., & Hellstrom, A. (2003). Swedish adaptations of the Novaco Anger Scale 1998, the Provocation Inventory, and the State-Trait Anger Expression Inventory-2. *Social Behavior and Personality, 31,* 77. PAR. (2010d). *State-Trait Anger Expression Inventory-2 (STAXI-2)*. Retrieved June 10, 2010, from http://www4.parinc.com/products/product.aspx?Productid=STAXI-2

TEST SPOTLIGHT 15.1

Hogan Personality Inventory (HPI)

Joyce and Robert Hogan

Title	Hogan Personality Inventory (HPI)
Author	Robert Hogan and Joyce Hogan
Publisher	Hogan Assessment Systems 2622 East 21st Street Tulsa, OK 74114 www.hoganassessments.com
Purpose	Since its inception, the HPI has been a measure of normal personality designed specifically to predict employment success. The Hogans began developing the HPI during the late 1970s using the California Psychological Inventory as their original model and the five-factor theory of personality as a theoretical basis for construct validity. After developing 420 questions, they tested more than 1,700 people, including students, hospital workers, U.S. Navy enlisted personnel, clerical workers, truck drivers, sales representatives, and school administrators. Analyses of these data led to a shortened inventory of 310 questions that made up the original HPI. Between 1984 and 1992, the HPI was administered to more than 11,000 people, most of whom were employed by organizations in the United States. The Hogans and others conducted more than 50 validity studies to assess criterion-related and construct validity. Based on these studies and factor analyses of the database of tests administered, the Hogans made revisions that yielded the revised edition currently in use.
Versions	The HPI is available for use in 30 languages.
Scales	The HPI contains 206 true/false statements (written at a fourth-grade reading level). The HPI has seven primary scales, six occupational scales, and a validity scale. The scale structure is supported by factor analytic research and generalizes across modes of testing, respondent cultures, and languages of translation. The primary scales and construct definitions are as follows: • *Adjustment*—confidence, self-esteem, and composure under pressure • *Ambition*—initiative, competitiveness, and leadership potential • *Sociability*—extraversion, gregariousness, and a need for social interaction • *Interpersonal Sensitivity*—warmth, charm, and ability to maintain relationships • *Prudence*—responsibility, self-control, and conscientiousness • *Inquisitiveness*—imagination, curiosity, and creative potential • *Learning Approach*—enjoying learning and staying current on business and technical matters

	The occupational scales and construct definitions are as follows: • *Service Orientation*—being attentive, pleasant, and courteous to clients and customers • *Stress Tolerance*—being able to handle stress, being even-tempered, and staying calm • *Reliability*—honesty, integrity, and positive organizational citizenship • *Clerical Potential*—following directions, attending to detail, and communicating clearly • *Sales Potential*—energy, social skill, and the ability to solve problems for clients • *Managerial Potential*—leadership ability, planning, and decision-making skills The HPI validity scale detects careless or random responding by the test taker. The validity referred to in the scale name is that of the test taker's response and does not provide information about the validity of the HPI itself.
Report	Reports are available in various formats that differ in content, scope, and complexity. All the most up-to-date reports for the Hogan Assessment can be found at hoganassessments.com/reports.
Reliability and Validity	The test manual for the HPI reports internal consistencies for the seven primary scales and subscales, obtained by testing 960 employed adults, ranging between .29 and .89. According to Joyce Hogan (personal communication, November 21, 2005), test–retest reliability coefficients range between .74 and .86. In general, subscale reliabilities are within the acceptable range and indicate substantial stability over time. Meta-analyses of HPI scales (published in peer-reviewed journals) indicate that the estimated true validities for the scales for predicting job performance are as follows: Adjustment, .43; Ambition, .35; Interpersonal Sensitivity, .34; Prudence, .36; Inquisitiveness, .34; and Learning Approach, .25 (Hogan & Holland, 2003). Early research indicated no adverse impact by race/ethnicity or gender. The HPI has been used in more than 200 validation studies to predict occupational performance across a range of jobs and industries. Jobs studied represent 95% of the industry coverage of the *Dictionary of Occupational Titles* (Coutsoukis & Information Technology Associates, 1995–2003).
Reliability and Validity	Since 1995, Hogan Assessment Systems has provided an Internet assessment platform to support the administration, scoring, and reporting functions of the inventory. Validation evidence continues to be collected from working adults in organizations around the world. Current norms are based on hundreds of thousands of adults who are representative of the occupational distribution in the U.S. workforce.
Sources	Coutsoukis, P., & Information Technology Associates. (1995–2003). *Dictionary of occupational titles.* Retrieved June 10, 2010, from http://www.occupationalinfo.org Hogan, R., & Hogan, J. (1992). *Hogan Personality Inventory manual.* Tulsa, OK: Hogan Assessment Systems. Hogan, J., & Holland, B. (2003). Using theory to evaluate personality and job-performance relations: A socioanalytic perspective. *Journal of Applied Psychology, 88,* 100–112. Hogan, J. (2005, November 21). Personal communication.

TEST SPOTLIGHT 15.2

Wonderlic Basic Skills Test (WBST)

E.F. Wonderlic

Title	Wonderlic Basic Skills Test (WBST)
Author	Eliot Long, Victor Artese, and Winifred Clonts
Publisher	Wonderlic 1795 North Butterfield Road Libertyville, IL 60048–1380 www.wonderlic.com
Purpose	The WBST provides a short measure of adult language and math skills designed to measure the job readiness of teenagers and adults. Job readiness is defined as having sufficient language and math skills to successfully carry out the written and computational requirements of the job. It is often used as part of a career school's admission testing program.
Versions	There are two equivalent forms for each WBST subtest.

Scales	The WBST contains 95 items that provide measurements on Verbal, Quantitative, and Composite scales. The Verbal Scale has three subscales: Word Knowledge, Sentence Construction, and Information Retrieval. The Quantitative Scale has three subscales: Explicit Problem Solving, Applied Problem Solving, and Interpretive Problem Solving. In addition, the test estimates GED subscale scores. (GED levels refer to the U.S. Department of Labor system for describing job requirements in terms of six levels of ability, covering all ability levels through the completion of college, and on three dimensions: Reasoning, Mathematics, and Language.)
	
	You may find these sample questions and others on the Wonderlic website (www .wonderlic. com):
	
	Sample Question 1
	
	Choose the verb that correctly completes the sentence.
	
	Saundra _____ yesterday.
	
	    A. exercise
	    B. exercises
	    C. exercised
	    D. exercising
	
	Sample Question 2
	Choose the answer that most nearly means the same as the underlined word.
	Cautious means
	
	    A. thrifty
	    B. careful
	    C. boring
	    D. strong

Sample Question 3

$56 \div 4 =$

    A. 16

    B. 9

    C. 14

    D. 23

SOURCE (for sample questions): Wonderlic. (n.d.). *WBST sample questions.* Received July 12, 2010, from http://www.wonderlic.com

Report	The computer-generated Individual Score Report compares the examinee's scores with the skill-level requirements of the designated job. It also reports grade-equivalent scores, and GED skill levels achieved. See below for sample report.

SOURCE (for sample questions): Wonderlic. (n.d.). *WBST sample questions.* Received July 12, 2010, from http://www.wonderlic.com

WONDERLIC BASIC SKILLS TEST
INDIVIDUAL SCORE REPORT

☑ Timed
☐ Untimed
☐ Retest

Organization Name: **Sample School**   Report Date: 10/03/2008
Organization Number:

Name: **Sample Student**   Program/Job Name:
Social Security Number: DOT Code:
Basic Skills Test Date: 10/3/2008   Program/Job Code:

Required GED Level: Verbal 2; Quantitative 2

SUMMARY	Total	GED Level Achieved	GED Level Required	Score at Required GED	Grade Level Indicated *
Verbal Skills	140	1	2	125	<6
Quantitative Skills	235	1	2	125	7.5
Skills Composite	188	1			<6

VERBAL SKILLS FORM VS2

	0	100	200	265	300	400	500
Total Verbal Score			140				
GED Level 1					290		
REQUIRED GED Level 2			125				
GED Level 3	0						
Word Knowledge				250			
Sentence Construction		80					
Information Retrieval		65					

QUANTITATIVE SKILLS FORM QS2

	0	100	200	265	300	400	500
Total Quantitative Score				235			
GED Level 1							500
REQUIRED GED Level 2			125				
GED Level 3	0						
Explicit					295		
Applied			150				
Interpretive	0						

SKILLS COMPOSITE

	0	100	200	265	300	400	500
Total Composite Score			188				
GED Level 1						395	
GED Level 2			125				
GED Level 3	0						

Wonderlic, Inc. • 1795 N. Butterfield Rd. • Libertyville, IL • 60048 • 800.323.3742

(Continued)

(Continued)

Reliability and Validity	Test–retest alternate form correlations for the Verbal Scale were .86 (n = 46) and .79 (n = 64). Test–retest alternate form correlations for the Quantitative Scale were .90 (n = 38) and .84 (n = 58). Internal consistency reliabilities (Cronbach's alpha) for the Verbal and Quantitative tests averaged approximately .92. The developmental history of the WBST, particularly its linkage to the job and skill descriptions in the *Dictionary of Occupational Titles*, suggests strong evidence of validity based on test content validity. The test content focuses on skills identified as job requirements rather than on curriculum taught.
Sources	Donlon, T. (2001). Wonderlic Personnel Test. In B. S. Plake & J. C. Impara (Eds.), *The fourteenth mental measurements yearbook*. Lincoln, NE: Buros Institute of Mental Measurements. Hanna, G. S. (1998). Wonderlic Basic Skills Test. In J. C. Impara & B. S. Plake (Eds.), *The thirteenth mental measurements yearbook*. Lincoln, NE: Buros Institute of Mental Measurements.

Appendix B

Guidelines for Critiquing a Psychological Test

To make informed decisions about tests, you need to know how to critique a test properly. A critique of a test is an analysis of the test. A good critique answers many of the following questions. Your instructor may have additional ideas about what constitutes a good critique.

General Descriptive Information

- What is the title of the test?
- Who is the author of the test?
- Who publishes the test, and when was it published? (Include dates of manuals, norms, and supplementary materials)
- How long does it take to administer the test?
- How much does it cost to purchase the test? (Include the cost of the test, answer sheets, manual, scoring services, and so on)
- Is the test proprietary or nonproprietary?

Purpose and Nature of the Test

- What does the test measure? (Include scales)
- What does the test predict?
- What behavior does the test require the test taker to perform?
- What population was the test designed for (for example, age, type of person)?
- What is the nature of the test (for example, maximal performance, behavior observation, self-report, standardized or nonstandardized, objective or subjective)?
- What is the format of the test (for example, paper-and-pencil or computer, multiple choice or true/false)?

Practical Evaluation

- Is the test manual comprehensive (does it include information on how the test was constructed, its reliability and validity, composition of norm groups, whether it is easy to read)?
- Is the test easy or difficult to administer?
- How clear are the administration directions?
- How clear are the scoring procedures?
- What qualifications and training does a test administrator need to have?
- Does the test have face validity?

Technical Evaluation

- Is there a norm group?
- Who comprises the norm group?
- What types of norms are there (for example, percentiles, standard scores)?
- How was the norm group selected?
- Are there subgroup norms (for example, by age, gender, region, occupation, and so on)?
- What is the test's evidence of reliability?
- How was reliability determined?
- What is the test's evidence of validity?
- How was validity determined?
- What is the standard error of measurement?
- What are the confidence intervals?

Test Reviews

- What do reviewers say are the strengths and weaknesses of the test?
- What studies that use the test as a measurement instrument have been published in peer-reviewed journals?
- How did the test perform when researchers or test users, other than the test developer or publisher, used it?

Summary

- Overall, what do you see as being the strengths and weaknesses of the test?

Appendix C

Ethical Standards for Assessment

9.01 Bases for Assessments

(a) Psychologists base the opinions contained in their recommendations, reports, and diagnostic or evaluative statements, including forensic testimony, on information and techniques sufficient to substantiate their findings. (See also Standard 2.04, Bases for Scientific and Professional Judgments.)

(b) Except as noted in 9.01c, psychologists provide opinions of the psychological characteristics of individuals only after they have conducted an examination of the individuals adequate to support their statements or conclusions. When, despite reasonable efforts, such an examination is not practical, psychologists document the efforts they made and the result of those efforts, clarify the probable impact of their limited information on the reliability and validity of their opinions, and appropriately limit the nature and extent of their conclusions or recommendations. (See also Standards 2.01, Boundaries of Competence, and 9.06, Interpreting Assessment Results.)

(c) When psychologists conduct a record review or provide consultation or supervision and an individual examination is not warranted or necessary for the opinion, psychologists explain this and the sources of information on which they based their conclusions and recommendations.

9.02 Use of Assessments

(a) Psychologists administer, adapt, score, interpret, or use assessment techniques, interviews, tests, or instruments in a manner and for purposes that are appropriate in light of the research on or evidence of the usefulness and proper application of the techniques.

(b) Psychologists use assessment instruments whose validity and reliability have been established for use with members of the population tested. When such validity or reliability has not been established, psychologists describe the strengths and limitations of test results and interpretation.

(c) Psychologists use assessment methods that are appropriate to an individual's language preference and competence unless the use of an alternative language is relevant to the assessment issues.

9.03 Informed Consent in Assessments

(a) Psychologists obtain informed consent for assessments, evaluations, or diagnostic services, as described in Standard 3.10, Informed Consent, except when (1) testing is mandated by law or governmental regulations; (2) informed consent is implied because testing is conducted as a routine educational, institutional, or organizational activity (e.g., when participants voluntarily agree to assessment when applying for a job); or (3) one purpose of the testing is to evaluate decisional capacity. Informed consent includes an explanation of the nature and purpose of the assessment, fees, involvement of third parties, and limits of confidentiality and sufficient opportunity for the client/patient to ask questions and receive answers.

(b) Psychologists inform persons with questionable capacity to consent or for whom testing is mandated by law or governmental regulations about the nature and purpose of the proposed assessment services, using language that is reasonably understandable to the persons being assessed.

(c) Psychologists using the services of an interpreter obtain informed consent from the client/patient to use that interpreter, ensure that confidentiality of test results and test security are maintained, and include in their recommendations, reports, and diagnostic or evaluative statements, including forensic testimony, discussion of any limitations on the data obtained. (See also Standards 2.05, Delegation of Work to Others; 4.01, Maintaining Confidentiality; 9.01, Bases for Assessments; 9.06, Interpreting Assessment Results; and 9.07, Assessment by Unqualified Persons.)

9.04 Release of Test Data

(a) The term *test data* refers to raw and scaled scores, client/patient responses to test questions or stimuli, and psychologists' notes and recordings concerning client/patient statements and behavior during an examination. Those portions of test materials that include client/patient responses are included in the definition of test data. Pursuant to a client/patient release, psychologists provide test data to the client/patient or other persons identified in the release. Psychologists may refrain from releasing test data to protect a client/patient or others from substantial harm or misuse or misrepresentation of the data or the test, recognizing that in many instances release of confidential information under these circumstances is regulated by law. (See also Standard 9.11, Maintaining Test Security.)

(b) In the absence of a client/patient release, psychologists provide test data only as required by law or court order.

9.05 Test Construction

Psychologists who develop tests and other assessment techniques use appropriate psychometric procedures and current scientific or professional knowledge for test design, standardization, validation, reduction or elimination of bias, and recommendations for use.

9.06 Interpreting Assessment Results

When interpreting assessment results, including automated interpretations, psychologists take into account the purpose of the assessment as well as the various test factors, test-taking abilities, and other characteristics of the person being assessed, such as situational, personal, linguistic, and cultural differences, that might affect psychologists' judgments or reduce the accuracy of their interpretations. They indicate any significant limitations of their interpretations. (See also Standards 2.01b and c, Boundaries of Competence, and 3.01, Unfair Discrimination.)

9.07 Assessment by Unqualified Persons

Psychologists do not promote the use of psychological assessment techniques by unqualified persons except when such use is conducted for training purposes with appropriate supervision. (See also Standard 2.05, Delegation of Work to Others.)

9.08 Obsolete Tests and Outdated Test Results

(a) Psychologists do not base their assessment or intervention decisions or recommendations on data or test results that are outdated for the current purpose.

(b) Psychologists do not base such decisions or recommendations on tests and measures that are obsolete and not useful for the current purpose.

9.09 Test Scoring and Interpretation Services

(a) Psychologists who offer assessment or scoring services to other professionals accurately describe the purpose, norms, validity, reliability, and applications of the procedures and any special qualifications applicable to their use.

(b) Psychologists select scoring and interpretation services (including automated services) on the basis of evidence of the validity of the program and procedures as well as on other appropriate considerations. (See also Standards 2.01b and c, Boundaries of Competence.)

(c) Psychologists retain responsibility for the appropriate application, interpretation, and use of assessment instruments, whether they score and interpret such tests themselves or use automated or other services.

9.10 Explaining Assessment Results

Regardless of whether the scoring and interpretation are done by psychologists, by employees or assistants, or by automated or other outside services, psychologists take reasonable steps to ensure that explanations of results are given to the individual or designated representative unless the nature of the relationship precludes provision of an explanation of results (such as in some organizational consulting, preemployment or security screenings, and forensic evaluations) and this fact has been clearly explained to the person being assessed in advance.

9.11 Maintaining Test Security

The term *test materials* refers to manuals, instruments, protocols, and test questions or stimuli and does not include test data as defined in Standard 9.04, Release of Test Data. Psychologists make reasonable efforts to maintain the integrity and security of test materials and other assessment techniques consistent with law and contractual obligations and in a manner that permits adherence to this Ethics Code.

Appendix D

Code of Fair Testing Practices in Education

*T*he *Code of Fair Testing Practices in Education* (Joint Committee on Testing Practices, 2004) is a guide for professionals in fulfilling their obligation to provide and use tests that are fair to all test takers regardless of age, gender, disability, race, ethnicity, national origin, religion, sexual orientation, linguistic background, or other personal characteristics. Fairness is a primary consideration in all aspects of testing. Careful standardization of tests and administration conditions helps to ensure that all test takers are given a comparable opportunity to demonstrate what they know and how they can perform in the area being tested. Fairness implies that every test taker has the opportunity to prepare for the test and is informed about the general nature and content of the test, as appropriate to the purpose of the test. Fairness also extends to the accurate reporting of individual and group test results. Fairness is not an isolated concept, but must be considered in all aspects of the testing process.

The *Code* applies broadly to testing in education (admissions, educational assessment, educational diagnosis, and student placement) regardless of the mode of presentation, so it is relevant to conventional paper-and-pencil tests, computer-based tests, and performance tests. It is not designed to cover employment testing, licensure or certification testing, or other types of testing outside the field of education. The *Code* is directed primarily at professionally developed tests used in formally administered testing programs. Although the *Code* is not intended to cover tests prepared by teachers for use in their own classrooms, teachers are encouraged to use the guidelines to help improve their testing practices.

The *Code* addresses the roles of test developers and test users separately. Test developers are people and organizations that construct tests, as well as those that set policies for testing programs. Test users are people and agencies that select tests, administer tests, commission test development services, or make decisions on the basis of test scores. Test developer and test user roles may overlap, for example, when a state or local education agency commissions test development services, sets policies that control the test development process, and makes decisions on the basis of the test scores.

The *Code* has been prepared by the Joint Committee on Testing Practices, a cooperative effort among several professional organizations. The aim of the Joint Committee is to act, in the public interest, to advance the quality of testing practices. Members of the Joint Committee include the American Counseling Association (ACA), the American Educational Research Association (AERA), the American

Psychological Association (APA), the American Speech-Language-Hearing Association (ASHA), the National Association of School Psychologists (NASP), the National Association of Test Directors (NATD), and the National Council on Measurement in Education (NCME).

Many of the statements in the *Code* refer to the selection and use of existing tests. When a new test is developed, when an existing test is modified, or when the administration of a test is modified, the *Code* is intended to provide guidance for this process.*

The *Code* provides guidance separately for test developers and test users in four critical areas:

A. Developing and Selecting Appropriate Tests
B. Administering and Scoring Tests
C. Reporting and Interpreting Test Results
D. Informing Test Takers

The *Code* is intended to be consistent with the relevant parts of the *Standards for Educational and Psychological Testing* (AERA, APA, & NCME, 1999). The *Code* is not meant to add new principles over and above those in the *Standards* or to change their meaning. Rather, the *Code* is intended to represent the spirit of selected portions of the *Standards* in a way that is relevant and meaningful to developers and users of tests, as well as to test takers and/or their parents or guardians. States, districts, schools, organizations, and individual professionals are encouraged to commit themselves to fairness in testing and safeguarding the rights of test takers. The *Code* is intended to assist in carrying out such commitments.

* The *Code* is not intended to be mandatory, exhaustive, or definitive, and may not be applicable to every situation. Instead, the *Code* is intended to be aspirational and is not intended to take precedence over the judgment of those who have competence in the subjects addressed.

A. Developing and Selecting Appropriate Tests

Test Developers

Test developers should provide the information and supporting evidence that test users need to select appropriate tests.

1. Provide evidence of what the test measures, the recommended uses, the intended test takers, and the strengths and limitations of the test, including the level of precision of the test scores.

2. Describe how the content and skills to be tested were selected and how the tests were developed.

3. Communicate information about a test's characteristics at a level of detail appropriate to the intended test users.

4. Provide guidance on the levels of skills, knowledge, and training necessary for appropriate review, selection, and administration of tests.

5. Provide evidence that the technical quality, including reliability and validity, of the test meets its intended purposes.

6. Provide to qualified test users representative samples of test questions or practice tests, directions, answer sheets, manuals, and score reports.

7. Avoid potentially offensive content or language when developing test questions and related materials.

8. Make appropriately modified forms of tests or administration procedures available for test takers with disabilities who need special accommodations.

9. Obtain and provide evidence on the performance of test takers of diverse subgroups, making significant efforts to obtain sample sizes that are adequate for subgroup analyses. Evaluate the evidence to ensure that differences in performance are related to the skills being assessed.

Test Users

Test users should select tests that meet the intended purpose and that are appropriate for the intended test takers.

1. Define the purpose for testing, the content and skills to be tested, and the intended test takers. Select and use the most appropriate test based on a thorough review of available information.

2. Review and select tests based on the appropriateness of test content, skills tested, and content coverage for the intended purpose of testing.

3. Review materials provided by test developers and select tests for which clear, accurate, and complete information is provided.

4. Select tests through a process that includes persons with appropriate knowledge, skills, and training.

5. Evaluate evidence of the technical quality of the test provided by the test developer and any independent reviewers.

6. Evaluate representative samples of test questions or practice tests, directions, answer sheets, manuals, and score reports before selecting a test.

7. Evaluate procedures and materials used by test developers, as well as the resulting test, to ensure that potentially offensive content or language is avoided.

8. Select tests with appropriately modified forms or administration procedures for test takers with disabilities who need special accommodations.

9. Evaluate the available evidence on the performance of test takers of diverse subgroups. Determine to the extent feasible which performance differences may have been caused by factors unrelated to the skills being assessed.

B. Administering and Scoring Tests

Test Developers

Test developers should explain how to administer and score tests correctly and fairly.

1. Provide clear descriptions of detailed procedures for administering tests in a standardized manner.

2. Provide guidelines on reasonable procedures for assessing persons with disabilities who need special accommodations or those with diverse linguistic backgrounds.

3. Provide information to test takers or test users on test question formats and procedures for answering test questions, including information on the use of any needed materials and equipment.

4. Establish and implement procedures to ensure the security of testing materials during all phases of test development, administration, scoring, and reporting.

5. Provide procedures, materials, and guidelines for scoring the tests and for monitoring the accuracy of the scoring process. If scoring the test is the responsibility of the test developer, provide adequate training for scorers.

6. Correct errors that affect the interpretation of the scores and communicate the corrected results promptly.

7. Develop and implement procedures for ensuring the confidentiality of scores.

Test Users

Test users should administer and score tests correctly and fairly.

1. Follow established procedures for administering tests in a standardized manner.

2. Provide and document appropriate procedures for test takers with disabilities who need special accommodations or those with diverse linguistic backgrounds. Some accommodations may be required by law or regulation.

3. Provide test takers with an opportunity to become familiar with test question formats and any materials or equipment that may be used during testing.

4. Protect the security of test materials, including respecting copyrights and eliminating opportunities for test takers to obtain scores by fraudulent means.

5. If test scoring is the responsibility of the test user, provide adequate training to scorers and ensure and monitor the accuracy of the scoring process.

6. Correct errors that affect the interpretation of the scores and communicate the corrected results promptly.

7. Develop and implement procedures for ensuring the confidentiality of scores.

C. Reporting and Interpreting Test Results

Test Developers

Test developers should report test results accurately and provide information to help test users interpret test results correctly.

1. Provide information to support recommended interpretations of the results, including the nature of the content, norms or comparison groups, and other technical evidence. Advise test users of the benefits and limitations of test results and their interpretation. Warn against assigning greater precision than is warranted.

2. Provide guidance regarding the interpretations of results for tests administered with modifications. Inform test users of potential problems in interpreting test results when tests or test administration procedures are modified.

3. Specify appropriate uses of test results and warn test users of potential misuses.

4. When test developers set standards, provide the rationale, procedures, and evidence for setting performance standards or passing scores. Avoid using stigmatizing labels.

5. Encourage test users to base decisions about test takers on multiple sources of appropriate information, not on a single test score.

6. Provide information to enable test users to accurately interpret and report test results for groups of test takers, including information about who were and who were not included in the different groups being compared and information about factors that might influence the interpretation of results.

7. Provide test results in a timely fashion and in a manner that is understood by the test taker.

8. Provide guidance to test users about how to monitor the extent to which the test is fulfilling its intended purposes.

Test Users

Test users should report and interpret test results accurately and clearly.

1. Interpret the meaning of the test results, taking into account the nature of the content, norms or comparison groups, other technical evidence, and benefits and limitations of test results.

2. Interpret test results from modified test or test administration procedures in view of the impact those modifications may have had on test results.

3. Avoid using tests for purposes other than those recommended by the test developer unless there is evidence to support the intended use or interpretation.

4. Review the procedures for setting performance standards or passing scores. Avoid using stigmatizing labels.

5. Avoid using a single test score as the sole determinant of decisions about test takers. Interpret test scores in conjunction with other information about individuals.

6. State the intended interpretation and use of test results for groups of test takers. Avoid grouping test results for purposes not specifically recommended by the test developer unless evidence is obtained to support the intended use. Report procedures that were followed in determining who were and who were not included in the groups being compared and describe factors that might influence the interpretation of results.

7. Communicate test results in a timely fashion and in a manner that is understood by the test taker.

8. Develop and implement procedures for monitoring test use, including consistency with the intended purposes of the test.

D. Informing Test Takers

Under some circumstances, test developers have direct communication with the test takers and/or control of the tests, testing process, and test results. In other circumstances the test users have these responsibilities.

Test developers or test users should inform test takers about the nature of the test, test taker rights and responsibilities, the appropriate use of scores, and procedures for resolving challenges to scores.

1. Inform test takers in advance of the test administration about the coverage of the test, the types of question formats, the directions, and appropriate test-taking strategies. Make such information available to all test takers.

2. When a test is optional, provide test takers or their parents/guardians with information to help them judge whether a test should be taken—including indications of any consequences that may result from not taking the test (e.g., not being eligible to compete for a particular scholarship)—and whether there is an available alternative to the test.

3. Provide test takers or their parents/guardians with information about rights test takers may have to obtain copies of tests and completed answer sheets, to retake tests, to have tests rescored, or to have scores declared invalid.

4. Provide test takers or their parents/guardians with information about responsibilities test takers have, such as being aware of the intended purpose and uses of the test, performing at capacity, following directions, and not disclosing test items or interfering with other test takers.

5. Inform test takers or their parents/guardians how long scores will be kept on file and indicate to whom, under what circumstances, and in what manner test scores and related information will or will not be released. Protect test scores from unauthorized release and access.

6. Describe procedures for investigating and resolving circumstances that might result in canceling or withholding scores, such as failure to adhere to specified testing procedures.

7. Describe procedures that test takers, parents/guardians, and other interested parties may use to obtain more information about the test, register complaints, and have problems resolved.

Working Group

Note: The membership of the working group that developed the *Code of Fair Testing Practices in Education* and of the Joint Committee on Testing Practices that guided the working group is as follows:

Peter Behuniak, PhD

Lloyd Bond, PhD

Gwyneth M. Boodoo, PhD

Wayne Camara, PhD

Ray Fenton, PhD

John J. Fremer, PhD (Cochair)

Sharon M. Goldsmith, PhD

Bert F. Green, PhD

William G. Harris, PhD

Janet E. Helms, PhD

Stephanie H. McConaughy, PhD

Julie P. Noble, PhD

Wayne M. Patience, PhD

Carole L. Perlman, PhD

Douglas K. Smith, PhD

Janet E. Wall, EdD (Cochair)

Pat Nellor Wickwire, PhD

Mary Yakimowski, PhD

Lara Frumkin, PhD, of the APA, served as staff liaison.

The Joint Committee intends that the *Code* be consistent with and supportive of existing codes of conduct and standards of other professional groups who use tests in educational contexts. Of particular note are the *Responsibilities of Users of Standardized Tests* (Association for Assessment in Counseling and Education, 2003), *APA Test User Qualifications* (2000), *ASHA Code of Ethics* (2001), *Ethical Principles of Psychologists and Code of Conduct* (1992), *NASP Professional Conduct Manual* (2000), *NCME Code of Professional Responsibility* (1995), and *Rights and Responsibilities of Test Takers: Guidelines and Expectations* (Joint Committee on Testing Practices, 2000).

Appendix E

Table of Critical Values for Pearson
Product–Moment Correlation Coefficients

	a Levels (two-tailed test)				
df	.10	.05	.02	.01	.001
	a Levels (one-tailed test)				
(df = N − 2)	.05	.025	.01	.005	.0005
1	.98769	.99692	.999507	.999877	.9999988
2	.900000	.95000	.98000	.990000	.99900
3	.8054	.8783	.93433	.95873	.99116
4	.7293	.8114	.8822	.91720	.97406
5	.6694	.7545	.8329	.8745	.95074
6	.6215	.7067	.7887	.8343	.92493
7	.5822	.6664	.7498	.7977	.8982
8	.5494	.6319	.7155	.7646	.8721
9	.5214	.6021	.6851	.7348	.8371
10	.4973	.5760	.6581	.7079	.8233
11	.4762	.5529	.6339	.6835	.8010
12	.4575	.5324	.6120	.6614	.7800
13	.4409	.5139	.5923	.6411	.7603
14	.4259	.4973	.5742	.6226	.7420
15	.4124	.4821	.5577	.6055	.7246
16	.4000	.4683	.5425	.5897	.7084
17	.3887	.4555	.5285	.5751	.6932
18	.3783	.4438	.5155	.5614	.6787
19	.3687	.4329	.5034	.5487	.6652
20	.3598	.4227	.4921	.5368	.6524
25	.3233	.3809	.4451	.4869	.5974
30	.2960	.3494	.4093	.4487	.5541
35	.2746	.3246	.3810	.4182	.5189
40	.2573	.3044	.3578	.3932	.4896
45	.2428	.2875	.3384	.3721	.4648
50	.2306	.2732	.3218	.3541	.4433
60	.2108	.2500	.2948	.3248	.4078
70	.1954	.2319	.2737	.3017	.3799
80	.1829	.2172	.2565	.2830	.3568
90	.1726	.2050	.2422	.2673	.3375
100	.1638	.1946	.2301	.2540	.3211

SOURCE: Data from Fisher, R. A., & Yates, F. (1963). *Statistical tables for biological, agricultural, and medical research.* Edinburgh, UK: Oliver & Boyd. Copyright © 1963 by Addison Wesley Longman Ltd., Pearson Education Limited, Edinburgh Gate, Harlow Essex CM20.

NOTE: To be significant, the *r* obtained from the data must be equal to or larger than the value shown in the table.

Glossary

360° feedback: A method of performance appraisal in which employees receive ratings from their supervisors, peers, subordinates, and customers as well as from themselves.

absolute decisions: Decisions that are made by seeing who has the minimum score needed to qualify.

abstract attributes: Attributes that are more difficult to describe using behaviors because people disagree on which behaviors represent the attribute; examples include personality, intelligence, creativity, and aggressiveness.

achievement tests: Tests that are designed to measure a person's previous learning in a specific academic area.

acculturation: The degree to which an immigrant or a minority member has adapted to a country's mainstream culture.

acquiescence: The tendency of some test takers to agree with any ideas or behaviors presented.

adaptive testing: Using tests developed from a large test bank in which the test questions are chosen to match the skill and ability level of the test taker.

administrative policy decisions: Decisions that are typically made by testing specialists, educational administrators, or committees.

age norms: Norms that allow test users to compare an individual's test score with scores of people in the same age group.

alternate forms: Two forms of a test that are alike in every way except for the questions; used to overcome problems such as practice effects; also referred to as parallel forms.

Alzheimer's disease: A progressive brain disorder that gradually destroys a person's mental functioning and ability to carry out day-to-day activities.

anchors: Numbers or words on a rating scale that the rater chooses to indicate the category that best represents the employee's performance on the specified dimension.

anonymity: The practice of administering tests or obtaining information without obtaining the identity of the participant.

aptitude tests: Tests that are designed to assess the test taker's potential for learning or the individual's ability to perform in an area where he or she has not been specifically trained.

area transformations: A method for changing scores for interpretation purposes that changes the unit of measurement and the unit of reference, such as percentile ranks.

artistic individual: One of the six types in Holland's Self-Directed Search; likes to work with creative ideas and self-expression more than with routines and rules.

assessment center: A large-scale replication of a job that requires test takers to solve typical job problems by role-playing or to demonstrate proficiency at job functions such as making presentations and fulfilling administrative duties; used for assessing job-related dimensions such as leadership, decision making, planning, and organizing.

attention deficit hyperactivity disorder (ADHD): A disorder characterized by excessive daydreaming and distraction; not considered to be a learning disability.

authentic assessment: Assessment that measures a student's ability to apply in real-world settings the knowledge and skills he or she has learned.

behavior: An observable and measurable action.

behavior observation tests: Tests that involve observing people's behavior to learn how they typically respond in a particular context.

behavioral checklist: When a rater evaluates performance by rating the frequency of important behaviors required for the job.

behavioral interviews: Interviews that focus on behaviors rather than on attitudes or opinions.

behaviorally anchored rating scales (BARS): A type of performance appraisal that uses behaviors as anchors; the rater rates by choosing the behavior that is most representative of the employee's performance.

beta: The slope of the regression line and amount of variance the predictor contributes to the equation.

biochemical assessment: Analysis of blood gases to determine the concentration of oxygen and carbon dioxide at the tissue level.

bivariate analyses: Analyses that provide information on two variables or groups.

categorical data: Data grouped according to a common property.

categorical model of scoring: A test scoring model that places test takers in a particular group or class.

central tendency errors: Rating errors that result when raters use only the middle of the rating scale and ignore the highest and lowest scale categories.

certification: A professional credential based on the holder meeting specific training objectives and passing a certification exam.

class intervals: A way of grouping adjacent scores to display them in a table or graph.

clinical assessment: A broad set of information-gathering and interpretive skills used by a professional counselor-therapist to determine a person's state of health or make a diagnosis.

clinical interview: A primary tool for gathering information about the client that involves a discussion between the client and the assessor—often a clinical psychologist or counselor—during which the assessor observes the client and gathers information about the client's symptoms or problems.

cluster sampling: A type of sampling that involves selecting clusters of respondents and then selecting respondents from each cluster.

coefficient of determination: The amount of variance shared by two variables being correlated, such as a test and a criterion, obtained by squaring the validity coefficient.

cognitive impairments: Mental disorders that include mental retardation, learning disabilities, and traumatic brain injuries.

cognitive tests: Assessments that measure the test taker's mental capabilities, such as general mental ability tests, intelligence tests, and academic skills tests.

Cohen's kappa: An index of agreement for two sets of scores or ratings.

comparative decisions: Decisions that are made by comparing test scores to see who has the best score.

computerized adaptive rating scales (CARS): Testing in which the computer software, as in computerized adaptive testing, selects behavioral statements for rating based on the rater's previous responses.

computerized adaptive testing (CAT): Testing in which the computer software chooses and presents the test taker with harder or easier questions as the test progresses, depending on how well the test taker answered previous questions.

concrete attributes: Attributes that can be described in terms of specific behaviors such as the ability to play the piano.

concurrent evidence of validity: A method for establishing evidence of validity based on a test's relationships with other variables in which test administration and criterion measurement happen at roughly the same time.

confidence interval: A range of scores that the test user can feel confident includes the true score.

confidentiality: The assurance that all personal information will be kept private and not disclosed without explicit permission.

confirmatory factor analysis: A procedure in which researchers, using factor analysis, consider the theory associated with a test and propose a set of underlying factors that they expect the test to contain; they then conduct a factor analysis to see whether the factors they proposed do indeed exist.

construct: An attribute, trait, or characteristic that is abstracted from observable behaviors.

construct explication: Three steps for defining or explaining a psychological construct.

construct validity: An accumulation of evidence that a test is based on sound psychological theory and therefore measures what it is supposed to measure; evidence that a test relates to other tests and behaviors as predicted by a theory.

content areas: The knowledge, skills, and/or attributes that a test assesses.

content validity: The extent to which the questions on a test are representative of the material that should be covered by the test.

content validity ratio: An index that describes how essential each test item is to measuring the attribute or construct that the item is supposed to measure.

convenience sampling: A type of sampling in which an available group of participants is used to represent the population.

conventional individual: One of the six types in Holland's Self-Directed Search; likes to follow orderly routines, meet clear standards, and avoid work that does not have clear directions.

convergent evidence of validity: One of two strategies for demonstrating construct validity showing that

constructs that theoretically should be related are indeed related; evidence that the scores on a test correlate strongly with scores on other tests that measure the same construct.

correlation: A statistical procedure that provides an index of the strength and direction of the linear relationship between two variables.

correlation coefficient: A statistic that provides an index of the strength and relationship between two sets of scores; a statistic that describes the relationship between two distributions of scores.

correlation matrix: A table in which the same tests and measures are listed in the horizontal and vertical headings and correlations of the tests are shown in the body of the table.

counseling and guidance decisions: Decisions that are typically made by testing specialists, educational administrators, or committees.

criterion: The measure of performance that we expect to correlate with test scores.

criterion contamination: When the criterion in a validation study measures more dimensions than those measured by the test.

criterion-referenced tests: Tests that involve comparing an individual's test score with an objectively stated standard of achievement such as being able to multiply numbers.

criterion-related evidence of validity: Evidence that test scores correlate with or predict independent behaviors, attitudes, or events; the extent to which the scores on a test correlate with scores on a measure of performance or behavior.

cross-validation: Administering a test another time following a validation study to confirm the results of the validation study; because of chance factors that contribute to random error, this second administration can be expected to yield lower correlations with criterion measures.

cumulative model of scoring: A test scoring model that assumes the more the test taker responds in a particular fashion, the more the test taker exhibits the attribute being measured; the test taker receives 1 point for each "correct" answer, and the total number of correct answers becomes the raw score.

cut scores: Decision points for dividing test scores into pass/fail groupings.

database: A matrix in the form of a spreadsheet that shows the responses given by each participant (row) for each question (column) in the survey.

decennial census survey: A survey that is administered by the U.S. Census Bureau every 10 years, primarily to determine the population of the United States.

descriptive research techniques: Techniques that help us describe a situation or phenomenon.

descriptive statistics: Numbers calculated from a distribution that describe or summarize the properties of the distribution of test scores, such as the mean, median, mode, and standard deviation.

diagnosis: Identification of the client's problem or disorder; also referred to as screening.

diagnostic assessment: Assessment that involves an in-depth evaluation of an individual to identify characteristics for treatment or enhancement.

diagnostic decisions: Decisions that are frequently made by classroom teachers.

differential treatment model: The model of assessment in which psychological tests provide definitive answers as to whether clients as a group have responded positively to a particular therapy or intervention.

differential validity: When a test yields significantly different validity coefficients for subgroups.

discriminant evidence of validity: One of two strategies for demonstrating construct validity showing that constructs that theoretically should be related are indeed related; evidence that test scores are not correlated with unrelated constructs.

discrimination index: A statistic that compares the performance of those who made very high test scores with the performance of those who made very low test scores on each item.

distracters: The incorrect responses to a multiple-choice question.

double-barreled question: A question that is actually asking two or more questions in one.

e-learning: Curricula that allow students to learn at their own pace using web-based lessons.

electroencephalogram (EEG): A continuous written record of brainwave activity.

electrophysiological assessment: The monitoring of vital signs such as heart rate and spontaneous electrical activity of the brain.

emotional intelligence: An individual's ability to understand his or her own feelings and the feelings of others and to manage his or her emotions.

empirically based tests: Tests in which the decision to place an individual in a category is based solely on the quantitative relationship between the predictor and the criterion.

employee assistance programs (EAPs): Programs provided as an employee benefit to help employees with problems not related to the workplace.

enterprise services: Online standardized tests offered by companies for large numbers of test takers at multiple sites.

enterprising individual: One of the six types in Holland's Self-Directed Search; likes to persuade or direct others more than to work on scientific or complicated topics.

equal interval scales: Level of measurement in which numbers are assigned with the assumption that each number represents a point that is an equal distance from the points adjacent to it.

essay questions: Popular subjective test items in educational settings that are usually general in scope and require lengthy written responses by test takers.

ethical dilemmas: Problems for which there are no clear or agreed-on moral solutions.

ethical standards: A set of professional practice guidelines or codes that are voted on and adopted by members of professional societies.

ethics: Issues or practices that influence the decision-making process in terms of "doing the right thing."

ethnocentrism: The inclination to believe that one's culture is superior to other cultures and to use it as a frame of reference for judging people from other cultures.

event-related potential (ERP): A record of the brain's electrical response to the occurrence of a specific event.

experimental questions: Test questions that are being tried out and that do not contribute to the test taker's final score.

experimental research techniques: Research designs that provide evidence for cause and effect.

experts: Individuals who are knowledgeable about a topic or who will be affected by the outcome of something.

exploratory factor analysis: A method of factor analysis in which researchers do not propose a formal hypothesis but instead use the procedure to broadly identify underlying components.

face validity: The perception of the test taker that the test measures what it is supposed to measure.

face-to-face surveys: Surveys in which an interviewer asks a series of questions in a respondent's home, a public place, or the researcher's office.

factor analysis: An advanced statistical procedure based on the concept of correlation that helps investigators identify the underlying constructs or factors being measured.

factors: The underlying commonalities of tests or test questions that measure a construct.

faking: The inclination of some test takers to try to answer items in a way that will cause a desired outcome or diagnosis.

false positive: When an innocent test taker mistakenly is classified as guilty.

field test: An administration of a survey or test to a large representative group of individuals to identify problems with administration, item interpretation, and so on.

five-factor model: A widely accepted personality theory that proposes there are five central personality dimensions: surgency, emotional stability, agreeableness, conscientiousness, and intellect or openness to experience.

focus group: A method that involves bringing together people who are similar to the target respondents in order to discuss issues related to the survey.

forced choice: A test item format that requires the test taker to choose one of two or more words or phrases that appear to be unrelated but are equally acceptable.

forced distribution: A method of ranking employees that requires the supervisor to assign a certain number of employees to each performance category.

forced ranking: A method of performance appraisal in which managers rank employees in terms of predetermined dimensions or criteria.

formative assessments: Assessments that help teachers determine what information students are and are not learning during the instructional process.

frequency distribution: An orderly arrangement of a group of numbers (or test scores) showing the number of times each score occurred in a distribution.

generalizability theory: A proposed method for systematically analyzing the many causes of inconsistency or random error in test scores, seeking to find systematic error that can then be eliminated.

generalizable: When a test can be expected to produce similar results even though it has been administered in different locations.

goodness-of-fit test: A statistical test of significance that provides evidence that the factors obtained empirically in a confirmatory factor analysis are similar to those proposed theoretically.

grade norms: Norms that allow test users to compare a student's test score with scores of other students in the same grade.

grading decisions: Decisions that are frequently made by teachers when awarding grades.

graphic rating scale: A graph for rating employees' performance that represents a dimension, such as quality or quantity of work, divided into categories defined by numbers, words, or both.

halo effect: A rating error that occurs when raters let their judgment on one dimension influence judgments on other dimensions.

heterogeneous test: A test that measures more than one trait or characteristic.

high-fidelity test: A test that is designed to replicate the job tasks and settings as realistically as possible.

high-stakes test: A test where student performance significantly impacts educational paths or choices.

histogram: A bar graph used to represent frequency data in statistics.

homogeneity of the population: How similar the people in a population are to one another.

homogeneous test: A test that measures only one trait or characteristic.

hosted services: Server space, web design, and maintenance provided by companies for the purpose of instruction and assessment.

hypotheses: Educated guesses or predictions based on a theory.

hypothesis confirmation bias: A form of bias in which decision makers form hypotheses about the behavior of others and then search for and elicit information to confirm their hypotheses.

individual decision: A decision that is made by the person who takes the test using the test results.

individually administered surveys: Surveys that are given by a facilitator to individual respondents to complete alone.

information-gathering model: The model of assessment in which psychological tests provide standardized comparisons and allow the assessor to make predictions about the client's behavior outside the assessment setting so as to identify disorders and design an individualized treatment program.

informed consent: Individuals' right of self-determination; means that individuals are entitled to full explanations of why they are being tested, how the test data will be used, and what the test results mean.

institutional decisions: Decisions that are made by an institution based on the results from a particular test or tests.

instructional decisions: Decisions made by classroom teachers.

instructional objectives: A list of what individuals should be able to do as a result of taking a course of instruction.

integrity tests: Tests that measure individual attitudes and experiences toward honesty, dependability, trustworthiness, reliability, and pro-social behavior.

intelligence tests: Tests that assess the test taker's ability to cope with the environment but at a broader level than do aptitude tests.

intercept: The place where the regression line crosses the y axis.

interest inventories: Tests that are designed to assess a person's interests in educational programs for job settings and thereby to provide information for making career decisions.

interitem correlation matrix: A matrix that displays the correlation of each item with every other item.

internal consistency: The internal reliability of a measurement instrument; the extent to which each test question has the same value of the attribute that the test measures.

interrater agreement: The consistency with which scorers rate or make yes/no decisions.

interscorer agreement: The consistency with which scorers rate or make decisions.

interview questions: The traditional subjective test questions in an organizational setting that make up the employment interview.

intrarater agreement: How well a scorer makes consistent judgments across all tests.

intrascorer reliability: Whether each clinician was consistent in the way he or she assigned scores from test to test.

investigative individual: One of the six types in Holland's Self-Directed Search; likes to explore and understand things or events rather than to persuade others or sell them things.

ipsative model of scoring: A test scoring model that compares the test taker's scores on various scales within the inventory to yield a profile.

item analysis: The process of evaluating the performance of each item on a test.

item bias: Differences in responses to test questions that are related to differences in culture, gender, or experiences of the test takers.

item characteristic curve (ICC): The line that results when we graph the probability of answering an item correctly with the level of ability on the construct being measured; the resulting graph provides a picture of both the item's difficulty and discrimination.

item difficulty: The percentage of test takers who answer a question correctly.

item nonresponse rate: How often an item or question was not answered.

item response theory (IRT): A theory that relates the performance of each item to a statistical estimate of the test taker's ability on the construct being measured.

job analysis: A systematic assessment method for identifying the knowledge, skills, abilities, and other characteristics required to perform a job.

learning disability: A hidden handicap that hinders learning and does not have visible signs.

leniency errors: Systematic rating errors that occur when raters give all employees better ratings than they deserve.

levels of measurement: The properties of the numbers used in a test—nominal, ordinal, equal interval, or ratio.

linear regression: The statistical process used to predict one set of test scores from one set of criterion scores.

linear transformations: A method for changing raw scores for interpretation purposes that does not change the characteristics of the raw data in any way, such as z scores and T scores.

literature reviews: Systematic examinations of published and unpublished reports on a topic.

low-fidelity tests: Tests that simulate the job and its tasks using a written, verbal, or visual description.

mail surveys: Surveys that are mailed to respondents with instructions for respondents to complete and return them.

mean: The arithmetic average of a group of test scores in a distribution.

measurement: Broadly defined, the assignment of numbers according to rules.

measurement error: Variations or inconsistencies in the measurements yielded by a test or survey.

measures of central tendency: The mean (arithmetic average), median, and mode that provide information about the middle of a set of test scores.

measures of relationship: Statistics that describe the relationship between two sets of scores, such as correlation coefficient.

measures of variability: Numbers that represent the spread of the scores in the distribution, such as range, variance, and standard deviation.

median: The middle score in a distribution.

mode: The most frequently occurring score in a distribution.

motor impairments: Disabilities that hinder physical movement, such as paralysis and missing limbs.

multicultural backgrounds: Experiences of those who belong to various minority groups based on race, cultural or ethnic origin, sexual orientation, family unit, primary language, and so on.

multiple choice: An objective test format that consists of a question or partial sentence, called a stem, followed by a number of responses, only one of which is correct.

multiple regression: The process in which more than one set of test scores is used to predict one set of criterion scores.

multitrait–multimethod design: A design for test validation that gathers evidence of reliability, convergent evidence of validity, and discriminant evidence of validity into one study.

multivariate analyses: Analyses that provide information on three or more variables or groups.

nature-versus-nurture controversy: A debate that focuses on whether intelligence is determined by heredity or develops after birth based on environmental factors.

neurobehavioral assessment: Diagnostic methods in which practitioners elicit reflexes, such as the Moro, Babinski, and tonic neck reflex, to assess the functioning and maturity of an infant's central nervous system.

neuropsychology: A special branch of psychology that concentrates on the relation between how the brain functions and the behavior it produces.

nominal scale: The most basic level of measurement, in which numbers are assigned to groups or categories of information.

nomological network: A method for defining a construct by illustrating its relation to as many other constructs and behaviors as possible.

nondirective clinical interview: A clinical interview that has few predetermined questions; instead, the assessor's questions are more likely to be determined by the client's responses.

nonhosted services: Instructional and assessment services that run on local area networks or private websites.

nonprobability sampling: A type of sampling in which not everyone has an equal chance of being selected from the population.

nonsampling measurement errors: Errors associated with the design and administration of a survey.

nonstandardized tests: Tests that do not have standardization samples; more common than standardized tests.

norm group: A previously tested group of individuals whose scores are used for comparison purposes.

norm-based interpretation: The process of comparing an individual's score with the scores of another group of people who took the same test.

norm-referenced tests: Tests that determine how well an individual's achievement compares with the achievement of others and that distinguish between high and low achievers; standardized tests that have been given to a large representative group of test takers from which scores have been used to create norms.

normal curve: A symmetrical distribution of scores that, when graphed, is bell-shaped.

normal probability distribution: A theoretical distribution that exists in our imagination as a perfect and symmetrical distribution; also referred to as the normal curve.

norms: A group of scores that indicate the average performance of a group and the distribution of scores above and below this average.

objective criterion: A measurement that is observable and measurable, such as the number of accidents on the job.

objective test format: A test format that has one response that is designated as "correct" or that provides evidence of a specific construct, such as multiple-choice questions.

objective tests: Tests that are structured and require test takers to respond to structured true/false questions, multiple-choice questions, or rating scales.

operational definitions: Specific behaviors that define or represent a construct.

order effects: Changes in test scores resulting from the order in which tests or questions on tests were administered.

ordinal scales: The second level of measurement, in which numbers are assigned to order or rank individuals or objects from greatest to least (or vice versa) on the attribute being measured.

outliers: Scores that are exceptionally higher or lower than other scores in a distribution.

parallel forms: Two forms of a test that are alike in every way except questions; used to overcome problems such as practice effects; also referred to as alternate forms.

Pearson product–moment correlation coefficient: Represented by *r,* a correlation coefficient that measures the linear association between two variables, or sets of test scores, that have been measured on interval or ratio scales.

peers: An individual's colleagues or equals, such as other employees in a workplace or other students in a class or school.

percentages: A linear transformation of raw scores obtained by dividing the number of correctly answered items by the total number of items.

percentile rank: An area transformation that indicates the percentages of people who scored above and below the transformed score.

performance appraisal: A formal evaluation of an employee's job performance.

personal interviews: Surveys that involve direct contact with the respondents in person or by phone.

personality tests: Tests that are designed to measure human character or disposition.

personality traits: Characteristics or qualities of a person (e.g., kind, optimistic); ongoing cognitive constructs.

phi coefficient: A statistic that describes the relationship between two dichotomous variables.

pilot test: A scientific investigation of a new test's reliability and validity for its specified purpose.

placement assessments: Assessments that are used to determine whether students have the skills or knowledge necessary to understand new material and to determine how much information students already know about the new material.

placement decisions: Decisions that are typically made by testing specialists, educational administrators, or committees to determine the appropriate program or job for the test taker.

polygraph: A physiological measure associated with evaluating how truthfully an individual responds to questioning; also known as a lie detector test.

population: All members of the target audience.

portfolio: Collections of an individual's work; used to highlight student learning and assess student performance.

practical test: A test in which a test taker must actively demonstrate skills in specific situations.

practice effects: When test takers benefit from taking a test the first time (practice) because they are able to solve problems more quickly and correctly the second time they take the same test.

predictive evidence of validity: A method for establishing evidence of validity based on a test's relationships with other variables that shows a relationship between test scores obtained at one point in time and a criterion measured at a later point in time.

pretesting: A method for identifying sources of nonsampling measurement errors and examining the effectiveness of revisions to a question(s) or to an entire survey or test.

probability sampling: A type of sampling that uses a statistical procedure to ensure that a sample is representative of its population.

proctor: A person who supervises a testing location; similar to a test administrator.

prognosis: An estimation of the length of treatment and the likelihood of a successful outcome. The hypothesis and prognosis are for the assessor's use and are not necessarily shared with the client.

program and curriculum decisions: Decisions that are typically made by testing specialists, educational administrators, or committees regarding the content of a program or curriculum.

projection: A defense mechanism that relieves anxiety by allowing a person to attribute thoughts or emotions to external events or individuals.

projective drawing: A psychological test in which the assessor directs the test takers to draw their own pictures.

projective hypothesis: The assumption that when people attempt to understand ambiguous stimuli, their interpretations of the stimuli reflect their own personal qualities or characteristics.

projective storytelling: Psychological tests that require respondents to tell stories in response to ambiguous stimuli.

projective technique: A type of psychological test in which the response requirements are unclear so as to encourage test takers to create responses that describe the thoughts and emotions they are experiencing; three projective techniques are projective storytelling, projective drawing, and sentence completion.

projective tests: Tests that are unstructured and require test takers to respond to ambiguous stimuli.

protected class: Persons in a group, such as ethnic class or gender, who are protected from discrimination by federal law.

psychological assessments: Tools for understanding and predicting behavior that involve multiple methods, such as personal history interviews, behavioral observations, and psychological tests, for gathering information about an individual.

psychological tests: Instruments that require the test taker to perform some behavior; the behavior performed is used to measure some personal attribute, trait, or characteristic that is thought to be important in describing or understanding behavior, such as intelligence.

psychometrics: Quantitative and technical aspects of mental measurement.

qualitative analysis: When test developers ask test takers to complete a questionnaire about how they viewed the test and how they answered the questions.

quantitative item analysis: A statistical analysis of the responses that test takers gave to individual test questions.

random error: The unexplained difference between a test taker's true score and the obtained score; error that is nonsystematic and unpredictable, resulting from an unknown cause.

random responding: Responding to items in a random fashion by marking answers without reading or considering the items.

range: A measure of variability calculated by subtracting the lowest number in a distribution from the highest number in the distribution.

ratio scales: The level of measurement in which numbers are assigned to points with the assumption that each point is an equal distance from the numbers adjacent to it and there is a point that represents an absolute absence of the property being measured, called zero (0).

raw score: The basic score calculated when an individual completes a psychological test.

realistic individual: One of the six types in Holland's Self-Directed Search; likes to work with things more than with people.

reliability: The consistency with which an instrument yields measurements.

reliable test: A test that consistently yields the same measurements for the same phenomena.

response rate: The number of individuals who responded to a survey divided by the total number of individuals who received the survey.

response sets: Patterns of responding to a test or survey that result in false or misleading information.

restriction of range: The reduction in the range of scores that results when some people are dropped from a validity study, such as when low performers are not hired, causing the validity coefficient to be lower than it would be if all persons were included in the study.

sample: A subset of a population used to represent the entire population.

sample size: The number of people in a sample.

sampling error: A statistic that reflects how much error can be attributed to the lack of representation of the target population due to the characteristics of the sample of respondents.

scientific method: A process for generating a body of knowledge that involves testing ideas and beliefs according to a specific testing procedure that can be observed objectively.

scorer reliability: The degree of agreement between or among persons scoring a test or rating an individual; also known as interrater reliability.

screening: The identification of a client's problem or disorder.

selection decisions: Decisions that are typically made by testing specialists, educational administrators, or committees regarding admission to a program or hiring for a job.

self-administered surveys: Surveys that individuals complete themselves without the presence of an administrator.

self-fulfilling prophecy: A phenomenon in which the researcher's expectations influence the behavior of respondents and lead them to meet the researcher's expectations.

self-report tests: Tests that rely on test takers' reports or descriptions of their feelings, beliefs, opinions, and/or mental states.

semistructured interview: An interview that contains predetermined questions, but the format also allows the assessor to ask some open-ended questions and follow-up questions to clarify the interviewee's responses.

sensory impairments: Disabilities that hinder the function of the five senses, such as deafness and blindness.

sentence completion: Psychological test item format in which the assessor administers partial sentences, verbally or on paper, and asks the test taker to respond by completing each sentence.

severity errors: Systematic rating errors that occur when raters give all employees worse ratings than they deserve.

simple random sampling: A type of sampling in which every member of a population has an equal chance of being chosen as a member of the sample.

single-group validity: When a test is valid for one group but not for another group, such as valid for Whites but not for Blacks.

slope: The expected change in one unit of Y for every change in X on the regression line.

social desirability: The tendency of some test takers to provide or choose answers that are socially acceptable or that present them in a favorable light.

social–emotional functioning: An area of assessment that includes tests that measure temperament, personality, intelligence, academic achievement, language development, visual and tactile perception, and sustained and selective attention.

social individual: One of the six types in Holland's Self-Directed Search; likes to help, teach, and counsel people more than to engage in mechanical or technical activity.

split-half method: A method for estimating the internal consistency or reliability of a test by giving the test once to one group of people, making a comparison of scores, dividing the test into halves, and correlating the set of scores on the first half with the set of scores on the second half.

standard deviation: A measure of variability that represents the degree to which scores vary from the mean.

standard deviation unit: A number that represents how many standard deviations an individual score is located away from the mean.

standard error of measurement (SEM): An index of the amount of inconsistency or error expected in an individual's test score.

standard scores: Universally understood units in testing, such as z scores and T scores, that allow the test user to evaluate a person's performance in comparison with other persons who took the same test or a similar test.

standardization sample: People who are tested to obtain data to establish a frame of reference for interpreting individual test scores.

standardized tests: Tests that have been administered to a large group of individuals who are similar to the group for whom the test has been designed so as to develop norms; also implies a standardized procedure for administration.

state: A temporary mood or characteristic.

stem: A statement, question, or partial sentence that is the stimulus in a multiple-choice question.

stratified random sampling: A type of sampling in which a population is divided into subgroups or strata.

structured clinical interview: An interview that has a predetermined set of questions in which the assessor assigns numbers or scores to the answers based on their content.

structured interview: A predetermined set of questions that the assessor asks the respondent; the assessor then scores the answers based on their content to arrive at a diagnosis or a hiring decision.

structured observations: Observations that are guided by forms or instructions that instruct an observer in collecting behavioral information, such as using a form to document the play behaviors of children on a playground.

structured record reviews: Forms that guide data collection from existing records, such as using a form to collect information from personnel files.

subgroup norms: Statistics that describe subgroups of the target audience, such as race, sex, and age.

subjective criterion: A measurement that is based on judgment, such as supervisor or peer ratings.

subjective test format: A test format that does not have a response that is designated as "correct"; interpretation of the response as correct or providing evidence of a specific construct is left to the judgment of the person who administers, scores, or interprets the test taker's response.

subtle questions: Questions that have no apparent relation to the test purpose or criterion.

summative assessment: Assessment that involves determining what students do and do not know; these are typically used to assign earned grades.

survey objectives: The purpose of a survey, including a definition of what it will measure.

survey research firms: Companies that specialize in the construction and administration of surveys and analysis of survey data for purposes such as marketing, political opinion assessment, and employee organizational satisfaction.

survey researchers: People who design and conduct surveys and analyze the results.

surveys: Research tools that collect information to describe and compare people's attitudes (how they feel), knowledge (what they know), and behaviors (what they do).

systematic error: When a single source of error can be identified as constant across all measurements.

systematic sampling: A type of sampling in which every nth (for example, every fifth) person in a population is chosen as a member of the sample.

T scores: Standard scores, which have a mean of 50 and a standard deviation of 10, that are used to compare test scores from two tests that have different characteristics.

telephone surveys: Surveys in which an interviewer calls respondents and asks questions over the phone.

test bank: A large number of multiple-choice, true/false, and short-answer questions that assess knowledge of a subject or group of subjects.

test format: The type of questions on a test.

test item: A stimulus or test question.

test of significance: The process of determining what the probability is that a study would have yielded the observed results simply by chance.

test plan: A plan for developing a new test that specifies the characteristics of the test, including a definition of the construct and the content to be measured (the testing universe), the format for the questions, and how the test will be administered and scored.

test security: Steps taken to ensure that the content of a psychological test does not become public knowledge.

test specifications: The plan prepared before test development that documents the written test or practical exam.

test taker: The person who responds to test questions or whose behavior is measured.

test user: A person who participates in purchasing, administering, interpreting, or using the results of a psychological test.

testing environment: The circumstances under which a test is administered.

testing universe: The body of knowledge or behaviors that a test represents.

test–retest method: A method for estimating test reliability in which a test developer gives the same test to the same group of test takers on two different occasions and correlates the scores from the first and second administrations.

tests of maximal performance: Tests that require test takers to perform a particular task on which their performance is measured.

therapeutic model: The model in which the goal of therapeutic assessment is to provide new experiences and new information that clients can use to make changes in their lives.

traditional interview: Pre-employment interview in which the interviewer pursues different areas of inquiry with each job.

trait: An ongoing part of a person's personality.

transportability: One strategy used for test validity generalization in which a case is made that a test that has been shown to be valid for one job is also valid for

a different job based on evidence that the jobs are substantially similar in their requirements.

true/false: A test item that asks, "Is this statement TRUE or FALSE?"

univariate analyses: The computation of statistics that summarize individual question responses.

user qualifications: Standards that the test purchaser or test user must meet to purchase the test and use the test results, such as certification or experience.

valid test: A test for which there exists evidence that the interpretation of the scores are appropriate for their intended purpose.

validity: Evidence that the interpretations that are being made from the scores on a test are appropriate for their intended purpose.

validity coefficient: The correlation coefficient obtained when test scores are correlated with a performance criterion representing the amount or strength of the evidence of validity for the test.

variance: A measure of variability that indicates whether individual scores in a distribution tend to be similar to or substantially different from the mean of the distribution.

virtual time: The time that a computer records elapsing during a test, which might not be equal to the actual time passed during test administration.

vocational tests: Tests that help predict how successful a person would be at an occupation before training or entering the occupation.

within-group norming: The practice of administering the same test to every test taker but scoring the test differently according to the race of the test taker.

work sample: A small-scale assessment in which test takers complete a job-related task such as building a sawhorse or designing a doghouse.

written test: A paper-and-pencil test in which a test taker must answer a series of questions.

z scores: Standard scores, which have a mean of zero (0) and a standard deviation of 1, that are used to compare test scores from two tests that have different characteristics.

References

Albanese, M. A. (2001). Review of the Mini-Mental State Examination. In B. S. Plake, J. C. Impara, & R. A. Spies (Eds.), *The fifteenth mental measurements yearbook*. Lincoln, NE: Buros Institute of Mental Measurements.

Albers, C. A., & Grieve, A. J. (2007). Test review: Bayley N. (2006). Bayley scales of infant and toddler development—third edition. *Journal of Psychoeducational Assessment, 25,* 180–198.

Allan, J. M., Bulla, N., & Goodman, S. A. (2003). *Guidelines for computer-administered testing*. Louisville, KY: American Printing House for the Blind. Retrieved May 21, 2010, from http://www.aph.org/tests/access/index.html

Alzheimer's Association. (2009). *2009 Alzheimer's disease facts and figures*. Retrieved May 19, 2010, from http://www.alz.org/national/documents/report_alzfactsfigures2009.pdf

Alzheimer's Disease International. (2009). *Common questions*. Retrieved May 19, 2010, from http://www.alz.co.uk/alzheimers/faq.html

American Counseling Association. (2005). *ACA code of ethics*. Retrieved May 20, 2010, from http://www.counseling.org/Files/FD.ashx?guid=ab7c1272-71c4-46cf-848c-f98489937dda

American Educational Research Association, American Psychological Association, & National Council on Measurement in Education. (1999). *Standards for educational and psychological testing*. Washington, DC: American Psychological Association.

American Psychiatric Association. (1987). *Diagnostic and statistical manual of mental disorders* (3rd ed., rev.). Washington, DC: Author.

American Psychiatric Association. (1994). *Diagnostic and statistical manual of mental disorders* (4th ed., rev.). Washington, DC: Author.

American Psychiatric Association. (2000). *Diagnostic and statistical manual of mental disorders* (4th ed., text rev.). Washington, DC: Author.

American Psychological Association. (1953). *Ethical standards of psychologists*. Washington, DC: Author.

American Psychological Association. (1954). *Technical recommendations for psychological tests and diagnostic techniques*. Washington, DC: Author.

American Psychological Association. (1985). *Standards for educational and psychological testing*. Washington, DC: Author.

American Psychological Association. (2000). *Report of the Task Force on Test User Qualifications*. Washington, DC: Author.

American Psychological Association. (2005). *Testing and assessment*. Retrieved May 20, 2010, from http://www.apa.org/science/programs/testing/index.aspx

American Psychological Association. (2003). *Ethical principles of psychologists and code of conduct.Washington, DC:* Author. Retrieved November 3, 2005, from www.apa.org/ethics/code2002.html#principle Copyright by the American Psychological Association.

American Psychological Association. (2010a). *Ethical principles of psychologists and code of conduct*. Washington, DC: Author. Retrieved May 20, 2010, from http://www.apa.org/ethics/code/index.aspx

American Psychological Association. (2010b). *FAQ/finding information about psychological tests*. Retrieved June 13, 2010, from http://www.apa.org/science/programs/testing/find-tests.aspx#findinfo

American Psychological Association Science Directorate. (1991). *Questionnaires used in the prediction of trustworthiness in pre-employment selection decisions: An APA task force report*. Washington, DC: American Psychological Association.

Ames, L. B. (1989). *Arnold Gesell: Themes of his work*. New York: Human Sciences Press.

Anastasi, A., & Urbina, S. (1997). *Psychological testing* (7th ed.). Upper Saddle River, NJ: Prentice Hall.

Anton, W. D., & Reed, J. R. (1991). *CAS: College Adjustment Scales professional manual.* Odessa, FL: Psychological Assessment Resources.

Archer, R. P. (1992). Review of the Minnesota Multiphasic Personality Inventory-2. In J. J. Kramer & J. C. Conoley (Eds.), *The eleventh mental measurements yearbook.* Lincoln, NE: Buros Institute of Mental Measurements.

Arenson, K. W. (2003a, October 16). Black and Hispanic students lag on Regents, group says. *New York Times*, p. B5.

Arenson, K. W. (2003b, August 30). Scores on math Regents exam to be raised for thousands. *New York Times*, p. B3.

Arenson, K. W. (2003c, October 9). State lowering bar on Regents exams needed to graduate. *New York Times*, p. A1.

Arvey, R. D. (1979). Unfair discrimination in the employment interview: Legal and psychological aspects. *Psychological Bulletin, 86*, 736–765.

Association of Test Publishers. (2005). *ATP computer testing guidelines.* Washington, DC: Author.

Axelrod, B. N., Goldman, B. S., & Woodard, J. L. (1992). Interrater reliability in scoring the Wisconsin Card Sorting Test. *The Clinical Neuropsychologist, 6*, 143–155.

Bailey, D. S. (2004, October). Approaching ethical dilemmas. *Monitor on Psychology*, p. 62.

Bandura, A. (1977). Self-efficacy: Toward a unifying theory of behavioral change. *Psychological Review, 84*, 191–215.

Bandura, A., Barbaranelli, C., Caprara, G. V., & Pastorelli, C. (1996). Multifaceted impact of self-efficacy beliefs on academic functioning. *Child Development, 67*, 1206–1222.

Baños, J. H., & Franklin, L .M. (2000). Factor structure of the Mini-Mental State Examination in adult psychiatric patients. *Psychological Assessment,14*, 397–400.

Barlow, D. H., & Durand, M. V. (2009). *Abnormal psychology: An integrative approach.* Belmont: CA: Wadsworth Cengage Learning.

Barrett, G. V., Phillips, J. S., & Alexander, R. A. (1981). Concurrent and predictive validity designs: A critical reanalysis. *Journal of Applied Psychology, 66*, 1–6.

Barrett, G. V., Polomsky, M. D., & McDaniel, M. A. (1999). Selection tests for firefighters: A comprehensive review and meta-analysis. *Journal of Business and Psychology, 13*, 507–513.

Barrick, M. R., & Mount, M. K. (1991). The Big Five personality dimensions and job performance: A meta-analysis. *Personnel Psychology, 44*, 1–26.

Bartlett, C. J., Bobko, P., Mosier, S. B., & Hannan, R. (1978). Testing for fairness with a moderated multiple regression strategy: An alternative to differential analysis. *Personnel Psychology, 31*, 233–241.

Bartram, D. (1995). The predictive validity of the EPI and 16PF for military flying training. *Journal of Occupational and Organizational Psychology, 68*, 219–236.

Bayley, N. (1993). *Bayley Scales of Infant Development* (2nd ed.). San Antonio, TX: Psychological Corporation.

Beck, A. T., & Steer, R. A. (1987). *Beck Depression Inventory manual.* San Antonio, TX: Psychological Corporation.

Beck, A. T., Steer, R. A., & Garbin, M. G. (1988). Psychometric properties of the Beck Depression Inventory: Twenty-five years of evaluation. *Clinical Psychology Review, 8*, 77–100.

Bennett, D. (2004, September 12). Against types. *The Boston Globe.* Retrieved May 19, 2010, from http://www.boston.com/news/globe/ideas/articles/2004/09/12/against_types?mode

Berkshire, J. R., & Highland, R. W. (1953). Forced-choice performance rating: A methodological study. *Personnel Psychology, 6*, 355–378.

Berliner, D. C., & Biddle, B. J. (1995). *The manufactured crisis: Myths, fraud, and the attack on America's public schools.* Reading, MA: Addison-Wesley.

Betz, N. E., & Hackett, G. (1986). Applications of self-efficacy theory to understanding career choice behavior. *Journal of Social and Clinical Psychology, 4*, 279–289.

Binet, A., & Simon, T. (1905). Methodes nouvelles pour le diagnostic du niveau intellectuel des anormaux [New methods for the diagnosis of the intellectual level of subnormals]. *L'Année Psychologique, 12*, 191–244.

Blouin, A. (1987). *Computerized Diagnostic Interview Schedule (C-DIS).* Ottawa, Ontario, Canada: Ottawa Civic Hospital.

Bolton, B. (1992). California Psychological Inventory–revised edition. In J. J. Kramer & J. C. Conoley (Eds.), *Eleventh mental measurements yearbook.* Lincoln, NE: Buros Institute of Mental Measurements.

Bond, L. (1987). The Golden Rule settlement: A minority perspective. *Educational Measurement: Issues & Practice, 6*, 18–20.

Boomsma, D., Anokhin, A., & de Geus, E. (1997). Genetics of electrophysiology: Linking genes, brain, and behavior. *Current Directions in Psychological Science, 6*, 106–110.

Booth, A., Johnson, D., & Edwards, J. N. (1983). Measuring marital instability. *Journal of Marriage and the Family, 44*, 387–393.

Borman, W. C., Buck, D. E., Hanson, M. A., Motowidlo, S. J., Stark, S., & Drasgow, F. (2001). An examination of the comparative reliability, validity, and accuracy of performance ratings made using computerized adaptive rating scales. *Journal of Applied Psychology, 86*, 965–973.

Botwin, M. (1995). Review of the revised NEO Personality Inventory. In J. C. Conoley & J. C. Impara (Eds.), *The twelfth mental measurements yearbook.* Lincoln, NE: Buros Institute of Mental Measurements.

Bouchard, T. J., Lykken, D. T., McGue, M., Segal, N. L., & Tellegen, A. (1990). Sources of human psychological differences: The Minnesota study of twins reared apart. *Science, 250,* 223–228.

Bowman, M. L. (1989, March). Testing individual differences in Ancient China. *American Psychologist, 44,* 576–578.

Brennan, R. L. (1998). Misconceptions at the intersection of measurement theory and practice. *Educational Measurement: Issues and Practice, 17*(1), 5–9.

Brown, M. B. (2004). Review of the Self-Directed Search (4th ed.). In J. J. Kramer & J. C. Conoley (Eds.), *The eleventh mental measurements yearbook.* Lincoln, NE: Buros Institute of Mental Measurements.

Buchan, B. D., DeAngelis, D. L., & Levinson, E. M. (2005). A comparison of the web-based and paper-and-pencil versions of the Career Key interest inventory with a sample of university women. *Journal of Employment Counseling, 42,* 39–46.

Butcher, J. N. (1997). Introduction to the special section on assessment in psychological treatment: A necessary step for effective intervention. *Psychological Assessment, 9,* 331–333.

Butcher, J. N., Graham, J. R., Williams, C. L., & Ben-Porath, Y. S. (1990). *Development and use of the MMPI-2 content scales.* Minneapolis: University of Minnesota Press.

Camara, W. J., & Schneider, D. L. (1994). Integrity tests: Facts and unresolved issues. *American Psychologist, 49,* 112–119.

Camara, W. J., & Schneider, D. L. (1995). Questions of construct breadth and openness of research in integrity testing. *American Psychologist, 50,* 459–460.

Campbell, D. T., & Fiske, D. W. (1959). Convergent and discriminant validity by the multitrait–multimethod matrix. *Psychological Bulletin, 56,* 81–105.

Campbell, J. P., Dunnette, M. D., Arvey, R. D., & Hellervik, L. V. (1973). The development and evaluation of behaviorally based rating scales. *Journal of Applied Psychology, 57,* 15–22.

Campbell, V. L. (1990). A model for using tests in counseling. In C. E. Watkins, Jr., & V. L. Campbell (Eds.), *Testing in counseling practice (pp. 1–7).* Hillsdale, NJ: Lawrence Erlbaum.

Cannell, C. F., Miller, L., & Oksenberg, L. (1981). *Research on interviewing techniques.* Ann Arbor: University of Michigan, Institute for Social Research.

Carter, R. D., & Thomas, E. J. (1973). Modification of problematic marital communication using corrective feedback and instruction. *Behavior Therapy, 4,* 100–109.

Cascio, W. F. (1991). *Applied psychology in personnel management* (4th ed.). Englewood Cliffs, NJ: Prentice Hall.

Cascio, W. F., Alexander, R. A., & Barrett, G. V. (1988). Setting cutoff scores: Legal, psychometric, and professional issues and guidelines. *Personnel Psychology, 41,* 1–24.

Cattin, P. (1980). Estimation of the predictive power of a regression model. *Journal of Applied Psychology, 65,* 407–414.

Censeo. (2007). *360-degree feedback survey response scales.* Retrieved from June 15, 2010, http://www.censeocorp.com/downloads/whitepapers/360-degree-feedback-survey-response-scales.asp.

Center for Applications of Psychological Type. (n.d.). *The forms of the MBTI instrument.* Retrieved July 6, 2010, from http://www.capt.org/mbti-assessment/mbti-forms.htm

Center for Public Education. (2006). *A guide to the No Child Left Behind Act.* Retrieved May 17, 2010, from http://www.centerforpubliceducation.org/site/apps/nlnet/content3.aspx?c=lvIXIiN0JwE&b=5125033&ct=6857877

Charney, D. S., Heninger, G. R., & Breier, P. I. (1984). Noradrenergic function in panic anxiety: Effects of yohimbine in healthy subjects and patients with agoraphobia and panic disorder. *Archives of General Psychiatry, 41,* 751–763.

Charter, R. A. (2003). A breakdown of reliability coefficients by test type and reliability method, and the clinical implications of low reliability. *Journal of General Psychology, 130,* 290–300.

Chibnall, J. T., & Detrick, P. (2003). The NEO PI-R, Inwald Personality Inventory, and MMPI-2 in the prediction of police academy performance: A case for incremental validity. *American Journal of Criminal Justice, 27,* 233–248.

Chun, K. T., Cobb, S., & French, J. R. P. (1975). *Measures for psychological assessment: A guide to 3,000 original sources and their applications.* Ann Arbor, MI: Institute for Social Research.

Ciechalski, J. C. (2001). Mathematics Self-Efficacy Scale. In B. S. Plake & J. C. Impara (Eds.), *The fourteenth mental measurements yearbook.* Lincoln, NE: Buros Institute of Mental Measurements.

Clark, E. (2001). Review of the Wisconsin Card Sorting Test, Revised and Expanded. In B. S. Plake & J. C. Impara (Eds.), *The fourteenth mental measurement yearbook.* Lincoln, NE: Buros Institute of Mental Measurements.

Cleary, T., Humphreys, L., Kendrick, S., & Wesman, A. (1975). Educational use of tests with disadvantaged students. *American Psychologist, 30,* 15–41.

Cofresi, N. I., & Gorman, A. A. (2004). Testing and assessment issues with Spanish–English bilingual Latinos. *Journal of Counseling and Development, 82,* 99–106.

Cohen, J. (1960). A coefficient of agreement for nominal scales. *Educational and Psychological Measurement, 20,* 37–46.

Cohen, M. J., Branch, W. B., Willis, W. G., Weyandt, L. L., & Hynd, G. W. (1992). Childhood. In A. E. Puente &

R. J. McCaffrey (Eds.), *Handbook of neuropsychological assessment: A biopsychosocial perspective* (pp. 49–79). New York: Plenum.

Cohen, R. J., Swerdlik, M. E., & Phillips, S. M. (1996). *Psychological testing and assessment: An introduction to tests and measurements* (3rd ed.). Mountain View, CA: Mayfield.

Cohen, S. L. (1978). Letter from the editor. *Journal of Assessment Center Technology, 1*(1), 1.

College Board. (2008). *SAT scores stable as record numbers take test.* Retrieved May 19, 2010, from http://www.college board.com/press/releases/197846.html

College Board. (2010). *SAT for the press.* Retrieved May 17, 2010, from http://www.collegeboard.com/about/news_info/sat/

Colligan, R. C., Osborne, D., Swenson, W. M., & Offord, K. P. (1983). *The MMPI: A contemporary normative study.* New York: Praeger.

Consulting Psychologists Press. (2009). *Myers–Briggs Type Indicator interpretive report: Report prepared for Jane Sample.* Retrieved June 9, 2010, from http://www.cpp.com/images/reports/smp261144.pdf

Cook, T. D., & Campbell, D. T. (1979). *Quasi-experimentation: Design and analysis issues for field settings.* Chicago: Rand McNally.

Coombs, W. T., & Holladay, S. J. (2004). Understanding the aggressive workplace: Development of the Workplace Aggression Tolerance Questionnaire. *Communication Studies, 55,* 481–497.

Costa, P. T., Jr., & McCrae, R. R. (1992). *NEO Personality Inventory–Revised (NEO PI-R).* Odessa, FL: Psychological Assessment Resources.

Council of American Survey Research Organizations. (2009a). *Surveys and you.* Retrieved May 24, 2010, from http://www.casro.org/survandyou.cfm

Council of American Survey Research Organizations. (2009b). *Who are we: What we do.* Retrieved June 4, 2010, from http://www.casro.org/whatis.cfm

Coutsoukis, P., & Information Technology Associates. (1995–2003). *Dictionary of occupational titles.* Retrieved June 10, 2010, from http://www.occupationalinfo.org/

Cox, A., Thorpe, G., & Dawson, R. (in press). Review of the Personality Assessment Inventory. In R. A. Spies, J. F. Carlson, & K. F. Geisinger (Eds.), *The eighteenth mental measurements yearbook.* Lincoln, NE: Buros Institute of Mental Measurements.

Coyne, I. (2005). *International guidelines for test-use: Version 2000.* Retrieved May 20, 2010, from http://www.intestcom.org/test_use.htm

CPP. (2009). *The CPI assessments.* Retrieved June 4, 2010, from https://www.cpp.com/products/cpi/index.aspx

CPP. (n.d.). *California Psychological Inventory: Talent.* Retrieved June 4, 2010, from https://www.cpp.com/products/catalog/CPI434_2008.pdf

Crandall, V. C., Crandall, V. J., & Katkovsky, W. (1965). A children's social desirability questionnaire. *Journal of Consulting Psychology, 29,* 27–36.

Crawford v. Honig, 9th Cir. 37 F.3d 485 (1994).

Creative Research Systems. (2007–2010). *Sample size calculator.* Retrieved June 4, 2010, from http://www.surveysystem.com/sscalc.htm

Crocker, L., Llabre, M., & Miller, M. D. (1988). The generalizability of content validity ratings. *Journal of Educational Measurement, 25,* 287–299.

Cronbach, L. J. (1951). Coefficient alpha and the internal structure of tests. *Psychometrika, 16,* 197–334.

Cronbach, L. J. (1988). Five perspectives on the validity argument. In H. Wainer & H. Brown (Eds.), *Test validity* (pp. 3–17). Hillsdale, NJ: Lawrence Erlbaum.

Cronbach, L. J. (1989). Construct validation after thirty years. In R. Linn (Ed.), *Intelligence: Measurement, theory, and public policy* (pp. 147–171). Urbana: University of Illinois Press.

Cronbach, L. J., Gleser, G. C., Nanda, H., & Rajaratnam, N. (1972). *The dependability of behavioral measurements: Theory of generalizability scores and profiles.* New York: John Wiley & Sons.

Cronbach, L. J., & Meehl, P. E. (1955). Construct validity in psychological tests. *Psychological Bulletin, 52,* 281–302.

Crowne, D. P., & Marlowe, D. (1960). A new scale of social desirability independent of psychopathology. *Journal of Consulting Psychology, 24,* 349–354.

Crowne, D. P., & Marlowe, D. (1964). *The approval motive: Studies in evaluative dependence.* New York: John Wiley & Sons.

Crum, R. M., Anthony, J. J., Bassett, S. S., & Folstein, M. F., (1993). Population-based norms for the Mini-Mental State Examination by age and educational level. *Journal of the American Medical Association, 18,* 2386–2391.

Czubaj, C. A. (1996). The Wechsler Adult Intelligence Scale–Revised, revisited. *Education, 117,* 271–273.

Darley, J., & Fazio, R. (1980). Expectancy confirmation processes arising in the social interaction sequence. *American Psychologist, 35,* 867–881.

Dawes, R., & Corrigan, B. (1974). Linear models in decision making. *Psychological Bulletin, 81,* 95–106.

Derogatis, L. R., Rickels, K., & Rock, A. F. (1976). The SCL-90 and the MMPI: A step in the validation of a new self-report scale. *British Journal of Psychiatry, 128,* 280–289.

Derr, W. D. (2005). Envisioning EAP's future by reflecting on its past. *Behavioral Health Management, 25*(2), 13–17.

Detrick, P., Chibnall, J. T., & Rosso, M. (2001). Minnesota Multiphasic Personality Inventory-2 in police officer selection: Normative data and relation to the Inwald Personality Inventory. *Professional Psychology: Research and Practice, 32,* 484–490.

Di Milia, L. (2004). Australian management selection practices: Closing the gap between research findings. *Asia Pacific Journal of Human Resources, 42,* 214.

Dillman, D. A. (1978). *Mail and telephone surveys: The total design method.* New York: John Wiley & Sons.

Dillon, S. (2003, July 16). Before the answer, the question must be correct. *New York Times,* p. B9.

Distefano, M. K., Pryer, M. W., & Erffmeyer, R. C. (1983). Application of content validity methods to the development of a job-related performance rating criterion. *Personnel Psychology, 36,* 621–631.

Doak, C. C., Doak, L. G., & Root, J. H. (1996). *Teaching patients with low literacy skills.* Philadelphia: J. B. Lippincott.

Doe, C. G. (2005, May–June). A look at . . . web-based assessment. *MultiMedia & Internet@Schools,* pp. 10–14.

Donlon, T. (2001). Wonderlic Personnel Test. In, B. S. Plake & J. C. Impara (Eds.), *The fourteenth mental measurements yearbook.* . Lincoln, NE: Buros Institute of Mental Measurements.

Dowd, T. E. (1998). Review of the House–Tree–Person and Draw-A-Person as measures of abuse in children: A quantitative scoring system. In J. C. Impara & B. S. Plake (Eds.). *Thirteenth mental measurements yearbook. Lincoln, NE: Buros Institute of Mental Measurements.*

Dreher, G. F., Ash, R. A., & Hancock, P. A. (1988). The role of the traditional research design in underestimating the validity of the employment interview. *Personnel Psychology, 41,* 315–327.

DuBois, P. H. (1970). *The history of psychological testing.* Boston: Allyn & Bacon.

Dunst, C. J. (1998). Review of the Bayley Scales of Infant Development: Second edition. In J. C. Impara & B. S. Plake (Eds.), *Thirteenth mental measurements yearbook.* Lincoln, NE: Buros Institute of Mental Measurement.

Durand, V. M., & Barlow, H. B. (2006). *Essentials of abnormal psychology* (4th ed.). Belmont, CA: Thompson Wadsworth.

Dutch, S. (2009). *Killing the messenger: Attacks on the SAT.* Retrieved May 19, 2010, from http://www.uwgb.edu/DutchS/PSEUDOSC/DENYSAT.HTM

Eberhard, W. (1977). *A history of China.* Berkeley: University of California Press.

Educational Testing Service. (1996). *ETS publications catalog.* Princeton, NJ: Author.

Educational Testing Service. (2005). *Interpreting your GRE scores.* Retrieved June 10, 2010, from http://www.gistguide.com/guide/gre/srinfo.pdf

Educational Testing Service. (2009). *Guide to the use of scores.* Retrieved June 10, 2010, from http://ets.org/Media/Tests/GRE/pdf/gre_0910_guide.pdf

Educational Testing Service. (2010). *Frequently asked questions about the GRE.* Retrieved June 10, 2010, from http://ets.org/gre/general/about/faq/

Edwards, J. E., & Thomas, M. D. (1993). The organizational survey process: General steps and practical considerations. In P. Rosenfeld, J. E. Edwards, & M. D. Thomas (Eds.), *Improving organizational surveys* (pp. 3–28). Newbury Park, CA: Sage.

Edwards, M. C., Schulz, E. G., Chelonis, J., Gardner, E., Philyaw, A., & Young, J. (2005). Estimates of the validity and utility of unstructured clinical observations of children in the assessment of ADHD. *Clinical Pediatrics, 44,* 49–55.

Eells, K., Davis, A., Havighurst, R. J., Herrick, V. E., & Tyler, R. (1951). *Intelligence and cultural differences: A study of cultural learning and problem-solving.* Chicago: University of Chicago Press.

Eggers, W. (2005). *Government 2.0.* Lanham, MD: Rowman & Littlefield.

Eisenberg, B., & Johnson, L. (2001, March). Being honest about being dishonest. *Staffing Management.* Available from http://www.shrm.org/Publications/StaffingManagementMagazine/Pages/default.aspx

Elert, G. (2005). The SAT: Aptitude or demographics? *E-World.* Retrieved July 6, 2010, from http://hypertextbook.com/eworld/sat.shtml

Elliott, R., & Strenta, A. C. (1988). Effects of improving the reliability of the GPA on prediction generally and on comparative predictions for gender and race particularly. *Journal of Educational Measurement, 25,* 333–347.

Ellis, K. (2004, September). The right track. *Training,* pp. 40–45.

Elmore, C. (1988, April). An IQ test almost ruined my son's life. *Redbook,* pp. 50–52.

Embretson, S. E. (1996). The new rules of measurement. *Psychological Assessment, 8,* 341–349.

Emory, E. K., Savoie, T. M., Ballard, J., Eppler, M., & O'Dell, C. (1992). Perinatal. In A. E. Puente & R. J. McCaffrey (Eds.), *Handbook of neuropsychological assessment: A biopsychosocial perspective* (pp. 15–48). New York: Plenum.

Exner, J. E. (1974). *The Rorschach: A comprehensive system (Vol. 1).* New York: JohnWiley & Sons.

Exner, J. E. (1976). Projective techniques. In I. B. Weiner (Ed.), *Clinical methods in psychology* (pp. 61–121). New York: John Wiley & Sons.

Exner, J. E., & Weiner, I. B. (1982). *The Rorschach: A comprehensive system. Vol. 3: Assessment of children and adolescents.* New York: John Wiley & Sons.

Eyde, L. D., Moreland, K. L., Robertson, G. J., Primoff, E. S., & Most, R. B. (1988). *Test user qualifications: A data-based approach to promoting good test use* (Issues in Scientific Psychology). Washington, DC: American Psychological Association.

Faggen, J. (1987). Golden Rule revisited: Introduction. *Educational Measurement: Issues and Practice, 6,* 5–8.

Fay, C. H., & Latham, G. P. (1982). Effects of training and rating scales on rating errors. *Personnel Psychology, 35,* 105–116.

FBI Director Freeh orders stepped-up polygraph tests. (2001, March 1). *Wall Street Journal,* p. A12.

Financial Times. (2009). *Online MBA 2009 listing.* Retrieved May 26, 2010, from http://rankings.ft.com/exportranking/online-mba-2009/pdf

Fink, A. (2002). *The survey kit* (2nd ed.). Thousand Oaks, CA: Sage.

Fink, A. (2003). *The survey handbook* (2nd ed.). Thousand Oaks, CA: Sage.

Finn, S. E., & Tonsager, M. E. (1997). Information-gathering and therapeutic models of assessment: Complementary paradigms. *Psychological Assessment, 9,* 374–386.

Fischman, J. (2005, June 26). A very precious gift of time. *U.S. News & World Report.* Retrieved May 18, 2010, from http://health.usnews.com/usnews/health/articles/050704/4alzheimer.htm

Fisher, R. A., & Yates, F. (1963). *Statistical tables for biological, agricultural, and medical research* (6th ed.). Edinburgh, UK: Oliver & Boyd.

Fitzgerald, S. (2003, March). Stolen profits: Customer and employee theft contribute to shrink, resulting in huge losses to retailers already operating on tight margins—Clearly, the problem isn't going to go away, so what's a retailer to do? *Canadian Grocer,* p. G7.

Florida Department of Education. (2005). *Fact sheet: 2005–2006 FCAT.* Retrieved June 7, 2010, from http://fcat.fldoe.org/pdf/fcatfact.pdf

Florida Department of Education. (2008). *FCAT achievement levels.* Retrieved July 5, 2010, from http://fcat.fldoe.org/mediapacket/2008/pdf/08pressPacketGR4_10_page2.pdf

Florida Department of Education. (2009). *Understanding FCAT reports 2009.* Retrieved June 15, 2010, from http://fcat.fldoe.org/pdf/ufr_2009.pdf

Ford, J. K., & Wroten, S. P. (1984). Introducing new methods for conducting training evaluation and for linking training evaluation to program design. *Personnel Psychology, 37,* 651–665.

Fowler, F. J., Jr. (1988). *Survey research methods.* Newbury Park, CA: Sage.

Fowler, F. J., Jr. (1993). *Survey research methods* (2nd ed.). Newbury Park, CA: Sage.

Fowler, F. J., Jr. (2002). *Survey research methods* (3rd ed.). Thousand Oaks, CA: Sage.

Franke, W. (1960). *The reform and abolition of the traditional Chinese examination system.* Cambridge, MA: Harvard Center for East Asian Studies.

Frankenburg, W. K., Dodds, J., Fandal, A., Kazuk, E., & Cohrs, M. (1975). *Denver Developmental Screening Test, reference manual, revised 1975 edition.* Denver, CO: LA–DOCA Project and Publishing Foundation.

Frazier, K. (2003, November/December). Polygraph testing to be scaled back at national labs. *The Skeptical Inquirer,* pp. 6, 8.

Freeman, S. J. (2003). Review of the State–Trait Anger Expression Inventory-2. In B. S. Plake, J. C. Impara, & R. A. Spies (Eds.), *The fifteenth mental measurements yearbook.* Lincoln, NE: Buros Institute for Mental Measurements.

Fritzsche, B. A., & McIntire, S. A. (1997, January). *Constructing a psychological test as an undergraduate class project: Yes, it can be done!* Poster presented at the annual meeting of the National Institute on the Teaching of Psychology, St. Petersburg, FL.

Gael, S., Grant, D., & Richie, R. (1975). Employment test validation for minority and nonminority clerks and work sample criteria. *Journal of Applied Psychology, 60,* 420–426.

Garrison, C., & Ehringhaus, M. (2007). *Formative and summative assessments in the classroom.* Retrieved June 7, 2010, from http://www.nmsa.org/Publications/WebExclusive/Assessment/tabid/1120/Default.aspx

Gatewood, R. D., & Feild, H. S. (1997). *Human resource selection* (4th ed.). Fort Worth, TX: Dryden.

Gaugler, B. B., Rosenthal, D. B., Thornton, G. C., III, & Bentson, C. (1987). Meta-analysis of assessment center validity. *Journal of Applied Psychology, 72,* 493–511.

Geertsma, R. H. (1972). Observational methods. In R. H. Woody & J. D. Woody (Eds.), *Clinical assessment in counseling and psychotherapy* (pp. 86–118). Englewood Cliffs, NJ: Prentice Hall.

Geisinger, K. F., Spies, R. A., Carlson, J. F., & Plake, B. S. (Eds.). (2007). *Seventeenth mental measurements yearbook.* Lincoln, NE: Author

Ghiselli, E. E. (1964). *The concept of reliability of measurement: Theory of psychological measurement.* New York: McGraw-Hill.

Gibbs, N. (1995, October 2). The EQ factor. *Time,* pp. 60–68.

Goh, D., & Fuller, G. B. (1983). Current practices in the assessment of personality and behavior by school psychologists. *School Psychology Review, 12,* 240–243.

Goldberg, L. R. (1970). Man versus model of man: A rationale plus evidence for a method of improving clinical inference. *Psychological Bulletin, 73,* 422–432.

Goldman, B. A., Mitchell, D. F., & Egelson, P. E. (Eds.). (1997). *Directory of unpublished experimental measures* (Vol. 7). Dubuque, IA: William C. Brown.

Goodenough, F. (1926). *Measurement of intelligence by drawing.* New York: World Book.

Goodwin, L. D., & Leech, N. L. (2003). The meaning of validity in the new *Standards for Educational and Psychological Testing:* Implications for measurement courses. *Measurement and Evaluation in Counseling and Development, 35,* 181–183.

Gootman, E. (2004, February 8). Now the Regents Math test is criticized as too easy. *New York Times,* p. I29.

Gottfredson, L. S. (1991). When job-testing "fairness" is nothing but a quota. *Industrial–Organizational Psychologist, 28*(3), 65–67.

Gottfredson, M. R., & Hirschi, T. (1990). *A general theory of crime.* Stanford, CA: Stanford University Press.

Gough, H. G. (1987). *California Psychological Inventory administrator's guide.* Palo Alto, CA: Consulting Psychologists Press.

Gould, S. J. (1982). *A nation of morons.* Retrieved May 19, 2010, from www.holah.karoo.net/gouldstudy.htm

Grant, C. A., & Sleeter, C. E. (1986). Race, class, and gender in education research: An argument for integrative analysis. *Review of Educational Research, 56,* 195–211.

Grasmick, H. G., Tittle, C. R., Bursik, R. J., & Arneklev, B. J. (1993). Testing the core empirical implications of Gottfredson and Hirschi's general theory of crime. *Journal of Research in Crime and Delinquency, 30,* 5–29.

Greer, M. (2004, October). Handling an ethical bind. *Monitor on Psychology,* p. 63.

Gribbons, B. C., Tobey, P. E., & Michael, W. B. (1995). Internal-consistency reliability and construct and criterion-related validity of an academic self-concept scale. *Educational and Psychological Measurement, 55,* 858–867.

Gronlund, N. E. (1998). *Assessment of student achievement* (6th ed.). Boston: Allyn & Bacon.

Gronlund, N. E., & Waugh, C. K. (2008). *Assessment of student achievement* (9th ed.). Boston: Allyn & Bacon.

Groth-Marnat, G. (1997). *Handbook of psychological assessment* (3rd ed.). New York: John Wiley & Sons.

Groves, R. M. (1989). *Survey errors and survey costs.* New York: John Wiley & Sons.

Guernsey, L. (2000, August 6). An ever changing course: Taking admissions tests on computers. *New York Times,* p. A32.

Guion, R. M. (1966). Employment tests and discriminatory hiring. *Industrial Relations, 5,* 20–37.

Haak, R. A. (1990). Using the sentence completion to assess emotional disturbance. In C. R. Reynolds & R. W. Kamphaus (Eds.), *Handbook of psychological and educational assessment of children: Personality, behavior, and context* (pp. 147–167). New York: Guilford.

Hafenbrack, J. (2010, March 10). Bill would tie teacher pay to performance, student test scores. *Sun Sentinel.* Retrieved July 28, 2010, from http://articles.sun-sentinel.com/2010-03-10/news/fl-teacher-merit-pay-20100310_1_broward-teachers-union-teacher-tenure-weed-out-bad-teachers

Hafenbrack, J. (2010, March 10). Florida Senate OKs merit pay, tougher graduation rules. Orlando Sentinal. Retrieved July 28, 2010, from http://articles.orlandosentinel.com/2010-03-24/news/os-education-reforms-senate-03-25-2010-20100324_1_merit-pay-plan-rank-and-file-teachers-public-school

Hammer, A. L., & Schnell, E. R. (2000). *FIRO-B: Technical guide.* Palo Alto, CA: Consulting Psychologists Press.

Hammer, E. F. (1975). *The clinical application of projective drawings* (4th ed.). Springfield, IL: Charles C Thomas.

Haney, W. (1981). Validity, vaudeville, and values. *American Psychologist, 36,* 1021–1034.

Hanna, G. S. (1998). Wonderlic Basic Skills Test. In J. C. Impara & B. S. Plake (Eds.), *The thirteenth mental measurements yearbook.* Lincoln, NE: Buros Institute of Mental Measurements.

Harcourt Assessment. (2006). *Bayley III Scales of Infant Development Caregiver Report.* Retrieved June 10, 2010, from http://www.pearsonpsychcorp.com.au/userfiles/1440370509BayleyIII%20Infant%20Dev%20Caregiver%20SampleReport.pdf

Harrington, G. M. (1975). Intelligence tests may favour the majority groups in a population. *Nature, 258,* 708–709.

Harrington, G. M. (1976). *Minority test bias as a psychometric artifact: The experimental evidence.* Paper presented at the annual meeting of the American Psychological Association, Washington, DC.

Hartigan, J. A., & Wigdor, A. K. (1989). *Fairness in employment testing: Validity generalization, minority issues, and the General Aptitude Test Battery.* Washington, DC: National Academy Press.

Hartnett, R. T., & Willingham, W. W. (1980). The criterion problem: What measure of success in graduate education? *Applied Psychological Measurement, 4,* 281–291.

Hattrup, K. (2003). Review of the California Psychological Inventory, third edition. In B. S. Plake, J. C. Impara, & R. A. Spies (Eds.), *The fifteenth mental measurements yearbook.* Lincoln, NE: Buros Institute of Mental Measurements.

Haymaker, J. D., & Grant, D. L. (1982). Development of a model for content validation. *Journal of Assessment Center Technology, 5*(2), 1–8.

Haynes, S. N., Leisen, M. B., & Blaine, D. D. (1997). Design of individualized behavioral treatment programs using functional analytic clinical case models. *Psychological Assessment, 9,* 334–348.

Haynes, S. N., Richard, D. C. S., & Kubany, E. S. (1995). Content validity in psychological assessment: A functional approach to concepts and methods. *Psychological Assessment, 7,* 238–247.

Heaton, R. K. (1981). *A manual for the Wisconsin Card Sorting Test.* Odessa, FL: Psychological Assessment Resources.

Heaton, R. K., Chelune, G. J., Talley, J. L., Kay, G. G., & Curtiss, G. (1993). *Wisconsin Card Sorting Test manual: Revised and expanded.* Odessa, FL: Psychological Assessment Resources.

Heifetz, J. (2003, July 12). A Regents moratorium. *New York Times,* p. A10.

Helmstadter, G. C. (1970). *Research concepts in human behavior.* New York: Appleton-Century-Crofts.

Heneman, H. G., III, Heneman, R. L., & Judge, T. A. (1997). *Staffing organizations.* Middleton, WI: Mendota House.

Herrnstein, R. J., & Murray, C. (1994). *The bell curve: Intelligence and class structure in American life.* New York: Free Press.

Hess, A. K. (2001). Review of Wechsler Adult Intelligence Scale, third edition (WAIS-III). In S. Plake & J. C. Impara (Eds.), *Fourteenth mental measurements yearbook.* Lincoln: University of Nebraska, Buros Institute of Mental Measurements.

Hess, A. K., Zachar, P., & Kramer, J. (2001). Review of the Rorschach. In B. S. Plake & J. C. Impara (Eds.), *The fourteenth mental measurement yearbook.* Lincoln, NE: Buros Institute of Mental Measurements.

Hiller, J. B., Rosenthal, R., Bornstein, R. F., Berry, D. T. R., & Brunell-Neulib, S. (1999). A comparative meta-analysis of Rorschach and MMPI validity. *Psychological Assessments, 11,* 278–296.

Hilliard, A. (1984). *Historical perspectives on black families.* Paper presented at the National Urban League/National Association for the Advancement of Colored People Summit Conference on the Black Family, Nashville, TN.

Hogan, J., & Holland, B. (2003). Using theory to evaluate personality and job-performance relations: A socioanalytic perspective. *Journal of Applied Psychology, 88,* 100–112.

Hogan, R., & Hogan, J. (1992). *Hogan Personality Inventory manual.* Tulsa, OK: Hogan Assessment Systems.

Hohenshil, T. H. (1996). Assessment and diagnosis in counseling. *Journal of Counseling and Development, 75,* 64–76.

Holland, J. L., Fritzsche, B. A., & Powell, A. B. (1996). *SDS: Technical manual.* Odessa, FL: Psychological Assessment Resources.

Holland, J. L., Powell, A. B., & Fritzsche, B. A. (1994). *SDS: Professional user's guide.* Odessa, FL: Psychological Assessment Resources.

Holman, T. B., Busby, D. M., & Larson, J. H. (1989). *PREParation for Marriage (PREP-M).* Provo, UT: Marriage Study Consortium.

Holman, T. B., Larson, J. H., & Harmer, S. L. (1994). The development of predictive validity of a new premarital assessment instrument: The PREParation for Marriage Questionnaire. *Family Relations, 43*(1), 46–52.

Holmberg, K., Rosen, D., & Holland, J. L. (1997). *SDS: The leisure activities finder.* Odessa, FL: Psychological Assessment Resources.

Hopkins, C. D., & Antes, R. L. (1979). *Classroom testing: Construction.* Itasca, IL: F. E. Peacock.

Horan, D. J. (2003, December). Controlling theft by key holders. *Chain Store Age,* p. 166.

Horel, J. A., Keating, E. G., & Misantone, L. J. (1975). Partial Kluver–Bucy syndrome produced by destroying temporal neocortex or amygdala. *Brain Research, 94,* 349–359.

Horowitz, M., Shilts, M. K., & Townsend, M. S. (2004). EatFit: A goal-oriented intervention that challenges adolescents to improve their eating and fitness choices. *Journal of Nutrition Education and Behavior, 36,* 43–44.

Houck, J. E., & Hansen, J. C. (1972). Diagnostic interviewing. In R. H. Woody & J. D. Woody (Eds.), *Clinical assessment in counseling and psychotherapy (pp. 119–186).* Englewood Cliffs, NJ: Prentice Hall.

Howell, D. C. (1995). *Fundamental statistics for the behavioral sciences* (3rd ed.). Belmont, CA: Duxbury.

Hucker, C. O. (1978). *China to 1850: A short history.* Stanford, CA: Stanford University Press.

Huebner, E. S. (1991). Initial development of the Student Life Satisfaction Scale. *School Psychology International, 12,* 231–240.

Human Resources Certification Institute. (n.d.-a). *Code of ethical and professional responsibility.* Retrieved May 20, 2010, from http://www.hrci.org/Page.aspx?id=51

Human Resources Certification Institute. (n.d.-b). *Our certifications.* Retrieved May 20, 2010, from http://www.hrci.org/HRCertification.aspx?id=2147483806

Human Sciences Research Council. (n.d.-b). Retrieved June 13, 2010, from http://www.hsrc.ac.za

Hunt, M. (1993). *The story of psychology.* New York: Doubleday.

Hunter, J. E., & Hunter, R. F. (1984). Validity and utility of alternative predictors of job performance. *Psychological Bulletin, 96,* 72–98.

HyperStat Online. (n.d.). *The effect of skew on the mean and median.* Retrieved June 24, 2010, from http://davidmlane.com/hyperstat/A92403.html

Indian Statistical Institute. (n.d.). *Psychology research unit.* Retrieved June 13, 2010, from http://www.isical.ac.in/~psy

International Test Commission. (2000). *International guidelines for test use.* Retrieved May 20, 2010, from http://www.intestcom.org/upload/sitefiles/41.pdf

International Test Commission. (2005). *International guidelines on computer-based and Internet-delivered testing.* Retrieved May 20, 2010, from http://www.intestcom.org/Downloads/ITC%20Guidelines%20on%20Computer%20-%20version%202005%20approved.pdf

IPAT. (n.d.). *The 16PF Questionnaire.* Retrieved May 17, 2010, from http://www.ipat.com/about/16pf/Pages/default.aspx

Jackson, D. N. (1986). *Computer-based personality testing.* Washington, DC: American Psychological Association, Scientific Affairs Office.

Javeline, D. (1999). Response effects in polite cultures. *Public Opinion Quarterly, 63,* 1–28.

Jensen, A. R. (1969). How much can we boost IQ and scholastic achievement? *Harvard Educational Review, 39,* 1–123.

Johnson, G. (2004, May). The good, the bad, and the alternative. *Training,* pp. 24–30.

Johnson, T. (2006, May 3). Can your personality get you hired or fired? *ABC News.* Retrieved July 5, 2010, from http://abcnews.go.com/GMA/TakeControlOfYourLife/Story?id=1915016

Joint Committee on Testing Practices. (2004). *Code of fair testing practices in education.* Washington, DC: Author. Retrieved May 21, 2010, from http://www.apa.org/science/programs/testing/fair-testing.pdf

Jones, J. W., & Youngblood, K. L. (1993, May). *Effect of a video-based test on the performance and retention of bank employees.* Paper presented at the annual meeting of the Society for Industrial and Organizational Psychology, San Francisco.

Jones, R. N. & Gallo, J. J. (2000). Dimensions of the Mini-Mental State Examination among community dwelling older adults. *Psychological Medicine, 30,* 605–618.

Jordan, J. D. (2010, February 24). Every Central Falls teacher fired, labor outraged. *The Providence Journal.* Retrieved July 1, 2010, from http://www.projo.com/news/content/central_falls_trustees_vote_02-24-10_EOHI83C_v59.3c21342.html

Kahn, R. L., & Cannell, C. F. (1957). *The dynamics of interviewing.* New York: John Wiley & Sons.

Kamin, L. J. (1995, February). Behind the curve [book review]. *Scientific American,* pp. 99–103.

Kane, M. T. (1994). Validating interpretative arguments for licensure and certification examinations. *Evaluation & the Health Professionals, 17,* 133–159.

Kaplan, R. M., & Saccuzzo, D. P. (1997). *Psychological testing: Principles, applications, and issues* (4th ed.). Pacific Grove, CA: Brooks/Cole.

Karr, A. R. (1988, July 1). Law limiting use of lie detectors is seen having widespread effect. *Wall Street Journal,* p. A1.

Katzell, R. A., & Austin, J. T. (1992). From then to now: The development of industrial–organizational psychology in the United States. *Journal of Applied Psychology, 77,* 803–835.

Keith-Spiegel, P., Wittig, A. R., Perkins, D. V., Balogh, D. W., & Whitley, B. E., Jr. (1994). *The ethics of teaching: A casebook.* Muncie, IN: Ball State University Press.

Kennedy, D. (2003). Committed to the best science? *Science, 300,* 1201.

Klecker, B. M. (2003). Review of the State–Trait Anger Expression Inventory-2. . In B. S. Plake, J. C. Impara, & R. A. Spies (Eds.), *The fifteenth mental measurements yearbook.* Lincoln, NE: Buros Institute for Mental Measurements.

Kleinmuntz, B. (1989). Review of the Computer Anxiety Scale. In J. C. Conoley & J. J. Kramer (Eds.), *The tenth mental measurements yearbook.* Lincoln, NE: Buros Institute of Mental Measurement.

Kline, P. (2000). *The handbook of psychological testing* (2nd ed.). London: Routledge.

Knobloch, H., Stevens, F., & Malone, A. F. (1980). *Manual of developmental diagnosis: The administration and interpretation of revised Gesell and Amatruda Developmental and Neurologic Examination.* New York: Harper & Row.

Knowles, E. F., & Bean, D. (1981). St. Louis fire captain selection: Litigation and defense of the selection procedures. *Journal of Assessment Center Technology, 4*(1), 9–22.

Ko, C. C., & Cheng, C. D. (2004). Secure Internet examination system based on video monitoring. *Internet Research, 14,* 48–61.

Kobrin, J. L., Patterson, B. F., Shaw, E. J., Mattern, K. D., & Barbuti, S. M. (2008). *Validity of the SAT for predicting first-year college grade point average.* Retrieved May 17, 2010, from http://professionals.collegeboard.com/profdownload/Validity_of_the_SAT_for_Predicting_First_Year_College_Grade_Point_Average.pdf

Kolb, S. J., Race, K. E. H., & Seibert, J. H. (2000). Psychometric evaluation of an inpatient psychiatric care consumer satisfaction survey. *Journal of Behavioral Health Services and Research, 27,* 75–86.

Korea Institute for Curriculum and Evaluation. (n.d.). Retrieved June 10, 2010, from http://www.kice.re.kr/en/index.do

Kouzes, J. M., & Posner, B. Z. (2003). *Leadership Practices Inventory: Leadership development planner* (3rd ed.). San Francisco: Pfeiffer.

Kracke, E. A. (1963). Region, family, and individual in the examination system. In J. M. Menzel (Ed.), *The Chinese civil service: Career open to talent?* (pp. 67–75). Boston: D. S. Heath.

Krall, V. (1986). Projective play techniques. In A. I. Rabin (Ed.), *Projective techniques for adolescents and children* (pp. 264–278). New York: Springer.

Kronhold, J. (2005, March 8). For the new SAT, perhaps you need a new study device. *The Wall Street Journal.* Retrieved May 20, 2010, from http://www.tilcoweb.com/wallstreetjournal01.htm

Krug, S. E., & Johns, E. F. (Eds.). (1990). *Testing in counseling practice.* Hillsdale, NJ: Lawrence Erlbaum.

Kryspin, W. J., & Feldhusen, J. F. (1974). *Developing classroom tests: A guide for writing and evaluating test items.* Minneapolis, MN: Burgess.

Kubiszyn, T., & Borich, G. (2007). *Educational testing and measurement: Classroom application and practice* (8th ed.). New York: HarperCollins.

Kuder, G. F., & Richardson, M. W. (1937). The theory of estimation of test reliability. *Psychometrika, 2,* 151–160.

Kuder, G. F., & Richardson, M. W. (1939). The calculation of test reliability coefficients based on the method of rational equivalence. *Journal of Educational Psychology, 30,* 681–687.

Kurlowicz, L., & Wallace, M. (1998). *The Mini-Mental State Examination.* Retrieved July 6, 2010, from http://www.suffolkhealthplan.com/Appendix%20Provider%20Manual/013MiniMentalState.pdf

Kush, J. C. (2005). *Review of the Stanford-Binet Intelligence Scales: Fifth Edition.* In R. S. Spies & B. S. Plake (Eds.), *The sixteenth mental measurements yearbook.* Lincoln, NE: Buros Institute of Mental Measurements.

La Rue, A. (1992). Adult development and aging. In A. E. Puente & R. J. McCaffrey (Eds.), *Handbook of neuropsychological assessment: A biopsychosocial perspective* (pp. 81–119). New York: Plenum.

Larzelere, R. E., Smith, G. L., Batenhorst, L. M., & Kelly, D. B. (1996). Predictive validity of the Suicide Probability Scale among adolescents in group home treatment. *Journal of American Academy of Child and Adolescent Psychiatry, 35,* 166–172.

Laurent, J., Catanzaro, S., Joiner, T. E., Jr., Rudolph, K., Potter, K., Lambert, S., et al. (1999). A measure of positive and negative affect for children: Scale development and preliminary validation. *Psychological Assessment, 11,* 326–338.

Lawshe, C. H. (1975). A quantitative approach to content validity. *Personnel Psychology, 28,* 563–575.

LeDoux, J. E., Thompson, M. E., Iadelcola, C., Tucker, L. W., & Reis, D. J. (1983). Local cerebral blood flow increases during auditory and emotional processing in the conscious rat. *Science, 221,* 576–578.

Lee, C., & Bobko, P. (1994). Self-efficacy beliefs: Comparison of five measures. *Journal of Applied Psychology, 79,* 364–369.

Lemann, N. (1999). *The big test.* New York: Farrar, Straus, & Giroux.

Liebert, R. M., & Spiegler, M. D. (1994). *Personality strategies and issues* (7th ed.). Pacific Grove, CA: Brooks/Cole.

Lilienfeld, S. O. (1993, Fall). Do "honesty" tests really measure honesty? *Skeptical Inquirer,* pp. 32–41.

Lilienfeld, S. O., Alliger, G., & Mitchell, K. (1995). Why integrity testing remains controversial. *American Psychologist, 50,* 457–458.

Lim, R. G., & Drasgow, F. (1990). Evaluation of two methods for estimating item response theory parameters when assessing differential item functioning. *Journal of Applied Psychology, 75,* 164–174.

Lindqvist, J. K., Daderman, A. M., & Hellstrom, A. (2003). Swedish adaptations of the Novaco Anger Scale 1998, the Provocation Inventory, and the State-Trait Anger Expression Inventory-2. *Social Behavior and Personality, 31,* 77.

Linn, R. (1982). Ability testing: Individual differences, prediction, and differential prediction. In A. Wigdor & W. Garner (Eds.), *Ability testing: Uses, consequences, and controversies* (pp. 335–388). Washington, DC: National Academy Press.

Linn, R. L. (1990). Admissions testing: Recommended uses, validity, differential prediction, and coaching. *Applied Measurement in Education, 3,* 297–318.

Linn, R. L., & Drasgow, F. (1987). Implications of the Golden Rule settlement for test construction. *Educational Measurement: Issues & Practice, 6*(2), 13–17.

Lippmann, W. (1922a). A future for tests. *New Republic, 33,* 9–11.

Lippmann, W. (1922b). The mental age of Americans. *New Republic, 32,* 213–215.

Lippmann, W. (1922c). The mystery of the "A" men. *New Republic, 32,* 246–248.

Lippmann, W. (1922d). The reliability of intelligence tests. *New Republic, 32,* 275–277.

Lippmann, W. (1922e). Tests of hereditary intelligence. *New Republic, 32,* 328–330.

Longshore, D., Turner, S., & Stein, J. A. (1996). Self-control in a criminal sample: An examination of construct validity. *Criminology, 34,* 209–228.

Lopez, M. N., Charter, R. A., Mostafavi, B., Nibut, L. P., & Smith, W. E. (2005). Psychometric properties of the Folstein Mini-Mental State Examination. *Assessment, 12,* 137–144.

Luther, C. (2009). *UCLA considering more than 55,000 applicants for 2009 freshman class.* Retrieved June 7, 2010, from http://newsroom.ucla.edu/portal/ucla/more-than-55-000-applicants-under-78627.aspx

Lyman, H. B. (1998). *Test scores: And what they mean* (6th ed.). Boston: Allyn & Bacon.

Maloney, M. P., & Ward, M. P. (1976). *Psychological assessment: A conceptual approach.* New York: Oxford University Press.

Marcoulides, G. A. (1985, November). *Developing measures of computer anxiety.* Paper presented at the annual meeting of the California Educational Research Association, San Diego.

Marcoulides, G. A., Stocker, Y., & Marcoulides, L. D. (2004). Examining the psychological impact of computer technology: An updated cross-cultural study. *Educational and Psychological Measurement, 64,* 311–318.

Marczyk, G., DeMatteo, D., and Festinger, D. (2005). *Essentials of research design and methodology.* Hoboken, NJ: John Wiley & Sons.

Martin, B. L. (1998). *Computer Anxiety Levels of Virginia Cooperative Extension Field Personnel.* Doctoral Dissertation. Virginia Polytechnic Institute and State University.

Martin, C. (n.d.). *The sixteen types at a glance.* Retrieved June 9, 2010, from http://www.capt.org/the_mbti_instrument/type_descriptions.cfm

Martin, W. A. P. (1870). Competitive examinations in China. *North Atlantic Review, 111,* 62–77.

Matarazzo, J. D. (1990). Assessment involving objective and subjective components. *American Psychologist, 45,* 999–1017.

McCall, C. H. (2001, November). *An empirical examination of the Likert scale: Some assumptions, development, and cautions.* Paper presented at the California Educational Research Association Conference, South Lake Tahoe, CA. Retrieved May 26, 2010, from http://faculty.pepperdine.edu/cmccall/CERAFinal.pdf

McCrae, R. R., & Costa, P. T., Jr. (1997). Personality trait structure as a human universal. *American Psychologist, 52,* 509–516.

McGraw-Hill. (1970). *Examiner's manual for the California Achievement Tests, Complete Battery, Level 2, Form A.* New York: Author.

McIntire, S. A., Bucklan, M. A., & Scott, D. R. (1995). *The job analysis kit.* Odessa, FL: Psychological Assessment Resources.

McLellan, M. J. (1995). Review of the Sixteen Personality Factor Questionnaire, Fifth Edition. In J. Conoley & J. C. Impara (Eds.), *The twelfth mental measurements yearbook.* Lincoln, NE: Buros Institute of Mental Measurements.

McPhee Andrewartha. (n.d.). Retrieved June 13, 2010, from http://www.mcpheeandrewartha.com.au/

Meade, A. W. (2004). Psychometric problems and issues involved with creating and using ipsative measures for selection. *Journal of Occupational and Organizational Psychology, 77,* 531–552.

Meehl, P. E. (1954). *Clinical versus statistical prediction: A theoretical analysis and review of the evidence.* Minneapolis: University of Minnesota Press.

Meglino, B. M., DeNisi, A. S., Youngblood, S. A., & Williams, K. J. (1988). Effects of realistic job previews: A comparison using an enhancement and a reduction preview. *Journal of Applied Psychology, 72,* 259–266.

Melchert, T. P., Hays, V. A., Wiljanen, L. M., & Kolocek, A. K. (1996). Testing models of counselor development with a measure of counseling self-efficacy. *Journal of Counseling & Development, 74,* 640–644.

Meyer, G. J. (1997). Thinking clearly about reliability: More critical corrections regarding the Rorschach Comprehensive System. *Psychological Assessment, 9,* 495–498.

Meyer, J. H., Woodard, P. G., & Suddick, D. E. (1994). The descriptive tests of mathematics skills: Predictive validity for an elementary mathematics concepts and structures course. *Educational and Psychological Measurement, 54,* 115–117.

Michael, W. B., & Smith, R. A. (1976). The development and preliminary validation of three forms of a self-concept measure emphasizing school-related activities. *Educational and Psychological Measurement, 38,* 527–535.

Michael, W. B., Smith, R. A., & Michael, J. J. (1989). *Dimensions of Self-Concept (DOSC): A technical manual* (rev. ed.). San Diego, CA: EdITS.

Miller, L. A., Mullin P. A., & Herrmann, D. J. (1990). Memory processes in answering retrospective survey questions. Paper presented at MNEMO '90, the International Symposium on Human Memory Modelling and Simulation, Varna, Bulgaria.

Miller, W. (1975). Psychological deficit in depression. *Psychological Bulletin, 82,* 238–260.

Millon, T. (1994). *Manual for the MCMI-III.* Minneapolis, MN: National Computer Systems.

Mindgarden. (2005–2009). *Mathematics Self-Efficacy Scale.* Retrieved June 10, 2010, from http://www.mindgarden.com/products/maths.htm

Morey, L. C. (1991). *Personality Assessment Inventory.* Odessa, FL: Psychological Assessment Resources.

Morey, L. C. (2001). *Personality Assessment Inventory.* Retrieved on April 1, 2009, from http://www3.parinc.com/uploads/ppt/PAI.ppt

Mueller, J. (2010). *What is authentic assessment?* Retrieved June 7, 2010, from http://jonathan.mueller.faculty.noctrl.edu/toolbox/whatisit.htm

Murphy, C. A., Coover, D., & Owen, S. V. (1989). Development and validation of the Computer Self-Efficacy Scale. *Educational and Psychological Measurement, 49,* 893–899.

Murphy, K. R., & Davidshofer, C. O. (1994). *Psychological testing: Principles and applications* (3rd ed.). Englewood Cliffs, NJ: Prentice Hall.

Murphy, K. R., & Davidshofer, C. O. (2005). *Psychological testing: Principles and applications* (6th ed.). Upper Saddle River, NJ: Pearson/Prentice Hall.

Myers, I. B. (1998). *Introduction to type* (6th ed.). Palo Alto, CA: Consulting Psychologists Press.

Myers, I. B., McCaulley, M. H., Quenk, N. L., & Hammer, A. L. (1998). *MBTI manual: A guide to the development and use of the Myers–Briggs Type Indicator* (3rd ed.). Palo Alto, CA: Consulting Psychologists Press.

National Association of School Psychologists, Professional Standards Revision Committee. (2000). *Principles for professional ethics: Guidelines for the provision of school psychological services.* Bethesda, MD: Author.

National Board for Certified Counselors. (2005). *Code of ethics.* Retrieved May 20, 2010, from http://www.nbcc.org/AssetManagerFiles/ethics/nbcc-codeofethics.pdf

National Board for Certified Counselors. (2009). *About us.* Retrieved May 20, 2010, from http://www.nbcc.org/whoWeAre/About.aspx

National Center for Fair and Open Testing. (2001). *The SAT: Questions and answers.* Retrieved July 6, 2010, from http://www.fairtest.org/facts/satfact.htm

National Education Association. (2002–2010). *Study finds test scores up since NCLB, but cause remains unclear.* Retrieved June 15, 2010, from http://www.nea.org/home/16231.htm

National Institute of Child Health and Human Development. (2010). *Learning disabilities.* Retrieved June 19, 2010, from http://www.nichd.nih.gov/health/topics/learning_disabilities.cfm

National Institute of Neurological Disorders and Stroke. (2010). *NINDS learning disabilities information page.* Retrieved June 19, 2010, from http://www.ninds.nih.gov/disorders/learningdisabilities/learningdisabilities.htm

Negy, C., & Snyder, D. K. (1997). Ethnicity and acculturation: Assessing Mexican American couples' relationships using the Marital Satisfaction Inventory–Revised. *Psychological Assessment, 9,* 414–421.

Neisser, U., Boodoo, G., Bouchard, T. J., Jr., Boykin, A. W., Brody, N., Ceci, S. J., et al. (1995). *Intelligence: Knowns and unknowns.* Retrieved May 19, 2010, from http://www.michna.com/intelligence.htm

Nelson Education. (n.d.). *General Aptitude Test Battery.* Retrieved May 19, 2010, from http://www.assess.nelson.com/group/gp-gatb.html

Net Industries. (2010). *Employee theft: Legal aspects-estimates of cost.* Retrieved May 19, 2010, from http://law.jrank.org/pages/1084/Employee-Theft-Legal-Aspects-Estimates-cost.html

Newberry, M. K., & Parish, T. S. (1987). Enhancement of attitudes toward handicapped children through social interactions. *Journal of Social Psychology, 127,* 59–62.

Newman, P., & Sweet, J. (1986). The effects of clinical depression on the Luria–Nebraska Neuropsychological Battery. *International Journal of Clinical Neuropsychology, 7,* 109–114.

Norcross, J. C. (2000). Clinical versus counseling psychology: What's the diff? *Eye on Psi Chi, 5*(1), 20–22. Retrieved June 7, 2010, from http://www.psichi.org/Pubs/Articles/Article_73.aspx

Nunnally, J. C. (1978). *Psychometric theory* (2nd ed.). New York: McGraw-Hill.

Nunnally, J. C., & Bernstein, I. H. (1994). *Psychometric theory* (3rd ed.). New York: McGraw-Hill.

O'Connor, R. (2008). Teen suicide. *Focus Analytic Service.* Retrieved June 2, 2010, from http://www.focusas.com/Suicide.html

Oetting, E. R. (1985). Oetting's computer anxiety scale. In J. V. Mitchell, Jr. (Ed.), *The ninth mental measurements yearbook.* Lincoln, NE: Buros Institute of Mental Measurements.

Ones, D., Dilchert, S., Viswesvaran, C., & Judge, T. (2007). In support of personality assessment in organizational settings. *Personnel Psychology, 60,* 995–1027.

Ones, D. S., Viswesvaran, C., & Schmidt, F. L. (1993). Comprehensive meta-analysis of integrity test validities: Findings and implications for personnel selection and theories of job performance. *Journal of Applied Psychology, 78,* 679–703.

Orsillo, S. M., & McCaffrey, R. J. (1992). Anxiety disorders. In A. E. Puente & R. J. McCaffrey (Eds.), *Handbook of neuropsychological assessment: A biopsychosocial perspective* (pp. 215–261). New York: Plenum.

Osman, A., Barrios, F. X., Longnecker, J., & Osman, J. R. (1994). Validation of the Inventory of College Students' Recent Life Experiences in an American college sample. *Journal of Clinical Psychology, 50,* 856–863.

Pajares, F., & Miller, M. D. (1995). Mathematics self-efficacy and mathematics performances: The need for specificity of assessment. *Journal of Counseling Psychology, 42,* 190–198.

PAR. (2010a). *NEO Personality Inventory-Revised (NEO PI-R).* Retrieved June 9, 2010, from http://www4.parinc.com/products/product.aspx?Productid=NEO-PI-R

PAR. (2010b). *Qualification levels.* Retrieved May 20, 2010, from http://www4.parinc.com/Faqs.aspx?FaqCategoryID=20#Qualification%20Levels

PAR. (2010c). *Rorschach Interpretation Assistance Program: Version 5 (RIAP5).* Retrieved June 9, 2010, from http://www4.parinc.com/products/product.aspx?Productid=RIAP5

PAR. (2010d). *State-Trait Anger Expression Inventory-2 (STAXI-2).* Retrieved June 10, 2010, from http://www4.parinc.com/products/product.aspx?Productid=STAXI-2

PAR. (2010e). *Wisconsin Card Sorting Test (WCST).* Retrieved June 7, 2010, from http://www4.parinc.com/Products/Product.aspx?ProductID=WCST

PAR. (2010f). Personality Assessment Inventory. Retrieved June 25, 2010, from http://www4.parinc.com/Products/Product.aspx?ProductID=PAI_INTERP_GDE

PAR. (n.d.). *Mini-Mental State Examination.* Retrieved July 6, 2010, from http://www.minimental.com/

Parish, T. S., Ohlsen, R. L., & Parish, J. G. (1978). A look at mainstreaming in light of children's attitudes toward the handicapped. *Perceptual and Motor Skills, 46,* 1019–1021.

Parker, K. (1983). A meta-analysis of the reliability and validity of the Rorschach. *Journal of Personality Assessment, 42,* 227–231.

Pearson Assessments. (2009). *MMPI-2 (Minnesota Multiphasic Personality Inventory-2).* Retrieved June 10, 2010, from http://www.pearsonassessments.com/tests/mmpi_2.htm

Pearson Education. (2009). *Wechsler Adult Intelligence Scale–Fourth edition (WAIS-IV).* Retrieved May 20, 2010, from http://psychcorp.pearsonassessments.com/HAIWEB/Cultures/en-us/Productdetail.htm?Pid=015-8980-808&Mode=summary

Pearson Education. (2010). *Effective January 1, 2007—Qualification levels and requirements.* Retrieved May 20, 2010, from http://www.pearsonschool.com/index.cfm?locator=PSZ3Fb

Piotrowski, Z. (1957). *Perceptanalysis.* New York: Macmillan.

Pirazzoli-t'Serstevens, M. (1982). *The Han civilization of China.* Oxford, UK: Phaidon.

Ployhart, R. E., Weekley, J. A., Holtz, B. C., & Kemp, C. (2003). Web-based and paper-and-pencil testing of applicants in a proctored setting: Are personality, biodata, and situational judgment tests comparable? *Personnel Psychology, 56,* 733–752.

Pond, M. (1927). Selective placement of metalworkers. *Journal of Personnel Research, 5,* 345–368, 405–417, 452–466.

Popham, J. W. (1975). *Educational evaluation.* Englewood Cliffs, NJ: Prentice Hall.

Popham, W. J. (2000). The mismeasurement of educational quality. *School Administrator, 57*(11), 12–15.

Poskey, M. (2005). Myths of psychological testing for candidate selection. *Recruiter Magazine Online.* Retrieved June 19, 2010, from http://www.recruiter.com/magazineonline/120702_feature_pm_022803_2.cfm

Potosky, D., & Bobko, P. (2004). Selection testing via the Internet: Practical considerations and exploratory empirical findings. *Personnel Psychology, 57,* 1003–1034.

Powers, R. (n.d.). *ABCs of the ASVAB.* Retrieved May 19, 2010, from http://usmilitary.about.com/cs/joiningup/a/asvababcs.htm

Probst, T. M. (2003). Development and validation of the Job Security Index and the Job Security Satisfaction Scale: A classical test theory and IRT approach. *Journal of Occupational and Organizational Psychology, 76,* 451–462.

Profiles International. (n.d.). *Step One Survey II.* Retrieved July 6, 2010, from http://www.profilesinternational.com/product_sosii.aspx

Prometric. (n.d.). *Prometric.* Retrieved May 24, 2010, from http://www.prometric.com

Psychological Assessment Resources. (2009). *Mini-Mental State Examination.* Retrieved June 29, 2010, from http://www.minimental.com/

Puente, A. E., & McCaffrey, R. J. (1992). *Handbook of neuropsychological assessment: A biopsychosocial perspective.* New York: Plenum.

Rabin, A. I. (1986). Concerning projective techniques. In A. I. Rabin & M. Haworth (Eds.), *Projective techniques for adolescents and children* (pp. 3–11). New York: Springer.

Reardon, R. C. (2001). *The Self-Directed Search interpretive report.* Retrieved July 5, 2010, from www.self-directed-search.com/sdsreprt.html

Riverside Publishing. (n.d.). *Stanford-Binet Intelligence Scales (SB5) Fifth Edition.* Retrieved July 6, 2010, from http://www.riverpub.com/products/sb5/index.html

Rodzinski, W. (1979). *A history of China.* Oxford, UK: Pergamon.

Rogers, B. G. (2001). Review of the Wechsler Adult Intelligence Scale–third edition. *Fourteenth Mental Measurements Yearbook.* Available from http://search.epnet.com/

Rogers, T. B. (1995). *The psychological testing enterprise: An introduction.* Pacific Grove, CA: Brooks/Cole.

Rojdev, R., Nelson, W. M., III, Hart, K. J., & Fercho, M. C. (1994). Criterion-related validity and stability: Equivalence of the

MMPI and the MMPI-2. *Journal of Clinical Psychology, 50,* 361–367.

Rollins College. (2008). *Rollins announces SAT and ACT test scores optional.* Retrieved June 7, 2010, from http://news.rollins.edu/07testsoptional.shtml

Rorschach, H. (1921). *Psychodiagnostik.* Bern, Switzerland: Bircher.

Rosen, L. D., Sears, D. C., & Weil, M. M. (1987). Computerphobia. *Behavior Research Methods, Instruments, & Computers, 19,* 167–179.

Rosenberg, M. (1965). *Society and the adolescent self-image.* Princeton, NJ: Princeton University Press.

Rosenberg, M. (1986). *Conceiving the self.* Malabar, FL: Krieger.

Rossi, R., Van den Brande, I., Tobac, A., Sloore, H., & Hauben, C. (2003). Convergent validity of the MCMI-III personality disorder scales and the MMPI-2 scales. *Journal of Personality Disorders, 17,* 330–340.

Rotter, J. B. (1966). Generalized expectancies for internal versus external control of reinforcement. *Psychological Monographs, 80,* 1–28.

Rotto, P. C. (1995). Review of the Sixteen Personality Factor Questionnaire, Fifth Edition. In J. Conoley & J. C. Impara (Eds.), *The twelfth mental measurements yearbook.* Lincoln, NE: Buros Institute of Mental Measurements..

Ruhlman, M. (2000). *The soul of a chef: The journey toward perfection.* New York: Penguin Books.

Ruscio, J. (2005, January/February). Exploring controversies in the art and science of polygraph testing. *The Skeptical Inquirer,* pp. 34–39.

Sabatelli, R. M. (1984). The Marital Comparison Level Index: A measure for assessing outcomes relative to expectations. *Journal of Marriage and the Family, 46,* 651–662.

Salgado, J. F., & Moscoso, S. (2003). Internet-based personality testing: Equivalence of measures and assessees' perceptions and reactions. *International Journal of Selection and Assessment, 11,* 194–205.

Saulny, S. (2005, March 25). State changing math standards in high schools. *New York Times,* p. B1.

Savage, D. G. (2009, June 30). White firefighters were unfairly denied promotions, Supreme Court rules. *Los Angeles Times.* Retrieved May 19, 2010, from http://articles.latimes.com/2009/jun/30/nation/na-court-firefighters30

Schmitt, N. (1996). Uses and abuses of coefficient alpha. *Psychological Assessment, 8,* 350–353.

Schoenberger, C. R. (2004, May 10). The insider. *Forbes,* p. 82.

Scott, W. D. (1915). The scientific selection of salesmen. *Advertising and Selling, 5,* 5–7.

Segal, D. L., & Coolidge, F. L. (2004). Objective assessment of personality and psychopathology: An overview. In M. J. Hilsenroth & D. L. Segal (Eds.), *Comprehensive handbook of psychological assessment: Volume 2, personality assessment* (pp. 3–13). Hoboken, NJ: John Wiley & Sons. Retrieved May 18, 2010, from http://media.wiley.com/product_data/excerpt/26/04714161/0471416126.pdf

Seligson, J. L., Huebner, S., & Valois, R. F. (2003). Preliminary validation of the Brief Multidimensional Students' Life Satisfaction Scale (BMSLSS). *Social Indicators Research, 61*(2), 121.

Sen. Pete Domenici introduced a bill to limit polygraph testing of personnel at DOE nuclear weapons facilities. (2001, August 6). *Inside Energy,* p. 11.

Sharpley, C. F., & Ridgway, I. R. (1993). An evaluation of the effectiveness of self-efficacy as a predictor of trainees' counseling skills performance. *British Journal of Guidance and Counseling, 21,* 73–81.

Sherer, M., Maddux, J. E., Mercandante, B., Prentice-Dunn, S., Jacobs, B., & Rogers, R. W. (1982). The Self-Efficacy Scale: Construction and validation. *Psychological Reports, 51,* 663–671.

Shore, M. F. (1972). Psychological testing. In R. H. Woody & J. D. Woody (Eds.), *Clinical assessment in counseling and psychotherapy.* Englewood Cliffs, NJ: Prentice Hall.

Simonson, M. R., Maurer, M., Montag-Torardi, M., & Whitaker, M. (1987). Development of a standardized test of computer literacy and computer anxiety scale. *Journal of Educational Computing Research, 3,* 231–247.

Skuse, D., Warnington, R., Bishop, D., Chowdhury, U., Lau, J., Mandy, W., & Place, M. (2004). The developmental, dimensional, and diagnostic interview (DI): A novel computerized assessment for autism spectrum disorders. *American Academy of Child and Adolescent Psychiatry, 43,* 548–558.

Smith, E. V., Jr. (2001). Mathematics Self-Efficacy Scale. In B. S. Plake & J. C. Impara (Eds.), *The fourteenth mental measurements yearbook.* Lincoln, NE: Buros Institute of Mental Measurements.

Smith, J. E., & Merchant, S. (1990). Using competency exams for evaluating training. *Training & Development Journal, 44,* 65–71.

Smither, R. D. (1994). *The psychology of work and human performance* (2nd ed.). New York: HarperCollins.

Society for Human Resource Management. (2010a). *About the Society for Human Resource Management.* Retrieved May 17, 2010, from http://www.shrm.org/ABOUT/pages/default.aspx

Society for Human Resource Management. (2010b). *SHRM testing center: Online testing solutions.* Retrieved June 19, 2010, from http://www.shrm.org/TemplatesTools/AssessmentResources/SHRMTestingCenter/Pages/index.aspx

Society for Industrial and Organizational Psychology. (2003). *Principles for the validation and use of personnel selection procedures.* Bowling Green, OH: Author.

Society for Industrial and Organizational Psychology. (2009). *Types of employment tests.* Retrieved May 19, 2010, from http://www.siop.org/Workplace/employment%20testing/testtypes.aspx

Spanier, G. (1976). Measuring dyadic adjustment: New scales for assessing the quality of marriage and similar dyads. *Journal of Marriage and the Family, 38,* 15–28.

Spies, R. A., Carlson, J. F., & Geisinger, K. F. (Eds.). *The eighteenth mental measurements yearbook.* Lincoln, NE: Buros Institute of Mental Measurements.

Stassen, H. H., Lykken, D. T., Propping, P., & Bomben, G. (1988). Genetic determination of the human EEG. *Human Genetics, 80,* 165–176.

Stevens, S. S. (1946). On the theory of scales of measurement. *Science, 103,* 677–680.

Stevens, S. S. (1951). Mathematics, measurement, and psychophysics. In S. S. Stevens (Ed.), *Handbook of experimental psychology* (pp. 1–49). New York: John Wiley & Sons.

Stevens, S. S. (1961). The psychophysics of sensory function. In W. A. Rosenblith (Ed.), *Sensory communication* (pp. 1–33). New York: John Wiley & Sons.

Strauss, E., Sherman, E. M., & Spreen, O. (2006). *A compendium of neuropsychological tests: Administration, norms and commentary* (3rd ed.). New York: Oxford University Press

Strenta, A. C., & Elliott, R. (1987). Differential grading standards revisited. *Journal of Educational Measurement, 24,* 281–291.

Sylvan Learning. (2010). *Why Sylvan works.* Retrieved on May 17, 2010, from http://tutoring.sylvanlearning.com/sylvan_tutoring_service_advantage.cfm

Szajna, B. (1994). An investigation into the predictive validity of computer anxiety and computer aptitude. *Educational and Psychological Measurement, 54,* 926–934.

Tam, S. (1996). Self-efficacy as a predictor of computer skills learning outcomes of individuals with physical disabilities. *Journal of Psychology, 130,* 51–58.

Ter Laak, J., de Goede, M., Aleva, A., & van Rijswijk, P. (2005). The Draw-A-Person test: An indicator of children's cognitive and socioemotional adaptation? *Journal of Genetic Psychology: Child Behavior, Animal Behavior, and Comparative Psychology, 166,* 77–93.

Terwilliger, J. S. (1996, April). *Semantics, psychometrics, and assessment reform: A close look at authentic tests.* Paper presented at the annual meeting of the National Council on Measurement in Education, New York. ERIC Document Reproduction Service No. ED397123.

Thorndike, R. M., Cunningham, G., Thorndike, R. L., & Hagen, E. (1991). *Measurement and evaluation in psychology and education.* New York: Macmillan.

Thorne, B. M., & Henley, T. B. (2001). *Connections in the history and systems of psychology* (2nd ed.). Boston: Houghton Mifflin.

Tipton, R. M., & Worthington, E. L., Jr. (1984). The measurement of generalized self-efficacy: A study of construct validity. *Journal of Personality Assessment, 48,* 545–548.

Tobin, M., & Hoff, K. (2007). Review of the Bayley Scales of Infant and Toddler Development (3rd ed.). In K. F. Geisinger, R. A. Spies, J. F. Carlson, & B. S. Plake (Eds.), *The seventeenth mental measurements yearbook.* Lincoln, NE: Buros Institute of Mental Measurements.

Tomsho, R. (2006, March 23). More districts pay teachers for performance. *Wall Street Journal,* p. B1.

TONI-4: Test of Nonverbal Intelligence. (n.d.). Retrieved May 17, 2010, from http://www.proedinc.com/customer/ProductView.aspx?ID=1383&sSearchWord=

Tourangeau, R. (1984). Cognitive science and survey methods. In T. Jabine, M. Straf, J. Tanur, & R. Tourangeau (Eds.), *Cognitive aspects of survey methodology: Building a bridge between disciplines* (pp. 73–199). Washington, DC: National Academy Press.

Tree Foundation. (n.d.). *CAT: Computer-adaptive tests.* Retrieved June 19, 2010, from http://www.treefoundation.gr/cat.htm

Trevisan, M. S. (2003). Review of the Wisconsin Card Sorting Test—64 card version. In B. S. Plake, J. C. Impara, & R. A. Spies (Eds.), *The fifteenth mental measurements yearbook.* Lincoln, NE: Buros Institute of Mental Measurements.

Trochim, W. M. K. (2001). *The research methods knowledge base* (2nd ed.). Cincinnati, OH: Atomic Dog.

Tseng, M. H., Henderson, A., Chow, S. M. K., & Yao, G. (2004). Relationship between motor proficiency, attention, impulse, and activity in children with ADHD. *Developmental Medicine and Child Neurology, 46,* 381–388.

Uniform guidelines on employee selection procedures. (1978). *Federal Register, 43,* 38290–38315.

University of Cambridge, Psychometrics Centre. (2008). *Psychometrics Centre.* Retrieved June 13, 2010, from http://www.psychometrics.sps.cam.ac.uk/

University of Missouri. (1993–2010). *Listening: Our most used communication skill.* Retrieved June 19, 2010, from http://extension.missouri.edu/publications/DisplayPub.aspx?P=CM150

U.S. Bureau of Labor Statistics. (n.d.). *Labor force statistics from the current population survey.* Retrieved June 4, 2010, from http://www.bls.gov/cps/home.htm

U.S. Census Bureau. (n.d.). *The Hispanic population in the United States: 2006 detailed tables.* Retrieved May 21, 2010, from http://www.census.gov/population/www/socdemo/hispanic/cps2006.html

U.S. Congress, Office of Technology Assessment. (1990). *The use of integrity tests for pre-employment screening* (OTA-SET-442). Washington, DC: Government Printing Office.

U.S. Department of Education. (2004). *Overview: Four pillars of NCLB.* Retrieved May 17, 2010, from http://www.ed.gov/nclb/overview/intro/4pillars.html

U.S. Department of Health and Human Services. (n.d.*). Beck Depression Inventory–Second Edition (BDI-II), 1996.* Retrieved July 6, 2010, from http://www.acf.hhs.gov/programs/opre/ehs/perf_measures/reports/resources_measuring/res_meas_phic.html

U.S. Department of Labor. (n.d.). *Uniform guidelines on employee selection procedures.* Retrieved June 8, 2010, from http://www.dol.gov/dol/allcfr/title_41/part_60-3/toc.htm

U.S. General Accounting Office. (1993). *Developing and using questionnaires.* Retrieved June 4, 2010, from http://archive.gao.gov/t2pbat4/150366.pdf

Usdan, S. L., Schumacher, J. E., & Bernhardt, J. M. (2004). Impaired driving behaviors among college students: A comparison of web-based daily assessment and retrospective timeline followback. *Journal of Alcohol and Drug Education, 48,* 34–50.

Van de Vijver, F. J. R., & Phalet, K. (2004). Assessment in multicultural groups: The role of acculturation. *Applied Psychology: An International Review, 53,* 215–236.

Van Hutton, V. (1994). *House–Tree–Person and Draw-A-Person as measures of abuse in children: A quantitative scoring system.* Odessa, FL: Psychological Assessment Resources.

Vispoel, W. P., Boo, J., & Bleiler, T. (2001). Computerized and paper-and-pencil versions of the Rosenberg Self-Esteem Scale: A comparison of psychometric features and respondent preferences. *Educational and Psychological Measurement, 61,* 461–474.

Von Mayrhauser, R. T. (1987). The manager, the medic, and the mediator: The clash of professional psychological styles and the wartime origins of group mental testing. In M. M. Sokal (Ed.), *Psychological testing and American society* (pp. 128–157). New Brunswick, NJ: Rutgers University Press.

Walker, E., Lucas, M., & Lewine, R. (1992). Schizophrenic disorders. In A. E. Puente & R. J. McCaffrey (Eds.), *Handbook of neuropsychological assessment: A biopsychosocial perspective* (pp. 309–334). New York: Plenum.

Waller, N. G. (1995a). Review of the Beck Anxiety Inventory. In J. C. Conoley & J. C. Impara (Eds.), *Twelfth mental measurements yearbook.* Lincoln, NE: Buros Institute of Mental Measurements.

Waller, N. G. (1995b). Review of the Beck Depression Inventory (1993 revised). In J. C. Conoley and & J. C. Impara (Eds.), *Twelfth mental measurements yearbook.* Lincoln, NE: Buros Institute of Mental Measurements.

Wanek, J. E., Sackett, P. R., & Ones, D. S. (2003). Towards an understanding of integrity test similarities and differences: An item-level analysis of seven tests. *Personnel Psychology, 56,* 873.

Ward, S. (2001). Review of the Mini-Mental State Examination. In B. S. Plake, J. C. Impara, & R. A. Spies (Eds.), *Fifteenth mental measurements yearbook.* Lincoln, NE: Buros Institute of Mental Measurements.

Wasserman, R. C., Kelleher, K. J., Bocian, A., Baker, A., Childs, G. E., Indacochea, F., et al. (1999). Identification of attentional and hyperactivity problems in primary care: A report from pediatric research in office settings and the ambulatory sentinel practice network. *Pediatrics, 103,* E38.

Waterman, J. A., & Rogers, J. (1996). *Introduction to the FIRO-B.* Palo Alto, CA: Consulting Psychologists Press.

Watson, C. G., Detra, E., Kurt, L. F., Ewing, J. W., Gearhart, L. P., & DeMotts, J. R. (1996). Comparative concurrent validities of five alcoholism measures in a psychiatric hospital. *Journal of Clinical Psychology, 51,* 676–684.

Weinberg, R. S., Gould, D., & Jackson, A. (1979). Expectations and performance: An empirical test of Bandura's self-efficacy theory. *Journal of Sport Psychology, 1,* 320–331.

Weinberger, D. R., & Berman, K. E. (1988). Speculation on the meaning of cerebral metabolic hypofrontality in schizophrenia. *Schizophrenia Bulletin, 14,* 157–168.

Weinberger, D. R., Berman, K. E., & Zec, R. W. (1986). Physiologic dysfunction of dorsolateral prefrontal cortex in schizophrenia: I. Regional cerebral blood flow evidence. *Archives of General Psychiatry, 43,* 114–125.

Weiss, D. J. (2004). Computerized adaptive testing for effective and efficient measurement in counseling and education. *Measurement and Evaluation in Counseling and Development, 37,* 70–84.

Weiss, R. I. L., & Heyman, R. E. (1990). Observation of marital interaction. In F. D. Fincham & T. N. Bradbury (Eds.), *The psychology of marriage: Basic issues and applications* (pp. 87–117). New York: Guilford.

Wheeler, V. A., & Ladd, G. W. (1982). Assessment of children's self-efficacy for social interactions with peers. *Developmental Psychology, 18,* 795–805.

Wherry, R. J. (1931). A new formula for predicting shrinkage of the coefficient of multiple correlation. *Annals of Mathematical Statistics, 2,* 440–457.

Whipple, G. M. (1910). *Manual of mental and physical tests.* Baltimore, MD: Warwick & York.

Wigdor, A. K. (1990, Spring). Fairness in employment testing. *Issues in Science and Technology,* pp. 27–28.

Wiggins, G. P. (1993). *Assessing student performance: Exploring the purpose and limits of testing.* San Francisco: Jossey-Bass.

Wiggins, J. S. (1973). *Personality and prediction: Principles of personality assessment.* Reading, MA: Addison-Wesley.

Wise, S. L. (1989). Review of the Computer Anxiety Scale. In J. C. Conoley & J. J. Kramer (Eds.), *The tenth mental measurements yearbook.* Lincoln, NE: Buros Institute of Mental Measurement.

Wohl, A., & Kaufman, B. (1995). *Silent screams and hidden cries: A compilation and interpretation of artwork by children from violent homes.* London: Taylor & Francis.

Wood, J.W., Nezworski, M. T., & Stejskal,W. J. (1997). The reliability of the comprehensive system for the Rorschach: A comment on Meyer. *Psychological Assessment, 9,* 490–494.

Wood, J. M., Nezworski, M. T., Lilienfeld, S. O., & Garb, H. N. (2003). The Rorschach Inkblot Test, fortune tellers, and cold reading. *The Skeptical Inquirer, 27*(4), 29–33.

Woody, R. H. (1972). The counselor-therapist and clinical assessment. In R. H. Woody & J. D. Woody (Eds.), *Clinical assessment in counseling and psychotherapy* (pp. 1–29). Englewood Cliffs, NJ: Prentice Hall.

Worchel, F. F., & Dupree, J. L. (1990). Projective storytelling techniques. In C. R. Reynolds & R. W. Kamphaus (Eds.), *Handbook of psychological and educational assessment of children: Personality, behavior, and context* (pp. 70–88). New York: Guilford.

Yam, P. (1998, Winter). Intelligence considered. *Scientific American,* pp. 4, 6–11.

Yerkes, R. M. (1921). Psychological examining in the United States Army. In *Memoirs of the National Academy of Sciences* (Vol. 15). Washington, DC: Government Printing Office.

Young, J. W. (1994). Differential prediction of college grades by gender and by ethnicity: A replication study. *Educational and Psychological Measurement, 54,* 1022–1029.

Zimmerman, D. W., Zumbo, B. D., & Lalonde, C. (1993). Coefficient alpha as an estimate of test reliability under violation of two assumptions. *Educational and Psychological Measurement, 53,* 33–49.

Zulig, K. J., Huebner, E. S., Gilman, R., Patton, J. M., & Murray, K. A. (1994). Validation of the Brief Multidimensional Students' Life Satisfaction Scale among college students. *American Journal of Health Behavior, 29,* 206–215.

Photo Credits

Chapter 1

Page 10. © Wang Sanjun/Istockphoto.

Page 15. © Robert Mizerek/Istockphoto

Chapter 3

Page 64. © Istockphoto

Page 78. © Istockphoto

Chapter 4

Page 102. © Tan Kian Khoon/Istockphoto

Chapter 5

Page 124. © Istockphoto

Chapter 6

Page 153. © PMSI Web Hosting and Design/Istockphoto.

Chapter 7

Page 204. © Lisa Gagne/Istockphoto

Chapter 8

Page 214. © Kati Neudert/Istockphoto

Chapter 9

Page 244. © Scott Maxwell/Istockphoto

Chapter 11

Page 312. Five images of international flags. © Istockphoto

Page 316. © Bonnie Jacobs/Istockphoto

Page 330. © Richard Leloux /Istockphoto

Chapter 12

Page 340. © Christoph Ermel/ Istockphoto

Chapter 14

Page 418. Stockbyte/Thinkstock

Page 422. © Istockphoto

Page 423. Lewis J. Merrim / Photo Researchers, Inc.

Page 430. © Istockphoto

Chapter 15

Page 448. © Sharon Dominick/Istockphoto

Page 462. © Lise Gagne/Istockphoto

Appendix A

Page 475. Photo of Gale H. Roid. Photo by Palmer Photography, Salem, Oregon.

Page 479. Photo of Katherine Cook Briggs and Isabel Myers Briggs. Reprinted by permission of CAPT Archives.

Page 485. Photo of Hermann Rorschach. http://en.wikipedia.org/wiki/File:Hermann_Rorschach.jpg

Page 491. Photo of Marshal Folstein. Taken by Mark Morelli in *Tufts Journal,* December 2001. Reprinted by permission of Tufts Office of Publications, and photographer Mark Morelli.

Page 503. Photo of Nancy Bayley. Institute of Human Development, University of California, Berkeley

Page 505. Photo of Will Schutz. Ethan Schutz, the Schutz Company

Page 512. Photos of J. C. McKinley and Starke R. Hathaway. Courtesy of University Archives, University of Minnesota, Twin Cities

Page 519. Photo of John Holland. Reprinted with permission of Dr. John Holland.

Page 525. Photo of Raymond Cattell. Reprinted by permission of the Cattell Family.

Page 527. Photo of Aaron Beck. Reprinted by permission of Dr. Aaron T. Beck.

Page 530. Photo of Charles Spielberger. Reprinted with permission of Charles D. Spielberger.

Page 534. Photo of the Hogans. Reprinted with permission of Joyce Hogan, Hogan Assessment Systems.

Page 536. Photo of E.F. Wonderlic. Reprinted with permission of Wonderlic, Inc.

Author Index

Subject Index

About the Authors

Leslie A. Miller, PhD, PHR, has broad experience in consulting, teaching, and researching in the area of organizational and educational assessment, measurement, and development. Currently the owner of her own consulting business, LanneM TM LLC, she provides her clients with pragmatic and affordable talent management solutions—solutions to help them acquire, develop, and retain the talent they need to achieve desired business results today and in the future. Her expertise includes designing performance improvement/management tools and knowledge tests, customizing and facilitating leadership training programs, providing assessment-based executive coaching, and designing and implementing business impact evaluation and return on value studies. She also spends a significant amount of her time teaching graduate business, organizational behavior/leadership, and human resource courses at Rollins College and for the School of Advanced Studies at the University of Phoenix as well as mentoring doctoral learners through the dissertation process. Previously the vice president of leadership development/human resources at the Central Florida YMCA, she was responsible for contributing to the strategic plans of the organization by leading the association's talent management initiatives—recruiting, developing, and retaining the association's talent. Prior to joining the YMCA, she was employed by Wilson Learning Corporation (WLC), a performance improvement company, where she served as the director of business solutions, a senior project manager, and a business solutions consultant. In these roles, she was responsible for conceptualizing, designing, managing, and implementing traditional and technology-based assessment, measurement, and training performance improvement solutions for client organizations.

Prior to joining WLC, she served as the assistant dean of admissions at Rollins College, where she was also a faculty member of the psychology, organizational behavior, and human resources programs. Before joining Rollins College, she was a senior research psychologist for the U.S. Department of Labor, Bureau of Labor Statistics, in Washington, D.C. At the Bureau, she designed, researched, and analyzed the results of some of our nation's most important surveys. In her current and previous roles, she has worked with various leading organizations in the high-tech, financial, pharmaceutical, and transportation industries. With a PhD in educational psychology from the University of Maryland, she has an extensive list of publications.

Sandra A. McIntire, PhD, received her bachelor's and master's degrees in psychology and her doctor of philosophy degree in industrial/organizational psychology from the University of South Florida. She began her career in the human resources department of the city of Clearwater, Florida, and moved into consulting with Wilson Learning Corporation (WLC) as a senior project manager. At WLC, she developed the first retail video selection test, the Teller Selection Program (TAP). She also consulted with

Fortune 500 companies such as Citibank NA, United Technologies, IBM, and General Motors. In 1991, she accepted a tenure track professorship in the department of psychology at Rollins College in Winter Park, Florida. In addition to teaching social science statistics, research methods, and tests and measurements, she served as director of the psychology program for nontraditional students in Rollins's Hamilton Holt School. She has collaborated on three books: The Job Analysis Kit, Organization Development: Strategies for a Changing Environment, and Foundations of Psychological Testing (first and second editions). In addition, she has served as a book reviewer for Personnel Psychology. She has collaborated on peer-reviewed research and made numerous presentations to national organizations such as the American Society for Training and Development, the American Psychological Association, and the Southeastern Conference on Teaching of Psychology. Dr. McIntire is now retired from Rollins College.

Robert L. Lovler, PhD, has over 30 years of experience working both as an internal and external consultant to Fortune 500 companies in the areas of employee assessment and selection, organizational development, strategic human resource consulting, and training design and delivery. His career began at CBS Inc. where he served in several roles including Director of Training for their retail consumer electronics unit, then moving up to Vice-President of two different units within the CBS Publishing Group. He is currently Vice-President of Human Resources and Practice Leader for Selection and Assessment at Wilson Learning Corporation, a consulting firm which focuses on human performance improvement. During his career, he has had the opportunity to design and implement a wide range of organizational interventions both domestically and internationally, working in Japan, China, Korea, Hong Kong, England, and Italy. In the U.S., he supervised the development and implementation of the assessment center used to select candidates for entry into the Environmental Protection Agency's Senior Executive Service Development Program, presenting the results in Washington D.C. to Governor Christie Todd Whitman, the EPA Administrator. He also developed the selection system used to help select commercial airline pilots for a major U.S. airline and worked with former Senator Warren Rudman to develop and implement a nationwide survey of sales practices in the rent-to-own industry. He has served as a testing consultant to the California Bar Association, the state of Pennsylvania, and oversaw the development of the licensure examinations for medical physicists in the state of Texas. He has been on the adjunct faculty of the State University of New York at Farmingdale, Hofstra University, and the University of Central Florida. He holds master's and PhD degrees from Hofstra University and is a member of the Society for Industrial & Organizational Psychology.